ERNIE PYLE • OTTO

1984

BERT L. MATTHEWS

RY ALLEN • RAYMOND

OR • KAY BOYLE • JOHN STEINBECK

• WEBB MILLER • ERNEST HEMINGWAY

LLIAM H. STONEMAN • EDGAR SNOW

RD W. BEATTIE. JR. • LOUIS ADAMIC

CHALL • ANNE O'HARE McCORMICK

AGNES SMEDLEY • VINCENT SHEEAN

. LIEBLING • EDGAR ANSEL MOWRER

OS • J. M. BROWN • DREW MIDDLETON

DERICK OECHSNER • MAURICE HINDUS

• A. A. MICHIE • RAYMOND CLAPPER

HAROLD DENNY • QUENTIN REYNOLDS

RTHA GELLHORN • DOROTHY THOMPSON

T. WHITAKER • HANSON W. BALDWIN

JOHN LARDNER • WALTER GRAEBNER

MAS B. MORGAN • ERNEST K. LINDLEY

JAMES B. RESTON • BEN ROBERTSON

OHN SPIVAK • CYRUS L. SULZBERGER

TH • JAY ALLEN • RALPH INGERSOLL

*THEY WERE THERE*

# THE STORY OF WORLD WAR II

# THEY WERE THERE

## THE STORY OF

# WORLD WAR II

## AND HOW IT CAME ABOUT

BY AMERICA'S FOREMOST CORRESPONDENTS

EDITED BY CURT RIESS

GARDEN CITY PUBLISHING CO., INC., GARDEN CITY, N. Y.

1945
GARDEN CITY PUBLISHING CO., INC.

# CONTENTS

ON CORRESPONDENTS *by Curt Riess*  xv

PROLOGUE 1922: HOW IT BEGAN *by Vincent Sheean*  3

## *Part I:* EUROPE ON THE EVE

FEAR IN GERMANY *by Bruce Bliven*  5

THE ROAD TO HITLER *by Louis Fischer*  8

WINTER 1931-1932 *by H. R. Knickerbocker*  11

DEPRESSION *by Edgar Ansel Mowrer*  13

FIRST INTERVIEW WITH REICH CHANCELLOR ADOLF
 HITLER *by H. V. Kaltenborn*  17

THE FIRE *by John Gunther*  20

PERSECUTION OF THE JEWS *by Edgar Ansel Mowrer*  25

THE BLOOD PURGE *by Frederick T. Birchall*  27

"SOMETHING IS ROTTEN...." *by Dorothy Thompson*  31

DOLLFUSS ASSASSINATED *by G. E. R. Gedye*  35

STRESA: END OF AN ERA *by Seymour Berkson*  40

THE PARTY IN CONTROL *by Louis P. Lochner*  41

THE SHAME OF NUREMBERG *by Ralph W. Barnes*  43

UNDERGROUND 1935 *by John L. Spivak*  47

FASCISM IN THE WEST *by Johannes Steel*  52

## *Part II:* THE LIGHTS GO DOWN

GERMANY PREPARES FOR WAR *by Louis Fischer*  57

THE MOSCOW TRIALS *by Walter Duranty*  60

THE POGROM *by Otto D. Tolischus*  65

THE JEWISH CHILDREN *by Westbrook Pegler*  69

*ETHIOPIA*

THE INVASION *by Webb Miller*     71
BADOGLIO ENTERS ADDIS ABABA *by Herbert L. Matthews*     76

*SPAIN*

FRANCO'S REVOLT *by Reynolds and Eleanor Packard*     80
MADRID BOMBED *by John Dos Passos*     83
A DAY IN SPAIN *by Lillian Hellman*     87
INTERNATIONAL BRIGADE *by Vincent Sheean*     90
ITALY'S FIRST DEFEAT *by Herbert L. Matthews*     92
THE LOYALISTS *by Ernest Hemingway*     97
THE SIEGE OF BARCELONA *by William P. Carney*     101
THE BITTER END *by Janet Flanner*     103
NEITHER GUNS NOR BUTTER *by Thomas J. Hamilton*     105

*AUSTRIA*

"ANSCHLUSS" *by William L. Shirer*     108
ONE YEAR LATER *by Anne O'Hare McCormick*     112

*CZECHOSLOVAKIA*

CHAMBERLAIN IN BERCHTESGADEN *by Ernest R. Pope*     114
PRAGUE, SEPTEMBER 1938 *by Raymond Gram Swing*     118
MUNICH *by Frederick T. Birchall*     123
PEACE IN OUR TIME *by Joseph Driscoll*     124
THE PROTECTOR *by Edward W. Beattie, Jr.*     126

*Part III:* THE PHONY WAR

EUROPE HOLDS ITS BREATH *by Edward W. Beattie, Jr.*     130
THE PARTNERS *by Walter Duranty*     133
WAITING FOR DER TAG *by Louis P. Lochner*     140

GERMANY AT WAR *by Wallace R. Deuel*      141

ENGLAND GOES TO WAR *by Oswald Garrison Villard*      145

BLITZKRIEG *by Otto D. Tolischus*      149

INSIDE WARSAW *by Joseph W. Grigg*      154

LOGIC AND DEATH *by Joseph C. Harsch*      155

A BOMB EXPLODES, *by Ernest R. Pope*      157

AT THE FINNISH FRONT *by Martha Gellhorn*      161

DEFEAT *by Virginia Cowles*      165

BLACKOUT IN BERLIN *by W. B. Courtney*      167

CHRISTMAS IN THE MAGINOT LINE *by A. J. Liebling*      169

FRENCH REASONING *by Edmond Taylor*      172

FRENCH MORALE *by Clare Boothe*      174

LAST DAY OF THE PHONY WAR *by Edward R. Murrow*      176

## Part IV: THE DEBACLE

WAR IN NORWAY *by Leland Stowe*      178

ALLIES EVACUATE NAMSOS *by Edmund Stevens*      186

THE BREAK-THROUGH AT THE MEUSE, *by M. W. Fodor*      187

ON A PARIS RAILWAY STATION *by Dorothy Thompson*      192

SURRENDER OF HOLLAND *by Beach Conger*      194

FALL OF SEDAN *by G. H. Archambault*      195

DUNKERQUE *by Raymond Daniell*      196

THE STAB IN THE BACK *by Herbert L. Matthews*      197

REFUGEES *by Robert J. Casey*      201

WITH THEIR HANDS IN THEIR POCKETS *by Demaree Bess*      206

ON THE ROADS OF FRANCE *by Sonia Tomara*      209

COMPIEGNE *by William L. Shirer*      212

ORAN *by Edward Angly*      215

FRANCE UNDER THE NAZI HEEL *by Glen M Stadler*      217

THE MAN WHO QUIT *by Jay Allen*      219

THE MAN WHO DIDN'T QUIT *by Quentin Reynolds*      221

UNDERGROUND FRANCE *by Richard de Rochemont* 223

THE FIGHTING FRENCH *by Dudley Harmon II* 226

THE SILENT WOMEN *by Kay Boyle* 228

THE WAR LORD *by Frederick Oechsner* 231

*Part V:* FROM THE BATTLE OF ENGLAND TO THE
BATTLE OF GERMANY

LONDON IN FLAMES *by Robert J. Casey* 235

THE BLITZ *by Ben Robertson* 241

THEY COULD TAKE IT *by W. L. White* 244

WHEN THE RAIDS WERE OVER *by Raymond Daniell* 247

THE BATTLE OF THE ATLANTIC *by Vincent Sheean* 250

CONVOY *by Harry T. Brundidge* 256

TEAMWORK *by William H. Stoneman* 258

DIEPPE *by Quentin Reynolds* 261

ON THE WAY TO MURMANSK *by Robert Carse* 266

LONE WOLVES OF THE RAF *by Jack Alexander* 272

TARGET: BERLIN *by James McDonald* 277

END OF THE BEGINNING *by James B. Reston* 281

*Part VI:* WAR IN THE EAST

THE GREEKS MEANT BUSINESS *by Thomas B. Morgan* 284

FASCISM DIED THERE, TOO *by John T. Whitaker* 286

THE COUP *by Robert St. John* 289

BOMBS OVER BELGRADE *by Ray Brock* 295

GREEK TRAGEDY *by Leland Stowe* 298

CONQUEST OF CRETE, *by Frank Gervasi* 300

RUSSIA AND JAPAN *by John Scott* 303

RUSSIA INVADED *by Margaret Bourke-White* 306

LUFTWAFFE OVER MOSCOW *by Erskine Caldwell*    308

SCORCHED EARTH *by Alice-Leone Moats*    311

HITLER'S "VICTORY" by *Howard K. Smith*    313

FROM MOSCOW TO KUIBYSHEV *by Wallace Carroll*    318

SEVASTOPOL *by Larry Lesueur*    321

MR. CHURCHILL GOES TO MOSCOW *by Henry C. Cassidy*    325

WENDELL WILLKIE IN THE KREMLIN *by Walter Graebner*    328

THE NAZIS ENTER STALINGRAD *by Ralph Parker*    331

COUNTERATTACK! *by James E. Brown*    332

REBIRTH OF STALINGRAD *by Henry Shapiro*    335

SHAKEUP IN THE GENERAL STAFF *by George Axelsson*    336

ANNIVERSARY *by W. H. Lawrence*    337

THE HANGING OF ZOYA *by Maurice Hindus*    339

## Part VII: THE FAR EAST

THE MANCHURIAN INCIDENT *by Wilfrid Fleisher*    345

ASSASSINATION OF A PRIME MINISTER *by Hugh Byas*    348

HELL IN SHANGHAI *by Carroll D. Alcott*    351

FALL OF NANKING *by A. T. Steele*    353

THE GREAT MIGRATION *by Jerome Beatty*    354

BURMA ROAD *by Vanya Oakes*    359

RUSSO-JAPANESE CLASH *by Relman Morin*    362

CHINESE GUERRILLAS *by Agnes Smedley*    363

THE DRAGON LICKS HIS WOUNDS *by Edgar Snow*    367

CHUNGKING *by Brooks Atkinson*    376

"MADE IN JAPAN" *by Joseph Newman*    378

INDO-CHINA *by Hallett Abend*    381

FROM SAIGON TO SINGAPORE *by Carl Randau*    383

A TOPIC OF CONVERSATION *by Leane Zugsmith*    388

BEFORE THE DELUGE *by Otto D. Tolischus*    390

## Part VIII: UNITED STATES AT WAR

FROM THE WHITE HOUSE *by Forrest Davis and Ernest K. Lindley* 396

TOKYO: DECEMBER 7th *by Otto D. Tolischus* 400

MANILA *by Clark Lee* 402

MACARTHUR *by Henry C. Wolfe* 404

THE LAST OF THE *REPULSE by Cecil Brown* 409

UNCONDITIONAL SURRENDER *by George Weller* 415

JAPANESE GENERALS *by John Hersey* 419

THE FATE OF THE DUTCH EAST INDIES *by John McCutcheon Raleigh* 421

FAREWELL TO BATAAN *by Melville Jacoby* 424

WE HAVE DONE OUR BEST *by Carlos P. Romulo* 426

RETREAT WITH STILWELL *by Jack Belden* 432

NEW GUINEA *by John Lardner* 435

PANAMA PATROL *by Walter Davenport* 437

HONG KONG 1942 *by Gwen Dew* 442

CITY IN PRISON *by Joseph Alsop* 446

THE *LEXINGTON* GOES TO GLORY *by Stanley Johnston* 449

BATTLE OF MIDWAY *by Robert J. Casey* 452

MISSION OVER KISKA *by Corey Ford* 455

FIRST GUADALCANAL NOTES *by Richard Tregaskis* 459

HEROES *by John Hersey* 462

THE FIFTH BATTLE OF THE SOLOMONS *by Ira Wolfert* 463

FLIGHT TO GUADALCANAL *by Hanson W. Baldwin* 466

BUNA VICTORY *by Pat Robinson* 472

PT'S TO THE FRONT *by Charles A. Rawlings* 474

TOUR OF DUTY *by Walter Winchell* 477

ALEUTIAN CAMPAIGN *by Keith Wheeler* 479

TARAWA *by Robert Sherrod* 484

AUGURY OF DEATH *by Raymond Clapper* 488

## Part IX: AFRICA

BRITISH VICTORY AND DEFEAT *by Allan A. Michie*    491

HELLFIRE *by Frank Gervasi*    495

PRISONER OF THE AXIS *by Harold Denny*    498

TOBRUK LIBERATED *by Russell Hill*    501

ROMMEL IN TOBRUK *by Alan Moorehead*    503

FEAR COMES TO CAIRO *by Frank Gervasi*    506

MEDITERRANEAN FLEET *by Larry Allen*    510

ALGIERS *by John A. Parris, Jr.*    513

THE WOUNDED ARE WAITING *by Leo Disher*    517

AMERICAN PARATROOPERS *by Lowell Bennett*    520

BRITISH FIRST ARMY *by Ned Russell*    524

AND NOT A TEAR WAS SHED *by Wes Gallagher*    527

CASABLANCA CONFERENCE *by John A. Parris, Jr.*    531

GERMAN COUNTERATTACK *by Phil Ault*    534

THE PLAINS BEYOND GAFSA *by Ralph Ingersoll*    538

HILL 609 *by Drew Middleton*    542

WE TAKE TUNIS AND BIZERTE *by Frank L. Kluckhon*    544

TWO WORLDS *by Erika Mann*    547

THE NAZIS CRACK *by Pierre J. Huss*    552

THIS MAN ROMMEL *by Richard D. McMillan*    555

"THANKS, PAL" *by Ernie Pyle*    558

## Part X: THE INVASION OF EUROPE

DESTINATION: SICILY *by John Mason Brown*    562

GOING ASHORE *by George Sessions Perry*    566

BALANCE SHEET OF A LIGHTNING CAMPAIGN *by Ned Russell*    571

MUSSOLINI'S FALL *by H. R. Knickerbocker*    573

ADVENTURE OF AN AMERICAN REPORTER *by Aldo Forte*    574

SALERNO *by Quentin Reynolds*     577

IT WAS DARK AS HELL *by John Steinbeck*     584

REPORT FROM SWITZERLAND *by Daniel T. Brigham*     586

DEATH OF A LIBRARY *by Herbert L. Matthews*     587

POLITICAL STRATEGY *by Frederick Kuh*     589

BLACK EAGLE GOES TO WAR *by Edgar T. Rouzeau*     591

BATTLE OF VOLTURNO *by Homer Bigart*     594

THE SYSTEM OF ATROCITIES *by Reynolds Packard*     595

THE ALBANIANS FIGHT BACK *by Henry T. Gorrell*     597

WHAT THE SOLDIERS THINK *by Helen Kirkpatrick*     598

ITALY'S POLITICAL SITUATION *by Don Hollenbeck*     599

PLANNED DESTRUCTION *by John O'Reilly*     601

SIDELIGHTS *by Tom Treanor*     601

THE STORY OF THE PARTISANS *by Daniel De Luce*     604

TITO'S ARMY *by C. L. Sulzberger*     608

A DYING GUERRILLA'S TESTAMENT *by Louis Adamic*     617

EPILOGUE: HOW IT WILL END *by Herbert L. Matthews*     620

AUTHORS     623

INDEX OF SOURCES     658

ACKNOWLEDGMENTS     664

# ON CORRESPONDENTS

*by Curt Riess*

## I

EVERY generation discovers the world all over again.

In our time that discovery is no longer achieved by means of sailing ships or expeditions. Our world is being explored and discovered by physicists, chemists, mathematicians, psychiatrists, and to no small degree by newspapermen.

Only twenty years ago we believed that there was a definite solution to every problem of humanity, a way to settle each difficulty by applying one or another political doctrine or economic principle. Only a dozen years ago we believed that we were living in a civilized world which could never again fall back into the barbarous ways of the Middle Ages. All this was illusion. We know today that our world is still far from being the best of all possible worlds. We know that it is full of misery and injustice, we know that we will have to work hard to make it a better world.

Discovering this world of yesterday and of today is the work of newspapermen, especially of the various foreign correspondents of our time. Without them we would know even less about the world we live in; it would be even more filled with mysteries and would seem even more senseless.

Correspondents have done much more than bring to the public attention a great number of daily events. They have succeeded in seeing and reporting to us what was hidden behind the events. They have explained what caused the happenings and have analyzed the motives of the persons and powers involved. They have understood and made plain to us the inner logic of seemingly unrelated and illogical sequences of happenings and showed us their common denominator. They told all of us who wanted to read and to listen what was bound to come and why it was bound to come. They predicted the disaster toward which the world was rushing, long before it actually took place.

They knew and made it known to us—the millions all over the world who were not aware of the impending catastrophe, who went about their business as usual, their lives full of hope and worry, happiness and despair. The correspondents understood that it was not the "historic personalities" but these "little people" who really mattered, who were the real heroes of our time, though they were to be tragic heroes.

Somerset Maugham wrote of one of these correspondents, Raymond Daniell of the *New York Times*: "It is such men as this who are the ambassadors of good will. For by being what they are they show the people of the country in which they are temporary sojourners that notwithstanding superficial differences all men under their skin are very much alike."

Ambassadors of good will. And why not? Why shouldn't the men who discovered the world of the little people be the friends of the little people —in the countries from which they came as well as in the countries to which they were sent—and thus become interpreters or messengers of a sort, a connecting link? Ambassadors, and perhaps better ones than those who were professional diplomats. That, at least, was the opinion of Frazier Hunt, who in 1938 declared, "During the last twenty years the American reporter abroad has been a lot closer to the facts than the American diplomat abroad." And Secretary of State Cordell Hull, without going into this question, said shortly afterward that foreign correspondents are "part and parcel of the foreign service."

All this went far beyond their "assignments." All this was more than they had been hired for by their newspapers, magazines, and book publishers. They gave more because the variety of what they had looked for when they went out did not seem to tell the whole story. It did not seem enough to them because they themselves had changed during their discovery of the world. Or perhaps, while discovering this world they had rediscovered themselves.

The result of all these discoveries: the disclosure of many events which seemed unrelated, the unearthing of connections and relations between them and of the strange and sinister logic behind them during the last ten and twenty years, the discovery of the people who lived in this world and who go on living: all these things were presented in different forms: it might have been a short cable dispatch in the early edition of a morning paper, or an article in a weekly, or ten minutes in front of a microphone far away, or a book. Some of it was destined for the day and did not survive it. A lot of it was of value for a long time afterward. Some of it will live for generations to come.

## II

We in America know more about the world around us and what happens in this world than is known by people in any other country. We boast of being the best-informed country in the world; and, indeed, we are. And we are so used to learning everything which goes on, and learning it with such lightning speed, that we take it for granted. It is necessary to have been abroad in order to get an idea of the superiority of our news services. During the thirties neither in France nor in England (not to speak of Central Europe or the Balkans) were people so well-informed about what went on in their own country or threatened their own country as we were in America. The last crises in Europe before the outbreak of World War II —Hitler's invasion of Austria; the Czechoslovakian crisis of May, 1938; Munich and the events of August, 1939—were often withheld from the people whose lives they directly affected; or at least the real meaning was withheld from them for weeks, sometimes for months. There was nothing in Europe comparable to the roundup broadcasts on which we heard numerous foreign correspondents in different countries reporting and analyzing a crisis as quickly and as precisely as though they were delivering a blow-by-blow description of a prize fight. Nowhere in the world was there anything comparable to our news services and the foreign correspondents of our newspapers.

America may have been, then as well as later, full of what were termed isolationists. It may have believed itself isolated from the rest of the world by two oceans. In a news sense, in the sense of knowledge, America was the least isolated country in the world.

This is, of course, to the credit of our great newspapers, of our news syndicates, of our broadcasting companies, which literally covered the world. And this, of course, was only small-time coverage compared to what would come when the war began.

But even the most efficient organization, even the expenditure of countless millions which made such coverage possible, would not have brought about the results achieved, if the American foreign correspondent had not proved himself equal and superior to any task.

For the last twenty years American foreign correspondents have gathered the most reliable information and have transmitted it to us with the utmost rapidity. This presented difficulties which often could only be overcome by more than average courage, more than average imagination.

We are, perhaps, too accustomed to such accomplishments. Abroad they are admired and envied. The American correspondents enjoy enormous prestige with their colleagues as well as with the general public abroad. They are considered the best, the most honest, and the fastest in the world. Indeed, all this is such an old story that no American correspondent would touch it any more.

### III

News is something relative. What is news to one man may not be news to another. News is what you don't know.

People have always wanted to find out things they did not know. That is why newspapers came into existence.

The journalist had many ways of presenting his material. He could content himself with giving only the interesting story, the sensation. He could try to record the invisible, or at least that which is not visible at first glance, the idea, the causes behind the event. He could write with sentiment, or he could state the case unemotionally.

The approach the journalist chose never depended upon him alone or upon his good will. There are limitations. He is dependent upon his employer and upon the public for which he writes. And he is limited more than he knows by his nationality, by the fact that he was born and educated in a particular country.

It is a fairy tale that journalism is international. How could a writer born and raised in America ever look at any event or at any problem in the same way as, let us say, a man born and raised in Japan? Their historical perspectives are too different. The way in which their minds work is too different. Their ideas of what is good or bad, desirable or undesirable, are too unlike.

Furthermore, journalism in every country has developed in a somewhat different way: in every country there are certain forms and formulas which can be disregarded by none, certain recipes according to which the journalistic meal is cooked. The public has become too used to these formulas and recipes to stand for a radical change.

The German reporter *"erstattet Bericht."* He makes his report. That is the closest translation of the phrase. Note the military flavor. The expression was, indeed, taken over originally from military usage. And not only this expression but the whole of German journalism is somewhat military in tone. Or at least it is matter-of-fact. (There have always been German journalists who tried to avoid the matter-of-fact, but they were exceptions to the rule.) The military tone has become even more dominant during the last ten years. The man who makes his report is no longer the *Berichterstatter,* but simply the *Berichter.* This particular innovation on the part of the Nazis is a literal translation of the word "reporter," but it is a word which had not been used in modern German for more than a hundred years and which possesses an even stronger military flavor.

The French reporter *"fait un papier."* He writes a paper. The idea is that he writes something; or rather, practically anything. The paper consists of his impression of what happened—not of what actually did happen. The event as such is of secondary interest compared with what the writer saw and how he felt about it. French journalism went pretty far in this sort of thing. French reports on international political conferences written by well-known correspondents gave the reader the idea that the reporter had not been present to observe the statesmen, but that the statesmen had really come to chat with the correspondent. Accounts of the Spanish Civil War which appeared in the Parisian Boulevard papers went into minute detail regarding the correspondent's traveling inconveniences, the shortcomings of his hotel room in Madrid, the inedibility of the food he was forced to eat, and the dangers under which he had to live. The war itself was going on somewhere in the background, and the reporter didn't seem to care much about it one way or the other.

The American correspondent "covers a story." The very phrase indicates that he or his newspaper aspires to completeness. Every angle must be treated; everything having to do directly or indirectly with the event to be covered should be presented. The reader must feel that he was there, that he had a hundred eyes and ears and thus saw and heard everything.

American and English reporting have much in common. Perhaps some differences can be explained by the fact that the great English press has never been entirely independent of the powers behind the government. It falls down on its job of disseminating the news if the news tends to embarrass "influential" circles. Its complete silence on the Mrs. Simpson affair almost up to the moment of the abdication of Edward VIII, or its almost

xviii

unanimous approval of the Munich agreement—though English reporters knew better—are cases in point.

American newspapers are not entirely independent. Upton Sinclair criticized them and their methods severely in his book *The Brass Check,* believing that they "represent private interest and not public interest." Even he admitted, though, that there existed exceptions to that rule. I think that the American press's handling of world events over the last ten or fifteen years may well be termed such an exception. Almost the entire American press fought against the threat of fascism from the very start—something which cannot be said of the English press.

The decisive difference between English and American journalism, therefore, cannot be explained entirely by a difference in their ownership. It seems to me that it can best be explained by the obvious fact that Americans and Englishmen are different.

## IV

Curiosity, which was the beginning of all journalism, is still predominant in the American correspondent. America is a relatively young world, and the American reporter is the journalistic representative of this young world. Vincent Sheean wrote that during his journalistic career he was always dominated by "a feeling that I must hurry, that the world might perish very soon and I with it before I could find out what it was like." In Europe one is older, more cautious, and somewhat less curious. In Europe everything has already happened before.

To quote Somerset Maugham again: he writes about American correspondents in England during the first months of World War II, "They grimly said that the most imposing monument to the departed that would be erected after the war would be that of the correspondents who had died of boredom at Dover."

The American correspondents were, indeed, impatient during the phony war. They wanted the war which they had been sent there to report to begin. When it started, they jumped into it without regard to personal danger. They could not understand that a reporter could feel differently, and they had only scorn for their more cautious colleagues. They resented those who preferred a more conservative *modus operandi,* as, for instance certain Swedish correspondents who thought it enough to describe the Norwegian campaign from safe places behind the front—and who missed the real story completely. They preferred safety to finding out "what it was like."

The American wants to find out for himself what everything is like. That is why he wants to be on the spot, wants to be as near the event as he can, wants to cover it from every angle.

Leland Stowe's wife knew it well. When her husband was about to leave to report on World War II, she remarked resignedly: "Of course you have to go. You'd be miserable staying home and reading about it."

Many American foreign correspondents have come up the hard way. Most of them started where most American newspapermen start: on the sport page. It may be admitted that a man may know a lot about a right hook or a curve and still not know anything about foreign politics. But one thing is certain: he can write about a curve only if he *sees* it. And it is not very easy to *see* a curve, or a right hook, or, as a matter of fact, anything which happens in sports. This has to be learned. Once the reporter has learned it, once he has learned to keep his eyes open and see what's going on, it is not likely that he will ever overlook anything, no matter whether it has to do with sports or politics or economics.

The American reporter was able to see what he went out to see. Again one must have had experience abroad, one must have made the acquaintance of journalism in other countries, in order to know how many newspapermen have been traveling all over the world and still have not seen what happened before their very noses, because they had never learned to see.

The accent, then, was on seeing. And, naturally, reporters in general and foreign correspondents in particular vied with each other to see more than their rivals, to see better stories than their rivals, to discover the unexpected, the unbelievable. Thus, American reporting, and especially American foreign reporting, developed to a point where the unexpected, the unbelievable, the sensation, became the main objective. And, of course, before a sensation could be reported, it had to be discovered.

The American foreign correspondent thus went out in search of the sensation. A figure who was representative of this fad (I oversimplify intentionally) was Richard Harding Davis, who among other things reported the Spanish-American War, the South African War, the Russo-Japanese War, and World War I. He was never one to be much interested in the causes behind these events or in political and economic problems. He was principally interested in the events themselves; that is, in action, which he described in colorful and exciting language.

A reporter (or a generation of reporters) looking for sensations progressed almost automatically to creating them, putting himself right in the midst of adventure and danger. Precisely that was done by Richard Harding Davis and even more by Floyd Gibbons. Thus the reporter, who up to that time had only been the means to an end, himself became the end of the story. He who had been going to so much trouble to get the story now became part of the story, or in some cases the whole story.

The latest representative of this species was, though involuntarily, the young Vincent Sheean who went out to find Abd el Krim in 1925. By no means did he search out Abd el Krim because he was looking for danger, but because it seemed pertinent to him, in face of the unreliable French and Spanish reports on the Riff situation, to get that man's point of view. However, the accounts of that trip became enormously successful mainly because they were written under dangerous circumstances. The reporter's employers were somewhat disgruntled when later Vincent Sheean sent articles giving a thorough analysis of the Chinese revolution, written in the relative security of a Hankow hotel room. They immediately cabled him, "What we expect of you is something quite different and we want you now to have personal adventures."

Notwithstanding the fact that the American foreign correspondent has for some time given up the adventure and sensation story, the popular idea of the foreign correspondent is still that he is a daredevil, always in trouble, less concerned with finding news and transmitting it than with making news himself.

The foreign correspondent in fiction and in the films is less often drunk than the local reporter in books and movies, less badly educated and less obnoxiously dressed. On the other hand his achievements are even more colossal. He has truck only with ministers or prime ministers (while the real foreign correspondents are lucky if they get near one of the secretaries of the propaganda ministry or an employee of an information bureau). Wherever he appears, hell breaks loose. He immediately takes a hand, and he prevents important international crimes or thwarts international conspiracies. We do not dare imagine what would happen if he didn't appear in the nick of time. Important plans would undoubtedly be stolen by an "enemy power." There would be international complications: at least revolutions, probably wars—not to speak of political assassinations and kidnapings of prominent personalities.

It is not quite that way in reality.

If you look over articles and books regarding the activities of American foreign correspondents between 1930 and 1940, you might even at first get the impression that they led an easy, comfortable, and almost luxurious life. At first glance you might think that they never moved out of the luxurious grand hotels all over the world.

They were sitting in the Hotel Breidenbacher Hof in Duesseldorf while the French moved into the Ruhr, and in the Majestic Hotel in Shanghai while the Chinese started their revolution. They were at the Majestic in Barcelona when Franco waged his war against Spanish democracy, and in the Basque Hotel Imatz in Hendaye when that democracy collapsed. They shifted to the Hotel Bristol in Vienna when Hitler's gangsters forced the Jews there to wash the streets, and to the Alkron Hotel in Prague when Mr. Chamberlain sold, nay, gave away the Czechs. They were in the Hotel Europeiski in Warsaw when the Germans invaded Poland, and in the Ritz in Paris when Hitler mounted the Eiffel Tower. They lived in the Athénée Palace in Bucharest when German tourists invaded the Balkans, and in the Grand Hotel in Oslo when Norway was betrayed.

In fact, hotels played such a large role in the lives and reports of foreign correspondents during the twenties and thirties that after the outbreak of World War II, H. L. Mencken made a point of hailing the arrival of a new correspondent—Daniel De Luce of the Associated Press—who camped and lived with the troops and not in hotels.

But even so, these hotel-room correspondents often were in danger of sudden death, even while the "peace in our time" still held. Dorothy Thompson, for instance, slipped into Poland in an evening dress in order to report on Pilsudski's *coup d'état* in 1926, and she came out alive only because she refused to pay a ransom price for the taxi which other journalists had rented to drive them to Warsaw. The taxi and its passengers later were found riddled by bullets.

And in the Spanish Civil War many American correspondents risked their lives almost daily. They did not do so because it seemed glamorous to them, not as an end in itself, not to make a story by getting into danger and out of danger again, but because risk was concomitant with getting the story, a story which was bigger than the one of personal danger. They no longer needed to search for adventure. Rushing from peace conferences to general mobilizations, from revolutions to pogroms, they became eyewitnesses to world history in the making.

## V

To write the story of these last twenty years was difficult enough even when the correspondents chose (wherever they could choose) not to get involved in dangerous situations for the sake of good copy.

Before World War I life had been easy for most American foreign correspondents. Almost everywhere their main task had been to report on Americans who happened to visit the station of their assignment. Such reporting could be done easily by covering the more luxurious hotels. The fruit of such labor consisted mainly in columns of gossip. The correspondents whose newspapers had the ambition to be informed politically got most of their news from local newspapermen or—and this recipe was quite popular —by attending teas given by ladies of the diplomatic corps.

After the war all this was out. After the war the world changed completely. The news that a famous or wealthy American had arrived in or from any given country was no longer the most important news. The accent now was on difficult problems of a political, social, and economic nature. Correspondents who wanted to understand what was going on could not depend on their ability to converse with ladies of the diplomatic corps. They had to work hard to understand the world which grew from the ruins of the First World War and which was being shaken by strange convulsions.

The world during these last twenty years was full of mysteries and secrets. Who knew what precisely went on? Most governments didn't even know what went on in their own country, let alone in other countries. Even the best intelligence services failed miserably. In every second country revolutions and counterrevolutions were in the offing. Conspiracies bloomed everywhere. The steadily rising scale of unemployment and depression, and the increasing despair among the people, made insecurity the only factor on which a foreign correspondent could rely securely. It was a world full of secrets, a world which wanted to keep those secrets, which guarded them jealously against inquiring correspondents, which went to great pains to prevent them from exercising their profession.

Needless to say, Japanese officials or certain members of the Weimar republican government, and even such French leaders as Minister Georges Bonnet, went out of their way to prevent foreign correspondents from seeing what really went on. Dr. Goebbels went much further. He understood that foreign correspondents, especially the Americans, were not exactly in favor of National Socialism, and he did everything possible to undermine their standing in the eyes of the world. He started systematically to disseminate false news. In many cases he did it via one of the little countries of Europe. When the correspondents used such news, he proceeded to tell the world that they were liars.

From 1935 on, American journalists in Germany were almost completely isolated. Their German friends had, of course, long since fled abroad or had been put into concentration camps. A German who gave them information did it at the risk of his life.

The time came when Berlin hotels threw the correspondents out. Their telephone conversations were listened in on. Censorship became tighter. And there was an invisible or, rather, unofficial censorship which decreed that journalists found to be "indiscreet" could be expelled or arrested as spies.

Once, shortly before America entered the war, a group of foreign newspapermen wanted to visit a German munitions factory where an explosion had taken place. They were viewed with suspicion, and it was suggested that they might be spies. When they showed their credentials as correspondents they were told: "That is even worse."

Soviet Russian censorship for a long time was handled in such a way that almost no story at all could get out. Thus the somewhat erroneous impression was created that everybody was happy there. George Seldes complained bitterly about it in his book, *You Can't Print That,* and said—this was in 1929—"It is not true that the people of Soviet Russia are happy or that the people of Italy are happy with their dictatorships." Many correspondents were expelled from Soviet Russia. The Moscow correspondent of the *New York Times,* G. E. R. Gedye, was recalled in the fall of 1940 because "obstructionism on the part of Soviet official news agencies effectually prevents foreign correspondents from sending out any news that matters." Things are considerably changed now—for the better.

From Italy a number of correspondents were expelled, especially those of the *New York Times.* Bud Ekins of the United Press was forced to leave only a few weeks after he had arrived because he had been bold enough to report on the state of health of the Duce—a matter which evidently was considered a military secret even in peacetime. John T. Whitaker (from the *Chicago Daily News*) was expelled with the somewhat original explanation of having had "access to too many highly placed Italians."

In France, once the war had started, foreign correspondents were almost completely stymied. Robert J. Casey tells us how he spent days and days filling out forms, having his picture taken, submitting to interviews, and getting nowhere. Quentin Reynolds finally was able to get to the front because he pretended to be the nephew of President Roosevelt and wrote out a cable in which he asked his uncle to intervene for him with the French authorities. (The telegram, incidentally, was sent by the French to the White House, where it must have caused some surprise.)

Neither was life easy for the American correspondents in China. After the Japanese invasion started, transportation facilities broke down and telephones did not function. News conferences with Chinese officials—up to 1941—brought few results. The censorship was extremely severe. Later, things eased up a bit.

At the beginning of the war in Europe, the American correspondents had to work under annoying handicaps in London. There, too, the censorship was handled foolishly, and the dissemination of news through the Ministry of Information left much to be desired. While the authorities in London learned fast, those in the Far East didn't want to learn at all. Military censorship there was in the hands of old Tories who tried to cover up their enormous military blunders by gagging those who wanted to report the situation. Correspondents like E. R. Noderer of the *Chicago Tribune* or Cecil Brown of the Columbia Broadcasting System were finally told that they would no longer be recognized as correspondents.

The Japanese knew, of course, just as well as the Nazis that the American correspondents would never fall in love with them. There was, according to Frank Smothers of the *Chicago Daily News,* a "thinly veiled hostile atmosphere" in which they had to work. The nearer Pearl Harbor approached, the less was that hostility veiled.

## VI

These, then, were the difficulties under which American foreign correspondents operated before America entered the war. Their lives were made difficult because they saw what happened, and they wrote what they saw. And because powerful men or cliques in all these countries, and often enough governments themselves, wanted to keep secret precisely the things they saw and wrote about.

John Gunther wrote—in 1930—about the material at the disposal of a foreign correspondent in Europe as "news among the 600 million odd people who never get into print."

Since 1930 a lot of news about those 600 million odd people has been printed. For the American correspondents understood that it was those 600 million odd people in Europe and the 2,000 million odd people all over the world who were the main actors in the tragedy which was being played before their eyes.

And the American correspondents showed us the perplexity and the confusion of the inhabitants of this ever-changing world in which so many things happened for which they had not been prepared, in which they were thrown to and fro by unknown powers over which they had no control.

John Whitaker wrote about the little Italian soldier in Ethiopia who didn't know whether he should fight or not. Mussolini had told him to fight. His priest had told him that war was evil.

Maurice Hindus told us about the people in Prague during the time after Munich. Almost every day new maps would be exhibited in shop windows showing the shrinking frontiers of an ever-smaller Czechoslovakia. Passers-by would gather, stare at the maps in bewilderment, wonder. They couldn't understand what had happened to their country. Why was it steadily growing smaller and smaller?

Louis Fischer told about a scene in an English railway station. There was a man and his son. The father had been in the First World War, the son was now in the R.A.F. The father spoke about his experiences in 1917 in France. "It was sad to think that the generation which fought the 'war to end wars' and then fathered sons and daughters to live in peace was now fighting a second world war in company with those sons and daughters."

Leland Stowe told us how the people in Oslo reacted when a few hundred Germans marched in and took over. They just looked on, incapable of understanding what was going on. What should they do? What could they do? They were much too dazed to try resistance, though resistance would have been easy in the circumstances. The American asked a young student why he didn't join the army. "But I've never had any military training," the answer was. "I don't know anything about being a soldier."

Louis Lochner told us about the prominent Jewish businessman who had proved himself a better patriot in many respects than most of his "Aryan" contemporaries, and who, after Hitler came to power, was sitting in his office waiting to die. "And now they say I am not a German," he kept repeating pathetically. "I just can't understand."

They couldn't understand. It was too confusing. It was confusing even to people who were used to understanding everything and who wanted to "be intelligent" about everything. Clare Boothe sketched such people sitting and waiting in the Ritz in Paris during the phony war—they themselves didn't know what they were waiting for—extremely well informed and still not knowing a thing.

And when the last English correspondent had left Paris and the Germans were on the point of entering the town, French workers appeared at the Reuters office to paint it. Robert J. Casey described the scene. The painters who, probably months before, had been told to do the job proceeded with it. They didn't understand that it was a bit pointless.

The little people. They didn't know what was happening. They only felt that they were no longer secure, if indeed they ever had been secure. And they still hoped that nothing would happen, that they would be safe somehow from the impending disaster. They were hoping against hope that by some miracle they would not be touched, that they would not be destroyed, that perhaps while a neighbor's house went up in flames they themselves might get away unhurt.

## VII

In Austria they had hoped, till the very moment Hitler's troops marched in, that something would happen to prevent the Germans from coming and taking over their country; G. E. R. Gedye wrote about it. H. R. Knickerbocker reported about the last hours in Prague before the Pact of Munich became known, when people still wouldn't believe that they had been sold down the river. William Shirer and Louis Lochner told us about how relieved the man in the street in Germany felt, once the Munich Pact was signed, because for a little while longer the peace was saved. In Paris Dorothy Thompson reported that thousands of people waited for Daladier's plane returning from Munich. Daladier was certain that they wanted to kill him for signing away French honor. To his amazement the masses were jubilant. Anything, anything but war! Anything, as long as one could go on living as usual.

And then the storm broke. The inevitable happened. There could no longer be any hope that the disaster could be avoided. The suffering was indescribable. There were the atrocities against Jews in Vienna, and terror against Czech students in Prague, the extermination of the Polish population, the bombing of Rotterdam after the armistice, the strafing of fleeing civilians with machine guns.

Life went on. The war raged, but people had to live. Howard K. Smith told us of the average German in Berlin going on with his little everyday business while German armies proceeded from one victory to the next. The little people no longer seemed much interested, and it was difficult if not impossible to arouse enthusiasm among them.

War. What was war? Robert St. John wrote: "War today is that curly-haired girl in the hospital in Argos, Greece, whimpering in the dark all night because her right arm hangs in blackened tatters and she wants her mother who is dead."

What was war? William Shirer jotted down in his *Berlin Diary* that after the destruction of Maubeuge a soldier from southern Germany told him in a disgusted voice: "It was the Prussians who destroyed the town.... Always the poor people who get it."

What was war? Hostages were shot. Ships with civilian passengers were sunk. A weeping old woman in Shanghai tried to pick up from the filthy street the spilled rice which represented her evening meal and was run over by a military car.

In ever-growing measure the world became peopled with refugees. First there had been those who fled from Germany into neighboring countries. Then there had been those who left Czechoslovakia for Poland and the Balkans, and then there were refugees from every European country ... from Poland, Holland, Belgium, France, Spain, Yugoslavia, Greece ... all of them trying to escape the almost inescapable.

Countless stories about these flights all over Europe were written by American correspondents. Robert J. Casey described the flight of the French population only a few days, sometimes a few hours, ahead of Hitler's mechanized columns. Fear, panic, despair. Once he asked why everybody was running away. After all, Hitler could not possibly have every Frenchman murdered. The people who were questioned only shook their heads. How could they know who would be let alone? They could not be certain. William Shirer tells how the Belgian refugees returned to the ruins of their cities, resigned and beaten. The American reporters asked them questions. They didn't answer. Was there anybody left whom they could trust?

During the exodus from Paris somebody asked Vincent Sheean if he had observed the scenes around the railway stations. Sheean shrugged. He had observed them: in China, in Madrid, in Barcelona, in Vienna, in Karlsbad, in Prague.

Carl Randau and Leane Zugsmith reported (in the newspaper *P.M.*) a story about Jewish refugees stranded in Kobe waiting for a visa to go somewhere—anywhere. "A year earlier some of them had been refugees in Lithuania from German-occupied Poland. They were on the move once more. . . ."

Refugees. A whole world of refugees. A world which had become too small for these refugees.

But there were not only refugees. Not only people running away in fright and panic. Nor did all those who stayed on resign themselves to taking everything the enemy dealt out. War wasn't only fatalism.

War was also the Basque peasant, whom Leland Stowe described, saying good-by to his wife and children and walking away into the fight, turning a last time, and then marching on because he knew that there was no other road to freedom. War was a young Australian about whom Relman Morin told us, a chap who had a nice job in Shanghai and who had forgotten all about his homeland and who then suddenly enlisted. "I got to reading about the R.A.F. . . . You know, a few of those guys taking on the whole bloody German air force. . . . Yeah, it got me all right."

War was the awakening of the little man all over the world and his resistance against the powers that wanted to enslave him forever. War was the English who came back from Dunkirk for more, who could take it, no matter how often they were bombed, who never lost their courage or their hope. War was the beginning of resistance in France, the resistance of the little man who began to understand that he was not only threatened by Hitler but also by those friends of Hitler, no matter whether they were Schneider from Creuzot or Petain, Laval, and Weygand, no matter whether they worked for Hitler or for the ideas Hitler represented. War was passive resistance in all the occupied countries, carried out heroically by little people often without leadership. They did not need colorful slogans, they did not need big words, they did not make grand gestures. During the London blitz an American correspondent went to the Savoy to find out whether the band leader played "There Will Always Be An England." The band leader said, "We know there will be, without playing that song."

This was the world at war, described by American correspondents. This was the front of the little people. Wendell Willkie went around the world and then wrote that there was really only one world. American foreign correspondents knew it before, knew it without going around the world, knew it wherever they were sent. Vincent Sheean expressed it in one classic sentence: "The Ebro River is flowing down Oxford Street."

## VIII

"My duty is to speak. I have no wish to be an accomplice. My nights would be haunted by the specter of the innocent being, expiating under the most frightful torture, a crime which he never committed. . . ."

These words were written in 1898 by Emile Zola, the great French novelist, after he had decided to take up the fight for a man he did not know, a Captain Alfred Dreyfus convicted of high treason. They were part of an open letter to the President of the French Republic bearing the title, *"J'accuse,"* published by the newspaper *l'Aurore*.

Zola did not fight merely for a man who had been wrongly convicted. He fought for something more important. His cause was justice. "My nights would be haunted. . . ."

The past twenty years there have seen more than just one Dreyfus case. The world was full of crimes and injustices committed everywhere and the sufferings of little people. Dorothy Thompson commenting on the fact that most of the onlookers seemed almost undisturbed exclaimed that the world had lost the "faculty of moral indignation." The world had lost it because it was more convenient to keep silent. And foremost among those who felt it more convenient to keep silent were the European newspapermen. Zola had, indeed, few successors among them.

Aside from the newspapers belonging to political parties, which of course had to defend or fight for the party programs; aside from men of politics (Lenin, Trotzky, or Churchill) who used journalism in order to reach their political goal; aside from a few courageous outsiders, the European journalism that fought for a principle or an idea, that fought against governments or other powers or machines, the traditional journalism that fought for a cause, had collapsed completely, long before totalitarian governments made their appearance.

That collapse was perhaps most painful and most grotesque in the country where civil liberties were born, in France. French newspapers no longer held up any ideals for which to fight. They were either the property of very rich industrialists who needed newspapers only to fight for laws which were advantageous to their interests and against laws that were not, or to influence public opinion for other selfish reasons. Or they were bribed and bought by anybody who had money; for instance, by Mussolini or Hitler. But these briberies (they called them subsidies) were by no means practiced exclusively in the field of political journalism. There was almost no Parisian paper whose amusement page or sport page could not be bought, and this not at all in an underhanded way but quite officially.

In Germany, too, fighting journalism had almost completely vanished by 1930. And that in spite of the fact that the great German newspapers had risen to importance (toward the end of the last century) only because they had fought for democratic liberation and against reaction. But now they had become important, they had become too big and too fat, and it seemed to them a nuisance and undignified to continue the fight. The rise of Hitler must be blamed partly on the great majority of German liberal papers which, had they been consistent, should have fought him to the last. Instead of fighting him, they tried to compromise.

By 1930, fighting journalism in Europe had largely disappeared. There were, of course, exceptions, particularly in England (*Manchester Guardian*); but by and large the press tried to be cautious, to be considerate, to compromise, to appease.

This state of affairs may be blamed primarily on those who owned the newspapers. But 90 per cent of the writing newspapermen never protested. They just went along. They betrayed their profession, which had become great because it had been a fighting profession. They preferred to keep their jobs and remain silent.

In some cases they were bribed. In most cases they were just indifferent. The European newspapermen who covered the League of Nations during the twenties, who were sent to report on the numerous international conferences, all realized at an early date that peace and collective security were doomed because they were being sabotaged everywhere. Those newspapermen knew a lot about what went on backstage. And it sufficed them to know what went on; they were content to be informed themselves while the rest of the world was not informed. They never wrote the real accounts. They were guilty of embezzlement—embezzlement of news which they should have handed over to their public.

## IX

Tradition has it that the American reporter should not have a cause. According to T. Campbell-Copeland, who in 1889 wrote "The Ladder of Journalism": "the first thing a reporter has to learn is to keep his eyes and ears open and his mouth shut."

Still, it didn't always work out exactly as Mr. Campbell-Copeland suggested.

There was an American journalism which devoted itself to a cause at the beginning of this century. In a way, the muckrakers who revealed the corruption of American city administrations and police departments, who broke the scandals in the oil business, were the true heirs of classic fighting journalism. Such writers as Ida Tarbell, Lincoln Steffens, David Graham Phillips, Thomas W. Lawson, Samuel Hopkins Adams, and Upton Sinclair were the logical successors of Voltaire, Jonathan Swift, John Adams, Benjamin Franklin, Gotthold Ephraim Lessing, Armand Carrell, Ferdinand

Lassalle, Giuseppe Mazzini, Karl Marx, Georges Clemenceau, Theodor Herzl, Emile Zola, Leo N. Tolstoy, and others.

But in spite of the magnificent accomplishment of the muckrakers the recipe of Mr. Campbell-Copeland was still considered an excellent one by most editors and publishers. In regard to the foreign correspondent, too. Particularly in regard to the foreign correspondent. He was paid to see and hear things and write them down, but not to write down why these things happened. And by no means what he thought about them. No one gave a damn about what he thought. In September, 1939, the publisher of the *Chicago Daily News,* F. W. Knox, told his correspondent, Leland Stowe, who was leaving for the theater of war, "All we want you to do is report the facts, and we'll write our editorials here in Chicago."

But the American correspondents did not keep silent. They retained the "faculty of moral indignation" and they made passionate use of it.

Shortly before America entered World War II the Italian journalist Virginio Gayda told an American correspondent: "You American correspondents are much more difficult than European ones. They are all friendly and try to say the things that will improve relations between Italy and their own country, while you, you are ever the critics and the makers of trouble."

The American correspondents were indeed "more difficult" than their European colleagues.

This state of affairs became clear on the very first day of the Conference of Versailles, with the first story that American correspondents cabled back home. It became even more evident during the innumerable conferences that followed; for instance, during the one of Genoa in 1922, to which Soviet Russia was invited for the first time.

Among the American correspondents was the former police reporter, Sam Spewack. His complete ignorance concerning forms and etiquette made his European colleagues gasp. They were shocked that he did not know how a correspondent should behave on such occasions. But it was Spewack who saw the real story which they either didn't see or didn't care to see: the real story that the British government was determined to continue the war of intervention against Soviet Russia with other, more "peaceful," means; the story that the men around Prime Minister Lloyd George were less interested in rebuilding Europe than in Turkish oil. It was this former police reporter who wore the wrong kind of clothes on the wrong occasions, who approached Chicherin and Litvinoff and from them got the first news about the German-Russian Treaty of Rapallo, which was to change European history decisively during the following years.

The unmasking of the Conference of Genoa as an attempted conspiracy was by no means the last time that American correspondents unmasked European statesmen who occupied the stage, who acted as though world affairs were their own private bailiwick, as though world history would write itself at their direction.

American foreign correspondents almost equal G. B. Shaw in the art of showing up heroes for what they really are. What was Mussolini after they were through with him? Was he the great man who made trains run on time, who had made his country bigger and better? American journalists simply wrote about a tennis match which Mussolini played, or rather the few sets which he played, and reported that he had lost more than he had won. They described how he broke off the game and declared himself "proud to have won." And the American public saw him for what he was— a show-off, a vain man, a ham actor.

Ernest Pope told us (in *Munich Playground*) about how the Nazi big shots found recreation in the company of nude dancers, guzzling down wine and beer. And just by setting forth these plain facts he reduced the supermen to their proper stature and showed them up for what they really were: stupid, base, and brutal human beings who thought themselves invincible because they had not encountered any resistance.

Wilfrid Fleisher, Joseph Newman, and Hallett Abend described the military and political leaders of the Rising Sun as they were in everyday life, and they were no longer frightening. They were representatives of a small clique, of a tiny caste which believed that it could govern the world because it had not enough imagination to understand that the world extended far beyond their own horizon from which they saw the sun rising.

The American reporter abroad also showed us how small, how stupid, or how corrupt were the men who seemed destined to lead the world against the so-called supermen. They showed the English Tories, led by Mr. Chamberlain or leading Mr. Chamberlain, striving at any cost (which others were to pay) for peace in their time, peace and the status quo.

American correspondents found out, long before the actual collapse occurred, that the French Republic was doomed. They saw its doom as the logical consequence of corruption, treason, and cowardice among the political leaders. And they said so. They showed up Edouard Daladier for what he was, a man too weak to make up his mind, who preferred to get drunk at times of supreme political stress rather than to fight. They showed up Paul Reynaud for what he was, a man completely in the hands of his mistress, who was too stupid a woman to know what it was all about. They proved that Leon Blum was guilty of the death of the Spanish Republic because he dreamed while his opponents acted. They showed Marshal Pétain to be, not exactly a venerable old man, but a conspirator against the republic which he served at a time when the excuse of his being senile could not have been put forward—if, indeed, it was ever an excuse.

Shortly before Italy entered the war, the Chamberlain government tried one last rapprochement with Italy. It desired that this undertaking should not become known to the public, and the English correspondents obliged by keeping silent. The American ambassador in Rome asked the American correspondents to visit him and, without saying how he personally felt about it, transmitted to them the wish of the British government. The Americans, too, were not supposed to let out anything about the negotiations. The American correspondents unanimously declined to oblige.

They did not keep silent on that particular occasion. They never kept silent. They did not care if they were called tactless or indiscreet. More than once, and for more than one of the American correspondents, the temptation not to write everything he saw must have been rather attractive. Or the temptation to write what he did not see, but what certain people wanted him to write. His life could have been so much more pleasant.

But the American correspondents did not want to lead pleasant existences. Consciously they continued the classic tradition of journalism by reporting more than just what appeared on the surface, by examining the causes, by taking up their position in the fight.

X

Walter Duranty tells us that after having spent many successive years in Russia, he reached a point where he had become too used to what was happening around him to discover any stories which might be worth reporting. Only after his return to America was he again able to see Russian affairs with the eyes of the American reader. He decided then and there that he would never again spend more than two years in succession in any one country.

Duranty's experience is not unusual. All foreign correspondents at one time or another have left the United States for some foreign assignment, and of course their point of view, their mentality at the time, was a hundred per cent American. Everything they saw in the beginning seemed strange, astonishing, and exciting. But after having spent some time abroad, many of them got used to the strange new things, which no longer seemed astonishing but instead became matters to be taken for granted. America and American readers receded farther and farther away from them. Time became distance. It happened almost automatically.

But even when they returned to the United States after a certain period, as Duranty did, even when they changed the scene of their activity from time to time, even if they never lost contact with America and if they never became quite at home in the country of their assignment, something strange and almost indescribable had happened to most of them. They were no longer at home anywhere. They had become eternal travelers far beyond the physical sense of the word. They had become small islands in themselves, situated somewhere, anywhere, between America from where they had set out and the countries in which they were stationed and about which they had to give an account. Where did they belong? To those back home or to those among whom they lived and about whom they wrote?

To none and, in a way, to both.

Lincoln Steffens wrote, toward the end of his Autobiography: "The world ... has changed me. It took a war, a peace, a couple of revolutions to do it, but it was done."

What Steffens said is true of practically every foreign correspondent of the last twenty years. They all changed. The sum of thousands of small incidents left traces which could never be wiped out. Those who changed perhaps did not realize it at first. When they became aware of it, they were astonished; they wondered, they became thoroughly upset, they began to think about themselves, and this self-analysis found its logical expression in their writings. They tried to find out exactly where they stood, and the only way writers can find out is by writing about it. A number of books were thus written, books which were supposed to be chronicles of what had gone on around the correspondent, but which also—or perhaps foremost—became accounts of what had gone on inside the correspondent. In this category belong *The Autobiography of Lincoln Steffens, Personal History,* by Vincent Sheean, *Men and Politics* by Louis Fischer, the books of Walter Duranty, Robert J. Casey, G. E. R. Gedye, Leland Stowe, Ray Brock, Robert St. John, and to a certain degree those of Quentin Reynolds.

## XI

Trying to find out exactly where they stood was not a tactless attempt to push their own personalities into the foreground. The confessions of American correspondents only served to clear up the enormous confusion of the many ideas, the political and economic doctrines fighting for recognition all over the world, by projecting them into the mind of a living witness—into the mind of the correspondent himself. Thus the ideas, the trends, the leading forces behind the events became visible, were clarified far beyond their incidental and accidental occurrence in actual events. Instead of giving only the actual facts, which in the last analysis would have constituted merely a résumé of unrelated photographs, the reporters gave us a panorama, a comprehensive aspect of affairs, a high relief.

Thus, the attempt of the reporter to find out where he stood, his crusade in search of his own soul, became—in its very translation into words, in its very transcription into pictures—a sounder, because less accidental, portrait of our time than a purely mechanical photograph, a bald enumeration of events, could have been.

How far could he go in thus rearranging reality for the purpose of making it truer than the truth? There is no doubt that it is permissible to cut out accidental happenings if they are not true reflections of what is behind them. May the reporter also add? Can he tell a story even if, by chance, he has not been a witness of the particular event? In a word, can he be allowed to tell the story he has to tell as though he had been the ideal spectator, always present when something important (because significant) took place?

Here the correspondent goes far beyond corresponding, the reporter far beyond reporting. He forms as an artist forms. He substitutes for the endless summary of seemingly fortuitous events something which has continuity. The accidental testimony is replaced by a survey organically developed. Is this permissible? The inner truth, the inner necessity of the account, becomes the only criterion of whether the writer has changed or colored the reality arbitrarily or has pictured a reality truer than the one which happened to become fact. Or, as Anatole France put it: "To write history ... requires imagination."

Lincoln Steffens, I think, was wrong when he said, "My writing is not important ... and finding out things is very important." He was wrong because only through his writing, through the reflection of what he saw in his mind, did we, the public, "find out" what we never could have found out if he had given a photographic account of the process of finding. Great reporting is never photography of reality. It is, to borrow a phrase Emile Zola used to define his naturalistic novel, "a corner of life seen through a temperament."

Where, then, does reportage end, where does literature begin? Perhaps there are not always well-defined boundaries.

## XII

A writer who tries to find out where he stands (and, in a sense, this is the eternal business of the writer) will always attempt to ascertain if what he writes expresses what he stands for (which, too, is the eternal business of a writer). This was something which many foreign correspondents wondered about.

Vincent Sheean writes about his own early journalistic development: "As months and years passed ... political interest deepened to political passion and I came in time to 'take sides' and have opinions, feel them as deeply and express them as violently as an amateur." That is how they all came to feel. It is by no means a coincidence that only a few American reporters who were assigned to the Spanish Civil War covered it on Franco's side. Whoever could choose from which side to cover it knew that he had no choice. He went where he knew he belonged.

Louis Fischer later described how, toward the end of that conflict, he talked with fellow correspondents, and how every one of them indicated what he would give to assure the victory of the Loyalists. Louis Fischer, who is not a man to make big gestures, thought that at that time he would gladly have given his life if, by his doing so, the Spanish Republic could have been saved.

He was not the only one who felt that way. Ernest Hemingway proved a true heir of Emile Zola when he jumped into the middle of the fight, risking his prestige, giving his entire fortune for a struggle which, as the American writers understood it, was not only for the Republic of Spain or for the Spanish people but for the future of the world.

The Ebro River was flowing down Oxford Street—and Broadway, too. There was only one world, only one front; and long before we entered the war, they knew that it was our front, too.

Was there still a possibility for the American correspondent to be impartial? A world was burning. Human beings were perishing in the flames. Was this something called neutrality still possible? To be sure, some of the American correspondents were still clinging to the illusion of neutrality. When Leland Stowe and Robert J. Casey in September, 1939, arrived in London they were still willing, even eager, to be neutral. They had some heated discussions with their colleagues H. R. Knickerbocker and John Gunther, who were convinced that America belonged in the war and that America should enter it without delay. A few months later Stowe and Casey were of exactly the same opinion.

*Only the Stars Are Neutral* was the title of a war book by Quentin Reynolds, a *Collier's* correspondent. Was there still something called neutrality? American reporters who covered London during the blitz knew that it was an illusion. A bomb doesn't respect a neutral press card.

Was there still something called neutrality? Joseph Grigg of the United Press covered Berlin at a time when his family was living in London, which was being bombed daily and nightly by the Germans. American corre-spondents who were in London during the blitz quite rightly felt the Germans were enemies. (And the owner of the Grand Hotel in Dover considered his hotel to be in particular danger because Hitler was aware that many American correspondents made it their headquarters.) But American correspondents covering Berlin were not upset by the R.A.F. raids, even when it meant danger for them. They were overjoyed whenever the British sent over a few bombers. Naturally, they could not say so.

And how much can a correspondent say? Walter Duranty, in a book called *I Write As I Please,* tells us that once when he was desperately ill he made up his mind to do just that. Later he found that he couldn't do it. "There are always limitations."

The most forceful of these limitations, perhaps—paradoxical as this may seem—is the correspondent himself. Or, to be more precise, his conscience. What, exactly, does his conscience tell the newspaperman? It tells him to write what he sees and hears. It tells him to write about it "objectively." But doesn't objectivity mean neutrality? Can one take sides and still be objective? And if one can't, how could the American correspondents be objective, since they could not be neutral, since they had convictions, since they saw the dangers, since they knew who was the enemy and who the friend?

Still, they wrote objectively. They reported objectively the terror regime of Hitler; they wrote an objective report on the pogroms in Germany and in Austria; they recorded objectively the bombing of Warsaw, Rotterdam, and Athens; they gave an objective account of a tennis match in which Mussolini participated, and of a putsch in Belgrade. And in every single instance, the clear, simple, objective report had more force, carried more conviction, was more persuasive than any editorial. The report itself became a condemnation.

# XIII

The American foreign correspondents were soldiers in the fight against the dark forces long before this war began.

They fought by warning. The record of their warnings is impressive enough to become part of the history of our time. American reporters abroad predicted almost everything as it came true, many years before it came true.

As early as 1933, the year Hitler came to power, Leland Stowe wrote a book entitled *Nazi Germany Means War*. Edgar Ansel Mowrer that same year wrote *Germany Puts the Clock Back*, predicting that the Third Reich would try to make the world revert to barbarism. He didn't think much of this wave of the future. Herbert Matthews, after having served as a correspondent during the Ethiopian and the Spanish wars, wrote *Two Wars and More to Come,* pointing out that the two wars were only the prologue to a world-wide conflict. Ralph W. Barnes said, on June 19, 1940, in a Berlin dispatch that a Russian-German war was but a question of time. Dorothy Thompson, Hamilton Fish Armstrong, John Whitaker, Louis Fischer, H. R. Knickerbocker, and countless others continually sounded the warning against Hitler and Mussolini, while Edgar Snow, Carroll Alcott, Relman Morin, Hugh Byas, and others predicted what Japan was going to do. If one looks through the correspondents' books written in the early thirties, if one glances at the thousands of articles that appeared in newspapers and magazines about what went on in the world, one finds them crammed with such warnings.

American correspondents proved better judges of the situation than the so-called experts. The flier, Charles Lindbergh, pronounced Russian air power worthless. The reporter, Walter Duranty, did not think so. The Chamberlain government believed that it could buy peace in our time, at least in the West. Vincent Sheean, Dorothy Thompson, William Shirer, and many others knew that it could not be done. Senator Borah insisted that war would not break out in 1939. G. E. R. Gedye, Louis Fischer, Frederick T. Birchall predicted that it would. Senator Wheeler and his friends believed America could keep out. John Whitaker knew that Lincoln's words still held true: *"We cannot escape history."*

But American reporters throughout those years were like the prophet in the desert. In many cases the home office was not exactly pleased by the alarming reports sent in by the correspondents. Sometimes, when the dispatches sounded too pessimistic, they were not printed at all. And the correspondents were accused of having been "influenced." Toward the end of the twenties, when isolationism was almost unanimous in the United States, some newspaper publishers became almost hysterical with fear that their correspondents would be "influenced." In one case—George Seldes tells it—a news syndicate sent to Europe a correspondent who could not speak the language of the country to which he was assigned, the idea being that therefore he could not possibly be "influenced."

The public, or at least a large part of it, invariably suspected "propaganda." People did not want to find out what was happening; they did not want to learn something they didn't know, because they did not want to be made uneasy; they wanted to go on with their wishful thinking, they wanted to be told that everything was all right and, reading it, say to themselves, "I knew it."

Free-lance correspondents such as Louis Fischer, for example, who wanted to write about something which according to their judgment would come to pass in the near future, would inevitably discover that the editors were not interested because the public wasn't interested. Dorothy Thompson, who never stopped writing about Hitler and against Hitler during the thirties, though she knew quite well that many of her readers considered this steady harping on one theme a nuisance, was finally denounced as a warmonger. After the beginning of World War II—in fact, during the whole twenty-seven months before we entered it—every reporter who stated his conviction that it was America's war, too, was considered a paid propagandist of the Allies. In many cases foreign correspondents had to content themselves with writing between the lines, not so much on account of censorship abroad as because they did not want to be branded as influenced, bribed, or agitating for war. As late as June, 1940, shortly before the fall of France, American broadcasting companies refused to let Dorothy Thompson and Vincent Sheean speak from Paris. The writers were informed that such broadcasts would not be considered "neutral."

The American correspondents all tried to warn us. And it was tragic how few listened to their warnings. It was their tragedy as well as ours. If we had listened, events might have taken a different course.

## XIV

Many American reporters abroad, knowing that the war was inevitable, wanted to do more than warn the people at home. It did not seem enough to them to point out the abyss. They wanted to do something about it. They wanted to help fight the battle.

Robert St. John, at the time a "neutral" correspondent in London, learned what had been done by the Germans to friends of his in Poland and Rumania. He decided it was not enough to write about it. He became a worker in a British munitions plant.

The last volunteer to join the International Brigade in Spain was the very young correspondent, Jim Lardner, son of Ring Lardner, who had been sent to Barcelona by the *Paris Herald*. Soon after his arrival he became pensive. He decided it was rather superfluous for still another correspondent to cover Spain, since so many older and more experienced journalists were already on the spot. He was by no means especially talented or equipped for soldiering; he was not physically strong, nor had he had any training, and he was nearsighted on top of it. At the time he decided to join up, the war was going badly for the Loyalists. The International Brigade was not accepting new recruits. Lardner's American friends, the other reporters, implored him to give up what they termed his foolish plan. But he couldn't give it up or forget about it. And finally he managed to become a full-fledged member of the Brigade. He had overcome all the obstacles, and he was profoundly happy. Shortly before the brigade dissolved, he was killed in action: the last American volunteer, the last American to fall.

Vincent Sheean has written Jim's Lardner's story. It was he, together with Ernest Hemingway, who had tried every possible argument to change the young man's mind. When he heard about Lardner's death, he could not help but feel that a valuable force had gone to waste. And it was the same Vincent Sheean who wrote in the spring of 1942: "The pattern of the associated effort by Russia, England, China, and the United States was becoming more real every day. The task of each man who believed in its validity was to contribute to it, each in a different way, each with the chosen instrument in the same general direction."

The chosen instrument. Vincent Sheean, who had tried to keep young Jim Lardner from joining up, volunteered in the American air force in the summer of 1942. He had made the same decision as his friend.

## XV

The war reporting of World War II became as different from war reporting during World War I as foreign correspondents in general after the first conflict had been different from foreign correspondents before.

World War I fell into the period of sensation and adventure journalism. Reading through newspapers and magazines between 1914 and 1918, we find a great number of disconnected stories: excellent reporting such as the piece by Richard Harding Davis on the German march through Brussels, or Irving Cobb's dispatches from the German front, or Floyd Gibbons' account of the sinking of the *Laconia* by a German U-boat. Life for most correspondents was "adventurous." Some of them were even captured and held as spies, though soon afterward they were released. In one instance American reporters even wrote a letter to the Kaiser. Ring Lardner was sent to Europe by the *Chicago Tribune* to cover the humorous aspects of the World War.

But there was no complete coverage. There was hardly an attempt at coverage. The stories obtained by the reporters at the front, in the trenches, had little connection with one another.

World War II brought perhaps not as many glamorous stories and certainly not as many scoops on the part of a few shrewd and fortunate lone-wolf correspondents. But there is a general coverage which gives the reader a fairly accurate idea of how the war is proceeding. This coverage is obtained by a great number of newspapermen who are assigned to the capitals of the countries at war, and whose job is not the mere collection of handouts but involves sieving them, establishing some kind of order and relation between important and unimportant news.

During the First World War there was an almost complete absence of the analytical type of article with its searching inquiry into the strategic, political, economic, and social background of world events. The war correspondents of that time were not prepared for that type of job. They knew little of military matters, not much about economic or political problems and trends. The foreign correspondents who came up after World War I, they who are today's war reporters, are well prepared to write the background story of this war, since indeed they have done nothing else for the last ten years before the war.

The decisive difference, however, between war correspondents of that earlier conflict and those of today lies in the fact that this war is a total war. During World War I the public, the readers of the dispatches, were sitting pretty far away. They were perhaps passionately interested spectators, but spectators nevertheless, who wish to be told exciting and adventurous stories. This war has no spectators. This war has only fronts, at home as well as abroad. That means that the war correspondents no longer have to entertain, they have mostly to inform. And they have to inform people who feel themselves part of the struggle. War correspondents have become intelligence officers who communicate news from one part of the front to another.

## XVI

For the American foreign correspondent, the war did not start with Pearl Harbor. Many were reporting on war long before: in Ethiopia, in Spain, in Finland, in Norway, Belgium, France, England, the Balkans, Russia. Now were added the theaters of war in the Pacific, the trips in the Flying Fortresses and on PT boats and aircraft carriers, the commando and task-force raids, the wandering through the jungle and the desert.

Cecil Brown said: "In the army if a soldier reports to sick bay when fever hits him he is hospitalized immediately. A war reporter, however, has no authority to report to but his own conscience. You damned near have to kill him before he gives up on his job."

This necessity to be on the job twenty-four hours a day every day perhaps does not lend itself to glamorous descriptions of the war correspondent's life. But it is nevertheless the hardest part of his profession. His, of course, is a dangerous profession as well. The war reporter wears a uniform but carries no arms. A bullet or a bomb can hit him just as well as the soldier next to him. To get his story, he must take many chances—and he takes them.

That doesn't mean that he takes unnecessary risks. "A dead correspondent sends no news," is a truth every reporter knows. He does not think of his profession in terms of high adventure as did his predecessor of World War I. If he goes along on air raids or commando forays, he doesn't do it as a stunt but because by so doing he gathers necessary information.

The risks that the former foreign correspondents—now war correspondents—have taken in this war, the dangers through which they have passed, would fill a book. According to official statistics (spring, 1943) the casualty rate among correspondents since Pearl Harbor has been three times as high as that of the army; they gave their lives to write about those who risked their lives.

Many gave their lives even before Pearl Harbor. There was Webb Miller, head of the United Press in Europe, who was killed in a blackout in London.

There was Ralph W. Barnes. He met his death when he took part in an R.A.F. raid during the Greek-Italian campaign. He was one of the truly great journalists of our time because he was one of the most conscientious. When he was assigned to a new country, he would arrive there with an assortment of books on the history of the country, its particular problems, the character of its natives.

Before he took off on his last fateful flight, his fellow reporters warned him that it was dangerous. For a moment he seemed undecided. He had a wife and children and after all, he would learn the next morning in any case about the result of the raid. Then he shook his head. No, he would not learn as much if he stayed behind. He could write a better story if he went along, if he were on the spot.

He was there, but he never wrote the story.

Almost identical was the fate of Robert Post of the *New York Times,* who took part in a bomber raid over Bremen and never returned.

There was Ben Robertson, who was killed in a clipper crash near Lisbon, and Melville Jacoby, who died in an equally senseless plane accident over Australia after escaping the dangers of Bataan.

There was Jack Singer of the International News Service, who was aboard the aircraft carrier *Wasp.* He took off in a torpedo plane not far from the Solomon Islands, wrote a blow-by-blow account of the air battle and the sinking of a Japanese warship by his plane. Soon afterward the *Wasp* was attacked by Japanese torpedo planes. Singer had repaired to the wardroom, and in the midst of the indescribable inferno he had started typing his story on the battle which was raging around him. A torpedo hit the ship, smashed through the wardroom, and killed Singer. Naval officers found the typewriter with the half-finished manuscript in it. Before the *Wasp* went down, they took the paper along with them and abandoned ship. When they finally landed in Honolulu, they wrote the rest of the story, to be published under the by-line of Jack Singer.

Then there was Byron Darnton of the *New York Times,* who was killed in New Guinea. In his last dispatch, printed on the day his obituary appeared, he wrote: "The correspondent in this war, unlike his predecessor of 25 years ago, can find manifold evidence that victory will be well used.... Young men who are doing our fighting are, to a surprising extent, thinking about the war's end. Not only in terms of getting back home to their wives and sweethearts and getting away from danger and discomfort. They are thinking also in terms of what kind of world we shall have after peace comes. They are thinking realistically.... The politician who preaches 'normalcy' at the end of this war will find some hardheaded opposition.

xl

"From the high hill near the airdrome a man can see his countrymen building with blood, sweat and toil the firm resolution that their sons shall not die under bombs but shall have peace, because they will know how to preserve peace.... It is stirring to see this change in attitude. It makes the dust all right, the flies all right, the heat all right."

This was the last story of Byron Darnton.

A life for a story. Is any story, are any number of stories worth a life? Are they worth the lives of the many correspondents who have been killed or wounded? The columnist Raymond Clapper went out of his way to cover parts of the Pacific theater of war, and particularly the great assault on the Japanese occupied Marshalls. He died in a plane crash. Was the story worth the price?

Perhaps the question is badly posed. More than just one story is involved. Major General Lewis H. Brereton said it as he handed over the air medal to Hank Gorrell, correspondent for the United Press: "His actions have been typical of the work of a free press fighting for a free world. On occasions like this, democracy has good reason to be proud of itself."

A free press fighting for a free world. That is what American foreign correspondents have brought about—as other Allied soldiers, and long before the others. Knowing for what they fight, fighting and dying so that we should know.

## XVII

In the newspaper business they say yesterday's story is no longer important today, and today's story will be dead tomorrow.

But is that true? It may be true for a murder committed yesterday, a sport record established today. But are there—among the political and military developments of the last ten or twenty years—any stories which could be termed yesterday's or today's?

It seems to me rather that there is only one story which was broken off yesterday, which will be broken off today, which will be continued tomorrow.

Do we even know when this story really began? Do we know when World War II began? Was it on Armistice Day in November, 1918? Was it in Versailles or when the French marched into the Ruhr? Was it when the Japanese rolled into Manchuria or when Hitler came to power? When Mussolini assaulted Ethiopia or when Hitler took over Austria? One thing is certain: it did not start on the official date of September 1, 1939. And who can venture to say when it will end?

On any single day only a very small part of the story of World War II can be told and consumed. That does not mean that even this very small part was written only for this one day. It has meaning far beyond this day. It cannot be understood, even on the day when it is printed, without knowledge of a thousand small items told on previous days. It must live on, together with those other small parts, if only to clarify what will happen tomorrow, next week, next month, next year. Only when these many small parts are put together, assembled as in an enormous picture puzzle, can we see the continuity, have a true perspective, a real understanding. Even if some of the parts are still missing, we will have something approaching a true picture.

Thus, the story which made yesterday's deadline or a deadline some months ago or a year since, together with tomorrow's story and the one that will make the deadline a year hence—all this together will be history.

History writing is perhaps a more important job today than ever before. Future mankind will be studying the story of our time, incapable of understanding how it was possible for a handful of gangsters to come so close to throwing civilization back to the Middle Ages, how, indeed, it was possible for gangsters who played with open cards to get anywhere near disturbing the peace of the world.

The gangsters are perfectly conscious of the role they will play in the eyes of future mankind. Therefore they are using their present power in many attempts to influence future history writing; they have been busy falsifying records and documents.

But those who thus attempt to deceive posterity have not been able to deceive their own contemporaries. Even while the scoundrels were at the height of their power, the true history of our time was being written. To no small degree this has been and is still being done by American reporters everywhere in the world. They write history while it is still unfolding, they set down a day-to-day account important beyond the day and the deadline against which it is being written.

Ironically enough, it was a German historian—Leopold Ranke—who, criticizing history writing, in the last century declared: "I see a time coming when new history will be built up from the reports of eyewitnesses and the most genuine immediate documents." It may be assumed however that he hardly thought of American correspondents as eyewitnesses and aides of future historians.

## XVIII

This book attempts to tell the history of our time, or part of it, in the words of those who saw it happen. Those who wrote for American newspapers and magazines, who spoke over the radio, who put their experiences and observations into book form.

This volume begins, somewhat arbitrarily, with the time shortly before Hitler's rise to power. It ends ... it does not end, because there is no end in sight yet. This book, which is composed of stories written for the day, the week, the month, is to be continued in stories which will appear tomorrow, the next week, the next month. Its deadline is infinity.

There were hundreds of books from which to select passages, thousands of magazine articles, newspaper stories, dispatches, and broadcast manuscripts.

The entire material divided itself into many categories. There were stories dealing with only one particular event; there were stories dealing with a certain phase of our time; there were others dealing with the fate of certain countries. There were still others concerning personal experiences of the authors; and finally there were those that analyzed the trends, the political background, any one of the numerous problems of a particular country or of the world at large.

The guiding principle in putting this book together was to give something approaching a running chronicle of the last twenty years, and at the same time a representative cross-section of American foreign reporting. To do that, valuable material of analytical, reflective, and editorializing nature had to be dispensed with. Also a great number of stories which upon their publication seemed to be of great and lasting significance had to be cut out; they no longer were so important from the perspective of many years afterward. On the other hand, some stories which passed almost unnoticed when they first appeared took on new significance and, therefore, found a place in this volume. It may also be added that a few stories were included that were written not by professional correspondents but by writers who for a certain time and for certain reasons stepped momentarily into the role of newsmen. Needless to say, completeness could not be achieved within the limits of two covers. It could not have been achieved within the limits of ten or fifteen volumes. Future historians will write libraries on points only touched upon here. What was attempted here was nothing but a running account of the most important trends and events, in the very words as they were originally handed over to us.

The running story of our time, written while the events took place, written in all parts of the world by those who were there, by those who saw it happen, by American foreign correspondents.

The running story of our time—the unmasking of our time and of the sad figures which dominated and welded it and transported it back to the Middle Ages. The truth, the whole truth, and nothing but the truth. Will it serve only as source material for future historians? Will it only cause future generations to shudder and wince with disgust? Could it not be that it will make our sons and grandsons wonder how all this came about, will it not decide them to find ways and means to prevent its ever happening again? Will it not move them and fill them with compassion and chasten them and make them better men? The running story of our time....

Thus, these accounts lend a new significance to the dark days in which we live. Thus, they may help to create a better world, better because wiser through the knowledge of the unspeakable suffered in our time.

... And let me speak to the yet unknowing world
How these things came about: so shall you hear
Of carnal, bloody and unnatural acts,
Of accidental judgments, casual slaughters,
Of deaths put on by cunning and forced cause,
And, in this upshot, purposes mistook
Fall'n on the inventors' heads: all this can I
Truly deliver.

WILLIAM SHAKESPEARE, *Hamlet* V, 2

# THEY WERE THERE

THEY WERE THERE

*Prologue 1922*

# HOW IT BEGAN

### *by Vincent Sheean*

AS THE weeks passed and my exploration of the richly unscrupulous character of my landlord continued, I made acquaintance with some of the details of his business. The first thing he did in any city was to pay a large sum to the local Fascio. The Fascisti were then little more than a national organization of hoodlums. I knew nothing about them beyond the facts that they wore black shirts, sang loudly off key, and obeyed the orders of an ex-Socialist politician named Mussolini. Every town had its Fascio, originally a sort of club of ex-soldiers, men who had fought in the war. The Fascio of Venice (like other Fascii) made a practice of smashing windows, beating up old men, and creating disturbances in the street. It was this strange new form of banditry that the Baron regarded as more important than police or municipalities.

"But why in the world should you pay money to the Fascisti?" I asked. "What have they got to do with you?"

"They have everything to do with everything," said the Baron. "If I did not pay my two thousand lire every month to the Fascio di Venezia my windows would be smashed, my furniture broken up, and my roulette and baccarat tables thrown into the canal."

"Who are these Fascisti, anyway? What right have they got to interfere?"

"All the young men who have nothing else to do are Fascisti," said the Baron. "There are thousands of them in every city. They think nothing of beating people up, burning their houses, killing them, if necessary. They have some kind of idea about the government, too—I don't quite know what it is. But one thing I do know: they get money from every gambling house and brothel and cabaret and bar in the country. I've paid them a lot in the past two years."

I was diverted from my interest in the Baron's profession by this new discovery—that a band of young men in black shirts terrorized the country.

"It sounds like a form of the Ku-Klux Klan," I said. "That was a thing they had in America years ago. They used to murder Negroes, and they were never punished. Do the Fascisti carry arms?"

"Yes," said the Baron. "In Milan they have killed many people. They don't like Socialists, so they kill them. That is their own affair, but I wish they would leave me alone. *Ahimè!* Everybody is afraid of the Fascisti; the police and the magistrates are just as afraid of them as I am. But Venice is better than Milan. They don't kill people here, much. Sometimes they

3

give them castor oil to drink. It is not pleasant, castor oil. Madonna! I pay them my two thousand lire promptly on the first of every month, I can tell you."

The Fascisti became interesting to me after the Baron had told the story of his two thousand lire. They presented, on the whole, an unprepossessing appearance in those days. They were almost all boys, many of them dirty, ill-grown and without discipline or soldierly bearing. They were cocky and quarrelsome to the highest degree, loud of voice and eager for trouble. To see them hustling some unfortunate citizen who had displeased them out of the Piazza San Marco was not a pleasant sight. They were approaching the crisis of their existence, encouraged into hysteria by the appeals of their leaders; the March on Rome was near. Little as I knew then about their leader or his ideas, there was something ominous about a rabble army existing so boldly outside the law, terrifying the magistrates and possessing the streets. I had an idea that one fine day they would have to be suppressed by a strong government, and the suppression would not be pretty. That they would themselves—these half-grown boys from the gutters of Milan and Turin and Venice—suppress the government and the constitution, suspend the laws and abolish every principle of the democratic system, never occurred to me. I left Venice without a premonition of that not inconsiderable event, the Fascist Revolution.

# *Part One:* Europe on the Eve

JANUARY 28, 1930: *Widespread rioting occurred among the more than 2,000,000 unemployed in many German industrial centers.*

MARCH 15: *President Hindenburg accepted the Young Plan of reparations payments for Germany.*

JUNE 30: *The French evacuated the Rhineland, five years in advance of the time set in the original peace agreement.*

SEPTEMBER 14: *In the general elections held in Germany the National Socialists increased their representation in the Reichstag from 12 to 107.*

NOVEMBER 27: *The former Allies in the League of Nations refused to agree to anything less than complete armament for themselves, and complete disarmament for Germany.*

APRIL 14, 1931: *King Alfonso was forced to abdicate, and he fled to France. Spain proclaimed herself a Republic.*

JUNE 23: *Josef Stalin, Secretary of the Executive Committee of the Communist Party, outlined a new five-year economic policy for the Soviet Union.*

JULY 20: *A seven-power conference for German relief opened in London.*

## FEAR IN GERMANY

*by Bruce Bliven*

NOVEMBER 18, 1931—It should go without saying that no foreigner can come to a country and, after a brief visit, speak with any authority about the state of mind of its people. I think I am well outside this prohibition, however, when I say that Germany is badly frightened today. Government officials, native and foreign journalists, casual conversations with all sorts of people, the whole tone of the press, all bear witness to it.

What do they fear? Most immediately, of course, the suffering which they foresee for many of their people during the coming winter. Next, perhaps, the possibility of an attempted revolution by the Right or the Left, the Nazis or the Communists—though this fear is less lively than it was a few weeks earlier. They dread, more vividly than anyone in any other

5

country can possibly do, the possibility of another financial collapse and a repetition of the wild, unlimited inflation of the currency which once before brought such suffering. In the past, the Germans have clung to a belief that if only France, England and the United States would experience a unanimous change of heart, the troubles of the Fatherland would soon be over. They no longer believe so today. As matters stand this autumn, they feel that England and America have troubles of their own so serious that even if they had the will, they have not the power to be of substantial aid to Germany. They consider that they must in reality deal with France alone, and that she will drive a desperately hard bargain.

The grave troubles Germany has experienced under the Hoover moratorium have helped to clear the air regarding the influence of reparations payments upon her economic life. Heretofore it has been the habit to blame everything upon the exhausting drain of these payments, overlooking the fact that Germany's borrowings abroad have about equaled what she has handed over to the Allies. No one in Germany with whom I have talked has much expectation that reparations payments will ever be resumed, or at least, that any future payments will be large enough to be important. They also recognize that the era of large loans from abroad has come to an end. It is generally admitted that much of this money was foolishly spent on needless public works and on overequipment for Germany's industrial organization. The official explanation is that this was done to find work for the unemployed; but the real reason no doubt was Germany's determination to salt away a great deal of wealth in a form which could not under any circumstances be taken away from her. At any rate, she is now experiencing, like the United States, the headache of the morning after. Her banking system is operating in the narrowest margin of reserve capital; her people are hard up and able to buy but little; her foreign trade is suffering from the competition of England and the Scandinavian countries—which now have an advantage in costs because of their depreciated currencies.

It was fear which, in the opinion of competent observers here, was responsible for the victory of Chancellor Bruening and his government on the last day of the Reichstag session, in the middle of October. It wasn't that very many people had faith in him, although he is generally considered Germany's strongest leader and just now almost her only one. It was merely that there seemed no hope of doing any better with anyone else. The Reichstag will not meet again until the end of February, and the present government will therefore presumably last until then—unless there is a Communist or Nazi revolution in the meantime. And at the moment, as I have said, there seems somewhat less likelihood of either than there was a few weeks ago.

Germany is talking today, and very seriously, of two sorts of inflation. The first is involuntary, the result of being forced partly or completely off the gold standard. The second is "limited and controlled" inflation for the purpose of stimulating industry by an automatic reduction of wages, and the better to compete in foreign markets with the countries which have

6

lately devaluated their currency. Very few people at present seem to believe that Germany will be able to remain on the gold standard, unless perhaps the situation is saved by a sudden and drastic improvement in world business conditions. The flight from the mark continues, and despite every sort of new rule in regard to it, the leaks go on. Actual gold and jewels are smuggled out of the country. German securities owned abroad are sold there and the proceeds do not come back. "Dollar bonds," of which there are large amounts outstanding in Germany, are sent abroad to be sold. Perhaps most important of all, exporters leave their profits in the countries where they have been earned.

Germany's very large "favorable" trade balance in recent months actually is not a sign of health, but the flush of fever. It means that Germans cannot afford to buy foreign goods, thus curtailing imports, and that exporters, as just mentioned, are leaving their profits outside Germany, despite the drastic penalties levied against those who are caught doing this. Sufficient proof that this is the case is found in the ironical fact that this "favorable" balance comes at the very moment when the nation's gold resources are dwindling so ominously.

Despite the dark future in Germany, there is very little change in at least the surface conditions of life. Germans have gone through so much in the past seventeen years that they have learned to enjoy themselves while they may; if your money is in danger of becoming worthless tomorrow, why not spend it tonight? The cost of living in Berlin is almost as high as in America, with the exception of a few items, yet cafés, theaters and other places of public assemblage find an astonishing number of patrons, not merely among foreigners or profiteers, but among the solid German bourgeoisie. In a huge popular café on a Sunday night, the crowd was so great that it was almost impossible to get in or out. The streets are filled with privately owned automobiles; the pedestrians look no more shabby or depressed than an equal number of persons in New York. These casual surface observations, to be sure, are almost valueless in themselves; but they would have great significance if they tended in the other direction.

The saddest sight I have seen in Berlin was one which was not regarded by its active participants as in the least gloomy. On a rainy midnight, walking down an empty street near the Brandenburger Tor, I heard far away the unmistakable clatter of military hobnails on hard pavement. They came two abreast in the uniform of Hitler's Nazis—mere children, boy scouts who looked to be not more than sixteen or seventeen on the average and certainly could not have been more than twenty. There were hundreds of them, very proud and cheerful, stepping briskly along on their way to the mass demonstration next day at Brunswick, where 100,000 of them marched for six and one-half solid hours past their leader (and afterward went and killed three workingmen and beat some seventy more). The Nazis have no real plan, as I have said; their philosophy is madness, their mental horizon is that of the Ku Klux Klan, an organization which, indeed, they strikingly resemble in several ways. Yet despite their sterility and de-

7

spair, the Nazi leaders have managed to kindle some sort of spark in the breasts of these young Germans so that here they were, marching at midnight in the rain, joking in undertones like any other boys the world over.

Within a few months, there is an excellent chance that some of the boys who marched past me will be dead, spitted on French or Polish bayonets in a hopeless, suicidal war of Hitler's making, or shot by German government troops in the course of an attempted revolution. Many of these boys were only two or three years old when the Great War began; few of them could have been more than seven when it ended. The experience of those terrible years means nothing to them. All that blood was shed, all that misery was endured, in vain, at least in so far as there was any effort to prevent similar experiences for these boys and the many millions of others who, throughout the world, are today wearing military uniforms for one reason or another. Looking at these youngsters marching, these seemed to me sad thoughts. But then, perhaps I am sentimental.

# THE ROAD TO HITLER

## by Louis Fischer

HOW did Hitler come to power in Germany? Hitler's policy, at home and abroad, has always been to reveal his plans. Hyper-suspicion of propaganda, however, led many people to doubt what he said. The Nazis boasted that they would rule Germany, and Hitler painted a picture of his future game. "Heads will roll," he said. He would destroy democracy. Yet democracy tolerated him and helped him take office in order to destroy democracy. This peaceful death of German democracy is one of the strangest chapters in history, and it is of special interest because the suicidal propensities of democracy are not uniquely German. German democracy marched to its grave with eyes wide open, and singing, "Beware of Adolf Hitler."

Democracy is temperate. Its foe is extremism. In Germany, extremism was the thermometer of a sick social system and an ailing economy. The two extremes in Germany were the communists and the Hitlerian National Socialists—the Nazis. Both fought democracy and urged dictatorships.

The voting strength of the Communists and Nazis rose and fell with bad business and unrest. In the elections of May, 1924, the Nazis won thirty-two seats in the Reichstag. But in December, 1924, the domestic calm following the adoption of the Dawes reparations plan reduced the Nazis to fourteen. In May, 1928, they had only twelve.

The Communists had sixty-three Reichstag deputies in May, 1924, but only forty-six in December, 1924, and fifty-four in May, 1928. Came the 1929 economic crisis. On September 14, 1930, the Nazis went up to one hundred and seven seats, the Communists to seventy-six. These polls were the temperature of the patient, Democracy.

What shook and finally upset the German Republic was the struggle for stability. The German craved stability because he liked it and lacked it. More than most people the German enjoys discipline. He prefers the calculable. I was in a Berlin barber shop one day and heard the barber ask a square-headed Prussian customer how he wanted his hair cut. "Make it two millimeters in the back and four in the front," the Prussian replied. Meticulousness is congenial to the German. President Hindenburg was shaved every day for forty years by the same barber who came each morning at the same minute, stayed the same length of time each day and departed at the same tick of the clock. Germany is a country of straight lines. I have flown over it many times. The scene from the plane is usually one of geometric form. Nature is occasionally permitted to add soft curves. Every patch is carefully tilled, every hedge neatly trimmed. (So different from the rambling English countryside.) German forests and woods look like painfully tended parks. No fence may be nonchalant. Everything wild is tamed by man—except man himself.

Life on a given territory does mold national character, and Germans in the between-wars era were nervous, uncertain, and tired, and they yearned more than ever for a strong hand to guide them. In the relatively tranquil years—1925 to 1930—President Hindenburg, dull and stolid, with flat-topped head and very broad shoulders, towering above all men around him, was a symbol of solidity, slow change, and loyalty to the past and the law, and he sufficed as a reassuring, stabilizing force. In the midst of the whirl of cabinets he stood still, the source of authority, the peg that held the whole structure. Behind him were the Reichswehr and the Junker landowners; the industrialists marched in step.

But in 1930 came confusion. The timbers creaked. Little pilots lost their direction and looked for some beacon to help them ride out the storm. Hindenburg was no longer enough, for he backed the Owen D. Young reparations plans and summoned the nation to unity behind the democratic Republic—for which "sins" Hermann Goering, Nazi, viciously attacked him. In time of turmoil, people turn to the parties of despair which aver that they have the only solution and that it lies in new men, new methods, new institutions. This seems logical to those who are suffering from the failure of the old. Mounting difficulties thus proved to be wind in the sails of the Communist and Nazi extremists.

On March 6, 1930, bloody riots of unemployed took place in Berlin. The next day Reichswehr Minister Groener issued a decree prohibiting Nazi cells in the army. On March 19, the Reichstag passed a law providing for fines on persons who insulted the Republic, the Republican flag, or the Republican government. On March 27, the cabinet of Chancellor Hermann Mueller resigned, chiefly because it lacked Parliamentary support to enact the federal budget. Three days later Heinrich Bruening was appointed Chancellor in Mueller's place.

Bruening was forty-five when he became head of the German government. He was a conservative Catholic. He concentrated on financial problems that brooked no delay, and was apparently too busy to see or to cope with the tremendous changes taking place in German life. He was stern, matter-of-fact, and honest. Those are important virtues, but they did not constitute adequate equipment to ride the German storm.

Chancellor Bruening faced a new budget deficit on July 1. His attempts to cover it by additional taxation found no Reichstag majority. He thereupon warned Parliament that under Article 48 of the Weimar Constitution, the President of the Republic could decree emergency legislation without a Reichstag majority.

Now the fun—and disaster—begin!

On July 16 Hindenburg issued a presidential edict providing fresh sources of revenue. Within forty-eight hours the Social Democratic Party, resenting this attack on parliamentary government, moved a resolution in the Reichstag to annul the President's decree. The motion passed by 236 to 221 votes. Who voted for it? The Nazis, Communists, and Nationalists—all enemies of parliamentary democracy. They were glad to intensify the political confusion. Bruening then persuaded Hindenburg to disband the Reichstag and order new elections. This is just what the Nazis wanted.

In July the government of the state of Prussia issued an order prohibiting its officials from joining Nazi or Communist organizations. This was a wire stretched across a torrent. During the months of July, August, and September, Germany seethed with an ugly election campaign filled with recrimination, violence, threats of dictatorship, and avowals of patriotism.

Fifteen parties participated in the national elections of September 14, 1930. Ten of them won fewer than 30 seats in the Reichstag. The remaining five fared as follows: the Social Democrats dropped from 153 to 143; the Nationalists dropped from 73 to 41; the Catholic Center rose from 62 to 68; the Communists jumped from 54 to 76, and the Nazis polevaulted from 12 to 107.

The Berlin stock market collapsed. The world press was shocked. The Social Democrats promised to support Bruening as the sole hope of de mocracy. Bruening again became Chancellor.

At this point, I stopped in a bookstore on the Kurfuerstendamm and brought an armful of Nazi literature, including *Mein Kampf*. I found this Hitler opus wild, disjointed, written in bad German, and completely unimportant as a political book. It was important only because a man who now controlled 107 Reichstag deputies had written it—in prison.

The economic situation deteriorated with increasing rapidity. Factories in the Ruhr shut down. Capital fled abroad in fear of internal disorders. The government endeavored in vain to reduce prices. Employers reduced wages.

The new Reichstag opened on October 13. The 107 Nazi deputies entered Parliament in brown semi-military uniforms, marching in goosestep. Stormy scenes accompanied the election for speaker. Nazi Deputy Heines, known to have murdered political opponents, repeatedly played on a fife. A Communist deputy countered with loud whistling. Communists and Nazi legislators rushed at one another at frequent intervals. Newspapers referred to the sessions as "a carnival parade," and "a barbarian performance." Social Democrat Loebe was elected speaker.

On November 12 Gutehoffnungshuette, Germany's giant steel corporation, declared a ten per cent dividend. In 1929 it had a seven per cent dividend. Rheinmetall, another steel company, likewise announced bigger dividends.

December 15: 3,977,000 unemployed.

Throughout December a film based on Erich Remarque's *All Quiet on the Western Front* was being shown in many theaters in Berlin and other cities. Incensed by its pacifist implications, Nazis attacked spectators as they entered the theaters, smashed electric signs outside the movie houses, and threw stink bombs inside. Nazis paraded in uniform to places where the picture was being shown. There was so much Hitler pressure that the government finally banned the film. The *Berliner Tageblatt* wrote, "This was done not on the basis of the law but at the command of the street. This affair too proves that the only danger which threatens Germany is not the growth and mouth-heroism of Nazism but the flabbiness, the spirit of retreat, and the vacillation of the so-called 'bourgeoisie.'" The *Berliner Tageblatt* itself was bourgeois.

The disease was correctly diagnosed. The spread of the disease worried the doctors. But the plague marched on.

# WINTER 1931-1932

### by H. R. Knickerbocker

THE midnight moon in the Froebel Strasse stood high over the gas tanks, shed silver on the blocklong bulk of Berlin's Night Refuge for the Homeless. A lamp burned in the warden's office. Not another light showed in the building. Too late to enter.

It was no lark to spend a night as a homeless tramp in Berlin, and the exploration of the question "How great is Germany's poverty?" ceased to be amusing when the winter wind cut through my rags. Max and Hans and Otto and I hurried past long lines of barracks. In them were part of the army of Germany's jobless.

Today there are approximately 5,000,000 of them. The public treasury, the Federal Government, the States, the communes and the cities spend around $750,000,000 a year for the support of the 5,000,000 and their families and the 1,200,000 short-time workers who, earning less than the dole, are furnished the difference to enable them to live.

Through Berlin's famous "model slum" district we wandered. The streets do not look like slum streets. They are wide and clean. From the outside they are streets of luxury compared to the East Side tenement streets of New York. In the "Ruecker Klause," a tavern, music clanged loudly. A piano player beat the keys of an upright without a front; a violinist and a drummer belabored their instruments heavily. At the tables sat groups of hard-eyed youths and girls.

The girls snatched the beer from our hands. Nobody else had a glass before them on the table. A "comrade" came over and explained that this was a resort of fugitive reformatory inmates, all under age, all jobless, all, he declared, hungry.

In the "Mulack Klause" two old women begged our coffee from us. Further down the Mulack Street, in a refuge and inn for members of a smiths' guild, the back room was full of men, reading tattered sheets of newspapers or just sitting. None had a drink or anything to eat before him. A band of three musicians came in, a French horn, a cornet and clarinet. They blew lustily a pre-war military march, but when they finished nobody had a pfennig for them.

The Mulack Refuge had beds only for union members. In the "Zarowka," low-ceilinged cellar across the street from the Schlesischer Bahnhof, a squat, dark woman showed us beds. Five to a room, the beds were filthy, had no sheets. A mark—25 cents—apiece was too expensive. We moved on to the "Hotel Metropole," stood shivering before a dark hall until the porter answered our ring.

"Got fifty-four guests," he muttered, "eighty pfennigs apiece. See for yourself." He tossed us a key.

We climbed five flights of stairs, found room ninety-six, observed five beds, considered the bedclothes gray with dirt, noted a cracked jar, remarked it would be a good room for a suicide, and departed. It was 3 o'clock.

Before Max's dwelling he paused to show us where he had hung a huge red banner of defiance to the police the day the shooting started. In Max's kitchen, scrubbed, clean, neat, his wife rolled the youngest member of the household into the hall, and essayed to explain how she managed to feed her husband, her five children, aged four months, four, six, nine and eleven years, and herself on her husband's unemployment dole of 15 marks 35 pfennigs, $3.80 a week. While she made a pot of imitation coffee, she talked.

"First, what I have to take out before food: Max gets 85 pfennigs a week for tobacco. We have to pay 3 marks a week back rent; 70 pfennigs for gas; 50 pfennigs a week for installment payments on a sweater for Max, and 30 pfennigs a week for rent towels; 1 mark 30 for newspapers and 1 mark party dues. That makes 6 marks 80 pfennigs and leaves 8 marks 20 pfennigs —$1.95 a week to feed seven people."

"But why," I exclaimed, "why 1 mark 30, nearly 10 per cent of your income, for newspapers?"

"There is the *Rote Fahne,* the *Rote Post* and the *Arbeiter Illustrierte Zeitung.* As good Communists, we must read the party press."

This seemed to me the most remarkable example of several things. But most remarkable of all was the utterly matter of fact way she mentioned that out of an income of fifteen marks eighty-five pfennigs, two marks thirty, or 15 per cent went to the party.

12

"And how do you buy food for seven people a week with eight marks, twenty pfennigs?"

"Bread and potatoes," she replied. "Mostly bread. On the day we get the money we buy sausage. Can't resist the temptation to have a little meat. But the last two days of the week we go hungry. That is, mostly it's Max that goes hungry."

It is pertinent to observe that Max's unemployment dole amounting to a round sixty-three marks a month is, because of the five children, considerably above the average. According to the Labor Office, Neukoelln, the average dole received throughout the Reich by an unemployed worker with wife and child is fifty-one marks a month. According to this official source, rent, light, heat and indispensable incidentals come to an iron minimum of 32 marks 50 pfennigs a month. This leaves 18 marks 50 pfennigs, or $4.16 for food for three persons a month.

Until I undertook this investigation I shared the opinion widely held at home that the German dole provided a living for its recipients. It even seemed probable that a good many persons would prefer to live on the dole than to go to work. I also held the opinion that the Russian employed worker had less to eat than the German unemployed worker. All these opinions have been revised in the face of the observed facts in Berlin. The dole at its present level in Germany is not enough to live on; too little to die on.

# DEPRESSION

## by Edgar Ansel Mowrer

THE German people came out of the revolution in a great wave of democratic enthusiasm. "No more war" was the slogan of the hour. War, the sinister work of an ancient ruling class, now fortunately eliminated forever! The belief in a new social and political order took on an almost religious fervor among the masses. To be sure, the disillusionment over the Armistice terms, the Peace Treaties, the reparation burden, was considerable and bitter and there were some who sought to profit by the moment to restore the old regime—as in the Kapp Revolt of 1920. But the masses were not with them. Not the humiliation at Versailles but the construction of a new and better society and a fairer State was the preoccupation of the hour. Socialists, Liberals and even Conservatives really never doubted that this State would be "social." It would incorporate a measure of justice and mercy and wisdom such as never before had been seen on earth.

Germany had had enough of war!

There was a gulf between the generations. The old were conservative and patriotic, the youth radical and pacifistic. The astonishing Social-Democratic success in the election to the National Assembly in 1919 was largely due to

13

the votes of young people of the same age as those who twelve years later swelled the legions of the reactionary demagogue, Adolf Hitler!

Inevitably the Republic, that imitation of a resolute State, lost caste through its failure to get the war burdens lightened. That it tried to do so as few governments ever had, tried to the point of bleeding its middle class to extinction, was hardly even admitted.

Equally dangerous to democracy in Germany was the ambiguity of the revolution. In a material sense, what occurred was no revolution at all. The victors did not even disarm their opponents! But on the plane of ideas it combined two revolutions at once: a democratic revolution that took power away from the feudal agrarian, official and military castes and gave it to the capitalist majority; and a working-class revolution that, leaping over the middle class, poured favors upon the organized manual workers.

Thanks to the influence of social-democracy, the workers in "oppressed Germany" achieved a higher living standard than in "victorious France and Belgium" and furthermore, through the extension of insurance of various kinds, actually realized a high degree of economic security. Yet it is notable that this increasing share in the profits of industry was not made at the expense of capital. The larger industrialist combinations grew along with the increased wages; the entire economic life was dominated by a monopolistic set of trusts, groups, cartels and holding companies, the like of which had been seen nowhere else in the world. The Social-Democratic leaders, blinded by their Marxian dogmas, seem to have accepted and even approved this concentration of wealth and economic power in the hands of the few, with the idea that it led "inevitably" to socialism.

The artisans and small merchants and employees had always been the champions of what little democracy Germany possessed. But what could they do with a State that consciously—one might almost say, deliberately— planned their exploitation for the benefit of organized workmen and organized capital?

The currency inflation was the worst blow to democracy in Germany. The economic superiority of the lower middle class over the manual workers was hardly a question of superior education or wages; it lay primarily in the possession of some productive capital, possession of a house, investments or savings. This economic basis the inflation completely annihilated. A portion of the rich became richer, and soon afterwards the workmen began to improve their standard of living. All the farmers without exception fared well during the currency boom, but the middle class, the professional people, the educated elite, were reduced to potatoes and in many cases, to beggary.

The responsibility lay with the rulers who, on the advice of men like Hugo Stinnes more or less consciously committed the country to a hopeless policy of passive resistance to the French in the Ruhr, in the name of patriotism.

Now the German is a marvelous thinker, but he believes what he is told by his "betters." He was told that "foreigners" were responsible for the inflation by their cruel greedy demands on Germany; he was not told that the German leaders alone could be held responsible for their lunacy in trying to fight a more powerful opponent with the savings of the middle class, while allowing the large industrialists actually to profit by the fight.

Furthermore, the German does not habitually see what is before his eyes, which accounts for a great many of what are called his deficiencies in taste. When he chooses to see, his taste, as exemplified in show windows and theatrical settings—to quote but a few instances—is second to none. But habitually he prefers to think about matters rather than to look at them, and will gladly debate half an hour about the weather rather than look out of the window. Therefore when the industrialists and their hirelings told him that "Germany's prosperity" had been destroyed by foreigners and German Socialists, he somehow did not notice the castles with motorcars and the grand style in which the said employers continued to live in spite of their vaunted "penury."

The result of inflation was a sharp movement away from liberal democracy and toward patriotic reaction. In the elections immediately following currency stabilization, the German Nationalists scored more heavily than at any other time before the reactionary avalanche.

In the years between 1925 and 1929, when Germany was enjoying prosperity on credit, salaries rose steadily and foreign politics fell into partial abeyance. The foreign policy was in the Fulfillment Period and, with the exception of a few ultra-nationalists and their incredible press, chauvinism was low-toned. So long as public opinion could be canalized toward the pursuit of wealth, the latent xenophobia native to a proud, defeated people hardly appeared upon the surface of things.

But the Republicans were committing a costly error: by their policy of frozen wages and prices and their encouragement of wholesale mechanization of industry, they contributed to produce even during a business boom, a permanent unemployment not unlike the one in Great Britain. The chief victims of this situation were the young people.

These children of disorder, war and inflation, neglected by parents, allowed to grow up unassisted in a world with no sustaining certainty, needed the particular care of society. Instead of which, they, the tender, the unorganized, were the first victims of social readjustment. As they reached the years of activity, they found to their dismay, no places open to them. The young chemist, engineer, teacher, lawyer, doctor, specialist in any branch, even the artisan, found the road blocked by his father and elder brother. In the resulting cut-throat struggle for employment, the inexperienced inevitably lost. And the hatred of the disinherited swelled monstrously—hatred against the father (according to Sigmund Freud, the most fundamental of all hatreds), hatred against a social system that had no place for its young, a system that had accepted from the victorious Allies a Treaty that (according to the Nationalists) inevitably meant the castration of Germanism. Here was splendid material for political radicalism. Without the Versailles Treaty these young men would unquestionably have turned against the economic beneficiaries of the system and perhaps succeeded in eliminating them. As it was, with sixty per cent of each new university graduating class out of work

(March, 1932), with over half of all Germans between the ages of sixteen and thirty unemployed, with a dole system that favored the elder jobless at the expense of the (presumably) protected youth, young Germany was an easy victim for the patriotic demagogue.

A new group, the National-Socialists, had the clever idea of uniting the militarism desired by the *Reichswehr,* the anti-Republican hatred of the reactionaries, the anti-Socialist aims popular among the capitalists, with a new, generous, vaguely social fascism.

This group paid to the young that special attention that the State authorities should have given them. And it worked upon their still unformed character with all the art of high-powered salesmanship at the service of a so-called Nationalist idea. It succeeded in making them hate foreigners, despise the Republic and its liberal thought, and oppose organized labor, in the name of a higher patriotism. The older generation—the men of Ypres and of the Somme—had generally had enough of militarism; their ears were deaf to war legends. But the pacifism they had learned through awful experience became to their sons an object of scorn. Every people must be trained to arms —said the officers in the *Reichswehr,* most of whom were too young to have heard the explosion of an enemy seventy-five! War again became romantic, an affair not of blood and mud and excrement, but of heroic charges and glorious triumphs. After all, peace had little to offer these embittered lads. At worst, they could but die. "Rather a terrible end than an endless terror!" became their watchword.

Adolf Hitler saw the young Germans and won them to his banner, chiefly because he found them at the moment of their deepest material and spiritual despair. To their empty lives he gave a meaning, however meretricious.

Thanks to such a general situation German youth became dangerously Nationalist and the German middle class hysterically reactionary. Admittedly there were other causes than those enunciated here. The larger capitalists obviously hoped, by supporting the Nationalist-Socialists to stab to death the trade unions and annul the costly privileges of labor. The jobless princes and their monarchical adherents, all the born adorers of class and privilege, clearly sought, by their fight against the "treaty of shame," to creep back into their former place of power and undo the criminal "November revolution." The Army was obviously trying to strengthen militarism among the youth for motives that soldiers throughout the world will understand. But their success would have been questionable except for the fact of new and sudden poverty, nationwide, crushing, stupefying.

By about 1931, the need for a "strong foreign policy" and a truculent attitude toward France and Poland had become public property. Few protested against the inordinate political influence of the Army and the spread of its ideals to the civilian population. Pacifism, international concilation and cooperation, personal liberty, as ideals simply faded before renascent Prussian conceptions of autocracy (disguised as leadership), blind obedience, patriotic frenzy, militarism. An entire nation's youth began to play soldiery and they were encouraged and assisted by the various authorities, with the obvious intention of preparing a future when, treaties or not, the Germans would again become "capable of defence"—ready, trained, not for the stern heroic tasks of human progress (a conception at which these new Germans merely laughed), but for the task of collective sacrifice to national vainglory.

In such an atmosphere the maintenance of the democratic Republic was obviously superfluous. Germany followed the band.

\* \* \*

BERLIN, Jan. 30, 1933 (International News Service): Adolf Hitler, Nazi chieftain who began life as a house painter and street sweeper, achieved his life's ambition today when he was appointed Chancellor of the Reich.

\* \* \*

# FIRST INTERVIEW WITH REICH CHANCELLOR ADOLF HITLER

*by H. V. Kaltenborn*

FEBRUARY 15, 1933—It is extremely difficult for American correspondents to see Hitler. He has a deep-rooted suspicion of them all. It was only after I had been passed upon by the press department of the National Socialist party that I was permited to visit the new Chancellor at his summer "Brown House" a hundred or so miles from Munich. Here he was living with his secretaries and his bodyguards, seeing the many callers who flocked to his house daily.

His greeting, when I was introduced to him, was perfunctory, suggesting latent hostility, and my first question brought this forth into full flame. I had asked him whether his anti-Semitism concerned Jews everywhere or whether he had something specific against German-Jews as such.

"In America you exclude any would-be immigrants you do not care to admit," he said emphatically. "You regulate their number. Not content with that, you prescribe their physical condition. Not content with that, you insist on the conformity of their political opinions. We demand the same right in Germany. We have no concern with the Jews of other lands, but we are very much concerned about the anti-German elements within our country. We demand the right to deal with these elements as we see fit. Jews have been the intellectual proponents of subversive anti-German movements, and as such they must be dealt with."

On foreign affairs Hitler proved uncompromising. In spite of the concessions which Germany had recently received at Lausanne, he considered

France to be playing the bully, holding down a helpless opponent and choking him to death.

"How can we have friendly relations with France while this attitude continues?" he asked. He referred to· separatist movements in Germany which he evidently feels are receiving aid from French sources. He summed up his comment with this sentence: "The existence of our sixty-five million people is a fact with which France must reckon; they want to live!"

Germany's relations with Russia are always important and I asked him what a National Socialist government would do about that country.

"It is possible, of course, to differentiate between a government and its policies," he said. "The Fascist government of Italy has dealings with Soviet Russia and at the same time carries on vigorous prosecution of Communists in Italy. But it is impossible for any country to have really good relations with Russia if it has a large number of Communists within its own borders."

Some National Socialists visualize a block of Fascist states extending from the Mediterranean to the Baltic. Such a grouping might include Albania, Italy, Hungary, Austria, Germany, Finland, Esthonia and Latvia. Hitler's reaction to the suggestion of this possibility was interesting. "There will be no Fascist block of states," he said. "But remember that Europe is accustomed to being governed by systems which extend over many countries. Many times in the past governmental systems and ideas have crossed frontiers, acquired local color and flourished. Mussolini once said that Fascism was not an article of export. I would say the same thing of our National Socialism.

"Europe," he continued, "cannot maintain itself, riding the uncertain currents of democracy. Europe must have authoritarian government. In the past this authoritarian leadership was provided by the monarch or by the Catholic Church. The form which the authority takes may differ. But parliamentarianism is not native to us and does not belong to our traditions. Yet because the parliamentary system has not functioned we cannot substitute brute force. Bayonets alone will not sustain any government for any length of time. To be viable a government must have the support of the masses. A dictatorship cannot be established in a vacuum. Any government that does not derive its strength from the people will fail the moment it confronts a crisis. The soldier and the policeman do not constitute the substance of a state. Yet dictatorship is justified if the people declare their confidence in one man and ask him to lead."

Hitler's mind is resourceful, but not flexible. Its operations are not under complete control. For some minutes his statements may be logical, then suddenly he runs off on a tangent and gets away from the matter in hand. He speaks with such force and torrential speed that it is difficult for an interviewer to interject questions.

Sometimes his logic is hard to follow. He insisted that with little more than one-third of the German vote he had the right to complete control. Here is his argument: "Under the rules of democracy, a majority of 51 per cent has the right to control the country. I now have 37 per cent of all the votes. That is 75 per cent of the necessary power. I am entitled to three-fourths of the power and my opponents to one-fourth. In the run-off election for President I stood alone and won thirteen million votes. That is my hard-earned capital. I slaved for it and risked my life for it. Without my party, no one can govern Germany today. Let us consider the German government as though it were a business. I am bringing into this business 75 per cent of the total capital investment. Whoever furnishes the rest, whether it is the President or the political parties, is only contributing 25 per cent of the total capital. Moreover, every unit of the 75 per cent investment which I make is worth twice as much of that of the others. I have the bravest, the most energetic, yes, and the best disciplined Germans in my ranks. That is why I don't have to march on Berlin—I am already there. The only question is, who will have to march out of Berlin. My fifteen million voters are actually worth thirty million. That is no mean capital investment. It can be put to work in the business of governing Germany forthwith without any majority votes, without commissions or committees. It can be put to work on the say-so of one man—myself."

This last sentence allowed me to put this question: "Which is more important to the success of a movement, the personality of its leader or the policies of his party?" To which he replied, "There is no fundamental sense in which you can separate the leader from his party. They are identical. It is only after the period of organization has passed, after party ideas have been translated into governmental action and after this action has been tested by experience, that you can dispense with the leader, or remove him if he should be guilty of transgressions.

"No idea can be launched without a leader. You cannot separate Fascism from the personality of Mussolini. Had Frederick the Great died prematurely, there would have been no state of Prussia. If Bismarck had died in 1869, there would have been no German Empire. Ten years later he might have been dispensed with. Only after a movement has been under way for a long time can it develop the historic background, and the traditions that would enable it to carry on without a strong leader."

The National Socialist party platform has had much to say about the iniquities of Big Business. Department stores were to be socialized, interest was to be reduced or abolished, land was to be confiscated for social purposes and income without labor was to be abolished. The only part of this program specifically mentioned in Hitler's radio appeal to the German electorate is compulsory labor service. Nor was there much radicalism in Hitler's answer to my question as to why he opposed Big Business. "I do not oppose Big Business in all cases," he replied. "I am well aware that you cannot build an ocean liner or a locomotive without business organization. But we believe in the wide distribution of wealth. We live next door to a country that has abolished private property. We do not wish to do that, but we must see to it that the average man has a chance to acquire property. In your country everyone still carries the marshal's baton in his knapsack.

Not so in Germany. Yet I cannot tell sixty-five million Germans that they should be satisfied with nothing because fifty thousand Germans happen to have a great deal. The more millions of our people own property, the better it will be for our whole nation and the less temptation there will be for our people to follow the Russian experiment. The collectivist idea cannot mean real progress. There must be competition. But the competition must promote individual welfare."

Hitler reveals a much sounder social and economic philosophy in private conversation than when he speaks in public. He has the orator's instinct for exaggeration and popularization, and is utterly conscienceless about speaking for effect. He knows the mob mind, and has gone out to win it. In speaking with me, he indicated that he would never take the chancellorship unless and until he had the power to enforce his party program. But he has now accepted power with crippling handicaps. Von Hindenburg, von Papen, Hugenberg, Defense Minister von Blomberg, Foreign Minister von Neurath are every one opposed to many of his policies and principles. Yet they are his associates in the government of Germany. He is sworn to obey the Constitution and is likely to do so. The time for a Fascist coup d'état is past. Hitler himself had definitely lost prestige and power before he won the chancellorship. Whatever the result of the March fifth election, it will not give Adolf Hitler the opportunity to establish his long-heralded *Drittes Reich*.

MARCH 5, 1933: *In the Reichstag election the Nazis and their nationalist allies won 330 seats out of a total of 647.*

# THE FIRE

### by John Gunther

ON the night of February 27, 1933, a few days before the March 5 elections which were to confirm Hitler's chancellorship, the building of the German Reichstag in Berlin was gutted by fire. This fire destroyed what remained of the German republic. It not only burned a public building; it incinerated the communist, social democratic, Catholic, and nationalist parties of Germany. It was discovered at about nine-fifteen on a winter evening back in 1933; but its embers are burning yet.

The Reichstag fire ruined a couple of million marks' worth of glass and masonry. It also ruined some thousands of human lives. Logically, inevitably, the fire produced the immense Nazi electoral victory of March 5, the savageries of the subsequent Brown Terror, the persecution of the Jews, the offensive against Austria, the occupation of Czechoslovakia, the invasion of Poland, and the enormous process of *Gleichschaltung,* or forcible assimilation, which steam-rollered over Germany.

The fire turned an imposing edifice to dust and ashes. Also it turned to dust and ashes the lifework of many thousands of pacifists, liberals, democrats, socialists, decent-minded people of all sorts and classes. But for the fire the Nazis would never have gained so sweeping and crushing a victory. In the flames of the Reichstag fire disappeared the old Germany of Bismarck, William II, and the Weimar constitution. In its smoke arose Hitler's Third Reich.

"When Germany awoke," Douglas Reed wrote, "a man's home was no longer his castle. He could be seized by private individuals, could claim no protection from the police, could be indefinitely detained without preferment of charges; his property could be seized, his verbal and written communications overheard and perused; he no longer had the right to foregather with his fellow countrymen, and his newspapers might no longer freely express their opinions."

The actual course of events the night of February 27 is quickly told. Smoke and flames were seen from the windows of the Reichstag, in the heart of Berlin near one end of the Unter den Linden, at about nine-fifteen P.M. The fire brigade was there by nine-twenty-five. The main hall was already a roaring caldron. The ramparts of the building were saved but the interior was gutted. Incendiarism was soon suspected. The fire had started simultaneously in a great number of places—between twenty and thirty in all, according to a subsequent official report. Goering and Hitler arrived within an hour and at once said the fire was the work of communists. "A sign from Heaven!" Hitler exclaimed, as he surveyed the ruins.

The background of these events may also be briefly sketched. Hitler, as we know, had become Reichskanzler. He had only three Nazis in the cabinet as against eight belonging to Papen-Hugenberg, but he had not the faintest thought of playing second-string to them. To accomplish supremacy a great increase in Nazi votes in the March 5 elections was necessary. Hitler desperately needed what he had never had before, a clear majority of Reichstag seats. Papen-Hugenberg were equally determined to prevent this. There was much bad feeling between Hitler and the nationalists. Fighting on a common front, they were fighting each other in reality, because each wanted to dominate the ensuing government.

Things were not going too well with Hitler. Hindenburg still distrusted him. There were wild rumors that Hitler would seek to depose him by force. The Nazis feared that they were going to lose votes. Only one thing might save them by giving them a clear majority. There would be, it was estimated, about six hundred deputies in the new Reichstag, and the communist party was bound to get about one hundred of them. The Nazis claimed about two hundred and fifty. Well, two hundred and fifty is not a clear majority of six hundred; but it was half of five hundred. Therefore, suppress the communist party and wipe out those critical one hundred seats, and all was won.

At first the Nazis decided to raid the Karl Liebknecht house, the communist party headquarters in Berlin, incriminate the communists in conspiracy to revolt, and thus obtain a pretext to suppress them. The raid was carried out, but it was a failure. The date for the elections was rapidly approaching. Tension between Hitler and Papen-Hugenberg increased. The Nazis had to think of something else—in a hurry. They did.

The fire produced exactly what the Nazis hoped for. This we have seen. The one hundred communist deputies were arrested. A state of virtual siege was proclaimed. The provisions of the constitution guaranteeing individual liberty were suppressed. Plans for a communist outbreak were "revealed." Germany rose with a roar. There was intense public excitement. The Nazis stormed the country, and Hitler was able to maneuver himself into a dictatorship for four years, affix himself to power immovably, unshakably.

The true story of the fire is not so well known today as it might be. The Nazis did their job so well that, whereas everyone well informed instantly suspected them of complicity, there was much puzzlement as to details. Even today there are mysteries, subsidiary mysteries, not entirely clear. Let us deal with them.

During the night of the fire a Dutch half-wit named Marinus Van der Lubbe was arrested when police found him in the burning ruins. There were no witnesses except the police to his arrest. The first statements about the Dutchman, issued by Goering, were false. It was said that he had a membership-card of the communist party on his person, a leaflet urging common action between socialists and communists, several photographs of himself, and a passport. Obliging fellow! He did possess the passport, but not the other documents, as the trial subsequently proved.

His career and movements were closely traced. He had set three other fires—minor ones—in Berlin just before the Reichstag fire. In 1929 he had joined something called the Dutch Communist Youth Organization, a secessionist group. Two years later he was expelled from this as a worthless and stupid fellow. He never belonged to the communist party itself. Van der Lubbe's itinerary the few days before the fire was well established. As late as the night of February 17-18 he slept at Glinow, near Potsdam. He could not have got to Berlin before the 19th or 20th. Yet inside a week he, an unknown hobo, either (a) so insinuated himself into the graces of the rigidly articulated communist party as to be given the dangerous and delicate job of firing the Reichstag, or (b) was hired to do it by someone else.

When it became clear, even in Germany, that the Van der Lubbe explanation simply would not hold water, the mystery thickened. The police got to the point of having to admit that Van der Lubbe had confederates. But how, carrying incendiary material, could enough of them possibly have penetrated the Reichstag walls, doorways, or windows in the middle of Berlin without being seen?

The German authorities themselves let the cat out of the bag, and an astounding cat it proved to be. It was announced that the incendiaries had presumably entered and escaped from the building by means of an underground tunnel leading from the Reichstag basement to the palace of the speaker of the Reichstag—Goering—across the street. Originally this tunnel was part of the Reichstag's central heating system. Until an official *communiqué* revealed its existence not a dozen persons in Berlin had ever heard of it. So one aspect of the mystery was solved. The incendiaries, whoever they were, got in and out of the Reichstag building—through Goering's back yard. Incredible information!

An ostrich sticks its head in the sand—well-meaning but stupid ostrich. There is an obverse of the ostrich process. A man may naïvely and stridently call attention to something he wishes to conceal, hoping thereby to lessen interest in it. A squirrel hides a nut under a tree. Then he squats and points at it, showing where it is. Disingenuously a man may reveal what is embarrassing to him, hoping thus to modify the terms of the embarrassment.

Long before the trial opened the accusation that the Nazis themselves had burned the building had impressed the world. A mock trial was held in London. The *Brown Book,* telling part of the story—but inaccurately —was published by *émigrés* and widely circulated. Moreover, a secret nationalist memorandum, written to the order of a prominent deputy named Oberfohren, was passed from hand to hand. Oberfohren was a nationalist, a Junker, one of Papen's men. He asserted flatly that the Nazis were the incendiaries. In June, a Nazi detachment searched his flat; mystery for some time surrounded Oberfohren's whereabouts. Then it was announced that he had "shot himself."

The half-wit Van der Lubbe was not the only person arrested. Ernst Torgler, chairman of the communist *bloc* in the Reichstag, gave himself up to the police when he heard the announcement incredible to his ears that he was accused of complicity; subsequently three Bulgarian communists, Dimitrov, Popov, and Tanev, were arrested, when a waiter who had served them in a Berlin café told the police that their activities had been "suspicious." Dimitrov was in Munich, not Berlin, on the night of the fire, as an incontrovertible alibi proved; nevertheless he was held for five months until the trial, without a scrap of evidence against him.

I covered the trial in both Leipzig and Berlin during its first six weeks. The court sat for fifty-seven days, and provided superlative drama. The trial was neither a farce nor a frame-up. The behavior of the police and judicial authorities before the trial was outrageous, but once the proceedings reached the court-room there was a difference. The court got itself into a curious dilemma, of having to pretend to be fair even while exercising the greatest animus against the defendants, and little by little this necessity —caused mostly by the pressure of foreign opinion—to simulate justice led to some modicum of justice in the court-room.

When the trial opened, I think, the judges like many people in Germany genuinely thought that Van der Lubbe was a communist and that the communists were guilty. The prosecution thought so too and assuming that the trial would be quick it made no serious effort to fabricate a "good" case. As the hearings went on it became evident even to the judges that there was no case at all. The evidence of the prosecution was a colossal confusion of inaccuracies, confusions, contradictions, and plain lies. But once the trial started, it couldn't be stopped. With dreadful pertinacity, with true Teutonic thoroughness, the court plodded on, deeper every day in a morass of evidence that ineluctably proved just what it didn't want proved—the innocence of the accused. The prosecution, rattled, began to produce incredible cranks as witnesses, whom even the judges couldn't stomach; the judges, rattled, threw Dimitrov out of court whenever his questions became too intolerably pointed—which was often.

No one, of course, counted on the brilliant gallantry of Dimitrov. This Bulgarian revolutionary had, moreover, brains. Unerringly he picked every flaw in the testimony of a crooked witness; unerringly he asked just those questions most damaging to the prosecution. He turned the trial into a public forum. The trial started as an attempt to pin the guilt of the Reichstag arson on the defendants. Dimitrov turned it before long into an action precisely opposite: one desperately seeking to clear the Nazis of the same charge.

When the judge rebuked him for making communist propaganda, Dimitrov pointed to Goering—on the witness-stand—and said with a subtle combination of impudence and perfect courtesy: "But he's making National Socialist propaganda!" No one who saw him will ever forget Dimitrov pointing to Lubbe and exclaiming, in his picturesque Balkan German: "This miserable Faust! Who is his Mephistopheles?" Nor the climax to his final speech when, imperturbable as ever with the executioner's ax or Goering's private vengeance facing him, he demanded of the court "compensation for his wasted time!"

Once the court was forced into calling every relevant witness, like porters and workmen in the Reichstag building, the flood-gates were open. Hot little clues dodged out. Lubbe, inert, apathetic, testified—in one of his few lucid moments—that he had been "with Nazis" the night before the fire. A gateman testified that a Nazi deputy, Dr. Albrecht, left the burning building, in great excitement, as late as ten P.M. A servant in Goering's house, Aldermann, testified that he heard, on several nights before the fire, mysterious sounds in the underground tunnel. Thus the fire—got hot.

The court had no option but to acquit Torgler, Dimitrov, Popov, and Tanev; Van der Lubbe was sentenced to death and presently decapitated. (Torgler, one should interpolate, was held in "protective custody" for two years after the trial, though the court declared him innocent.) The Dutchman died with his lips sealed, and with him to the grave went one secret—how exactly he and the incendiaries had worked together.

APRIL 1, 1933: *The Hitler government began a planned campaign of anti-semitic persecution, boycott of the Jews, and issuance of the first Aryan laws.*

# PERSECUTION OF THE JEWS

## by *Edgar Ansel Mowrer*

THE elimination of Jews from German public life (if not from Germany altogether) was one of the chief promises of National-Socialist propagandists and apparently rarely failed to elicit approval. Gregor Strasser promised (October 31, 1931) that the National-Socialists would put an end to Jewry in Germany. Pastor Peperkorn told the Prussian Diet that the Jews must get out. Deputy Kube announced to the same august body (June 2, 1932) that "when we clean house, the Exodus of the Children of Israel will be a child's game in comparison." The so-called Boxheimer documents seized by the police on National-Socialists announced the preparation of obligatory service for all but Jews, and food only for those who served. Clearly, the Jews were to starve.

The important National-Socialist, Captain Hermann Goering, gave an interview to an Italian newspaper in which he explained that while only those Jews who had in any way injured the German State would "be punished," those who entered Germany after August, 1914, were to be shown the door and all remaining Jews, irrespective of origin, to be turned out of responsible positions in the press, in the theater, in moving pictures, in the schools and universities, as well as from every official position, honor or position from which they may conceivably exert "their decomposing, anti-national, international or at best non-national influence to the detriment of the German people." While in the words of deputy Bauer of the Prussian Diet, "The Third Empire will treat Jews like plant lice."

As a result of such encouragement, young fanatics and rowdies for a considerable period made a practice of defiling and desecrating Jewish cemeteries and synagogues—in all, 109 of them up to the summer of 1932—and announced that more synagogues would soon burn. The house and shop windows of Jews were repeatedly broken. Nationalist heroes, more or less directed, swept along Kurfürstendamm in Berlin on Jewish Easter, 1932, and, twenty to one, attacked persons whom they suspected of Semitic blood. They were young lads, and racially inexperienced. A Hindu and a Frenchman, both of whom I knew personally, were surrounded. The Hindu was knocked down and his nose broken, the Frenchman saved himself only by a volley of Gallic curses which betrayed his origin.

A Jewish organization published a long list of attacks on isolated Jews. In Pustutten, men of the Third Empire set dogs on a Jewish merchant. Smearing Jewish walls with taunts, obscenities and swastika symbols had become the pastime of thousands of children. In many schools Jewish children were enduring hell at the hands of their merciless Christian companions. Many a small merchant was hounded from the small town where his family had lived for generations, by unceasing boycott and persecution.

25

At one moment the Nationalist students at the University of Berlin coolly demanded the dismissal of all Hebrew students.

And the courts? Surely all decent Germans protested against such villainy and severely punished the offenders? They did not.

The German magistrates decided that "Jew" as a taunt was no cause for resentment and that the democratic State might be called "Jew Republic" with impunity by any that so desired. A gentleman who called the Berlin Police President a "Jewish bastard" was acquitted. A great many of those who desecrated Jewish cemeteries and synagogues got off free or with the mildest of sentences. No wonder that in the summer of 1932 a number of prominent Jews wrote a letter to the German Chancellor asking if the Government had the intention of giving its Jewish citizens the protection that they had a right to expect. An official answered, promising protection, but requesting that his answer be kept secret!

The police authorities persuaded the Association of Jewish Boy Scouts (*Jüdischer Pfadfinderbund Deutschlands*) to give up the idea of an open-air camp (summer of 1932) because they could not guarantee the personal safety of the campers against the attacks of racial rowdies. A pretty index of a situation.

The various published appeals for the boycott of Jewish shops, Jewish physicians, Jewish lawyers, proved clearly that this Aryan propaganda was not entirely disinterested. It is difficult to imagine that the leaders believed a tenth of what they said, still less to gauge how much of their threats they would have put into effect had they had a chance. A suspicion arises that Adolf Hitler himself accepted anti-semitism with his characteristic mixture of emotionalism and political cunning. Many doubted if he really desired pogroms.

At first too the masses could hardly have swallowed the attempt to make the "Jid" shopkeeper they had known all their life a drinker of Christian blood. But with the increase of poverty and unemployment, assertions at first accepted as jokes, began to stick. Germany became a yeast-bed of racial hatred.

What could the Jews do? It had all happened often enough before, every detail, every lie. For more than two thousand years. It would not change for anything they did. Anti-semitism is an Aryan, not a Jewish problem.

When the Jews in Germany were taunted with their Jewish national feeling, they became German patriots and roared with the rest in 1914. Yet Germany was a country which by the Delbruck Act specifically allowed its natives to take on a second nationality without losing their right to be German. What hypocrisy was here?

Then the Jews were accused of keeping socially apart, and in answer they sought assimilation. Only to be told that the Germans did not accept mixture with their inferior blood. Then they were reproached with their religion, but most of them had lost their religion. Half of them were by history and habit more German than the bulk of the population east of

26

the River Elbe and, what is more, they had contributed considerably more to German culture.

What could the Jews do?

> JUNE 12, 1933: *A concordat was signed for the Vatican and Germany by Vice-Chancellor von Papen and the Papal Nuncio, Cardinal Pacelli.*
>
> JULY 14: *Germany passed a law forbidding the formation of any new political parties.*
>
> OCTOBER 14: *Germans withdrew from the Disarmament Conference and from the League of Nations, and at the request of Chancellor Hitler President Hindenburg dissolved the Reichstag.*
>
> JANUARY 30, 1934: *Abortive Nazi* putsch *in Vienna.*
>
> FEBRUARY 12: *Socialist uprisings in Austria.*

\*    \*    \*

BERLIN, June 30 (Associated Press): Chancellor Adolf Hitler...smashed a revolt in the Third Reich today....In a day of summary punishment for those who challenged his authority...the Chancellor "liquidated" leaders of a threefold opposition.

\*    \*    \*

# THE BLOOD PURGE

## *by Frederick T. Birchall*

THE telephone at my bedside in the hotel in Berlin rang early in the morning of Saturday, June 30, 1934, and kept on ringing. This was annoying because I did not want to get up. It had been a late night and this was probably only someone who wished to ask me to lunch. But duty being duty, and since it is never safe to despise a telephone call, especially in Germany, I answered.

"Better wake up and get busy," said the voice of the office, "something doing here. It may be revolution or counter-revolution or what have you, but apparently a lot of people are being shot."

Within an hour I was very busy indeed, collecting the news of Adolf Hitler's "purge," which left bloodstains throughout the greater part of the Reich and sent a thrill of horror through the civilized world.

All that day lorries filled with armed police and Hitler's black uniformed guards rushed through the Berlin streets on mysterious errands. Police were out in force, carrying rifles and with the chin-straps of their shakos down,

27

sure sign of disturbance. People living near the Lichterfelde police barracks, in the outskirts, reported continuous fusillades within it, but it was impossible to learn what was going on inside. Strangely enough, the storm troops seemed to be in eclipse. Not a brown shirt was visible in the streets of Berlin; nor were there any Reichswehr soldiers to be seen. The Reichswehr, it was said, was confined to barracks. The eclipse of the storm troops went unexplained.

After a while editions of the evening papers came out, each with a new sensation. They were grabbed up so eagerly that the news vendors could hardly hand them out fast enough. "Chief of Staff Roehm dismissed," said one big headline. Then more startling still "Roehm shot!" (It was not true then, but came true later.) Ernst, leader of the Berlin storm troops, shot. Heines, the Breslau bully and former Fehme assassin, shot; this was the Heines who in the Reichstag fire trial had boasted: "I now admit that I dispatched a traitor to the place where traitors belong." Now he too had been dispatched there—why? More and still more storm-troop leaders shot in Munich and Berlin, including Spreti—"Count Pretty" everybody called him —Roehm's curly-haired, good-looking young secretary who had shared his carousings.

Then more serious news still. General von Schleicher shot, and his wife with him; and with this a weird tale about Schleicher's having been in a plot with the executed storm-troop leaders and "a foreign power"—which was absurd. Schleicher disdained Roehm and his kind. And there were Catholics among the dead, men known to everyone for their high purpose and stainless lives: Bose, Papan's adjutant and secretary; Dr. Klausener, the learned head of Catholic Action. These at first were labeled suicides, but when it came out that Herr von Bose's body showed six bullet wounds, that pretense was hastily dropped and the explanation given that they were killed "in attempting to resist arrest"—Dr. Klausener in the Ministry of Communications with the minister in the next room, and Bose in Papen's office!

Herr Jung, Papen's collaborator, who was reputed to have written for him the speech Papen had delivered at Marburg, had been caught in the bathroom of his apartment and killed there. Papen himself was said to be under arrest in his house until judgment could be passed on him—or until it could be certain that Hindenburg would not avenge him if he was killed. Göring went later to Papen, sent away his captors, and apologized to him. Hindenburg, out in Neudeck, was still President and must not be antagonized.

This evidently was no action against rebellious storm troops. It looked more like a general clearance of all the elements opposed to the Nazi regime or disliked by those in it, as indeed it proved to be. A story came out later of a district leader in Silesia who, hearing that old scores were being paid off, gathered in four Jews he disliked and shot them.

The massacre, initiated early in the morning in Munich by Hitler himself, was continued in Berlin by Göring at noon and spread thereafter throughout the country. It continued for three days, and before it ended more than a thousand persons lost their lives. They included such different personalities as the aged General von Kahr, who had suppressed Hitler's futile putsch in Munich in 1923 and was living in retirement in Bavaria, and Captain Scheringer, a much younger Bavarian who had been Hitler's disciple but had left him, disillusioned. To say that a thousand lives were lost is probably an understatement. At least that many died, though an official statement said: "Although the number of traitors shot is under fifty, grotesque figures are being circulated," and Hitler in his later statement to the Reichstag put the total at exactly seventy-seven.

These things came out piecemeal in the course of the next few days. That day we knew very little except that Hitler had flown with Goebbels from Bonn to Munich before dawn and, arriving there before anyone was up, had summoned to him various storm-troop leaders. Stripping them of their party decorations, he had ordered them arrested and shot. After that he had motored out to Bad Wiessee, had arrested Roehm in his bedroom and ordered him to prison. Heines, who had been found sleeping with a male companion, had then and there been hustled into the garden and before a firing squad.

Much was made of this Heines case, and of the unsavory record of Roehm, in the various explanations of the purge. It was said to have filled Hitler with horror. Since the habits of both men and of other Nazi leaders had never been any secret—Roehm's letters from Bolivia, in which he told all about it, had even been published in the newspapers under the Republic—this was disingenuous, to put it mildly, and aroused some surprise and not a little skepticism. I remember accompanying a colleague to his apartment, on the day of general explanation, to get some documents. The old janitor of the apartment house was sitting in his armchair in the sunny courtyard, devouring the afternoon newspaper. Suddenly he burst into shrieks of laughter.

"Whatever have you found there?" asked my friend.

"Wonderful! Wonderful!" gasped the old janitor. "So they've finally discovered that Roehm was a so-and-so. Isn't that marvelous?"

Karl Ernst, tall blond commander of the Berlin storm troops, the former hotel bellboy who had become Jew-baiter and bully *par excellence,* had been caught with his bride in Bremen on their honeymoon as they were about to sail for Madeira. He had been brought back, handcuffed, by airplane to the Lichterfelde barracks and shot there, not knowing what it was all about. Believing it was a counter-revolution and disdainful of it, he had thrown up his arm in salute shouting: "Heil Hitler!" as the volley brought him down. He had been married only two days before and Hitler had been at his wedding. A week later, before a specially assembled Reichstag, with elite guards in steel helmets lining all the aisles and two standing at attention on each side of the President's chair, Hitler gave his own version of what he had done. He spoke for an hour and a half, quivering with emotion and emphasizing with his clenched fist the turpitude (of the conspirators) he described. The tale he told was long and involved. We know it now for the tissue of lies and humbug it was, but at that time it sounded plausible enough. The Reichstag and the crowded galleries listened spellbound.

29

Roehm, said Hitler, had sought control of the army. When Hitler turned him down, he plotted with other Gauleiters in the storm troops to put Hitler out of the way and seize control of the government. Hitler gave details of Roehm's plan and the hours at which it was to be executed. At five o'clock on Saturday afternoon in Berlin, the storm troops, mustered by Ernst an hour earlier, were to seize all government buildings and the government ministries. Hitler himself was to be arrested and held until he could be disposed of, objections being silenced by pretense that this was his own wish, so that he could avoid being involved. Nevertheless, the man to kill him had already been chosen—Standard Bearer Uhl, who had "confessed a few hours before his death." The action in Berlin was to be followed at nine o'clock by similar action in Munich. Learning this, Hitler himself had struck.

"I was responsible for the destiny of the German nation. I had only one course open—ruthless and bloody intervention. Therefore during twenty-four hours the Supreme Court of the German people consisted of myself."

The Reichstag rose in a frenzy of cheers at that. Women in the galleries split their gloves applauding. Reichswehr officers thundered "Hoch!" for this angel of vengeance, who spared not traitors.

Hitler gave his own list of the killed: seventy-seven in all—sixty-one persons executed, comprising nineteen higher storm-troop leaders, thirty-one subordinate leaders and members, five party members, three special guard leaders, and three special guard members "shot for mistreating prisoners"; thirteen "including some civilians," killed while resisting arrest; and three suicides.

It sounded plausible until the known dead were totaled. He brought into the plot also the "foreign power" involved, hinting that it was France. And he concluded:

"I am ready before history to take the responsibility for the twenty-four hours of the bitterest decision of my life, during which fate has again taught me to cling with every thought to the dearest thing we possess—the German people and the German Reich."

How they cheered him, again and again, as he sank back in his seat, head bowed over his desk as if to hide his emotion! Cabinet members, party leaders, and officials from the upper benches crowded around him, shaking his hand and assuring him of their loyalty. Two little girls in the uniform of the Hitler Mädchen brought him flowers. Only Hugenberg, the Nationalist, a lone stodgy figure in civilian gray amid the sea of brown uniforms, did not join in the applause. Perhaps he wondered how he had escaped. Papen was not present.

Göring led the procession of congratulation. They stood face to face on the dais for almost a minute, hand grasping hand, looking into each other's eyes while the flashlights popped for this affecting scene which would be a front-page feature in all of tomorrow's newspapers. Perhaps we may be permitted to conjecture now what the eyes really said.

"You put it over, Führer. You are a wonder!"

And the response: "Hermann, you said it!"

Coldly analyzed, the speech was an accounting without vouchers, assertion without proofs or promise to supply them, a report supported solely by the emotion with which it was rendered. We know now that there was no plot. Would leaders of a mutinous army which was to seize Berlin at five o'clock in the afternoon and Munich at nine the same night be sleeping peacefully at a Bavarian watering-place hours away from both places at seven o'clock that morning? How came it that Ernst, whom Hitler named as the actual leader of the Berlin revolt, was taken off a ship in Bremen on which he was starting on his honeymoon? And the "foreign power" faded out of the plot that day; for after the Reichstag speech had made the charge official, the embassies began inquiring which of them had been guilty, and France demanded details and was reassured. The newspapers were ordered to print the indignant denial which came promptly from the French government, and which called the allegation a "nonsensical fable." After that, the "plot" and the "foreign power" were never mentioned again.

The bodies of most of the victims were cremated and all that came back to their families was their ashes. No details of the deaths were ever vouchsafed, nor was any list of them ever forthcoming. The funeral services for Schleicher and his wife were forbidden by the police, and the wreaths placed on their graves were removed. Kinsfolk of all the dead were forbidden to talk of how they came to their end. The account was declared closed with Hitler's speech.

The German people accepted it all as part of a strange new system which would have to be endured, and Hitler's declaration as clearing him of all blame. At the end of the speech, Göring had risen to say that it was now the Reichstag's duty to approve the declaration and thank the Leader for the courage and energy with which he had stamped out a menace to his country. That was done with one voice, the entire audience rising, members and galleries alike, and they sang the "Horst Wessel Lied," with arms upraised in tribute, for emphasis.

# "SOMETHING IS ROTTEN. ..."

## by Dorothy Thompson

WHEN I reached Berlin [July 1934] I went to the Adlon. It was good to be there, like home. There was Fix in the bar, with his shining black hair and his shining smile and his good Dry Martinis. There was the big porter who can always get anything you want—reservations when the airplane is sold out and money when the banks are closed. There was the manager who always remembers how many people there are in your family and what room you had last time. Oh, I was glad to be back! The French doors were open into the garden and the fountain was sparkling and the little lawn was as smooth as the finest broadloom, and a man in an apron was actually sweeping it with a broom. It was all the courtesy, all the cleanliness, all the exquisite order which is Germany.

I sent my luggage up and went out and walked round the block and down another street and round another corner. The newspapermen had said, "Don't telephone from the hotel. Hotel 'phones are watched." I saw a cheap beer saloon with a telephone booth in the back, went in, and called up Anna. She recognized my voice; I knew because she said, "Oh, so you are back!" I asked where I could find The Little One. We call him "The Little One" because he is six feet two. The Little One is a Storm Trooper and I wanted to see him more than anyone. "Come to Maria's this afternoon at three," she said.

A girl I know came to lunch, a stenographer who works in a state bank. She has a nice German face with a high, unpowdered forehead and eyes as candid as water. When you look at her you know she never told a lie in her life. We didn't talk about politics at all at first, but after a while she said shyly, "Do you find that it's so bad here as the outside world seems to think?" I said that was what I had come to find out. She said, "I wasn't a Nazi at first. But in my bank everything is different since Hitler came. We don't get such high wages as we used to, but the ones who get the lowest wages are cut least. And the directors are cut most of all. They used to get fees for attending meetings, and now they have to turn them all in to the bank, and they aren't allowed in our bank to get more than two hundred and fifty dollars a month. And they treat us much better, as though we were all equals. Nobody is ashamed now to be poor or not to have as good clothes as anyone else. It's as though we all belonged to a big family. It's good to know where you belong. Before we were never sure. There were so many political parties and they all had different ideas. It is quieter in Germany than I can ever remember it."

I asked her how people took the news that there might be food cards this winter, and that there would be substitutes for textiles. "It doesn't matter so long as we have work," she said. "Everybody is willing to make sacrifices. It would be bad if people were out of work."

I asked her about June thirtieth. She flushed. "That was an awful shock," she said. "We never dreamed of anything like that. We thought the Nazi leaders were different because they always talked about how corrupt the old leaders were. But then, on June thirtieth, we saw that lots of them were just like everybody else, wasting money that didn't belong to them and acting dreadful. That is why Hitler had to execute them."

"In my country we think there should be a trial," I said.

"But if the whole people are in danger?" she asked wonderingly.

It was funny. I never met anyone in Germany except a few intellectuals, who minded that those people did not have a trial. It was as though they had forgotten that there had ever been such a thing as law.

After lunch I went out and looked up a mechanic to go over my car. I told him what the stenographer had said. "Bunk!" he said. "A man can't live on the wages he gets now; he can eat, but he can't buy a suit of clothes.

And there are plenty of people still spending money. There's money for flags and propaganda and for all the shoe leather men have marched off their feet in the last year." He looked round, and lowered his voice. "This country's a prison," he said. "This won't last. It will collapse."

"And then what?" I asked.

He shrugged his shoulders.

In the afternoon I went to Maria's. I took a taxi and then a street car, and then I walked several blocks. I went right up to the apartment. The Little One was there. He wasn't wearing his uniform. I hadn't seen him for over a year but he looked years older.

"What happened on June thirtieth?" I asked.

He looked at me steadily. "Hitler sold us out," he said. "That's what happened. There wasn't any plot. No one was treasonable to Hitler. The conservatives wanted to reform the Cabinet. They wanted to put in some of the old gang that the outside countries have confidence in. That was because the industries couldn't get credits and were busted. There was lots of discussion going on. Different people meeting in different houses. They sounded out some of the foreign embassies. Hitler knew all about it. They talked it over with him. Everyone wanted to keep Hitler. But some of them wanted to get rid of Goebbels and some didn't like Goering. That Mr. A, that Hitler mentioned in the speech in the Reichstag, that was Werner von Alvensleben. He went to Hitler with various proposals. I heard Hitler told him he had been reading about Napoleon and about how Napoleon always went his own way and made his own decisions. So this man Alvensleben told him he'd better remember that after all Napoleon ended up on St. Helena. Hitler wouldn't forgive that. He never forgets anything or forgives it.

"Roehm, the chief of the Storm Troops, was sore at Hitler, and Hitler was sore at Roehm. That's true. But they'd been sore at each other before, lots of times. Roehm knew that the army was pushing at Hitler to dissolve the Storm Troops, and Roehm wanted Hitler to make the army take the Storm Troops in. Roehm wanted a Nazi army. It was always in our program that we were to have a people's army in place of the professional one. But the army wouldn't give in, and neither would Roehm. He promised us he wouldn't give in. We had been ordered on leave for the whole of July, and we were going; but Roehm promised that when we reassembled in August we would make a big demonstration that would show that we were the real strength and backbone of the revolution and couldn't be pushed aside by the Reichswehr that used to fight us.

"We went off duty everywhere on Friday the twenty-ninth. Ten days before that, here in Berlin, we had got orders from Karl Ernst, the Berlin group leader, that we were to be relieved of all duties during July and were to spend the month quietly. I saw the orders, and what I tell you is true. Ernst was going on a holiday to Madeira. He was all excited about it. He was leaving Saturday—that was the thirtieth—from Bremen. On Friday, he heard that the army had been ordered to stand by, and he called up both General Blomberg and General Goering and asked if anything was up. They said it was nothing, so he started as he planned, on Saturday morning. The SS troops who were with the army arrested him near Bremen and brought him back here and shot him in the Lichterfelde Barracks. They beat him so hard they had to prop him against the wall in order to shoot him, after he went down on his knees and swore he was innocent.

"They must have shot sixty or seventy men in that barracks. It was a shambles. They had a firing squad of eight, Hitler's personal bodyguard, and the firing order was, 'On the wish of the Leader: hail, Hitler! Fire!'

"Do you know about Sandor? He was Ernst's chief of staff. He heard Ernst had been arrested but didn't know he had been shot. He took an airplane and flew to Munich with copies of Ernst's orders to show to Hitler and thus prove his innocence. They arrested him and brought him back and shot him too. And Gerth. He was Ernst's adjutant. He went to Group Headquarters on Saturday and was arrested. They stood him up before a firing squad twice. Once he was reprieved and then, two hours later, they shot him. His mother made such a scene in Goering's office that they put her out, and then she stood in the Unter den Linden screaming and crying. My God, it was awful! Men didn't know why they were shot; I'm telling you they didn't have an idea. Some of them thought that there was a conspiracy of the SS against Hitler, and they were dying for Hitler. They held up their arms and shouted, 'Hail, Hitler!' as the squad fired. What I'm telling you is true."

I don't know whether it was like that but I could see he believed it. "What will happen now?" I asked.

"There are two and a half million Storm Troopers. How do you think they feel?" he asked.

"I'm asking you," I said.

"It used to be that we were the fighters for the revolution. Hitler still says so. He says it was only a handful that were traitors. But it used to be that we were the men who saved Germany. When we passed people saluted. When we went in a restaurant, we got the best seats. Now people look the other way. It's no honor any more to wear an SA uniform. The people who know the truth are mostly dead, and if you talk you get sent to concentration camp. The top leaders are almost all dead. Lots and lots of the subleaders are in prison."

"How many did they shoot?" I asked him.

"About three hundred," he said. "But the papers never printed it. Hitler said seventy-seven."

"What will happen?" I asked.

He shrugged his shoulders. "It will be a hard winter," he said. "We'll see how the people stand it. It will never be the same again with Hitler. That's true. The heart's gone out of the revolution."

"Hitler sits on a throne more powerful than all the Caesars," I said.

The Little One looked at me sidewise. "Hitler stands on a tightrope," he said.

I was still in my room in the morning when the Secret Police called. The porter rang up from the desk. "Good morning, madam, there is a gentleman here from the secret state police." That is Goering's organization to snuff out discontent, sedition, plots and treasonable activities.

"Send him up," I said. He was a young man in a trench coat like Hitler's. He brought an order that I should leave the country immediately, within forty-eight hours, for journalistic activities inimical to Germany.

Well, it was too bad. I hadn't been long in Germany. In such a short time you don't see much. I packed my things after a while and went downstairs. I stood for a few minutes in the lobby. Lord, how familiar it all was. In this lobby I had met my husband for the first time. Out there in the garden we had had that birthday party.

"What, you are leaving us already?" asked the manager. "Has everything been all right?"

"Perfect," I said, "thanks ever so much. Thanks for everything."

The porter helped me with my luggage. I went into the bar. *"Auf wiedersehen, gnaedige Frau,"* said Fix.

*"Auf wiedersehen,"* said the little page. *"Come again soon, gnaedige Frau. Auf baldiges wiedersehen."*

# DOLLFUSS ASSASSINATED

## *by G. E. R. Gedye*

THE newspaper public abroad was tiring of the daily catalogue of Nazi outrages in Austria which (with a short interval after the February Counter-Revolution) had been going on for nearly eighteen months. The dog days of August were approaching when even the wire-pullers in Berlin and Munich would find it hard to stir up Nazis in Vienna to cause much trouble. February and its aftermath had been pretty much of a strain, and on July 25th, 1934, I came out of the French travel bureau at midday with a ticket-of-leave in my pocket which would give mc a fortnight to recuperate in the sun and forget the slow but steady march of the Austrian tragedy. A sleeper to the Riviera, to a country where speech and thought were still free, sounded pretty good to me, and when I saw policemen, revolvers in hand, taking pot shots at the back of a building the entrance to which was in the Johannesgasse, I was not unduly disturbed. After all, there was a two-front war always in progress underground, and a few revolver shots or bombs more or less seemed no reason to change my holiday plans. But in the Johannesgasse itself I found steel-helmeted storm detachments of police taking cover and opening rapid fire with carbines and machine-guns on the Ravag, the building of the Austrian broadcasting company. I telephoned through to my office, and was told that an announcement had just been broadcast that Dollfuss had resigned and Rintelen formed a Government. Within five minutes I had handed back my sleeper to the Riviera. I settled down to cover the Nazi rebellion from behind the shelter of shrubs surrounding the terrace of Naumann's Restaurant in the Johannesgasse until an enraged policeman rushed at and tried to club me with his carbine, and afterwards from such vantage points as I could find during the hours that the hellish din of machine-guns and hand-grenades in and around the Ravag building continued.

At ten minutes past 12, Marek, one of the two detectives sent to the Siebensterngasse, telephoned to Major Wrabel that troops and police in uniform and young men in civilian clothes were gathering in the gymnasium. At 12.15 he telephoned that they were loading up lorries with various articles, and at 12.30, while he was telephoning that other lorries had arrived, he was seized by the police conspirators and taken with them to the attack on the Chancellery. At 12.15 Secretary of State Karwinsky telephoned the Police President Dr. Seydl to send reinforcements to the Chancellery and to the Siebensterngasse. At 12.30 he telephoned again to ask whether his instructions had been carried out. The Police President admitted they had not, and told some story of having concentrated defensive measures on the Michaelerplatz, close to the Chancellery, where an attack was allegedly planned to be made on the Chancellor when he should leave the Ballhausplatz. At 12.35 Karwinsky telephoned once more, urging that alarm detachments should be sent without an instant's delay to the Chancellery and to the Siebensterngasse. At last, at 12.40, the police began to move—after the four motor-lorries loaded with conspirators—soldiers, police and civilians—had already left the Siebensterngasse for the Chancellery. Meantime, Secretary of State Kerwinsky had ordered Inspector Goebel (in charge of the Security Service in the Chancellery) to close the great gates of the building; this was also about 12.35. The order was not obeyed, the excuse subsequently being given that at 12.50 the guard had to be changed. At 12.53, on the heels of the new guard in came the four lorries, loaded with armed rebels, and the gates were at last closed—by the rebels themselves, from the inside.

Despite the political situation and the repeated warnings, neither the guard nor their officers had drawn ammunition, and were promptly disarmed by the rebels, without resisting. The rebel commanders wore officers' uniform, and the guards were under the impression that the whole army had revolted against Dollfuss and that they were confronted by a *fait accompli*. The seizure of the building had been carefully worked out, and the rebels broke up into groups, each of which had its allotted tasks—to arrest willing or unwilling police and detectives and to drive the various civil servants and Government officials encountered out into one of the courtyards. One group of rebels, headed by ex-Sergeant-Major Otto Planetta, made for the Chancellor's apartments. As Karwinsky was trying to persuade the Chancellor to leave his room and go into the adjoining building containing the State Archives, from which there was still a free exit on to the street, the Planetta detachment broke in through another door. Planetta rushed at the little Chancellor without a word and fired two shots into his body. With a weak cry for help Dollfuss flung up his hands to his head, half turned, and crashed over backwards on the floor. This happened a few minutes after 1 o'clock. For the moment the Chancellor was left lying on the floor in a pool of blood; how long he remained so, nobody knows. The first authentic news of him after the shooting is to be found in the statements of two policemen, who were allowed to try to bandage his wounds at a quarter to two. The Chancellor asked several times to see Schuschnigg, a priest and a doctor. Some time later Fey was allowed in to see him alone. The Chancellor was now lying on a divan with some cotton-wool placed on the two wounds in his neck, from which the blood was still oozing. He seems to have been persuaded by the rebels that the whole army, police force and the country had risen against him. In this heartbreaking belief, after lingering two hours and three-quarters without medical aid, he died at about 3.45 in the hands of his utterly callous Nazi captors—less than twenty-four hours after he had sent to the gallows the young Socialist Gerl for doing what thousands of Nazis had for months been doing almost with impunity—trying to damage railway property with explosives.

In Vienna the Nazi Putsch was a complete failure. I saw hundreds of young Nazis in their white stockings standing around on the Ringstrasse while their leaders were besieged in the Chancellery, doing nothing. In the provinces, where the Nazis were stronger, things were different and fighting broke out which lasted for a week. The fact is that the Nazis had confidently expected the job to be done for them by Adolf Hitler through invasion, as was to be the case nearly four years later. In July 1934, as everybody knows, Mussolini rushed troops to the Brenner and warned Hitler in Berlin that the first German move across the frontier would be countered by the descent of his own troops from the Brenner. This would not have been all, for Jugoslavia, fearing to see Italy circumvent the barrier of the Karawanken Alps and be in a position to invade her from Southern Styria, rushed troops to the Maribor area, ready to cross the frontier and seize the high ground on the other side the moment the Italians left the Brenner. Czechoslovakia was prepared to push forward troops in the direction of Vienna to secure defensive positions against a German Nazi invasion.

There was nothing much to the credit of the Clerico-Fascist regime in the way it disposed of the 144 Putschists in the Chancellery. They surrendered under an unconditional written guarantee of safe conduct to the German frontier. When they came out of the building, instead of being conducted to their spiritual home as they expected, they were taken to the police barracks in the Marokkanergasse. Thirteen were hanged, the others sentenced to imprisonment and later amnestied. Here is how the Vienna correspondent of the pro-Heimwehr Budapest newspaper *Magyarszag* describes what he saw and heard outside the Chancellery that afternoon.

"4 P.M. Fey appears on the balcony, pale-faced and trembling. The commander of the besieging forces with an escort is admitted by the rebels for negotiations. At 4.15 the escort returns and says: 'Fey says that no

37

unauthorized attack must be made.' 5 P.M. The besieging Heimwehr tell us 'Rintelen has been made Chancellor.' 5.15 P.M. Police-Inspector Eibel tells us that Dollfuss is dead. 5.20 P.M. Neustaedter-Stuermer shouts to Fey on the balcony: 'If the Chancellery is evacuated, we guarantee safe-conduct for all across the German frontier.' 6.10. Fey appears on the balcony, his face whiter than before, and says: 'Please extend the time limit for evacuation until 7 P.M.' Neustaedter-Stuermer: 'No—until 6.30 P.M. only. I re-affirm the safe-conduct with my word of honor as an officer. Not a hair of their heads shall be injured.' 7 P.M. Secretary of State Karwinsky (a prisoner of the rebels) appears at a barred window and says: 'Fey and I have promised that the German Minister, Dr. Rieth, shall come and speak with the rebels.' Fey comes out. 7.15 P.M. Dr. Rieth arrives. 8 P.M. The police enter the building."

The Austrian official Brown Book quotes a reliable witness who listened in to the conversation which Holzweber, the commander of the rebels in the Chancellery, had on the telephone with Dr. Rieth. Beginning: "This is Captain Friedrich" (his alias), "the Commander-in-Chief of the Rebels," the conversation fully established that the German Minister must have known all about the Putsch in advance.

My colleague Nypels of the *Allgemeene Handelsblad* relates how at 4.18 P.M. a police officer, on instructions, asked the rebels whether it was any use to send for a doctor for Dollfuss and reported the reply to his superior officer—"It is no longer necessary." At his trial Holzweber said uncontradicted that at 2.30 P.M. he had allowed Fey to telephone to the Ministry of War that Dollfuss was dying. At the trial of Planetta and Holzweber both Fey and Karwinsky admitted in court that the promise of safe-conduct was made unconditionally. When Dr. Rieth arrived and remarked with cynical jocularity to Neustaedter-Stuermer, "Crazy business, this!" Neustaedter-Stuermer said, "Excellency, I find it very remarkable that you have no other words for this terrible event. The blood guilt for what has happened here lies on the other side of our frontier," and added that they had granted a safe conduct to Germany to "the whole of the armed men inside the Chancellery"; this was confirmed by Fey. Then this German diplomat went in to confer with the Austrian rebels and murderers, witnessing their guarantee of safe conduct, although told by Neustaedter-Stuermer that his intervention was not desired.

The Austrian Clerico-Fascists were responsible for a second breach of faith, this time with Dollfuss' murderer himself. Unable to discover who had fired the fatal shot, Police-President Skubl told them that if the murderer would give himself up, he would be hanged, but that all the others should go free to Germany. When Planetta stepped forward and confessed, the promise to hang him was very properly kept; the other promise was ignored. One London newspaper commented on the conduct of the Security Minister: "Major Fey has lost all prestige—and could only have retrieved it if he had resigned his office at once—by giving promises at the point of the pistol which he was not able to perform."

The Government's excuse for not observing the safe conduct—that it was given before it was known that Dollfuss had been murdered—is quite untenable in face of all the evidence. Instead of making the only permissible offer to the men whom they knew had murdered their leader—that of a public trial if they surrendered without resistance, otherwise the storming of the building at the point of the bayonet and a rope for every single man if their prisoners were touched—the Clerico-Fascists showed themselves apt disciples of Nazi morality by giving and immediately violating a solemn promise of safe conduct to the whole gang. The latter had even less than the usual gangsters' armaments, and would have been quite incapable of withstanding a proper military assault.

\* \* \*

BERLIN, August 2, 1934 (Associated Press): Adolf Hitler ... made himself absolute dictator of Germany today. He concentrated in his own hands the functions of President and of Chancellor as soon as the aged President ... Paul von Hindenburg, had died at Neudeck.

\* \* \*

SEPTEMBER 18: *Russia entered the League of Nations.*

\* \* \*

MARSEILLES, Oct. 9 (United Press): King Alexander I of Yugoslavia was assassinated today as he arrived in France on one of the most important missions since the World War. Louis Barthou, Foreign Minister of France, also was slain.

\* \* \*

GENEVA, Jan. 15, 1935 (Associated Press): Return of the Saar territory to Germany was assured by an overwhelming majority in Sunday's plebiscite, it was officially announced at the League of Nations' Secretariat today....

\* \* \*

MARCH 16: *Hitler restored universal military service.*

# STRESA: END OF AN ERA

### by Seymour Berkson

STRESA, April 14—England, France and Italy, in a six-point declaration ending the historic Stresa conference, today swung the diplomatic door wide open for Germany to collaborate in a new set of European peace pacts.

These pacts, as outlined in the three-power declaration, will include an aerial non-aggression pact in Western Europe, a non-aggression pact for Eastern Europe (the so-called "Eastern Locarno" proposal) and a Danubian pact for Central Europe.

Censuring Chancellor Hitler of Germany politely but firmly for Germany's rearmament in violation of the Versailles Treaty, the three powers joined in a warning that any further unilateral repudiation of treaties will be opposed with severe measures.

They invited Hitler to join in an international agreement on limitation of armaments, which is expected to be the subject of a later conference.

Translated from the technical language of the declaration, the six points which British Prime Minister MacDonald, French Premier Flandin and Premier Mussolini of Italy agreed on are:

1—A common line of conduct to be pursued on France's protest against German rearmament, which is to be heard by the League of Nations Council in Geneva tomorrow.

2—Pursuance of negotiations to accelerate an Eastern Locarno non-aggression pact.

3—Summoning of a new conference at Rome May 20, to conclude a Central European agreement among France, Germany, Italy, Austria, Hungary, Poland and the Little Entente countries, which may later be supplemented by a Mediterranean peace pact among France, Italy, Greece and Turkey.

4—The three governments agreed to proceed with the proposed air pact for Western Europe to embrace England, France, Germany, Italy and Belgium in an agreement of mutual assistance in event of air attack by any of the signatory powers.

5—England, France and Italy affirmed their earnest desire to sustain peace and join in every effort for promoting an international agreement on limitation of armaments.

6—Representatives of the three governments considered the right of Austria, Hungary and Bulgaria to increase their armaments but it was decided this question should be further examined in collaboration with adjoining Little Entente nations (Rumania, Czechoslovakia and Yugoslavia).

In addition to those six points, there was included an important Anglo-Italian declaration in which these countries "formally reaffirm their obligations under the Locarno treaty, and declare their intention, should need arise, faithfully to fulfill them."

Reaffirmation of the Locarno obligations was regarded as a definite guaranty of peaceful intent toward Germany.

Hitler has signified his willingness to join in the Eastern Locarno providing he does not have to pledge mutual military assistance; to join the aerial pact for Western Europe if a satisfactory draft is made, and to consider a Danubian pact if an acceptable definition of "non-interference" in Austria is found.

> JUNE 18, 1935: *Germany signed a treaty with England by means of which Germany gained a U-boat tonnage equal to that of Britain.*

# THE PARTY IN CONTROL

### *by Louis P. Lochner*

"GIVE me four years' time," was Hitler's slogan when he took over. It needed far less than that to erect in Germany the most complete dictatorship known in modern history.

When the Nazis came into power, they possessed themselves of virtually all the government offices and wrecked the trade unions. That first impact was so terrific that the country was completely dumbfounded and dazed, and one position of influence after another was abandoned, often without even a struggle.

But filling pivotal positions with Nazis could not alone have guaranteed the continuance of the Nazi regime. The Gestapo saw to it that the German people were kept sufficiently in terror not to attempt to conspire against it without fully counting the costs.

Before Himmler took over the secret service, I asked his predecessor Regierungsrat Rudolf Diels why, now that all other parties had been abolished and the Nazis were in full control, organizations like the SA and SS were still maintained. Why couldn't everything be left to the regular organs of the police?

"The value of the SA and SS," he said, "seen from my viewpoint of inspector-general responsible for the suppression of subversive tendencies and activities, lies in the fact that they spread terror. That is a wholesome thing."

When, therefore, my American friends sometimes ask me, "If the German people, or at least some of them, are opposed to Nazism, why did they ever stand for its fastening itself so completely upon the country?" I can only point to the bestiality of the Nazi concentration camp; to the efficacy of the Gestapo in ferreting out every person who tried to maintain inde-

41

pendence of thought and action; and the utter impossibility, once a German fell into the meshes of its ubiquitous organization, of ever extricating himself.

These innumerable groups suddenly learned that they did not have the proper *Weltanschauung*. It followed logically that if they lacked this prerequisite to healthful living in the new Nazi state, they could not possibly be good stamp collectors, entymologists, bowlers, etc. So a Führer, with the proper philosophical attributes was imposed on them—on all, that is, which were allowed to exist. Many a time-honored institution fell by the wayside.

Step by step, the Nazis were eliminating whatever or whoever did not suit them. Even justice—the garden variety of justice, not its palpable perversion, the Gestapo system—had to be dovetailed into the fundamental conception of Nazism, "Whatever is useful to the national socialist state, is right." Moreover, like every other institution, it had to be subordinated to the will of one man, Adolf Hitler.

A judge whom I knew well gave me the following picture:

"Suppose a case of larceny or embezzlement or manslaughter is brought before me for trial. I hear the case, examine the witnesses, scrutinize the evidence, and study up the law as it applies in the particular instance. I announce that I am taking the case under final advisement.

"That same night, likely as not, I am visited by the local party boss. He tells me that the defendant is a man who has rendered certain services to the party which must be taken into account when deciding upon his guilt or innocence. In short, the party demands an acquittal.

"Or suppose I have finished a case in one sitting and have meted out punishment in accordance with the law. Likely as not the party will step in and demand a revision if not a commutation of the sentence.

"'I simply could not stand it any longer, and hence applied for a post as military judge. There, at least, the party cannot interfere—at least not yet!'"

At a luncheon in the Kaiserhof Hotel, Dr. Roland Freisler, Secretary of State for Justice, remarked:

"Justice, like everything else in Germany, emanates from our Führer. He is not only the supreme executive and the supreme legislator, but also the supreme judge. Whatever our Führer wills, gentlemen of the legal profession, whether you be judges, court officials, department of justice specialists, or attorneys, you must carry out.

"If our Führer decides that so-and-so is guilty, then, *meine Herren Richter* (Judges), you must find him guilty. There are no two ways about it. Our Führer's word here as in everything else is law."

There was one other sector of German life upon which the Nazis seized eagerly the moment they came into their own. Youth was regarded as the most important group in the entire German nation for perpetuating national socialism....

I asked Baldur von Schirach, the Reich's Youth Leader, to receive me for a talk. I quote from the interview, as approved by von Schirach and published in his *Reichs-Jugend-Pressedienst* on April 3, 1935:

"I am not concerned in questions of faith. If I keep demanding of our youth that it overcome thinking in terms of a particular religious faith this does not constitute an attack against Protestantism or Catholicism, but it is an offensive against the spirit of disunion which was ever the cause of setbacks in the history of our German people. It caused the tragic death of Arminius the Cheruscan quite as much as it did the collapse of 1918....

"As an educator of youth I have indeed certain apprehensions regarding some passages of the Old Testament, in which pornographic and indecent incidents are narrated in a manner that must necessarily be a source of danger to the youthful mind....But it is not my function to take over responsibilities of the church....

"Never in all my life have I thought of attacking the Christian faiths, but of course I was yesterday, am today, and shall ever be of the opinion that the confessional youth organizations in their present-day structure and tendency are to be disfavored....

"As to the question of quasi-military training and the allegation that such training leads to the militarization of youth, my reply is: I would favor quasi-military education even if Germany were surrounded by disarmed neighbors, for the simple reason that the tendency of such training is peaceful and humane. We want nothing except to make our youth healthy and happy. To attain this ideal we need bodily training. Our soldierly attitude has nothing in common with militarism....

"When you claim that our youth assumes an attitude of superiority toward parents and teachers, you must remember that naughty juveniles existed at all times and ever will exist.

"At the same time, it is not the task of the Hitler Jugend to develop 'model' children....It is a good thing that the German youth of today possesses more self-confidence than the young generations that preceded. I have always found that those people got farthest in life who even in their youth were taught to master their fate....

"You must understand that the political development of Germany has not increased our respect for old people, and for this reason we have the excusable conceit of believing that in decisive political situations more depends upon youthful aggressiveness than upon the experience gathered in seventy years of living...."

# THE SHAME OF NUREMBERG

*by Ralph W. Barnes*

NUREMBERG, Germany, Sept. 15, 1935—Stringent new laws depriving German Jews of all the rights of German citizens and prohibiting marriages between Jews and "Aryans" (Gentiles) were decreed by a subservient, cheering Reichstag here tonight, after an address by Chancellor Adolf Hitler.

In addition, the swastika banner of German Fascism, described to the Reichstag by General Hermann Wilhelm Goering as "the anti-Jewish symbol of the world," was declared to be the sole national flag of the Reich. The black-white-red emblem with its imperial implications, was abolished in its present form.

Tonight's decrees are considered among the most sweeping measures taken since the Nazis came into power two and a half years ago.

That proclaiming the swastika flag as the national banner was occasioned in part by the rioting on the liner *Bremen* in New York in July, when the Nazi flag was torn down, and by Magistrate Louis B. Brodsky's subsequent characterization of the swastika standard as a "black flag of piracy," it was indicated by General Goering.

He declared: "It is regrettable that the American people recently tolerated an impudent Jewish insult to our flag, which has been to us a holy symbol, under which we have fought and suffered, and under which Germany will stand once and for all throughout eternity."

Under the new statutes, Jews in Germany will be put back abruptly to their position in Europe during the Middle Ages and the Renaissance.

The laws constitute a signal victory for the violent anti-Jewish wing of the Nazi party, led by Julius Streicher.

The new anti-Jewish laws, which go into effect January 1, constitute realization of nearly the whole anti-Semitic portion of the Nazi program.

They are described as "laws for the protection of German blood and German honor." As read before the Reichstag by Goering, president of the legislative body, they follow:

1. Marriages between Jews and German citizens are forbidden;
2. Extra-marital relations between Jews and Germans are forbidden;
3. Jews are not permitted to employ in their household German servants under the age of forty-five;
4. Jews are forbidden to hoist the swastika emblem (now the sole national flag);
5. Jews are permitted to hoist a racial flag of their own with assurance of official protection.

Violation of any of the first three articles, concerning marriage, sexual relations and employment of servants, is punishable by imprisonment at hard labor. Violation of the fourth article is punishable by simple imprisonment.

Goering thereupon spoke at length, explaining the new anti-Jewish and citizenship laws.

"We must preserve," the Air Minister and Prussian Premier said, "the Germanic and Nordic purity of the race, and must protect our women and girls with every means at our disposal. In this pure blood stream will blossom forth a new era of Germanic happiness.

"An example of our idea of men sound to the core is found in the men (100,000 Storm Troopers) who marched before Der Fuehrer today. That is purity of race. Never again will we let our Germanism be infected and ruined by Jewish infiltration.

"Every Nazi German finds in his race and in his people the highest fulfillment of his individual being, and is ready to give up his whole life for both. We hereby acknowledge our fealty to this principle of right, which is itself dictated by nature."

Goering then turned to the question of the flag.

"Our newly won freedom," he said, "requires a new symbol. It is fitting that the new symbol should be the one under which we won our new freedom. The old black, white and red flag belongs to a glorious period, but a period of the past. This symbol of the Second Empire [Bismarck's empire, from 1871 to the end of the World War] was dragged into the dirt during our period of shame and degradation [the post-war period up to the Nazi assumption of power].

"A soldier from the front lines, Adolf Hitler, pulled us out of the dirt and brought us back to honor. At the same time we can have no compromise now. The swastika has become for us a holy symbol. It is the anti-Jewish symbol of the world."

Here Goering referred to "impudent Jewish insults in the United States to our flag."

Tonight's session of the Reichstag was summoned unexpectedly by Hitler after the Nazi party congress had convened here last week. All but two or three of the 600 members are Nazi party men, so they were ready at hand when the session was announced.

The Reichstag, which is now nothing more than a rubber stamp, was called to order by Goering at 9 P.M. in the auditorium of the German Cultural Union. On the platform besides Hitler were Rudolf Hess, deputy Nazi party leader; Baron Konstantin von Neurath, Foreign Minister; General Werner von Blomberg, War Minister, and other government officials.

After speaking of the three laws, Goering asked the Reichstag for unanimous approval. Six hundred-odd men, the bulk of them in brown uniforms, leaped to their feet.

At various points during the speeches of Hitler and Goering there was enthusiastic cheering.

A roar of laughter arose when Goering proposed that Jews should not be permitted to employ in their households "Aryan" servants under the age of forty-five.

With the violently anti-Jewish wing of the Nazi party now apparently in the saddle, further anti-Semitic measures, supplementing those decreed by the Reichstag here last night withdrawing citizenship from Jews and forbidding Jewish-"Aryan" (Gentile) marriages, are expected to be enacted soon.

Re-establishment of the ghetto is now under way, as is manifest in the recent decision to establish separate schools for Jews. Two months ago Julius Streicher, anti-Semitic Nazi leader of Franconia, urged on the government the ghetto policy with all its implications. Streicher had his way in the matter of the schools, and again last night in the enactment of the anti-Jewish laws.

There are definite indications that Chancellor Adolf Hitler is prepared to go much further along the lines which Streicher and others of his crew are pointing out, with elimination of all the Jews in Germany as their ultimate aim.

Just now there is much speculation as to how the gradual realization of a ghetto policy will affect Jews in business. Although stringent legal as well as extra-legal measures are intended to eliminate Jews from the professions, direct interference with their business activities has been confined largely to anti-Jewish boycotts and anti-Jewish riots of a type which now are frowned on even by Streicher.

Hitler repeated in his speech before the Reichstag last night a passage of his proclamation at the opening of the Nazi party congress here—that if the agencies of the state proved incapable of dealing with the "enemy," including the Jewish "enemy," the task would be delegated by law to the Nazi party.

The Fuehrer mentioned in this connection the foreign boycott of German goods, indicating that revision of the Nazi policy in the direction of more stringent methods would be needed if the foreign boycott of German products were to continue. Hitler's forceful declarations to this effect are considered additional proof of his ruthless determination to "put the Jew in his place," regardless of opinion abroad.

Breathless wonder was expressed tonight at the announcement by official news agencies that the new anti-Jewish laws referred only to full-blooded Jews. If this interpretation were to be followed, hardly more than 600,000 persons, and perhaps fewer, would be affected. Of this number about 50,000 are Christian converts. In some circles it is thought, however, that courts will interpret the new marriage laws as applying to all persons with any Jewish blood.

It should be mentioned that for several months the authorities have followed a policy of barring Jewish-Gentile marriages, so that the law passed last night merely gives a legal basis for decisions already in effect. In fact, a court in Breslau recently went so far as to say that an "Aryan" who maintained intimate social relations with a Jew short of cohabitation was guilty of "race defilement."

Exceptions are made by the courts for business relations. Hence the forthcoming law, which is to define the rights and duties of a "member" of the Reich as distinguished from a citizen, is awaited with much interest. This law, it is thought, may throw some light on the question of what business activities of Jews are to be interfered with directly.

46

# UNDERGROUND 1935

## by John L. Spivak

THREE strong muscle-men were throwing one another about in what I immediately suspected was a funny act when I walked into the smoke-laden Alkazar cabaret on Reeperbann in the St. Pauli district in Hamburg and found a vacant table at a corner of the dance floor. The place was crowded with men and women, some in evening clothes, and a good sprinkling of Nazis in black and brown and the greenish-gray of the air forces despite the Nazi Party prohibition to men in uniform frequenting night clubs.

It was ten-thirty and though I had been told to be there at eleven o'clock, I arrived a little earlier lest all the corner tables be taken. I ordered a liqueur and sat there sipping it and wondering whether I was on a wild goose chase. Two months before in Paris I had met some Communist refugees who had fled Germany when heads began to roll and I had expressed a desire to be put in touch with the Communist underground movement. I knew I was making a dangerous request, dangerous not so much to me but to the Communist who would meet me, should I be followed. But, everyone expects the Communists to seize control of Germany when Hitler collapses, yet few, even among the best-informed refugee circles, know the actual Communist strength and what they are thinking of doing in such an event. The activities of the underground movement is so befogged with rumors and patently exaggerated assertions that some real information from an official source seemed to me worth the risk.

So here I sat in this sumptuously furnished cabaret heavy with the scent of wines and perfumes and expensive tobacco, uncertain whether to feel like a conspirator or a fool. An appointment made two months ago to meet a person I did not know and who did not know me sounded a little silly, but it had the thrill of mystery, so I sat there smoking and sipping the liqueur and wondering whether anyone would really show up.

"Just be sure you are not followed," they had impressed on me in Paris and I made so sure, by walking, driving along deserted streets and changing taxis for two solid hours that the thought of going through that procedure again for possibly two more nights was very disturbing.

Pleasure seekers kept strolling in with Aryan women on their arms. There were very few women with dark hair I noticed. The place was pretty well filled and I looked at my watch, feeling a little foolish for it was eleven-thirty and no one had appeared. Six beefy girls, with the whole dance floor to themselves, were raising tired legs in what I assumed was a dance. At an adjoining table was an S.A. man, an officer of high rank who was having a grand time flirting with a really gorgeous blond of the tea-and-cabaret type. They had taken their table about a half hour earlier and their proximity caused me a bit of uneasiness for if whoever was to get in touch with me saw him there, the chances of his appearing would be slim. I had agreed to be there for three successive nights and I gave myself up to brooding over the whole matter when the Nazi officer, after searching his pockets for a match, turned to me and politely asked if I had one.

"The waiter is not around," he explained apologetically.

I offered him my cigarette lighter and he lit the blond's and his own gold-tipped cigarette.

"You are waiting for someone?"

"No," I said casually. "I had nothing to do tonight so I thought I'd spend a little time here."

"Ach, so! Well, why not join us?" he invited me cheerfully.

He wouldn't listen to my protests. He rose, clicked his heels and introduced himself and the beautiful blond.

"My name's Spivak," I muttered.

The waiter brought a bottle of wine. The music played a soft waltz and couples strolled out onto the floor.

"To the new Germany," said my host, clinking glass against mine.

We drank to the new Germany. I decided that I might just as well salvage something from the evening by talking with him since my appointment for that evening at least was now ruined, when I was startled by a voice saying in English:

"I believe we have an appointment here?"

It took me a moment or two to realize that it was the Nazi officer who was talking. Luckily the lights had been dimmed for the dance. I don't know what my expression was, but the beautiful Aryan lady of the perfect tea-and-cabaret type laughed in a soft, well-modulated voice and the Nazi officer grinned boyishly.

"I beg pardon?" I said.

"An appointment for eleven o'clock tonight at the Alkazar, arranged by some friends in Paris?"

I looked at him again. He nodded slowly, his boyish grin growing more pronounced.

"You want to know something about the underground movement in Germany?" he asked quietly, leaning towards me a trifle. "What do you wish to know?"

"But—" I stared at the rank on his uniform.

"There are many of us in Nazi uniforms," he smiled.

He raised his glass again.

"Shall we drink again to the new Germany?" he asked, and this time I understood.

While he talked he toyed with the long stem of his wine glass, smiling in that boyish manner as though he were telling naughty stories and I, too, listening had to keep reminding myself to smile and nod appreciatively while the blond Aryan of the tea-and-cabaret type (I hope, should she ever read this, that she realizes I mean this as a very high compliment) kept her eyes constantly on people approaching or passing our table the

48

while she occasionally nodded her head as though somewhat amused by the funny stories.

"Are many of the Communists in the Nazi Party now?"

"No. Some of us are—a very few. Most Party members are in the labor front—among the industrial and agricultural workers. Surely we want to carry on propaganda among the Nazis and also among the workers and the farmers. Of course, it is necessary for some of us to be in the Nazi Party—so we are. Before Hitler got in power we had between five and six million Communist sympathizers. That is history. After the Nazis got the government many of those sympathizers were won away from us. Hitler made serious inroads among some workers, who were swayed by propaganda and actually thought that a form of socialism would be effected. However, as time went on and instead of socialism they discovered it was one of the worst forms of fascism, the left wing of the Nazi Party became active. They and the people talked of a 'new revolution' to achieve socialism. It was then that the Blood Purge came on June 30. The left wing was shattered and the S.A. which had been powerful, lost its importance.

"The Blood Purge had a very beneficial effect. It showed the workers precisely where Hitler stood and ended their dream of a 'new revolution.' Workers whom Hitler had won two years ago were greatly disappointed and swerved away from the Nazis though, of course, they dare not show it too openly.

"During this entire period, Communists were still being arrested due to the host of spies still in the underground movement. When one least expected it, some active Communist was whisked away to a concentration camp."

"How extensive is your propaganda and how effective?"

"Our best propagandist is Hitler and his Nazis," he smiled. "Hitler is doing a great deal to develop Communist sympathizers. So far as our own work is concerned, you know, of course, about the literature that's smuggled in like books, pamphlets, etc. The circulation of these smuggled papers is quite small and its effectiveness is difficult to gauge. They are probably not very effective in themselves, but we cannot judge by the effectiveness of one means. They are all little rivulets which eventually add up to a stream.

"Then we have our own mimeographed newspapers which come out at irregular intervals. Here in Hamburg we have three. In Berlin we have eight. The number varies according to the size of the center. The circulation of these papers, too, is very small, but in their own way they are quite effective. Then there are other propaganda methods; which, necessarily, are constantly being changed. At present, for instance, we are scattering round bits of paper and cardboard which look exactly like money when on the ground. We see to it that they are scattered particularly in places where women have to stand in line for their quarter of a pound of butter, for instance. These women are already irritable and are voicing their displeasure at the food shortage quite openly. When they see what seems to be a coin they pick it up only to find a legend on it like 'Death to Hitler' or 'Demand food instead of armies' and so on. No one dares to hold on to the paper, so they drop it again where it lies ready for the next person to pick it up. A trifle, of course. But when a people is irritable, suggestions pounded in day in and day out produce a profound effect in the long run. Our best work, of course, is being done in the industrial centers where, despite the inroads made by the Nazis among the workers, the nucleus of the Party remained pretty much intact. The groups are smaller, of course, but we are more solidified."

"Are the tortures today as brutal as when Hitler first took power?"

"That depends on the region and the people in charge. The German people are not sadists; they are really a kindly people and the tortures inflicted on the Communists in the early period of the Nazi regime have revolted many a German. Today there are still vicious, inhuman tortures. But they have learned that Communists will not talk; they have developed a feeling of admiration for the stoical suffering that many Communists have undergone."

"Is the Nazi strength great among the people?"

"I should say that there are about 100,000 persons in Germany who really believe in the Nazi principles. The rest are Nazis because they got good jobs out of the regime and considerable graft."

"That being the case, with the Nazis losing the people's sympathy and the Communists gaining, how long can Hitler last?"

"Barring a war—for a very long time."

I looked at him a little surprised.

"But the financial condition of the country is very precarious. Hitler has enough money to last another year. Then comes inflation, more unemployment. People are grumbling. Will the people stand for it?"

He smiled a little grimly:

"The Nazis have the army and the army has the guns. It would be suicide at present to attempt to seize the government. We would be slaughtered. In the event of war, when soldiers are dissatisfied and a lot of us sympathizers have arms and can lay hands on machine guns, munition, bombs, planes—then it becomes a different story."

"But what happens when Hitler cracks?"

"That depends upon a great many circumstances—the economic and world political conditions at the time. At present it looks like the dictatorship will be assumed by the military who already show a tendency toward the restoration of the Hohenzollerns. Should that happen, there will be, of course, concessions to the dissatisfied populace, like elections and so on—probably a monarchy patterned after the one in England, but with not so much freedom. The Reichswehr is far more shrewd than the Nazi Party. The General Staff is composed of scholars who know not only the military situation but the political and economic as well. They know what is happening. But, though the General Staff is very competent, its cleverness is limited. They want to maintain the present economic system and it is this disintegrating system which will defeat them in the long run. We Communists can only confine ourselves to preparing the workers and the farmers to seize and hold power when the upholders of the system have been so weakened by its disintegration that the soldiers upon whom the General Staff depends, will also rebel and be ready to turn against them."

"You have not had a drink for some time and you are not looking at the show," the beautiful Aryan reminded us again.

He smiled quickly at her. We raised our glasses, touched them to one another and drank silently.

"Conditions make for revolutions, not Communists," he continued quietly. "The period Germany is passing through today is but another step in our direction. Before Hitler is through he will have helped considerably to wreck the already weak capitalist system here."

"But when Hitler goes, there will be chaos. What will the Communists do then?"

"Why will there be chaos?" he asked gently. "The strings of government are never suddenly thrown to the wind. Those in power know when they are about to collapse and those seeking power also know it and have prepared for it—for a long time. There may be some chaotic conditions for a while, but some group will control the army and that is the group that will emerge in control. It is not, of course, inevitable that when Hitler goes Communism follows. The people are not quite ready for a Communist attempt, the conditions are not ripe and though we gain sympathizers rapidly (this is even more important) we are not ready."

"But a war seems to be likely in the next two, possibly three years. Will the Communists launch a civil war which will hasten the disintegrating process?"

"That depends on conditions. We are not rushing into anything. If the war is against the Soviet Union, as from all indications it will be, then it may become necessary. Otherwise we may just continue to work quietly."

"Are you so organized that you could tear the country apart by civil war immediately after a war began?"

"No. It would take at least half a year before we could do effective work along that line."

"It is past two," the beautiful Aryan reminded him.

We rose. The woman offered her hand.

"Charming evening, *nicht?*" she said in her best social tone.

He clasped mine in a firm grip. "We shall meet again one day I'm sure." *"Auf wiedersehen,"* they said.

I sat staring at their departing backs. A new act was on, some more beefy girls raising tired, fat legs. When the fifteen minutes were up, I drained the rest of the wine in my glass—to them:

*"Auf wiedersehen*—in a happier Germany!"

# FASCISM IN THE WEST

*by Johannes Steel*

I

MARCH, 1934—England, like all other countries where society is organized in defense of capitalism, will soon pass through a phase of fascism. One of the major and most tragic reasons for this will be the absence of any real opposition to fascism. The official British Labor Party is intellectually and spiritually just as corrupt and decadent as the Social Democratic Party of Germany was in the middle of 1932, when, in spite of the fact that it had complete control over the well-trained police forces, it abdicated in Prussia without any resistance on being politely requested to do so. The English Labor Party will suffer the same ignominious fate. That Labor for the first time in English politics has just conquered the London County Council and routed the London Conservatives means only that the good people of that city consider the Labor Party "safe" and disinclined to "unconstitutional experiments," and believe that it can be depended on to pursue a liberal middle course. Indeed, there is very little that is Socialist and nothing that is revolutionary about the official British Labor movement of today. Using the old obsolete terminology, its leaders talk of the "gradualness" of social and political evolution—the same talk that I have heard from German Social Democrats for the last ten years. In all its aspects and aspirations the British Labor Party is thoroughly bourgeois; its leaders are tired old men who feel that they cannot take any risks, and like their German colleagues, they have neither the mental agility to face issues with political realism nor the courage to assume responsibility for the grave and sudden decisions which will soon become necessary. These leaders have grown accustomed to the comparative comfort and prestige they have enjoyed for the last ten years and they intend to remain strictly constitutional in order to retain these privileges. They admitted as much when on March 1 of this year the National Executive Committee of the Labor Party refused the Independent Labor Party's invitation to take part in an "immediate consultation between the representatives of all sections of the working classes" for the purpose of planning common action against fascism.

In his reply to this invitation the Right Honorable Arthur Henderson, secretary of the Labor Party, said: "Your suggestion ... is one which in the considered opinion of the National Executive of the Labor Party cannot result in any agreed policy of common action in view of the *fundamental differences* which exist, for example, between the Labor Party and the Independent Labor Party." To speak of "fundamental differences" between two parties which are both supposed to represent the interests of labor means of course that the leaders of the Labor Party intend to consolidate these differences as the basis of their own economic position and political and social career. In short, the British Labor Party is displaying the same lack of vision and of integrity of purpose that led the German Social Democrats into disaster when they failed to agree upon a course of common action with the more radical and aggressive Socialist elements.

But the next elections, always provided that they are held and that the National Government does not invent a state of emergency to prevent them, will also sweep a great number of fascists into Parliament. It is certain that Sir Oswald Mosley will test at the polls the strength of his movement, which he believes to be supported by not less than one million voters. All available figures indicate the correctness of Sir Oswald's estimate. In many rural districts, particularly, he is making converts every day: the violent interference of black-shirt gangs whenever the tax-collector attempted to foreclose or sell small farms for arrears of church tithes or other taxes was clever strategy. The impoverished middle classes are overwhelmingly in Mosley's favor, and he has, of course, had ample financial support from English industrialists, which has made it possible for his organization to establish branches in every important town and city of Great Britain. His party is run with the proverbial fascist efficiency and employs the same methods of organization and propaganda that the Hitlerites use. The London Chelsea Headquarters, where the party executive officers are trained, are staffed with experienced German Nazis who have been sent by Hitler to instruct Mosley's stalwarts in political terrorism. Moreover, Mosley has now a powerful press almost completely at his disposal. Lord Rothermere, who in the course of his checkered political career has asked the British public in his various papers to "take their hats off to France" and to "take them off to Hungary," and who produced the faked Zinoviev letter which resulted in a Conservative stampede, is now requesting his fellow-countrymen to "cry hurrah for the Black Shirts." Since his *Daily Mail* has a circulation of more than 1,750,000 and his various evening papers a combined circulation of not less than 3,000,000, there is no doubt that these opportunities for propaganda will be of considerable assistance to Mosley in his struggle for popular support. The Rothermere papers can be particularly useful because the Rothermere staff are past masters in the art of coloring news—after all, the most effective way to mold public opinion.

The Labor Party made a grave mistake when it underestimated the personality of the leader of the British fascists. Sir Oswald's own mother said of him that he "had intelligence, courage, knowledge, vision, and even genius, but that he lacked completely all balance and ballast." It was this lack of balance that made him turn fascist instead of drawing farther to the left when he could not satisfy his craving for action in the Labor Party. If Mosley comes to power it will be thanks to the stupidity and lethargy of Socialists like Snowden and Thomas, who in 1929 turned down their colleague Mosley's proposals for the reduction of unemployment and snubbed him for his urge "to do something."

But it will not be Mosley, or at least not Mosley alone, who will bring fascism to England. The English character will not permit fascism to take either the German totalitarian form with its ruthless regimentation or the Italian form with all its flamboyance. It will have to be something specifically British. The British brand of fascism, the result of the instinctive fear of a capitalist society that it will be unprepared for the coming struggle, is taking form, for example, in the militarization of the police and the creation of a police officer class not drawn from the ranks but from the universities; it is seen in the strengthening of the territorial army and in the training of thousands of "special constables" to be called in case of a "state of national emergency." In the event of a general strike these special constables will take over the functions of the workers in the key industries, such as power, light, transportation, and communications, in order "that everyday life may go on as if nothing had happened."

All these developments have the tacit support of such influential people as the young Conservative leader Lord Lloyd, the motor-car manufacturer Sir William Morris (England's Henry Ford), the Guinness family, and others, not to mention Sir Henri Deterding and a group of regular Conservatives who are thinking in terms of an aggressive British foreign policy. This group of Conservatives has definite pro-German sentiments. The Nazis, through Dr. Rosenberg and Dr. Schacht, with the aid of Deterding, Montagu Norman, governor of the Bank of England, and the City of London generally, have been able to convince them of the advisability of a great fascist alliance embracing England, Germany, and Japan. The Nazis have suggested that they could "guarantee in Europe the safety of the British possessions over seas." By this they mean they will "undertake to do all the necessary police work" to keep Central and Southeastern Europe free of socialism and communism, thus giving England a free hand to direct all its efforts toward the preservation of the Empire. Led most actively by Lord Lloyd, a very influential school of thought in England believes today that this is one of the ways to perpetuate British imperialism and that it would help to stem the rising tide of communism already engulfing the colonies generally and India in particular. The pro-Japanese feeling is the result of propaganda by British armament interests, which did not even stop their sales to Japan during the period of the ill-fated Simon arms embargo.

## II

OCTOBER, 1935—Premier Laval is preparing a Fascist coup d'état with the help of Colonel François de la Roque, commander of the Croix de Feu, Fascist army, your correspondent was told today by a person close to the Premier.

According to these sources, Laval is going to Geneva this week to pay lip service to the application of sanctions, while in effect, France is pledged, through Laval, not to make sanctions effective.

At the end of November the parliamentary situation will be such in France that Laval, if things take a normal course, would be overthrown

54

by the Chamber of Deputies and succeeded by a transition government, Georges Mandel, Edouard Herriot and ex-Premier Deladier to be in office until elections next May.

Laval, however, has decided not to cede power, because he believes that the moment for the realization of his admitted political dream of conservative dictatorship in France and the creation of a great Fascist European bloc has now come.

The Premier, therefore, will dare the attempt at which Gaston Doumergue failed in the summer of 1934 because of militant Left opposition.

Many important steps have already been taken to prepare this dictatorship. All diplomatic news sent abroad, as well as that of French newspapers, is severely censored. Having the secret funds of the office of Premier, as well as Foreign Minister, at his disposal, money is spent left and right on propaganda for the present Government.

Expressions of opinion against Italy are simply forbidden.

Laval already directs affairs of nation from his private Villa Said, and many decisions are taken without consultation of his Cabinet, in open defiance of democratic procedure.

The statesmen who gave this information to your correspondent added that anything is likely to happen in the next two or three weeks and anything might be expected from Laval, who has for a year now officially conducted a policy he doesn't believe in himself.

This goes particularly for the Franco-Russian treaty which he concluded.

Laval actually told Prince Paul, Regent of Yugoslavia, during the latter's visit to Paris last week, that he was opposed to a Yugoslavian treaty with Russia at this time, since he (Laval) would soon change France's pro-Soviet policy.

What, exactly, the outcome will be depends in the greatest measure upon a Front Commune (common front) of the Left parties, now paralyzed by lack of leadership and personal antipathy between Leon Blum, Socialist leader, and Deladier, head of the Radical Socialists, France's greatest party.

Meanwhile retail prices continue to rise and Laval's policy of deflation will soon have the people of Paris rioting again.

That these riots are expected is evidenced by the new concentration of 40,000 Gardes Mobile and two infantry regiments on the outskirts of Paris.

In short, the next few weeks will see probably the final defeat or victory of democracy in France, a development that probably will be accompanied with much bloodshed and the outcome of which will have serious consequences for the politics of Europe and ultimately the cause of war and peace.

Deaf to the protests of the Leftist press, Premier Laval keeps unswervingly to the course by which he intends to invest the French Government machinery with the character of Fascism.

Among 300 emergency laws promulgated on Saturday, Laval slipped in one decree of which his ministerial colleagues knew nothing.

It virtually abolishes the free press in France, for it provides that "any

55

writer who insults the heads of foreign governments or their foreign ministers is liable to fine and imprisonment."

In this case the word "insults" is to be interpreted as meaning the expression of displeasure.

Further, the Premier is postponing the convocation of the Chamber of Deputies, which must meet once more this year if it is to vote on the budget.

Also, Laval has delayed ratification of the treaty with Russia, hoping that by the end of this year the sentiment of the people and their representatives in Parliament may have changed. If a vote were taken in the Chamber now, ratification would be certain.

In the field of foreign affairs, Laval's efforts at conciliation of the British-Italian dispute have failed dismally.

Despite reports to the contrary, there is at present no basis for agreement between those two countries, and it is more than a possibility that war between England and Italy will be the eventual outcome.

# Part Two: The Lights Go Down

## GERMANY PREPARES FOR WAR

### by Louis Fischer

MARCH 1, 1936—The most important question I wanted my Berlin stay to answer was this: Will Germany's food and financial troubles seriously impair its ability to complete its armament program? I think the answer is in the negative.

German industrial production has reached a post-war high. But much of it can neither be eaten nor worn. Germany is freezing huge quantities of its capital in war materials. Experts estimate that 3,000,000 more persons are employed now than in January, 1933—there are 750,000 more office-holders, 750,000 more soldiers and sailors, and 1,500,000 more factory hands. But the volume of consumers' commodities remains relatively low. The technical apparatus of the German army—aeroplanes, guns, tanks, and so on—will reach its high point in 1936, when the army will be fully prepared for war.

In other respects, however, 1936 will not find Germany ready for war. Nation-wide military conscription has just commenced, and the Reichswehr's *cadres* are not sufficiently trained for a conflict with major powers. Nor have the enlarged officers' corps and staff had time to acquire the efficiency and knowledge demanded by modern warfare. The World War veterans are old, physically below par, and technically backward. Germany must wait till the new millions are molded into soldiers fit for long and trying battles. When will that be? Some specialists say 1937, most say 1938, some say 1939. The Reichswehr today probably numbers 800,000 commanders and men. In 1939 it will count 1,000,000 men under arms and 2,500,000 freshly drilled reserves. This is about the right amount of cannon fodder for a beginning.

The chief problem is raw materials. The American Socony-Vacuum Company, therefore, is building a refinery in Hamburg which will convert inferior oil into aviation lubricants. The plant will be finished this year.

Research laboratories are working on substitutes for steel, iron, copper, cotton, and sulphur. The authorities have a scientific record of all non-ferrous metals in private and industrial use. In time of war these reserves—underground telephone cables, for instance—would be requisitioned. Germany, moreover, is financing the production of soya beans in Hungary, bauxite in Yugoslavia, and tobacco in Bulgaria; the German Vereinigte Stahlwerke own 1,700,000 of the 3,000,000 shares of the Alpine-Montan Company, the largest metallurgical firm in Austria. Germany hopes to draw supplies from these sources when war breaks out.

57

The army's orders are the chief food of German heavy industry, and industry in turn subordinates its activities to military considerations. The army is supervising the erection of a big Opel automobile plant at Brandenburg. There are General Motors and International Telegraph and Telephone Company factories in Germany which, though American-owned, cannot be entered by any American; they are turning out war equipment.

All Germany is an armed camp. One who like myself returns to Germany after irregular absences notices the marked increase in the number of Reichswehr cars and uniforms. The ordinary army trucks which now pass through the streets of Berlin are painted with camouflage. This is a part of the practical preparation for war. But it is also part of the psychological preparation which goes on with unrelenting intensity every hour of every day in the press, radio, and schools.

Germany's mental mobilization is of supreme importance. Every nation is frantically increasing its armaments. This phenomenon has become so normal that few ever stop to think how many shoes, shirts, loaves of bread, pounds of meat and butter, medicines, comforts, and pleasures it steals from hundreds of millions of human beings every morning, afternoon, and evening. Sometimes one comes to the conclusion that a humanity which submits to such madness really deserves a war which will exterminate most of it. Germany, in fact, charges that Bolshevik Russia harbors aggressive designs, just as Rome charged that Abyssinia was the aggressor. The Germans contend that they are pacific, and Hitler has made several speeches which are quoted in Berlin as evidence of Germany's deep desire for peace. Can an objective truth be lifted out of this polemic?

The Germans, notoriously, have always been bad diplomats, and the reason is that they put little trust in diplomacy and therefore little effort into it. They respect force; they are cynical about words. Hitler came to power in January, 1933. Poland grew frightened. In the previous year equality in armaments had been conceded to Germany by the League, and Warsaw feared that a rearmed Germany ruled by super-nationalistic Nazis would seriously menace Danzig and the Corridor. In March, 1933, accordingly, the late Marshal Pilsudski concentrated five army corps near the German frontier and sounded France and England on the desirability of a preventive war against Fascist Germany. Rumor has it that General Weygand, then French Chief of Staff, lent an ear to the idea. In April Polish troops occupied the Westerplatte, a strip of Danzig territory. It looked like the beginning of war. On May 16, 1933, President Hindenburg wrote to his assistant, State Secretary Meissner, a note the facsimile of which was published in the Berlin *Deutsche Allgemeine Zeitung* of August 12, 1934. It said: "These days you can of course get in touch with me at any time of the day or night." The very next day Hitler summoned the Reichstag to listen to a long pacifist speech. "No new European war," the Chancellor declared wisely, "could create conditions better than the unsatisfactory conditions of today. . . . Germany is always ready to assume further security obligations of an international character. . . . Germany would be prepared to abolish its entire military establishment." The world at large did not know that these promises were designed to ward off an imminent war. The Western powers, however, were glad to take Hitler at his word because they did not want to fight. Paris vetoed Pilsudski's preventive war.

Chancellor Hitler made another pacifist speech on May 21, 1935. Every German with whom I have spoken recently quoted this address as the cornerstone of German foreign policy. The address had two motifs, one of which was friendship for England. Three weeks later the Anglo-German naval agreement was signed. Hitler wanted it very much. The speech of May 21 was a bid for it. The second motif was hostility to Bolshevik Russia. Hitler outdid himself in fiercely, wildly attacking Moscow. On the next day the German government offered the Soviet government a billion-mark long-term credit. Germany needs Soviet raw materials—oil, manganese, timber, and so on—and wants to put her unemployed plant to work. Even though Moscow must distinguish between business advantages and political sympathies, it has not accepted the proposal. Indeed, Hitler's presentation of May 21, 1935, warrants the fear that Germany has reserved for itself certain spheres of future conflict. One is Austria. Hitler stated that he wanted "self-determination" for Austria. A high German official said to me the other day that Germany wanted a plebiscite in Austria to determine whether or not Austria wished to adhere to Germany. Germany has been asked and has refused to guarantee Austria's territorial integrity. The second is Lithuania. "We are ready," Hitler declared on May 25, "to conclude pacts of non-aggression with all our neighbors except Lithuania." This may sound innocent, especially as Hitler added that if Lithuania adhered to the Memel statute which guarantees the rights of the German minority the exception could be removed. But this problem is a complicated one. It may remain open for a long time. And Lithuania is a step toward the Soviet frontier.

But perhaps, since Germany will not be ready for war until about 1938, there is no cause for immediate alarm. This would be a false and dangerous attitude. Until 1937 or 1938 or 1939 Germany will not be in a position to cope single-handed with a group of powers which includes France. But if Germany finds an ally in Japan or Poland or Hungary, the date may be advanced. Moreover, the weaker the probable coalition against Germany, the nearer the catastrophe. Innumerable Germans are convinced that Britain's preoccupation with Italy and the Far East and its dread of air attacks upon London will keep England out of the next war unless it is directly menaced. Would England be as ready to give battle for Austria, Czechoslovakia or Lithuania as it was for Abyssinia? The fate of European civilization may depend on the answer.

Everything, accordingly, depends on how many friends Germany can win and on the extent to which it can undermine the potential enemy. The outstanding and rather transparent purpose of German diplomacy at present is to separate France from Russia, France from England, and Russia from England. Simultaneously it strives to weave closer ties with London as a

59

preliminary to neutralization. But even this last all-important goal is subordinated to Germany's policy vis-a-vis Italy. A weakened Italy makes Germany's task in Austria easier. On the other hand a revisionist and embittered, because thwarted, Italy might be an ally in a world war. Yet Italy could also side with France against Germany. Italy's defeat in Abyssinia might end in Mussolini's fall, which would react to the detriment of German fascism, both at home and abroad. That defeat, if hastened by League collective action, would be a terrifying precedent for the next aggressor. Germany, therefore, watches the Ethiopian affair with hope, trepidation, and indecision. It does not wish to offend England by word or gesture, but it also does not want to alienate Italy. Hence the "neutrality" to which Germans point as proof of their pacifism. They are waiting to see how the wind blows.

Europe's great good fortune is that the period of highest tension in Italy, which produced the Abyssinian adventure, did not coincide with the same period in Germany. If the two periods had coincided, the two countries would be allies and Europe would be a shambles. European statesmen feel obliged to settle the Anglo-Italian-Ethiopian conflict before the German problem grows much riper. This is wisdom. It is also difficult.

\* \* \*

BERLIN, March 7, 1936 (International News Service): German troops marched into the demilitarized Rhineland zone today as Chancellor Hitler sensationally announced the smashing of this last big fetter of the Versailles Treaty....

\* \* \*

JUNE 4, 1936: *Leon Blum became Premier of France.*

SEPTEMBER 9: *Hitler announced to the Germans a four-year plan.*

NOVEMBER 28: *Germany and Japan signed anti-Comintern Pact.*

JANUARY 19, 1937: *New "Trotzkyist" trials in Moscow.*

# THE MOSCOW TRIALS

### *by Walter Duranty*

WHEN Trotsky was exiled to Turkey more than eight years ago, it seemed to most people in the USSR, including foreign observers, that the long Opposition struggle inside the Communist Party was definitely ended. In point of fact, as recent events have shown, the contrary was true; Trotsky's exile did not end the struggle but paved the way for its resumption in a new and more sinister form.

It is now clear that the Kremlin-Opposition conflict falls into three chronological phases. The first period covers the years from 1923, when the Bolshevik leaders first realized that Lenin's days were numbered, to January, 1928, when the Opposition, which by then had formed a somewhat disparate bloc under the leadership of Trotsky, was crushed and its adherents, great and small, were scattered in exile across Siberia and Central Asia. This may be called the phase of Open Controversy. There followed the phase of Reconciliation, from the latter part of 1928 to 1934, during which Trotsky's supporters in Russia recanted their heresies and paid abject lip service to the Kremlin. Many of them were restored to posts of high importance, although they had already shown that their previous recantations of error and promises of amendment in the future were not to be relied upon. During these years Trotsky found harborage on the Isle of Prinkipo in the Bosphorus, where his activities were somewhat hampered by Turkish supervision and where he appears to have confined himself to the preparation of a new campaign against his opponents on Soviet soil by the formation of the so-called Fourth International and by writing in order to raise funds. He established and maintained contact with his friends in the USSR and elsewhere, and by the end of 1932, when he was able to leave Prinkipo for a less restricted and more congenial sojourn in France, he had laid the foundations for a renewed attack on the Kremlin. This preliminary work was continued and developed in 1933 and 1934, coincidentally with a great extension of German activity in the USSR. At the end of November, 1934, Kirov, one of Stalin's closest henchmen, was assassinated in Leningrad. This marked the beginning of the third and present phase of Secret Conspiracy. This development was due: (a) to the character and ability of Trotsky himself, (b) to the international situation, with particular reference to Germany and Japan, and (c) to circumstances inside Russia.

Trotsky's expulsion from Russia was an act not of clemency alone but of policy. To begin with, the First Five-Year Plan was proving unexpectedly successful, all internal opposition seemed to have disappeared, and Trotsky's previous services to the Revolution were not forgotten. Second, it was felt that such early opponents of the Soviet regime as Kerensky, Martov and Dan had been politically sterilized by exile from Russia. They lost contact both with the undercurrents of Russian life and with the central stream itself and became little more than voices crying in the wilderness. Trotsky, however, is a man of different and far higher caliber. His career has shown that he combines great executive ability with brilliant intelligence. He has unlimited ambition, an absolute belief in the rightness of his own views and the most profound experience in and capacity for revolutionary organization. Finally, he has the double gift of leadership and of arousing the enduring loyalty of his friends and subordinates. It was not to be expected that this man who had shone so bright in the sun should be content to spend his declining years in spiteful twilight. There could be no rest for his boundless energy, no compromise with his fanatical conviction that Stalin had "betrayed the Revolution."

The fact of Germano-Japanese hostility to the USSR needs no demonstration; the archives of the State and Navy Departments in Washington can bear witness that more than once in 1932 and 1933 war between the USSR and Japan hung literally by a thread, and Hitler, from "Mein Kampf" to his speech at Nuremberg last September, from Nuremberg to the present day, has made no secret of his determination that Germany should atone for defeat in the World War by "eastward expansion" at the expense of the USSR. Hitler's own position, however, was not consolidated until 1933, and three more years were to elapse before he could feel that the German war machine was ready for a major struggle. In the meantime Japanese aggressiveness had been somewhat checked by American recognition of the USSR and was now directed toward China, in which it has gradually found itself more and more deeply involved. Second, there were signed pacts of mutual assistance between the USSR and Czechoslovakia and the USSR and France, which were regarded as tantamount to defensive alliances. Last but not least, the Red Army and the Soviet war industry gained prodigiously in efficiency and strength.

During the years 1933 to 1937, therefore, neither Germany nor Japan was yet ready to make a direct attack upon the USSR although they gave further evidence that they wished to do so by signing in 1936 a pact of mutual co-operation against Bolshevism, which the statesmen of Britain, France and Russia immediately recognized as a preliminary step toward joint action. In 1936, moreover, Germany's attention was diverted by an attempt in conjunction with Italy to set up a puppet fascist government in Spain and thus obtain access to the rich Spanish deposits of iron, copper and other minerals. It was thought at first that it would be easy to overthrow the Spanish government, but the latter showed sufficient powers of resistance and received enough material aid from France and Russia for the civil war to be undecided in ten months of bitter fighting. Hitler was infuriated to learn that the Russians were no longer content with the role of destined victim but had the temerity to thwart his plans in Spain, where the success of the Soviet planes and tanks caused a notable effect upon French opinion and reinforced the Franco-Soviet pact, which it was Hitler's aim to break. In short, the Red Army had become a positive adversary instead of a potential obstacle; it not only blocked the future but seriously menaced the present. In this juncture, circumstances within the USSR combined with the anti-Kremlin activities of Trotsky to play into Hitler's hands.

The details of Kirov's assassination at first pointed to a personal motive, which may indeed have existed, but investigation showed that, as commonly happens in such cases, the assassin Nikolaiev had been made the instrument of forces whose aims were treasonable and political. A widespread plot against the Kremlin was discovered, whose ramifications included not merely former oppositionists but agents of the Nazi Gestapo. As the investigation continued, the Kremlin's conviction deepened that Trotsky and his friends abroad had built up an anti-Stalinist organization in close collaboration with their associates in Russia, who formed a nucleus or center around which gradually rallied divers elements of discontent and disloyalty.

If one accepts these premises, it is obvious that both Trotsky and the foreign enemies would use every means in their power to deny and discredit the evidence produced at the trials. In this they have been aided by Western unfamiliarity with Soviet mentality and methods and, to no small degree, by Soviet unfamiliarity with Western mentality and methods. Thus at the very outset, the Western world was shocked by the harshness of the reprisals which followed Kirov's murder, and already the cry was raised abroad that this wave of killings and arrests was a sign of panic on the part of the Kremlin or that Stalin and his associates were taking advantage of an "accident" to rid themselves of political opponents.

The later "treason trials" of the Kamenev-Zinoviev and Pyatakov-Radek groups were used by Stalin's enemies to confirm these two assertions and to deepen the skepticism with which the extraordinary (to Western minds) nature of the confessions had been received abroad. In the fog of denials and declarations that the confessions were elicited by drugs, torture, pressure upon relatives, hypnotism or other nefarious devices of the GPU, foreign opinion lost sight of three important facts: first, that these same men had, individually and collectively, confessed their sins and beaten their breasts in contrition no less fully and abasedly on previous occasions; second, that the outline of the conspiracy was gradually taking shape; third, that through the maze of charge and counter-charge the thread of collusion with foreign enemies ran ever stronger and more clear. The second trial established the fact of personal contact between several of the accused and foreign, *i.e.*, German and Japanese, representatives. This in itself meant little because Pyatakov received dozens of foreigners every week in his official position, the accused railroad managers of the Far Eastern lines had similar official contact with Japanese consuls and business men, and Radek was a familiar figure at most of the diplomatic receptions in Moscow. Nevertheless the element of opportunity was thus introduced to buttress the prosecution's charge of treasonable and hostile motives that led to collusion.

Curiously enough, the most convincing piece of evidence was provided by no other than the Japanese War Minister himself, General Sugiyama, in reply to a question at a secret meeting of the budget committee of the Japanese Parliament early in February. The General was asked if he knew the carrying capacity of the Soviet Trans-Siberian Railroad. He replied that he did but that it was a military secret. To a further question, "How do you know?" the General said, "On information supplied by persons in Soviet Russia who are opposed to the Stalin regime." News of this incident "leaked" into a single Tokyo newspaper whose news editor was promptly dismissed and the managing editor fined and reprimanded. It was further stated that if any such leakage occurred, it would be more severely punished in the future. As far as the question of German and Japanese espionage in the

USSR is concerned, it is notorious that the secret services of almost every nation in the world have an espionage department that varies in importance and numbers according to the size of the country and the imminence of hostilities with some other power. Everyone knows, for instance, that England before the World War was honeycombed with German spies, many of whom had long been detected by the British Counter-Espionage Department, and who, as Sir Basil Thomson, the former Chief of Scotland Yard, relates in his memoirs, were immediately picked up at the outbreak of hostilities. There must be hundreds of German and Japanese spies on Soviet soil, and for that matter the Russians doubtless carry on similar work in Japan and Germany. In either case, one may be sure, these secret agents do their utmost to get into touch with disaffected elements in the country where they are working, with a view not merely to espionage but to sabotage as well. This self-evident truth, however, has been somewhat overlooked in the discussion of the Moscow trials.

That disaffected elements existed apart from the small devoted group of Trotsky's adherents, particularly among senior (in length of membership) ranks of the Bolshevik Party, is obvious and natural enough. There were those who grumbled that the growing tendency to regard Stalin as a superman had destroyed party democracy as they had known it in the old days.

It is further true that in totalitarian states no opposition can be permitted, because the idea of the state has been deified and opposition is therefore a Deadly Sin, which forces oppositionists to work underground and not only to become conspirators but to gravitate toward each other and toward a common center, if there is one. The Trotskyists offered such a center and in consequence, as in the case of the abortive revolt against Hitler in 1934, an odd lot of the most diverse elements became associated in common hostility toward the regime.

Thus one reaches a final synthesis, as follows:

a. Trotsky was fanatically determined to overthrow the Stalinist regime.

b. Hitler was fanatically determined to "expand eastwards" at the expense of the USSR.

c. Both Hitler and Trotsky had at their disposal efficient organizations to develop conspirative action, sabotage and espionage within the USSR and to conduct propaganda abroad.

d. Opportunities for contact between Germany (and Japan) and the anti-Stalinist conspirators both inside and outside the USSR were not lacking.

The conclusion is inevitable.

It cannot be negatived by foreign bewilderment over the "mystery" of the trials and of the confessions made by the accused, or by foreign belief that the morale of the Red Army has been gravely impaired and that the whole USSR is engulfed in a flood of hysterical witch-hunting. The Kremlin's enemies have used this belief and bewilderment to weaken, at a most critical period, the international prestige of the USSR, but that does not alter the fact that their Trojan horse is broken and its occupants destroyed.


NOVEMBER 7, 1938: *Herschel Grynszpan, a young Polish Jew, shot Ernst von Rath, German diplomat, in Paris.*

# THE POGROM

## by Otto D. Tolischus

BERLIN, Nov. 10—A wave of destruction, looting and incendiarism unparalleled in Germany since the Thirty Years War and in Europe generally since the Bolshevist revolution, swept over Great Germany today as National Socialist cohorts took vengeance on Jewish shops, offices and synagogues for the murder by a young Polish Jew of Ernst von Rath, third secretary of the German Embassy in Paris.

Beginning systematically in the early morning hours in almost every town and city in the country, the wrecking, looting and burning continued all day. Huge but mostly silent crowds looked on and the police confined themselves to regulating traffic and making wholesale arrests of Jews "for their own protection."

All day the main shopping districts as well as the side streets of Berlin and innumerable other places resounded to the shattering of shop windows falling to the pavement, the dull thuds of furniture and fittings being pounded to pieces and the clamor of fire brigades rushing to burning shops and synagogues. Although shop fires were quickly extinguished, synagogue fires were merely kept from spreading to adjoining buildings.

As far as could be ascertained the violence was mainly confined to property. Although individuals were beaten, reports so far tell of the death of only two persons—a Jew in Polzin, Pomerania, and another in Bunzdorf.

In extent, intensity and total damage, however, the day's outbreaks exceeded even those of the 1918 revolution and by nightfall there was scarcely a Jewish shop, cafe, office or synagogue in the country that was not either wrecked, burned severely or damaged.

Thereupon Propaganda Minister Joseph Goebbels issued the following proclamation:

"The justified and understandable anger of the German people over the cowardly Jewish murder of a German diplomat in Paris found extensive expression during last night. In numerous cities and towns of the Reich retaliatory action has been undertaken against Jewish buildings and businesses.

"Now a strict request is issued to the entire population to cease immediately all further demonstrations and actions against Jewry, no matter what kind. A final answer to the Jewish assassination in Paris will be given to Jewry by way of legislation and ordinance."

What this legal action is going to be remains to be seen. It is known, however, that measures for the extensive expulsion of foreign Jews are already being prepared in the Interior Ministry, and some towns, like Munich, have ordered all Jews to leave within forty-eight hours. All Jewish organizational, cultural and publishing activity has been suspended. It is assumed that the Jews, who have now lost most of their possessions and livelihood, will either be thrown into the streets or put into ghettos and concentration camps, or impressed into labor brigades and put to work for the Third Reich, as the children of Israel were once before for the Pharaohs.

In any case, all day in Berlin, as throughout the country, thousands of Jews, mostly men, were being taken from their homes and arrested—in particular prominent Jewish leaders, who in some cases, it is understood, were told they were being held as hostages for the good behavior of Jewry outside Germany.

In Breslau they were hunted out even in the homes of non-Jews where they might have been hiding.

Foreign embassies in Berlin and consulates throughout the country were besieged by frantic telephone calls and by persons, particularly weeping women and children, begging help that could not be given them. Incidentally, in Breslau the United States Consulate had to shut down for some time during the day because of fumes coming from a burning synagogue near by.

All pretense—maintained during previous comparatively minor anti-Jewish outbreaks—to the effect that the day's deeds had been the work of irresponsible, even Communist, elements was dropped this time and the official German News Bureau, as well as newspapers that hitherto had ignored such happenings, frankly reported on them. The bureau said specifically:

"Continued anti-Jewish demonstrations occurred in numerous places. In most cities the synagogue was fired by the population. The fire department in many cases was able merely to save adjoining buildings. In addition, in many cities the windows of Jewish shops were smashed.

"Occasionally fires occurred and because of the population's extraordinary excitement the contents of shops were partly destroyed. Jewish shop owners were taken into custody by the police for their own protection."

Berlin papers also mention many cities and towns in which anti-Jewish excesses occurred, including Potsdam, Stettin, Frankfort on the Main, Leipzig, Luebeck, Cologne, Nuremberg, Essen, Duesseldorf, Konstanz, Landsberg, Kottbus and Eberswalde. In most of them, it is reported, synagogues were raided and burned and shops were demolished. But in general the press follows a system of reporting only local excesses so as to disguise the national extent of the outbreak, the full spread of which probably never will be known.

On the other hand, the German press already warns the world that if

66

the day's events lead to another agitation campaign against Germany "the improvised and spontaneous outbreaks of today will be replaced with even more drastic authoritative action." No doubt is left that the contemplated "authoritative action" would have a retaliatory character.

Says the *Angriff*, Dr. Goebbels's organ:

"For every suffering, every crime and every injury that this criminal [the Jewish community] inflicts on a German anywhere, every individual Jew will be held responsible. All Judah wants is war with us and it can have this war according to its own moral law: an eye for an eye and a tooth for a tooth."

The wrecking work was thoroughly organized, sometimes proceeding under the direct orders of a controlling person in the street at whose command the wreckers ceased, lined up and proceeded to another place.

In the fashionable Tauenzienstrasse the writer saw a wrecking crew at work in one shop while the police stood outside telling a vast crowd watching the proceeding to keep moving.

"Move on," said the policemen, "there are young Volksgenossen [racial comrades] inside who have some work to do."

At other shops during the wrecking process uniformed Storm Troopers and Elite Guards were seen entering and emerging while soldiers passed by outside.

Generally the crowds were silent and the majority seemed gravely disturbed by the proceedings. Only members of the wrecking squads shouted occasionally, "Perish Jewry!" and "Kill the Jews!" and in one case a person in the crowd shouted, "Why not hang the owner in the window?"

In one case on the Kurfuerstendamm actual violence was observed by an American girl who saw one Jew with his face bandaged dragged from a shop, beaten and chased by a crowd while a second Jew was dragged from the same shop by a single man who beat him as the crowd looked on.

One Jewish shop owner, arriving at his wrecked store, exclaimed, "Terrible," and was arrested on the spot.

In some cases on the other hand crowds were observed making passages for Jews to leave their stores unmolested.

Some persons in the crowds—peculiarly enough, mostly women—expressed the view that it was only right that the Jews should suffer what the Germans suffered in 1918. But there were also men and women who expressed protests. Most of them said something about Bolshevism. One man —obviously a worker—watching the burning of a synagogue in Fasanenstrasse exclaimed, "Arson remains arson." The protesters, however, were quickly silenced by the wrecking crews with threats of violence.

To some extent—at least during the day—efforts were made to prevent looting. Crowds were warned they might destroy but must not plunder, and in individual cases looters either were beaten up on the spot by uniformed Nazis or arrested. But for the most part, looting was general, particularly during the night and in the poorer quarters. And in at least one

67

case the wreckers themselves tossed goods out to the crowd with the shout "Here are some cheap Christmas presents."

Children were observed with their mouths smeared with candy from wrecked candy shops or flaunting toys from wrecked toy shops until one elderly woman watching the spectacle exclaimed, "So that is how they teach our children to steal."

Foreign Jewish shops, it appears, were not at first marked for destruction and were passed over by the first wrecking crews. But in their destructive enthusiasm others took them on as well and even wrecked some "Aryan" shops by mistake.

Among the foreign wrecked establishments were three American-owned shops—the Loewenstein jewelry shop in Kanonierstrasse, near the office of the New York *Times,* the owner of which shop is now in America; the Leipzig fur shop in Rosenthalerstrasse, owned by C. G. Schultz, who is also in America, and the Rose Bach rug shop in the Hauptstrasse.

Also wrecked were the Warner corset shop on the Kurfuerstendamm, which is partly American-owned; a Jewish Ford dealer's on Unter den Linden, and a large, well-known department store that has considerable British capital invested in it.

The Leipzig fur shop displayed a large American flag in its window, but the manager reported that the wreckers had shouted that they did not care whether the place was American or not and went to work. This shop reported the loss of three silver fox capes and other furs; the Bach rug shop reported the loss of goods valued at 2,000 marks.

No photographing of the wreckage was permitted and Anton Celler, American tourist, of Hamden, Conn., was arrested while trying to take such pictures, although he was soon released. Members of a South American diplomatic mission likewise got into trouble on that account.

Grave doubt prevails whether insurance companies will honor their policies. Some are reported to have flatly refused to reimburse for the damage because of its extent, and, considering the standing the Jew enjoys in German courts today, there is little likelihood of his collecting by suing. But there still remains to be settled the damage done to "Aryan" houses and other property.

The National Socialist regime, through Dr. Joseph Goebbels, its Propaganda Minister, and other authorized spokesmen in declarations to the foreign press, in articles in its own press and in speeches to mass meetings, today openly sanctioned the wave of terrorism, destruction and incendiarism that swept over Germany yesterday.

That wave destroyed almost all Jewish business, burned most of the synagogues and landed thousands of Jews in jails and concentration camps, besides driving many to suicide.

It was denied that these "demonstrations" were organized and it was insisted that they represented the German people's "spontaneous reaction" to the murder of Ernst von Rath, third secretary of the German Embassy in Paris, by a young Polish Jew.

It was also denied that there had been any plundering except incidentally or that the police or fire brigades had failed to do their duty.

Finally, it was asserted that the government had done everything to end the demonstrations as rapidly as possible, and it was announced that there would be further anti-Jewish laws for a comprehensive solution of the Jewish problem in a manner "that will equalize the status of the Jews in Germany in conformity with popular anti-Semitic sentiment."

But in all the declarations there was no word of condemnation or regret for the excesses themselves.

# THE JEWISH CHILDREN

### by Westbrook Pegler

THE most pathetic victims of Adolf Hitler's slow massacre of the Jews in Germany are the children of the Jews who are too young to know what it is all about. These children are subjected to a method of torture far worse than the baby killing which was charged against the German infantry in the early days of the Great War in cartoons depicting little bodies wriggling on the bayonets of the marching armies.

It finally was shown that the German soldier, Michael, as he was called at home, was the soul of kindness, who often shared his rations with the waifs behind the Belgian lines, and reasonable people on the Allies' side of the fight ultimately admitted that the charge was false.

But it will be impossible ever to disprove the atrocities which are being perpetrated on the children of the Jews under the orders of Adolf Hitler as a policy of the German government of today.

The Chinese have a method of torture known as the death of a thousand cuts, in which the executioner is rated according to his ability to hack and mutilate the victim without permitting him to die until the maximum of suffering has been inflicted. They have a very good photograph of an execution by this method in the Chamber of Horrors in Madame Tussaud's Museum in London, but most people coming upon it unsuspectingly turn away revolted, and only the most morbid visitors linger for a second glance.

Hitler's torture of the Jewish children is even more ingenious, however, for he has invented a way to convert the period of childhood into a term of unrelieved sorrow, fear, dread and suffering. It is commonly accepted among the civilized peoples of the world that any man who would inflict suffering on a child, wantonly or for the purpose of avenging some offense, real or imaginary, attributed to the child's parents, or for any other reason, is not quite right mentally and ought to be put away.

We had a case of that kind in New York. An old man tortured and killed a little girl for the pleasure it gave him, and public opinion pretty well agreed that he was insane. But even in that case the suffering of the little girl was of short duration. Then she was dead. Hitler's little victims, however, are not allowed to die. They have no such luck. Hitler keeps them alive, and they suffer day after horrible day at the hands of a nation which constantly boasts of its honor and manhood, as a matter of national policy.

The German child who is a Jew is compelled to listen to the most unspeakable vilification of his parents, and the child's first attempts at spelling out public notices on the billboards will inform him that he is not a human being, like other children, but a beast whose parents were not human beings, either, but loathsome animals.

If the child lives in a country town where there are not sufficient Jewish children to warrant the establishment of a ghetto school in which to segregate little Jews, then the torture of the victim is even more artistic. In that case the child may be compelled to sit in the classroom and pay attention while the teacher explains that little Isadore or Rosie is a vile creature, a species of vermin and a menace to the German nation. If the teacher so desires, the Jewish child may be dismissed from the room during the lecture, in which case the Aryan children, with the characteristic cruelty of children plus the sadistic delight in the infliction of pain which is now being fostered in young Nazis, will catch the young Jew after class and tell Isadore or Rosie what the teacher said.

If the radio is turned on in the home of a Jewish family the children will hear an orator somewhere in Berlin or Munich explaining that their parents are beasts and that they are little beasts themselves.

A lone Jewish child in a small community must play alone, for the true Nazi children, of course, will not admit him to their company, and a Gentile child with pity in his heart would be afraid to offer the victim any sympathy. He would be ostracized.

And then, of course, it is fair sport for the Nazi children to kick and beat and throw rocks at the little Jews, because that is preliminary training for one of the highest functions of Nazi citizenship and manhood in days to come.

All children have a trusting attitude toward grown people, and a harsh word may leave an ineffaceable scar on the soul of the young one. The souls of the children of the Jews in Germany will be cross-hacked with a thousand cuts, for they will never know anything in childhood but insults to themselves and the foulest aspersions on the only adults to whom they can turn for comfort—their parents and other relatives.

It is absolutely certain that their childhood, the few hours of innocence which are given to all of us and which civilized people try to invest with beauty and joy, has been destroyed by a man with a mustache, adopted from the makeup of a famous comedian, who has been seriously nominated by some of his followers not for king, not merely for ruler, but for God the Redeemer of the German race. It would be a mistake to call him a baby-killer. You can't torture a dead child.

70

# ETHIOPIA

DECEMBER 14, 1934: *Ethiopia made a formal protest to the League that Italian troops at Ualual had violated the sovereignty of the country.*

JANUARY, 1935: *Ethiopia further complained that Italy was meditating aggression.*

FEBRUARY: *Italy demanded an apology and indemnity from Ethiopia for the frontier clash at Ualual, and began to mobilize.*

MAY 7: *Mussolini warned the other powers to refrain from intervention in Ethiopia.*

JUNE 22-24: *Anthony Eden conferred in Rome with Mussolini. The latter declared that it was now time for Italy to have more territory of her own in Africa.*

SEPTEMBER 11: *Great Britain, France, Russia, and the smaller members of the League, with the exception of Austria and Bulgaria, demanded that the League act against Italian aggression.*

SEPTEMBER 23: *Italy increased her army to 1,000,000, and mobilized 10,000,000 Fascisti. Great Britain sent her home fleet into the Mediterranean.*

# THE INVASION

## *by Webb Miller*

AT five o'clock on the morning of October 2 [1935] the thunderous roar of a column of motor trucks awakened me. I rose and went down to Asmara's main street, Viale Benito Mussolini. The procession of motor trucks continued hour after hour, manned by drivers sunburned to the color of old leather, dusty, begoggled, with their mouths and noses swathed in handkerchiefs to keep them from breathing the clouds of talcumlike dust. On some of the trucks was chalked the inscription, "Rome to Addis Ababa."

During the forenoon General De Bono and his headquarters staff moved from Asmara to field headquarters, established on the top of Coatit Mountain about eight miles from the Ethiopian frontier. In my description of the passage of the motor-truck columns I tried to convey the fact that General Headquarters moved toward the frontier. The censor deleted my indirect reference to it. However, he passed my mention of the general air of tension and excitement in Asmara and my appended personal message to Stewart Brown, our Rome bureau manager, in which I said, "Presume your arrangements perfected," which I hoped would tip him off that the war was about to start.

In my diary I made the following entry about nine o'clock on the night of October 2: "Church bells start ringing wildly. Searchlights criss-cross sky. Darkened streets are filled by throng of excited men. Everyone seems to realize invasion of Ethiopia starts tomorrow. Governor's residence and Fascist Club floodlighted by searchlights. Impromptu band marches up street playing 'Giovinezza,' the Fascist song. Hundreds of men in ferment of emotion follow shouting, singing, chanting, 'Il Duce, Il Duce.' They mass in front of Fascist Club, which is now press headquarters. Call repeatedly for Count Ciano, Mussolini's son-in-law. Finally get him out, seize him, tumultuously carry him on shoulders.

"In press headquarters we implore Count di Bosdari to tell us what time war will start. About eleven P.M. Bosdari comes into press room, where Gibbons and I and several Italian and French correspondents are hastily writing description of scenes in street. We crowd around him in breathless silence. 'Advance starts at five A.M. You can go to general headquarters at one A.M.,' Bosdari said. We rush to pack duffle bags, folding cots, blankets, nettings, canned eatables, water canteens, typewriters, paper, carbons, field glasses, et cetera."

At one A.M. with Count di Bosdari and Roman Fajans, correspondent of a Warsaw newspaper, I started to General De Bono's observation post on the brow on Coatit Mountain, from which we were to witness the start of the invasion of Ethiopia. It was an uncanny experience, motoring in comfort to witness the commencement at a fixed minute of a war started coldly and deliberately, to see a vast war machine grind into action at a word, to watch more than 100,000 men begin at an appointed minute the invasion of the last independent kingdom in Africa; to witness an action which would have unforeseeable repercussions. I tried to analyze my curious sensations; as nearly as I could define them they recalled somewhat the feeling of abhorrent fascination I always felt when witnessing men put to death by legal execution.

Bosdari and I were silently occupied with our own thoughts, but Fajans was excited to the verge of hysteria. He chattered continuously in French. Bosdari and I simulated sleep in an effort to shut him up, but then he talked to the driver. Finally I exploded with all the French curses I could muster and succeeded in silencing him. As we neared the front we passed long lines of motor trucks hurtling without lights along the twisting roads. I think more men were killed in accidents that night than on the first day of war.

About four A.M. we reached the stone barracks which was to be our headquarters and unloaded our gear into a bare room devoid of furniture or light. Raffaele Casertano, chief of the press section, shaved hastily by candlelight. Everyone spoke in subdued tones; some took hasty gulps of cognac. At about four-thirty we took our typewriters and set out for the observation post, a few miles away.

72

It occupied a flat space of about a quarter of an acre on the side of the mountain 2,600 feet above the Asamo plain. It was very dark; no lights were visible. In the low stone huts telegraph instruments clicked and officers talked on field telephones. A big table outside was covered with maps. We were introduced to several officers and then milled around smoking cigarette after cigarette, awaiting the dawn. I scribbled in my notebook as follows:

"Four-thirty-five A.M. Air quivers with suppressed excitement. Staff officer says down in Asamo plain half a mile below us General Biroli's column of about 40,000 men constituting central of three columns ready for advance. No spark of light shows in valley below although thousands of men on move.

"In the east horizon pales, showing jagged silhouette of mountains toward the Danakil, 'hell hole of creation.' Officers pace up and down, talking in undertones. Faint rose color in east. Birds begin to sing. Now detect few glimmers light in valley below. We synchronize watches with official time.

"Press officer announces we can send only five twenty-word bulletins each over military wires. Says wires clogged with urgent military messages. Our detailed descriptions must be sent by motorcycle couriers sixty miles back to wireless station at Asmara.

"Four-forty-five A.M. Sun suddenly springs up over chocolate-colored rim of mountains. General De Bono, tiny, spare, goat-bearded, aged 74 but remarkably alert, drives up. Goes into consultation with staff. Light enough to see maps on table. General Gabba, Chief of Staff, explains disposition of troops—General Santini's column of 35,000 men lies about thirty miles to our left; General Maravigna's column of about 35,000 thirty miles to our right; General Biroli's column of about 40,000 mostly Askaris, below us in the center. Says he hears Ethiopian troops mostly withdrawn from vicinity frontier.

"Through glasses we see curtains of dust miles long in plain below. On mountain terrace few hundred feet below, native shepherd drives out his goats to pasture—unconcerned with and probably ignorant of world-shaking event about to occur. I arrange typewriter on sand-bagged parapet on edge of plateau. De Bono and Gabba pace up and down, scan plain through glasses.

"Four-fifty-five A.M. I write first of series of bulletins for release at exactly five A.M.; only six words, 'Italians commenced invasion Ethiopia five A.M.,' addressing identical messages to New York, Rome, Paris, and London marked for transmission by different cable and wireless routes. These six words will set thousands of presses spinning in forty-nine countries, spewing out extras. World will awaken to learn another war started.

"Five o'clock! War is started. Telegraph operator clicks out my messages. Through glasses I watch gray-green figures about eight miles away wade shallow Belesa River, holding rifles high over heads. Simple fact of wading that stream constitutes act which will send reverberations through world.

(Later learned they sang 'Giovinezza,' cheered Mussolini; were not fired upon at any of three points where crossed frontier.)

"Had we not kept eyes on watches we should not have known from anything done or said at our observation post at five A.M. that war was officially started. General Debono and General Gabba continued slowly pacing, occasionally examining maps. No drama and no word spoken to signalize momentous act; nothing to mark difference between Ethiopia uninvaded at 4:59 and Ethiopia invaded at 5:01. I expected cheers, some gesture or word to distinguish moment when invasion commenced; there were none.

"Straddling sand-bagged parapet, Gibbons and I hammered out twenty-word bulletins, sometimes chiseling in a few extra words; the wind swirled dust eddies into typewriters and we batted at swarms of flies."

The hasty scrawls entered in my notebook from minute to minute, many now illegible, reveal that I worked under a severe strain.

At 6:30 A.M. the first airplane appeared from the direction of Asmara, apparently a scouting plane. Gabba told me that airplanes would drop proclamations in the Tigrina language announcing that civilians would be unharmed if they did not fire upon or hinder the troops. I wondered about the utility of the gesture because everyone knew that not one Ethiopian in ten thousand could read. Through glasses we saw long, serpentlike columns of dusty men, mules, and motor trucks pouring across the Belesa ford.

At 6:40 A.M. I heard the heavy drone of Caproni bombers far away to the right in the direction of Adowa, but could not pick them up with glasses. A pale rose light now bathed the fantastic saw-toothed peaks around Adowa, about forty miles away. At 8:03 A.M. I heard a series of heavy explosions from the direction of Adowa, like the clanging of huge iron doors; forty minutes later the air shook with concussions of thunderous explosions, this time from the direction of Adigrat. Both these towns lay at least forty miles away behind successive ranges of mountains but we could hear the sound of the air bombs. Within a few minutes nine huge, tri-motored Caproni bombers glistening in the early morning light droned back toward Asmara. Four days passed before I learned that the bombs had been dropped outside the cities—except for several small bombs which accidentally fell within the towns—and that only a few casualties resulted.

Scrappy reports over the field telephone announced that the three columns were advancing rapidly and without resistance except on the right where, according to an official announcement Maravigna's troops thrusting toward Adowa "overcame all resistance," but we were unable to obtain any details of the resistance. By 9:30 the sun was searing; the temperature had risen to 118 in the shade. We were exhausted from strain and lack of sleep.

Suddenly a staff officer announced that the military courier must start for Asmara within fifteen minutes and that our detailed descriptive stories must be ready or await the next courier late in the afternoon. We pleaded for more time but the officer said the courier carried urgent military messages and must go within fifteen minutes.

Here were Gibbons and I with the biggest newspaper story since the World War—a story of sitting on top of a mountain with a grand-stand seat witnessing the beginning of a war—and we had only fifteen minutes in which to write our story. It was a reporter's nightmare. We straddled the sand bags frantically, slammed down words, trying to pack as much of the picture as possible into a few hundred words. I wrote 620 words; about a column and a half with telegraphic abbreviations expanded. The motorcycle courier roared away.

We had been eyewitnesses of the start of a war; an experience unique, I think, in the history of newspapers. Floyd Gibbons and I were the only representatives of the American press on the spot. Our competitors of a dozen nationalities, still many days away, fretted aboard the *Vulcania* somewhere in the Mediterranean. But we were too tired for self-congratulation; we crawled into a near-by thatched mud hut, lay on the earthen floor, and fell asleep with exhaustion when the war was less than five hours old; and I became infested with fleas.

That afternoon and night I wrote occasional bulletins on the progress of the advance. By nightfall the three columns had occupied 2,000 square miles of Ethiopian territory; Santini's army had come within five miles of Adigrat and Maravigna's column twelve miles from Adowa. In mid-afternoon planes bombed a concentration of about three hundred Ethiopian soldiers at Mai Barai near Adowa; we heard the dull explosions of the bombs. The field wireless reported the panic caused among the populations of Adowa and Adigrat, most of whom had never seen an airplane or heard an explosion louder than a rifle shot.

Next morning Gibbons and I crossed the arid plain of Asamo in a car, forded the Belesa River, and succeeded in penetrating about ten miles into Ethiopia over a trail hacked out hastily by Italian engineers in twenty-eight hours. Ours was the first automobile that had ever used the trail. We passed herds of thousands of cattle streaming forward from Eritrea to provide meat for the troops. Every few hundred yards bodies of dead mules lay beside the trail, swarming with vultures tearing out their entrails. Working parties with rifles within arm's reach wrenched stones out of the trail to make a passage for motor trucks. The picturesque Askari camel corps carried goatskins full of water to the advance positions; thousands of Black Shirt troops slopped through dust inches deep.

Late that night back at General Headquarters at Coatit I received a telegram from my New York office informing me that I had achieved a worldwide "scoop" on the beginning of the war; that my cablegram announcing the commencement of the invasion of Ethiopia arrived forty-four minutes ahead of the news from any other source; that for forty-four minutes my message was the only news in the world announcing that the war had begun. Hundreds of newspapers in the United States and in forty-two countries which the United Press served had issued extras before the Italian government in Rome could announce the start of the war.

In the next few days I received twenty-nine telegrams of congratulation from all over the world. I had achieved what some of my colleagues were kind enough to describe as the greatest newspaper "scoop" since the World War. It was later to win for me honorable mention for the Pulitzer Prize in Journalism.

OCTOBER 22, 1935: *The Five-Power Committee of the League debated the question of military sanctions against Italy. Sir Samuel Hoare told the House of Commons he thought they could be avoided, and that economic sanctions would suffice.*

NOVEMBER 11: *Italy warned the nations that she would retaliate in kind against sanctions.*

NOVEMBER 18: *The League applied economic sanctions against Italy.*

DECEMBER 7: *Foreign Minister Sir Samuel Hoare of Great Britain and Premier Laval of France agreed on a plan to dismember Ethiopia according to Italy's wishes. This plan aroused great popular opposition in England.*

DECEMBER 11-15: *The League disregarded the Hoare-Laval agreement, but postponed levying oil sanctions against Italy.*

JANUARY 3, 1936: *President Roosevelt, in a speech to Congress, denounced dictatorships and aggressors.*

APRIL 30: *The defense of Addis Ababa was abandoned. Haile Selassie fled.*

# BADOGLIO ENTERS ADDIS ABABA

### *by Herbert L. Matthews*

IT was two o'clock in the afternoon. The road made a huge curve in front of us, and about a mile away I could see a group of officers talking. The Marshal was giving his last orders. The mechanical units and the Eritreans were told to commence taking the city, which they entered fifteen minutes later. The troops who were to pour in after Badoglio were gathered from behind us and waited in readiness. Any idea of the Marshal entering like a conquering hero on horseback had long been abandoned. There was no time for pomp and circumstance, although I learned months later that a very heated controversy developed in the world Press as to whether he had ridden into the city on a white or a brown charger. He rode into the city in nothing more romantic than a Ford limousine.

A whole hour was spent in those preparations, and then the order came to go. Branca had cleverly prepared that last dash. At the start of it we were a mile behind the Marshal and his staff. All the drivers had been warned to stick behind Branca as if we were tied together. It was a regular cross-country charge, but a completely successful one, and when the entrance to the capital was reached, our caravan was directly behind Badoglio's. He drove into the native quarter at four o'clock precisely, from which time the Italian occupation of Addis Ababa will date for future historians.

There was nothing spectacular about it—no shouting, no excitement, no cheering crowds, not the slightest ceremony. Yet it was one of the great moments of modern history, and it lacked no genuine element of drama and color. The setting was an imperial capital in ruins—buildings still burning, the stinking dead still lying about the streets, gutted houses and stores gaping blackly and emptily at us as we drove by. The men were a sullen and fearful lot, wondering what retribution Italy would take for the horrible orgy of the four previous days. But the women greeted the invaders with flowers and trilled their welcome in that curious, high flat note, which I first heard at Azbi, as I rode into the town a lonely and inadvertent conqueror.

And then there were the foreigners, happy at being delivered from a terrible danger. Whether purposely or not, the triumphal procession went by the British Legation, where barbed wire and trenches, the Sikh Guard and civilian volunteers had successfully defended the major part of the foreign colony. There were some hearty jeers from that direction, as we went past the gate. At one point a few dozen Ethiopians in uniform—policemen, we were told—saluted ostentatiously. No soldiers were in evidence, for military uniforms had been prudently hidden or burned before the Italians arrived. And so there was no surrender; just the passive occupation of a prostrate city.

It was a long drive to the Italian Legation, Badoglio's goal and his new headquarters. Although undefended during the pillaging, the natives, significantly enough, had not dared to touch it. There were enormous grounds, lovely gardens, and an attractive house set in a high, sheltered spot.

That was my goal, too—the point that knowingly, or unknowingly, I had been aiming at for seven long months: the end, for which I had left Nancie and the children, traveled by sea and air and land, suffered and rejoiced, through seemingly endless days. Yet I felt no exultation—only an unutterable weariness of flesh and spirit. My head ached dismally; my nerves were on edge; I cared for nothing but a little rest so that I could pull myself together and tell the greatest story since the World War ended.

It was not to be. Badoglio and his staff quickly entered the Legation, and the first thing the Marshal did was to send for us. He, at least, was glowingly happy. We stood around him in the reception room, as he talked. The words, alternately sarcastic and proud, put the seal on a great conquest.

"Following his great victories, the Negus has been obliged to flee from his capital. Following the defeats we received, we have arrived here. You have seen, in this march from Quoram to Addis, what tenacity and force

77

Italian soldiers are capable of. You have seen them work in the rain, make paths through mountains, drag trucks from the mud and across rivers—and all this with enthusiasm and vigor. Il Duce told me to reach Addis Ababa. I have been able to do so, because I have had the high honor to command Italian officers and soldiers. You have seen the welcome which the inhabitants gave us along the road. They feel themselves freed of the heaviest yoke. Now begins a new labor for us, as arduous as the war we won, to give civilization and progress to these people, through peace and tranquillity."

He might have said more, but just then Pibe fell in a graceful faint at his feet, expressing in that eloquent way the weariness and emotion we all felt. Outside it was pouring rain again. Branca abruptly announced that we must give him our stories in half an hour, otherwise he could not guarantee us that they would arrive that evening. So I sat in the old Fiat, typewriter on my knees, my head throbbing painfully, and wrote five hundred words of grand climax to the Ethiopian War while the Italian flag was being hoisted over the Legation, and the rain poured down in buckets. And now let it pour, indeed! The war was over, and the greatest potential enemy of them all had been beaten, too.

I turned my copy in, disgusted that the masterpiece I had planned should have turned into those few, hastily written words, but too tired to care much. Ten thousand miles away, in the wireless receiving room of *The New York Times,* an operator felt through the air for messages from Addis Ababa. Here, he had it! Unfamiliar Italian words came over, from the wave-length that must have been the capital. Then his pencil flew over the paper before him:

"Times roma may fifth date addis ababa matthews era of independence that lasted since biblical times ended four this afternoon when Italians occupied addisababa stop newer empire founded by menlik received its quietus same time and new epoch history this ancient country begins stop this story being typed automobile wherein your correspondent came to addisababa with badoglio...."

And so he wrote, and so *The New York Times* alone of American newspapers had a special story from Addis Ababa the next morning, for all Branca's efforts proved in vain, and our dispatches were not delivered in Rome until five or six o'clock in the morning.

My assignment was all but over. Ten days more and Ethiopia ceased to become news. The war was ancient history, and the reading public turned indifferently away to new excitements. There were some mildly interesting stories during that time: descriptions of the ruined city, of the dead, interviews with members of the foreign colony, the restoration of order. The foreigners were bitter at the Emperor for having left the city so soon to its terrible fate: the railway to Jibuti reopened: Ras Seyoum submitted with native obsequiousness: an amusing storm in a teacup raged over diplomatic privileges and immunities: the American Minister, Cornelius van H. Engert, and his family provided some excellent stories of bravery and charitableness in the face of great danger.

And so it went. On the ninth, Harrar was taken by Graziani, ending the remarkable southern campaign which had started at Mogadishu. On that same day Mussolini proclaimed the new empire, and Badoglio became the first Viceroy. We listened to the proclamation that night as it came four thousand miles through the air, stirring an emotion too deep for words in the officers and soldiers who listened with us. The proudest of them all, in our group, were Vittorio and Bruno Mussolini, the Duce's sons, and Count Ciano, his son-in-law, all of whom left the next morning for Rome.

Badoglio received us for the last group-interview on the day after he was made Viceroy. It was a pleasant talk of plans for the future, of that last dramatic dash for the capital, of nostalgia for the war that was already history. He had come through the ordeal strong, active, and immensely happy, and like all soldiers after the fight is over, he looked back wistfully upon the exciting days of combat which had passed forever.

"I want you all to go away from here," he told us, "with the memory of Italians as good soldiers who did their best for their country. And when, in future years, seated at your hearths with your families around you, you look back on the day of the taking of Addis Ababa, you will think of it— perhaps not with nostalgia—but at least as a pleasant recollection."

And how much more, I thought, how very much more!

On May 12 the victorious army marched proudly through the streets, reviewed by the Commander-in-Chief who had led them there. It was a conquerors' parade—the immemorial reward of all soldiers who have planted their flag in the heart of the enemy's country. The Italian tricolor was raised over the Imperial gibbi at nine in the morning while a cannon boomed twenty-one salutes. As the banner reached the top of the staff I could almost sense a thrill of pride and joy sweep over the rigid ranks, standing at attention, for that ceremony was the final, outward symbol of a new Roman Empire, after so many centuries of eclipse.

NOVEMBER 7, 1937: *Italy joined Germany and Japan in their pact against Communism, signing it in a ceremony at Rome.*

DECEMBER 7: *Italy withdrew from the League of Nations.*

# SPAIN

Madrid, July 19, 1936 (United Press): A new government was formed today, as the Leftist regime of President Manuel Azana took drastic measures to quell a rebellion which began in the Spanish Foreign Legion and other groups in the African protectorate of Morocco and spread to the Republic.

\* \* \*

# FRANCO'S REVOLT

### by Reynolds and Eleanor Packard

AN English D. H. Rapids cabin plane circled around the airfield at Santa Cruz de la Palma as the sun was sinking behind the corrugated-iron hangar. It made a perfect landing and taxied up to the customs shed. Two pretty young girls in light summer prints descended from the airplane, followed by a soldierly-looking middle-aged man in a linen suit, who immediately reached into his pocket, pulled out a pipe, and lighted up. Shortly afterwards, an English pilot climbed out of the cockpit and joined them. It was hardly the season for tourists to arrive in a winter resort like the Canaries, being July 14 and very hot, but the pipe-smoking Englishman, disdaining to make any attempt at speaking Spanish, asked the Civil Guards:

"Is there a good hotel along the beach here? We want to get in some bathing."

The Civil Guard muttered some answer in Spanish which none of the English group appeared to understand. A customs official, anxious to be helpful, rushed to their assistance. Once again the Englishman explained that they were looking for a hotel on the beach. The customs official told him in English that it was not the season in the Canaries but they would find accommodations at one of the smaller hotels which he recommended.

Examination of their passports, which were perfectly in order, showed that their itinerary had been: Croydon, from where they took off on July 11, Biarritz, Oporto, Lisbon, Casablanca, and Cape Juby, in the Spanish colony of Rio de Oro. While the pilot garaged his plane, the rest of the party passed through the customs without any difficulty and took a cab to the hotel. The crowd of Spanish mechanics, fliers, and customs officials who had gathered around to admire the two girls never dreamed of the role this innocent-looking party was to play in the destiny of Spain.

At the hotel, using their right names, they registered as Major Hugh Pollard, retired army officer, his daughter, Diana Pollard, and Miss Dorothy Watson. The pilot gave his name as Captain Cecil Bebb. That night, over a bottle of sherry in the hotel lobby, the Major and the two girls, with the aid of a tourist guidebook, and a road map of the islands, began to plan their sight-seeing for the next few days. The following morning the three of them took a passenger steamer and went to Santa Cruz de Tenerife, another Canary island across the bay. After a stroll during which they visited a number of curio shops where they bought appropriate souvenirs, they turned down a side street and stopped at the house of a lawyer. A Spanish servant ushered them into a living room, where they were soon joined by the lawyer.

The Major, speaking Spanish with a British accent, said to him: "Viva la muerte."

The lawyer turned pale, tugged at his black tie, and asked, "What did you say?"

"Long live death," the Major replied, this time in English.

The lawyer assured him that there must be some mistake, but the Major insisted that the phrase was a password. The Spaniard, still distrustful, told him to return within an hour when a friend of his who might be able to establish contact would be present. The three English people went to a café, where they had some of the inevitable sherry. Returning at the appointed hour, they met the lawyer's friend who, though suspicious, was much calmer than the lawyer.

After great difficulty, the Major finally convinced the two Spaniards he was the envoy that General Francisco Franco had been expecting. They advised him to return to his hotel at Santa Cruz de la Palma and await developments.

It was quite an adventure for the Major, who since his days as an intelligence officer during the World War, had done nothing more exciting than collect ancient firearms and edit the sports section of *Country Life*. An ardent Catholic, he had become interested in the situation of the Church in Spain following the advent of the Republic.

In the middle of the next night, the Major heard a knock on his bedroom door. There stood the second Spaniard. He admitted this time that he was General Franco's aide-de-camp and said that everything was in readiness. He wanted Pollard to arrange for immediate departure of his private plane.

The Major called the pilot, who hastily dressed, and the two of them, accompanied by the Spaniard, left the hotel and scrambled into a closed Cadillac. A short, chubby man and a rather tall, distinguished-looking woman were already in the car. They exchanged greetings in Spanish, and the car moved off. The woman was tearful and constantly called upon the Virgin Mary to protect her husband on the adventure he was about to undertake.

At the airfield, the Major was surprised at the ease with which Captain Bebb, who had been told nothing of the plot, obtained permission to leave in the private plane with Franco and his aide-de-camp. The Major and Franco's wife remained behind.

Later that day, Captain Bebb arrived at Casablanca, in French Morocco, some seven hundred miles away, where his two passengers hurried to a small hotel. They were greeted in a back room by a group of Spaniards who saluted their leader with great deference. They included the Marquis Pepe del Mérito, the Spanish sherry producer, who, along with Juan de la Cierva, the inventor of the autogiro, had bought the plane and financed the Pollard expedition, and Louis Bolin, London correspondent of the Madrid newspaper *ABC,* who as a personal friend had prevailed on Pollard to make the trip to the Canaries. They told Franco that the revolution had started at dawn in Spanish Morocco but that they had not as yet heard how it fared. It was July 17, 1936.

After a sleepless night, Franco took off the following morning for Ceuta, not knowing whether he would be shot as a traitor or acclaimed as a leader upon his arrival. He was acclaimed as a leader. In Spanish Morocco the revolution had succeeded. Blue-shirted Falangistas, red-bereted Carlistas, and green-bereted Alfonsistas were rising up on the mainland along with the army. The so-called Nationalist movement was underway. General Queipo de Llano, Military Governor of Seville, had turned against the Republican government, which he had once stanchly supported. Other cities in the south of Spain which immediately joined the revolution were Cádiz, Algeciras, Granada, Córdoba. In the north, where General Emilio Mola became the rebel leader, Burgos, Valladolid, Pamplona, Saragossa, Salamanca, Vitoria, Avilla, Segovia, and Vigo followed suit. In Madrid, Barcelona, and San Sebastián, small groups of revolutionaries, mostly army, were fighting losing battles from behind the walls of the buildings they had seized. The Canaries and the Balearic Islands, with the exception of Minorca, joined the revolt. Insurgent officers also took over the Spanish colonies and protectorates of Ifni, Rio de Oro, and Fernando Po.

Almost all of the naval officers joined the uprising, but in most cases, as aboard the battleship *Jaime 1* and the cruisers *Cervantes* and *Libertad,* the crews remained loyal and, overpowering their officers, threw them overboard. On the battleship *Espana* and the cruiser *Almirante Cervera,* the loyal crews were overpowered by the officers with the aid of land forces of El Ferrol, where they were being repaired.

The assassination in Madrid on July 13, 1936, of Calvo Sotelo, leader of the Monarchist party in the Cortes and Minister of Finance under Primo de Rivera in 1925, has frequently been cited as the cause of the revolt. But the fact that Major Pollard had taken off from Croydon two days before to deliver a plane to Franco proved that the uprising had been hatched previously. As a matter of fact, during the time we were in Franco Spain, we were told on all sides that the Sotelo assassination had harmed rather than helped the army plot. A number of Franco followers explained to us that it had, by whipping up political sentiment to such a pitch, forced the army to start the movement ahead of schedule—the original date having been set at July 22. General José Sanjurjo, who was to have been the leader of the entire movement, was, as a result, left behind in Portugal. It was not until July 20 that he was able to arrange for a private plane to take him to Spain. En route the plane crashed and he was killed, leaving the leadership open to Mola and Franco.

82

Queipo de Llano, most colorful, eccentric, and unpredictable of all Spanish generals, held the fate of the revolution in his hands. Without his support, Franco could never have brought over his Moors and Spanish Legionaries of the famed El Tercio to the mainland. Well known as a Socialist, and as a leader of the anti-Monarchist movement which had forced Alfonso to go into exile, Queipo had been entrusted by the Republican Cabinet to govern Seville. His change-over was made all the more difficult by the fact that the population under him was predominantly Socialist.

Not above tricking the people, Queipo de Llano used the small garrison of two hundred and fifty soldiers that he had at his disposal to convince the people of Seville that thousands of reinforcements were arriving hourly. He dressed them, in turn, in the uniforms of all the armed branches of Spain, which he took from the commissary storehouse, and rushed them in trucks through the principal streets of the town. For the final display, he made his two hundred and fifty soldiers stain their faces with walnut juice so that they looked like Moors beneath the turbans and baggy trousers with which he had masqueraded them. Over the radio he lied glibly, announcing that the revolution had succeeded throughout Spain, that Madrid and Barcelona had joined the movement. Through this ruse, he prevented hundreds of small towns that might have opposed the revolt on the first day from taking action. This gave the revolutionaries just enough time to take over many of these towns before the truth was known.

JULY 20 TO SEPTEMBER 27, 1936: *The Siege of Alcazar.*

JULY 25 TO AUGUST 9: *Rebel uprisings in Madrid and Barcelona were finally put down.*

AUGUST 5 TO 8: *Great Britain and France declared a policy of "non-intervention" in Spain, and laid an embargo on materials to that country.*

AUGUST 14: *Franco began to encircle Madrid. The heroic resistance of Madrid was to last for almost three years.*

AUGUST 15: *Germany and Italy now began to send men and materials to Franco.*

OCTOBER 1: *Franco was elected dictator by Rebel juntas.*

# MADRID BOMBED

### by John Dos Passos

I WAKE up suddenly with my throat stiff. It's not quite day. I am lying in a comfortable bed, in a clean well-arranged hotel room staring at the light indigo oblong of the window opposite. I sit up in bed. Again there's

83

the hasty loudening shriek, the cracking roar, the rattle of tiles and a tinkling shatter of glass and granite fragments. Must have been near because the hotel shook. My room is seven or eight stories up. The hotel is on a hill. From the window I can look out at all the old part of Madrid over the crowded tiled roofs, soot-color flecked with pale yellow and red under the metal blue before dawn gloaming. The packed city stretches out sharp and still as far as I can see, narrow roofs, smokeless chimney-pots, buffcolored towers with cupolas and the pointed slate spires of seventeenth-century Castile. Everything is cut out of metal in the steely brightening light. Again the shriek, the roar, rattle, tinkle of a shell bursting somewhere. The silence again, cut only by the thin yelps of a hurt dog, and very slowly from one of the roofs below a smudge of dirty yellow smoke forms, rises, thickens and spreads out in the still air under the low indigo sky. The yelping goes weakly on and on.

It's too early to get up. I try going to bed again, fall asleep to wake almost immediately with the same tight throat, the same heavy feeling in my chest. The shells keep coming in. They are small but they are damn close. Better get dressed. The water's running in the bathroom, though the hot's not on yet. A man feels safe shaving, sniffing the little customary odor of the usual shaving soap in the clean bathroom. After a bath and a shave I put on my bathrobe, thinking after all this is what the Madrileños have been having instead of an alarmclock for five months now, and walk downstairs to see what the boys are up to. The shells keep coming in. The hotel, usually so quiet at this time, is full of scamper and confusion.

Everywhere doors fly open onto the balconies round the central glassed over well. Men and women in various stages of undress are scuttling out of front rooms, dragging suitcases and mattresses into back rooms. There's a curly-haired waiter from the restaurant who comes out of several different doors in succession each time with his arm round a different giggling or sniveling young woman. Great exhibition of dishevelment and lingerie.

Downstairs the correspondents are stirring about sleepily. An Englishman is making coffee on an electric coffeepot that speedily blows out the fuse at the same time melting the plug. A Frenchman in pajamas is distributing grapefruit to all and sundry from the door of his room.

The shells keep coming in. Nobody seems to know how to get at the coffee until a completely dressed woman novelist from Iowa takes charge of it and distributes it around in glasses with some scorched toast and halves of the Frenchman's grapefruit. Everybody gets lively and talkative until there's no more coffee left. By that time the shelling has died down a little and I go back to bed to sleep for an hour.

When I woke up again everything was quiet. There was hot water in the bathroom. From somewhere among the close-packed roofs under the window there drifted up a faint taste of sizzling olive oil. Round the balconies in the hotel everything was quiet and normal. The pleasant-faced middle-aged chambermaids were in their neat aprons, quietly cleaning. On the lower floor the waiters were serving the morning coffee. Outside on

84

the Plaza de Callao there were some new dents in the pavement that hadn't been there the night before. Somebody said an old newsvendor at the corner had been killed. Yesterday the doorman at the hotel got a spent machinegun bullet in the thigh.

The midmorning sunlight was hot on the Gran Via in spite of the frigid dry wind of Castilian springtime. Stepping out of doors into the bustling jangle of the city I couldn't help thinking of other Madrids I've known, twenty years ago, eighteen years ago, four years ago. The streetcars are the same, the long-nose sallow Madrileño faces are the same, with the same mixture of brown bullet-headed countrymen, the women in the dark-colored shawls don't look very different. Of course you don't see the Best People any more. They are in Portugal and Seville or in their graves. Never did see many this early anyway. The shellholes and the scars made by flying fragments and shrapnel have not changed the general look of the street, nor have the political posters pasted up on every bare piece of wall, or the fact that people are so scrappily dressed and that there's a predominance of uniforms in khaki and blue denim. It's the usualness of it that gives it this feeling of nightmare. I happen to look up at the hotel my wife and I stayed in the last time we were here. The entrance on the street looks normal and so does the department store next door, but the upper stories of the building, and the story where our room was, are shot as full of holes as a Swiss cheese.

It's funny how the least Spanish building in Madrid, the baroque tower of Wall Street's International Tel and Tel, the symbol of the colonizing power of the dollar, has become in the minds of the Madrileños the symbol of the defense of the city. Five months of intermittent shellfire have done remarkably little damage. There are a few holes and dents but nothing that couldn't be repaired in two weeks. On the side the shelling comes from the windows of several stories have been bricked up. The pompous period ornamentation has hardly been chipped.

Inside you feel remarkably safe. The whole apparatus of the telephone service still goes on in the darkened offices. The elevators run. There's a feeling like Sunday in a New York downtown building. In their big quiet office you find the press censors, a cadaverous Spaniard and a plump little pleasant-voiced Austrian woman. They say they are going to move their office to another building. It's too much to ask the newspapermen on the regular services to duck through a barrage every time they have to file a story, and the censors are beginning to feel that Franco's gunners are out after them personally. Only yesterday the Austrian woman came back to find that a shell fragment had set her room on fire and burned up all her shoes, and the censor had seen a woman made mincemeat of beside him when he stepped out to get a bite of lunch. It's not surprising that the censor is a nervous man; he looks underslept and underfed. He talks as if he understood, without taking too much personal pleasure in it, the importance of his position of guardian of those telephones that are the link with happier countries where the civil war is still being carried on by means of gold credits on bank-ledgers and munitions contracts and conversations on red plush sofas in diplomatic anterooms instead of with six-inch shells and firing squads. He doesn't give the impression of being complacent about his job. But it's hard for one who is more or less of a free agent from a country at peace to talk about many things with men who are chained to the galley benches of a war.

There are trenches made with sandbags in the big recently finished Plaza de España. The huge straggling bronze statues of Don Quixote and Sancho Panza look out oddly towards the enemy position in Carabanchel. At a barracks building on the corner a bunch from the International Brigade is waiting for chow. French faces, Belgian faces, North of Italy faces; German exiles, bearded men blackened with the sun, young boys; a feeling of energy and desperation comes from them. The dictators have stolen their world from them; they have lost their homes, their families, their hopes of a living or a career; they are fighting back.

Up another little hill is the burned shell of the Montana Barracks where the people of Madrid crushed the military revolt last July. Then we're looking down the broad rimedge street of the Paseo de Rosales. It used to be one of the pleasantest places in Madrid to live because the four- and five-story apartment houses overlooked the valley of the Manzanares and the green trees of the old royal parks and domains. Now it's no man's land. The lines cross the valley below, but if you step out on the Paseo you're in the full view of the enemy on the hills opposite, and the Moors are uncommonly good riflemen.

With considerable speed the sightseers scuttled into a house on the corner. There's the narrow hall and the row of bells and the rather grimy dark stairs of the regular Madrid apartment house, but instead of the apartment of Señor Fulano de Tal on the third floor you open a ground glass door and find ... the front. The rest of the house has been blown away. The ground glass door opens on air, at your feet a well opens full of broken masonry and smashed furniture, then the empty avenue and beyond across the Manzanares, a magnificent view of the enemy. On the top floor there's a room on that side still intact; looking carefully through the half-shattered shutters we can make out trenches and outposts at the top of the hill, a new government trench halfway up the hill and closing the picture, as always, the great snowy cloud-topped barrier of the Guadarrama. The lines are quiet; not a sound. Through the glasses we can see some militiamen strolling around behind a clump of trees. After all it's lunchtime. They can't be expected to start a battle for the benefit of a couple of sightseers.

Walking back to the hotel through the empty streets of the wrecked quarter back of the Paseo we get a chance to see all the quaint possibilities of shellfire and airbombing among dwelling houses. The dollshouse effect is the commonest, the front or a side of a house sliced off and touchingly revealing parlors, bedrooms, kitchens, dining rooms, twisted iron beds dangling, elaborate chandeliers hanging over void, a piano suspended in the air, a sideboard with dishes still on it, a mirror with a gilt stucco frame glittering

86

high up in a mass of wreckage where everything else has been obliterated.

From the west came a scattered hollow popping, soft perforations of the distant horizon. Somewhere not very far away men with every nerve tense were crawling along the dark sides of walls, keeping their heads down in trenches, yanking their right arms back to sling a hand grenade at some creeping shadow opposite. And in all the black houses the children we'd seen playing in the streets were asleep, and the grown-ups were lying there thinking of lost friends and family and ruins and people they'd loved and of hating the enemy and of hunger and how to get a little more food tomorrow, feeling in the numbness of their blood, in spite of whatever scorn in the face of death, the low unending smolder of apprehension of a city under siege. And I couldn't help feeling a certain awe, as I took off my clothes in my quiet clean room with electric light and running water and a bathtub, in the face of all these people in this city. I lay down on the bed to read a book but instead stared at the ceiling and thought of the pleasant-faced middle-aged chambermaid who'd cleaned my room that morning and made the bed and put everything in order and who'd been coming regularly every day, doing the job ever since the siege began just as she'd done it in the days of Don Alfonso, and wondered where she slept and what about her family and her kids and her man, and how perhaps tomorrow coming to work there'd be that hasty loudening shriek and the street full of dust and splintered stone and instead of coming to work the woman would be just a mashed-out mess of blood and guts to be scooped into a new pine coffin and hurried away. And they'd slosh some water over the cobbles and the death of Madrid would go on. A city under siege is not a very good place for a sightseer. It's a city without sleep.

# A DAY IN SPAIN

### by Lillian Hellman

AT twelve o'clock on an October day in Valencia it is usually warm and sunny. I stopped at the flower market and bought a bunch of flowers and some green leaves I had never seen before. I went around the corner and down the street and felt good walking in the hot sunshine. Ahead of me was a cat and I don't think I paid any attention to what had happened until I saw the cat suddenly sit down in the middle of the street. While I stood there looking at him, I began to hear the sirens. A woman with a pushcart suddenly picked up a little girl, threw the child on the cart, and wheeled it swiftly away. I think a few people began to run, but most people stopped, suddenly, and then moved on again more swiftly. I knew afterwards, by the way my jaw felt, that I had been pressing my teeth together too hard. I turned, too, and began to walk, and told myself over and over again that as long as the sirens sounded the planes had not yet arrived. I didn't really believe that, but people were standing quietly in the open square, looking up. I went through the square quickly and towards my hotel and when I first heard the noise of the motors I didn't want to turn to see where they were. I thought: in that hotel room is a toothbrush, a clean nightgown, a cake of soap, an old coat and a box of lousy candy. Yet I am hurrying to it, it is where I am trying to go, it is the place where I have what belongs to me. And I knew, suddenly, why even the poorest women in Madrid wanted to stay with what was theirs.

But when I got to the corner of the hotel, the noise of the planes was close. I stopped at the corner and leaned against the wall. The planes were high in the east and flying fast. Next to me were two soldiers. One of them had a bunch of grapes in his hand. In a minute he said something to his friend and pointed in another direction. From the south four planes were flying towards us. They came up, swung around. Suddenly the soldier touched my arm and shouted, "They are ours." "There go ours." Then he pulled off some grapes, wiped them clean on his coat, and handed them to me. He said, "Our planes are up. It's all right, now." It wasn't all right. In the section around the port, three minutes later, the Italian bombers killed sixty-three people. But as we ate the grapes and smiled at each other, we didn't know that.

I drove up to the base hospital at Benacasim with Gustav Regler. Regler, who is a Jesuit-trained Catholic, was a fairly well-known novelist until Hitler came in. He was a captain in the World War and had been badly injured in this, the "little war," when his car was bombed to pieces going up to the front lines. Driving fast towards Benacasim, we talked about writers and writing and got excited and argued and had fun. We got to Benacasim at dinner time, and the Germans and the Americans were eating at one large table. Some of their wives were there with them and I thought what good-looking people they all were and how generous they were with their food and cigarettes. (There wasn't much food and it was very bad.) Later that night, lying on a straw bed next to the wife of a Czech army officer, I thought that these foreigners from everywhere were noble people. I had never used the word noble before, and it came hard, even to say it to myself. They had come a long way to Spain, most of them making the cruel sixteen-hour walk across the Pyrenees. When it was over, if they came out alive, or with enough arms and legs to seem alive, there would be no glory and no reward. They had come because they thought that if a man believed in democracy he ought to do something about it. That's all they would go home with—wherever home was. Lying there, I prayed, for the first time in many years, that they would get what they wanted.

The next morning the American, Dr. Busch, Regler, the political commissar and I went on a round of visits. In the third room we visited, there were two men. One was a Canadian. One was a New York boy with that small, pinched, pale face that is so common among poor people in New York. The Canadian had lost his foot and didn't know it yet. The American boy was lying on his left side, his face twitching with pain. He was so bad that I couldn't look at him, and, as Busch went over to the bed to examine him, I moved away. The political commissar was a fat little man who had just recovered from a bad spine wound. I heard the New York boy cry out in pain and I said to the political commissar, "What's the matter with him?" He said, "He was shot through the kidneys and through the thigh. The thigh wound is open." I said, "Can't you give him dope? Listen to him scream." The commissar nodded, "Sure. Busch will give him something. But don't mind the boy too much: he's a bad hypochondriac."

In the courtyard of the press office in Madrid, somebody has put a great many big statues. Nobody is very clear about how they got there, or what they are, or why they are there, but everybody agrees they are very bad statues indeed. Wednesday night, at about seven o'clock, a newspaper man said to me, "They're pretty awful. If they've got to shell, why can't they ever hit these things?" We reached the door to the street. "Can you find your way in the dark?" and I laughed and said sure, I was old enough not to be afraid of the dark. But when I opened the door and came out on the sidewalk, I knew that was a foolish thing to have said.

Without meaning to, I gasped. It is a terrible thing to see a city in complete darkness. A modern city is not meant to be without light at night: the buildings meet at the top in distorted triangles, and the sky seems too close to the earth. I went down the street, trying not to stumble, trying to find the curb of the sidewalks, trying not to step in holes. Twice I got lost, and once I turned my ankle and fell, and when I got up I was crying, and thought I was crying because my ankle hurt. But when I finally got to the hotel, I ran through it, feeling safe again. That was at seven o'clock. At eight-fifteen there was a sudden, whistling noise and then a far-off, muffled crash. A few minutes later, an English girl who worked in the Blood Transfusion Institute opened my door and came in to ask what I had done that day, did I like Madrid, did I want a drink, couldn't she— and stopped to listen and then to talk again quickly.

They were dropping forty shells a minute into Madrid and the whistling noise was growing very close. She turned to me, "Do you know what that is?" "Yes," I said, "shelling." "All right," she said. "I came up because I knew it was your first time. Come in the bathroom and you'll be able to tell how close it is." We went into the bathroom and she sat on the tub and watched me. In a few minutes the whistling went straight by the corner window and the crash this time was heavy, not sharp, and very close. She got up. "I'll go see if I can do anything. Go down to the dining room. It's in the center of the building." I said, "What good does that do?" She laughed, "Not much," and went out. I stood there looking out into the darkness. There were no sounds but the whistling, the flight of the shell and then a sharp or a dull crash. Suddenly there was a long heavy sound in the darkness—I think it was from a man—and through it a second sound. When the sound from the man ceased, the second sound came clear: a child was screaming, shrilly. In the hour and a half that Madrid was shelled that night there were many other sounds. Some of those sounds have no name in English.

This was the damage done that night: eighty people had been killed, two hotels had been hit, one grocery store and some houses in the poorest section of the town were gone, the press office had three shells in it, and the gentleman who didn't like the statues had been there to see two of the statues get two shells. In a kitchen back of my hotel, a blind woman was holding a bowl of soup that she came to get each night. She was killed eating the bowl of soup. Afterwards an Englishman said to me, "Not much sense to this kind of killing. They don't even try for military objectives any more, or for men. When I was on the Franco side, a few months ago, I heard the German technicians call this 'the little war.' They're practicing. They're testing, testing the guns. They're finding the accuracy of the guns, they're finding the range." Finding the range on a blind woman eating a bowl of soup is a fine job for a man.

NOVEMBER 18, 1936: *Germany and Italy recognized Franco.*

DECEMBER 1: *Germans numbering 5,000 were reported to have landed at Cadiz to aid the Rebels.*

DECEMBER 4: *England and France extended their policy of "non-intervention" to volunteers to Spain.*

JANUARY 5, 1937: *Great Britain and France asked Italy and Germany to cease giving aid to Spain.*

JANUARY 13: *The U.S. State Department warned citizens against serving in Spain.*

# INTERNATIONAL BRIGADE

## *by Vincent Sheean*

I SUPPOSE the existence of the internationals—of all the International Brigades then contained in the 35th and 45th divisions of the 5th Corps of the Spanish army—was suddenly proved to me with startling reality. I knew their story, roughly. The first of them (mostly Germans) had appeared at Madrid in November, 1936, and many had died there in Madrid's defense. The French had been next in time and number; the anti-Fascist Italians, the Yugoslavs and other southeastern Europeans (including a good many Czechs) and the British, Americans and Canadians had appeared first during the first dreadful winter. The American battalions (there were two to start with) had fought in the campaigns of Jarama and Brunete (for Madrid), in the Quinto campaign (for Aragon), at Teruel and now in this second and disastrous Aragon campaign. But knowing their story, on paper or by hearsay, was not at all the same thing as seeing them there as they returned from the catastrophe, after three weeks of the most ghastly punishment that overwhelming superiority of aviation and artillery could inflict upon them. They had seen their friends butchered; they had been in such acute danger that it is a wonder any of them got across the Ebro again; they had been hungry and cold for a long time, and their clothes were in tatters. A certain number of them had been, of course, dispirited by such a succession of calamities, and there was plenty of grumbling to be heard here and there, as well as some evidences of shell shock and demoralization. There had been (or so I heard) some desertions. But most of the ones I saw—and I wandered about among them pretty freely—startled me by their indomitable spirit, their refusal to recognize even implicitly that this defeat might affect the outcome of the war, their easy, cheerful and implacable resolution. I had been in Pennsylvania only a few weeks before, and I had visited Valley Forge on a day of thick white snow when it was easy to imagine what the state of the Continental army must have been in the winter of 1777-78. These boys made me think of Washington's words inscribed on the national arch at Valley Forge: "Naked and starving as they are, we cannot enough admire the incomparable patience and fidelity of the soldiery." They owed this particular strength to their political convictions. The whole Spanish army was political; the system of commissars was instituted partly because the army was of political origin—not a professional soldiery—and partly to make it even more political, since it was clear from the beginning that the professional soldiers, in an enormous proportion, were partisans of the military chieftains who had revolted against the Republic in the service of Fascism, and that the strength of the Republic, if it was ever to have a formidable armed strength, must come from the convictions of its men. In the poverty of materials to which the sinister farce of "nonintervention" had condemned the Republic, the strength of the anti-Fascist cause had to come first of all (and sometimes only) from the willingness of its men to die for it.

In this matter the internationals had already passed through an apprenticeship by enlisting at all. It was difficult for them to get to Spain. All their own governments discouraged it. Their passports were not valid for Spain; the French were busily attempting to keep them from crossing the border; they were promised nothing but hardship and death when they got there. And yet they had come, from all the ends of the earth, from China, Mexico, California, Devonshire, Illinois, Texas and Croatia, in disobedience to their own civil authorities, to cross the Pyrenees on foot in the snow and fight for the Republic. In so doing they expressed their conviction that the struggle of the Spanish Republic against its rebellious generals and their German and Italian masters was in fact the struggle of common humanity against the black forces that everywhere threatened to overwhelm it. This conviction had been sometimes formalized into membership in the Communist party, as the most militant body at hand; a large proportion of the Americans, for example, were Communists. But they were by no means all Communist; there was every form of liberal idealism among them; and the vital thrust of their effort was magnificent. The cause for which they fought in Spain was not Communism, but the right of the Spanish Republic to find its own peaceful solutions to its internal problems—that, and the necessity of raising a shield in time to defend ordinary mankind against the deadly reaction called Fascism. They had international minds, most of them ("What is Chamberlain going to do?"). They knew that Spain today is certainly no farther from London than Sevenoaks was in 1800. They were nearly all young, products of the age of communication, aware of the whole world as much as of their particular segment of it; they were young enough to do what they had to do in high spirits and (whenever possible) with a laugh. In the darkest moments of the whole dark year of 1938—even in Prague in September—I could think of the International Brigades in Spain and be sure that courage and generosity still existed somewhere on this planet. In such as these is the hope of the world; I think the only hope.

MARCH 22, 1937: *The Loyalists gained a decisive victory at Brihuega.*

# ITALY'S FIRST DEFEAT

## by Herbert L. Matthews

CONSIDERING its preliminaries and the completion of the action afterwards, the Battle of Brihuega lasted fifteen days. I felt at the time, and now that seven months have passed I feel even more strongly, that it will rank as one of the twelve or fifteen decisive battles of history. In my opinion, nothing more important has happened in the world since the European War than the defeat of the Italians on the Guadalajara front. It will be a symbol and a turning point for history in the years to come. What Bailen was to Napoleonic imperialism, Brihuega was to Fascism, and it will be that whatever may be the outcome of the Civil War.

I am not ordinarily addicted to such bold and sweeping statements. We journalists are always chary of "getting out on a limb" in any case, but I have thought often and deeply about what happened in those fifteen days and that is my considered opinion. I am going to set down here whatever slight contribution I can make, as a personal observer, to those historic days.

It is always so trite to say that "the darkest hours come before dawn"— but always so true. One had to be hopeful indeed not to appreciate how desperate the Government's situation was. They did have one great advantage, however, although none of us, and the Spanish General Staff least of all, thought for one moment that the Italian thrust would be allowed to come alone. There could have been no greater tactical error on the part of the insurgent command and it demonstrated an internal dissension whose significance is only now beginning to be appreciated.

The Guadalajara drive could so easily have been timed to coincide with the Jarama River push! In that case nothing could have saved the Government. They were only separated by a few weeks' time and it would have been the simplest thing in the world for the Spanish rebels to wait and strike together with the Italians. There is only one satisfactory explanation for their refusal to do so—jealousy and a desire to win the war without the aid of the hated foreigners. For the Italians are hated in Spain, even on the rebel side—let there be no mistake about that.

At any rate, when the Italians started on a front more than sixty miles from Madrid it seemed incredible that they could have entertained hopes of encompassing the downfall of the capital all by themselves. We ordinary people, who have nothing to do with the running of nations and of the world, cannot help feeling that our rulers must have infinitely more intelligence, and more knowledge, than we. The conception of them making obvious and foolish mistakes is something beyond us. If they seem foolish to us we feel there must be some rational explanation hidden by our lack of knowledge.

So it was with the Guadalajara drive. The Italians literally tried the impossible. There was no chance of their plan of campaign succeeding. I am not making this statement for the first time. Anyone who wants can consult the files of *The New York Times* for the early days of the drive and find it all there. It was so obvious to us here who knew the opposition which the Italian force would meet! That is why we and the Spanish staff from Miaja down simply could not believe that we were seeing it. It was a colossal error based on ignorance—nothing less than that.

We all know now what the Italian plan of campaign was. In three days they expected to take Guadalajara, then push swiftly down the level plain to Alcalá de Henares, at which point the capital would be virtually cut off. As if Madrid were Malaga, as if this dangerous, hard-fighting Popular Army could be swept aside like chaff! Incredible, simply incredible—and yet there they were, trying it with the utmost confidence!

Of all the things we wondered about that night (and thoughtful Spaniards must have been doing the same) the most persistent question was: "What will Mussolini do now?" By then there could be no minimizing the loss of prestige which the events of that week entailed for the Italian Army. By one of the choicer ironies of fate, it so happened that in going through five cases of documents captured in Brihuega a message from Il Duce to General Mancini of the Italian force was found and copies distributed to the press that night, as well as read over the radio, by the Information Department of the Spanish Army. Mancini had ordered the distribution of copies to all commands and all troops on the Guadalajara front, which was done in a memorandum signed by First Adjutant Major Luigi Bernardi.

93

The message read as follows:

"On board the *Pola,* on my way to Libya, I have received your dispatches in connection with the great battle which is going on in the direction of Guadalajara. I am following the incidents of the battle with unshakable confidence because I am sure that the impetus and daring of our Legionaries will break the enemy's resistance. To crush the International forces will be a great success, including the political aspect. Tell the Legionaries that I follow their action hourly and that their efforts will be crowned with victory."

The message, which was signed "Mussolini," was dated March 13, the day that the Internationals recaptured Trijueque, and it was distributed to the troops on March 16, two days before the fall of Brihuega.

The next day was one of the most memorable of my life. The realization of what had happened was gradual but before mid-afternoon I was overwhelmed by what I had seen. We entered Brihuega at about two o'clock, marveling to find it so little damaged. The air communiqués had foolishly kept announcing the terrific bombardment of the town, so that we expected to find it ground to dust. Actually, the pilots had received orders not to bomb the town itself, but the Italian positions around the town. There were shell holes in some of the houses, but that was all.

The civilian population never had had time to evacuate it. When the Italians entered, they just fled to their cellars. Some were routed out, some came out of their own free will, while others stayed down there, not daring to make their presence known. One woman told Gorrell and me that she had taken her baby and stayed in the cellar of her house for eight days, never seeing an Italian and only emerging when the Loyalists retook the town. Forty of the inhabitants, men, women, and youths, had been imprisoned and were under sentence to be shot. Seven, in fact, had been executed, but before the other sentences could be carried out the Government troops entered.

Two sisters, eighty-two and eighty-six years old, had stuck it out with the rest, and were now happily pottering around their house. We walked around assessing the damages and talking to people. All of them assured us that the invading troops had been Italian, with the exception of a few interpreters and liaison officers. One of the churches had been employed as a stable, and militiamen were busy collecting dozens of fine, new mule-saddles that had been left behind. The post office was completely sacked. On a wall opposite one of the churches was painted, *"Viva Mussolini! Arriba España!"* Farther up the same street, on another house, the inscription *"Viva el Generalissimo Franco!"* had been scrawled.

We soon drove on toward Budia, through terrain that a few days before had been full of Italians. A small part of the captured war material had been piled in there—cannons, mortars, machine guns, hand-grenades, rifles, and other things. Under ordinary circumstances it could have been considered a large haul, but the Loyalists had taken so much that what we saw was unimportant. However, before lunching we went over the material

94

carefully, verifying from the markings and names that it was all Italian.

All day, at every place we stopped and no matter whom we talked to or what we saw, there was only one label—Italian. The dead bodies, the prisoners, the material of every kind, the men who had occupied Brihuega and then fled, were Italian and nothing but Italian.

About a mile out of Brihuega on that road running north there was a depot of at least 300 cases of cartridges, each containing 2,000 bullets. And all along the road on both sides we saw more full cases—surely 200 more—which would give a total of a million cartridges abandoned in that stretch alone, while the officers with us claimed they had knowledge of another million in all found elsewhere. On three occasions I descended from the car to read the labels on the boxes and make sure that the material was Italian. There were dead along that road, many abandoned trucks, heaps of 75-millimeter shells, about half a dozen field pieces.

And so it went until we reached the front lines just short of Yela. That town had been occupied a half hour before without a shot being fired. The Commander came over to talk to us. Under his arm he had a pile of documents which he showed us. They were all Italian—passports, carnets, private letters, official documents—taken from four prisoners who were found hiding in Yela.

The Commander told us about a terrific bombardment carried out during the morning by some eighty Government planes on the Aragon highway beyond Algora, where a train of about a thousand trucks carrying soldiers and material was surprised. Six hundred and fifty bombs were dropped on them, and then the combat planes swooped down, machine-gunning the soldiers.

Nobody knew where the main body of Italians could be. The Commander's guess (which proved true) was that they had fled to the high town of Bujalaro, north of the Aragon road. It is true that a few miles beyond we were stopped by guards and warned that if we proceeded farther we would come under cannon fire, but that merely meant that the Italians were covering their retreat with artillery. At that point we were even with Kilometer 92.

Back in Brihuega for the last time we were just turning on to the main road when a group of women and children and an old man ran screaming toward us, holding out their hands imploringly. On stopping, a woman with a baby in her arms begged us weeping to take them back to Guadalajara. Their house had been destroyed in the bombing and they all had barely escaped with their lives by running into a neighbor's cellar a moment before the disaster. We somehow managed to squeeze six into our car while another automobile took the remaining two.

The children were whimpering when we started, but soon calmed down and it was from one of them, a lad of seven, that I heard the only sane remark of that whole astonishing day.

"What do you think of all this?" I asked.

"*Muy bueno,*" he answered happily. "The bombs destroyed our school!"

The military operation had not been terminated yet, for it was necessary to secure the left flank, still menaced by the presence of the original Spanish line along the Soria road. That had held firm, making too great an advance along the Aragon highway dangerous. The Loyal command decided that after having regained the ground lost on March 8 and 9 they would fortify the strongest positions along the front so that it could be held against any future attack. On March 20, 21, and 22, as the Lister Brigade advanced steadily and easily along the Aragon road, the Eleventh Brigade, with the Pi y Margall and Largo Caballero Battalions of the Thirty-fifth Brigade cleaned up the towns of Muduex and Utande along its left flank.

The Battle of Brihuega was over.

Mussolini hastily abandoned his trip to Libya and rushed back to Rome to take things in hand. In London, Ambassador Grandi firmly announced that the Italian "volunteers" would remain in Spain. In fact, the international implications of the defeat were so great and it is so important that future historians should have a firm basis for their interpretations, I would like to sum up briefly the reasons for stating that the force defeated by the Loyalists was entirely Italian.

These are the facts which must be considered:

*First,* all prisoners, deserters, and dead identified themselves or were identified as Italians by their documents;

*Second,* all of the enormous amount of war material captured on that front was Italian;

*Third,* all documents found on men or in houses or camps or recaptured towns were either Italian or referred to the Italian action;

*Fourth,* Spanish officers, soldiers, and the civilian populations of the recaptured towns unanimously bore witness to the fact that the men they fought or who occupied their towns were all Italians, with the exception of a few interpreters, liaison officers, and police who did not take part in the fighting.

*Fifth,* the military tactics used were typically Italian.

The existence of these facts is not dependent upon statements by the Government or by partisans of the Government, for every foreign newspaperman here had ample proof for his own eyes and ears. My own case was typical. I saw at least a hundred prisoners and deserters and talked in Italian to dozens of them, chosen by myself or found at the front. I saw hundreds of documents so personal—such as letters, postcards, identity cards, photographs—that there could be no possibility of forgery. I talked to many dozen Spanish and International soldiers and officers at the front who fought against the Italians. They were of the most varied type and nationality and it was inconceivable that they were all fabricating their stories. I also talked in Brihuega with civilians who stayed in that town during the eight days of the Italian occupation. They were simple peasant folk who had been approached by nobody—and they, too, told the same story. I saw with my own eyes a huge quantity of abandoned material which I examined —boxes of cartridges, shells, field pieces, tanks, trucks, machine guns, and

96

so forth. All of that material was Italian and bore the name of Italian makers. Finally, I had seen Italian troops in action in Ethiopia and I knew how they fought, and to me the tactics used in the original advance were typically Italian.

The Government's addition to these facts in the book of documents presented to the Council of the League of Nations in Geneva is available to all historians, as are the documents, for that matter. They in themselves tell a story that admits of no contradiction.

# THE LOYALISTS

## *by Ernest Hemingway*

### ON THE ARAGON FRONT

WHEN we got up with the Americans they were lying under some olive trees along a little stream. The yellow dust of Aragon was blowing over them, over their blanketed machine guns, over their automatic rifles and their anti-aircraft guns. It blew in blinding clouds raised by the hooves of pack animals and the wheels of motor transports.

But in the lee of the stream-bank, the men were slouching fearful and grinning, their teeth flashing white slits in their yellow-powdered faces.

Since I had seen them last spring, they have become soldiers. The romantics have pulled out, the cowards have gone home along with the badly wounded. The dead, of course, aren't there. Those who are left are tough, with blackened matter-of-fact faces, and, after seven months, they know their trade.

They have fought with the first Spanish troops of the new government army, captured the strongly fortified heights and town of Quinto in a brilliantly conceived and executed fashion, and have taken part with three Spanish brigades in the final storming of Belchite after it had been surrounded by Spanish troops.

After the taking of Quinto, they had marched twenty miles across country to Belchite. They had lain in the woods outside the town and had worked their way forward with the Indian-fighting tactics that are still the most life-saving that any infantry can know. Covered by a heavy and accurate artillery barrage, they stormed the entry to the town. Then for three days they fought from house to house, from room to room, breaking walls with pickaxes, bombing their way forward as they exchanged shots with the retreating Fascists from street corners, windows, rooftops and holes in the walls.

Finally, they made a juncture with Spanish troops advancing from the other side and surrounded the cathedral, where 400 men of the town garrison still held out. These men fought desperately, bravely, and a Fascist

97

officer worked a machine gun from the tower until a shell crumpled the masonry spire upon him and his gun. They fought all around the square, keeping up a covering fire with automatic rifles, and made a final rush on the tower. Then, after some fighting of the sort you never know whether to classify as hysterical or the ultimate in bravery, the garrison surrendered.

Robert Merriam, former California University professor and chief of staff of the Fifteenth Brigade, was the leader in the final assault. Unshaven, his face smoke-blackened, his men tell how he bombed his way forward, wounded six times slightly by hand-grenade splinters in his hands and face, but refusing to have his wounds dressed until the cathedral was taken. The American casualties were 23 killed and 60 wounded out of a total of 500 of all ranks who took part in the two operations.

The total government casualties given in the entire offensive were 2,000 killed and wounded. The entire garrison of 3,000 troops in Belchite was either captured or killed except for four officers who succeeded in escaping from the town during the last night before the final assault.

### MADRID

They say you never hear the one that hits you. That's true of bullets, because, if you hear them, they are already past. But your correspondent heard the last shell that hit this hotel. He heard it start from the battery, then come with a whistling incoming roar like a subway train to crash against the cornice and shower the room with broken glass and plaster. And while the glass still tinkled down and you listened for the next one to start, you realized that now finally you were back in Madrid.

Madrid is quiet now. Aragon is the active front. There's little fighting around Madrid except mining, counter-mining, trench raiding, trench-mortar strafing and sniping, in a stalemate of constant siege warfare going on in Carabanchel, Usera and University City. The cities are shelled very little. Some days there is no shelling and the weather is beautiful and the streets are crowded. The shops are full of clothing; jewelry stores, camera shops, picture dealers are all open and the bars are crowded.

Beer is scarce and whiskey is almost unobtainable. Store windows are full of Spanish imitations of all cordials, whiskies and vermouths. These are not recommended for internal use, although I am employing something called Milords Ecosses Whiskey on my face after shaving. It smarts a little, but I feel very hygienic. I believe it would be possible to cure athlete's foot with it, but one must be very careful not to spill it on one's clothes because it eats wool.

The crowds are cheerful and the sandbag-fronted cinemas are crowded every afternoon. The nearer one gets to the front, the more cheerful and optimistic the people are. At the front itself, optimism reaches such a point that your correspondent, very much against his good judgment, was induced to go swimming in a small river forming a no-man's land on the Cuenca front the day before yesterday.

The river was a fast-flowing stream, very chilly and completely dominated by Fascist positions, which made me even chillier. I became so chilly at the idea of swimming in the river at all under the circumstances that, when I actually entered the water, it felt rather pleasant. But it felt even pleasanter when I got out of the water and behind a tree.

At that moment, a government officer who was a member of the optimistic swimming party shot a watersnake with his pistol, hitting it on the third shot. This brought a reprimand from another, not so completely optimistic officer member, who asked what he wanted to do with that shooting—get machine guns turned on us?

We shot no more snakes that day, but I saw three trout in the stream which would weigh over four pounds apiece; heavy, solid, deep-sided ones that rolled up to take the grasshoppers I threw them, making swirls in the water as deep as though you had dropped a paving stone into the stream. All along the stream, where no road ever led until the war, you could see trout; small ones in the shallows and the biggest kind in the pools and in the shadow of the bank. It's a river worth fighting for, but just a little cold for swimming.

At this moment, a shell has just alighted on a house up the street from the hotel where I am typing this, A little boy is crying in the street. A Militiaman has picked him up and is comforting him. There was no one killed on our street, and the people who started to run slow down and grin nervously. The one who never started to run at all looks at the others in a very superior way, and the town we are living in now is called Madrid.

Brunete was not a last desperate effort by the government to relieve the siege of Madrid, but the first in a series of offensives launched on the realistic basis of regarding the war as of a possible duration of two years.

In order to understand the Spanish War, it is necessary to realize the Rebels are holding on to a single linked-up line of trenches on an 800-mile front. They are holding fortified towns, often unconnected by any defenses; but those which dominate the country around them, much as castles did in the old feudal days, must be passed, turned, encircled and assaulted as the castles were in olden times.

Troops that had been on the defensive for nine months, waiting to attack, learned their first lessons in April in Casa del Campo, that frontal assaults in modern war against good machine-gun positions are suicidal. The only way an attack can overcome the superiority machine guns give defense, if the defenders are not panicked by aerial bombardment, is by surprise, obscurity or maneuver.

The government first began to maneuver in a counter-offensive that beat the Italians at Guadalajara. At Brunete, the government troops were not yet experienced enough to turn and take their objectives on time so that the whole front could advance. But they held and threw back a counter-offensive that cost the Rebels more men than they could afford to lose. The Loyalist casualties were estimated at 15,000. The Rebel counter-offensive across that bare terrain, lacking any element of surprise, must have cost them many more than that.

While Franco's troops have been advancing this week in the Asturias, the government troops have just completed another nibbling offensive in the extreme north of Aragon which brings them within striking distance of Jaca. Just now they are in striking distance of Huesca, Saragossa and Teruel. They can fight on in this way indefinitely, improving their positions in a series of small offensives, with limited objectives, designed to be carried out with a minimum of casualties, while teaching their army to maneuver in preparation for operations on a grand plan.

While this goes on, Franco is constantly forced to divert troops to meet these small offensives. He can continue to take "name" towns of no ultimate strategic importance, working along the coast and thus improving his international position with obvious cashable successes, or he can face the unavoidable, though postponable, necessity of again attacking Madrid and its lines of communication with Valencia.

Personally, I think Franco got himself into a fix when he advanced into Madrid and failed to take it, a situation from which he can never extricate himself. Sooner or later he must risk everything in a major offensive on the Castilian plateau.

### LOYALIST ARMY HEADQUARTERS, TERUEL FRONT

For three days, all Teruel's communications had been cut and the government forces had taken successively Concud, Campillo and Villastar, important defensive towns guarding the city from the north, southwest and south.

Friday, while we watched from a hilltop above the town, crouching against boulders, hardly able to hold our field glasses in the fifty-mile gale which picked up the snow from the hillside and lashed it against our faces, government troops took the Muela de Teruel Hill, one of the odd thimble-shaped formations like extinct geyser cones which protect the city.

Fortified by concrete machine-gun emplacements, and surrounded by tank traps made of spikes forged from steel rails, it was considered impregnable, but four companies assaulted it as though they never had had explained to them by military experts what impregnable meant. Its defenders fell back into Teruel, and, a little later in the afternoon, as we watched, another battalion broke through the concrete emplacements of the cemetery, and the last defenses of Teruel itself were squashed or turned.

In zero weather, with a wind that made living a torture, and intermittent blizzards, the army of the Levante and part of the new army of maneuver, without the aid or presence of any International Brigades, had launched an offensive which was forcing the enemy to fight at Teruel when it was a matter of common knowledge that Franco had planned offensives against Guadalajara and in Aragon.

When we left the Teruel front last night for the all-night drive to Madrid to file this story, the presence of 1,000 Italian troops drawn from the Guadalajara front was signaled north of Teruel, where their troops, trains and transport had been bombed and machine-gunned by Loyalist aircraft. Authorities estimated that 30,000 Fascist troops were already massing on the Catalayud-Teruel road for a counter-offensive. So, regardless of whether Teruel is captured, the offensive has achieved its purpose of forcing Franco's hand and breaking up plans for simultaneous Guadalajara and Aragon offensives.

Across a country cold as a steel engraving, wild as a Wyoming blizzard or a hurricane mesa, we watched the battle which may be the decisive one of this war. In the Peninsular War, Teruel had been taken by the French in December and there was good precedent for an attack on it now. On the right were snowy mountains with timbered slopes, below was a winding pass which the Rebels held above Teruel on the Sagunto Road, from which many military authorities had expected a Franco attack to the sea to be launched. Below was the great yellow battleship-shaped natural fortification of Mansueto, the city's main protection, which the Loyalists had slipped past to the northwards, leaving it as hopeless as a stranded dreadnaught.

Close below were the spire and ocher-colored houses of Castralvo, which government troops entered as we watched. On the right, by the cemetery, there was fighting and shell bursts plumed up, while beyond, the city, neatly ordered against its fantastically eroded background of red sandstone, stood quiet as a tethered sheep too frightened to shiver when wolves are passing.

What Franco's Italians and Moors will do in the present situation of weather conditions in Teruel remains to be seen. Horses could never have stood up under the conditions of this offensive. Cars had their radiators frozen and their cylinder blocks cracked. But men could stand it, and did. One thing remains. You need infantry still to win battles, and impregnable positions are only as impregnable as the will of those who hold them.

SEPTEMBER 20, 1937: *Spain lost her seat in the League Council. Russia warned the League that "non-intervention" in Spain increased the danger of a general European war.*

JULY 25, 1938: *The Loyalists retreated across the Ebro.*

# THE SIEGE OF BARCELONA

## by *William P. Carney*

WITH insurgent troops, before Barcelona, Spain, Jan. 24, 1939—Republican [Loyalist] troops have failed to prevent Generalissimo Francisco Franco's forces from crossing the Llobregat River. A colonel on General Franco's headquarters staff told your correspondent the fate of Barcelona had been decided today.

General Juan Yague's Moroccan troops captured Barcelona's airdrome at

Prat de Llobregat and late this afternoon were within one mile of the suburbs of the city. No serious obstacle remained in their path.

Nationalist [Insurgent] artillery concentrated on the harbor, putting up a terrific bombardment in an attempt to prevent the Republicans from escaping by sea.

General Yague's Moors have marched twenty miles a day this last week, and the rope-soled slippers of many are now in ribbons.

The railway between Sitges and Barcelona runs through a number of tunnels cut into the precipitous coast near Garraf. The Republicans, on retreating, blocked one of these tunnels by setting fire to a freight train including several tank cars of gasoline. The train was still blazing and huge columns of smoke pouring out of the tunnel mouth when the Nationalists arrived.

General Franco's troops are excitedly cheering. Everyone is eager to be in the first column to enter Barcelona.

Artillery has been rushed up and has Barcelona under direct fire from the Plain of Llobregat. Huge trimotored bombers drone overhead, adding to the constant menace to Republican troops still inside the city. I counted thirty of these bombers, high up in the sky, circling the outskirts of Barcelona but not dropping their deadly loads.

Barcelona appears tense in the distance, awaiting the decision in the next twenty-four hours which will determine whether the city will fall without its defenders firing a shot or only after sanguinary street fighting and sniping from roofs.

General Franco today has been moving along the whole southern sector, encouraging his men by his appearance among them. Many of his troops are almost played out after a week's rapid advance, some carrying machine guns and ammunition belts. Mule columns strung along the roadside are resting at every available moment, while engineers rush up bridges.

The Republicans have destroyed every bridge, and some of the temporary military structures hastily erected by the Nationalists to enable troops and transport to move forward are nightmares to cross. Some small bridges I crossed today with my car had to be supported by troops while I got over.

Cars with broken springs have been abandoned in ditches, as everybody is eager to enter Barcelona.

General Garcia Valino this afternoon completed his flanking movement around Manresa on the north and forced the Republicans to surrender that town almost without a shot. The Republican troops' resistance in that area has now collapsed completely, and Manresa fell after a few minor affrays between the retreating Republican rear guard and the Nationalists' vanguard.

Manresa is an important textile town and engineering center.

Columns of Navarrese and Italian and Spanish legionnaires who crossed Llobregat River penetrated to the outskirts of Tarrasa, a town of 10,000 population only ten miles northwest of Barcelona.

The biggest problem General Franco now faces is to enter Barcelona without fighting. With this object, he is closing all exits from the city, leaving open only the roads leading northward through Granollers and Gerona.

JANUARY 26, 1939: *Franco's army entered Barcelona.*

FEBRUARY 27: *Great Britain and France recognized Franco.*

# THE BITTER END

## *by Janet Flanner*

MARCH 1, 1939—There has never been anything in modern history like the recent flight of the Catalonian army and civilian population into France. Since the exodus was without precedent, nobody was prepared to take care of it. When the French frontier roads were finally opened, about three hundred thousand Spaniards—soldiers, civilians, women, and children, all hungry, exhausted, and in a panic—swept down on the two hundred thousand French inhabitants of the Pyrénées-Orientales who, though they were at peace and at home, found themselves living in what was practically occupied territory. The Spaniards, entering as a horde of homeless guests, found themselves living largely as prisoners of war. The discomfort and confusion for both French and Spanish have been bitter.

Certainly the Spanish militiamen believed that if they stayed in their own land they would be killed. They are now alive—behind barbed wire—in France. It would seem that between the two extremes of life and death everything else to them is relatively unimportant.

When we were in Perpignan, there were still two hundred thousand refugees, mostly soldiers, in the two largest concentration camps on the sandy wastes of St. Cyprien and Argelès, and about sixty thousand, more lucky, in smaller camps, like Amélie-les-Bains. The little camps are better situated, mostly have hills for protection and trees for firewood, and are, naturally, easier to run. In the three sectors of the Amélie camp we saw about twenty-five thousand men, of whom six thousand were milling on a football ground in what looked like misery but was the envy of the other camps. The men were under the surveillance of the Garde Mobile, who shooed them around like chickens when they spread out too thickly on the highroad. Mimosa was blooming on the hillside, but the air was cold. Most of the men had brought a blanket, their sole possession, and wore it all day draped like a giant scarf over their shoulders. There was no shelter. The refugees sat, slept, and waited on the brown ground. The camp, being near the snow-topped Canigou peak, afforded pine boughs for firewood; smoke hung like a flat, low second sky over the scene. The French government was giving two pounds of bread daily to every twenty-five men, who, as a unit, were cooking their stew, beans, and rice soup when and how they chose or could in washboilers, buckets, or iron pots. Much of the food was contributed by the Front Populaire or by neighbors. Some of the meat lying in newspapers on the ground came from Spanish cows or horses which the refugees had brought with them and butchered. Amélie is ordinarily a watering place, favored by modest English visitors. One elderly British lady with an anachronistic parasol came daily with baskets of raw mutton chops for the soldiers, and also daily complained that she couldn't cook properly on a slab of sheet iron balanced on boulders.

Behind the football ground is a little rocky river, where the men, stripped to the waist, were washing when we were there. During the first three dreadful days, the refugees, out of fear of pollution, were driven away from the river. They stood in line all day waiting to get water from a spigot with a trickle as wide as your thumb. Now bad water is general and dysentery is commonplace in all camps. The main hospital tent at Amélie was full when we visited it but seemed well run and didn't smell. It contained about seventy patients bedded on straw pallets, each wedged into a sort of window frame set on the ground. Most of the men had minor wounds. One grizzled Goyaesque peasant with the ague shook all four patients boxed around him. The pharmacist, doctors, and internes were picked from among the refugees. Fifteen days after the camp opened, it was excellently run by the Spaniards themselves, the manager being a former Barcelona impresario. While there, we watched three contingents of the younger and bolder men march off, singing and shouting, to join the French Foreign Legion—if they weren't shipped to Franco, as one officer predicted they would be.

In the arid countryside between Amélie and St. Cyprien, the refugees have left three tragic traces. First are the ruined valley vineyards, where, before the Spaniards were dispersed to camps, they helplessly rested; burned whatever came to hand, to keep from freezing; and wrecked the land. Second are the thousands of abandoned jalopies, battered trucks, and semismart sedans. And finally there are the tens of thousands of slowly moving, deserted Catalonian horses and mules, herding together in hunger, idleness, and misery, and constantly edging, with strange sociability, toward human habitations. The day we were there, a vast troop of these beasts, attracted to the St. Cyprien camp, were being rounded up by the unpopular Spahis, who waved their sabers and shouted Arabic from their squealing little stallions—men and animals all rushing in a dark cloud of wind-driven sand and dust that turned the pale sun into a red harvest moon. Inside the barbwired camp we saw the hated, surly Senegalese guards, with their scarlet fezzes, rubber truncheons, and unfraternal faces. In general, what we saw was a maze, miles long, of dun-colored shapes which, when viewed close up, turned out to be white men—walking, standing, sitting on sand, sleeping on sand, breathing and eating sand as it blew on food and faces, men living by the thousand on a treeless beach, on the edge of a muddy, soiled sea. Because of the flying sand, all St. Cyprien refugees have, in addition to their other troubles, conjunctivitis. From the camp center, a loudspeaker called the names of men who had mail, gave orders, asked questions. Some men who had been issued sheets of corrugated iron were laying them out on the sand and digging holes underneath to form a home. The latrines were unsheltered, saucer-shaped declivities scooped in the sand; the kitchens were any spot out of the wind where a man could find wood. The whole scene was an unforgettable one except to those living in it. They had been in the war itself and seemed to notice nothing. The one bright feature was the intelligent, unsentimental work being done by the International Commission for the Assistance of Child Refugees, largely an English and American Quaker group aided by Swiss volunteers.

In the International Brigade sector at St. Cyprien, a German soldier asked us to mail a postcard to his home, written in French. It began, "Dear Family: Since several days I find myself in France and I find myself in good health and now I find myself in a concentration camp."

\* \* \*

MADRID, March 28, 1939 (Associated Press): Shell-torn Madrid, symbol of Republican resistance during thirty-two months of civil war, passed into the hands of Nationalist Generalissimo Francisco Franco today ...

\* \* \*

# NEITHER GUNS NOR BUTTER

### by Thomas J. Hamilton

THE blundering attempt to impose a totalitarian economy was all the worse because Spain was traditionally the land of special privilege. Franco's success in restoring these privileges therefore produced a singularly vicious combination: the rich stayed rich, if they did not get richer, and the poor were even hungrier than they had been in the worst days of the civil war.

This misery is in sorry contrast to the cry of social justice raised by the early Spanish fascists. It was all the more deplorable when contrasted with the fine idealism of a few of Franco's supporters, who believed he would win them a better Spain. These hopes have been bitterly disappointed. In few countries of the world is there such grinding, soul-destroying hunger and such luxury for the favored of fortune.

Even with equal rights for all and special privileges for none—a principle which does not exist in the bright lexicon of "young" and fascist nations— some hardships would have been inevitable as a result of the civil war and the mistaken economic policy which followed it. But the suffering was increased immeasurably by the restoration of the old privileges; despite the steadily increasing misery of the poor, the wealthy managed to obtain vir-

105

tually everything that they needed. And a new class of parvenus, who had made their money by special "favors" obtained from the government officials in charge of operating the faltering economic machine, spent their profits with an abandon which was one failing that could not be charged against the old families.

The Franco regime had, in fact, loaded still more privileged classes upon a suffering country. In order to hold its two most valuable supporters, the Army and the Phalanx, special arrangements were made for officers of both to obtain food from government commissaries. Even the common soldier ate far better than the ordinary citizen, while the food supplied to officers of the Army and the Phalanx, and to the more important officials of the government, more than compensated them for their comparatively low salaries. By 1941 the Phalanx had instituted its own separate rationing system for the rank-and-file members of the party, thus setting any kind of fascist above the general population.

An excuse for this practice was found in the special arrangements that were made to enable members of the diplomatic corps to live just as comfortably as though neither the civil war nor the greater war which followed had taken place. Despite the general misery, each embassy and legation was given a special monthly quota of sugar, potatoes, coffee, rice, lentils, and other staples which was far in excess of the amounts that the diplomats were able to obtain through the usual ration cards—although they were allowed to use these as well.

The object, presumably, was to prevent the diplomatic observers from realizing just how badly off Spain was, and it succeeded to some extent. When the American community was raising funds to equip the Vallecas orphanage, the wife of a member of our Embassy proposed a benefit party. She suggested that each American family donate eight dozen sandwiches for refreshments, just as at home. The wives of American private citizens were astonished, for they were finding it difficult to obtain even the one small roll a day per person to which they were entitled under the rationing scheme. Finally they realized that although bread had been rationed for some time, the fact was not known generally among diplomats, who had ample flour with which to make their own white bread.

The weight of circumstance finally compelled the Franco regime to reduce these quotas of the diplomatic corps, but during the first two years after the civil war many diplomats had more of the staple goods, at least, than they could eat. This was particularly true in the case of those who had foreign exchange with which to buy still more food, imported duty-free, from Gibraltar, Portugal, Argentina, and the United States. I knew several diplomats who had storerooms crowded with between five hundred and a thousand dollars' worth of food—enough, as they boasted, to enable them to live a year or more even if they were besieged in their apartments and could not obtain a single loaf of bread or after-dinner mint from hungry Spain.

Diplomats also were permitted to purchase meat, the most difficult of all foods to obtain, from the same government butcher shop which supplied Franco, Serrano Suñer, and other chiefs of the realm. I knew one chargé d'affaires who complained bitterly because he received only 132 pounds (60 kilos) a month for himself, his wife, and the persons whom they entertained. Criticisms of the regime by American and British diplomats did not omit their claim that the Axis representatives not only obtained the best cuts of meat, but received a special ten per cent discount besides. There was general regret early in 1941 when a dispute between the government butcher and the Serrano Suñer cook, who complained that he had been given beef instead of veal, resulted in the closing of the butcher store. It reopened after a time, but has never regained its old free and easy style of operating.

The wealthy classes of Spain did not have such official privileges, but as they had recovered their lands and their factories intact, they were able to buy what they needed. Apart from food obtainable on the black market, there was a considerable supply of non-rationed articles available, of course at extremely high prices. Until 1941 there were no restrictions except the size of one's pocketbook upon purchases of fish, chicken, game, ham, sausage, liver, tripe, kidney, and similar foods. Visitors passing through from France, Holland, and other occupied countries used to walk past the butcher shops marveling that such abundance still existed in the world.

For inexplicable reasons, comparable to our own failure to convert the automobile industry to war production until months after Pearl Harbor, it was years before the Franco regime could bring itself to restrict consumption of other foods that were even more essential to the health of the Spanish working classes than meat. Until early in 1941, for example, pastry shops were allowed to operate just as usual, and while the poor stood in line for their pitiful daily ration of uneatable bread, the wealthy continued their pleasant custom of stopping off on their way home from Mass to consume some of the admirable Spanish éclairs or *mille-feuilles;* it was not until the famine had long since reached its acute stage that the government finally ordered pastry shops to use wheat flour on only one day a week. On other days almond paste had to be used instead of flour, but consumption of sugar, chocolate, and shortening was still not checked. And until I left Spain you were still free to buy all the candy you liked despite the shortage of the materials used in making it. I can remember only two occasions during our residence in Madrid when chocolate was distributed on the ration cards, and although an American could not use the dark, greasy stuff, the Spanish poor considered it a great treat. It was the same with ice cream, soft drinks (Coca-Cola was hard to get because of the shortage of bottles, not for lack of sugar), sandwiches in Madrid's numberless cafés, and other luxury articles.

Any kind of food that was adjudged *de lujo,* in fact, was not subject to rationing or price-fixing regulations; therefore we were able occasionally to buy sweet potatoes, which sold for two or three times the price of Irish potatoes, and sometimes eggs. Butter, being as clearly *de lujo* as it was rancid, was not rationed though it was always scarce; the usual practice was to

107

give Leonese's or some other fancy grocery store a large order for sherry, almonds, and so forth, then threaten to cancel it if the clerk made any difficulties about sending along half a pound or so of butter. Almost always there were ample supplies of green peas, tomatoes, and various kinds of fruit, which were not rationed until the winter of 1941. Except for bread, wealthy families could get along quite satisfactorily with the help of purchases in the black market.

Eternal vigilance, however, was the price that all had to pay for keeping sufficient supplies of food in the larder. In Madrid and Barcelona, therefore, many wealthy families did not think it worth while to reopen their town houses, took suites in the big hotels, and let the restaurant-keepers do the worrying. This was, to be sure, practicable only in the two great cities. Elsewhere it was difficult to obtain eatable food even in the most expensive restaurants; in the government-operated tourist inn at Merida, for example, dinner sometimes consisted of fish cooked in rank olive oil, and fruit. The bad and insufficient food available in luxurious hotels, where there were lackeys to anticipate one's every desire, was as ironic a contrast as one could find even in Spain.

# AUSTRIA

FEBRUARY 12, 1938: *The Austrian Chancellor Kurt von Schuschnigg went to Berchtesgaden to discuss Austria's future with Hitler.*

# "ANSCHLUSS"

## by *William L. Shirer*

VIENNA, *March 11-12* (4 A.M.)
THE worst has happened! Schuschnigg is out. The Nazis are in. The Reichswehr is invading Austria. Hitler has broken a dozen solemn promises, pledges, treaties. And Austria is finished. Beautiful, tragic, civilized Austria! Gone. Done to death in the brief moment of an afternoon. This afternoon. Impossible to sleep, so will write. Must write something. The Nazis will not let me broadcast. Here I sit on one of the biggest stories of my life. I am the only broadcaster in town. Max Jordan of NBC, my only competitor, has not yet arrived. Yet I cannot talk. The Nazis have blocked me all night. I have argued, pleaded, fought. An hour ago they ushered me out with bayonets.

To begin at the beginning of this day of nightmare, if I can:

The sun was out and spring was in the air when my train got into the Südbahnhof at eight this morning. I felt good. Driving to Ploesslgasse I noticed the streets littered with paper. Overhead two planes were dropping leaflets.

"What is it?" I asked the taxi-driver.

"Plebiscite."

"What plebiscite?"

"The one Schuschnigg ordered." He did not trust me and would say no more.

I climbed the stairs to our apartment puzzled. I asked the maid. She handed me a stack of newspapers for the last three days. Over breakfast I caught up on the news. On Wednesday night (March 9) Schuschnigg, speaking at Innsbruck, had suddenly ordered a plebiscite. For this Sunday. The question: "Are you for an independent, social, Christian, German, united Austria? *Ja oder Nein.*"

About eleven A.M. I took a taxi into town and went to the Schwarzenberg Café on the Schwarzenbergplatz to see what was up. Fodor and Taylor and some Austrian newspapermen were there. They were a little tense, but hopeful. The plebiscite would go off peacefully, they thought. And Schuschnigg, assured of the support of the workers, would win, hands down. That would hold Hitler for a while. I felt better. Someone turned on the radio. The announcer was reading a proclamation calling up the class of 1915 to active service. That's merely to police the election, we agreed. One of the Austrians was called to the phone. When he came back he said something about the Nazis having just smashed the windows of the Monarchist offices near the Stefansplatz. For some reason, I remember now, everyone laughed. I had in mind to phone Colonel Wolf, the Legitimist leader, with whom I've been negotiating for a broadcast by Otto von Habsburg. But I didn't.

Shortly before four P.M. I set out for the hospital to see if Tess was any better. Crossing the Karlsplatz to catch a subway train I was stopped by a crowd of about a thousand people. They were Nazis and it was a bit comical. One lone policeman was yelling and gesticulating at them. And they were giving ground! "If that's all the guts the Nazis have, Schuschnigg *will* win, hands down," I mused. "And he's arming the workers. That'll take care of the Nazi toughs." I hurried along to my train.

About six o'clock I emerged from the subway to the Karlsplatz. What had happened? Something! Before I knew it I was being swept along in a shouting, hysterical Nazi mob, past the Ring, past the Opera, up the Kärntnerstrasse to the offices of the German "Tourist" Bureau, which, with its immense flower-draped portrait of Hitler, has been a Nazi shrine for months. The faces! I had seen these before at Nuremberg—the fanatical eyes, the gaping mouths, the hysteria. And now they were shouting like Holy Rollers: *"Sieg Heil! Sieg Heil! Sieg Heil! Heil Hitler! Heil Hitler! Heil Hitler! Hang Schuschnigg! Hang Schuschnigg! Hang Schuschnigg! Ein Volk, ein Reich, ein Führer!"* And the police! They were looking on, grinning. What had happened? I was still in the dark. I shouted my question into the ears of three or four jammed against me. No response. Couldn't hear. Finally a middle-aged woman seemed to get me. "The plebiscite!" she yelled. "Called off!"

There was no need to learn more. That was the end of Austria. I extricated myself from the swirling dervishes and made my way down the Ring to the Hotel Bristol. Taylor was there. He introduced me to his wife, Vreni, pretty, brunette, intelligent-looking, who had just arrived. He confirmed the news. It had been announced an hour before on the radio, he said. We took a taxi to the American Legation. John Wiley was standing before his desk, clutching his invariable long cigarette-holder, a queer smile on his face—the smile of someone who has just been defeated and knows it.

"It's all over," he said quietly. There had been an ultimatum from Berlin. No plebiscite, or the German army marches. Schuschnigg had capitulated.

"You'll hear more on the radio shortly," John said. "Stick around."

I left to put in a call for Murrow, who's in Warsaw. Going out of the Legation I stumbled into Gedye, very excited. Home, I put in a call for Ed, my radio playing softly a Viennese waltz. Hateful, it sounded. It stopped abruptly. "Attention! Attention!" a voice said. "In a few minutes you will hear an important announcement." Then the ticking of a metronome, the Ravag's identification signal. Maddening, it sounded. Tick . . . tick . . . tick . . . tick. I turned it down. Then a voice—Schuschnigg's, I recognized—without introduction.

"This day has placed us in a tragic and decisive situation. I have to give my Austrian fellow countrymen the details of the events of today.

"The German Government today handed to President Miklas an ultimatum, with a time limit, ordering him to nominate as chancellor a person designated by the German Government and to appoint members of a cabinet on the orders of the German Government; otherwise German troops would invade Austria.

"I declare before the world that the reports launched in Germany concerning disorders by the workers, the shedding of streams of blood, and the creation of a situation beyond the control of the Austrian Government are lies from A to Z. President Miklas has asked me to tell the people of Austria that we have yielded to force since we are not prepared even in this terrible situation to shed blood. We have decided to order the troops to offer no resistance.

"So I take leave of the Austrian people with a German word of farewell uttered from the depth of my heart: God protect Austria."

Towards the end you feel his voice will break; that there will be sobbing. But he controls it to the last. There is a second silence. And then the national anthem played from an old record. It is the tune of *Deutschland über Alles,* only in the original and slightly different version as Haydn first composed it. That is all. That is the end.

The rest of this evening? A little later the rasping voice of Judas. Dr. Seyss-Inquart is saying something, saying he considers himself responsible for order, saying the Austrian army is not to offer resistance. This is the first we hear of the German invasion. The ultimatum, Schuschnigg says, said capitulate *or* invasion. Now Hitler has broken even the terms of his own ultimatum.

I cannot get Ed in Warsaw. His hotel keeps saying he's out. It is still early. I call the Austrian Broadcasting System to see about my broadcast. No answer. I start downtown. In the Karlsplatz there's a tremendous crowd. Someone is shouting a speech from the steps of the Karlskirche. "Hess and Buerckel," a storm trooper near me whispers. His uniform gave off a stench of moth balls. "Hess and Buerckel! They're here." But I could not get near enough to see.

I fought my way out of the crowd towards the Kärntnerstrasse. Crowds moving about all the way. Singing now. Singing Nazi songs. A few policemen standing around good-naturedly. What's that on their arm? A red-black-white Swastika arm-band! So they've gone over too! I worked my way up Kärntnerstrasse towards the Graben. Young toughs were heaving paving blocks into the windows of the Jewish shops. The crowd roared with delight.

Over at the Café Louvre Bob Best of U.P. is sitting at the same table he has occupied every night for the last ten years. Around him a crowd of foreign correspondents, male and female, American, English, Hungarian, Serb. All but Best in a great state of excitement, running to the phone every five minutes to get some news or give it. The most fantastic rumors. Bob reads over to me his dispatches. He is called away to the phone. He comes back. Schuschnigg has been recalled as chancellor and the Nazis are out, he says. He is optimistic; things are not over yet. A few minutes later: it's a false report. The Nazis have taken over at the Ballhausplatz. We sprint over to the Ballhausplatz, Metternich's Ballhausplatz ... Congress of Vienna. ... Twenty storm troopers are standing on one another before the building, forming a human pyramid. A little fellow scampers to the top of the heap, clutching a huge Swastika flag. He pulls himself up to the balcony, the same balcony where four years ago Major Fey, held prisoner by the Nazis after Dollfuss was shot, parleyed with the Schuschnigg people. He unfurls the flag from the balcony and the *Platz* rings with cheers.

Back to the Louvre. Martha Fodor is there, fighting to keep back the tears, every few minutes phoning the news to Fodor. Emil Maass, my former assistant, an Austro-American, who has long posed as an anti-Nazi, struts in, stops before the table. "Well, *meine Damen und Herren,*" he smirks, "it was about time." And he turns over his coat lapel, unpins his hidden Swastika button, and repins it on the outside over the buttonhole. Two or three women shriek: "Shame!" at him. Major Goldschmidt, Legitimist, Catholic, but half Jewish, who has been sitting quietly at the table, rises. "I will go home and get my revolver," he says. Someone rushes in. Seyss-Inquart is forming a Nazi government. It is a little after eleven P.M. Time to go over to Broadcasting House. Five P.M. in New York.

In the Johannesgasse, before the Ravag building, men in field-gray uniforms stand guard with fixed bayonets. I explain who I am. After a long wait they let me in. The vestibule and corridor are full of young men in army uniforms, in S.S. and S.A. uniforms, brandishing revolvers, playing with bayonets. Two or three stop me, but taking my courage in my hand I bark at them and make my way into the main hall, around which are the studios. Czeja, the *General-Direktor* of Ravag, and Erich Kunsti, program director, old friends, stand in the middle of the room, surrounded by excited, chattering Nazi boys. One glance. They are prisoners. I manage to get in a word with Kunsti.

"How soon can I go on the air?" I say.

He shrugs his shoulders. "I've ceased to exist around here," he laughs. He beckons towards a scar-faced chap who seems to be the boss, for the moment anyway. I explain my wants. No impression. I do it again. He doesn't get me.

"Let me talk to your chiefs in Berlin," I say. "I know them. They'll want me to broadcast."

"Can't get through to Berlin," he says.

"But you will, some time tonight," I say.

"Well, maybe later. You can come back."

"Not a chance," Kunsti whispers. A couple of guards, fingering their revolvers, edge me out. I wait outside in the hall, barging in every so often to see if Scarface has Berlin on the phone. Around midnight a broadcast comes through from the Ballhausplatz. A new government is to be announced soon. I dash over there. Spotlights (from where?) play on the balcony. A dozen men are standing there. I make out Seyss-Inquart, Glaise-Horstenau. . . . Judas is reading his new Cabinet list. He himself is Chancellor.

# ONE YEAR LATER

## *by Anne O'Hare McCormick*

A YEAR ago yesterday, on Friday, March 11, 1938, following the forced resignation of Dr. Schuschnigg, German troops crossed the Austrian frontier. On Saturday the vanguard was in Vienna. That was the day when Hitler stood on a balcony at Linz, capital of the province where he was born, and in a characteristic flash of decision, inspired by the delirium of the crowd, made up his mind that the hour had come for the annexation of Austria to the Reich—at one stroke instead of by gradual steps.

And on that day, cheering her conqueror, Austria died. By March 15, when the Austrian corporal rode in triumph through the avenues of the capital, which had been widened for the imperial processions of the Habsburgs, the bloodless occupation was complete. The rump of the old empire, with its limp insignia, its last gasps of defiance, its helpless and deserted government, was buried under the red banners and gray armies of the new German Empire, for the first time breaking through its historic frontiers.

The full importance of that break was not appreciated until September, when a second frontier fell. Then it was realized that Vienna held the key position in Europe. The fall of Vienna destroyed all hope of recreating an economic Austrian empire, except under German auspices. It weakened Prague more than the hammering of the Sudetens. It shook Budapest, Belgrade, Zagreb, Bucharest. For these cities Vienna was the fount of politics, the center of trade, fashion and banking, the focus of civilization.

A young Central European diplomat recently recounted to the writer a conversation he had with Hitler about Austria. He confirmed reports that the Reichsfuehrer is not at all satisfied with conditions in the Ostmark. Hitler does not like the lagging enthusiasm of the people, steadily declining from the high mark established in the first days in Linz and Graz and Vienna, when the shouting crowds expressed great expectations that have not been fulfilled. He does not like the inefficient administration of the Austrian Nazis—malcontents, adventurers and unemployed riffraff who were good enough to undermine the former government but no good for responsible jobs.

More and more these Austrians are being displaced by Germans, and this does not improve the situation. It embitters the local Nazis, who did not take risks and suffer imprisonment and exile in order to make jobs for Germans. It increases the disorder, because Austrian methods cannot be Germanized without a clean sweep of the civil service. And it feeds the sullen resentment of Austrians in general against the German assumption of superiority. "The stupidest clerk I had," says a Viennese business man, "is now a high party official. Of course he is unfit to fill an important administrative post. But that is no reason why we, who trained officials to administer an empire, should suffer imported Prussians to run us as a colony."

A more or less liberal economy, supported by foreign loans, has given place to a completely planned and rigidly supervised system. Austrians miss their imported goods. They still enjoy more variety and abundance of food than other Germans, but good things are dearer, they complain, and cheap things of inferior quality.

A comparatively free society, greatly impoverished but within its narrow range retaining vestiges of the old order, is being rapidly leveled down. A year ago, for instance, the audience at the opera showed traces of its oldtime brilliance. The annual Vienna Ball went off in a last spurt of splendor. This year's ball was an odd mélange of people never invited before. On ordinary nights the audience at the opera is reminiscent of Moscow—Nazis in the imperial box, and in the loges and parquet a sprinkling of officers among rapt crowds of plain people from offices and shops who carry sandwiches and drink beer in the grand foyer during the entr'acte. One night a week the house is reserved for workers of the "Strength Through Joy" movement.

The diplomats are gone. There are practically no foreigners. Even Balkan travelers no longer come to Vienna. Germans are the only visitors in the almost empty hotels. Germans are everywhere. Where the Austrian Parliaments once sat Reich Commissar Joseph Buerckel of the Saar presides over the offices engaged in forging the politico-economic bonds tying the Ostmark into the Reich. While his former chief, Dr. Schuschnigg, a white-bearded and broken man, waits in a cell-like room on the top floor of the Metropole, Staathalter Arthur Seyss-Inquart, the only Austrian in command, proceeds with his appointed task of liquidating Austria. Reduced to the simplest terms, this is the conflict spreading over Europe. After a year of Anschluss, Austria is gone, but there is no certainty that the ferment stirring in this small theater in the heart of the continent may not turn out to be the leaven that will work changes in a lump that must become less solid as it expands.

# CZECHOSLOVAKIA

APRIL 24, 1938: *Konrad Henlein, leader of the Sudeten Nazis, made a speech at Carlsbad, demanding a revision of Czechoslovakia's foreign policy, which, he declared, had led the country into the ranks of Germany's enemies.*

MAY 21: *The German press started a campaign against the Czechs, speaking of "intolerable provocations." In Paris, Foreign Minister Georges Bonnet assured the foreign press that France would fulfill her obligations "if the occasion demands."*

JULY 22: *Britain and France rejected Germany's proposal of a four-power settlement of the Sudeten problem, on the grounds that Czechoslovakia would be excluded from the discussion.*

AUGUST 3: *Lord Runciman arrived in Prague to "advise in the settlement of the Sudeten dispute." The visit had been suggested by the British cabinet.*

AUGUST 18: *Runciman conferred with Henlein.*

AUGUST 23: *Runciman called briefly on Benes.*

SEPTEMBER 7: *France called up reservists to man the Maginot Line. The Sudeten party broke off negotiations with the Czechs. The National Socialist Party meeting opened at Nuremberg.*

# CHAMBERLAIN IN BERCHTESGADEN

*by Ernest R. Pope*

AFTER a week of this bedlam [the Nuremberg Congress] reporting inflammatory speeches, covering theatrical Teutonic ceremonies and mock warfare that revealed some of the Reich's latest war machines, reporting new Nazi exhibitions, attempting to ferret out Nazi policies being formed behind the scenes, discovering Henlein and other carefully guarded guests of the Führer, struggling with Nazi mobs, Black Guards, miserable telephone service, and irate Nazi officials, and finally hearing Adolf beat the war drums over the Czech situation in his violent concluding address to all of the members of his government and party—I was glad to return to Munich for a rest, leaving Hitler to climb his mountain to plot the rape of his eastern neighbor. I was just crawling into my first warm bath in ten days when my telephone rang. London calling.

"Listen, Pope old boy, get down to Berchtesgaden as fast as you can. Reserve several rooms, if possible at the Grand Hotel. 'Phone us the moment you get there. Chamberlain is flying from Croydon tomorrow morning to see Hitler!"

I hurriedly made arrangements for my assistant to cover the Prime Minister's arrival at Munich, threw on some clothes, and hopped into my little roadster. No chance for a bath or meal until I had prepared the ground in Berchtesgaden. "Chamberlain is flying to see Hitler!" droned around in my head as my car chewed away at the monotonous, straight kilometers of Hitler's Munich-Salzburg highway. "The British Mountain coming to the Nazi Mohammed! What next?"

Journalistic reinforcements from all parts of Europe began flocking into the little mountain village. Star reporters from the big London dailies even had chartered a special 'plane to follow the Prime Minister's glistening craft. Our Reuters team consisted of four men, one of whom arrived after the conference was over. I was compelled to bulletin Chamberlain's arrival single-handed. That was what I was paid for: to be first on the Bavarian scene, before competition was able to invade the territory.

What a strange contrast between this peaceful Bavarian mountain resort and the turbulent world that one of its residents had pushed to the brink of chaos! It was hard to believe that the Prime Minister of the world's greatest empire and the Supreme Commander of the world's strongest army were about to stand face to face for the first time in their lives in this little village, to decide the fate of all Europe. Hard to imagine that thousands of newspaper editors all over the globe were waiting breathlessly for the feeble electric vibrations of a few thin wires emanating from the local telephone exchange. Yet, in Berlin, Goebbels was pumping stories of "Czech Outrages" into the vast distributing system of his propaganda machine. A hundred miles from this idyllic Alpine retreat, arrogant Sudeten Germans and sullen Czechs were at swords' points, burning each others' farms or committing actual physical violence; embassies and state departments of all civilized nations were beehives of activity, buzzing with the latest speculations and reports about the Berchtesgaden meeting. Konrad Henlein had just fled into Germany, and from the safety of his powerful big brother had issued a proclamation demanding the annexation by Germany of the Sudeten territory in Czechoslovakia.

How ironical that one of America's newest airplanes upon which Great Britain was to base her hopes for defeating Hitler a year later, was the machine in which England's Prime Minister placed his trust to enable him as soon as possible to shake hands with the Führer of the Third Reich. It was a twin-motored Lockheed Electra, recently purchased from America by the British Airways, that flew Neville Chamberlain to Munich on Thursday morning, September 15, 1938. The 'plane arrived at the birthplace of National Socialism at 12:30 P.M. Swastikas and Union Jacks decorated the Oberwiesenfeld Airport. Reich Foreign Minister von Ribbentrop received Chamberlain, and whisked him to Hitler's waiting, bomb-proof train. Had the band not blared so loudly at the airport, Chamberlain could have heard the roar of hundreds of airplane motors at a near-by factory, being tested before their installation in the Nazi bombers.

In Berchtesgaden, my first view of the famous, tragic appeaser was against a somber, portentous background. Six black-uniformed, steel-helmeted giants with fixed bayonets clicked to attention as Chamberlain alighted from his car and entered the hotel. A soulless guard of honor with six bayonets—to watch over one gaunt, trusting old man with an old black umbrella.

The British Ambassador to Berlin, Sir Nevile Henderson, Chamberlain's two flying companions—William Strang of the British Foreign Office and Sir Horace Wilson, chief industrial adviser to the British Government—and the Munich Consul occupied the English quarters of the Grand Hotel. Twenty minutes after he had entered the hotel, the British Prime Minister and his Anglo-German entourage were driven to Hitler's villa.

"How swiftly the car climbs!" Chamberlain remarked to von Ribbentrop as they sped up the steep, winding trail to the Berghof. (How swiftly Ribbentrop climbed over his own precipitous, winding agreements!)

Hitler was waiting for his distinguished guest on the steps of his mountain home. The forty-nine-year-old dictator was wearing black trousers, a double-breasted brown jacket, a white shirt with stiff collar and brown four-in-hand tie as he came down the steps to salute the sixty-nine-year-old democratic leader at five o'clock that afternoon.

Tea was served in the spacious hall of Hitler's villa. For twenty-five minutes the British and Nazi delegations conversed together. Then Hitler conducted Chamberlain to his study on the second floor. Here, closeted alone with Dr. Paul Schmidt, the Reich's official interpreter for the Foreign Office, the two statesmen laid their cards on the table. The historic interview lasted two hours and thirty-five minutes. At 8:15 P.M., tired but smiling, Neville Chamberlain returned to the Grand Hotel. His collar was wilted, his mustache disheveled. He looked like a ruffled, but unscathed Daniel emerging from the Lion's den. About thirty of us correspondents stood at a respectable distance in the lobby. The Prime Minister lingered a moment. Press photographers' bulbs flashed. Then Chamberlain retired to his suite.

Outside, the drenching rain came steadily down. The mountains were cloaked in misty Alpine clouds. A true Shakespearean motif! Nature fitting the mood of the drama. We knew that mountain peaks were there. We knew that Chamberlain had risen to new heights in his talk with Hitler.

But the outline of the conversation was hidden from us as impenetrably by official silence as the Berchtesgaden mountains enveloped in the heavy fog.

At nine o'clock, Sir Nevile Henderson came down to the lobby. He gave us the text of the official communique issued after the Berchtesgaden meeting. The total fruits of the three-hour dramatic visit handed to the press were the following three sentences:

"The Führer and Reich Chancellor had a discussion today with the British Prime Minister at Obersalzberg in which a full and frank exchange of views on the situation took place.

"The British Prime Minister will return to England tomorrow to consult the British Cabinet. A new conversation will take place in a few days!"

Even this terse communique was wolfed by the foreign correspondents, and disappeared in a flash down the long gullet of international press wires, to be digested by ravenous editors and statesmen all over the world. Where would the dictator and the democratic leader meet again? Berlin? Munich? Frankfort? The Führer had told Chamberlain that he would meet him halfway. At last it leaked out that Godesberg on the Rhine would be the scene of the next epochal conference.

When I had sent my last message through the bottleneck of the Berchtesgaden telephone exchange, I returned to the lobby of the Grand to join my colleagues' post-mortem of the unprecedented day's events. Neville Chamberlain, worn out by his long and unaccustomed flight, and the strain of arguing with Adolf Hitler, was fast asleep upstairs. Nevile Henderson was not asleep. But he might just as well have been. For the scene I witnessed through the glass doors of the private dining room left an uncomfortable impression on my mind, which became justified a year later.

The British Ambassador to Berlin, dapper as any English gentleman could be, a red carnation in his buttonhole, was sitting among his German associates of the Nazi Foreign Office. Champagne flowed. Laughter was frequent and protracted. Everything seemed very jolly. But I could not help feeling that the laughter of Ribbentrop's henchmen was at the expense of this slim, boyish-looking diplomat. As I saw Henderson chatting with the heavy-set, scar-faced veteran of several German regimes, State Secretary Dr. Otto Meissner, I thought instinctively of a cat playing with a mouse. Just a week ago, Meissner had kicked an SS Bodyguard all the way down the stairs of the Deutscher Hof in Nuremberg because the Guard had not stepped out of his way quickly enough. If a member of the Nazi Foreign Office could be so brutal and ruthless to one of his own men, what lay in store for a member of the British Foreign Service the moment he should attempt to hold back the juggernaut of Third Reich policy?

SEPTEMBER 18, 1938: *Daladier and Bonnet arrived in London to consult with the British. They agreed to demand that Czechoslovakia accept Hitler's demands.*

SEPTEMBER 21: *The Czech cabinet accepted this ultimatum.*

# PRAGUE, SEPTEMBER 1938

## by Raymond Gram Swing

KNICK was at the telephone, speaking in his crisp Texan German when I walked in unannounced. He jumped up, for we are the oldest of friends, dropped the receiver and greeted me. I had just flown from London by way of Geneva. "I'll call you back," he spoke into the telephone, and put it down.

"They're going to fight. They've got to fight. If they won't fight for themselves, nobody will fight for them. They'll deserve what they're going to get."

Knick—his full title is H. R. Knickerbocker, foreign expert for the International News Service—had only a few phrases on seeing an old friend, and launched into exposition.

"Benes is as clever as they make them. This morning he called in the British and French ministers and told them the Prague government accepted. Accepted unconditionally. Then he called in the coalition leaders, and they said they wouldn't accept, not unless parliament was called and voted on it. So he told the British and French that he was powerless. After all, Czechoslovakia is still a democracy. You see he has to play for time. He must make Hitler attack. That's the whole idea, to force the Germans to attack. Then the French will have to fight."

The phone rang. Another talk in German began. Knick grabbed for a pencil.

"Are you sure of that?" His voice was anxious. He hung up and put in an urgent call for his Paris office.

"The British and French have told Benes that he must accept unconditionally—without delay—or they will be regarded as the guilty party."

"You mean the aggressor," I threw in.

"That's it. He called back the party leaders. They debated back and forth. They've finally decided to accept. The government has just handed a note to the British and French ministers accepting."

He was rolling a sheet of paper into his typewriter and went to pounding the keys vigorously. The phone rang. It was Paris. Knick dictated a flash into the recording machine at the Paris office.

Fodor came in (*Chicago Daily News* and *Manchester Guardian*), then John Whitaker (*Chicago Daily News*). Fodor occupied the adjoining room. He put in a Paris call, and began writing. Maurice Hindus (*Humanity Uprooted*) came in. He was to broadcast to New York later in the evening.

Down in the street people were shouting. I went to the balcony. Men and women were marching, calling out short fierce phrases.

"Maurice, go down and get what they're shouting, won't you?" Knick asked, for Hindus was the only one who could understand the language. Knick went on, hanging over my shoulder, looking down on the crowd.

"This is the first demonstration there's been in Prague. They must have heard the news by word of mouth, for they've not had a word of what's happened from any newspapers. Those people down there want to fight." He put in another urgent call for Paris. Another sheet of paper rolled into the typewriter. Fodor was yelling a dispatch to Paris in the next room.

I watched the marchers, trying to estimate how many there were. Not more than three or four hundred, I thought. They shouted, but not in unison. It was different from the college-cheer shouting of the Nazis and fascists, who call out their "Sieg-Heils" and "Duce," as though a youth in a white sweater with a megaphone were leading them, and the ball was on the five-yard line.

The shouts from the street came up in an angry counterpoint. People lined the streets and clapped their hands.

Hindus came back. "They're calling 'Long Live the Army!' 'Down with Chamberlain!' 'Down with Hitler!' 'Shame on France!' 'The Army into Power!' that's significant—and 'Long live Syrovy!'"

I asked, "Who is Syrovy?"

"The one-eyed general inspector of the army. In the 15th century the Czechs had a one-eyed king who never lost a battle. He lost his other eye, but he went on fighting blind. He is the Czech legend, for even blind he never lost a battle. Syrovy was a legionnaire; he made the march to Vladivostok. With his one eye, he is the symbol of national survival. The people believe he will be able to hold off Hitler."

The phone rang, and Paris received another flash. The shouting rose louder from the street, and I went to the balcony. The marchers were following a route which brought them past the hotel recurrently. This time their numbers had grown, at least five times. The sidewalks were packed. The marchers were shouting and waving their arms in emphasis, like mass orators making gestures. By now there must have been 2,000 or more. The sidewalks were filled, and the shouts were heard against a steady clatter of applause.

The hotel is on Wenceslaus Square, the widest boulevard in Prague, leading up to the stately National Museum. Wenceslaus, for whom it is named, is the man in the Christmas carol, "Good King Wenceslaus," who helped the beggar gathering "winter fuuuuu-el." Now thousands of feet were beating the pavement of his square calling for war, demanding the right of modern martyrdom.

Inside the room the radio was going. Knick had tuned in London for the news bulletin. A newspaper correspondent still travels with a typewriter, but he also must have a radio, since only the ether can bear the news across today's European frontiers.

The British news bulletins were the most authentic and complete. The London announcer reads everything with a standardly pleasant manner. He uses the same cheering inflection for a cabinet meeting or a forecast of rain. Bad news comes to the brain wrapped in his polite cellophane, and there has to be opened up to the emotions it deserves. This night London gave some reports of opposition to the Anglo-French plan, both from the Liberal and Labor parties in England, and from the United States. London had the news of the acceptance of surrender by the Czech government.

When the London announcer began telling about the injury of a British racing car on the Utah salt flats, the radio was switched over to the Deutschland-Sender, which was telling about "menacing communist demonstrations" in Prague.

Then the marchers began to boom past the hotel again. I went out on the balcony. By now the wide expanse of the square was well filled, and the shouting was a steady roar. Fodor looked down. "A hundred thousand, I should say." My eye ran over the dense throngs, which seemed like an election night crowd in Times Square. But I thought it could not be more than 50,000. They were not communists, for Prague does not have so many. There are only 30 communists in parliament, ten per cent of the total, and perhaps 30,000 in Prague.

The crowds were not holding aloft the clenched fist, the salute of the united front. A cheering group went past, the applause from the sidewalks grew loud. Marchers had seized a Czech army officer and were bearing him off shoulder-high. But it was an orderly crowd, with hardly a policeman in sight.

We went back into the room. Would it be war after all? Would the crowd grow still larger? Would it become violent, call for military dictatorship, war?

"If they don't fight," someone in the room said, "then we're all lost. They have to fight for us, for our children."

Fodor, the wisest correspondent in Eastern Europe, paced back and forth. He went out to the balcony and came back, paced some more. His wide, round face was grave. Finally he made his pronouncement.

"That is not a revolutionary crowd. I can tell a revolutionary crowd." No consulting diagnostician on a serious case ever spoke with more scientific certainty and sense of responsibility. The crowd now was roaring so loud the balcony door had to be kept shut if we wanted to converse.

The phone kept ringing. Paris; the office of the Prague newspaper where Knick's assistant was keeping him informed; the military attaché of a democratic power, who called up to say that mounted guards had been thrown around the British and German legations, also Premier Hodza's palace. Why not the French legation? Was the government willing to have that mussed up a little? Someone repeated the remark of a leading politician that afternoon, who had said: "And when we are all Nazis, WILL I BE DELIGHTED when it comes to fighting France!"

A new noise came from the street, a tremendous voice. I thought it was from a sound van, but it was the public-address system laid in the downtown area. With it, the government can speak to its people whenever occasion arises. A great solemn voice was booming the words of a monstrous metallic giant. None of us could translate it. Hindus came in at the end, but he caught only one phrase, which he thought meant: "We shall never give in."

Knick called his assistant to let him have the text. It proved to be the first public pronouncement of the Prague government about its surrender. It was couched in terrible words:

"It is not cowardice which has moved our leaders to their decision, a decision which has pierced our hearts. Even the bravest man must retreat before the fury of an avalanche. God knows that it often requires more courage to live than to commit suicide. God knows that not an honest man can say that we were frightened and cowardly when we authorized the foreign minister to tell France and Britain: 'We have chosen to sacrifice ourselves for the peace of the world, just as the Savior sacrificed himself on the cross for the welfare of mankind.'"

The phone rang; Paris again. More flashes were read into the Paris receiving machines. The room filled. An unhappy looking man hung about hoping for a word with Knick, wanting intervention at the American consulate to expedite his American visa. Knick begged him to come back after the crisis. The waiter brought a huge tumbler of cracked ice for the whisky and sodas. Vincent Sheean was talking in a corner with Whitaker about a trip to Sudetenland in the morning. The radio, tuned low, supplied a background of dance music. The shouts sounded more defiantly from the street. The loud-speakers boomed over everything their giant, metallic words.

New York was calling Knick, then canceled the call. Hindus came back from his broadcast grumbling about the censorship. He had been forbidden to refer to any demonstrations, or to mention the reluctance of the Agrarian Party, the largest in the country, to appeal for Soviet help. The Agrarians, it seemed, preferred to be ruled by Hitler to being saved by a red army. Hindus went off to telephone the facts to New York, and came back to say that none of his broadcast had been received, perhaps because of Prague censorship, but probably because of the hurricane in New York.

Then came a telegram read from Paris. Knick had scooped the world on the cabinet decision, and the brown eyes twinkled in his angular face. Fodor, to my question as to where he would go if Hitler entered Prague, said his next stop was Budapest. He is conducting a personal retreat before the Nazis that reads like a train schedule. Vienna, Prague, Budapest, Belgrade or Bucharest. But when Hitler came to Bucharest Russia would fight, he said, and that would be the European war, if it hadn't come sooner. He was pacing up and down relentlessly.

From the street came the roar of shouting. I went to the balcony and looked down on the crowd. Its earlier movement had almost stopped, as the flood had been dammed by the people who waited at the loud-speaker across the broad boulevard. The wide space was dense with men and women, and their shouts merged into a continual uproar. From the loud-speakers poured exhortations to the crowd to go home, to trust the government, to believe that their leaders knew better than they what was good for them. In their restless pressing forward and in their shouts they voiced their displeasure at this advice. Slowly the pressure of the throngs worked past the loud-speaker and the noisy march began again. "Down With

Hitler!" "The Army into Power!" they called. An officer was hoisted onto the shoulders of young men and the crowd cheered deliriously. "Down with Chamberlain!" "Shame on France!" "Long Live Syrovy!" "The Army into Power!" It was a scene of passion, and the measure of that passion was to decide the destiny of Czechoslovakia, and affect the destiny of the whole world. For if that passion had swept onto the government buildings, if it had demanded the downfall of the men who that day had surrendered to the bullying of France and Britain, if it had placed in power men who should cry "No!" to Hitler's demands, and prepare to defend the soil of the ancient Bohemian state, history would have taken a strangely different turning on that September night. There would have been war, perhaps victorious, perhaps lost; war that might have swept Hitler from power; war that might have loosed the forces of revolution over all Europe; war that might have ended in the restoration of the ethics of peace, in which democracies might survive and thrive; war that might have left Europe smoldering in ruins and unable to raise its head for half a century. These were the issues being decided by the power of the passion that moved the feet and lifted the voices of that Prague crowd that night.

A cabinet minister was pleading through the loud-speaker: "Go home and trust your government." Syrovy himself, the one-eyed hero of the nation, added his dignified, curt appeal, which cut the night air, a soldier's command: "Go home and trust your government!"

Passion disbelieves reason, but reason also undermines passion. The conflict between the two played itself out in the brains and the bodies of that marching crowd. And slowly passion waned and reason prevailed. In half an hour the crowd was thinning. The shouts were distinguishable, they were no longer lost in the vast roar. In an hour the broad spaces of Wenceslaus Place were beginning to empty. And after the turn of midnight the storm of human feelings had died.

The fate of Czechoslovakia and of Europe was to be decided in other places, in the conference rooms at Berchtesgaden, Godesberg and Munich, to be decided by a few leaders working in secret, beyond the reach of the men and women whose destiny they were forming. But that night in Prague, men and women had their chance to make their own destiny. And the history of Europe was written as much in the slowing tramp of their feet and wane of their shouting, as in the secret bargaining of the new Directory of Europe. They went home that night still believing that all was not lost. They woke the next morning to demonstrate again. But having once submitted to exhortations, once having curbed their passions by their reason, they were unable to push themselves to the point of overt action. The life of Czechoslovakia had been measured in the heat of their collective feeling.

And it had not been enough.

SEPTEMBER 22, 1938: *Chamberlain flew to Godesberg to see Hitler again.*

122

SEPTEMBER 23, 1938: *Hitler increased his demands on the Czechs. Chamberlain agreed to submit them to the Czechs. The Czechs ordered general mobilization.*

SEPTEMBER 25: *The Czech Government notified London and Paris that it could not accept Hitler's last proposals.*

SEPTEMBER 27: *Britain mobilized its fleet.*

SEPTEMBER 28: *Chamberlain reported to the House of Commons on the Czech situation. His speech was interrupted by a message from Hitler, asking him to come to Munich the following day.*

# MUNICH

## *by Frederick T. Birchall*

MUNICH, Sept. 30.—The four-power conference to decide the fate of Czechoslovakia and avert a general European war by bringing pressure to bear on her to accept its decisions has met here, reached an agreement and adjourned.

In something less than nine hours of actual conversation time it has settled everything to the satisfaction—more or less—of the conferees.

It may be said at once that the decisions give Germany just about all she has demanded except the total extinction of Czechoslovakia as an independent State, which has never in fact been among her formulated demands, although that has been implied.

The decisions indicate, moreover, that the Poles and Hungarians will receive their shares of the spoils of Czechoslovak dismemberment.

The only change discernible from Chancellor Adolf Hitler's Godesberg memorandum is in the period allowed for the fulfillment of the demand. That has been slightly extended and beginning tomorrow the predominantly German territories are to be evacuated and occupied progressively until October 10.

The agreement to this effect was signed by the four powers in the conference room at the Fuehrerhaus, Chancellor Hitler's personal headquarters in Munich, at 1 o'clock this morning [7 P.M. Thursday, Eastern standard time]. The leave-taking afterward was most cordial.

Herr Hitler, "on behalf of the German people," thanked Prime Minister Neville Chamberlain of Britain and Premier Edouard Daladier of France for their efforts for European peace. They responded in kind and will return home by air later today. Premier Benito Mussolini of Italy has already departed by special train.

Mr. Chamberlain spent an hour in the early morning discussing the agreement with two Czech representatives sent from Prague at his suggestion to receive it.

Much stress is laid on the unanimity obtained in the conference and the mutual friendliness exhibited by the conferees.

"I am not going to quibble about a village," Herr Hitler is said to have told the others when doubtful areas were being discussed and the main points of his demands had been conceded.

A duplicate of the agreement has been prepared for the Czechs and their two representatives will carry it to Prague by air this morning. No doubt seems to exist about their accepting it. What else could they do?

From its outset this conference has proceeded with a smoothness and celerity that must have surprised its participants as much as it has astonished neutral observers. Agreed upon in desperation when the threat of war hung over Europe more threateningly than at any time since 1914, it has been marked by a spirit of mutual accord inconceivable forty-eight hours ago.

It was the first time the two great European democracies had faced the two leading dictatorships at a conference table. It was Mr. Chamberlain's first meeting with Signor Mussolini and only his third with Herr Hitler. It was the first meeting of M. Daladier with either of the two.

Yet all four seem to have worked together with a thoroughness of purpose and speed in execution that restore to the practice of conferences some of its lost prestige.

One effect of this gathering now beginning to be perceptible is that Premier Mussolini's dream of a four-power combination to try for a general European settlement has been brought appreciably nearer. It really seems that not only has the peril of immediate war been removed but the general atmosphere is being cleared for a much larger adjustment.

# PEACE IN OUR TIME

### by Joseph Driscoll

LONDON, Sept. 30.—Prime Minister Neville Chamberlain, returning tonight to receive a grateful welcome from hundreds of thousands of peace-loving Britons, brought from Munich not only the four-power agreement which authorizes Nazi Germany to take over Czechoslovakia's Sudetenland by gradual stages, but an Anglo-German pact of friendship, by which the two nations resolve never to go to war against each other and to settle all disputes by consultation and negotiation.

When his American Lockheed airliner brought him back to English soil at Heston Airport this afternoon Chamberlain received his first hearty welcome, which was followed by stirring street scenes the like of which had not been equaled in London since Armistice Day, 1918. The Prime Minister responded by reading, for the benefit of the newsreels and television apparatus, the text of the peace pact to which he and Hitler had affixed their signatures.

Chamberlain came back from a bloodless two-day war, fought out over tea and beer and sandwiches by the "big four" who have taken over the direction of European affairs from the League of Nations—Chamberlain, Hitler, Premier Benito Mussolini of Italy and Premier Edouard Daladier of France.

Germany won the diplomatic war, in that she was permitted to march into Bohemia tomorrow to dispossess the Czechs, but all Europe and the world were victors to the extent that there has been averted, at the eleventh hour, a repetition of the World War of 1914-18, in which more than 8,000,000 were killed.

Standing on the balcony of his home at 10 Downing Street, Chamberlain told the cheering thousands below: "My good friends, this is the second time in our history that there has come back from Germany to Downing Street peace with honor. I believe it is peace for our time."

No one need be surprised if Chamberlain follows up the Anglo-German pact by arranging another conference in the near future, in which Britain will attempt to appease Germany's hunger for a colonial empire by offering Hitler an African colony or two. France also may be called on to make a colonial contribution to the Chamberlain project for general settlement of old feuds which have prevented the reconciliation of Hitler's Germany with Britain and France.

News of this monumental pact, which Chamberlain and Hitler signed after breakfast at Munich, and which may mean peace for a generation or may turn out to be just another scrap of paper, had preceded the Prime Minister from the airport to his next stops—Buckingham Palace and Downing Street.

Only on Armistice Day, 1918; abdication night, 1936, and coronation night, 1937, had there been comparable outpourings of the London citizenry into the streets, and only 1918 quite equaled today's assemblages. Half the populace of London seemed to have left home to celebrate the end of a "war" fought without the loss of a single British life.

Despite drenching rain, thousands and thousands of men, women and children had packed the pavements around Buckingham Palace long before the Prime Minister drove up, accompanied by his wife. While the throngs waited patiently, nature presented in the skies a symbolic story of the ordeal from which Europe was emerging. For some time dark clouds lay unbroken across the horizon, as the war clouds had lain over the Continent for weeks. Then came a sudden transformation—the sinking sun dramatically broke through the clouds and projected in the east the arch of a perfect rainbow —the sign of hope.

Mrs. Chamberlain was obviously moved by the reception, and her husband seemed deeply affected as he crossed and uncrossed his thin hands. There was an even wider burst of cheering as Chamberlain turned to his wife and clasped her hand in his.

After the ovation had lasted five minutes, the Prime Minister waved a farewell to the demonstrators. The King waved his hand for the first time, and he, too, left the balcony. The crowd sang "God Save the King" before dispersing.

After twenty-five minutes with their majesties, the Chamberlains drove on to Downing Street by way of Birdcage Walk and Whitehall. Never within living memory has Downing Street been the scene of such a welcome. Rain or no rain, spectators by the thousands and tens of thousands had waited for hours to greet their elderly hero. The dull stretches were enlivened with the singing of "Land of Hope and Glory, "Oh God, Our Help in Ages Past" and "Rule Britannia."

Four American sailors from the United States cruiser Honolulu, which was rushed here to evacuate refugees from the expected war, got a tremendous reception from the crowd as they came up the center of Downing Street and shouldered along through police lines. The police awarded them front-row standing room alongside No. 10's doorway.

At 7 o'clock thunderous cheers drifted up from Whitehall as mounted police cantered ahead of a limousine which everybody assumed to be Chamberlain's. The crowd roared and broke through the cordons to climb on the running boards. The car's occupant was only cherubic Sir Kingsley Wood, the Air Secretary, who bounded out of the car like a frightened rabbit and popped into the haven at No. 10.

OCTOBER 5, 1938: *Eduard Benes resigned as president of Czechoslovakia.*

MARCH 14, 1939: *Hungary invaded Ruthenia.*

MARCH 15: *German troops entered Prague. Bohemia and Moravia were made part of the Reich.*

# THE PROTECTOR

### by Edward W. Beattie, Jr.

THE murder of Czechoslovakia is just a little red-inked stamp on page 19, [of my passport], with the date March 14, 1939 and the word *Prejezd,* which I guess must mean entry. There is no exit stamp because the German army marched in next day, and it took a military pass to leave Prague.

I reached the city in the late evening. All the way up from the German border there had been a tension around the dark little stations. There were a couple of Czech businessmen in my compartment, returning from a trip to Berlin, and we talked spasmodically about what might be going to happen.

When I told them we had heard in Berlin that the Reich would march next morning, one shrugged and said:

"Well, we have expected it since Munich. Now we go underground again."

He said he had worked in Bohemia throughout the World War for the secret Czech organization which helped overthrow the Hapsburgs.

The man who stamped my passport at the border had been in the Czech Legion, which had fought for Russia against the Austro-Hungarian Empire and had finally battled its way back from the middle of Asia when the Bolsheviki took control. We asked him if he knew anything definite. He could only tell us that there had been movements the other side of the border, and that planes had been flying along it most of the day.

There was little gaiety in Prague that night. In the streets people stood in crowds and a few hotheads made speeches. There had been one or two minor demonstrations. A small group bowed their heads at the grave of the Czech Unknown Soldier by the ancient City Hall, and the light of the flame rippled over their set faces. At the raucous Sekt Pavillon there were no tired businessmen to buy champagne for the hostesses. Everyone knew that President Hacha had been "invited" to Berlin, and waited hopelessly for the result. At that very moment he was being browbeaten into a state of collapse.

The lobby of the Hotel Ambassador was back in form. A lot of the old crowd had gone, but there was still the same babel of rumor and the same crush for the telephones. Nobody had much doubt that it was Czechoslovakia's last night of liberty.

I was introduced to a young Englishman, who turned out to be an officer in the tank corps. He seemed pretty drunk and was most annoyed that his "central European vacation" had been interrupted. He stayed more or less drunk for most of the next week, and nobody could have been more open and above-board. When he finally left, he got some very useful plans and documents out with him, and he told me later in London that he had enjoyed his ride across Germany very much. He is now in the R.A.F.

I was awakened early next morning by a loudspeaker mounted in the Waclavske Namesti, which repeated over and over again a plea to all Czechs to be calm and accept the blow which had fallen during the night. It has been officially announced that Czechoslovakia had "requested" a protectorate and that German troops would march in at dawn.

Nobody knew then how the people would react. The army was still capable of bitter resistance. There were tremendous possibilities for riots and sabotage. The Czechs took the blow with a cold fatalism which was the product of centuries of strife, in which they had been more often dominated than free. It became fashionable for other small nations in Europe to face the threat of Nazi expansion with a half-frantic cry of, "We are not Czechs." Let it be said that nobody who was in Prague when the Germans marched in thinks the Czechs are cowards.

There was a blinding snowstorm, and the taxi driver said driving would be impossible on the road to the border. Finally he admitted that he was afraid there might be fighting, and didn't want to lose his car. I showed him enough dollars to change his mind.

We met the Germans just across the frontier, at a bend in a village street. They were moving steadily through the snow, a light scouting force of fifty men or so on bicycles and motorcycles mounting machine guns, with one small car towing an antitank gun. They didn't stop in the villages as we trailed them in toward Prague. That was the job of the heavy units behind them. They were on the lookout for resistance, and they had been ordered to keep the road clear.

When we met them head on, the driver tried frantically to turn. It was too late. The unit began passing us. The officer in command leaned out over the side of the scout car. I thought he was going to ask for identification, but all he said was:

"From now on in this country you drive on the righthand side of the road."

The occupation was as easy as that.

There are a lot of things which are vivid in mind from those days in Prague: the Jewish suicides; the look on the face of a German refugee when two of his former warders in concentration camp walked into the Ambassador; the arrests; the German officers gorging themselves on the good Czech food, and cleaning out the shelves of the bulging shops with their big wads of marks; the Czechs, who had eaten better than the Germans for years, ignoring the convoy of huge Nazi food kitchens which had rolled in filled to bursting with watery soup and propaganda. I remember the Czechs who stood silently at the grave of the Unknown Soldier and placed little bouquets there, and the German sentries who stood a decent distance away to give them privacy.

I remember sitting in the Embassy night club in the basement of the hotel, the second night of the occupation, singing *Tipperary* and *Madelon* and *Over There* and a dozen other Allied war songs with a bunch of other foreign correspondents. The band played anything we wanted, and kept a straight face, and a couple of dozen German officers at other tables got more and more restless.

It was a futile and rather stupid gesture on our part; but, like sitting on the yellow benches marked "J" in the Berlin parks, it served as a safety valve.

Finally two officers a short distance away pounded for silence, and one of them came over and demanded that we stop "insulting the German Army." Later in the evening, when everyone was drinking pretty heavily, he drew me to one side and said, "You don't think we like this sort of thing too much, do you? For God's sake, let us try to make this occupation as decent as possible." (The army's part in the occupation *was* decent in every way. Of course, the Gestapo and the S.S. arrived later.)

I remember the long lines of flatcars waiting on railroad sidings, loaded with tanks and antiaircraft guns and hundreds of heavy Skoda howitzers, all destined to strengthen the Germany Army.

I remember that Hitler came to Prague the first night, against the advice of his lieutenants, because he wanted "to be with my troops." But it was no triumphal entry in the Nazi grand manner. He slipped in unobtrusively and, except for a look out the palace window, never saw the town at all.

But the one scene which was most poignant was the entry of the first heavy German column into the Waclavske Namesti in midmorning of March 15.

Dense snow slanted down over the great baroque buildings at the head of the plaza and over the big stores and the tramway lines where the cars stood deserted. It beat on the bared heads of thousands of Czechs who waited there for the symbolic act which would destroy their freedom once again.

The crowd was jammed so close that it was almost impossible to move, and there was only one narrow lane down the center for the Germans to march in. The people stood in silence, and tears streamed down their faces.

Then a rumble grew down the side street, and the first German tanks and armored cars, their crews sitting tight-lipped with sub-machine guns at the ready, turned into the square. As they clattered across the pavement, a wave of sound swept with them and grew into a chorus of thousands of voices, as the Czechs sang their national anthem into the mouths of the German guns.

# *Part Three:* The Phony War

* * *

KAUNAS, LITHUANIA, March 22, 1939 (United Press): The Lithuanian government this morning announced that the Memel territory has been surrendered to Germany ... The surrender was in answer to an implied ultimatum from Germany....

WARSAW, POLAND, March 29 (Associated Press): Poland, reluctant to join France and Britain in a bloc against Germany, has started talks with the Nazis, to settle the future status of the Free City of Danzig....

LONDON, March 31 (Associated Press): Prime Minister Chamberlain announced in the House of Commons today that Great Britain and France would back with arms the independence of Poland while pursuing means of stabilizing the European situation.

* * *

APRIL 7: *Italian troops invaded Albania. King Zog fled.*

APRIL 13: *France and Great Britain, alarmed at Italy's thrust toward the Balkans, gave guarantees to Rumania and Greece.*

MAY 3: *Germany and Italy signed a military alliance.*

AUGUST 16: *Germany demanded that Danzig be returned to her.*

# EUROPE HOLDS ITS BREATH

## *by Edward W. Beattie, Jr.*

ENGLAND in the summer of 1939 was like a customer who takes time to roll up his sleeves for a bar fight when the saloonkeeper is already hefting the bung starter in his hand. Like the customer, she was still busy on the first sleeve when she was clouted on the head. Thanks to an extraordinary ability to take punishment, she has kept on her feet but, having lost the initiative, she still can't trade blow for blow.

Chamberlain succeeded that summer in putting through peacetime conscription, to the dismay of a great clamorous group which shouted about invasion of the rights of free Englishmen without ever stopping to think that failure to stop Hitler was the sure way to forfeit those rights.

The Navy was unchallenged, and there were more and bigger ships on the ways.

The air situation was a serious one, but nobody knew how serious. There was tremendous fear of bombing, but everyone hoped the Germans would be too busy on the Continent to pay much attention to objectives farther afield.

Some people dug shelters of their own design, most of which immediately filled with water. Others did nothing whatever about it, serene that the government would take care of everything. The government, meanwhile, was "surveying facilities" or something similar.

Lots of facts were ignored in England during the summer of 1939. The cabinet ignored the fact that, whatever progress had been made in production, 1939 was a year for super, hundred per cent, all-out effort, to overcome the ghastly arms deficit which had been inherited from the years of side-stepping and I-am-holier-than-thou-ism at Geneva. It ignored the fact that virtually every essential activity was being hamstrung by industrialists' bullneckedness, the reactionary deadwood of the civil service, or muddle-headed administration.

The one convincing excuse for the allied disaster at Munich would have been a concerted drive for material and moral rearmament in the year which intervened before the Dorniers swept down on Warsaw. It would have been proof of a grasp of what lay ahead, and of a play for time. It just wasn't there. England complacently went about "business as usual," or whatever it was called, that summer.

Of course there were a few strident voices which broke in from time to time on the pleasing spectacle of the world's greatest empire preparing itself step by ponderous step for the annihilation of another continental upstart. But they came from men like Winston Churchill, who had been warning England for years and who didn't ever seem to like what the government had done in foreign policy, and who some people thought was a traitor to his class and his party.

The average Englishman reacted after his own fashion and without much regard for the official muddleheadedness or editorial hashish. He certainly didn't realize how badly prepared he was going to be when war started, or how systematically prepared for everything the enemy was going to be. He trusted the government to look out for that part of it. He was pretty well convinced that war was going to come and looked on it as a disagreeable job which had to be done.

The King and Queen went to Canada and then the United States, and everyone sympathized with them for the heat which the newspapers described, degree by degree, and the strange things like hot dogs which they took in stride. Everyone was hugely pleased at the obvious hit they made everywhere they went.

When the King and Queen returned to London, uniforms had grown much more numerous in the streets, and in particular there were many more men in the blue-gray of the RAF, which had never been very noticeable before. The shelter trenches in the parks were longer, and sandbagged gun positions had been prepared.

In the paint shop at the London Zoo there was a sign ready to be nailed to a tree. The sign was both a directive and a wry commentary on the Europe of 1939. It bore a large black arrow, and the caption read: "To Air Raid Shelter In Monkey House."

In Paris the summer sun slanted down through the thick foliage to lay a peaceful patina over the café terraces and the graceful streets. To a casual visitor everything was completely normal. "Les Guards" came over from London to march in the Bastille Day parade in emphasis of Franco-British solidarity and were cheered by the crowds only slightly less heartily than the Legion. There were a few heavy antiaircraft guns mounted for propaganda purposes at the Invalides and elsewhere. But such things clashed only briefly with the feel of pleasant normalcy.

In the factories of the north and east, desperate efforts were being made to gear a rickety and torpid production machine to meet the emergency. In the Maginot Line the troops exercised with the guns, and supplies were piled up below the ground against the day when the enemy, if he came, would waste himself against the steel-ribbed frontier hills. In Paris all that was hardly noticeable.

In Belgium, people were realists. If war came, they would be invaded, probably by Germany. They had a good fortified line on the eastern frontier, and Liége and Namur would stand firm. The Ardennes had been made "almost impregnable." But of course they would need help.

Meanwhile, it was better to be gay if you could, and enjoy the superb Brussels food, and stroll in the Bois under the soft afternoon sky.

In Holland, the army was trying out a new technique of wrapping the roadside trees with girdles of dynamite, to be exploded if an enemy came. There were little holes in the roads themselves, where mines could be laid. Canal bridges would be quickly dynamited. There was much talk of the classic defense of inundation.

But in the big mercantile cities, such as Amsterdam and Rotterdam, nobody believed war was coming, and everyone said that, if it did come, nobody would attack peaceful Holland. Things would be, at the worst, just as they were in the last war.

A few Dutchmen admitted it was wishful thinking.

Poland in the summer of 1939 was preparing for war like a knight donning a white-plumed helmet to go out and smite the heathen. It was tragic for Poland that the heathen was equipped with swarms of fast planes and a crushing phalanx of tanks which mounted three-inch guns and others of the more modern weapons.

Close to one gate of the Foreign Office in Warsaw, was scrawled in chalk:

"We want another Grunwald."

132

At Grunwald, in 1410, the Poles and Lithuanians had crushed the Order of Teutonic Knights, last great victory over the Germans in Poland's embattled history. The inscription was typical of the Warsaw atmosphere.

Taxi drivers talked of the "Battle of Berlin," which would inevitably come if Germany ever attacked.

The city Poles wanted to fight because they were fatalistic about Hitler's demands. They knew he would not relax them. They knew that to yield, and to present Germany with Danzig and a free zone across the Corridor, would be the first step to economic dependence. Czechoslovakia had shown what came after that. A war was better. And the west would surely and devastatingly come, somehow, to Poland's aid. Nobody wanted help from Russia, the ancient enemy.

In the countryside out to the west of Warsaw, around Lodz and off far to the southward, the grain stood high in the fields, and the harvest promised to be the best in years. The peasants said that such a harvest always came in the year of war. It had been the same in 1914.

In a night club in ancient Cracow, burial city of the Polish kings, I ran into a dozen or two young reserve officers who were off to join their regiments. Their names read like a list of the Polish nobility. All were in the cavalry.

I asked whether the cavalry was motorized. Even in England the old traditional regiments were being dismounted and put into tanks that summer. The officers were indignant. Certainly not. A gentleman's place was in the horse cavalry, and the horse cavalry would be the spearhead of Poland.

Three months later the horse cavalry was counterattacking the German panzer divisions gallantly and desperately, and in gory futility.

\* \* \*

Moscow, August 24, 1939 (Associated Press): Germany and Soviet Russia early today signed a non-aggression pact binding each of them for ten years not to "associate itself with any other grouping of powers which directly or indirectly is aimed at the other party...."

\* \* \*

# THE PARTNERS

### by Walter Duranty

IN the spring and summer of 1939, France and England took it for granted that the rulers of Germany and Russia meant precisely what they said when they called each other names. (As recent history has now shown, the alternately friendly and hostile relations of Alexander I and Napoleon might teach a lesson to modern statesmen.) England, if not France, was at that

133

time somewhat preoccupied by the rather hasty guarantee given to Poland I mean, it was hard to make valid that pledge with real effectiveness unless the U.S.S.R. would implement it too. It therefore seemed useful and wise to bring the Russians into the anti-Nazi pool, which then seemed easy enough to do. But the English had not understood the true purpose of Stalin's pledge to the Communist Party Congress on March 10. Stalin inveighed strongly against "aggressors"—which the outside world naturally and perhaps rightly then interpreted as meaning Nazi Germany of the "axis." But Stalin also said that the U.S.S.R. was opposed to all "firebugs of war"—an unlovely phrase which is current in Soviet Russia. What the English and French failed to understand was that when Stalin talked about war he meant not only war in general, which might or might not be discordant with Soviet views, but specifically war in which the U.S.S.R. would be engaged to fight another great power. For that kind of war the Kremlin had little use.

When negotiations began between Russia, England, and France, the Russians seemed to believe that the aim of those talks was a pact which might serve as a countersignal to Hitler, to warn him that three nations—France, Britain, and the U.S.S.R.—would join to resist aggression in any place or form. I believe that the Kremlin then thought such a warning would be sufficient, and with this thought in mind it sent to London, in the third week of April, a reply to the Franco-British proposal which was tantamount to acceptance. To the Kremlin's surprise and to the ruin of the Soviet Foreign Minister, Litvinov, who had assured the Kremlin that the pact was now as good as signed, London made new and different proposals, from which the Kremlin drew the unwelcome deduction that Britain and France no longer wanted to prevent war, but wished rather to coerce the U.S.S.R. into the war against Germany which the Russians had already suspected was one of the aims of Munich.

From that moment I should say there was little hope of a pact between the U.S.S.R. and France or Britain, because the Russians had acute suspicions of France, believed that Poland could not hold out against Germany, and saw themselves in consequence as the father-mother victim of the German wolf after the Polish baby had been devoured. It is true that in the subsequent conversations with France and England, both civil and military—and one can say it in all sincerity—the Russians took on themselves a guarantee against Germany in the shape of the right to bring troops under their own command into Poland and, if necessary, to vote "measures of protection" against a possible German aggression in the Baltic States. Whether the Russians honestly wanted this arrangement, or whether, as the Franco-British believe, their purpose was obstructive, has little importance now, although it is interesting to remember that the Kremlin at that time was still uncertain about Germany and to all appearances nailed its flag to the anti-Nazi mast.

It may also be true that France and Britain missed their pact with the U.S.S.R. by slighting the Soviet *amour-propre*, already thoroughly wounded by Munich, in sending a competent but lowly functionary to conduct a transaction with Stalin. At any rate, proceedings dragged on in an atmosphere of mutual doubt and suspicion until that sudden and startling day in August when Hitler's necessity proved Stalin's opportunity.

It may reasonably be argued that Hitler's system of government by easy triumphs—the Rhineland, Austria, Munich, Memel, Prague—which in a sense corresponds to the Roman maxim of "bread and circuses," made it *necessary* for him to regain Danzig and the former German territory in West Poland. As previously, he attempted to attain his ends without fighting. But by the middle of August he saw that Poland was standing firm and that France and Britain seemed equally determined. Italy showed no great signs of eagerness to engage in war for Danzig; indeed, it is clear that the Italo-German diplomatic conversations at that time expressed Italy's desire to restrain any violent action on the part of Germany. Hitler thereupon extricated himself from what might have proved an awkward position by playing his Russian card. The result for twenty-four hours was stupefaction in France and England.

If Hitler had meant from the first to fight, that was the time to attack. Instead he waited, hoping no doubt that his *coup de théâtre* would modify the situation in his favor either by terrifying Poland or by inducing France and England to bring pressure on Poland to yield. The event proved otherwise, and, as a device to avoid war by causing his opponents to back down, the treaty with Russia failed Hitler. Yet once more he let time pass while his propaganda department used every means in its power to convince the world and the German people that the Russo-German agreement was far more than it appeared: an alliance, to say the least, which aimed not merely at the partition of Poland and the division of Eastern Europe between the two "allies," but a union of the Red and Brown autocracies to dominate Europe and Asia. On the side of the Russians there was serious delay in ratifying the treaty, and it seemed that they, like Hitler, were waiting for a last day's weakening in the camps of France and England and Poland. No such weakness occurred; the supreme chance of Russia passed, and the next morning Hitler struck.

At this point certain deductions can be made: first, that the treaty was what it purported to be on paper—that is, an agreement by which Germany obtained the benevolent neutrality of the U.S.S.R. in war. In that case it is not difficult to estimate what Germany wanted and received. To begin with, the U.S.S.R. was to move from the ranks of potential enemies; and the danger of obstruction no longer existed, or at least it was lessened. This point alone might to Hitler warrant any sacrifice in personnel or any loss of prestige and moral standing in Japan, Spain, and Italy. Because, however much the offensive power of the Red Army might have been discounted on the side of the Allies, it not only would have facilitated Allied aid to Poland, thereby diminishing the chances of success of a *Blitzkrieg*, but would have established an eastern front of wide and increasing extent.

135

One must not forget, moreover, that the agreement was initially sent to and hailed by the German people as a step to ensure peace. The Moscow press and Communist newspapers abroad advanced the same thesis. This must have been done on the assumption that France, England, and Poland would be bluffed into acceptance of Hitler's demands; and it was only later, when Hitler saw that the Allies did not accept, that the German masses were told they would henceforth be able to receive Russian food and raw materials. This is surely important, because, although foreign observers in Germany are inclined to agree that the recent and present restrictions on the sale of food and commodities have not yet greatly affected the health and morale of the German people, the fact remains that the memory of the "hunger years"—1917-1919—is still vivid in Germany. It is therefore most encouraging to Germans to think that the treaty with Russia has not only removed the danger of military encirclement and long-drawn hostilities on two fronts but also provided and effected a permanent breach in any hunger blockade.

One may say, then, that a Russo-German agreement which involved no more than Soviet neutrality has served Hitler's purpose admirably. If one supposes that he really did not want war—or rather that he hoped, as before, to attain his immediate objective, in this case Danzig, without war—the agreement was a valuable card in his game of nerves and bluff. As the event proved, his adversaries refused to be bluffed, and war resulted; but the agreement lessened the military danger and strengthened the German morale.

There exists, however, the possibility of a second deduction, that the Russo-German treaty was not merely a pact of neutrality, however benevolent on the part of the U.S.S.R., but a far-reaching scheme of co-operation in which the U.S.S.R. should take an active part and receive a share of the spoils. This thesis is undoubtedly supported by the Soviet occupation of East Poland, by Soviet action in the Baltic States, and by the Soviet attempt to make Finland accept similar terms. From the outset the Germans did their utmost to make the world believe that this is the true purpose and inward meaning of the agreement. The day after it was signed the French and British press was sprayed with messages from its Berlin correspondents about the projected partition of Poland, the Soviet plans to dominate the Baltic, and the Soviet threat to Bessarabia.

We have seen that the U.S.S.R. went forward on these lines, and therefore it is natural to suggest that Russia and Germany are indeed to all intents and purposes allies. Nevertheless, I am reluctant to believe it, if only for the reason that it is the view which the German Propaganda Bureau has been so eager to advance.

It still is asked why Germany should wish to make a treaty with the U.S.S.R., but it is less easy to determine Stalin's motives. Before going any further, one must understand that the U.S.S.R. considers solely the interests of the U.S.S.R. and nothing else. The great English statesman,

Lord Palmerston, once remarked: "In the final instance the policy of England is dictated by English interests." The same may be said of the Soviet Union today, except that in its case there is still a question whether the interests of the U.S.S.R. are purely Russian interests or the interests of the Bolshevik Revolution and the Third International, and the destruction of capitalism throughout the world. Stalin's conduct of policies has given support to the view that he is concerned chiefly with the interests of Russia as such. In other words, Lenin's dream of Russia as the nucleus and fatherland of a world socialist state has been supplanted by the Stalinist reality of Russia as one world power among others. That means the replacement of internationalism by nationalism, and implies that the only difference between Hitler's Germany and Stalin's Russia is that one is national-socialist and the other socialist-national.

To all outward seeming this is true, but although the idea of world revolution and internationalism may for the moment be thrust into the background of Stalin's mind and policy, it nevertheless is still there and may at any moment be brought forward. Lenin, Stalin's master, was an opportunist. In 1921 he threw overboard the practice of Communism in Russia by establishing the economic policy—the N.E.P.—which restored private production and ownership. Lenin said this was only a temporary retreat. It is possible that Stalin, Lenin's disciple, may also be making no more than a temporary concession to nationalism as Lenin did to economic individualism.

The Russians pride themselves upon their realistic and objective view of policies. To suggest to them that they acted unbecomingly in making a deal with Hitler at the time they were negotiating with his adversaries would only provoke them to laughter. They did not like England and France. They suspected what Stalin had said in his program speech at the party conference on March 10: that France and England would attempt to use them as cat's-paws against Germany. But they also thought Hitler had based his whole philosophy and policy upon opposition to them, and therefore must be their enemy. They thought that Hitler's conduct was provocative of war; and war they wished to avoid because they wanted and needed peace to develop their own resources.

Then Hitler changed his mind and offered a deal to Russia. As I see it, Hitler found himself in a difficult position and made his offer for the combined purposes of bluff and business, as explained earlier in this article. The Russians accepted because it not only kept them out of western war but renewed their friendship with Germany. Secondly, the treaty gave them a much freer hand in the Far East, where the Soviet interest is great. Thirdly, Hitler's conduct of negotiation showed an understanding of Soviet psychology and put balm on the pride of Russia which had been wounded by Munich. It is significant that the Soviet press and radio maliciously stressed Anglo-French discomfiture in their first comments on the treaty.

There remains a more sinister explanation which is widely accepted in Europe. When, at about the end of April, the Russians became convinced that France and Britain meant war, there emerged, so to speak, from the back of the Soviet mind a dormant and "cold storage" idea of world revolution. It has been a Soviet tenet that the next world war would produce a Soviet revolution in Eastern Europe. Accordingly, it is suggested, the Russians conceived a Machiavellian plan to precipitate war and keep out of it themselves.

At this point there is some divergence about Russia's ultimate purpose, even in the minds of the most convinced anti-Russians. Some argue that the Stalinists and the Hitlerian régime are practically indistinguishable, and that the dictators started a general alliance for the conquest of Europe and Asia. They admit, however, that the Russians have double-crossed the Germans just as they double-crossed the French and British. Anyhow, it is agreed that the partnership began about May, and its fruits were the dismissal of Litvinov, who represented the Franco-British tendency and an obstacle to the Kremlin's rapprochement with Hitler. Henceforward the French and British served simply as bait to lead on the Germans, because, according to this theory, it was Russia and not Germany which initiated the conspiracy.

The French and British were fooled into considering the hope of Russian support and committing themselves, beyond withdrawal, to aid Poland. At the psychological moment the Russians threw off the mask and accepted Hitler's terms, thus assuring war in Europe, which not only eliminated their old bogey of a European combination against the U.S.S.R., but made it certain that a victorious Germany—or victorious Allies—would be so weakened in comparison with the U.S.S.R. as to leave the latter master of Europe for revolution or conquest. Meanwhile, the U.S.S.R. would swallow the Baltic States, East Poland, and Bessarabia with relative ease, and through its augmented support to China, or by actual war with Japan, become the master of Asia also.

I think this is too far-fetched in cunning. It savors more of Radek than of Stalin, although Radek may still be alive and Stalin has shown himself crafty on occasion. At any rate it remains as an interesting and possible hypothesis which gains, I am forced to allow, some support from the Soviet action in forcing war upon Finland, in the alleged instance of the "Finnish legal government"—that is to say, a Bolshevik revolutionary group or movement. And no matter what one thinks about the motives and possible scope of the German-Soviet agreement, whether it was loose or tight, general or specific, sincere or false, the paramount question today is how it can be, is being, and will be carried out politically, economically, and militarily.

As matters now stand between Germany and the U.S.S.R., political collaboration is felt to be, and in all probability is, mutually useful. Quite recently we have seen that, while Russia was blaming Sweden for its wish to give aid to Finland, the German official press began a campaign of threats against any Swedish attempt to "overstep the balance of neutrality." In their attitude toward France and England, the German and Russian spokesmen talked the same language. Both Allied countries are accused of having provoked the war in the first place "by inciting Poland to fight" and now of trying to expand the war by similar incitations of neutrals—Holland, Belgium, and the Scandinavian countries. In this case, however, it is rather Russia who calls the tune while Germany joins in harmony, whereas earlier it was Germany who voiced the claims of the "partnership" while the Russians acquiesced.

Even here one may ask, moreover, whether sometimes the tune does not sound false. For instance, when the German war against Poland was drawing to a victorious conclusion, the Soviet press was full of warnings to the Allies that they had better make peace with Germany or else. . . . And almost simultaneously the U.S.S.R. was affirming its position as a neutral and its right to conduct trade negotiations with England. In short, the "or else" was little more than bluff. Similarly, when Germany threatened Sweden about the infringement of neutrality in aid to Finland, there was reason to believe that the Swedes were given assurances from Berlin that they could do pretty much what they wanted, provided they did it in a decorous and not too overt manner.

In the rôle of economic collaboration, one can only see that there has been a lot more talk of plans and projects than results. In the Baltic States, indeed, there is greater evidence of competition than of co-operation. The Russians have taken from the Baltic commodities like foodstuffs, cellulose, and lumber, which Germany clearly needs. They are importing into the Baltic cotton and oil products, which Germany also needs; and, to make matters worse, they are paying for some of their purchases in the Baltic States with *valuta*—to be exact, American dollars—which can only mean that the Baltic States are thus in a measure relieved from the limitations imposed upon them by the German blockade of their commerce with England, which formerly was their principal support of "free" money.

That Russia is a great potential source of the things Germany most needs—grain, oil, cotton, manganese, and arms—is obvious enough. But that Germany has received any great quantity of these goods has yet to be proved. Russia needs them all herself, and that need will not be diminished by the Russo-Finnish conflict. There arises, too, the question of transport, which foreign observers are unanimous in believing to be the weakest link in the somewhat overstrung chain of the Soviet system. Last but not least, one may ask how collaboration in any field can be rapidly and successfully established between Germany and the Russians, who have demonstrated to the world in recent years a singular lack of ability to collaborate with one another. What I say is harsh, I admit, but how else can one interpret the "purge" and its effects?

In military matters there are two sides to any collaboration. The U.S.S.R. gave Germany no help during the German campaign in Poland, and the Soviets in Finland have found no aid or solace from Germany. One cannot but feel that this lack or omission is one of the most significant factors in any attempt to appraise Russo-German relations and is almost sufficient by itself to negative the view that the two countries are united by anything more tangible than a temporary community of interests and a joint dislike of others, which is surely a slender foundation on which to build a permanent edifice.

To conclude, then, it can be said that the German-Soviet agreement may be everything or nothing, as fate or circumstances provide, but it is much more reasonable to say that it is neither everything nor nothing, but something in between. In other words, not black or white, but gray.

# WAITING FOR DER TAG

### by Louis P. Lochner

ON August 26, Professor Karl Bomer, then head of the Propaganda Ministry's foreign press department, said during the daily conference that in the event of war the Foreign Press Section of the Propaganda Ministry would be in charge of the foreign correspondents as usual. Many workers in industrial plants were suddenly called for in official vehicles and even taxis, to be mobilized. The annual party convention at Nürmberg, scheduled for early September, was officially called off. Ration cards for eggs, textiles, shoes, and soap were given out. Private airplane flying was forbidden. Various annual conventions, such as that of the German pharmacists, were indefinitely postponed.

On August 27, I saw many soldiers on the streets, accompanied by their wives and children to the railway stations. Their faces were serious and there was no cheering.

Our young lady neighbor's trim car was requisitioned like so many others.

On August 28, my informant B. brought me the new zero hour for the attack on Poland—dawn during the night of August 31 to September 1. At the British Embassy everybody was busy packing. There were no more trains to France. Long queues were forming before textile and food shops. There was a panicky feeling among the German people.

That day my Japanese colleague K. called to tell me his government would re-evaluate its relations to Germany. Japan felt let down by Hitler, as Ribbentrop told the Japanese ambassador about the pact with Russia only thirty minutes before he started for Moscow to sign it.

On August 29, one could hear on every side, "Another Munich is about to materialize. The British government will yield." The British Embassy itself seemed to think a peaceful settlement was in the offing.

On August 30, general mobilization was ordered in Poland. A Propaganda Ministry spokesman stated that Germany welcomed Queen Wilhelmina's offer of mediation, and added that Britain must now take the initiative and get the Poles to come to Berlin. Colonel Jozef Beck, the Polish Foreign Minister, ought to be on his way now.

On August 31, the optimism displayed in the Wilhelmstrasse only two days before in regard to "another Munich" had given place to pessimism. The Polish delegation had not come and apparently was not coming.

That day I learned confidentially that during the early hours of the morning, Henderson was given Hitler's Sixteen Points for the settlement of the Polish issue by Ribbentrop who merely read them aloud without handing Henderson a copy. The Sixteen Points were released to the press late that afternoon.

Summarized, these points were that Danzig was to be returned at once to the Reich; Gdynia was to remain Polish; a Plebiscite, under international supervision, would decide the fate of the Polish Corridor within twelve months; only those who resided in the region before January 1, 1918, were to vote; both Germany and Poland would have free access, under the plebiscite, to certain roads in the Corridor; if the Corridor voted for Poland, Germany was to obtain a corridor across it to East Prussia, while if it fell to Germany, there was to be an exchange of population; complaints in regard to the treatment of minorities were to be submitted to an international commission.

The great news of that day, August 31, however, was the publication of the fact that Great Britain was mobilizing.

\*    \*    \*

WARSAW, August 31, 1939 (Associated Press): Polish sources asserted tonight that German patrols had crossed the border into Polish territory at several points. . . .

BERLIN, Sept. 1 (Associated Press): Herr Hitler today accepted the Free City of Danzig into the Reich.

\*    \*    \*

SEPTEMBER 1: *German armies invaded Poland.*

# GERMANY AT WAR

## *by Wallace R. Deuel*

A PALE, demonic man with a comedian's mustache, wearing a field-gray tunic and black trousers, stood in the speaker's rostrum of the Kroll Opera House in Berlin and told the world that there was war again.

It was hot in the Opera House that morning of September 1—very hot, and humid. The dark-red walls and maroon carpets and the great, bright, lighted eagle rampant on the silver backdrop there behind the man made it seem even hotter, even more humid. Perspiration stood out on the faces of the severally uniformed deputies who filled the main floor seats, men thick and savage and intent, like wild boars just before a kill. There was perspiration on the faces of the cabinet ministers and their aides, all of them uniformed, too, on the benches that flanked the man on either side; on the face of Field Marshal Goering, baleful in the president's place above and behind the man, and on the faces of the diplomats and guests in the boxes and balconies. But the heavy, humid air ached with the tension of the most terrible of all tragedies. Few thought to wipe the perspiration off.

"Since 5:45 o'clock this morning," Hitler said, "the fire has been returned. . . ."

This, then, was Apocalypse. This was war. No matter what else might come, the world would never be quite the same again after those words had been spoken, this deed done. The world of 1939 was gone, just as the world of 1914, too, had gone, and all the other worlds that wars had destroyed.

The deputies and the guests and diplomats listened—listened for their lives.

There had been reports in the outside world that Hitler was "weakening." These reports, too, were part of the nightmare. There had always been such reports in every crisis. This time they were even more false than they always had been before. Weakening? The man had plunged the whole world into war. It was a strange kind of weakness.

In what Hitler said, too, were the repetitiousness and unreality of the nightmare. He began, as he had begun a thousand times before, by denouncing the Treaty of Versailles. The ideas were the same, the words were the same, the voice was the same. Then he denounced the clauses of the Treaty dealing with Danzig and the Polish Corridor in particular. He had made proposals to Poland for the revision of these clauses, he said. The Poles had rejected his proposals. He had warned the Poles. The Poles had defied him. Defied by Poles! Outrage blared in the man's voice. The Poles had attacked Germans, had attacked the Reich itself, the man said, just as he had said the Czechs had done—the Czechs and the others, each in their turn. And so, the man said, "I therefore determined to speak to the Poles in the same language as that in which they had been speaking to us for months!"

He had no claims to make on Western Europe, Hitler said: "I have given formal assurances, and I repeat, that we demand nothing from the Western Powers and that we shall never demand anything."

Again the air of nightmare repetitiousness and nightmare unreality. How many times had assurances like these been heard before by these same dark-red walls, by this same great, bright eagle, by these same listeners?

Then a muted echo of 1914; once again the Italian ally stood aside. "I should like above all, here," the Chancellor said, "to thank Italy, which has supported us throughout this entire time. You will understand, however," he said, "that I do not wish to appeal for foreign help for the conduct of this struggle."

"There shall be no privation in Germany which I myself do not also accept," Hitler said. "My whole life belongs to my people from now on in a new sense. I wish nothing other than to be the first soldier of the German

142

Reich. I have therefore put on that tunic which once before was the dearest and most sacred to me, and I shall take it off only after victory has been won—or I shall not live to experience the end."

He meant it all, this strange, demonic man. That made it worse. It was morbid and tormented and agonized, this open flaying of nerves, this public, exhibitionist orgasm of a soul.

There was something incredible about it, too. There stood the pale man in the field-gray tunic, calling down the lightning of war, and directly opposite him in the diplomatic gallery sat the representatives of the powers in the West (the Pole was already gone from the gallery) on which he called it down. From that moment, these men were consecrated to each other's destruction. This was war. There was no way out. Yet the proprieties were sacred, were inviolate: the lightning would strike, but it would strike later. It was not time for it yet.

Hitler spoke for 34 minutes. It seems to have been the shortest recorded speech he ever delivered to a Reichstag.

That night, the lights went out. "The lamps are going out all over Europe," Sir Edward Grey had said in 1914; "we shall not see them lit again in our lifetime." It had been a figure of speech then; now it was a statement of literal fact, too.

Busses ran with only single, ghoulish blue lights. Street cars had faint illumination on their route numbers, but inside all the lights were shrouded in black cloth hoods. Automobile headlights were blackened except for narrow slits. A faint square of paleness glowed here and there through darkening material that was not quite opaque on a window. Street arc lamps showed only minute green flames on amber mantles. The only bright sparks in the blackness were the fiery red tail lights of the cars and the blinding blue flashes from an occasional trolley.

When France and England declared war two days later, it was almost a relief. People had not liked the waiting.

It was at twenty-nine and one-half minutes after 1 o'clock on a still, hot, sunny Sunday afternoon that the Germans finally learned that they were at war with England again. They learned it from the radio. Played by the Hamburg station orchestra, a program of classical music was being broadcast on a national network. At 1:22 o'clock, midway through the Liszt's "First Hungarian Rhapsody," the music faded out. A man's voice, urgently: "Attention! Attention! In a few minutes we shall make an important announcement." The voice stopped, and the music faded in again. The orchestra finished the "Rhapsody." Then came the announcement:

"The British government, in a note to the Reich government, has made the demand that the German troops which have advanced into Polish territory be withdrawn to their original positions," the voice said. "At 9 o'clock this morning the British Ambassador in Berlin informed the Reich government in a provocative note that if a satisfactory answer was not received by 11 o'clock, England would consider itself in a state of war with Germany...."

143

Outside, the trees stood still in the sun. The light shimmered on the leaves as though reflected from a quiet stream. A street car clacked through a switch. A bird scolded and a child cried.

Inside, there came from the radio the voice that said war. The ultimatum had expired at 11 o'clock. The Ambassador had called at the Chancellory shortly after 11 to ask for his passports.

It was the Sabbath, the Lord's Day. All the church bells of the city must have been ringing for morning service as the Ambassador went down the Wilhelmstrasse.

Once again it all seemed incredible, unreal. War? It was impossible. It was a dream, a nightmare. It had not happened, it was not happening; it had happened to somebody else, somewhere else, at some other time.

And yet the voice went on. It really was war. There were the times, the places, the people, the papers. Everything was quite in accordance with protocol. All the proper formalities had been observed. All the proper honors had been rendered. All the proper courtesies had been exchanged.

Only the people in the streets still did not seem to believe it. The sidewalk cafés along Kurfuerstendamm were well filled. There were no more uniforms than usual to be seen. A car with a diplomatic license, piled high inside with clothes and rugs, stopped at an intersection, and a man called out from the sidewalk, "You'd better get out of here!" But nobody paid any attention to either the man or the car. A few feet away a fat, berouged and painfully corseted woman of 50 did not even take her greedy eyes off a new model evening gown in a shop window to see what was happening.

In the Tiergarten, the people in their Sunday clothes walked slowly along the paths pushing their baby buggies and leading their dogs on leashes like any other Sunday crowd. The only gatherings of people in the park were those watching the spindly-tailed red squirrels begging for nuts.

There was a crowd in the Wilhelmstrasse, but it was a quiet, subdued and orderly crowd, moving as slowly as fish in a tank, and with as little sign of feeling, looking with only blank interest, at the big, canary-yellow painted stone British Embassy with the lion and the unicorn on the double doors, and standing silently across from the Chancellory down the street.

There was a hush of waiting and suspense along the Western Front that week end of Apocalypse, too, waiting and suspense for the guns to speak, for the bombers to fly. They did not speak or fly that week end. They were not to speak or fly in real earnest for more than eight long months. But neither Paris nor Berlin knew in advance how long they would be still and silent, and so the civil population on both sides were evacuated from their homes.

The Germans along the Rhine were allowed to stay, but those in a Red Zone of presumably greater danger in the Saar-Pfalz had to go. More than half a million human beings were moved out on the German side that week end. The sick and infirm, the aged and the children under 10, were evacuated in special trains beginning Friday. All the others between 10 and 60 had to go on foot. Orders for their evacuation were issued at 3 o'clock Sunday afternoon. The people were given two hours to lock up their homes and get to the appointed gathering places, leaving most things as they were. War had been declared, the orders said, and there was no time to lose.

But if war had been declared, then where were the bombers and why were the guns still silent—the bombers that everybody knew were waiting in hundreds at their bases, the guns that everybody had seen in the fields and everybody had guessed were in the new "farm houses" and "barns" the army engineers had built so thickly through the countryside? The guns were silent, the skies empty. Here at the Front, too, the war was unreal.

But the people had to go, anyway. The uprooting of humanity had begun —although only just begun. The peoples were on trek.

It was all organized down to the last detail. Roads and rails were choked with the troops moving up to the Front, but two trains were reserved for the last of those who could not walk, and two highways were kept open a few hours for the escape of those who went on foot.

It was hot and sultry in the Red Zone up to midafternoon that Sunday. Then, just before the time set for departure, the skies dulled and darkened and a cloudburst struck. Bowed under the torrent and the weight of their possessions, drenched, sodden and buffeted by the storm, the half million trudged to their meeting places; they huddled there until their turns came and they set out for the interior: men, women, young people, carrying as much as they could, leaving their homes and fields and setting out on foot into a future none could foresee. Most of them had to walk 10 to 15 miles that afternoon and evening through the storm to reach the points from which they were sent on by bus and train to their temporary homes.

Army engineers had already laid charges of high explosive at the bridges. As the last refugee train was about to leave Merzig, lightning struck one of the charges and blew up the bridge over the Saar.

SEPTEMBER 3, 1939: *State of war existed between Great Britain and Germany since 11 A.M., between France and Germany since 5 P.M.*

# ENGLAND GOES TO WAR

### *by Oswald Garrison Villard*

CRIMINAL lunacy on the one hand and almost incredible ineptness and weakness and diplomatic folly on the other have brought about a new World War. No man today can foresee when or how it will end, or what it will produce. We only know that another deadly train of events has been started. Whether the present capitalist system or, indeed, civilization itself will survive this struggle depends chiefly on how long it lasts. Stanley

Baldwin told a group of London business men and bankers in 1935 that if another war of nations took place there will be "few of our stripe left." And what of the rest?

Today we can only see clearly how unnecessary the resort to arms is. Its coming has been carefully prepared ever since 1931—yes, ever since 1919 and the Treaty of Versailles—and was made inevitable by Munich and the subsequent handling of international affairs. It is too early to pass judgment upon what happened in the last seventy-two hours. As at the same stage in 1914, there are points still to be cleared up. Why did the French seek to delay matters at the end; was the published explanation that France needed more time to perfect its preparations the proper one? Why was the expiration of its ultimatum set for a different hour from that of England? Just how far did Mussolini go with his five-power-conference proposals? Why was Parliament so obviously in bad temper with Chamberlain on Saturday and so angry that he postponed until Sunday the announcement of a state of war? Was there perfect co-operation between Warsaw and London? These are things upon which we need more light.

Certainly this war by itself will cure nothing. If the Allies win and repeat Versailles, the consequences will be even worse than before. The danger will be that the desire to make impossible another recurrence of this struggle will create an irresistible demand for exemplary vengeance. Already one hears talk of the necessity of separating North Germany and South Germany once and for all. Hence it is gratifying to find in today's London *Times* an appeal from Dr. Maxwell Garnett, formerly secretary of the League of Nations Union, for an immediate statement of England's actual war aims—without, let us hope, any secret treaties in the background—and for them to be so shaped that a genuine new world order will arise. To this is added a demand from A. A. Milne that England continue to differentiate between the German people and the German government, precisely as was done, notably by President Wilson, in the last war. These are hopeful signs. Will they disappear as the horrors of the war pile up, as grief and rage at the losses warp men's minds? Surely the Germans have set a swift pace by the abominable sinking of the *Athenia*.

All these things lie in the future, behind the most awful of clouds, the darkest of nights. The mind cannot today forecast; it merely reviews the years 1914-18 in tortured night hours and wonders what greater horrors we shall see. My only relief is to watch what is going on under my eyes here in London. For what I see is wonderful—a calm, a resolution, a resignation, a certainty of the right that compel one's complete admiration. I should unqualifiedly say that this is humanity at its best did not one thought force itself upon me: if these indomitable people would only bring their great qualities to bear upon their government and foreign policy and demand greater and wiser statesmanship, such calamities would not befall them. As I sat in Parliament on Friday, September 1, to hear Chamberlain announce that war was at hand unless the Germans accepted his ultimatum—and he was sure, he said, that they would not—I could not help recalling how many such fateful scenes had taken place in that historic chamber, how many times English leaders had ordained there the deaths of multitudes of their fellow-citizens because of their own stupidities and blunders or in order to carry on imperialistic policies of their own, long since pilloried by history.

It was a scene to remember as long as I live. Yet I believe I have seen in that very House of Commons moments of greater excitement, of more profound emotion. Mr. Chamberlain spoke earnestly, sincerely, at times passionately in his justified indignation. Munich was far behind him. Yet neither his address nor those of Arthur Greenwood for Labor and Sir Archibald Sinclair for the Liberals sounded emotional depths, nor did the last two stir their parliamentary hearers to more than perfunctory applause. It was all over in twenty-five minutes. And it left me far from feeling that I had witnessed one of the most fateful scenes in all history; I have surely, at other times, seen a larger attendance of members—perhaps a number are already in service—and the London *Times* was incorrect in saying the galleries were crowded, for the side galleries were in the main empty.

As for the public at large, whether it is stunned, or numbed by the months of expectancy of the worst, or lacks imagination, or is trained to accept what its political leaders hand down to it, or whether it is inspired by a glorious courage and traditional faith, its attitude moves you to tears. I was near tears when I visited two stations to watch the evacuation of the children, and saw the quiet, unobtrusive sorrow of the mothers saying good-by. For the children it was a grand excitement—no more school and an adventure in the country. I wondered once more whether we should honor the Wright brothers for teaching us to fly or bewail their fatal invention of a machine which brings death to whole populations.

Fifteen minutes after I heard Neville Chamberlain announce over the radio that a state of war existed, the sirens screamed and people ran for the air-raid shelters. At the first one I came to, it was "women and children first"; the second, near my hotel, was full, so I sat outside, convinced that it was a trial alarm. Soon after the "all's well" we had another alarm. Last night I was waked at 2:45 A.M. with the insistent demand that I descend to the cellar at once, and when I refused to hurry a porter came for me: "It's orders, sir." So there we sat in a cellar hallway, in all kinds of costumes, with gas masks on laps (except a few of us), but everybody calm and cheerful and no one showing any trepidation. Indeed, in the daytime the only persons to show concern are the mothers whose children are still here —far too many remain in the city. The spirit of co-operation is really wonderful; everyone wants to do his or her share, and everyone is so courteous that it seems quite unnecessary to post signs telling what constitutes good manners in an air-raid shelter!

The streets are full of new constables; all, old and new, wearing "tin hats," the new men still in "cits" but with armbands. There are innumerable new auxiliary firemen, fine-looking fellows in dark blue uniforms, and a thousand taxicabs have been supplied with trailers and transformed into quite powerful fire-engines equipped with axes, hose, rope ladders, and the like. There are air-raid protection wardens galore. Every other car has a sticker to show that it belongs to the fire service, or A.R.P., or the transport or evacuation branches. Signs everywhere call for volunteers to fill the sandbags —millions must have been filled already. The sky is full of beautiful silver-gray balloons, the "balloon barrage" that is counted on to entangle any invading aircraft in the steel cables which hold them in place. At least fifty can be seen from my window as I write. Nothing else is overhead; not an airplane ever passes.

If there is much to cheer and hearten, if the thoroughness of the organization is astounding, if there is every evidence that England begins this war as far along as it was, say, in 1915, and even later as to conscription, ominous signs of what is to come are on every hand. You cannot help starting when you read the placards telling you where to get gas masks for "children under two." You get a shock when you unexpectedly pass a first-aid station and read the notice, "Walking casualties this way." And you cannot get used to seeing store windows blocked out by sandbags or completely boarded over. But what moved me most was a visit to a great 700-bed hospital from which every patient who could be moved has been moved. All its scientific work has stopped; its whole life has been made over; and here it stands, empty but in such complete readiness that it gives you a sinking at the pit of your stomach: in the front hall are thirty tables for the first to come, with a huge morgue not far away. It was night when I visited it, and the building of course was dark. The chief nurse radiated joy over the completeness of everything—even over the rubber boots the staff will wear when the gas cases come in.

Two kindly surgeons took me up on the roof. There was London in the dark—incredibly more majestic, more thrilling than by day or with its usual lights; more mysterious, more questioning of the why and wherefore. A hundred feet above the street, we could see only a few light spots and the faint, will-o'-the-wisp lights of buses and motors. "I wonder," I said to myself, "whether London has been as dark as this since Will Shakespeare walked the Strand." My astonishment never ends that I walk the streets of London with a shaded flashlight to find my way as if I were on a Berkshire hill. I wonder if I too should be able to pilot a car through the dark with only parking lights and those well wrapped, while the "Stop" and "Go" greens and reds and ambers have shrunk to little shaded crosses. Every night not London alone but all England down to the smallest village is blacked out. Just now every place of amusement is closed. Piccadilly Circus is as quiet as a hamlet in Kent. And in these black and murky streets everybody is eager to help everyone else, to put the stranger in the right bus, on the right road.

"We shall win," said my doctor friends on that hospital roof. To the west tremendous flashes of lightning, the rumbling of thunder gave just the atmosphere the moment called for. "We shall win," said the doctors, "because every man and woman in this hospital is at his or her post in the dark—quiet, determined, efficient, prepared for the worst, uncomplaining, certain that we shall win in the end. And as they are, so is England."

\* \* \*

Budapest, Sept. 6, 1939 (Associated Press): Diplomatic dispatches from Warsaw early today said the German Army was shelling the Polish capital after a lightning advance from the north. Warsaw ... was described as partly destroyed under the heavy bombardment.

Berlin, Sept. 14 (International News Service): The rich seaport of Gdynia, Poland's only outlet to the sea, surrendered and passed into German hands today.

Berlin, Sept. 17 (United Press): A spokesman for the Propaganda Ministry announced that Russian troops had marched into Poland today....

\* \* \*

# BLITZKRIEG

### by Otto D. Tolischus

NOWOGROD, Poland, Sept. 26.—The victorious German Army, which early this month broke through the supposedly impregnable Polish Narew fortifications within 48 hours, today evacuated all the territory east of the Pissa and Narew Rivers, which form the German-Russian demarcation line in the north. The Germans left it and its population, like the larger part of all Poland, to the Soviet Russian troops and the bolshevist régime.

Now this army of veterans is moving toward the west to face the French and British. All roads in East Prussia are crammed with lines of military transports many miles long. Some of these trains are apparently heading west along the land routes; others move northward to Baltic ports, from which they are being transshipped west by German ocean liners.

The evacuation was scheduled to coincide with the arrival of the Russians at the Narew at noon today, but as the Russians were late a group of foreign correspondents, including this writer, were still able to penetrate to the ruins of what once was called Nowogrod on the Russian side of the demarcation line to view the scene of one of the decisive battles of the Polish campaign. They could also learn from German officers who participated in the battle how the Polish "national line" was broken and could witness the flight and dread of the abandoned population.

Perhaps one of the most significant things learned on the trip was that, although Berlin official quarters still speak of a merely temporary military demarcation line, the armies look at it as a matter of course only as the new border. In fact, army circles seem surprised that it is called anything else, and this perhaps has something to do with Foreign Minister Joachim von Ribbentrop's projected visit to Moscow.

Incidentally, contact between the German and Russian armies did not take place without the classic accident. Russians mistook the earth-brown uniforms of the German Labor Service, now part of the army, for Polish troops and unleashed an artillery barrage that killed nine German labor soldiers and wounded four. Three German armored cars were smashed before the misunderstanding was cleared up. Since then, the two armies have main-tained a certain distance between them.

Impressive as was the quick German victory on the Narew, even more impressive is the army that achieved it. This army today passed, so to say, in review before the correspondents. For this army was a living triumph of military motorization, which in the German view at least now has demon-strated its superiority over any other form of locomotion on every kind of terrain and in any weather.

According to the German testimony, the modern motor has been able to conquer ground where no motor was supposed to go before—even on Polish roads, which in part, however, proved to be better than their reputation—and motors received direct credit for the speed of the German victory.

The entire northern army is completely motorized. Infantry no longer marches, but rides in trucks; even horses have become a rarity. Thousands of motor vehicles of all kinds—all up to date—take the place of long columns of infantry.

There are light 7-ton and heavy 24-ton tanks, light and heavy armored cars for the so-called "fast divisions," light motorized field artillery and heavy motorized 15-centimeter fortification howitzers, motorized anti-tank guns, motorized pioneer troops and motorized communication troops, regi-ments of motorcyclists and even bicycle troops, but only one lonely horse-drawn field battery could be discovered on the road and marching troops could be seen only in garrison towns.

The particular army group that broke through the Narew line at Nowo-grod first came west out of East Prussia to conquer the fortress of Graudenz (Grudziadz) and then turned East against the Narew on Sept. 7. The Narew was fortified for 35 kilometers by a line of "bunkers" or huge steel and concrete pill-boxes, which protected every possible crossing not pro-tected by swamps. A dozen such bunkers were just outside Nowogrod, built only this year according to the latest French and Czech models and located in terrain ideal for defense.

The Germans advanced on the Narew on Sept. 8, and one company even crossed it in rubber boats without one shot being fired. But then the Poles opened up with machine-gun fire from the bunkers and from artillery be-hind them, with the result that the German advance company was cut off and the Germans stalled.

All the next day heavy fighting continued. German artillery concentrated on pounding the bunkers but without noticeable effect. Largely from the revelations of prisoners, the positions of Polish artillery were located and the guns silenced. The Germans also succeeded in pounding Nowogrod into ruins and silencing the heavy Polish machine-gun fire from the town. All further attempts to cross the Narew, however, failed because rubber boats were shot to pieces from the bunkers, which also made bridge-building impossible.

Thereupon, during the night of the tenth, the Germans moved up heavy artillery right to the river's edge, concentrating their fire on individual bunkers from a distance of only 3,000 feet. Even then, as shown by an inspection today, not one shot actually penetrated through the steel and concrete into the bunkers themselves. But, according to German officers, the impact of the rain of shells was such that the Polish crews were made to feel the whole pill-boxes were turning around and it "drove the soldiers inside crazy."

Some of the bunker crews came out and surrendered; others had to be "smoked out." For that purpose a German advance company, which meanwhile had dug itself in, "ran under" the machine-gun fire; that is, ran through the fire so close to the bunkers that the machine guns could not be trained on them. Then they used flame-throwers or hand grenades to finish the crews inside or drive them out.

Desperate counterattacks by the Poles on Nowogrod came too late and collapsed under German machine-gun fire, which virtually exterminated whole regiments. On the evening of Sept. 10 the impenetrable Polish lines had been penetrated.

In the view of German officers, the Narew line would have been really impenetrable but for two things. One was the break in the morale of the Polish troops, who had no notion of modern artillery fire and could not stand up to it although they fought bravely otherwise. The second and most important, however, was insufficient Polish artillery backing. Had the Poles possessed enough artillery to keep the German guns from advancing too closely to the bunkers and keep the German planes from bombing them, the Germans feel that they might be fighting there yet.

Meanwhile, the whole town of Nowogrod looks like a burned forest of smokestacks that somehow still stand erect. Only one house in the market place had been left miraculously without a scratch. Some few inhabitants were returning today, possibly to search the ruins of their homes for any small belongings that may have escaped the shells and flames. They are a terror-stricken, bewildered lot who have saved only what they could carry on their backs, and that was not much. Hunger is written on their faces, fear lurks in their eyes. The children especially have acquired almost an animal look, furtive and savage because of the brutal experiences they do not comprehend.

With the German Army, Before Warsaw, Poland, Sept. 28.—The German campaign in Poland came to an end today when the fortress of Modlin followed Warsaw in surrendering unconditionally at 7 o'clock this morning. At the same time the bulk of the German army had returned to the western side of the German-Russian demarcation line, which army circles regard as the new Reich border.

With that surrender of the last fort defending the city, Germany has attained her war aims in the East, namely, the partition of Poland, in exactly four weeks. She is already at work organizing the newly-won territory in order to enhance its agricultural and industrial resources.

But German army quarters are perfectly well aware that this new aggrandizement has been obtained at a high price that is not measured by German casualties, which are comparatively small, but by the fact that, in place of weak Poland, Germany has again put powerful Russia on her eastern flank. Army circles are so aware of this new situation that they frankly declare:

"Germany must now be stronger than ever, not only to win the conflict with France and Britain but also to prepare for the inevitable dispute with Soviet Russia that must come some day."

In fact that is the consolation the German army offers the conquered foe remaining on the German side of the demarcation line who still fear National Socialist Germany less than they do Bolshevist Russia.

The final dramatic scenes of Warsaw's and Modlin's surrender were witnessed by this writer together with a group of other foreign correspondents who arrived at the German front line on the edge of the capital yesterday afternoon to find Warsaw in flames and Modlin still being bombed and shelled to pieces.

We stood at the same spot on the Warsaw-Modlin road where General Werner von Fritsch fell and where a Polish army officer with a white flag had appeared a few hours earlier to offer the surrender of the city.

Around us stood German troops in their first line positions and there also lay the Polish dead. In front of us some 250 yards away, stood the Polish advance guards in the shelter of a gateway, guns in hands, silently and suspiciously watching every move on their enemy's front.

Where they stood began the sea of houses that was Warsaw. Dense columns of smoke rose high above the Polish capital, which the evening sun painted with a rosy glow that turned blood red. Behind us, in the background, was Modlin, where fighting still continued and which was just being shelled and bombed by a German air attack. The roar of cannon, the bursting of bombs could be heard plainly, to be followed a little later by the roar of the engines of the attacking planes. Appropriately enough, Modlin was overhung by sinister-looking storm clouds into which the evening sun put enough reflected light to convert them into an autumnal background for the columns of smoke and dust rising from the bursting bombs.

When we arrived at the front line firing had ceased, but the Germans still watched enemy movements as closely as did the Poles. For only today, after the "stop firing order" had been sounded for 9:30 in the morning, some misunderstanding arose as a result of which the Poles resumed fire with rifles, grenades, mine-throwers and machine guns about 11 A.M. The Germans replied with artillery until a few more houses went up in flames.

What most interested veterans of former wars in our party, however, was the fact that despite motorization and other mechanical improvements on the war machine, modern warfare had really changed little and that its quintessence, as represented by the front line, was still mud holes.

A weapon more modern even than firearms, propaganda, was also being used right at the front line. A large poster displayed by the Germans announced in Polish:

"Poles! Come to us. We will not hurt you. We will give you bread."

As explained by German staff officers, Warsaw was first treated as an open city and only military objectives were bombed or shelled. Then, however, General Czuma, commander of the defense, restored the old Warsaw forts, such as Modlin, the last to hold out, and established defense lines around the city. Whereupon the German army command announced it would treat Warsaw as a fortress and shell and bomb it.

But this threat failed to weaken the city's defense. The Germans then offered a truce to evacuate diplomats and the civilian population and called for the Polish representative to appear at a designated point to negotiate.

After this the Germans sent airplanes over Warsaw, throwing millions of leaflets calling on the city to surrender, promising soldiers would be sent home instead of being made war prisoners, and that in view of their brave defense, officers would be permitted to keep their swords. The appeal to the officers was considered especially important because, in the German view, the backbone of the defense consisted of officers who had left their surrendering troops outside and had rallied within Warsaw in regiments consisting for the most part of officers only. When that failed, two truces were arranged—one for evacuating foreign diplomats, who arrived in Königsberg, East Prussia, recently, and another for evacuating sixty-two Soviet diplomats after the Russian occupation of Eastern Poland.

Only then, according to German officers, did the real bombardment start. The forts, and especially the old citadel, were heavily bombed and shelled, as were the barracks, airport and such inferior points as had been observed. As a result, many buildings also were damaged, including, it is understood, the former royal palace. A Polish truce officer, as well as others from Warsaw, asserted that, in fact, a large part of the city is merely "heaps of ruins."

Finally, late Tuesday night a Polish officer bearing a white flag appeared at the German front line and asked for a truce to evacuate the civilian population and the wounded. This was refused and the final unconditional surrender was announced early yesterday morning.

Today German heavy artillery and munitions trains already are moving westward again, carrying Polish flags and eagles as trophies and bearing on trucks and caissons short inscriptions such as:

"To hell with Poland and England" or "Warsaw-Paris express."

Details of how General von Fritsch was killed in action just before the Polish-German War came to an end were learned here at the front today.

According to this account, General von Fritsch had helped in front-line observation posts throughout the campaign and did so again last Friday in a major reconnaissance attack undertaken with infantry, artillery and bombers to test out the Polish line's strength. Suddenly from a house where no enemy previously was observed, the Poles started a heavy machine-gun fire. A bullet hit General von Fritsch in the thigh and severed an artery. A lieutenant accompanying him tried to bind up the wound but the general merely said:

"Please do not bother!"

These were his last words. Two minutes later he was dead. Despite a heavy fire, the lieutenant carried the body of his commander to the rear.

\* \* \*

BERLIN, Sept. 27 (International News Service): Beleaguered Warsaw surrendered unconditionally tonight following twenty days of ceaseless pounding by Nazi artillery and aerial bombs, it was announced by the German Army Headquarters here.

\* \* \*

# INSIDE WARSAW

## by Joseph W. Grigg

I WAS a member of the first group of foreign newspapermen to reach Warsaw. We arrived there on October 5th, the day on which Hitler held his victory parade amid the ruins of the former Polish capital. Such devastation would be difficult to imagine. The whole center of the city had been laid in ruins by the two-day fury of the German bombardment and air bombing. Dead horses still lay rotting in the parks, their carcasses half hacked up by starving Polish troops during the siege. New graves bulged the grass along side street car tracks. Bomb craters made it difficult to drive along some of the main streets. The brand new central railway station was scarcely recognizable. The Polish population looked bewildered and stunned.

For an hour we stood alongside Hitler as tank after tank, motorized infantry, guns, and more tanks thundered past along the tree-lined avenue where most of the foreign embassies and legations are situated. No Pole saw that victory parade. The street where Hitler stood and those along which the gray German columns rolled had been cordoned off and no Pole was allowed nearer than a block distant. The tanks were clean and in parade-ground condition. The troops were fresh and clear-eyed. The dull steel armor of the new Nazi *Wehrmacht* had scarcely been dented by its first blitz campaign.

That was the lesson of the conquest of Poland. Overwhelming superiority in tanks, overwhelming superiority in the air from the outset, use of the dive bomber as the new "super-artillery" of the future, and complete coordination between Army and Air Force. And the new strategy—lightning attack to gain the advantage of surprise and use of the swift, overlapping armored spearheads to split the enemy, encircle him and crush him in an iron ring from which there is no escape.

Later that afternoon on the Warsaw airport a dozen or so foreign newspapermen were presented to Hitler. His face was pallid and unhealthy-looking but his mood was that of a triumphant conqueror.

"Gentlemen," he said, "you have seen the ruins of Warsaw. Let that be a warning to those statesmen in London and Paris who still think of continuing this war."

With a quick Nazi salute he turned from us and walked towards the plane that was to carry him back to Berlin. He had used this chance meeting with our small group of foreign correspondents to send back to London and Paris the warning: "Remember the ruins of Warsaw. Remember what your own fate may be."

# LOGIC AND DEATH

### by Joseph C. Harsch

NATIONAL Socialist Germany prides itself on its logic. It is sometimes a peculiar kind of logic which would scarcely stand up under the tests of objective thinking which the great intellectuals of Western civilization have established through the generations. But it is a kind of logic which will follow through a given Nazi course of action not only to a *reductio ad absurdum,* but sometimes even to a *reductio ad bestium* which recognizes no curbs of humanity, religion or reasonable compromise.

According to Nazi-party doctrine, the German is *per se* superior to an individual of any other so-called racial derivation. The idea of a special Germanic race, as has been pointed out before, is, of course, a scientific violation of fact, logic and common sense. But Nazism has laid down this arbitrary edict that there is a German race and that it is superior. On that unscientific and ridiculous premise they proceed to instruct French peasants in the art of tilling soil which the ancestors of those same peasants have tilled with loving and highly successful care for scores of generations. On that premise they presume to teach Dutch and Danish stockmen in the breeding of cattle. Because they can produce conquering armies they think they can produce superior culture, art, music, literature, science, animals and people. The amazing thing is how baldly public dogma asserts these inanities.

According to Nazi dogma, Germany, being superior, is destined to rule its allegedly inferior neighbors. Therefore, so their logic runs, any desire on the part of its neighbors to retain their own national identity is wrong and criminal. Therefore, any step taken to destroy the nationalism of those neighbors is right. Because Polish nationalism is the nearest competitor to German nationalism the Nazi considers it right and proper that any steps

155

necessary to stamp out Polish nationalism is right and proper and perfectly legal. That the Pole has a right which can compete or challenge a German right seems unthinkable and intolerable.

This attitude toward Poles, for example, is not even a monopoly of more fanatical Nazis. One of my acquaintances in Germany was a cultured, intellectual, Christian woman who considered herself to be anti-Nazi and who was deeply disturbed whenever I suggested that some of her ideas seemed to bear a familiar "Made-in-the-Propaganda-Ministry" trade mark. She expressed deep horror over tales of alleged atrocities committed by Poles against Germans. That Germans should suffer at the hands of Poles seemed to her horrible and wicked. But when I referred to widespread execution of Poles under the guise of retaliation she remarked in surprised innocence:

"But they are Poles."

It did not seem particularly horrible to her that in one Polish village 140 Polish men were lined up and shot because a single German soldier had been killed in the dark the night before. Nor could she feel that the beatings and executions of Czech students at Ruzyn on November 17, 1939, was particularly horrible. They were Czechs and therefore had no right to persist in singing the songs which express the ancient urge of the Czech people for independent existence, according to her mentality.

If even an ordinary German woman who does not consider herself a Nazi can take the executions of Poles so lightly it is no wonder that Nazi leaders can proceed with a deliberate policy of annihilating Polish nationalism by means which amount to deliberate mass murder and mass starvation. When it comes to destroying Poles, Nazi logic pursues its course with a ruthless consistency which knows no limits.

The same logic justifies them in their own eyes in using starvation as a deliberate instrument of national policy. There is no excuse whatever for food shortage in Poland. Poland has always, up until the conquest, been a net exporter of food. It raises enough to feed its own people. Yet agents of the Hoover Relief Commission report that there was actual widespread starvation in Poland during the past winter. Whether the Germans cut grain before it was ripe just to deprive Poles of food I cannot know of my own knowledge, never having been permitted by Germans to enter Poland after the occupation. But such is the report of American relief experts who did enter Poland to study conditions. And there is no secret made in Berlin of the fact that enormous quantities of food were taken from Poland.

The Nazi dogma of German superiority justifies them in their own eyes in taking food from other people to fatten their own larders. But their logic goes even farther. They make a fetish in their press of observing international law. Yet there is nothing in international law which justifies or even condones the deliberate use of food as a weapon of propaganda and war. When and if the history of the German occupations is ever written it will almost certainly show that they have controlled the movements of food as a means of punishing those regions where unrest is strongest and re-

156

warding those where the inclination to accept the German yoke is most active.

But in no field of action has their "logic" been invoked to justify such extreme measures as inside Germany itself toward those who, because of mental or physical disability, can no longer contribute to the efficiency of the German state. Nazi dogma decrees that the individual lives for the benefit of the state. Nazi logic concludes from this premise that any individual who is a burden on the state is undesirable. They have proceeded under this dogma to liquidate the aged, insane and infirm by the thousand. How many have actually been killed under the label of euthanasia, or "mercy killings," since the practice began sometime in the summer of 1940 no one knows outside of the Gestapo, which supervised the operation. Estimates by Germans with some personal knowledge of the affair who were in touch with American correspondents in Berlin have run as high as from eighty thousand to one hundred thousand. This seems a probable exaggeration. It may be nearer twenty thousand. But there can be no doubt of the fact that large numbers of persons have been taken from the sanitariums of Germany and destroyed.

There was, of course, a reason beyond the "logic" which is used as justification. In a highly socialized country such as Germany the hospital facilities which are devoted to aged, insane and infirm consume roughly one third of the total hospital facilities of the state. This does not seem logical to the Nazi mind. There may have been some other contributory reasons, such as saving food and perhaps even experimenting with various forms of taking life. And there is the ugly suspicion that political graft entered into the selection of victims. But it was probably the desire to free hospital facilities which provided the practical motivation for carrying the logic of efficiency to such an extreme.

# A BOMB EXPLODES

## by Ernest R. Pope

TWO months after the beginning of the war, a bomb explosion in the Bürgerbräu Beer Hall killed six Nazis and one waitress, injured scores of other Brown Shirts, but was timed to miss Adolf by eleven minutes. I happened to be the only American correspondent in Munich when the bomb went off. The Führer had been addressing his Old Guard in the beer hall, commemorating the anniversary of the night when, sixteen years previously, he had started the unsuccessful Nazi Putsch by firing a pistol into the same ceiling that crashed down too late to bury him in 1939.

Since journalists were barred from the Bürgerbräu meeting, I listened to Hitler's speech by radio. The only way to obtain further information on these annual celebrations was to corner one of the Old Guard Nazis in the

157

Gestapo-managed Vier Jahreszeiten Hotel, where the higher-up Nazis always stay when in Munich. The beer hall was as unapproachable on these nights as the Siegfried Line or Hitler's bedroom.

When the broadcast ended with a description of Hitler leaving the hall for the station, I drove to the hotel. But the Nazis were too busy to stop and chat. "We must hurry back to Berlin; this is wartime, you know," was all they contributed to this frustrated journalist, except to add that the Bürgerbräu jamboree "was the same as last year." So I comforted myself at a near-by bar and left my Berlin colleagues to worry about translating and dispatching the Führer's speech. The customary blackout shrouded Munich in complete darkness.

Suddenly the waiters began clearing the tables. I was requested to pay and leave. Since Munich had no curfew hours and it was only about 1:30 A.M., I asked, "Why all the rush?"

"Because of the police curfew," answered the waiter, pocketing my tip.

"Why is there a curfew tonight?"

"On account of the explosion."

"What explosion?"

"In the Bürgerbräu Beer Hall," the waiter finally confessed, but knew no more. He didn't need to urge me to leave!

Outside, the city lights glared brightly, while the nighthawks cheered and celebrated drunkenly. The bright lights which the police had switched on after the ambulances had removed the victims from the wrecked beer hall across the Isar River, had started a wild rumor that the war was over.

I raced to my Munich office after a police cordon had turned me back from the Bürgerbräu to file "blitz" calls to Berlin. (Blitz calls cost ten times as much as the ordinary long-distance rate. They are the only calls which assure you of an immediate connection with your party.)

While Berlin offices were relaying my first messages to America, I returned to the Bürgerbräu to resume my efforts at entering the building. The police always turned me back. But I could see the army engineers and Nazi labor service clearing away the wreckage, and noticed that the roof of the hall was gone. I left once more to send Berlin a follow-up description of the beer hall from the outside.

At 10 A.M. Jack Raleigh and Percy Knauth of the *Chicago Tribune* and the *New York Times* knocked at my door, frozen and hungry from a marathon dash on the Hitler Highway from Berlin to Munich in Percy's car.

Knauth left us for another November Nazi ceremony, while Jack followed me back again to the Bürgerbräu. My six years in Germany against Jack's three months naturally gave me the responsibility for doing most of the talking. But all my eloquence did not procure even a glimpse of the shattered hall, so Jack and I started for my car to get permission from Gestapo Headquarters. Just as we were driving off to the Lions' Den, a regular policeman and a diminutive plainclothesman stopped us and asked "What did the gentlemen wish?" I told them, whereupon the little fellow said, "Come along and I'll see what I can do."

158

In good faith we followed him through the courtyard of the Bürgerbräu and just outside the main hall where the explosion had brought down the roof, but our captor took us to a corner where we could see nothing but the entrance to the building. "Wait a minute," he said, placing us between two burly Gestapo colleagues. We cooled our heels for an hour, but at least could watch Adolf Wagner, Ritter von Epp, Julius Streicher, Reich Labor Service Leader Hierl, and other Nazi big shots enter the mysterious door to the hall while the Munich Police Chief, Herr von Eberstein, stomped around barking out arrest orders as liberally as a politician shouting promises in a campaign. Finally our Gestapo midget, an Austrian, returned. With a disarming smile he asked for our passports "for identification." He implied that this was the last step in getting permission for us to see what we wanted. Our two Gestapo book ends remained impassive as our SS Mickey Mouse popped back into a huddle somewhere among the sepulchral beer vaults.

Our heels had dropped almost to the freezing point before Mickey Gestapo returned, simulating deep chagrin. "Sorry, *Meine Herren,* but I'll have to take you to Headquarters"—all in the name of "Identification."

"Well, let's get a move on," I suggested impatiently. "It's past lunchtime, and I'm hungry," Jack's displeasure, as registered in his expressive face, made up for any failings in his mastery of south German dialects.

"You must wait; the car has not been sent yet from H.Q.," replied Mickey.

"We can get there quicker in my car," volunteered your correspondent.

"Yah, but how will I get back? I'm on duty here at the beer hall, you know," queried our half-pint guardian.

"I'll drive you back, my friend, since I promise you that we will get out of Gestapo Headquarters just as quickly as you will. Shall we go now?" I argued, this time with results, for Mickey led the way to my car.

"You can get in between us, since you're shorter. We won't bite you," I kidded, emboldened by hunger pangs.

"Aw, I ain't scared," retorted our plucky little dick.

For the first and last time in my life I was allowed to park my car in the awe-inspiring courtyard of grim Wittelsbacher Palace, which Gestapo Headquarters had "inherited" from Bavarian royalty shortly after Hitler had moved into his Brown House one block to the west. As we passed the armed SS sentry, Mickey Mouse waved his Gestapo pass and snapped, "These two men belong to me!"

In the course of three hours, we told the chief all about where we lived in Munich, in Berlin, in the United States; our sex; the color of our eyes and hair; why it could be plausible that a foreign correspondent might want to see the blasted remains of what just escaped being the tomb of the greatest dictator in the world; that we still wanted to see the hall; etc., etc.; and that we at least hoped he would release us in time for the *Kaffeestunde,* even if the ersatz coffee and cake wasn't as good as it is in America. Fortunately we were not searched. Jack had a hot story burning a hole in his pocket on its devious way out of the Reich. I had certain documents which would have required more explaining than I cared to tackle before supper.

At last, with an eloquent gesture, the SS Master Mind handed us back our passports, but no permission to see the junk pile. "The detectives are still at work in the debris," he explained apologetically, "but of course you, as members of the foreign press, will receive the first permission to view the interior of the Bürgerbräu." We never were given the permit, and while he was stalling us off, the *Völkischer Beobachter* already was going to press with a picture of the wreckage and a description of the scene by a trusted Nazi journalist.

There were many telltale indications that the Munich explosion was an inside Nazi job. Once more Goebbels' propaganda machine tripped over itself by asserting that Gestapo investigations revealed that "the preparations for the attempt on the Führer's life have been traced back to the month of August." If Goebbels had been up on his toes, instead of limping mentally as well as physically, he never would have credited England's secret service with the ability to work inside the Reich and Adolf's beer hall for almost four months without being discovered by the super-efficient Gestapo.

The immediate scapegoat accused of planting the bomb, Georg Elser, had never been heard of in Munich. If he had really been a British agent, determined to assassinate Hitler, he never would have been so foolish as to return to Munich from the German frontier, just to make sure that the bomb was still ticking. Yet the lurid Nazi version of his capture claimed that he had done this very thing.

I had returned to Munich from Berlin expecting fireworks of some sort at Adolf's November Eight Reunion. Listening to his speech with some friends that evening, I had remarked, "I wonder when we'll hear the 'Bang.'" I had thought it very possible that some irreconcilable anti-Soviet member of Hitler's Old Guard would shoot him on this occasion for concluding a pact with the arch-enemy Stalin since their last get-together in the Bürgerbräu. Lucky for me that my Gestapo hosts at Himmler's Munich headquarters were ignorant of my remark the next day, otherwise they might have spared themselves the trouble of digging up a Georg Elser!

My own opinion is that the Bürgerbräu explosion was a job inspired by Goebbels and executed by Himmler in order to make the Germans hate the British. The jubilation over the Polish conquest had expired, there was a dismal stalemate on the western front, and the disgruntled Germans were beginning to grumble more audibly about the blackout, the rationed food, and the freezing temperatures in their homes. They were still angry at Hitler for plunging their country into war, and had not yet been seriously bombed or attacked by the Allies, so had no reason to hate England. The Munichers especially remembered Chamberlain vividly as their angel of peace. Goebbels thought that six dead, petty Brown Shirts and one Munich waitress was a bargain price to pay for getting obstinate Germans to curse the British Prime Minister. But his project backfired, much to the embarrassment of his foreign-press contact men in the Wilhelmstrasse.

My theory about the propagandistic nature of the explosion was seconded by a prominent Municher, who expressed his own belief to me as somberly as this:

"After this explosion," he whispered, "we can expect anything. The next surprise will be British 'planes dropping poison gas bombs over Munich. They will be our own 'planes in disguise, with RAF markings. This will be Goebbels' method of switching the recalcitrant Bavarians' hate from the Führer to the British, and simultaneously will provide Hitler with an excuse to launch a gas attack against the Allies."

> NOVEMBER 28, 1939: *Russia denounced her non-aggression pact with Finland.*
>
> NOVEMBER 29: *Russia invaded Finland. Helsinki was bombed.*
>
> DECEMBER 12: *Russia refused to allow the League to mediate in the war between herself and Finland. The League expelled Russia from membership.*
>
> JANUARY 20-26, 1940: *Russians made unsuccessful assault north of Lake Ladoga.*
>
> JANUARY 28: *Russian troops began to crack the Mannerheim Line.*

# AT THE FINNISH FRONT

## *by Martha Gellhorn*

THE road was just wide enough for the car and here it narrowed at a bridge. The blued lamps of the car only dimly lighted the frozen snow four feet ahead. "Be careful," the soldier said to our driver.

We had been driving in low and now seemed barely to move. Suddenly the tail-light showed a red-painted pole to the left. The bridge felt different from the road, smoother and even more slippery. When we were across, the soldier let out his breath. "That's pretty dangerous," he explained. "Those mined bridges—if you skid, I mean. One of our men hit such a mine and we couldn't even find him. There's another to cross now." The car had cleared the side of the bridge by less than a foot.

Our civilian driver turned on his full lights; he wasn't crossing any more of those bridges in the dark. The black, close-growing pine forest stood out against the snow, and the ice on the road flickered. We crossed the second bridge and the driver sighed and the soldier offered me a cigarette. Ahead of us a staff car painted dead-white—the camouflage color here—blinked its lights twice, turned a corner and suddenly sped along a narrow road past an open, snow-covered field. We followed with full lights at a more sensible pace. The soldier muttered something, then the forest closed in again and the soldier spoke in a pleasant, conversational voice to the driver. The driver answered quickly. I asked what they were talking about. Finnish is not a language you can pick up in a short time. "He says," the driver translated, "that I really should not have kept my lights on going past that field, or else I should have gone faster. The Russians can see you from there, but he says they are poor marksmen and they have not managed to hit the road yet."

Nothing surprised me any more. This night war in snow and ice with unending forest hiding the armies was too fantastic to be true.

Our soldier guide, a lieutenant, wore a gray astrakhan cap and a romantic-looking but practical coat with astrakhan collar and trimming, and high, over-the-knee leather boots with turned-up toes, and he was twenty-one and answered to the nickname of Viskey. I had no idea where we were or where we were going because we had been driving for three hours since leaving Viipuri on these unmarked glassy roads.

Now Viskey said stop, and we piled out and joined the four staff officers from the car ahead. We spoke in whispers. Gun flashes from the Finnish batteries burned like summer lightning against the sky and the noise of the outgoing shells was very loud and blurred, and like an echo, we would hear the explosions as they landed. For an hour I had been waiting to hear the Russian batteries reply and still they were silent.

Ahead of us a line of soldiers loaded the small lightweight sledges they use for transport. Sledges are the nearest you can come to mechanized efficiency in these forests and on these roads. The line of soldiers stretched far forward into the darkness. I thought it was probably a company of 150 men but couldn't be sure; most of them, wearing white overalls over their uniforms, seemed part of the snow and the dark-dressed ones were lost against the dark trunks of the trees.

They moved fast but in absolute silence, and from time to time the gun flashes would light up a man bending to fix his boots or another slapping his hands for warmth.

Then a clear, crackling word was shouted down the line. It came from the leading officer commanding this action and was passed on by every twentieth man, and now it sang out over the road, and the sledges and men began to move forward. "Follow!" called a voice from the darkness. "Follow!" the other voices echoed.

This was the first big night operation of the war. The Russians were less than three quarters of a kilometer ahead, and all that day they had been maneuvered into a trap. The Finnish colonel in command of this sector believed there was an entire Russian division caught in the pocket.

Two battalions of soldiers with sledges, moving into the darkness, were to circle and pass the Russian lines and attack from the rear while other mobile units attacked from the front. So now we watched these go, and heard behind us the rumble of trucks and we stepped backward into the ditches to leave the road clear as heavy ammunition trucks, burning glow-worm lights, drove up and stopped. The road seemed to be blocked with incoming supplies.

An officer I had known for three hours, and who was therefore an old friend, loomed up and said, in German, "Get in your car. You must go back. This is the height of stupidity, and besides your cars are in the way." He said something sharply to Viskey, who laughed and took my arm.

Half-frozen and very tired, we reached the great bombed city of Viipuri at five-thirty in the morning. We had left Helsinki at five-thirty the morning before. That was the end of the night but all of it had been strange enough.

At eight o'clock, in the beginning of the night, we had come upon GHQ. It was on a large, rambling country estate with many barns, stables and out-buildings. We found staff headquarters and were ushered into a ballroom with pale blue walls, lace curtains, cut-glass chandeliers and a grand piano. From this we were led into a small, equally elegant salon where scale maps were pinned on the wall and a long, businesslike table was the only furnishing. The general, a gray, slender, shy man, came in presently from a trip to the front.

We connected with Viskey here and the next step was field headquarters, another tent equally warm and comfortable and lost in the woods. The colonel showed us positions on his scale map and answered questions and joked and all this time an attack was starting.

It is not usual to find a field headquarters so calm and good-humored when real business is under way. Only once division headquarters telephoned to ask how things were going, and the answer was, "Fine!" Meantime, the Finnish batteries, scattered through these woods, were preparing the attack with a fairly heavy bombardment. The sound of an outgoing shell is a cozy thing.

From this place you could see the sky marked with fire from burning villages, and we had passed on the road numerous small fires reflected in a lake. These small fires were from burning hay; the Finns systematically destroy anything that may be of use to the enemy, and the burning villages before the lines were either fired by occasional Russian shells or by the re-treating villagers themselves or by the Finnish army. The Russians come to a bare and unfriendly country where there is nothing to eat and little or no shelter.

Also in the dark, we had passed the Mannerheim Line; the Finnish army was still in front of its own fortifications.

The Mannerheim Line crosses the bottleneck of the Karelian Peninsula in a triplicate defense of granite border tank traps, barbed wire and trenches. But nature itself has provided the Finns with the best defense—the forest studded with rocks and broken with countless lakes, icy weather and a gray, cloud-thick sky. I don't know what is going on in the north, where it is no more than 125 miles from the Russian border to the Finnish coast of the Bothnian Gulf and the vital railway line that connects Finland with Sweden. Nor does anyone know what the Russian army has in store or what the Russian aviators can produce. But, those days on the southern front, I thought it would not be fun to be a Russian soldier.

At eight-thirty in the morning, after three hours' sleep, we heard the siren wail over Viipuri and we descended to the concrete-walled hotel garage.

Nothing happened. Then the snow started, soft and steady, and the day promised to be safe.

We went to the Viipuri prison to visit the captured Russians. The chief warden of this prison was a spare gray man with pince-nez and a stammer and the gentle manner of a professor. He was talking in Russian with a Soviet flier.

The flier was a man of thirty-two with a sad, tired face and two days' growth of beard, and he stood as straight as his fatigue would let him and answered questions in a humble, soft voice. I asked whether he had any family. He did not move and his voice did not change, but standing so, tears rolled down his face, and the warden and the jailers turned away because they did not want to look at this.

The flier said in the same soft voice that he had two children, one so high and the other so high, and his beloved wife and another child on the way. He simply stated these facts, not asking for pity, but his loneliness was terrible to see.

We walked down stone steps into the cellar and two Russian soldiers were let out of barred cells. They also stood in this tight, rigid manner, and I thought probably they expected to be shot every time they were called out of their cells. One was a tall man of thirty-seven, and the other a boy of twenty-three. They had had two and three months' military training respectively. They were very thin, their clothes were the crudest cotton pants and coats in this desperate climate, and the Finns were shocked because they were so louse-infested. These prisoners answered questions shiveringly also, and repeated what all the others had said: They were told Finland was attacking them, and so they were fighting to save Russia. The individual man, in trouble and alone and lost, is pitiful, and these were as pitiful as any I had ever seen. The warden allowed me to give them cigarettes, thus breaking a prison rule of seventeen years standing and proving also that he was a kind, unhating old man.

The roads are as ghastly by day as by night. The cars spin like coins, skidding on ice and gently descending into ditches. We arrived in the dark at the town where we were to sleep, and the next morning they gave a fine imitation of the best London fog. The Finns seemed very lucky in these matters. This town was a bombing objective for the enemy and an unhealthy place to be in clear weather.

I was taken to the great airfield of this sector, where fighting planes are stationed. Not much can be written about it. Even when you were on the field you could see nothing. The planes were hidden in the woods and in their own dugouts and all the vastly complicated organization work was carried on in dugouts which looked from the ground like snowdrifts. The planes—fast single-seater pursuits—were imported from Holland; some of them had been copied in Finnish factories.

We stepped over sweet-smelling pine boughs that camouflaged a dugout where the crack pursuit squadron of Finland has its quarters. As always, one is astounded by the age of the pilots; they ought to be going to college dances, you feel, or cheering at football games. Their dugout was warm and cheerful and one of the pilots played a guitar. The squadron commander, a new hero of Finland, answered questions for a time politely and then said, "Do you want to hear a sad Finnish love song?" I said I would be delighted, and one aviator sang while the blond one played his guitar and the squadron commander, when it was over, remarked with a lovely quick, humorous smile, *"Paris et l'amour."*

The flight lieutenant, a tall man of thirty with a beautifully chiseled face, brought down two planes in one day. The second one, from a distance of thirty meters, splashed him with oil as it fell. All these men were modest and jolly, the way the brave men are. I learned that they go up, alone or in twos, to fight off any number of oncoming bombers. The flight lieutenant on his big day had been fighting alone against thirteen Russian bombers. He told me, in passing, that some years ago he tried to get a job flying transport between New York and Boston but that he failed to get the job because the American company didn't think he was good enough. He said, of course, it was much easier to fly pursuit planes in war.

One cannot know what will happen in a war from one day to the next and certainly guessing is even more hazardous in a war between such unequal forces, but it is safe to say that the Finns have a trained army, helped by knowledge of the terrain; the soldiers are well equipped and wonderfully fed and the pilots are apparently, from results already shown, extra good. The army has that sound and comforting gaiety of good troops. It has confidence in its leaders. And it has the determination of those who fight on their own soil. The flight lieutenant spoke for them all when he said, "They will not get us as a present."

MARCH 1, 1940: *The Russians entered the key city of Viipuri.*

MARCH 13: *A peace agreement was signed between Soviet Russia and Finland, by which Russia obtained the Karelian Isthmus and naval bases at Hangoe.*

# DEFEAT

## *by Virginia Cowles*

WE ARRIVED in Stockholm on March 11. On the same day the Finns issued a communiqué admitting that peace discussions were being held in Moscow and that Sweden was acting as mediator. That was all. There were no details, and the lobby of the Grand Hotel was filled with journalists trying to get a "line" on the conversations. That night Gordon Young of Reuter's invited Eddie and me to dine with himself and Mr. Erkko, the Finnish Minister to Sweden. Erkko was non-committal, but genial; he gave us champagne and confided nothing. We told him we might return to Helsinki in a day or so, and, as it was impossible to secure seats on the plane without reserving them several days in advance, he offered to get them for us at an hour's notice.

The following day there were more peace rumors. I ran into a Danish journalist—I don't know his name—who told me he was positive an agreement had been reached in Moscow, but was unable to get official confirmation of it. He said that Sweden, intimidated by Germany, had refused to allow the transit of troops from England and France, and had forced the Finns to throw their hand in. Eddie and I had decided to return to Helsinki that night and rang up Mr. Erkko to arrange for the aeroplane seats. Not expecting a reply, but just a parting shot, Eddie said to him: "Is it true that an agreement has been reached in Moscow?" To our astonishment, Erkko replied that it was. (Why he admitted it to Eddie, I never discovered, for he spent the rest of the evening emphatically denying it.)

This gave Eddie a world-wide scoop. He sent a telegram to London which was read over the B.B.C. on the six-o'clock news—the first semi-official report that the Finnish-Russian War had come to an end. We arrived at the Stockholm aerodrome about seven o'clock—an hour later—and heard the people in the waiting-room discussing it. One of the passengers, a Finnish colonel, commented on it angrily. He turned to Eddie and said: "Did you hear the report the B.B.C. is putting out. That fellow—Ward Price, I think his name is—must be crazy. Peace! We'll make peace when the Russians withdraw every last soldier from Finland. And not before!" Eddie agreed and quickly moved away.

When we took off from the aerodrome the lights of Stockholm sparkled like diamonds against the snow and we wondered what price Sweden had paid to keep them blazing. It was a sad trip. Eddie and I were apparently the only passengers who knew what we were returning to, and somehow it seemed to make it worse. I looked at the faces around me, strong, confident faces, and dared not think what the following day would bring. The pilot was the same man who had flown me to Turku two months before. He took the usual precautions of wiring ahead to find if the way was clear, of circling the aerodrome and dropping his flares. In fact, everything was the same except that the trip was slightly more dangerous, for six or seven seats had been ripped out of the plane and the floor packed with boxes marked: "Explosives—Second Class."

We arrived at Turku about midnight and drove to Helsinki the following morning in a bus. Although it was March 12th, the day the peace terms were announced, people were still unaware of what was in store for them. The Turku morning paper carried headlines of the number of Russian planes shot down the previous day. The only item referring to the negotiations was a small box in the corner of the front page announcing that foreign radio stations were reporting a solution had been reached in Moscow. And this was encircled by a large question mark.

166

It didn't seem to attract much attention. The bus was packed with farm girls and road workers with white capes over their clothes, who read the papers casually; they appeared to find nothing unusual in them. We stopped at one of the villages for coffee and the driver told us if the air-raid alarm sounded to climb in the bus as fast as possible so that we could get under way once more before the police stopped us and forced us into a shelter.

We drove up in front of the Hotel Kämp at eleven o'clock, just as the radio was blaring out the announcement that peace had been made. But it was not until an hour later when the Foreign Minister, Mr. Tanner, spoke, that the people of Finland realized they had been defeated.

The shock was staggering. None of them imagined they were even approaching capitulation; and many actually thought it was the Russians who had been forced to come to terms. The people on the streets seemed completely dazed. The Finnish women in the press room broke down and wept and the men turned their faces away. None of the journalists knew what to do. Commiseration seemed hopelessly inadequate. I was so miserable I went downstairs and sat in a corner of the half-empty restaurant. A group of officers came in and took the table next to me. They had the latest edition of the morning paper in which the peace terms were published. They read it silently, then one of them crumpled it up angrily and threw it on the floor. No one spoke. They just sat there staring into space. I went out and walked down the street. The flags of Finland were flying at half-mast.

That same afternoon workmen began replacing the bulbs in the street lamps and ripping down the wooden protections from the shop windows. Otherwise, there was little change in Helsinki. You expect a national crisis to mark itself on the face of a city, but somehow it never does. War or peace, peace or war, life manages to drag on in a more or less routine fashion. People filled the shops, the restaurants, the cinemas, as they always did. The only real contrast was in the Press room. A few days previously it was a scene of wild confusion; now it was almost deserted. The slate which used to announce the time the communiqué would be released was wiped clean, but tacked above it was a slip of paper:

"BOMBING NEWS WILL BE GIVEN OUT AT TWENTY-THREE O'CLOCK."

No one bothered to take it down.

# BLACKOUT IN BERLIN

### by W. B. Courtney

DECEMBER 9, 1939—You came to Germany by a route that gave the sharpest contrast. Last night you were in Sweden, which boasts the largest per capita use of electricity in the world. Sweden has no feeling for back-street lighting; all her ways are great white ways. In her company are the other small neutrals who seek safety through intensified lighting to advertise the happy fact that they are just outside the shadow of war. To aviators, belligerent Europe is like a vast sea of darkness surrounded by a blinding shore of light—Sweden is even brighter than usual.

Today you crossed the mine-peppered waters to Sassnitz. Now, in the twilight, from a swift, clean train you safely behold the autumnal display of lovely Mecklenburg. Look where you may, there are no signs of war, only townspeople and farm people going about their homely tasks. In the vividly dyed bracken, in the fallen leaves scraping about with aimless, puzzled melancholy, in the fiery oaks, yellowing maples, russet-mottled basswoods and beeches, and in the high, flaming chestnuts there are thoughts of home for an American.

At first it all seems a familiar picture of autumnal dusk, but gradually you become aware that it isn't like any other twilight you have ever known. The habits and circumstances of your life heretofore have accustomed you to see lights appear in house and farm, village and city, street and highway, to frustrate the onset of darkness. Here you are watching the advance of night unresisted upon a great civilized nation.

The train slowed considerably when it became pitch-dark but runs steadily at a speed that in daytime would exasperate you but now is chilling. Try running pell-mell across an unlighted, unknown room some night if you want a graphic idea. It's like flying through an ink-pot. You peer and listen intently but there is absolutely no way of telling when you are arriving in Berlin, one of earth's largest and greatest cities. It's a half-hour before the expected time and you sit innocently until a weary conductor finds you with his blue lamp and says, " 'Raus. This is the Stettiner Bahnhof."

Within the station the stairs are ghost-lighted but once you pass into the outer limbo, existence for a forlorn and tongueless stranger becomes formidable. You are one of an amorphous horde bellowing "Taxi" and there are no taxis. Ghastly, luminescent caterpillars crawl by: trolley cars. Incandescent mausoleums roll from anywhere into nowhere: busses. Once every ten minutes something identifiable as a taxi seen by a pair of hang-over eyes zigzags up and becomes instantly the core of a riot in which language if not temperament unfits you for success. Bruised and breathless, even gory, you fear, you sit on your baggage and possess yourself of Yankee guile. Two marks to the paper vender and the night is won. He takes you to one side. *"Bleiben sie hier."* He vanishes. A few minutes later a taxi sneaks past the crowd and halts beside you. The paper boy jumps off the running board, hurls you and your bags in and slams the door. The taxi is off just in advance of the outraged mob that charges down, clutching windows, fenders and tires with wrathful fingers.

You are in Berlin.

Every Berliner has his favorite tale of black-out mix-ups. The blind date, familiar to American college sororities and fraternities, has actuality here. There was the fellow who met his fiancée at a dark corner without taking the trouble to pencil identification on her Gluehwuermchen. When he got her into a lighted café it was the wrong girl but he liked her better and married her.

And there was the married couple that came into the lobby of a famous hotel bickering and with long faces. It seems that in the darkness some passing woman heard his voice and called, "Walter, is that you?" Strangely enough, his name was Walter and he replied honestly. "Oh, darling," said the unseen charmer, "I left a package on the table for you." It was difficult for him to make his wife believe that it must have been some other Walter.

Still all is not comedy on these black streets. While you are enjoying the spirit of lark, adventure and romance that animates people in Berlin tonight, you are sometimes poignantly reminded that, after all, this is war.

As tonight, when you go down Unter den Linden to the Staatsoperhaus, the Rosencavalier is being sung, but you are late and the house is sold out. Under the marquee one faint blue lamp gives the hurrying operagoers the ghastly appearance of truant corpses. You cross the wide avenue, the handsome Via Triumphalis of Berlin, toward where the Doric columns of the Ehrenmal, the war memorial, shield a grotto bathed in an unearthly flush. As you pass in reverently, a woman is coming out. She is in deep widow's mourning. You accept her presence unthinkingly as in past years you have accepted all such women at such memorials, as the bereaved of the last war.

Then suddenly with a jarring shock, you become aware that she is a young woman. The dew of fresh agony lies on cheeks that have not known twenty summers; her tears under this sepulchral light glisten like a mist of crumbled sapphires. This is her war, *now, today*. This war, not the last war.

You are glad to hurry nervously back to your hotel.

# CHRISTMAS IN THE MAGINOT LINE

## by A. J. Liebling

I LEFT Paris on my first "mission" on December 23. I took the noon train to Nancy, which rolled at its peace-time express clip until nightfall, when, because of the dimmed signal lights, it dropped into a cautious crawl. Arriving at Nancy that night, I found the town blacked out completely. Luckily the hotel is directly across the street from the station, so I was able to reach it without any trouble. A woman at the hotel desk told me that the press officer had not arrived yet, but if I cared to step into the *brasserie* of the hotel I would find a number of other American and English correspondents awaiting him. I could immediately distinguish the correspondents in the *brasserie* because their uniforms were much more magnificent than those of the French military at the other tables. A particularly tailored-looking uniform on a photographer for *Life* had the French officers gnawing their mustaches with envy. The most lavishly accoutered man I have seen in France turned out to be an employee of the Columbia Broadcasting System. Since I was trying to get by in riding pants and a vaguely brownish topcoat, I felt like the only ship passenger in a lounge suit at the captain's dinner. I was cheered by the costume of Mr. Browne of the *Christian Science Monitor,* who had come to the war in tweeds. After one look at each other, Browne and I decided to stick together so that we wouldn't feel inferior.

When, early the next afternoon, we got to our station, we could see we had arrived at the war, because there were no women in sight. Here, against a background of brown, frozen earth and sleety roads, of trees covered with rime, and of the ugly, amorphous buildings of a railway junction town, there were only soldiers. Most of the men on our train were *permissionnaires* returning from furlough. They lingered around the railroad station unhappily, like students returning from a holiday, then moved off in the direction of their cantonments. Browne and I didn't bother to look for our officer; we were so incongruous in that crowd that he couldn't possibly miss us. After we had waited a while, an officer stopped in front of us. He had a square jaw and high Celtic cheekbones, and was about as big as a Brooklyn pitcher. "Lieutenant Sauvageon," he announced as he saluted, "aviation officer of the Divisional Staff." Sauvageon stepped aside and we could see another officer behind him, a slight, smiling man who carried a bamboo cane and maintained a monocle in his right eye. Introducing him to us, Sauvageon said, "Captain de Cholet is one of the few cavalrymen in our sector. He is on the staff also." "I have a horse," the Captain said, "but he is in Paris."

A soldier came up, took the one valise in which Browne and I had concentrated our possessions, and carried it to a 1936 Citroën that had a red-and-white-striped pennon on the forward end of the left mudguard. *"Fanion du Général,"* the soldier volunteered pleasantly, pointing to the pennon. The soldier's name, we learned, was Siegfried. It was a standing joke with the Captain and the Lieutenant that Siegfried, who was an Alsatian, had constructed the Siegfried Line. Browne and I rode in the rear with the Captain between us, and the Lieutenant sat in front with Siegfried, who drove. It was about three o'clock in the afternoon. The road was glassy and the mist was very heavy. "Evidently it is not a good day for observation," said the Captain. "Moreover, we are sufficiently distant from anything to observe. Therefore, Lieutenant, where can we buy a drink?" "Siegfried," said the lieutenant, "can you discover the mess of the balloonists?" Siegfried did not answer, but after ten minutes of blind navigation he landed us in front of a shuttered tavern.

We all walked into the taproom, which was decorated with a green tile stove, a Christmas tree, and enough antlers to fit out a small museum. At a heavy, bare table a half-dozen soldiers of the Balloon Corps sat with aniline-dyed apéritifs, wrangling over a card game. A young lieutenant got up from among them to greet us. The officers' mess was upstairs, he explained, but he was the only officer in the house, so he had come down to the bar for company. We invited the lieutenant to join us, and Siegfried took his hand at the card table. We all ordered hot grog, and the drink stimulated Browne to ask the balloonist if he had seen anything of a war which, according to the people in the United States, was at that moment in progress between France and Germany. The lieutenant, it seemed, had actually been under fire. The company had an observation balloon at a nearby field, and twice, when it was up, Messerschmitts had come after it. Both times the ground crew had pulled the bag down safely. Lieutenant Sauvageon said that several German machines had come down in the sector. "Curiously," he added, "three of them were undamaged. The pilots said they were air-sick. We reported them as shot down because we did not want their families to have any trouble in Germany."

We all went into the mess hall to wait for the Colonel, which, we were told, was the warmest place in the fort. There were two clusters of German lances on the wall, left behind by the Imperial Army when the French occupied Alsace. Captain de Cholet looked at them tenderly and said, "I left for the last war carrying a lance. I even managed once to stick a German with one, but later war ceased to be fresh and joyful." Sauvageon nodded sympathetically. Before long the Colonel walked in. He was tall, straight, and consciously prototypical. He wore a brown beret which was barely balanced on the side of his head, like Rodolfo's in "La Bohème." His cheeks were old rose and his eyes cobalt blue, and his long white mustaches did not droop, but descended in a powerful, rhythmic sweep, like the horns of a musk ox. He was an excellent colonel, we had been informed; he had commanded a large part of the heavy artillery in the campaign around Salonika twenty years ago. Between wars he was a banker in Paris.

"Gentlemen," the Colonel said, after we were introduced, "I welcome you to the humble barrack of a sick old man. It is not the Meurice. It is not the Plaza Athénée. The fare is not that of Au Cabaret or the Berkeley." We assured him that his fort would do us very well. A soldier then wheeled over a tea wagon holding about twenty bottles—Scotch, port, sherry, and various apéritifs. The Colonel took an obvious pride in his gamut of alcohols; it proved he could "defend himself." The verb *"se défendre"* has acquired a very broad meaning in the French Army; it signifies "getting along." An officer pulls a pair of old socks over his shoes so that he will not slip on the ice; a private meets a stray hen and wrings her neck because otherwise she might fly into Germany; soldiers going on patrol in wooded parts of no man's land set rabbit snares so that on their way back, if they come back, they may pick up a tasty breakfast—all these expedients are part of the French concept of self-defense. It follows logically that a colonel must defend himself on a grander scale than a subordinate, lest he lose face in this most reasonable of armies.

The dinner was polished off with businesslike haste because there was a full evening ahead of us. After coffee and armagnac, a Christmas mood began to seem less unattainable. We all walked along a corridor and down a flight of stairs to an unused powder vault which the soldiers had turned into a *salle de théâtre*. The walls of the vault had been painted to give a three-dimensional illusion of draperies, and at one end of the room there was a real curtain of the same color as the painted ones. A surgeon major said to me, "A Frenchman is a funny mechanism. He has a job, let us say, in a handbag factory. He is mobilized. You say to him, 'Fire a cannon.' He fires the cannon. 'Decorate a theater.' He decorates you a theater. 'A soup.' It's not bad, the soup. We are an adaptable people."

The party broke up at five o'clock in the morning. The only officer who seemed mildly unhappy was a gangling, thin-lipped captain, a transfer from the regular Army, who said to the Colonel doubtfully, "This is all very well, my Colonel, but it isn't really war." The Colonel, whose chest was covered with campaign ribbons and decorations from 1914-1918, stopped chuckling and looked at the captain steadily. "Sometime you may look back on this evening," he said, "and you will say, 'The days at the fort were the good ones.' What the devil! A fellow has to defend himself."

# FRENCH REASONING

## by Edmond Taylor

FEBRUARY 16, 1940—"Vreni and I dined this evening with my friend C. D., a young doctor. His reactions toward the war are very interesting. C. D. has always had strong Left-wing leanings—anarchist rather than communist—and a few years ago he was a militant pacifist, but he is not an apostle of non-violence. Before and after Munich he was violently *anti-Munichois;* during the Spanish war he favored intervention on the side of the loyalists. He is, moreover, completely honest, very well-informed, and extremely intelligent, a little impulsive in his judgments, but never naïve or bigoted. Brave also, I think. Therefore what he says carries considerable weight with me, when he is giving his opinion and when he is talking as an observer. Somewhat to my surprise, he is anything but enthusiastic about the war. Doesn't see victory except after frightful massacres which will leave Europe a shambles. It would be better to talk now than after two or three million men have been killed, he says. Only he is realistic about it, realizes the difficulties of a negotiation with Hitler. Seeing no way out of the dilemma, he pins his hopes, somewhat childishly, it seems to me, on America, not for intervention but for mediation. He questioned me a lot about Sumner Welles's forthcoming trip—as if I knew anything.

"In the provinces, where he has been mobilized since the beginning of the war, C. D. says people are not exactly defeatist, they just aren't interested in the war. If the war gets serious, he says, they will fight on as long as the generals can take it, but if there is a compromise peace there will be no complaints, *au contraire.*

"'What do they think of Bonnet?' I asked.

"'Bonnet is unpopular. They don't think of him as the man who wanted to compromise rather than fight, but simply as the man who failed to avert war.'

"'And Daladier?'

"'Daladier they think pretty highly of [a general sentiment in the country, as far as I can gather], but not because of the war, just because he has been tough with the Communists.'

"Here C. D. went into one of his impulsive flights, partly true but considerably exaggerated, I believe. According to him, hatred of communism is the strongest political force in France, stronger even than the conviction for war or the desire for peace. In the provinces they think of nothing else. The big war aim is not the smashing of Germany or even Russia, but the smashing of communism in France. They are not terribly excited about Soviet Russia and are only lukewarm for aid to Finland, they just want to go for the French Communists.

"'Daladier did the Communists a favor by putting them in jail,' C. D. says.

"Though he has always been rather anti-Communist himself, C. D. is disgusted with this movement, which he attributes to the ignoble fear, based on avarice, of the French peasant and *petit bourgeois*. I gather it is one of the reasons why he is fed up with the war.

"Regarding the English, whom he does not like particularly, C. D. says that in the early days of the war there was a great wave of anti-British sentiment throughout the country, but that it has largely died down, owing to the activity of the British fleet. Not so much the British naval victories as their disasters, their losses, are responsible for the improved feeling. 'After all, we are not the only ones who are getting killed in this war.'

"Interesting footnote on wartime psychology contributed by C. D.: there was one raid of German scouting planes in his region—the southwest. No one saw the planes, but they were picked up by sound-detectors. They were not fired upon or chased. Yet a few days later officers censoring the soldiers' outgoing mail fell upon scores of vivid descriptions of air battles, bombs falling all around them, etc.

"C. D. is the second respectable defeatist—what I call respectable—that I have met since the war. Rather I should say the third, counting in an English friend in Paris. The other one was also a doctor, a man of very similar formation to C. D. but older and a deeper student of the human mind. He was even more categorical than C. D. about the necessity of a negotiation.

"I find all this somewhat disconcerting. My own political convictions do not derive either from an unshakable faith in any particular ideology or from mass movements, but rather from the way in which certain of my friends, men whom I respect both for character and intelligence, apply the general principles, the world outlook which I share with them, to specific political situations. Now it seems that my friends are divided as to what to do about the war. Some think it must be fought to victory regardless of cost; others think it does not matter so much how it ends provided it ends quickly.

Fortunately, this division does not yet involve any great bitterness. When a defeatist meets a bitter-ender they do not even argue, merely express tangent points of view and trail off into a shrug. The reason: the bitter-ender does not feel proud in anticipation of his victory, and the defeatist does not feel proud of his negotiated peace. Each chooses what he considers the lesser evil."

# FRENCH MORALE

## by Clare Boothe

IN the final analysis the morale of the French was just a national attitude of confidence based on the reasonable expectation of victory. The morale of a surrounded garrison that dies to the last man, the morale of a Christian on the rack, the morale of missionary bands boiled in foreign oil in foreign lands by barbarian skeptics, *is* something different. One man in a thousand has that. We have words for such men: heroes and saints—and crusaders. A nation is never composed entirely of heroes and saints. And with the exception of the German nation's own perverse crusade for a thousand years of German *Kultur,* and German economy, there is today certainly no nation of crusaders. But the French have never prided themselves on being saints and heroes and crusaders. They are above all, as they will always tell you, *hommes raisonnables.* So when France's reasonable expectation of victory no longer seemed *raisonnable,* their morale vanished—and they laid down their arms and surrendered.

Now, what, in turn, was that "reasonable expectation" based on?

Three things: One, the popular uncritical belief that "History repeats itself," and that therefore the history of the last war would repeat itself. (And the history of the last war was that Time won for the Allies. In 1914 the Allies were disorganized and unprepared. But Time, working exclusively for them, ultimately assured them of victory. Now, better prepared, better organized, had not Time, the beneficent, omnipotent genie of Democracy, already been working for them on twenty-four-hour shifts for the seven months of the Sitzkrieg?)

Two, the less popular, more criticized, but still major faith in the *ultimate* efficiency of the traditional democratic-capitalistic economic process itself, even against that formidable new contender in the economic world—totalitarianism.

And, three, a blind confidence in France's army in being, and France's system of defense (in England, the counterpart of this was England's faith in the navy, and England's blockade system.)

An acceptance of these three tenets of faith added up to an even more than reasonable expectation of victory.

To be sure, the three tenets which made up the creed of victory were not separate articles of faith—they derived their power to convince, or to convert, syllogistically, one from the other: If you *believe* you have time, your doubts about the slow, bumbling nature of the democratic economic process are comparatively unimportant. If you *believe* in your present system of defense, these same doubts are still a pardonable heresy which time (in which you do believe) will cause you to recant. Believe in any *one* of these three tenets, and you find yourself eventually embracing all of them. The Frenchman who denied all three was either a Hitler agent, a defeatist, or, at best, *pas raisonnable*.

So everywhere in March you heard Frenchmen saying to one another and to Americans: "At the end of the last war we had ten times as many guns and raw materials—and even men—as we began with." But, you slyly asked (being American), where, at the end, did they come from? And they said: "From our own factories, slowly but inexorably mobilized for war industry, from the factories of our Allies—well, from America." And then at this point you were always told (as you pleasantly expected to hear) that the nation or nations which could command America's industrial output ("Never mind its man output, we'll never need it") were unconquerable. There was regrettably one immediate barrier to the Allies' free access to America's industrial output: the Johnson Act. But it was only a question of *time*, every Frenchman argued, before the Johnson Act would be repealed. "Why are you so sure it will be repealed?" you often heard yourself asking. And every Frenchman said: "Because in *time* you will realize this is your war!"

And right there you both stopped talking either current or future Allied war-industry output and began passionately to talk American domestic politics and American foreign policy.

Sometimes Frenchmen, instead of explaining to you why democratic economy must win the war in time, explained why totalitarian economy must lose it in time. Oil, iron, ore, timber, wheat, and butter fats were the theme song of all that. Hitler didn't have much now, couldn't get more, was gradually using up what he had (and if he became desperate enough to attack, would use them all up with fatal rapidity). With a paper and a pencil you could prove that on any French restaurant tablecloth, just the way people were proving it at home.

Look, if Rumania (oil) turned against him, if Stalin (wheat) made trouble in the Balkans, if Norway (timber), if Sweden (ore) or Holland (fat) veered further toward England, if Italy (the big leak in the blockade) could be bullied or bribed or merely awakened to its own "enlightened self-interest," well, the jig was up with Herr Hitler and Company. And as the first neutral went, so would go all the other neutrals. And weren't all these things, in March, well within the realm of possibility?

So many Frenchmen said: "Anyone can see that if Hitler doesn't attack now, at the peak of his strength, he's doomed." And when you asked: "Then why doesn't he attack now?" they replied, with vast logical Gallic shrugs: "Undoubtedly because he knows he's doomed anyway."

So, the stalemate on the western front was widely explained as "Hitler's realization of the economic impasse he's got himself into." His constant threat of an offensive was "just his last war of nerves; he hopes to wear us down nervously, and either force *us* to attack (which we won't do) or wait for French internal dissension (much overrated since the declaration of war) to breed a favorable atmosphere in which he can make peace overtures." In early March a Hitler-inspired peace, a Mussolini appeasement move, was very much the topic of indignant French conversation. The visit of my friend Mr. Sumner Welles, his over-cordial reception by Mussolini, his long hours with Hitler, gave much credence to this supposition. But these expected peace proposals, however violently debated, were questions of only academic interest to most Frenchmen. They were in no mood, in March, to discuss Mr. Hitler's peace proposals. *Il faut en finir* first was their motto. Afterwards "We talk peace—*our* peace," they said to you. Still, thinking on peace, with all its problems (which were, in March, infinitely more perplexing and numerous and even harrowing than the problems of war), you again began to talk Allied foreign policy and domestic politics.

And so while in March everybody posed the urgent question: "Will the coming of spring bring a great offensive on the western front?"—or "Hitler's much vaunted hammer blow," as the London *Times* called it—nobody really worried very much about the outcome of that offensive.

# LAST DAY OF THE PHONY WAR

### by Edward R. Murrow

LONDON, April 8, 1940:

Not for a long time has London had a day like today. That something-is-going-to-happen atmosphere that marked the early days of the war has returned. Gas masks, pretty well discarded during recent months, began to appear again this afternoon. The day's news, while it may not herald the beginning of a *Blitzkrieg,* certainly marked the end of the winter-long *Sitzkrieg.* The British press and radio are unanimous in approving the mining of Norwegian territorial waters. The Norwegians have protested. If Norway sweeps up the mine fields, Britain will plant them again. If the Germans try to clear a channel or initiate a naval engagement, well, nothing would please the British more. One thing is certain, and that is no matter how strongly Norway or any other neutral protests, the British aren't going to pick up those mines and bring them home again.

No one here seems to be particularly worried about the outcome of this new phase of the war. It's a job for the Navy and the confidence of the British in their Navy is supreme. It is admitted here that Britain has violated international law and that she had signed an agreement with Norway permitting that country to trade freely with Germany. But the British maintain that they had sufficient provocation for the action. They deny that the Allies desire to extend the war to Scandinavia. Norway, they say, did not defend her neutrality with sufficient vigor—and that's that.

This is not the first violation of neutral sovereignty, nor is it likely to be the last. Earlier wars were like boxing—hitting only with the fists and above the belt. This one is rapidly reaching the point where nothing is barred—teeth, feet, heads, toes, and fingers will be used by all belligerents; anything to get at a vulnerable part of the opponent's anatomy.

According to the latest reports received in London, a considerable German naval force, estimated at between ninety and one hundred ships, is moving out of the Baltic. This force is said to be composed mainly of mine sweepers and trawlers. Unofficially London claims that British submarines have accounted for two German ships today—a 12,000-ton tanker and a troop ship believed to have been carrying three thousand men; half of them were drowned. A German merchantman and a U-boat are also believed to have been accounted for. All these naval actions took place in or near Norwegian waters. There are unconfirmed rumors that Berlin has told Norway to sweep up those Allied mines or suffer the consequences. There are also rumors that the British fleet has entered the Baltic. But whether it has or not, and probably it hasn't, German planes bombed Scapa Flow again tonight.

Today in the British Foreign Office—that big, gray smoke-grimed building in Downing Street, just opposite Mr. Chamberlain's residence—eight British ambassadors have been meeting with Lord Halifax. The results of these talks with Britain's diplomats from Russia, Italy, and the Balkans will probably be conveyed to the House of Commons in its secret session on Thursday. But it is safe to assume that each man is asking for pretty much the same thing—more loans, more trade, more propaganda for the country to which he is accredited. Buy up the Balkans. If they're determined to remain neutral, Britain must do everything possible to prevent them from supplying Germany with goods. The doing of that will put a tremendous strain upon British economy, and even if it can be done, the price must be paid by a lowering of the standard of living of the masses of this country.

While the diplomats talk and the Navy stands guard over its new mine fields, a Gallup survey claims that the British public would prefer Mr. Anthony Eden above all others as Prime Minister if Mr. Chamberlain should retire. Winston Churchill is a close second, with Lord Halifax third. Clement Attlee, leader of the opposition, and Mr. David Lloyd George follow in that order. This survey, which claims to be an accurate cross section, shows that during the last year Churchill has gained and Eden has lost. The young ex-Foreign Secretary, who has been cautious and correct since he left office, leads Mr. Churchill by only 3 per cent as the nation's favorite successor to Neville Chamberlain.

# Part Four: The Débâcle

\* \* \*

LONDON, April 9, 1940 (Associated Press): A dispatch by the Reuters (British) News Agency today quoted the Oslo radio as announcing that German troops disembarked at Norwegian ports at 3 A.M.

\* \* \*

## WAR IN NORWAY

### by Leland Stowe

IT was the first week of April, 1940, and I had an airplane reservation to fly to Riga on Wednesday. Friends said Riga was wonderful in the spring and after the strain of Finland all I wanted was to go some place where there would be plenty of sunshine and nothing much would be likely to happen. Nevertheless, the Norwegians and the British were still arguing about the naval blockade business. Perhaps it would be wiser to go to Oslo first, just in case something should happen. I sounded out my foreign editor by cable and he was of the same opinion. So I'd have to wait awhile before discovering Riga in the spring, and Edmund Stevens of the *Christian Science Monitor* was in the same boat.

"I think we'd better get to Oslo first," I said to Steve. "Supposing we're bobbing around off the Norwegian coast when something pops loose in Oslo. Maybe the Norwegians will tell the British to go hang themselves. We won't know anything about it and we won't be able to file a story for days. I'm going straight to Oslo. If things quiet down we can come back by way of Narvik."

So Steve and I were in Oslo on Thursday night, April 4, and the only other American correspondent in Norway at that time, Otto Tolischus of the *New York Times*, assured us before leaving for Stockholm that the story was "all washed up" and we had arrived too late. We weren't so sure about that and anyway we wanted to find out about Norway's shipping problems, what the war had done to her cost of living, and lots of things like that. Prices were certainly high in Oslo, much the same as in Stockholm; but the young Norwegians seemed to be having a good time and the beer cellar of the Grand Hotel was crowded with finely built young men and with girls who maintained the Scandinavian standards for schoolgirl complexions and good looks. We noticed plenty of Germans were stopping at the Grand, too; much the same sort of mysterious businessmen and "tourists" we were accustomed to see in the Stockholm hotels, except that they appeared even more energetic here. One big, smartly dressed and handsomely proportioned fellow we noticed particularly. He was always buzzing in and out with a fat briefcase under his arm, and he had with him a sleek blonde fräulein who looked like a mannequin and acted like the first cousin of the Queen of Sheba. She was a blonde eyeful, in the fullest sense of the term, and whenever her boy friend introduced her to the Norwegians with whom he was constantly conferring she always attracted a proper amount of attention.

We remarked incidentals like these during the cocktail hours, but we kept busy interviewing people until Sunday evening.

The British mined the shore waters between Narvik and Bergen that same night. Lucky we hadn't taken the Narvik route. We were the only foreign correspondents in Oslo at that moment and Oslo was seething with excitement and anxiety.

At the Foreign Office that Monday morning a press spokesman cast official reticence to the winds. "After this, hell is let loose," he declared grimly. That evening we went to the Storting (parliament) and heard Dr. Koht, Norway's Foreign Minister, protest against Britain's "open violation" of Norwegian neutrality. Newspaper extras were hawked on the streets all day and all evening, but at midnight the dance halls were still crowded with students and youngsters improvising swing steps with gleeful abandon and astonishing gusto. Their gaiety, so strangely heedless of the day's news, actually increased our own feeling of uneasiness. "Maybe there'll be five hundred German bombers over this city before the week is out," I said. We were scarcely in bed when a terrific honking broke loose over the city and Steve came rushing in shouting: "You hear that? It's an air alarm." We waited for half an hour or more and nothing happened. Probably it was a test alarm intended to make Osloans more serious-minded. There was nothing we could do at this hour anyway. So we went to bed. The crazy honking alarm woke me up several times, but I had had enough sleep ruined by sirens and there would be too much work to do in the morning in any event. On that latter point I was certainly correct. This was the morning of April 9.

About seven o'clock another alarm destroyed my last effort to doze, but nothing could be seen in the sky from my bedroom window. I started down the corridor to get some papers and stumbled into Orho Toivola, formerly the Finnish press chief in Helsinki. Toivola was plenty excited.

"Have you heard the news? The Germans presented an ultimatum at five o'clock this morning. They're occupying all Norwegian ports. Parliament has just met."

"What? What in hell—?"

"Yes, yes. The King and the royal family are leaving. The government is evacuating to Hamar. Parliament has voted unanimously to resist. All hell has cut loose. They say they're fighting now down the fjord."

We woke up Steve, and then he and I pumped Toivola, who was leaving at once to follow the government. I ordered my breakfast and started to dress. Then came the familiar roar of big bombers, but louder and nearer than I'd ever heard them in Finland. It was seven forty-five A.M. I leaped to the window just as Steve ran in crying: "Here they are. Here they come. My God, look at them." They were five huge tri-motored planes with engines wide open, slicing down within five hundred feet of the rooftops across the park—straight toward our hotel. They roared like hungry lions. We could see the German crosses beneath their wings.

From that time on, the Nazi bombers, sometimes five but sometimes three or only one, roof-hopped over the city every fifteen or twenty minutes for the next three hours. All the while thousands of people stood in knots along the streets and watched curiously. They didn't seem to have any idea what one bomb could do. Something had happened that had never happened to Norwegians for more than a hundred years. War had come to Norway; and war was something utterly incomprehensible to these peace-loving people because they had never believed it could possibly happen to them. We could see this stunned look of incomprehension in their upturned faces. We saw it all that day and for several days to come.

One of the first things I did that morning was to telephone Mrs. Day Adams Morgenstierne, the young American wife of a Norwegian engineer. On the day before, I had made an arrangement for her to do newspaper translations for me and we had picked a wonderful hour for her to begin— nine o'clock on Tuesday morning, April 9. She had heard Foreign Minister Koht announce the government's departure by radio at eight thirty and she also told me the Norwegian Admiralty had an extraordinary communiqué on the air every fifteen minutes. "The Admiralty says that five large German warships and two small ones have forced their way through the outer fortifications of Oslo fjord," Mrs. Morgenstierne said breathlessly.

"But your people must have had mines out," I protested.

"Of course, you'd think so. But I don't know. Anyhow, the Admiralty says one German warship forced its way past the Oskarsborg fortress and then foundered at Digerud—"

"Foundered where? No, never mind. I'll check on that later. What else?"

"They say the Germans have seized Bergen and Narvik and it's possible they're in Trondheim."

"My God! How in the devil could they take Narvik and Trondheim? And even if it's true, why is the Norwegian Admiralty telling the whole country things like that?"

"I don't know, but that's what they say—and the radio is warning everybody in Oslo to fill every household receptacle with water, so as to be prepared to fight fires."

From that moment we heard nothing except an endless succession of the wildest rumors, but by eleven o'clock the skies were totally empty of planes. What did that mean? No one could figure it out. We kept waiting for squadrons and squadrons of Nazi bombers, but they never came. We had never seen more than five planes, and apparently the same five planes.

Where were the Germans? Nobody knew. The Norwegians were already asking: "Where are the British?" Only fourteen hours before, their government had been berating the British for violating Norway's neutrality by sowing mine fields to keep German ships from getting through to Narvik. Now people were asking: "Why don't the British come?" And so were Steve and I.

Coming out of the restaurant at half past two, I walked over to ask the porter about something and he said: "Aren't you going out to see the Germans come in?"

"What? What did you say? The Germans—"

"Sure. They're going to march up the Karl Johansgade any minute now."

I yelled to Irv and Steve and we rushed out the door into a mob which completely obstructed the sidewalk. I pushed my way through and landed smack up against a burly fellow in a field-gray uniform. The uniform was German all right and so was he. He looked and acted like Victor McLaglen suffering from an acute case of distemper. He was waving his arms and shouting orders at several big Oslo policemen. Well, his uniform was unmistakably German, but he was shouting in excellent Norwegian.

It was difficult to estimate, but by three o'clock we thought there must be twenty or thirty thousand people along this route. About ten minutes earlier two open trucks crept slowly up the Karl Johansgade. Each contained two machine-guns and behind each gun a German soldier was stretched out prone. They held the guns ready for action and looked eloquently business-like. The crowd, staring after them, had a full view of those narrow-mouthed little guns, and the murmur of their talk suddenly died away.

At three minutes after three the rumble of the crowd, far down the boulevard, suddenly warned us that the Germans were coming at last. We saw a thin column, marching three abreast, swing into the Karl Johansgade at the foot of the palace hill. Six mounted Norwegian policemen led the way. We could scarcely believe our eyes. They were escorting the Germans in, and here they came. Directly behind the mounted police strode a German general and two other officers. We later learned that the commander was General Nikolaus von Falkenhorst. The German regulars marched behind them—three abreast to make the line look longer—granite-faced and loaded with equipment. Some had machine guns on their shoulders and others carried rifles, also slung on their shoulders.

They were hard-muscled and they had lots of iron in their faces, the coolest cucumbers I have ever seen in uniform anywhere. Some of them could not restrain triumphant smiles. But what we noticed particularly was the fact that the three Nazi officers, out in front, occasionally acknowledged Hitler salutes from persons in the crowd. Evidently the Nazi advance agents were all on hand to welcome them, and there were plenty of up-raised palms on our own hotel balcony.

For a victory parade it was extremely short and over very quickly. Less than fifteen hundred German soldiers had occupied Norway's capital while thousands of dazed, bewildered citizens looked dumbly on. Not a bomb had been dropped inside Oslo. Not a shot was fired. Not a hand or a voice had been lifted—and not a single Nazi soldier had yet reached this captured city by ship. This handful of troops had arrived by air, since daybreak that morning. They had only small weapons—but absolutely incredible discipline and nerve. They were an amazingly tiny band of men, but they marched in like conquerors. They were.

About four thirty that afternoon we heard the radio announce the formation of a "Quisling national government" and then we heard Major Vidkun Quisling himself—the man who had significantly returned from Berlin on Saturday, when the plot was ready to be sprung; the man who was the foremost traitor of his country, just as Seyss-Inquart had been in Austria. Quisling's language was Norwegian, but his tone was electrifyingly that of Berlin. "This," he boomed forth, "is a responsible government which has deposed party politicians.... Anyone who does not comply will be considered a criminal."

Now the clock rolls back to shortly after one thirty on the morning of April 9. Three Norwegian naval ships lie off Horten's base in Oslo fjord. Their commander suddenly receives an urgent order, supposedly direct from the Norwegian government or from Foreign Minister Koht. (Just how this order was transmitted and by whose authority has never been definitely established, but its transmission cannot be doubted.) The commander is told that German warships are coming up the fjord very soon. He is ordered not to resist, but to put all his men ashore at once—without arms of any kind. Apparently the commander does not question the authenticity of this order. At any rate, he carries it out. But the order is for the three war vessels which persons in Oslo knew were lying off Horten. It does not include the mine-layer, *Olaf Trygvason,* because she had unexpectedly come in for repairs after nightfall on Monday night. Simultaneously, according to later testimony of Norwegian naval men, somebody in the naval control base at Oskarsborg disconnected the electric mines which were strewn in front of the narrows. Aside from the presence of the *Olaf Trygvason,* the first stage in the plot is functioning perfectly down Oslo fjord.

At half past three that morning a group of men assembles on the quay of Oslo's inner harbor, apparently without attracting the slightest attention from the capital's police. The group is headed by Dr. Brauer, Germany's Minister to Norway. Most of the German legation staff are with him, as well as expectant Nazi newspapermen who are eagerly waiting to obtain exclusive eyewitness accounts of a story that will astonish the world. They have been told that Germany's powerful cruiser, the *Blücher,* will dock in Olso harbor at four fifteen sharp; that she will bring a major general and the general staff of Germany's expeditionary force to Norway, together with fifteen hundred troops. According to Berlin's audacious plan, the Norwegian government will not receive the slightest warning about what has happened until after all troops have disembarked from the *Blücher.* Then King Haakon and the members of the government will be captured as they leap, startled and bewildered, from their beds. But four fifteen comes and the impatient German reception committee on the quay begins to have fearful doubts. By five o'clock it is clear that something has gone wrong. At last Dr. Brauer, boldly deciding to rely upon bluff as a last and only resort, calls upon Norway's Foreign Minister and delivers Berlin's ultimatum—just as if the *Blücher* and German troops were already in the city. Whatever may have gone strangely and inexplicably amiss down Oslo fjord, Dr. Brauer is certain that the plot must succeed in other Norwegian ports. In any case, the essence of a gigantic gamble is to gamble through to the very end.

But it is now four thirty A.M. down at Horten. The cruiser Emden and two German submarines steam confidently up toward the naval base. The three Norwegian war vessels give no sign of life. It looks as if the incredible plot would work to perfection. But over to one side, almost too small to notice, lies the little mine-layer—obviously of no consequence. So the *Emden* glides forward, sensing her overwhelming strength; glides forward until she is almost abreast of the *Olaf Trygvason*. Then the tiny *Olaf* lets go with her Bofors guns, a terrific point-blank blast of explosives. The *Emden* keels over and has almost disappeared when another round from the *Olaf* dooms one of the submarines. Then the astonished Norwegian commander orders the mine-layer to run up a white flag. Another warship, presumably the *Blücher,* comes up. About a hundred marines are landed; a brief one-sided exchange of shots, and Horten is captured. The Norwegian sailors, most of them unarmed, stand dumbfounded and helpless, asking one another: "Why did they tell us not to fight?"

Shortly afterward the *Blücher,* with its invaluable cargo of expeditionary corps commanders and approximately fifteen hundred men, proceeds into the narrows. Of course, that insignificant little mine-layer has caused a nasty hitch. Perhaps the German admiral on the *Blücher's* bridge is somewhat anxious now, but the mighty cruiser slips serenely into the narrows and all aboard are counting upon Oskarsborg's big guns having been spiked by treachery. Now the dark hulk of the *Blücher* looms straight in front of Oskarsborg, much closer than eight hundred yards. Inside the old but granite-padded fortress an unknown Norwegian artillery officer gives a sharp command. The guns belch deafeningly. Their shells strike just above the cruiser's waterline. In less than five minutes the *Blücher* plunges to the bottom, carrying with her all but fifty or sixty of the hundreds of Germans on board. The original commander-in-chief of the Nazi army of occupation is gone. So is his general staff. So is the admiral. So are the troops which should have captured Norway's King and Norway's capital. All because of a Norwegian officer, inside Oskarsborg, who remained faithful to his duty and could not be bought. The *Emden* and a German submarine are also gone, because the officers and crew of the *Olaf Trygvason* were too alert and courageous to be betrayed as other brave men had been betrayed. These two hitches in an otherwise perfect conspiracy have placed the Nazi invaders in a most dangerously tight place, but unfortunately for Norway, only the Germans know that this is true—and the Nazis long ago became experts in the game of bluff. Having failed to seize Oslo by sea, they do not need more than a few bombs and planes to seize Fornebu airport from the air. Then fifteen hundred men are landed from air transports in the course of a single morning and Oslo is occupied, through sheer nerve coupled with clocklike efficiency. So, for the first time, a nation's capital is taken by air-borne troops.

British troops had landed at Namsos. Mylander and I found ourselves at Asp, persuading a handsome, tired-eyed British major to give us passes to go into Steinkjer, which had just been plastered by Nazi planes a couple of hours earlier. Our borrowed car splashed, sloshed, and careened southward as fast as any human being could drive it under such conditions. In twenty-five minutes we rounded a curve on the brow of a hill and suddenly looked down upon a masterpiece of the twentieth century's newest art. There, along the tip of the fjord and tucked in the slanting palm of the spruce-covered, snowbound hills, lay the blackened and burning skeleton of Steinkjer. Until Sunday, which was yesterday, some four thousand peaceful Norwegians had lived here and no war had touched this town in several hundred years. Now not a soul remained inside Steinkjer. We looked down into the center of the town upon the scarred black fingers of scores of chimneys. To our right tongues of fire darted skyward along the water-front and billows of black smoke obscured the ice beyond.

A young British soldier, a Scot, was standing guard where the road dipped down into the town. Of course we had heard the shooting. The crisp crackle of machine-gun fire seemingly came from the hills below and beyond the smoking ruins. Sometimes a cannon boomed and the echoes rolled back and forth bafflingly. "The Jerries have got a destroyer or something over there and are shelling from the fjord," the soldier said, after he had examined our pass. "If you're going down into the town you'd better not stay there long. It's getting hot on the other side there." We climbed into the car. "Don't stay longer than just time enough to take the pictures," he warned.

Rubble and black ruins were on all sides of us. The odor, mixed with the smell of hundreds of burned-out buildings, gathered thickly in our nostrils. It was everywhere, heavy and repulsive. The Nazis had used plenty of incendiaries all right. We remained for more than half an hour. Then the dusk was too deep for any more pictures. At the top of the hill the Scots corporal was still standing guard alone and he came up to us with anxiety unconcealed on his face.

"You're going back to battalion headquarters, aren't you?" he asked. "Listen. This is terribly important. Please see Major Godfrey or Major Sinclair right away. Tell them the fighting is getting nearer all the time. Tell them only one lorry has come through. Say I'm waiting for instructions—that I'm still waiting for instructions and I need them immediately. Tell any officer you see. Go as fast as you can."

Then we started back up the road toward Kvam, where the Red Cross colonel had been assembling his cots in a movie hall, designed to become a base hospital. As we rode I scratched in my notebook: "Trondheim won't be captured soon." But I didn't begin to know how true that was at that time. We drove on until we must have been twenty miles from Steinkjer and, having lost more than an hour at Asp, it was now half past ten at night. Frequently we got stuck in mudholes and sometimes caught in a jam behind other cars which were bogged down. Finally we had to halt again, this time behind a truck full of soldiers. A British lieutenant jumped off the truck and came back to us. We could see his agitation in his walk and on his face. When I hailed him and explained I was an American newspaperman, he burst forth in a torrent of words.

"We've been massacred—simply massacred. It's the planes. We've got no planes. The Jerries have been bombing us all afternoon—and shelling us on our right flank from the fjord. It's been bloody awful, I tell you. ... Yes, we were fighting in front of Steinkjer, at Vist. We only had one battalion of 600. I think we must have had over 200 killed or wounded. I don't know how many we've got left. Maybe 150. We're fleeing. We're going north. We hope to re-form up there somewhere. There's nothing else to do."

Paul and I listened in stupefied amazement. We had left Steinkjer only a couple of hours before. These men had been fighting below Steinkjer. Now they were ahead of us, northbound on the road, and miles beyond their own battalion headquarters. They must have come right through Asp without stopping. Things must be in an awful state.... But another Britisher, a non-com, was talking feverishly now: "The Jerries would send over six planes. They'd drop signal flares. Then their artillery, on the destroyers in the fjord, knew all our positions. Then the Jerries would come back with bombs. We've got no anti-air guns and we have no field pieces. We could hear our wounded crying in the woods, but we couldn't get to them. It was bloody hell...." Now the lieutenant cut in once more: "We've got no proper clothes for these mountains. We've got no white capes. The Jerries could see us everywhere in the snow. They just mowed our men down. I tell you it's that bloody Chamberlain, and that bloody Oliver Stanley. They made Stanley Minister of War just because his father's got a title. I wish to God I could write a letter to the *Daily Telegraph*. We've got to have Hore-Belisha back."

Now half a dozen survivors of the battle at Vist were pouring forth the incredible details of their disaster. They said only two British battalions had been landed at Namsos, a battalion of Territorials and another battalion of the King's Own Yorkshire Light Infantry. Only one battalion had been in this engagement, and their officers thought at least one company had been cut off and captured. "It was just a bloody slaughter and it got worse after dark. There was nothing we could do but get out." I asked the lieutenant how long he had been in service. He replied that he'd been in since March of the previous year. "We're not regulars," he said. "I'm glad you're a reporter. For God's sake, tell them we've got to have airplanes and anti-air guns. Tell them everything we've said. That's the only thing that will do any good." I asked the lieutenant where the French were. "We don't know where the French are. We haven't seen any. We have no contacts," he said. And a young Territorial, covered with mud and grime, chimed in: "What can you expect with a bloody old fool like Chamberlain? If they don't get rid of him soon, we'll all be done in."

# ALLIES EVACUATE NAMSOS

### by Edmund Stevens

MAY 3, 1940—The re-embarkation and departure "for an unknown destination" of the Anglo-French expeditionary force at Namsos during the past 48 hours was announced here today.

This event, immediately following a similar withdrawal from Andalsnes in southern Norway appears to write a sudden finis to the Allied military fiasco in Norway.

True it is only one sector of the war as a whole. But it is the first major contest and the Allies have shown themselves no match for the German war machine either in the air or on land, while British naval superiority has proved powerless to affect the tactical issue.

The Allies left Andalsnes and Namsos because they were literally blasted out by the German air force. At Namsos the harbor was so completely wrecked by successive bombings that it was physically impossible to land guns, ammunition and supplies and the Allies' warships were prevented from entering and operating in Namsos-fjord by German flyers.

The Allied troops were thus placed in imminent danger of being cut off. The re-embarking operations were constantly harried by the German planes, which scored a direct hit on the British destroyer *Bittern*. An American eye-witness of this event with whom I talked by phone this morning said that 30 of the *Bittern's* men were killed and 60 injured. A party of foreign journalists who arrived in Namsos two days ago were surprised to find re-embarkations operations already in full preparation.

The journalists were arrested by the military authorities and later were released on parole, having promised they would not reveal the news until after the re-embarkation had been completed.

The first to leave were the French Chausseurs Alpins, who shoved off the night before.

The British departed last night.

Two American cameramen and an Associated Press correspondent left with the British forces and are now passengers aboard a British cruiser.

Today Namsos and Andalsnes are empty and all that remains of the Allies' "rapid and effective aid to Norway" is wreckage.

Yesterday the Swastika was hoisted over Andalsnes, but south of Namsos, where the road to Steinkjer skirts the shores of Snasen lake, Norwegian forces were still holding up the German avalanche.

It was the brave action of these Norwegian regulars under Colonel Getz that covered the Allies' re-embarkation operation. The Norwegians, thus abandoned to their fate, are naturally bitter, but this morning Lieutenant Dahl, in charge of the Norwegian press office, told newspapermen that the Norwegians in this district intend to continue their resistance.

However, with the Allies gone and the Germans now able to hurl the full force of their shock troops northward, the fate of these last Norwegian defenders is sealed. Thus the war in Norway is at an end except for the operations in the Narvik area.

\* \* \*

AMSTERDAM, May 10, 1940 (United Press): Germany invaded Holland and Belgium early today. Land troops being preceded by ... the landing of parachute troops at a number of points ...

PARIS, May 12 (Associated Press): ... The German High Command claimed the capture ... of Eben Emael, strongest fort in the Liége chain.

ROTTERDAM, May 11 (United Press): Tremendous fires blazed in this beleaguered city tonight.... Near the right bank of the Nieuwe Maas ... the Holland-American liner Statendam ... was on fire ... Parachute troops were dropped by the hundreds today....

\* \* \*

# THE BREAK-THROUGH AT THE MEUSE

## by M. W. Fodor

THE *Blitzkrieg* took us by surprise—but did it? And if so, why? We had had plenty of warning. Responsible French quarters had long known that the attack on France was certain to come, and that it would come across the Low Countries.

Why did France and the two Netherlands not attempt by all means in their power to forestall the German move? The answer is a tragic story of lack of statesmanship in the Low Countries, of the refusal of King Leopold of Belgium and Queen Wilhelmina of Holland to conclude alliances with the western Powers or to make suitable military arrangements between the respective general staffs. Other factors in the story were incompetence, inefficiency, treason, Fifth-Column activity in the Low Countries as well as in France.

For at least two years, the Low Countries had realized that they were continuously exposed to the danger of a sudden German attack. Nevertheless, they refused to treat, not only with each other, but also with the western democracies, concerning political and military aid.

As early as October, 1939, more than forty divisions of the German army were concentrated opposite the Low Countries, and by the end of October the number of these divisions was doubled. Moreover, twelve out of the seventeen German motorized divisions now were brought opposite Holland, Belgium, and Luxembourg. So tense was the situation at the beginning of November, 1939, that King Leopold, tipped off by German emissaries and by a German lady friend, rushed to The Hague to see Wilhelmina and to counteract the danger of an imminent invasion by a joint peace offer of the two sovereigns.

At the end of October and the beginning of November, 1939, I made repeated trips into Holland to see the Dutch fortifications and inundation works, also to observe changes in the disposition of German troops on the Dutch-German border.

During one of these frontier tours I could also establish that the soldiers opposite Holland were mostly elderly classes, and I found even two regiments of Slovak troops—certainly not fit for offensive purposes.

On November 4 I met with a nasty automobile accident. My Dutch friend who drove the car ran into two huge trees—one was not enough for him. The next few weeks I had to go around with a head completely bandaged, and my friends used to call me "the first casualty of the Dutch war."

Still with a bandaged head, I had to report on the meeting of the rulers of Holland and Belgium in The Hague, on November 6, 1939. One day later I noticed suddenly that steel-helmeted police, armed with carbines and revolvers, were guarding the public buildings in The Hague and in other Dutch cities. Two days later the leaders of the British secret service in Holland, Captain Stephens and Sigismond Payne-Best, were kidnaped from Venlo, a place on the Dutch frontier. Again two days later German troop concentrations on the Dutch border caused fear that an invasion of Holland was imminent. The situation was tense, and The Hague and Amsterdam were in a panicky atmosphere.

I telegraphed then to my paper, the *Chicago Daily News*:

"The Germans, as they did in Austria and Czechoslovakia, wanted to work by means of internal pressure as well, and a Dutch Nazi *Putsch* was engineered. This *Putsch* aimed at eliminating the present government and replacing it with a Dutch Nazi government that would have concluded a treaty with Germany. Since last Wednesday, however, public offices have been under guard by the Queen's auxiliary police, with steel helmets and bayonets.

"The nervousness was increased by the presence of the German army across the frontier.... German troops on the frontier are described as a special maneuver army trying out certain theories which, under peculiar conditions, could be best carried out under the protection of a neutral frontier. All this points to a temporary, if not a long, respite.... Germany will try to persuade Belgium and Holland to cede certain points and air-dromes peacefully. If this does not work, then force of arms may be used."

Before deciding on the final attack the Germans made several more rehearsal and feinting moves, attempting to divert attention from certain parts of their own defenses to other, less relevant parts. For this purpose, they staged a clever "incident."

A German airplane with two majors of the general staff made a forced landing in Belgium, not far from the German border, on the tenth of January, 1940. The landing was allegedly due to lack of gasoline. One major had in his possession the plans of a complete German scheme of attack against Belgium which was to take place three days later. The two majors made apparently desperate attempts to destroy the documents, but failed; the plans showed that the Germans contemplated an attack on Belgium, and intended to pierce the Belgian fortification lines on the Meuse between Huy and Andenne. The conversation of one of the majors with the German air attaché was listened in on by microphone, and the officer acted surprised; he swore even that he had destroyed the documents. This was all comedy! I immediately asserted that the plans were "phony," and were intended to divert attention from real plans. But this theatrical *coup* was staged so realistically that the Belgians were convinced and started to fortify the "threatened" section with great zeal, thus not paying enough attention to the lines to the right and left—where four months later the real attack was launched.

As the Marne was the famous river of the last World War, the Meuse is the tragic river of this war. Yet it was, and is, such a nice quiet river! Ever since the days of Jan van Eyck, its blue waters and green banks have been favorite subjects for Flemish and Belgian painters. Nevertheless, on the Meuse was decided the fate of Belgium and Holland, the fate of France, and perhaps that of civilization.

In the second half of April, 1940, accompanied by officers of the Belgian army and general staff, I visited the defenses of Belgium, both on the Albert Canal and on the Meuse. I was taken around the fortifications of Namur. On the highest hill the Belgians were busy completing one of the strongest of these forts, while in other parts soldiers were erecting more pillboxes, barbed-wire fences, and other entanglements and obstacles. Huge anti-tank barriers ran around the city and its fortifications, and the steep cliffs, dropping almost perpendicularly into the blue river, seemed an insurmountable obstacle for enemy divisions.

Less than a month later I saw Namur again. A large-scale German aerial bombardment had just reduced the peaceful homes and lovely gardens to smoldering ruins. It is true that Namur was a fortress town; yet it was also a city inhabited by peaceful people like you and me; people who never offended the Germans or anybody else. And today they are dead or in exile; their properties are reduced to débris and ashes.

As sudden as the destruction of Namur was the demoralization of the

Belgian army. When I visited the eastern suburbs of Brussels on the morning of May 11, the second day of the totalitarian war, I found them, to my great amazement, crowded with soldiers in full war equipment, loafing in the public thoroughfares, surrounded by large, curious crowds. These fugitive soldiers were spreading the tale of defeat, nay, more, of a catastrophe; and by exaggerating the magnitude of the defeat, they helped to create further uneasiness, bordering on panic, among the Brussels population, who were already terrified by the constant bombardment by German planes, claiming large numbers of civilian victims.

"What are the officers doing?" I asked a sergeant who was the loudest in a crowd.

"They were the first to run away," was the laconic answer.

Where was the proud Belgian army which only a few days ago had seemed cheerful and confident? These ragged, destitute-looking soldiers recalled to me Ernest Hemingway's brilliant description of the Italian *débâcle* at Caporetto, in *Farewell to Arms.* This was obviously another Caporetto, the consequences of which, however, proved to be more far-reaching than those of its Italian model. ...

A half-hearted attempt was made by the Belgian authorities to collect these demoralized troops on the Cinquantenaire exhibition grounds and to re-form them into fighting units. The demoralization of the Belgian army, however, had proceeded so far that all these attempts seemed in vain. At the exhibition grounds the soldiers cursed their officers and refused to go back to the inferno on the Meuse and the Albert Canal. When the officers appealed to their patriotism, they answered that they preferred servitude to sure death. Nobody thought in terms of the future; there were no soldiers who realized that the fate of civilization probably depended on the power of resistance of the Allies in Belgium. ...

While the Belgian forces on the Albert Canal and the Lower Meuse were in complete dissolution, the Germans did not forget to deal with the southern part of the Belgian front. The Belgian army was expecting a direct attack coming through the Ardennes, a hilly, rough country, with thick woods and winding rivers. The undulating hills there were believed to be extremely suitable for defense—the Belgian general staff thought that the army could hold the fortifications and pillboxes of the Ardennes for at least five days, while neutral observers calculated that at least two days would be required for the Germans to reach the Upper Meuse between Givet and Liége.

At the beginning of their "lightning war" the Germans did not concentrate their attack on the Ardennes fortifications. They once more resorted to their well-known tactics of turning the enemy's line. Thus they rushed their troops into undefended Luxembourg, which had an army of one hundred fifty-six men, and which had previously been pumped full of Fifth-Columnists in the form of tourists. Everybody in Brussels believed that the French could launch their divisions into Luxembourg as quickly as the Germans. Yet the Germans were able to occupy the Grand Duchy within a few hours without meeting any serious resistance, except in the extreme southern part. Luxembourg once occupied, they could rush their divisions into southeastern Belgium. With the aid of their artillery they mowed down the barbed-wire entanglements and other obstacles, and hundreds of German motorcyclists with machine guns in their sidecars rushed cross-country into Belgium, leaving forts and pillboxes behind to be dealt with by heavy tanks and artillery. The Ardennes sector thus was occupied within forty-eight hours, which, in turn, enabled the German troops to proceed with the attack on the upper reaches of the Meuse.

It was calculated by the Belgian and French general staffs that the French army could take over the Belgian section of the Meuse between Namur and Givet within forty-eight hours. And here happened the other tragedy of the present war, another drama on the Meuse River: the folding up of the French Ninth Army.

Napoleon used to inspect his troops personally during the night, taking good care that no omission in vigilance should be permitted. The leaders of the French Ninth Army had forgotten their great predecessor's maxims. There was no vigilance among its chiefs. Was it negligence, or was it more? In any case, we had all been expecting a German attack on the Belgian-French lines ever since May 6, and yet General Corap, commander of the Ninth Army, was absent when the Germans launched their motorized divisions against the Allied lines, and did not turn up for another twenty-four hours. He had been given orders to take over the Belgian front between Namur and Givet, on the Meuse, and also to defend the positions of the extended Maginot Line, from Givet to Sedan, along the Meuse. On May 12, when the French troops should already have been in position along the Meuse, only a fraction of the Ninth Army arrived to take over the Belgian positions. Six bridges on the Meuse were not blown up; their dynamite chambers were left untouched. Over these intact bridges, meeting only slight resistance, poured the German motorized and armored troops.

A river like the Meuse is still an important obstacle to tanks. Regular solid bridges are needed to support German heavy tanks, which weigh forty or fifty tons; no quickly constructed pontoon bridge can bear the weight of these steel giants. Moreover, guns placed on the other side of a river can hold off advancing tanks for a long time. Granted that there was a surprise element in the German attack, still there is no excuse for leaving six bridges intact; for the artillery to remain unused; for troops being one hundred hours behind schedule; for the failure of the air force to appear in time and in sufficient numbers.

Is it a wonder that the word "treason" was now whispered among the *poilus*, in the cafés of Sedan, in the restaurants of Lille? And it *was* treason. Even if the entire staff of General Corap can whitewash themselves from the charge of actual treason, their action, for all practical purpose, was treason to their country. They failed to carry through a minutely drafted defense plan of the French general staff. They failed to organize their units properly; they failed to observe that vigilance which is the first commandment of all army officers.

It will be difficult to erase the belief, firmly fixed among the French troops of the Ninth Army and whispered all over northern France, that treason, probably actual bribery of some officers, or of one staff officer (these were the versions related at the time in those parts), was the cause of the *débâcle* on the Meuse.

With the bridges undynamited, only one defense remained: metal against metal, either in the form of anti-tank guns with proper armor-piercing shells or the actual opposition of other tanks. But where were the French armored divisions? Where were the French tanks, the French anti-tank guns? France had hardly any. Behind her Chinese Wall, the Maginot Line, she had felt secure. But this line defended only part of France's frontier; on the part undefended by the Maginot Line, the Germans resorted to a modernized form of medieval warfare: the metal-protected warrior. The knights of the Middle Ages rode against each other in armor of forged steel, and tried to dislodge each other from the saddle either by their heavy lances or the sheer weight of their impact; the Germans now substituted a steel-plated tank for the war horse, and replaced the lance with the guns and machine guns of the tanks.

But the French had few armored warriors of their own; not enough tanks to oppose the sheer weight of the onrushing German metal. Valiantly the French infantry died before the devastating fire of the German tanks and low-flying airplanes. The few motorized units of the French army were quickly reduced to old junk—sometimes less than a hundred men of a motorized column survived the German assault. Heroically they tried to resume resistance, but in vain. The unblown bridges did their duty....

German armored and motorized divisions poured into France on May 12 through the breach created by the failure of Corap—a breach by then fifty miles wide and fifty miles deep. Tanks, spreading fire and destruction, supported by low-flying airplanes with which they were connected by radio, co-operated in advancing on French soil, while the bringing up of French reinforcements was impeded by the constant flow of refugees pouring towards Paris.

# ON A PARIS RAILWAY STATION

### by Dorothy Thompson

MAY 13—The soldier stands face to face with his girl, his hands on her waist, under her jacket. The officer holds his girl by her arms. The soldier kisses his girl unashamedly. The officer kisses his girl with his eyes. None of the four speaks at all.

"The French are a talkative people." On the crowded platform hardly a word is heard. What is there to say now that has not been said before?

192

What is apprehended that was not long since apprehended? What has come that was not awaited?

"Sincerely trusts" ... "Conscience of mankind" ... "Respects neutrality" ... "Rights of non-belligerents." ...

Hitler's troops without warning crossed the frontiers of Luxemburg, Holland and Belgium Friday, May 10, 1940, at dawn. They dropped into Holland in Dutch uniforms, from parachutes. Men from Mars.

"We shall breed a new race out of an élite, trained to hardness, cruelty, violence; supermen, leading masses. On them we shall found a new Reich that will last for a thousand years.

"The supermen will be ingenious, treacherous, masterful. The masses will be uniform, with arms that rise and fall rhythmically, voices that cry hoarsely, rhythmically, 'Sieg Heil!' "

"First the men from Mars, and then the masses. Breed them, mothers! Prizes for the most fertile! Equality for the illegitimate! Born in love or lust or for a bonus, all are equal, all alike, one folk, one Reich, one Fuehrer."

The soldiers on the Paris railway station are uniformed, but they are not uniform. Men of yesterday, why has each of you a different face? You, so diverse, so individual; you, with the ascetic bones and the cynical eyes; you, little soldier with the gleeful mouth of a peasant epicurean; you, lovers of books and you, lover of your girl, and you with the nervous lips—you have got to meet the man of tomorrow, No. 1135, type B.

The soldier holds his little girl on his shoulder; she has big, wet black eyes, like the eyes in a drawing by Laurencin. He strokes her hair—the hair of his individual little girl, a French child, precious, rare.

"The French birth rate is stable, the small family is the rule. The family is the basis of society. One has the number of children that one can support and educate."

"This one is clever and shall go to the lycée."

"Demographically speaking, the French are a dying race. There are 42,-000,000 French and 80,000,000 Germans. The Third Reich needs room for its growing population."

"Make room, little father, make room!" Nobody smiles, nobody sings. "What! No Tipperary? No Madelon?"

A woman in black holds her son in her arms. Tears flow down her face. His lip trembles slightly. The women of Sparta exposed their weakling children to the elements. They sent them into battle with the cry, "Return with your sword or on it!"

But Homer, whose name is given to the age of heroes, was blind.

"Man for man the French army is the best in the world."

The boy is nine years old. He stands apart, while his father and mother say something to each other, swift and low. He wears his Sunday suit. He cries bitterly but without noise.

"Nazi youth do not weep."

The whistle blows. The officer holds his girl's cheek to his. The soldier kisses his girl on the mouth. Just once more!

Nobody watches any one else. No one pretends. No one is pretending anything.

"Kill a Boche for me, darling." Didn't they say that in the last war?

No one says a word about Boche or killing. Not a word. Not a flag. Not a salute . . . not an au revoir. They pull apart, and the men crowd into the cars. They wear good woolen uniforms and good thick boots.

They look through the open windows—a thousand faces, a thousand different faces, not one like another, not one common expression, not one replaceable face. Now, at last, they smile, kindly, comfortingly, understandingly. The women and the girls stand together, but each alone, each surrounded by a little space of loneliness and separateness, each alone in her tears.

The train begins to move. The men wave. The women wave and weeping, smile.

No one calls "Vive la France!"

There goes France.

# SURRENDER OF HOLLAND

## by Beach Conger

AMSTERDAM, May 14.—Following merciless German bombings of Utrecht and Rotterdam, it was announced at 6:58 o'clock tonight over the radio that Holland's troops had been ordered to lay down their arms to prevent further bloodshed.

Foreign correspondents had foreseen this capitulation last night, following the flight of Queen Wilhelmina to England, despite the encouraging proclamations issued in her name and in that of Gen. Henri Gerard Winkelman, her commander in chief.

A grown Dutchman wept openly in front of my radio as the announcement was made. In a pitiful ceremony in the square in front of our hotel, thirteen civic guards marched up and unloaded their rifles and then marched off down the street to disband.

There had been grave faces last night when the Queen's departure was announced. Today the population did its best to reason that her trip to England had been for the best of reasons, but the complete absence of any soldiers or civic guards in the streets of Amsterdam, and the fact that at five spots the Dutch themselves set fire to oil tanks along the Amsterdam harbor as "defensive measures," was the only additional proof of surrender needed by foreign observers.

As this dispatch was being written at 7:10 P.M., the streets were almost completely deserted. Word had spread rapidly. "Tomorrow we will be German," another Dutchman said to me bitterly.

The local population experienced a slight panic today. Whole families in the Jewish section started to leave for the coast, hoping they might possibly find a ship for England. But there were so many of these refugees that the Mayor of near-by Ijmuiden stated on the radio that the town, being a naval base, was a dangerous spot, that there were no ships going to England and that all fleeing persons would be turned back. There were lines in front of the banks.

Another indication was the fact that without warning to Belgium or French subjects, the staffs of the French and Belgian Consulates left suddenly either last night or this morning and asked the American Consulate General to take over their interests. All day long these three offices were besieged not only by Belgian, French and British but also by German refugees, both Jewish and "Aryan," asking for help in getting out of the country.

# FALL OF SEDAN

## by G. H. Archambault

PARIS, May 14.—"The enemy is making a momentous effort with furious obstinacy and at the cost of heavy casualties." This sentence in the communiqué issued tonight by the Allied High Command indicates sufficiently what the coming battle will be.

The sentence relates specifically to the Sedan region, where, after occupying that French town, the Germans are seeking to bring about a rupture of the front. But it is becoming evident that such an effort will be applicable to every action by the Germans now.

People here are recalling the statement attributed to Adolf Hitler that he was prepared to sacrifice 1,000,000 men to break through the Maginot Line.

The "Battle of the Meuse," as it already is being called, spread along a 150-mile battlefront on Belgian and French soil, engulfing cities and towns laid waste when Kaiser Wilhelm sent his armies toward Paris over the same route in the August days of 1914. Perhaps a key to the outcome of the whole European war, the battle was fought by hundreds of thousands of men and thousands of tanks, airplanes, guns and armored cars.

Casualties were enormous on both sides.

The French admitted that the Germans were pounding southward through Belgium with amazing speed and had penetrated eight or ten miles into French territory at some points, but asserted that only the outer fringes of the Maginot Line had been reached.

The German High Command, according to French press dispatches, has ordered from 6,000 to 7,000 planes into action to blast a path for Adolf Hitler's mechanized forces in an unprecedented mass bombing.

The Belgian city of Namur, thirty-five miles southeast of Brussels, was reported in flames after aerial bombardment, and the Belgian fortress of Liége, now well behind the Nazi advance westward and southward, was bombed almost constantly for twelve hours.

Brussels and Antwerp were threatened by motorized German forces.

MAY 17, 1940: *The Germans entered Brussels.*

MAY 18: *General Maxime Weygand replaced General Gamelin as commander of the French Army.*

MAY 21: *The Germans had bombed their way through Antwerp to the Channel coast town of Abbéville, completely cutting off the Belgian and English forces.*

\* \* \*

PARIS, May 28 (Associated Press): Capitulation of the Belgian Army... on orders of King Leopold III ... was announced today by President Paul Reynaud of France....

\* \* \*

# DUNKERQUE

### by Raymond Daniell

THINGS looked very bad on May 29. The British and French Armies of the North were surrounded. For them there was only one way out. That was through the port of Dunkerque and its neighboring shallow beaches. Attacked from every side, the R.A.F. was at first hopelessly outnumbered in the air. The whole French First Army and all of the B.E.F. north of the gap the Nazis had broken through between Amiens and Abbeville seemed doomed.

Thus was the stage set for the evacuation from Dunkerque, one of the most dramatic episodes of this or any other war. Fighting a desperate rear-guard action the British and French fell back upon the beaches in a contracting arc against which all the strength the Germans could bring to bear was thrown. Nazi cannon raked the beaches on which the tired troops had swarmed. Formations of Nazi planes sprayed the sand dunes the British and French soldiers were trying to use for shelter. They bombed the single pier that remained, and they tried to close the seas by sowing magnetic mines. Submarines and fast little motor torpedo boats sought to frustrate the Titanic task of rescue that the Royal Navy, with the help of scores of vessels of all kinds, had undertaken. Hospital ships and ambulances bearing the wounded victims of the battle for Flanders were especial targets for Goering's lighthearted young men.

The full story of the rescue of the B.E.F. and their French comrades in arms is a book in itself. It was probably the first time in history that a civilian population ever went to the rescue of an army. But that is just what happened. The nearest thing to it in modern times occurred in the last war, when the taxicab drivers of Paris were mobilized to rush reinforcements to the front. This time it was the lifeguards, fishermen, river boatmen, and ordinary civilians who knew something about the sea who went to that little bit of hell on earth where more than 300,000 men were trapped.

Two hundred and twenty light warships steamed across the Channel and lent the weight of their guns to the artillery and the rifles fending off the Germans. Some 650 other vessels of various types were used in the evacuation. Flat-bottomed boats and vessels of shallow draft were especially needed to cross the shoals before the beaches, pick up the wading men, and ferry them out to the larger ships waiting to take them back to Blighty. Operating in bad weather along a treacherous coast, these little boats and big ships accomplished a miracle. In all, they snatched 335,000 French and British soldiers "out of the jaws of death and shame," as the Prime Minister himself phrased it in reporting the achievement to Parliament.

It was no easy task. At first the ships were not only at the mercy of mines and torpedoes but were under an almost ceaseless hail of bombs and shells. At the beginning the Nazis had complete mastery of the air above Dunkerque, but soon the R.A.F., by throwing a large part of the main metropolitan fighter strength into the breach, wrested it from them in a series of desperate encounters in which the Nazis paid fourfold for the losses they inflicted.

# THE STAB IN THE BACK

## by Herbert L. Matthews

ROME, April 9, 1940—Germany invades Denmark and Norway, and the next day I began my dispatch by saying: "The Allies are in graver danger in Southeastern Europe and in Italy today than at any period since the war started. The danger signals are so clear as to be almost visible. . . . The effect of the German victory and the Allied defeat has proved of enormous importance. . . . It must never be forgotten that Italy is looking out solely for her own vital interests. So long as those interests lie in nonbelligerency, Italy will stay out of the war, but if she becomes convinced that those interests will best be served by actively supporting a Germany that is either on the road to victory or in a position to gain a decisive victory with Italian aid, then one must expect Mussolini to take this country into the war on the side of the Reich."

Before a week passed the whole weight of Fascist propaganda had been placed on the Italian people. The German effort was glorified, and no word of sympathy or human feeling for the Norwegians was permitted. Sentiment and moral issues were rigidly excluded for a cold realism which was aimed at a certain effect—to convince Italians that their interests lay in supporting Germany. The whole object was not the winning of sympathy for Germany —that would have been a vain hope—but merely making the public believe that the Allies were beaten.

Mass demonstrations, organized and directed by the Fascist party, began in Milan April 16, and never ceased until Italy entered the war. The dregs of society were called in, real gangsters who had orders to use fists and clubs when necessary. Demonstrations in Italy were always a farce, never spontaneous, never expressions of popular feeling. They were instruments of official policy, and therein lay their importance.

It would be hard to say exactly at what point the Duce made up his mind to take the plunge. On April 21, in a talk to the hierarchs of the twenty-two Corporations, he said: "Do not think that Italy is not going to war."

On May 10 I wrote what was quite obvious, that "if the Allies get beaten in the Lowlands, or are in danger of defeat, they cannot expect Italy to remain nonbelligerent." Yet there was no mobilization, or even psychological preparation to enter the war immediately. On the contrary, unpreparedness was as complete as it could be. Senator Bocchini, head of the OVRA, the secret police, and one of the few men who dared to tell the Duce the truth about his own people, made a report to Mussolini in which he frankly demonstrated the desire for peace and the dislike of the Germans. As a result he was out of favor for several weeks. The evening before the invasion of Holland, two German officers in the Apollo cabaret tried to pay their check with a 20-mark bill. The waiter refused to accept it and one of the Germans said, "All right, I'll pay in lire now, but in a few months you will be using these, you may be sure." Two Italian officers rose and threw the Germans out, much to everybody's pleasure.

On May 11 Mussolini began the last part of his anti-British campaign. The report was published on the Allied blockade, calling it "literally intolerable." There were deliberately fostered anti-Ally demonstrations by Fascist thugs and scatter-brained students. Posters were plastered on walls throughout Italian cities and towns intended to make the Allies look ridiculous, and the newspapers exceeded themselves in scurrility and boasting. The demonstrations were farcical to see. Good-natured students laughed and shouted as if it were a great lark to them—and so it was. Then *Giornale d'Italia* came out with a lurid account of a great mass of indignant students and citizens moving "with spontaneous passion" to "protest vibrantly against the disgusting naval blockade exercised by the Allies." The report on the blockade was like a spark, said Gayda's newspaper, and "the generous hearts of our studious youth were inflamed with indignation."

By May 26 it was possible to write that "as things are going now, Italy will intervene before June 20—probably between the 10th and 20th." The

British and French by then were offering Mussolini virtually everything he wanted. The French ambassador, François Poncet, said to me that it was the first time any ruler deliberately chose to fight for what he could have taken peacefully. But *that* was Fascism. As I wrote in a dispatch at the time: "If only for the sake of Fascist prestige, and not to be reproached with winning such a bloodless war as the Allies are supposed to have tried to win, the Fascist regime would want to shed some blood." Such was the absurd but monstrous conclusion to which Fascist doctrine was leading.

Apparently, Mussolini had been clever. Italy was in the extraordinary position of being able to tell her future enemies quite plainly and simply that she was going to war against them when it best suited her, and when it would be most dangerous to them. These enemies not only could do nothing but were trying to buy off Italy with huge offers that were making no impression, since the Fascist leaders were completely convinced that Germany was going to win the war soon.

The Duce was making the greatest gamble of his career, although he did not recognize it to be such. There is plenty of evidence to show that he, and other Fascist leaders, were convinced the war was almost over. They gave it three months, at most, and they were sure the United States would have no time to intervene effectively. Roosevelt's speech June 10, the day Mussolini declared war, the speech with the famous phrase, "the stab in the back"—a phrase that will forever and with justice brand the Italian action—merely infuriated the Fascists. They knew we were their enemies, and now the war, Mussolini announced in his speech from the balcony of the Palazzo Venezia, was to be against "the plutocratic and reactionary democracies of the West."

At 4:30 in the afternoon of June 10, Ciano received the French ambassador at the Chigi Palace and told him that "His Majesty the King Emperor declares that Italy considers herself in a state of war against France, beginning tomorrow, June 11." Fifteen minutes later he communicated the same message to the British ambassador.

It had been a moderately exciting day—not very much so, for nothing can move the Roman deeply, and he did not consider this his affair especially. It was Mussolini who was declaring war; the ordinary Italian had no animosity whatever toward either the British or French; he had no desire to fight them or anybody else. The only deep sentiments he harbored were dislike of the Germans—with whom he was now being allied—and a longing to see the war end. It was taken for granted that Mussolini knew what he was doing, and a more or less bloodless victory would bring to Italy some benefits.

Only a small group of intelligent and decent Italians was profoundly ashamed of this indelible blot on Italy's name, but the average Italian did not care much one way or another. For a certain number of them, it was pure cynicism, or what they called "realism"; for the vast majority it was thoughtlessness, ignorance, indifference, a failure to understand what was happening and what its implications were. When they did realize what had been done in their name they repudiated it in the only way they could—by refusal to fight for the Axis, by political opposition, by plots against Fascism, by sabotaging the war effort, or, at the least, by a passive resistance which has baffled all Mussolini's efforts.

Nothing can too strongly condemn the Fascists who led Italy to that shameful pass. The chief accusation against the ordinary Italian is that he was willing to accept it. Had Mussolini guessed right, his people would have applauded his "cleverness." Even today, the failure of Fascism, for the average Italian, is a material one; morality and ethics have very little to do with it.

The attitude was clear enough on that fateful day June 10, 1940. There was an immense demonstration in front of the Palazzo Venezia for the Duce, and later for the King but it was entirely organized. The local Fasci had their orders to collect members, meet at a certain time, and proceed to the square. Fascists went around telling shopkeepers that they had to close at 5 o'clock. The radio kept announcing throughout the day that Mussolini was going to speak, and everywhere in Italy the citizens had to gather around loud-speakers to listen. There was not the slightest spontaneous feeling, and the only cheering came from those, especially the students, who had been brought into the center of the mob, under the balcony. Outside of that relatively tiny group of organized applauders, there was a light-hearted indifference which was really appalling, considering what was happening. I saw troops marching through nearby streets while the passersby did not even turn their heads to look at them.

The cycle of Fascism had taken a great turn to an old starting point—at least, the Fascists thought so. On the eve of the March on Rome, the proclamation of the Quadrumvirate said: "Urge on your spirits and your strength like Romans. We must conquer! We shall conquer!" [*Vinceremo!*]. And they did, indeed, go on to the conquest of Italy. Eighteen years had passed, and Fascism was on the eve of a still greater adventure.

"There is but one categorical watchword, binding on all," shouted the Duce from his balcony. "It has already penetrated and fired the hearts of all, from the Alps to the Indian Ocean: 'Conquer!' And we shall conquer!" [*Vinceremo!*].

Once again let it be written—if someone had only whispered in his ear: "Beware of Nemesis!" He was never a man to be perplexed by doubts, and he had none now. The French, defeated and demoralized, were falling back. The gallant rear-guard action of Dunkirk seemed merely a prelude to the final defeat. The United States was torn by isolationism—and 3,000 miles away. Germany had proved herself to be invincible. Russia washed her hands of the struggle. To defeat England might take two or three months, hardly more, and the Reich would, of course, do virtually all the fighting. Then Italy would collect her share of the spoils. It was all so simple!

The last shred of self-respect that might have remained to Italy was removed when Mussolini dared not even send his army against the weak French forces on the Alps until the Germans had advanced so far that the

French were caught, hopelessly, in a vise. There was not even that much courage left in Fascist Italy! The word passed around by Roman wits was: "Don't fire until you see the whites of their flags." And that was exactly what happened. It was not until four days after Pétain sued for peace that Mussolini sent his troops forward—only to have them severely mauled by the embittered French.

Newspapers jeered over the fall of Paris. *C'est Paris!* wrote *Lavoro Fascista* in an eight-column box. "Capitalists, Jews, Masons, and snobs, all over the world, are in mourning." "Stop crying for France," advised *Tevere*. "What more could they have done to merit our heel on their necks? Let that country of carrion learn, once and for all, in the torture of the direst defeat, to respect the honor of other peoples, and let them stay on their knees for centuries. As for the English, their turn will come."

Such sentiments, and the newspapers that expressed them, were typical "fruits" of Fascism. Let us remember that, for the record.

# REFUGEES

## by Robert J. Casey

AT a little after noon Monday, June 10, we came into Paris from the south. The roads were already pretty well congested with southbound traffic but there was as yet no sign of a collapse of the general morale. The cars leaving Paris were the big shiny ones, the cars of politicians and decorative women and retired industrialists and such.... But the politicians weren't the important ones or they would be on the road somewhere with the government. And the decorative women were not of the preferred stock, because they had started getting out of town when the Germans bombed Neuilly and slaughtered the children in the trench near Orly a week ago.

Up to this time we hadn't heard about the complete removal of the Government. We had known that a move was intended. Quarters had been blocked out for it at Tours as early as May 19. But for a week we had been living with people who couldn't think of any catastrophe that might endanger Paris, and if one accepted their ideas even with reservations, it had seemed that the Hôtel Continental in Paris would be just as safe a shelter for brass hats as Hôtel de l'Univers in Tours. But the Government had left. We found that when we tried to turn in our passes to the zone of the Alpine Army. The keeper of the estaminet across the street from the Continental in Rue du Mont Thabor was deeply grieved at the hegira, not because he felt that it signified anything untoward in the affairs of France but merely because it took business from him to places he could not follow.

Before we parted that night we carefully exchanged addresses and wrote down a schedule of where we should be each hour tomorrow starting at 8:00 A.M. We arranged to meet in front of the Café de la Paix at 10:30.

The first thing that a casual observer noticed on Tuesday morning was the beauty of the day, the exhilaration of the air. The second most noticeable item was the absence of taxicabs. Not only had the bracing atmosphere brought one the desire to live but the exodus of the city's most potent menace had made longevity possible. You didn't waste much time smiling at your own joke, however. You didn't have to be told that these taxicabs hadn't been recruited to turn anybody's flank in some new battle of the Marne. The smart boys of Paris had reached a unanimous decision about what was going on and their combined negative opinion of the prospects for the survival of the city was considerably more impressive than any broadcast message by Paul Reynaud. As nearly as I could interpret such portents as this, it wouldn't be long now.

I was first at the rendezvous in front of the Café de la Paix and sat for possibly half an hour in the weirdest sort of seclusion. I had never thought to see the day when I would look across the Place de l'Opéra and behold not one single soul. And in the other direction there weren't three people in the Boulevard des Capucines, including the waiter who leaned like a rubber man against a stanchion at the end of the deserted terrace. Almost as far as the Madeleine was an empty vista of shade and sun-splashes and thick-leaved chestnut trees. I looked at it with unbelieving eyes and wondered if anybody had seen Paris like this ever before.

There was nothing alarming about this sudden absence of life at what had once been very nearly the busiest corner in the world. Rather it was calming and restful. I leaned back in my chair and half closed my eyes and thought it would be very pleasant to stay here in this sunny isolation for a long time ... forever. Privacy on a terrace in the Place de l'Opéra was a novel experience and worth enjoying.

Presently a trickle of people began to come into the Place from somewhere north of the Opéra. First was a fine-looking old gentleman in frock coat and striped trousers and other accouterments of an haute monde that one did not expect to see afoot on such a day as this. He had a pair of gray gloves in his left hand and a cane tucked up under his right arm and his pace was in keeping with his decorative effect, like that of a boulevardier on an aimless stroll. After him—ten paces or more behind him—came a young woman carrying a baby. There was nothing remarkable about her or her clothes or the fat, sleepy child in her arms. These people moved on through the sunlight, as unreal as the atmosphere that they walked in ... figures out of some old silent moving picture escaped from a film vault. They were halfway across the square when I discovered what had kept me looking at them after a first casual glance: They were walking not on the sidewalk but in the middle of the street, shortcutting across that one-time death trap as one might follow a path in a park.

The disjointed parade went on. The strangers—the Frenchmen you had never before seen in France—continued to spill into the square in steadily increasing numbers. After a while you began to note more oddities of transport—single bicycles serving as suitcase carriers, bicycles hooked together catamaran fashion and used as pushcarts, and bicycles that were just bicycles —"triporteurs," the three-wheeled traffic menaces that generally looked after deliveries for small shops—baby cabs carrying all manner of quickly salvaged lares and penates including, sometimes, babies—varieties of handcarts, the French version of the soap-box gig—bundles slung from a pole carried on the shoulders of two men. . . . Several children went past on scooters, and one young woman who appeared to be having a fine time, flashed by the terrace on roller skates. . . . I wonder what ever happened to her.

Somehow none of these people looked like the ones you used to see about the cafés or even among the Sunday crowds in the Bois or on the boulevards. They probably were the city's submerged tenth, the class so rare in Paris as to be almost legendary, the stay-at-homes. They were rich in the basic French virtue of minding their own business. They were able to contrive amusements for themselves and for their families. They, in a word, were the richest people on earth, the contented and incurious ones. . . . As a class they were late in hearing of crises and later in doing anything about them. And there was no encouragement in that thought as they took their leisurely course down toward the Seine. If these people—the last to find out about things—were taking the road, what had become of that great majority party, the people who are the first to find out about things? I began to feel like a last survivor in a city where there had been about three million people.

We took a very roundabout course through the wood but it was sensible. In an hour we were outside of Paris and feeling our way somewhere to the west of the municipal garbage dump, trying to cut into Versailles without getting mixed up with the traffic on the main routes. Bill led the way in his car, picking roads that didn't show on the route maps. But even here we weren't alone. After a bit of maneuvering on a sunken road we came to the top of a gentle rise overlooking miles of grassy fields. Through this farmland wound six or eight minor roads like that we had just left and all of them had hoisted festoons of dust to show the passing of automobiles.

In a moment we, too, were trailing such a streamer, for we came to a barrier and turned off the narrow belt of asphalt onto a dirt path and a minute or two later were part of this section of the big parade. So far we weren't very crowded. This lane, which did not show on any of the route maps, was carrying only one-way traffic and, fortunately, the cars on it were moving along at a reasonable rate. It looked as if luck might travel along with us for several hours yet—until the dark had come down at least —and then the Heinkels came over.

The aeroplanes were close, too, and getting closer. The crescendo snarl of them had an inflection not so different from that of the alerte—the changing pitch as the machine dived from ten thousand feet to straighten out above the road. We saw one of them flash into a cloud and disappear until it was over the head of our column. But we counted distinctly the shriek of four others. Two bombs let loose not far away and from over in the direction of the alerte there was some anti-aircraft fire. It seemed to be about as effective as it was twenty-three years ago.

Even though we knew what was going on—it was so familiar that we seemed to have been plunged back a couple of weeks into the Belgian debacle—we didn't react as quickly as we might have to this situation. It may be that we didn't like to admit to ourselves that we were in a bad spot. It may be that we hoped by moving along a little bit that we might find some sort of side lane and run off the target. Anyway we continued to move along in the direction of the first bombs even after the planes had come out of the clouds into the sunlight—even after we saw the uprush of black smoke straight in front of us and heard the first burst of machine-gun fire.

After that we didn't need much advice, although, oddly enough we got plenty of it from civilian children who had been picking up soup-greens in a near-by ditch. They came running by, white-faced with panic and screaming that the Boches were coming.

Even though you know better, there is always something in you that makes you believe an open ditch will protect you from on top. It doesn't, of course. There is also a superstition that to stand still no matter where you are is a better policy than inviting the attention of a playful machine-gunner by running for cover. The success of that maneuver depends, I believe, on where you are standing in the first place.

Just how you protect yourself from bombing and machine-gunning on a public highway will always make an interesting subject for argument but, as I see it, the best thing to do is to scatter the choice of targets and then pray. That, however, wasn't the way we did it. We dived off the road into the lush meadowland, ran twenty or thirty feet through a stand of barley and then dived into a grassy ditch.

The planes came overhead—squarely overhead as we could see if we cared to raise our chins. They strewed the road with machine-gun bullets. They took altitude and dived and dropped their bombs. And we weren't hurt because the zone of error was all in the field north of the road instead of in the one to the south where we with a large contingent of frightened bedfellows had occupied the ditch. The damage such as it was had been up ahead of us, but when the planes had gone away and we carefully picked our way back to the cars we didn't think of the merciful distance—however far away this ground-strafe had been, it had been too close.

The Heinkels did not come back that night. They never did any promiscuous bombing, the Heinkels—not in our experience. They picked their objective and they slapped a crump onto it or they tore it to shreds with machine-gun bullets. . . . And they couldn't work at nights because it was too hard for them to find the roads where the fugitive civilians stood trapped and helpless in traffic jams. They worked in daylight and at low altitudes. From a height of a couple of hundred feet above the trees you could see the bombs burst among the automobiles and farm wagons. You could see men and women and horses and cars all dissolving ludicrously in the orange flame and the rolling black smoke. You could see the corpses falling spread-eagle on the farmlands along the road when you let the machine gun go. You had plenty of time to see the high comedy of panic as you dropped out of the sky with sirens blaring from your wingtips. You could feel almost godlike as you released a whistling bomb and watched the doomed ones scatter—jerking like puppets on a string—as they tried so foolishly to get away from certain death.

The sun went down in a haze. A bluish cloud was rolling down into the west from the direction of Paris. The thickening dusk found us with no more fear of slaughter from the air but well imbedded in the tangle of traffic that had been wandering over farm roads to a point of convergence near St. Cyr. We crawled into a sunken road just wide enough to accommodate two cars abreast and in that trap, just as a motorcycle squad came roaring through to line up all cars on the right of the road and permit two-way traffic, my engine coughed and died.

Every town proved to be a bottleneck no matter how complete its unimportance because all four-lane highways narrowed to two-lane highways in the towns and in spite of war or threat of bombardment or the more imminent menace of a mob that was getting tired and hungry and impatient, the local uses of these two-lane streets had to be respected before all others. ... The parked carts and bicycles and perambulators of the local populace remained parked on curves or on hills or wherever they happened to be. And the cars of the uninvited pilgrims from Paris could go around them one at a time and inch by inch no matter how loudly they might howl or how long it might take. More than once we thought that maybe the refugees in desperate wrath might do something at one of these traps. But apparently all of the wanderers felt as I was beginning to feel, numb, tired, miserable, hopeful of nothing better and unconcerned at the prospect of anything worse. We stopped. We started. We moved a little. We stopped again. We listened carefully for aeroplanes and were glad when presently a cold rain came and dismal clouds filled up the sky.

\*    \*    \*

PARIS, June 11, 1940 (Associated Press): ... The French Government fled from Paris last night....

\*    \*    \*

JUNE 14: *German troops occupied Paris.*

# WITH THEIR HANDS IN THEIR POCKETS

*by Demaree Bess*

WE watched the Germans, almost literally with their hands in their pockets, walk into Paris. On that warm morning of June fourteenth, they hung the swastika flag on the Eiffel Tower and on the Arc de Triomphe. They made military headquarters of the Hotel Crillon, next door to the American Embassy; and press headquarters of the Hotel Scribe, around the corner from the American Express. They staged their ceremonial review in the Place de la Concorde, where two German planes alighted spectacularly and delivered that morning's Berlin newspapers.

But very few Parisians witnessed the scenes of that historic day. Because the Germans had conquered an almost abandoned city. They had walked into a Paris whose population was less than it ever has been in modern times, into a city where most of the responsible men had run away from their responsibilities. And that is one reason why the Germans came.

It is not yet possible to tell the full story of what occurred in France during those five dramatic weeks between the launching of the German Blitzkrieg and the occupation of Paris. The heavy smoke screen of the French censorship obscured the march of events, hiding what went on not only from the outside world but also from the French people themselves. A score of years from now old men publishing their memoirs will still be giving us additional details.

At this time, we can only report what we personally saw and heard of the Blitzkrieg in Paris. We can tell how doubt and suspicion and fear grew in the minds of the people, as they were deserted by their employers, as they observed politicians resuming their bitter personal quarrels in the hour of France's great danger, and as they heard sinister rumors of incompetence and treachery in the high army command.

During those days we encountered bewildered French junior officers who had been stationed on the front beyond the Meuse River, where the German break-through came. They reported that, instead of attempting to stop this invasion, a general withdrawal order had been issued. They had seen with their own eyes that, during this retreat, vital bridges had not been blown up —and they could not understand why. They knew that a number of French officers on that front had been executed—for reasons which were not clear. And, in spite of the confusion which began to spread from those earliest days, they had seen their friends fighting bravely and going to their death.

It was stories of this sort which began to percolate through Paris before the King of the Belgians surrendered, before the campaign in Flanders ended. It was such reports which distracted the French soldiers, even before the Germans turned their powerful striking force against the army on the

Somme. It was these doubts and fears which laid the foundations for the panic which finally engulfed Paris.

The people of Paris were close to panic many times during those weeks. The war communiqués told them that their British allies were being driven across the Channel, that some of the finest troops of France were cut off in Belgium. They recognized that the stand on the Somme was a desperate hope, and that Paris would be one of the first German objectives. But in those days, the government took strong measures to stem the panic, and ordinary people responded courageously. They went about their business as cheerfully as they could, so long as their leaders stood by and directed their affairs. But when this leadership dissolved, Paris lapsed into chaos.

The evacuation panic started on June ninth. That night was black and sultry, uneasy with ominous lights and noises. There was the soft gulping sound of bomb explosions; the sharper barking of antiaircraft guns; the dull hum of cannon on the all-too-near battlefields. And each sound was accompanied by strange lights; sudden white brilliance each time a bomb exploded; orange-colored flashes each time an antiaircraft gun released its flame; and always the questing searchlights, sending long thin shafts of radiance, sweeping the skies, hunting for the enemy.

By dawn on Monday, the streets were thick with people. They had been packing their belongings all through that frightening night, and by four o'clock in the morning they were in full flight. Every vehicle with wheels was pressed into service. Some of the automobiles which passed our windows must have come from museums. Long queues stood at the taxi garages; there were two thousand people waiting at the depot nearest our hotel. But most Parisians had no motor vehicles, nor hope of hiring any. They left their homes on foot, pushing baby carriages and laden bicycles, carrying packs on their backs, leading a child by one hand, and clutching a dog or a gas mask with the other.

At twilight on Monday, Paris was blotted out by a blanket of black smoke. Was the wind blowing the cannon fumes from the adjacent battlefields? Was this smoke screen a clever device to protect our city? Or was the French army destroying its oil supply before it fell into German hands? No one knew. The French government itself had evacuated during the day, and no one remained behind to answer the anxious questions of the people.

There were no more guns or bombs the next day, but the pitiful procession of men with bundles and women with bread and babies continued endlessly. Where were they going? Many of them said they were going to their families on farms. Would they be able to reach these ancestral homes? Most unlikely. The trains were loaded beyond capacity and by this time no longer attempted to collect tickets. Reports came back that the roads around Paris were clogged not only with civilian refugees and thirsty cattle but also with wounded soldiers and the advancing German army. Then why were Parisians rushing out into this mad bedlam? Most of them did not know. Sheep without a shepherd, they followed one another, because no one directed them otherwise.

From what was happening in the small hotel which we occupied, we could tell what was happening in private enterprises everywhere in Paris that week. The owner of this hotel, its manager and its chief accountant had all been mobilized when war was declared in September. Although mobilization had thus deprived the organization of most of its brains, the hotel continued to operate during the winter on its inherited energy. Many of the staff had been on the job for years and they continued to function fairly well under the direction of the concierge, a wounded veteran of the last war. The concierge told us, in fact, that the hotel had never enjoyed such a busy winter season. The profits from this season were paid to the aged mother of the owner.

On June tenth, however, the old lady caught the contagion of fear which was infecting Paris. She sought advice from the municipal authorities, but none was to be had. Suddenly, deciding to seek safety in the country, she paid the hotel employees their wages and left them to fend for themselves. Most of the guests of the hotel were also departing, and this decision to close the hotel confirmed the doubts of any who had considered remaining. All joined the stampede southward.

But, as we had decided to remain in Paris, we asked permission to keep our own apartment in this otherwise sealed hotel, and this request was granted. We then recruited a maid and a cook and laid in a little supply of food for ourselves. Several other members of the hotel staff, when they heard that we were staying, begged us to provide work for them also, and we did set two of them to cleaning up the rooms of some of the guests who had departed, leaving their rooms in wildest confusion.

No one remotely guessed what actually did happen. No one foresaw that German troops would come into Paris as peacefully and quietly as they came into Copenhagen or Oslo. No one predicted that Parisians would watch the German entry with the same appearance of bewildered incomprehension the Danes and Norwegians had shown.

We first became aware that Germans were in occupation of the city when Paris fire trucks, manned by Frenchmen, stopped below our hotel on Friday morning and we watched them haul down the four big French flags which encircled the Rond-Point des Champs Élysées. Then they began to tear down posters which urged Frenchmen to buy armament bonds.

We went out then to meet the incoming troops, advancing along the Rue Lafayette, past the Madeleine into the Place de la Concorde. The German high command knew, of course, the conditions which awaited the arrival of their army in Paris. They knew they were coming into an almost empty city. They knew that French gendarmes had been left behind to guard against disorderly incidents.

Nevertheless, it was startling to observe the nonchalance with which those Germans marched through the heart of Paris. They were still at war with France, but they did not even bother to assign guards along the boulevards through which they advanced.

Those first German troops were young and alert and freshly shaved. They

208

had rested during the night in the suburbs and they did not seem tired. To the amazement of Parisians, who had read so much of Germany's mechanized army, those first units were all drawn by horses. We stood at the Madeleine on that sunny morning amid small clusters of Frenchmen and watched the Germans pass. They looked about them with a lively curiosity at the beautiful city which most of them were viewing for the first time. They might have been tourists, out to see the sights, for anything their manner showed. If they felt a sense of exultation, they carefully suppressed demonstrations of triumph. The French people around us watched the procession in silence, bearing themselves with that dignity and sang-froid which their authorities had recommended.

For several days after the occupation the German army authorities simply ignored the population of Paris. The disorganized French civil administration very slowly pulled itself together again. We had curfew at nine o'clock and the blackout continued. And Paris, for the first time since the war began, took on the appearance of a military city. There were continuous troop parades up and down the boulevards, there were military band concerts, there was the incessant roar of planes flying low over the city. We had seen none of these things in Paris during the previous nine months of the war.

On the afternoon of the second day of occupation, as we stood near the American Embassy, the first French prisoners went by in trucks through the Place de la Concorde. The crowds had become larger then, and they surged toward their defeated men. Girls and women ran after them, a few weeping, but most of them shouting encouragement and questions. The Germans did not attempt to hold them back.

Sunday the sixteenth, the third day of the occupation, was a cool sunny day. By this time Paris had become accustomed to the steady roll of army vehicles, carrying German troops and guns and supplies along the boulevards toward the battle lines in the south. We were incapable of astonishment now, even when we saw sight-seeing busses commandeered in Holland and Belgium and Northern France conveying infantrymen to the swiftly shifting front. They looked like some gigantic excursion party, and the eagerness with which the Germans soldiers snatched their brief view of Paris enhanced the illusion.

# ON THE ROADS OF FRANCE

## by Sonia Tomara

TOURS, France, June 14.—For four days and four nights I have shared the appalling hardship of 5,000,000 French refugees who are now fleeing down all the roads of France leading to the south. My story is the typical story of nine-tenths of these refugees.

I left Paris Monday night, June 10, in a big car which was to take me, my sister, Irene Tomara, and a Canadian doctor, William Douglas, who has been working with the American and civilian refugees. We loaded our car with whatever we could carry. We had enough gasoline to take us at least to Bordeaux. It was quite dark when we left. All day cars had been going toward the southern gates of Paris.

Just as we departed dark clouds rose above the town, obscuring the rising crescent of the moon. I thought at first it was a storm. Then I understood it was a smoke screen the French had laid down to save the city from bombing.

We drove across the Seine bridge and in complete darkness past the Montparnasse station, in which a desperate crowd was camping. We found the so-called Italian Gate and drove past it, risking all the time the chance of being hit by trucks. But all went well for about fifteen miles. Then, as we started up the first hill, the gears of our car refused to work and the car would not move.

We managed to pull off the road and park. We were in a small suburb of Paris. As nothing could be done during the dark hours, we rolled into our sleeping bags in a ditch alongside the road and tried to sleep. But cars roared by us incessantly. Then came an air-raid alarm. Then the cars started again.

When dawn came we tried to get the car going. It would not start. We waited for hours for a mechanic, while cars passed at the rate of twenty a minute. Then we learned there were no mechanics. They had all been called into the army. But the driver of a truck stopped and inspected the car. He said it could not be repaired on the road.

We tried to buy a little truck that could take our luggage. Finally the gendarmes on the road took pity on us and stopped a military truck, asking its driver to tow us. Fortunately we had a chain. We started off at noon on the road to Fontainebleau. At that time the road was a dense stream of army and factory trucks carrying big machines. We drove all day, and at 8 P.M. got into Fontainebleau.

In Fontainebleau we located a garage. The mechanic looked at the car and said it could not be repaired in less than two days. "We have no men to repair it, anyway," the manager of the garage said. "We work only for the army." We passed the night at a hotel and in the morning started to look for a truck that could tow us. Douglas found a youngster who had a country truck, but no gasoline. He was going back to Paris. We promised him gasoline and he said he would take us to Orleans and then drive to Paris.

We were abandoning our car, which was worth at least 40,000 francs (approximately $875), but money had ceased to have significance. We reloaded our bags on the truck, which had no top, and sat on them. It was 5 P.M. We drove five miles without difficulty and then got into a stream of refugees and army cars. Refugees blocked the road by trying to pass the main line of cars, thus interfering with oncoming traffic. At 10 P.M. we had driven less than fifteen miles from Fontainebleau. The boy driving our car was in despair. He wanted to turn back to Paris, but we would not let him. We saw thousands of cars by the roadsides, without gasoline or broken down.

We drove on in the night. Presently the road cleared, but we were off our route. Soldiers had detoured traffic to permit movement of military cars. We were driving south instead of toward Orleans. In a small village we turned off and started at a good speed through the dead of night, with lights turned off. It was fantastic. The clouds parted and the moon came up. The country seemed phantom-like. There were piles of stones in front of each village we passed, and peasants with rifles guarded these barricades. They looked at our papers and let us pass.

We arrived before the Orleans station at 3 A.M. on Thursday. After three nights and two days we had made only seventy miles. The scene near the station was appalling. People lay on the floor inside and the town square was filled. We piled our baggage and waited until daylight. There was nothing to eat in the town, no rooms in the hotels, no cars for sale or hire, no gasoline anywhere. Yet a steady stream of refugees was coming in, men, women and children, all desperate, not knowing where to go or how.

I walked around and found a truck that was fairly empty. I talked to the driver, offering him money to take me to Tours. He would take us near Tours. For food, we had only a little wine, some stale bread and a can of ham.

The scene of the refugees around the station was the most horrible I had ever seen, worse than the refugees in Poland. Fortunately, there was no bombing. Had there been any attacks it would have been too ghastly for words. Children were crying. There was no milk, no bread. Yet social workers were doing their best and groups were led away all the time, but new ones continued to arrive.

All morning we sought means of transportation. There was none. I decided to go to Tours. I started to walk in the rain with my typewriter and sleeping bag, at last getting a lift in a car which moved slowly through a mob of refugees moving in the opposite direction. In Tours, I learned that the government had left. Also gone were most newspapermen, but a Press Wireless operator and the French censor were still there.

As I finish this story there is a German air raid. The sound of bombs is terrific. I hope the German bombers have not hit at the road which leads to the south, for there refugees are packed in fleeing crowds. (Here eight words were censored.)

The catastrophe that has befallen France has no parallel in human history. Nobody knows how or when it will end. Like the other refugees, and there are millions of us, I do not know tonight when I shall sleep in a bed again, or how I shall get out of this town.

# COMPIEGNE

## *by William L. Shirer*

PARIS, June 21

On the exact spot in the little clearing in the Forest of Compiègne where at five A.M. on November 11, 1918 the armistice which ended the World War was signed, Adolf Hitler today handed *his* armistice terms to France. To make German revenge complete, the meeting of the German and French plenipotentiaries took place in Marshal Foch's private car, in which Foch laid down the armistice terms to Germany twenty-two years ago. Even the same table in the rickety old *wagon-lit* car was used. And through the windows we saw Hitler occupying the very seat on which Foch had sat at that table when he dictated the other armistice.

The humiliation of France, of the French, was complete. And yet in the preamble to the armistice terms Hitler told the French that he had not chosen this spot at Compiègne out of revenge; merely to right an old wrong. From the demeanor of the French delegates I gathered that they did not appreciate the difference.

The German terms we do not know yet. The preamble says the general basis for them is: (1) to prevent a resumption of the fighting; (2) to offer Germany complete guarantees for her continuation of the war against Britain; (3) to create the foundations for a peace, the basis of which is to be the reparation of an injustice inflicted upon Germany by force. The third point seems to mean: revenge for the defeat of 1918.

Kerker for NBC and I for CBS in a joint half-hour broadcast early this evening described today's amazing scene as best we could. It made, I think, a good broadcast.

The armistice negotiations began at three fifteen P.M. A warm June sun beat down on the great elm and pine trees, and cast pleasant shadows on the wooded avenues as Hitler, with the German plenipotentiaries at his side, appeared. He alighted from his car in front of the French monument to Alsace-Lorraine which stands at the end of an avenue about two hundred yards from the clearing where the armistice car waits on exactly the same spot it occupied twenty-two years ago.

The Alsace-Lorraine statue, I noted, was covered with German war flags so that you could not see its sculptured work nor read its inscription. But I had seen it some years before—the large sword representing the sword of the Allies, and its point sticking into a large, limp eagle, representing the old Empire of the Kaiser. And the inscription underneath in French saying: "TO THE HEROIC SOLDIERS OF FRANCE ... DEFENDERS OF THE COUNTRY AND OF RIGHT ... GLORIOUS LIBERATORS OF ALSACE-LORRAINE."

Through my glasses I saw the Führer stop, glance at the monument, observe the Reich flags with their big Swastikas in the center. Then he strode slowly towards us, towards the little clearing in the woods. I observed his face. It was grave, solemn, yet brimming with revenge. There was also in it, as in his springy step, a note of the triumphant conqueror, the defier of the world. There was something else, difficult to describe, in his expression, a sort of scornful, inner joy at being present at this great reversal of fate—a reversal he himself had wrought.

Now he reaches the little opening in the woods. He pauses and looks slowly around. The clearing is in the form of a circle some two hundred yards in diameter and laid out like a park. Cypress trees line it all round —and behind them, the great elms and oaks of the forest. This has been one of France's national shrines for twenty-two years. From a discreet position on the perimeter of the circle we watch.

Hitler pauses, and gazes slowly around. In a group just behind him are the other German plenipotentiaries: Göring, grasping his field-marshal's baton in one hand. He wears the sky-blue uniform of the air force. All the Germans are in uniform, Hitler in a double-breasted gray uniform, with the Iron Cross hanging from his left breast pocket. Next to Göring are the two German army chiefs—General Keitel, chief of the Supreme Command, and General von Brauchitsch, commander-in-chief of the Germany army. Both are just approaching sixty, but look younger, especially Keitel, who has a dapper appearance with his cap slightly cocked on one side.

Then there is Dr. Raeder, Grand Admiral of the German Fleet, in his blue naval uniform and the invariable upturned collar which German naval officers usually wear. There are two non-military men in Hitler's suite —his Foreign Minister, Joachim von Ribbentrop, in the field-gray uniform of the Foreign Office; and Rudolf Hess, Hitler's deputy, in a gray party uniform.

The time is now three eighteen P.M. Hitler's personal flag is run up on a small standard in the center of the opening.

Also in the center is a great granite block which stands some three feet above the ground. Hitler, followed by the others, walks slowly over to it, steps up, and reads the inscription engraved in great high letters on that block. It says: "HERE ON THE ELEVENTH OF NOVEMBER 1918 SUCCUMBED THE CRIMINAL PRIDE OF THE GERMAN EMPIRE ...VANQUISHED BY THE FREE PEOPLES WHICH IT TRIED TO ENSLAVE."

Hitler reads it and Göring reads it. They all read it, standing there in the June sun and the silence. I look for the expression on Hitler's face. I am but fifty yards from him and see him through my glasses as though he were directly in front of me. I have seen that face many times at the great moments of his life. But today! It is afire with scorn, anger, hate, revenge, triumph. He steps off the monument and contrives to make even this gesture a masterpiece of contempt. He glances back at it, contemptuous, angry— angry, you almost feel, because he cannot wipe out the awful, provoking lettering with one sweep of his high Prussian boot. He glances slowly around the clearing, and now, as his eyes meet ours, you grasp the depth of his hatred. But there is triumph there too—revengeful, triumphant hate. Suddenly, as though his face were not giving quite complete expression to his feelings, he throws his whole body into harmony with his mood. He swiftly snaps his hands on his hips, arches his shoulders, plants his feet wide apart. It is a magnificent gesture of defiance, of burning contempt for this place now and all that it has stood for in the twenty-two years since it witnessed the humbling of the German Empire.

Finally Hitler leads his party over to another granite stone, a smaller one fifty yards to one side. Here it was that the railroad car in which the German plenipotentiaries stayed during the 1918 armistice was placed—from November 8 to 11. Hitler merely glances at the inscription, which reads: "The German Plenipotentiaries." The stone itself, I notice, is set between a pair of rusty old railroad tracks, the ones on which the German car stood twenty-two years ago. Off to one side along the edge of the clearing is a large statue in white stone of Marshal Foch as he looked when he stepped out of the armistice car on the morning of November 11, 1918. Hitler skips it; does not appear to see it.

It is now three twenty-three P.M. and the Germans stride over to the armistice car. For a moment or two they stand in the sunlight outside the car, chatting. Then Hitler steps up into the car, followed by the others. We can see nicely through the car windows. Hitler takes the place occupied by Marshal Foch when the 1918 armistice terms were signed. The others spread themselves around him. Four chairs on the opposite side of the table from Hitler remain empty. The French have not yet appeared. But we do not wait long. Exactly at three thirty P.M. they alight from a car. They have flown up from Bordeaux to a near-by landing field. They too glance at the Alsace-Lorraine memorial, but it's a swift glance. Then they walk down the avenue flanked by three German officers. We see them now as they come into the sunlight of the clearing.

General Huntzinger, wearing a bleached khaki uniform; Air General Bergeret and Vice-Admiral Le Luc, both in dark blue uniforms, and then, almost buried in the uniforms, M. Noël, French Ambassador to Poland. The German guard of honor, drawn up at the entrance to the clearing, snaps to attention for the French as they pass, but it does not present arms.

It is a grave hour in the life of France. The Frenchmen keep their eyes straight ahead. Their faces are solemn, drawn. They are the picture of tragic dignity.

They walk stiffly to the car, where they are met by two German officers, Lieutenant-General Tippelskirch, Quartermaster General, and Colonel Thomas, chief of the Führer's headquarters. The Germans salute. The French salute. The atmosphere is what Europeans call "correct." There are salutes, but no handshakes.

Now we get our picture through the dusty windows of that old *wagon-lit* car. Hitler and the other German leaders rise as the French enter the drawing-room. Hitler gives the Nazi salute, the arm raised. Ribbentrop and

Hess do the same. I cannot see M. Noël to notice whether he salutes or not.

Hitler, as far as we can see through the windows, does not say a word to the French or to anybody else. He nods to General Keitel at his side. We see General Keitel adjusting his papers. Then he starts to read. He is reading the preamble to the German armistice terms. The French sit there with marble-like faces and listen intently. Hitler and Göring glance at the green table-top.

The reading of the preamble lasts but a few minutes. Hitler, we soon observe, has no intention of remaining very long, of listening to the reading of the armistice terms themselves. At three forty-two P.M., twelve minutes after the French arrive, we see Hitler stand up, salute stiffly, and then stride out of the drawing-room, followed by Göring, Brauchitsch, Raeder, Hess, and Ribbentrop. The French, like figures of stone, remain at the green-topped table. General Keitel remains with them. He starts to read them the detailed conditions of the armistice.

Hitler and his aides stride down the avenue towards the Alsace-Lorraine monument, where their cars are waiting. As they pass the guard of honor, the German band strikes up the two national anthems, *Deutschland, Deutschland über Alles* and the *Horst Wessel* song. The whole ceremony in which Hitler has reached a new pinnacle in his meteoric career and Germany avenged the 1918 defeat is over in a quarter of an hour.

# ORAN

### by Edward Angly

LONDON, July 4.—The British Navy seized, sank and crippled part of the French Navy in the Mediterranean yesterday afternoon. This startling stroke was taken to prevent ships which only a few weeks ago were allied with the Royal Navy from falling into German control under the terms of the French capitulation.

The largest of a series of actions in which the British attacked French naval vessels took place in the waters off Oran, on the Algerian coast. There, it was believed, two of the biggest and most modern ships of the French Navy were engaged. One of these was set afire.

The British Admiralty announced at 3:35 A.M. today that operations were still proceeding and that a statement would be made to Parliament later today by Prime Minister Winston Churchill.

Yesterday morning the British took control of all French men-of-war in British ports and, having tried to persuade captains of French vessels in Africa not to turn their ships over to the Germans, gave them an ultimatum to surrender by 3 P.M. yesterday.

When the commanders of certain French warships lifted anchor at Oran and started out of the harbor British warships pursued them and promptly at 3 o'clock opened fire. Several score of smaller French naval vessels were involved in the historic action, along with two major units.

Since the Pétain government of Premier Marshal Henri Pétain bowed to Adolf Hitler and deserted its British ally, the officers and men in the French Navy had, to this correspondent's knowledge, been approached on the sly and otherwise by agents threatening them and their families in France with all manner of threats should they fail to knuckle down to Germany's terms.

Surrender of the French fleet to Germany was to Britain a life or death matter, and Britain has given her answer. Whether the attack upon the French fleet will make it any easier for Hitler to arouse anti-British feeling among the French populace, and thus facilitate its plans to use France as a base for the battle of Britain remains to be seen.

Well-informed persons in London, after a night of expectancy as news of the naval battle in the Mediterranean trickled in—sometimes by airplane courier—seemed sure as dawn broke this morning that most of the French units brought into action had either surrendered to the British or been sunk.

Many hours before the Franco-British naval battle opened in the Mediterranean I learned from a trustworthy source of a "last order" in secret code which Admiral Jean Darlan, commander of the French Navy, had sent to the commanding officers of all French warships on the day after he became a member of the Bordeaux government of Marshal Pétain.

In that message he informed his commanders that he was giving them his last order, that all future orders signed with his name were to be ignored "because" the message explained, "I am no longer free."

"This last order," he wrote, "is that you shall not surrender your ship."

In the days of treachery and betrayal, of confusion and chaos, that immediately followed, it is my understanding—from French naval folk now in Britain—that Pétain removed the commanders of several French warships from their bridges and in their places put officers he could trust to capitulate to the Germans. Thus was written one more chapter in the recent tragedy of France.

The Admiralty communiqué issued this morning follows:

"It will be recalled that the French government, relying upon the promises of Germany and Italy not to use her fleet against France's former ally, undertook by the terms of the armistice to allow their fleet to pass into the hands of the enemy.

"His Majesty's Government, having lost all faith in promises made by the governments of Germany and Italy, felt that they were compelled, not only in their own interests, but also in the hope of restoring the independence of France and the integrity of the French Empire, to take steps before it was too late to insure that the French fleet should not be used against them by the common enemy.

216

"With this object in view, steps were taken in the early morning of July 3 to place all French men-of-war in British ports under British control."

* * *

Vichy, France, July 5, 1940 (United Press): The French Government of Marshal Henri Philippe Pétain today broke off diplomatic relations with Great Britain. . . .

Zurich, Switzerland, July 9 (United Press): France's democratic Parliament today voted itself out of existence in favor of a totalitarian dictatorship.

* * *

# FRANCE UNDER THE NAZI HEEL

### by Glen M. Stadler

A MONTH after the fall of Paris I walked down the Grand Boulevards, pushing my way through sweating Nazi soldiers and sauntering Frenchmen. It was Bastille Day. The strains of "The Woodpecker's Song" ground from the juke boxes of several sidewalk cafés. Wine and beer were plentiful. From outward appearances this tableau was not much different from any other lazy afternoon. To me it was evident that the French had not yet recovered from the apathy which struck them like a plague with the annihilation of their armies. Nor had they begun to feel, to a great extent, the economic and political catastrophe befalling them. I strolled from the Boulevard des Italiens to the Boulevards Montmartre, Poissonnière, Bonne-Nouvelle, St. Denis, St. Martin, Temple, Filles du Calvaire and Beaumarchais to the Place de la Bastille itself. Hawkers were peddling the latest lists of French prisoners of war. The square was almost deserted except for a small crowd in one corner. The German military governor had forbidden all public gatherings. Could it be possible, then, that this group had defied the decree and that French individualism had not been beaten into these very stones over which crazed mobs surged 151 years ago?

*"Mesdames! Messieurs!"* I heard the raucous voice cry.

Stretching high, I looked over the heads of the crowds and saw . . . a weight lifter trying to badger his spectators into tossing him francs instead of sous. War seemed a million miles away.

Bastille Day, 1941, also was hot, but there were fewer German soldiers, far less food and practically no wine. Nazi "purchases" and requisitions had almost exhausted the supplies. Every bit of French economy had been gobbled up by the Nazis. The bread ration was slightly less than half a pound a day per person, meat less than that a week—if available at all. Wine soon was to be rationed at a quart a week, or about the normal average daily consumption. Music drifting from the crowded cafés was mostly German: "Vienna," "Marlene," and "Bel Ami." Perhaps only a

217

hundred or so Frenchmen had been executed by the Gestapo in the past year. Lists of war prisoners no longer were sold. Everyone knew that more than 1,500,000 were in prison camps, many being forced to work for Hitler's total war.

Behind the conquering *Wehrmacht,* experts of the "Economic Mobile Units" followed like jackals, stripping industry. This system had a twofold purpose. First, since France was to be chiefly an agricultural tract in the master plan of the New Order, and an exporter of luxury items, she would not need this machinery. Second, the stuff that the French actually did need until the *Neuordnung* was accomplished could be used as barter goods to trade *back* to the rightful owners for concessions profitable to the Nazis. Of course, the factories which the Germans could utilize immediately were left intact. This Utopian scheme was explained to me in detail in the early days of the occupation by Dr. Helmuth Westphal of the Reich's Economic Ministry, whom I interviewed in the German-occupied Chamber of Deputies building. Speaking English he had perfected during five years' residence in the United States, he expounded his Fuehrer's version of *raison d'être.* He spoke with equal acumen of the roles that Norway, Sweden, Italy, Spain and Bulgaria would play.

"Every person and business must prove its right to exist," he explained. "For instance, if heavy industry because of the proximity of raw materials, fuel and the availability of transport, skilled labor and outlets, is more suited to the Ruhr, and agriculture has its *raison d'être* in France, then French industry must be moved up to the Ruhr, leaving the French unencumbered by mechanical things. The *Neuordnung* cannot tolerate misfits."

During the first days of the occupation men and boys were rounded up by Germans and taken to barracks where they were pumped full of propaganda designed to induce them to go to work in the Reich. The Vichy government protested and the men were released. Some did sign for German jobs, however, for want of something to do. Two years later Laval admitted that Germany planned to "requisition" French labor to obtain over 300,000 "volunteers" he had asked to work in German factories, so that some war prisoners would be released.

"A policy of entente and conciliation with Germany, whose victory I desire, is necessary to assure the salvation of the country and the future peace," Laval asserted.

Nazi authorities made it easier for French workers to decide about going to Germany by decreeing longer hours in French industry, throwing thousands out of work. During the spring and summer of 1942 about 1,300 French factories and artisan shops were closed because of lack of raw materials. An additional 1,600 were threatened with closure. Twenty-five employment offices opened in Paris after Laval's plea. Three were promptly bombed.

Two of France's most famous and profitable industries, fashions and champagne, probably have suffered more than any other under Nazi rule. Cut off completely from North and South American and British markets, *haute couture* was dealt a critical blow. But for the so-called fashion experts of Berlin and Vienna it was a golden opportunity. Frau Robert Ley, blond young wife of the *Arbeitsfront* chief, proclaimed that Germany would dictate the world's fashions. Soon materials began to become scarce and "wood-wool"—ersatz wool made from trees—was introduced. Vichy became alarmed and announced that henceforth Paris fashion houses would not be governed by clothing ration cards, so "France can retain her leadership in fashions." Five per cent added to each purchase went to the national relief fund.

Because the vineyards in the Champagne region were virtually abandoned in the exodus, production that year was 83 per cent below normal and there was no prospect of recuperation for three years. Actual war damage was slight; the harm was done by leaving the vines untended. During a visit to Rheims I learned that the Luftwaffe had violated the *Wehrmacht's* promise not to enter the city for a certain period and took 2,000,000 bottles of champagne before the Ribbentrop-appointed "Champagne Fuehrer" arrived to take charge. He was right at home: he had lived there many years before the war. Upwards of 12,000,000 bottles were requisitioned immediately. The estimated reserve at that time was 55,000,000 bottles. The Germans paid an average of forty francs a bottle—two marks—which was tantamount to seizure because of the artificial value of the mark in francs. A glass of weak beer at the Adlon Hotel bar in Berlin, for example, costs a mark. It's practically impossible to get French champagne in Berlin; if it is obtainable it costs about 100 marks, or forty dollars. The German people would like to know what happened to all the wines taken from France.

# THE MAN WHO QUIT

## by Jay Allen

MARSHAL PÉTAIN received me on December 17, 1940, in his apartment in the Hotel du Parc at Vichy, where he had taken refuge from the brutal cold of the unheated pavilion de Sevigné. He works in a spacious corner room filled with light, warmth and the serenity of its occupant. He wore a dark, double-breasted suit and as I entered, he got up from his working table in the middle of the salon and held out a big gnarled paw.

He talked with me for over an hour about conditions in France, of the great decisions he had taken in the midst of the catastrophe and of his "monster efforts of reconstruction." He spoke of the "national revolution" which is in the making, and of the unavoidable new organization of the European Continent.

It was the only interview he has given to any foreign newspaperman since he took the helm.

The Marshal talked sadly about the Armistice, but he spoke of it as one speaks of things long past. He said that if France had tried to carry on the war from North Africa, she would have paid dearly for it, for the entire country would have been occupied by the Germans. He said furthermore:

"No one knows how effective further resistance might have been. A nation vanquished cannot without presumption cherish too many hopes. But a nation vanquished has still the right not to regret what would have been an act of despair.

"My national revolution differs from the other French revolutions. It is a revolt not against political oppression but against an obsolete and outworn order. The beautiful tree of Liberty of 1789 replanted in 1848 has borne its crop. Its fruits have fallen to earth. What we have to do now is to create a new orchard within lesser bounds.

"In the Etat Français of 1940 the historical ideals of the late French Revolution—Liberté, Egalité, Fraternité—are to be pruned down as materially they have been scratched from many a public building already."

The Marshal sees the role of France in the future post-war Europe as the bridge between the New World and a new order in the Old World.

About his "revolution" Pétain uttered the following sentences:

"The French Revolution of 1940 is taking place in the aftermath of defeat, seven years after the German Revolution and eighteen years after the Italian Revolution. But my new order is entirely different in spirit from both of these historic revolutions. We broke sharply with the past in order to restore community discipline, to restore quality in labor, fecundity in family life and the more compelling pervasive sense of La Patrie. These ideals are nearer to the soil of France, more intimate to her true destiny. As yet this revolution has only just begun. Its true flowering will come in the harmonizing of social conditions and in the restoration of security for industrial worker and peasant alike.

"There," the Marshal cried, "you have a true revolution. Believe me, this revolution has need of liberty, but to a degree it excludes individualism. This revolution calls for equality, but for equality of sacrifice. It rejects demagogy. This revolution calls on the spirit of fraternity, but this spirit of fraternity it will organize to save the said revolution from temptations to deviate and from falling into a caricature of itself.

"France must first of all devote her efforts to her own reconstruction. Her will to accomplish this can be seen in the rapidity and the order with which she is co-operating with the authorities of occupation.

"Today we find ourselves having stood the trial. France has survived. She has recovered her unity, and those who in the worst days sought refuge on foreign soil are beginning to regret their departure."

# THE MAN WHO DIDN'T QUIT

## by Quentin Reynolds

THE man who didn't quit has a closely cropped mustache and he is tall and straight. When he speaks the words come out sharply and when he talks of the betrayal of his country the words are bits of rounded hail dropping on a tin roof. General Charles de Gaulle, today the mouthpiece and leader of all-free Frenchmen, is a very tough citizen indeed.

"France lost the war," he says with the confidence of a man who knows war tactics backwards, "for very definite reasons. These were: First of all, our military system did not bother to develop any mechanized strength in the air and on the ground; second, the panic which gripped our civilian population at the advance of the German mechanized units; third, the tangible effect the fifth column had on the minds of many of our leaders, and fourth, lack of co-ordination between us and our Allies."

In those few sentences de Gaulle told why a great nation was strangled to death in a few weeks. Behind each of his reasons lies one fundamental fault common to all—the horrible inefficiency of the general staff, which still thought of this war in terms of the last war. The general staff was proud of its Maginot Line. Its complacency communicated itself to the civilian population and finally to the Army.

France looked upon the Maginot Line as Americans still mistakenly look upon the Atlantic Ocean. It was a bulwark against invasion. France thought only in terms of defense. France believed that the war would be a war of position as was the last, not a war of movement, of quick, smashing forays by large armies of tanks and motorcycles.

Only de Gaulle saw the handwriting on the military wall. As late as last January he sent a long memorandum to General Gamelin, who was then trying to win the war on blueprints. De Gaulle condemned the policy of passive defense and foretold the disaster it brought about. He pleaded for more, bigger, faster and better-armored tanks; he got nothing but a rebuke for this impertinence.

"Germany can still be beaten, even now," de Gaulle says. "But we must make use of the same weapons which she has used so successfully. Germany won with six thousand tanks and five thousand planes. She must be beaten by twenty thousand tanks and twenty thousand planes."

By a strange paradox the military theories of de Gaulle helped to defeat the French Army in 1934. He published a book on mechanized warfare. De Gaulle was an obscure captain then known only for his personal bravery during the last war, when he was wounded three times. The General Staff frowned on the advanced theories he pronounced in his book. The book itself, *Vers l'Armée de Métier,* received scant attention except from a few of his colleagues who thought as he did.

But one German read it, the astute General Heinz Guderian, who was just beginning to organize the mechanized forces of the Reich. Guderian made it his bible and when he swept through northern France with his army of twelve tank divisions, he used the paralyzing tactics advocated by de Gaulle.

De Gaulle himself, during May, held command of the French tank army, but he had only one division. His tanks performed brilliantly at Abbeville, but he was only staving off the inevitable. He himself rode and issued commands by radio from one of the tanks.

He didn't have the enormous sixty-ton tanks used by the German Army. So confident was Guderian of the success of these tanks that many of them were armored only in front. From the beginning the Germans fought an offensive war with the possibility of retreat ruled out.

Today de Gaulle is the only articulate voice the free Frenchman has. Each day hundreds of weary French who managed, by some miracle, to escape from the cataclysm that engulfed their country go to his dingy suite of offices in St. Stephens house on Victoria embankment, asking to join his forces, pleading for a chance to strike a blow that might by some miracle breathe life into the corpse that is France. Within two months de Gaulle may be a half-forgotten name but if the miracle should happen he will emerge as the greatest and most patriotic of the French generals, the one man who refused to be a stooge for the miserable set of leaders who figured in the betrayal at Bordeaux. If de Gaulle's past is to be believed it is difficult to think that his future will be sterile.

In the beginning his career followed the military pattern. He graduated from St. Cyr as a lieutenant. He fought in the last war under the then Colonel Henri Pétain. He was wounded twice but each time returned to his regiment. Then, during the Verdun battle, he was wounded badly and taken prisoner by a German patrol. He made five abortive efforts to escape and each time had to endure the penalties for such failure.

His military career after the war was active except for a stretch at teaching in the military college at St. Cyr. During recent years his radical military theories received support from only one man in a high place, Paul Reynaud. During the first week of June he was recalled from the front by Reynaud to join the cabinet as Undersecretary of State for War. Reynaud felt that his colleagues were weakening under the pressure of both German military and fifth column strength; he wanted one additional strong voice to overcome the babble of the incompetent and the senile who through no fault of his had been put into the cabinet which he headed.

De Gaulle's tenure as a member of the cabinet was short-lived. When Reynaud was deposed at Bordeaux and Pétain put in, de Gaulle knew that it was all over but for the division of spoils. He hurried to London where he sent out an appeal to colonial generals for help.

One inducement was offered to French officers who fell in line with the Bordeaux government. The Germans promised them that their pensions would be safe if they behaved well. They held the safety of their families over their heads as another blackjack. Thousands of French officers made their choice. They picked what they thought would be financial security and continued health for their families. They threw in their lot with the Bordeaux group which, day by day, becomes more of a puppet government.

De Gaulle, with the reticence of a professional soldier, refuses to condemn or even comment upon the action of his fellow French officers. He condemns the politicians and the general staff bitterly, but he has not reproached the men who fought so brilliantly with him at Abbeville and at Cambrai during the nightmare of May. De Gaulle would rather discuss the lessons this war has taught the military world today. No country can say that distance protects it from the mechanized forces of another nation. He says, "To date the war has taught us that we have a real military revolution. If I were an American I would take these lessons to heart. America must be ready at any time with the necessary weapons to meet a modern attack, with mechanized forces of air, land and sea. If I were an American I would take for my slogan, 'We should do our utmost to save liberty in this world by all means and at any cost.'"

De Gaulle stood erect and strong; his face showed nothing but confidence. He terminated our talk with a short nod and a strong handshake.

Outside, in the badly lighted hall, men and women were waiting to see him. There were two small anterooms. In one a bespectacled lieutenant took the names of the callers, in another a Cockney lad answered a telephone. The shabbiness of the uncarpeted room and the derelict furniture, dimly lighted by uncertain bulbs, seemed a poor setting for bright dreams. But General Charles De Gaulle, the man who didn't quit, may emerge from the shabbiness of this old office building to make the dreams of hundreds of thousands of free Frenchmen come true.

# UNDERGROUND FRANCE

## by Richard de Rochemont

AUGUST 20, 1942—When Pierre Durand and I had last met, we were both still in Paris and the war had just begun.

After the fall of France, he had missed the last chance to get out to England and had stayed with his men until the demobilization. Within a month he had become fully aware of the treason that had accomplished France's downfall and had put himself at the head of a corporal's guard of men who, like De Gaulle, felt that France had lost a battle but not a war. With them he had plunged into the bitter, secret fight for freedom.

Today, two years later, he is the head of one of several organizations that compose the French Underground. His own outfit alone has 4,000 active armed members, and its sympathizers, still lacking arms but not faith, number in the hundreds of thousands. He is the editor in chief of an underground newspaper which is printed simultaneously in a dozen cities of France, with a total press run of over 50,000 and a hand-to-hand circulation among a half-million readers.

He can rarely show himself in a public place, either in Paris or the cities of the south of France, but a thousand houses open to his knock to give him food, shelter and concealment. Though the Church has never officially blessed the underground resistance of the French, hundreds of village rectories offer him food and comfort. Pierre Durand is one of perhaps a dozen men whom the Gestapo and Vichy's State Police most keenly desire to lay hands upon, yet in 20 big towns of France he can read secret reports, and of the prison registers kept by these same police. He was able to tell me that in May of this year 400,000 Frenchmen were behind bars for alleged political crimes, 120,000 of these in the so-called "free" zone.

To Pierre Durand come reports from Toulon, Mers-el-Kebir, Dakar and Bizerte on the material and moral dispositions of the much-discussed French Fleet—not diplomatic estimates but factual data gathered by quartermasters and machinist's mates.

"How do you get back and forth across the demarcation line between the two zones?" I asked.

"Sometimes by stealth, slipping over with a peasant guide," explained Durand, "but more often with a forged German travel permit and the identity papers to accompany it. On reasonable notice we can produce almost any sort of papers, including passports, birth certificates, police identity cards and so on. Sometimes we buy the papers from the Germans themselves."

Durand said that he had crossed the line of demarcation and the line into the forbidden zone of the coastal departments with a dozen different identities, including those of a Rumanian priest, a Swiss police official going to fetch an extradited criminal, a lawyer and an Italian consul returning to Milan.

Propaganda is more important to the Underground this year than sabotage or acts of terrorism, for the resisting groups still need recruits, funds and information. Therefore, all the groups have centered around their newspapers. In the Occupied zone, the organization called "Liberation" publishes a paper of the same name, while another group called "Liberation Française" publishes a paper called *Combat*. Other papers sponsored by smaller outfits appear sporadically, generally mimeographed, sometimes printed. The two principal papers mentioned above also appear regularly each week in Unoccupied France, where *Le Franc-Tireur*, the newest of the important weeklies, has also been brought out. Independently of these, the Communist party organ, *L'Humanité* appears in both zones, either printed or in offset. The total press run, including the Communist papers, is about 200,000 a week. Some are seized by the police or the Gestapo, but the clandestine circulation managers always attempt to replace the confiscated copies a day or two later.

After each issue is printed, type is distributed rapidly, plates are melted down, and the printing shop which did the work returns to its normal appearance and business, quite probably that of publishing a German-approved provincial weekly, or typesetting for books and pamphlets bearing the imprimatur of the censors of Vichy. One paper was run off for several weeks on the press which a big hotel, entirely occupied by Germans, used for printing its menus. The paper was moved finally, for fear the Germans would recognize the similarity of the hotel's one font of battered type with that of the underground sheet.

Most daring exploit of the outlaw publishers was the launching of a paper in German for the edification of the occupying forces, called *Unter Uns* (Among Ourselves), which was made up mainly of news from the Russian front. In March of this year the Gestapo finally ran down the two men who had been the ringleaders in the venture and shot them.

The clandestine papers are not impressive to look at. Yet to Frenchmen in whom the spirit of resistance is strong and who are sickened by the press of Paris and Vichy, they are a banner of hope and a handclasp of friendship and resolution. Their news is often something already heard on the British or American radio, their jokes something copied from old magazines, but their editorials are a force any American publisher would envy. They help slow down production of war material for Germany by their appeals to the French worker. They have effectively blocked the Laval-Pétain drive to recruit factory hands for work in Germany itself.

The Underground draws its support, Pierre Durand told me, from four principal sections of French society: the lower middle and "middle middle" classes, the university students and professors, the working class in its totality, and a great majority of the French peasants. The most violently combative groups are to be found in Lorraine and Alsace, Picardie and the Pas-de-Calais, and among the French Flemings of Dunkirk, Lille and Roubaix. All the coastal sections down to the Bordeaux region are in a state of ferment, probably because they see the R.A.F. at work, have seen or heard of Commando raids, and know that the Germans are not without fear. Working-class Paris is solidly against the regime, and took the British bombardment of its suburbs without a whimper. All classes of those resisting refuse to participate in the persecution of the Jews, and laugh at Hitler's racial theorizing.

The minor clergy, and particularly those of the Dominican Order, have taken a firm stand against collaboration, though most priests are careful to avoid outright rebellion. Some, however, have gone so far as to issue fake baptismal certificates to Jews to protect them from the racial laws. Today the liberal Catholic elements of France have their own underground paper, a well-edited, serious journal called *Témoignages Chrétiens* (Christian Testimony), which takes no pains at all to conceal its attitude toward Germans and Vichy alike, and which opposes collaboration by the Church.

The Protestant minority, with certain notable exceptions, has been united in its opposition to the invaders and usurpers. One of the wealthiest groups

225

in France, it has made considerable cash available to the workers of the underground movement.

I questioned Durand as to the relations of the Underground with General de Gaulle and the official Fighting French movement.

"In the year since you visited France," said Durand, "General de Gaulle has grown greater and greater in the eyes of the French. He is the only possible leader for the France that fights, and he has claimed no other right or authority. It is only a few months ago that our organizations gave full and official adherence to de Gaulle. He did not ask it. We gave it to him in response to a demand from our rank and file, and from that of the French labor movement. Then we asked the general to state his political position and submitted his statement to our membership. It was found to be wholly acceptable, and from that time on our union has been a total one," stated Durand.

# THE FIGHTING FRENCH

## by Dudley Harmon II

OCTOBER 3, 1942—When American troops passed through Free French Equatorial Africa recently on their way to Leopoldville, capital of the neighboring colony of the Belgian Congo, they were greeted with American flags. Some of these flags had six-pointed stars. Others had only 16 or 20 stars instead of 48. This was because the Frenchmen who sat up nights sewing on them in preparation for the arrival of an American mission last year were not quite sure what was correct. That the banners were there at all meant that the officers had spent days hunting down scraps of red, white and blue bunting in regions where every single article they use must be imported.

This incident is typical of the way the Fighting French are carrying on in the colonies of their scattered Empire, which ranges from craggy islands in the foggy North Atlantic to coral reefs in the South Pacific. It is a strange, patchwork Empire, numbering colonies about which many Frenchmen knew little or nothing before the war. The largest, French Equatorial Africa, is five times the area of France itself. One of the smallest, the island of Miquelon, has only a little more than 500 inhabitants. The other territories are the torrid Pacific island of New Hebrides, first to rally to General de Gaulle; the French islands in the Pacific, among them the Society Islands, best known of which is Tahiti; the French Protectorate in India, numbering 13 settlements; the rich Cameroons, the former German colony which adjoins Equatorial Africa, and Syria and Lebanon in the Middle East.

These colonies extend over three continents and comprise some 10,000,-000 people. Today their affairs are supervised from London instead of

Paris by cable and air mail. Minister of Colonies in General de Gaulle's National Council of Defense is René Pleven, a Breton who was a successful businessman before the war. His next in command, M. de Saint-Mart, was governor of the Ubangui-Chari province of Equatorial Africa before going to London.

In some instances, as in the French Protectorate in India, the Governors of the colonies are the same men who held these posts before the Armistice. In Syria, St. Pierre, and Miquelon, where Vichy sympathizers were in charge, de Gaullists have been installed. Governor of Syria is that outstanding Fighting French military figure, General Catroux, who before the Armistice was Governor General and Commander in Chief in Indo-China. In Syria he is concerned with civil, political and administrative questions, while in the event of military operations the British General Maitland Wilson is in charge.

The Negro Governor of Equatorial Africa, Felix Eboué, was transferred to his present post from the Tchad in recognition of his services in rallying that department to de Gaulle and his long experience in Africa. Governor of the Tchad today is M. Lapie, who went to England following the campaign of Norway and wrote a book on the French Foreign Legion at Narvik.

Since the 1,863,450 square miles of the Fighting French Empire boast little industry, the colonies are dependent on the world outside for most of their needs. Chief source of supply is the British Empire, with the United States second.

New Caledonia and other French Pacific islands which are half a world removed from Britain are now supplied exclusively from the United States. Vast deposits of nickel make this colony the richest one in the Fighting French Empire. The ore, vital in the prosecution of the war, is today being mined under the direction of American engineers, who by introducing new methods plan to greatly increase the regular output of 10,500 tons a year.

The United States also buys from Equatorial Africa copper and tin, though they could get even more if the French were able to introduce heavy machinery into their damp jungles. Most of the Fighting French colonial products are purchased by Great Britain, which arranged to keep the colonies going economically in an agreement signed between Winston Churchill and General de Gaulle. England pays for wood, cocoa, and palm oil from Equatorial Africa, though because of the shortage of shipping space some products are stored for distribution in France after the war.

Even more important than the copper, tin and nickel of the Fighting French Empire, however, is the strategic advantage offered by their situation. At Pointe Noire, Equatorial African port, the Americans are building a base where planes will be assembled and flown over the Tchad. In New Caledonia, which is only 625 miles from Australia, American troops are stationed, and the French are under the command of a United States officer, General Patch.

The Fighting French have drawn on all their colonies for their Army. Turbaned Spahis from the African desert continue to eat in London their favorite dish of boiled mutton and rice. Members of the Equatorial African army are kept supplied by the French with their main food, manioc, a root-like plant which they cook in iron kettles outdoors for breakfast, lunch and dinner.

The strange geography and peculiar climates of their remote colonies have raised problems for the Fighting French. At Camp d'Ornano in Brazzaville, soldiers begin their work at six in the morning to avoid the equatorial heat. A radio station is being built there with 400 tons of material manufactured in the United States.

# THE SILENT WOMEN

## by Kay Boyle

A FORMER major in the Austrian Army said to me the other day that when the Nazi régime will have been brought to an end in Europe, the concentration camp and the poison gas factory should be preserved as the most fitting monuments to that régime. The fitting monument to European woman should be, I think, the one which represents her sitting in absolute silence, her head bowed, her suitcase beside her, her hand across her eyes.

In a country where women never cease saying what they have to say on the lecture platform, on the radio, and in the press, it is strange to remember that there are women who sit silent, not speaking the words of despair because they have learned through grief and misery and privation the futility of protest, and not speaking the words of hope because they know that even words, once uttered, may be taken away. We who have lost nothing demand that things be said, that books be written, that explanations be made, but the women of Europe are silent, and it is their silence that we must seek to hear.

Perhaps it is true that people of any time and in any country must have the proper setting for greatness before great demands may be made upon them. Perhaps the wide, wild area of the West and the individual endurance it demanded shaped the integrity of the men and women who went there as pioneers. The West of those early days may have been the required *mise en scène* for the dramatization of that history of a great people—a drama for which there had been no dress rehearsal and which had never previously been played.

Thus it may be that the women of contemporary Europe, had there been no territorial invasion, no wholesale exile, and no racial persecution, would not have faced other and lesser issues with the same degree of dignity and courage. But all that we need to know today of them is the fierce, undefeated silence which they keep. They have kept it in evacuation and defeat, in concentration camps and in exile, and the rules of it are more difficult than those of any other language to learn.

Hear the silence of this woman whose husband, a former member of the Spanish Ministry of Public Instruction, writes from the Camp of Argeles in France:

"From this immense sea of sand which is constantly swept by the simoom, bed of eternal rest for many of us and for all of us a territory of inexpressible pain, I take the liberty of writing this letter. It may never reach you, but if it does, hear it as a cry of despair. Acute hunger, physical misery, and moral degradation of the most elementary of human principles have not yet broken my spirit, but my wife has contracted tuberculosis here, and this I can not and will not bear! No medical assistance is being given her, she is permitted no supplementary rations, the sea washes in at night across our platform where she lies in heroic, unprotesting silence on the boards. . . ."

Or the silence of Frenchwomen whose men—a million and a half of them—are prisoners of war in Germany. No newspaper prints their protests, no letters can contain their anguish, there is no vocabulary simple enough and moving enough to say: "This is my emotion, this is what I am feeling," as one might say: "What dress shall I put on today?" There is one letter, out of that national silence, which a French mother has written to Admiral Darlan. It says:

"French blood is flowing in Syria. Frenchmen are ordered to fight there against their former ally and against the French. Your noble career, Admiral Darlan, is stained with French blood. We do not like the English, but we respect them because they are continuing the fight for liberty. This is a fact that none of us forgets, so your propaganda has no effect. Men can forgive their executioners—Christ has been the living example of this—but they cannot collaborate with them."

It would make great music, it would make great poetry if the silence of these women could be brought to sound and speech.

Every man is in himself an expression of some portion of his nation's spirit. He is, voluntarily or not, a part of his nation's internal or external conflict. His deeds are his nation's deeds, his nation's acts are his acts, and he cannot evade the consequences of them. How tragically and how profoundly women are implicated in these consequences depends upon men. Last year, Frenchwomen stood silent in the streets, waiting the return of the defeated. Those who did not stand waiting were the women who knew, although no actual word had been communicated to them, that their men were active dissenters to that defeat and that they would not be returning home. When men make their escape to other countries, it is women who keep the secret, knowing that in choosing the nation's ideal they had for the moment at least to relinquish the nation's soil.

Women of the invaded territories have fled with their men, or have gone into concentration camps with them, or have stood by and seen their men go and not been able to follow where they went. There is one army of silent women that I can see clearly, and that is the army of women which assembles on the railway tracks before the troop-trains in the stations of German cities, massed there in living barrier so that the trains taking their men to Russia may not pass.

It is not to our credit if we feel that such women are strangers to us. It is we who should feel uneasy about our own feminine souls if they seem to us like characters out of a sensational play. They have fought several stages of our battle for us, and now the time has come for us to carry on with the same inviolability they have done. They are women who once had everything, as we now have everything, and from whom everything has been taken. They are women who have learned to resist, in Sigrid Undset's words, "... an army of marauders who came to live where they have not built, to reap where they have not sown, to rule over a people they have never served."

If we concede that man is representative of at least some element of his country's state, then we should define what part of the national spirit it is woman's part to give interpretation to. I should say that she interprets nothing of any value whatsoever as long as she continues to see a national event in its particular application rather than in a profounder and graver way. There is a responsibility that we must meet, and neither politicians nor armies can meet it for us. It resides in women's hands, and the women of Spain, the women of France, the women of Russia, and of the invaded countries have shown us what that responsibility is.

I remember a Frenchman saying to me during the war in France that if you listen to men talking in a barber shop, you will know the state of mind of that country's Army, and I have never forgotten it. If the truest picture of contemporary man's morale is to be found in the barber shop, then it is also quite likely that the hair-dresser's salon—precisely because of its essential multiformity—will give us the most authentic picture of womankind. The curtain which separates us each from the sight of the other is the screen on which the magic-lantern slide of the other's agony is shown.

I have listened with the greatest interest to some of the conversations I have overheard, and they are strange indeed to hear. One woman in the booth next to mine talked indignantly of the rationing of sugar in a country of such plenty, of the difficulty in finding good hot-water bottles, and the rise in price of rubber gloves.

"Look at my hands!" she said. "Just look at the condition of my skin! I have to wash the dishes without rubber gloves now that they've gone up in price," and I remembered a story told me recently by an American consular officer who was returning by Clipper to Switzerland. He was taking with him a dozen or so pairs of rubber gloves for a surgeon friend in Berne who required gloves for his operations and could no longer find them in a substantial enough quality over there. In the New York wholesale place where the consular officer bought them, the salesman said to him:

"If you are going abroad, perhaps you could tell me or find out for me the address of a doctor in Paris who ordered a great quantity of rubber

230

gloves from us about a year and a half ago. He paid us for them at the time he ordered them, but then France fell, and we didn't send them because we thought they'd never reach him."

The consular officer asked his name, and the clerk consulted his records. "Dr. Martel," the clerk said, and the consular officer said quietly: "He won't be needing them."

The name Martel may mean nothing to you now—at best the name of a cognac which the French aren't drinking any more—but eighteen months ago, it may have meant something for a brief moment. In all the welter of tragic foreign news, you may have read of the doctor in Paris' American Hospital who, the day the Germans walked into the city, took his own life and so put himself beyond degradation, as well as beyond any human need.

Perhaps, when great demands have been made upon us, as well, it will be difficult for us to speak as long and as loudly as we do now. I often think of the women of Europe sitting in silence with their suitcases beside them, and their heads bowed, and their hands across their eyes. Silence becomes a grave and vigilant posture, an incalculable strength, the clearest name for dignity and tenacity that we know.

# THE WAR LORD

## by Frederick C. Oechsner

IT IS more than likely that Hitler, being the egoist that he is, was relieved not to have to submerge his identity or his personality in so conventional a thing as marriage. Whatever propaganda value the role of husband, and perhaps father, might have had, it probably would not have equaled his identity as bachelor War Lord. So he gave himself entirely to this role, which is almost certainly what he has always wanted above everything else.

The propaganda machine, with the first Nazi invasion, switched over smoothly to glorifying Hitler as War Lord rather than as statesman. The build-up had actually started when Hitler took personal command of Germany's fighting forces in 1938, and after Poland it took on new proportions. Goebbels, in his capacity of propaganda chief, led the chorus, and myriad were the newspaper and magazine articles and photographs which reminded the Germans that Der Fuehrer was in the field.

It was Hermann Goering, however, who reached the epitome of acclaim when, on May 20th, 1940, he said that Hitler had attained heights of military genius achieved only once before in German history—by Frederick the Great. He gave Der Fuehrer unreserved and unqualified credit for conceiving, planning and directing the execution of the Nazi onslaughts on Poland, Norway and Western Europe.

"Who is responsible for the overwhelming success of these plans?" he

231

asked in a special press conference, and answered himself without pausing for breath: "Der Fuehrer. He is the originator of these plans. In long nights, for weeks and months, Adolf Hitler acquainted himself with every possibility of military developments and with all the eventualities of enemy counter-action. He even outlines all minor attacks down to the very last detail."

Goering went on to say that German tacticians had considered Fort Eben Emael, in the northeast corner of Belgium, at the juncture of the Albert Canal and the Meuse River, the strongest fort in the world, but that even that Allied stronghold guarding the gateway to Belgium was taken "in conformity with plans made by Der Fuehrer himself." He added that Hitler possessed an almost incredible knowledge of every type of arms.

"There is no warship, no gun, and no weapon in existence which Der Fuehrer cannot judge as to its effect on operations," Goering continued. "Not only has he intimate knowledge of weapons but also, as an old soldier on the front line during the World War, he knows the value of man power. His experience and expert knowledge enabled Der Fuehrer not only to make plans of operations but also to lead the armies himself. He is in continuous contact with everything that happens anywhere on the fighting fronts and consequently is able to make his dispositions accordingly. His enormous energy and exemplary discipline make every German officer and private strive to the utmost limit of what is humanly possible."

Such panegyrics about Hitler are not unusual for Goering. A large man, he pays large compliments. But the song of praise goes right on down the line. I remember well the eulogies of one General Staff officer who conducted a party that I was in on a five-day tour of the West Wall, Germany's great line of fortifications in the Rhineland. He was one of the Army's leading technical experts on the Wall and always conducted Hitler personally on his tours of inspection. This is what he told me: —

A book had been published in France by a certain high Army officer detailing what he considered to be the faults of the Maginot Line's construction. Apparently he was disturbed at the too great faith which was placed in the Line. The book was immediately suppressed in the interests of military secrecy, but one copy of it fell into German hands in Paris, whence it was immediately dispatched to the War Ministry in Berlin. It was shown to Hitler, who, realizing its importance to Germany, immediately had it translated verbatim into German. When the translation was delivered to Hitler he read it through without stopping, making voluminous notes. After a brief interval for digestion and reflection, Hitler sat down and dictated an exhaustive report on the book, which came to be the basis of the whole plan of Germany's own opposing line of fortifications, the West Wall, construction of which Hitler ordered on May 28th, 1938, when it became evident that his forcing of the Sudetenland solution might lead to war and that his western flank was totally unprotected.

"Not only did Hitler maintain an over-all supervision of the Wall's construction," said my General Staff informant in awe, "but he even sketched the design personally of some of the pillboxes down to the smallest detail, such as the thickness of the walls or the placement of the gun slits."

Corroboration that Hitler had taken this strong personal interest in the construction of the fortifications was given me by the engineer who built it, Dr. Fritz Todt, next whom I sat at luncheon in the spring of 1939. A simple, earnest, unassuming man, Todt, an early adherent of Hitler's, had been selected by him to construct the great network of federal auto highways, the *Reichsautobahnen*. That had been a big job of concrete construction and Todt had done it well. So Hitler gave him the West Wall assignment, with unlimited authority to get the work finished in the shortest possible time. In the face of an already shrinking labor supply, Todt got 500,000 workers out into the Rhineland by paying them higher wages, shanghaiing them, or whatever else it took, housed and fed them in cooperation with the Nazi Labor Front, commandeered 15,000 motor trucks and 8,000 railway cars, and got his concrete and steel put together in time for Goering, just five months later, to shout at the annual Party rally that Germany's western frontier had been made impregnable.

A year later, when I made my tour of the Wall, it was still abuilding, but Todt had unquestionably accomplished an astounding piece of work. After every tour of it Hitler ordered new pillboxes to be constructed, and by the time I traveled it from Aachen to Karlsruhe it was a viciously efficient-looking line of shark's teeth, perhaps as many as 10,000 individual pillboxes, staggered in a double, or even triple row, fifty miles in depth at some points. The entire thing is co-ordinated with anti-tank barriers. The individual pillboxes contain either artillery or machine-gun equipment and at special points are built in clusters in which each unit is in constant telephonic connection with every other. The pillboxes are set into hillsides or in the midst of woods so as to escape detection either from the ground or from the air. Scores of them are built and disguised to look like houses, either out in the fields or on the outskirts of towns. A few are even camouflaged as gas stations, and one, which cradled a ten-inch gun, is built to look like just that rustic inn where you have been planning to spend your week end. An even larger gun, nestling in the midst of the Black Forest, can be fired only on direct orders from Berlin. It has a crew of fifty men to run it.

Hitler's interest in military matters down to the smallest detail cannot be doubted. We have seen what a great part of his personal library is devoted to military literature. Moreover, he was always in direct contact with the problem of operations, visiting proving grounds, airfields and barracks and holding frequent conferences with his Chiefs of Staff even long before he went into war. I think all the claims by Goering and others that Hitler possesses an innate genius for military matters are exaggerated. I think that through reading and discussion he has developed a thorough knowledge of tactics and a sense of strategy. His naturally acute ability to sift and co-ordinate facts enables him then to take what his generals tell him, combine with it, or relate to it, his own acquired knowledge on the subject, weigh it all in the light of what he knows of the enemy's weakness and his own

233

strength, and then produce a synthesis which is pretty apt to be the right answer. His experience as a World War soldier could not be of great use to him as Supreme Commander, except in enabling him to know how the common soldier reacts. In four years of the World War, Hitler never progressed beyond the rank of lance corporal.

In military matters, as in political ones, Hitler's whole career has reflected his choice of the bold, audacious, dynamic policy rather than the cautious and conservative course, and he draws to himself and promotes men who think and act boldly. Of such a type are the men who are closest to Hitler today in waging war. They are men whom he has appointed to generalcies and field marshalships on the basis of their performance for him and he knows them all personally. Hitler has always made it a practice not only to meet his officers but to know them.

The last few years of Nazi "dynamism" and nerve war have taken their toll of the world's nerves and blood; they have taken their toll, too, of Hitler's nerves, though he is yet alive. Even shortly after the beginning of the invasion of Russia, Hitler was reported by persons who saw him to have grown extremely serious of expression and as showing signs of unusual sensitivity. Ribbentrop was among those who sought to spare him shocks and sternly forbade persons coming to make special political reports to him to say things that might smack of defeatism. It was at this time that Hitler began using sleeping sedatives, so that even his doctors cautioned him about them. The coldness of the nights, too, made him resort to an occasional hot grog, something unheard of in earlier days. I myself saw him twice at fairly close range in these months. His color was not good, his eyes had more than their usual sharp, glaring, not quite normal stare. He fidgeted in his chair, peered up at the ceiling, seemed to look through people near him. But as always, when the moment came for him to assert his personality and his dominance, to say a few words, he was in absolute command of himself: poised, assured, hard; acting Der Fuehrer as if born to the title.

# Part Five: From the Battle of England to the Battle of Germany

JULY 29, 1940: *Germany launched mass air raids over Britain.*

AUGUST 25: *First British air raid over Berlin.*

SEPTEMBER 7: *Hitler started all-out bombing of London.*

# LONDON IN FLAMES

*by Robert J. Casey*

LARRY RUE called up that morning. By some legerdemain and possibly a bit of foresight, he had salvaged one of the Chicago *Tribune's* cars out of France and he wanted me to go somewhere with him out of town for luncheon. We picked up Jack Brebner of the North American Section of the Ministry of Information and went to the Hindshead Inn near Maidenhead. Barry Neame, the manager, describes himself in the billing as "Mine Host," which is all you need to know about him. But the atmosphere of the place is not too atmospheric and the food is excellent. So we had a pleasant afternoon and started back to London refreshed, relaxed and completely out of rapport with a world that has air raids in it.

Jack went back to clean up some work at his office. I said he'd do better coming with us—to the St. Regis or the Savoy—inasmuch as his place might be classed as a military objective. Jack said he thought he'd be safe enough and Larry agreed with him. "Listen," Larry said to me; "you don't think the Germans are going to bomb the Ministry of Information, do you? You don't think they want to knock over the last allies they've got in London?"

On which high note we parted. We went over to the Savoy and met a few people including Stan Johnstone who had run the Press Wireless office in Amsterdam for correspondents in Finland, Norway, Sweden, Holland, Belgium and Luxembourg. He was now one of Rue's staff. There were quite a lot of reporters around the Savoy premises that evening which, come to think about it, was fairly remarkable. I don't recall ever before having seen a lot of newspaper people sitting right next door to the big story when it happened.

Of course, though at the time we paid no attention to their reading of the auguries, they had some reason for suspecting sensational developments in Hitler's blitz. There had been a lot of bombing during the afternoon, they

235

said. Hundreds of planes had been flying over the East End dropping incendiary stuff on the docks. A big gas storage tank and some warehouses were alight, they said. One who had just come back from there said that the fires were tremendous, completely out of control and getting bigger. He said he didn't think any power in London could ever put them out. But all of us took that with a little salt. Fires always look a lot worse than they are.

We dawdled about the lobby for a while and I got ready to go home. Larry suggested that we go over to the *Daily Telegraph* building, where his office was, and look at the fire. I went more to avoid argument than anything else. Because the attack had been so definitely localized I hadn't heard any planes overhead. I hadn't heard any fire engines. I hadn't even heard the alert. A dock fire in the East End wasn't likely to be anything worth the cable tolls.... Besides, it was Saturday night and we didn't publish on Sunday and ...

"I talked to Guy Murchie on the telephone," said Larry as we fumbled through the courtway and turned right, into the Strand. "He says it's a hell of a big fire...."

The crumps were slapping down into Fleet Street when we got there—not many but enough to make the going precarious and uncomfortable. The guard at the *Daily Telegraph* building stood away back in the entryway—as far as he could get without a pick and shovel. He said it was a nasty night and we agreed with him. We took the elevator straight to the roof and stepped out. We were looking at the biggest spectacle of its kind that the world had seen since the previous "Great Fire of London" in 1666.

"Good God!" said Larry. "This looks awfully like the end of London."

"Like the end of everything," I said.

London was burning down. London the glorious and irreplaceable would be ashes tomorrow. London the immortal would be dead.

The light of the pyre made a brilliant glow all across the eastern sky—and it was getting brighter. The dismal blackout was gone. From where we looked into the cavernous recesses of the City and over the elegant old wrecks of aristocratic Mayfair, along the mysterious river and beyond the spire of Westminster and the tower of the House of Parliament there didn't seem to be a single shadow left in London. The steeple of Bow Bells rose like a silver sword against the flame. The dome of St. Paul's, no less ethereal and fragile than it had ever been, was marked with a million glittering facets. The streets, to use a phrase of Ed Angly's, were scattered with gold.

London, about to die, had buckled on its most gorgeous armor to do the dying in.

("The wind," said the practical Larry, "may save us.... I wouldn't bet on it.")

Great cumulus formations of smoke billowed out of the raging east, rolled skyward and flattened southward. They did not look so much like smoke as rivers of slow-moving, white-hot slag, miraculously freed from restraint of gravity. Some of the fumes were working their way westward—although we couldn't see them save as misty blemishes on the bright metallic surface of the sky. But we were conscious presently of the deadly stagnation of the air. First it was merely hot and lacking oxygen. Then it was hot and scented with oil and burning wood. Then it was acrid, choking and almost unbreathable.

"I guess there must be half a million people down there in their fine, fireproof Anderson shelters," said Larry grimly. "I wonder how much longer they're going to be able to get air."

"How much longer do you think they're going to need air?" asked Stan Johnstone.

By this time there was plentiful evidence of the thoroughness of the raid. Hitler's effort, it appeared, wasn't directed solely toward the demolition of London's most populous slum—it was spread out to embrace congested areas south of the river and the night-club district in Piccadilly and the sacred pagodas of the rich and mildewed in the sainted West End. Queerly camouflaged by the thousand glittering reflections of the night, the planes hung high above the light and dropped their bombs with ease and precision on perfectly illuminated targets.

There seemed to be hundreds of them—probably were. The rhythmic growl and mumble of them seemed no farther away than the caps of the flues above our heads. We heard them bracketing Fleet Street and the Strand and the Embankment with sticks of bombs. . . . One . . . two . . . three . . . four . . . five. Some of the crumps were so close that they seemed to have been aimed at us, personally. We crouched in the dubious protection of the concrete parapet as the blasts went off below us and the rattle of tumbling masonry and glass continued when the echoes of the explosion had ceased. Distantly now and then I caught the familiar sound of ack-ack and now and then I could see the burst of anti-aircraft shells, weird blue stars above and beyond the glowing dome of red. But there wasn't much of it and I guessed why. London hadn't been expecting any such attack as this. London had talked about it and gravely discussed what course of action would be taken when fire should rain down out of the heavens and God's poor should be blown to atoms in the streets as they tried to escape their horrible destiny. London had gone through all the motions of providing an amateur fire department and had drilled a good many A.R.P. wardens in a lot of theory that seemed to include everything except the catching of dinosaurs. But London, whatever its conversation, had kept a sneaking belief that Hitler might still be a gentleman and play this foul game according to the rules. So the ack-ack had been spread out around purely military objectives. It had protected factories and ports and railroad centers and the like. . . . Heinie had a field day over London on September 7. He had a couple more pretty good days, but never anything quite equal to that one.

Along about midnight I went down into the street. The blaze in the east was wider and higher if anything than it had been when we first came onto the roof. But it was getting too public up there. I suspected that the big white rectangle presented to a pilot by the roof of the *Telegraph* building was attracting more crumps than might be reasonably expected as our share. (They later painted the *Telegraph* roof black.)

The din in the street was terrific—worse than it had seemed on the roof for the reason that the bursts were closer and your ears seem to get sharper —and more easily offended—when the danger gets more noticeable.

At first I stood back in the doorway with the porter trying to figure out where I was going to go and how I was going to go there. It occurred to me that I wasn't permitted to be out after midnight but that seemed likely to be the least of my worries. As I had studied the situation from above there didn't seem to be any choice of streets. Heinie was just sending plane loads of bombs to London and dumping them over the side apparently at the whim of the pilot. There was no partiality. You were quite as likely to get killed in Trafalgar Square as in the crippled children's ward of some hospital—although German accuracy altered that parity not long afterward. So I went out into Fleet Street and just walked away.

Down near the approach to the Waterloo Bridge a taxicab came slowly around the corner—slowly, not because of any habitual concern for pedestrians who might step down unexpectedly from curbs, but because Heinie's bombs had begun to leave noticeable craters in the streets. I didn't know whether the driver might be looking for custom or not—it seemed improbable. On the other hand I thought that if he were going in my direction (whatever it was) I might as well ride with him. So I stopped him.

He didn't want to take me. He was going home, he said, and he was in a hurry, only he had to be careful coming around blind corners into streets where the Nazis had been "knocking things abaht." He lived in the East End and he had a family out there and he was worried about them and he was going home right away. I said that would be all right with me. So I got in and we went out somewhere near the Elephant and Castle.

The ride, according to all the rules, should have been exciting. But it wasn't really. The bombs didn't sound any nearer than they had sounded in Fleet Street and over the rattle and crash of the cab the visiting aeroplanes could hardly be heard at all. We turned into a lot of byways and alleys flanked by what appeared to be warehouses so that we traveled most of the time in a sort of red twilight. I got a glimpse of the frightful glare on the sky only at street crossings.

I could tell when we got closer to the fire. The smoke was floating about in wisps like cotton batting, and the acrid, choking ingredients in it were thicker. Presently we got the roar of it, a sound like a whisper magnified a million times, the rush of the hurricane, the ear-numbing murmur of the blast furnace. The smash of the crumps came through this noise like the puny rattle of toy drums in a foundry. And you knew the aeroplanes were still working only when some house folded up ahead of you or a new and higher plume of sparks stood out from the hot background.

After a while we got to a place that looked like an earthquake in a brick-yard. There were ropes across the road and A.R.P. guards by the rope— black figures against the fiery background. The cab driver saw that he wasn't going to get any further, so he alighted and held the door open for me.

The meter read ten shillings. He thought that he ought to have two shillings above that price on account of unusual risks and difficulties. I gave him five extra because I put a higher value on the risks than he did. I gave him my card and told him to call our office and let us know about his family. But he never did. He may not have found any family when he got to his home, wherever it was. He may never have found his way there. The last I saw of him he had parked his car in an areaway and was setting out afoot.

I didn't know what direction to take into the mess that lay ahead of me, but apparently it didn't make much difference. The wreck looked to be complete in any direction. Crumps were still dropping regularly.... Heinie fed the fires all night. The air in this neighborhood got more and more stuffy and insufferably hot. A couple of big gas tanks let loose near by and for a long time the horror lay bared in front of you, stark and shameless.

Bill Stoneman and Helen Kirkpatrick and Dorothy Hewitt had been through the mill that night just as I had. Dorothy had a harrowing tale about the wiping out of a lower middle-class residence district. She thought perhaps five hundred people might have been killed. Helen had been bracketed between two paths of destruction. Two houses just around the corner from her place were gutted. A building across the street from Bill's flat in Chelsea had been hit. He didn't know whether he was going to stay out there or not. So far as he could see at the moment one place was just about as bad as another.

Bill and I went over to the Ministry of Information that morning—for reasons I cannot now recall any more than I can recall a reason for going to the Ministry of Information on any other day. We left fairly early, got a taxicab in front of the office and traveled through the park, so we didn't see much of the populace en route. We got back to Parliament Street about eleven o'clock just as the sirens turned loose and we flattened up against a wall to see what was going to happen. What did happen was the thing we had least expected to see.

Both of us had been abroad on the occasion of other alarms and had commented on the Londoner's instinctive command of himself. Everyone had gone to shelter at once, or at least had left the street, without any indication of panic or undue haste. We had pointed out to each other the fact that if any Londoner got bombed it would be in the most dignified manner possible. So as we stopped automatically for this alert we thought we could tell in advance what everyone would do. We were wrong about that.

There must have been a couple of hundred people where we could see them in Parliament Street and Parliament Square. Neither of us had noticed them particularly. We hadn't had much opportunity between the arrival of our cab and the arrival of the Nazi raiders. But I was conscious afterward that there hadn't been much movement. When we saw the black cross of a Junkers bomber up above us only a little higher than the barrage balloons it occurred to me to take another look at the street. I caught Bill's arm and called his attention to a spectacle that neither of us would care to look at again.

Nobody had moved. Nobody was moving now. The yammer of the siren had had no effect whatever on such of London as lay before us. Nobody was looking up at the aeroplanes. Men and women, wherever we turned our eyes, were standing at the curbs as immobile as plaster casts of themselves staring out of this noisy and troublesome world into far-distant nothingness. I looked at them and, frankly, for the first time since the beginning of the war, was thoroughly frightened. Hitler had succeeded after all. There weren't any six million people in London with the grit of the girl ambulance drivers, the A.F.S. and Tommy Thompson. Probably there weren't any more people like that anywhere. Anyway, the London that we were looking at now was spiritually beaten. It had been terrified beyond endurance, dazed at the sight of its treasures shattered and its loved ones murdered. It was punch-drunk, stupefied, out on its feet in a sort of mass shell shock. I didn't need anybody to interpret the symptoms for me. I had seen people standing like that in the streets, and looking like that, in Bordeaux the day they announced that France was going to ask for an armistice.

Several of the experts have figured out that Hitler had won the battle of Britain for a few hours on September seventh and eighth and they say that this was due to Britain's inability to get defenses organized in time against so vicious an attack. They knew the condition was there. They sensed it as everybody did but never yet have I seen one of them who put his finger on the cause as we saw it that morning. Weapons had nothing to do with it. Hitler had then and still has more weapons than anybody else in the world. But his only chance to conquer England was to break the English spirit. And for one brief moment he had it broken.

During the next two hours I toured for miles through metropolitan London. The bombers still darted about unheeded and virtually unhampered and everywhere the people were as they had been in Parliament Street, drugged with horror and surprise. And then, suddenly, as if a broken cinema film had been patched and started again the people in the streets began to move. They quit staring out into the blue and looked about them as if they had suddenly been awakened from sleep.... Not all at once nor all according to any program or pattern, but presently all of them were pursuing a normal gait and taking a normal interest in the things about them. The group hypnosis was finished and Hitler's psychological advantage was gone forever.

# THE BLITZ

## by Ben Robertson

WE DROVE on into Liverpool—huge, sooty, dirty Liverpool, tough and full of slums and poverty; and here as in Manchester and Birmingham we found people full of faith and courage. "I won't buy a new coat this winter," said a waitress to us in a restaurant. "What does it matter what we wear? Who cares what we look like, so long as we beat Hitler?"

"How does our bombing compare with London's?" the doorman inquired at the Adelphi, where we stopped (the Adelphi was across the street from the station). "Is London's bombing worse than ours?" By this time, we knew enough never to tell any Englishman that his town had been out-bombed anywhere; so we evaded the question with a question: "You've had a lot of raiding, haven't you?" With pride, he replied: "Had a hundred and forty-five—Jerry started on us a month before he started banging London." He then named three docks that had been damaged and a fourth near which a bomb had fallen. "Then they got the Custom House—got it right on the top—but it was an old building, and a lot of folks had been saying for fifty years it ought to be torn down; the street there's been needing widening since any of us can remember."

In the lift the elevator boy said: "They've damaged our new Cathedral—broke some of the windows—but we're going on with the construction just the same." As he took our suitcases he said: "It's appalling how bad the Germans shoot—you wouldn't believe anybody could be so unfortunate."

All that afternoon we drove about the city—saw the damaged Cathedral, saw warehouses that had been demolished, smashed railway lines, bombed churches, public houses, hospitals, parochial halls, homes, factories. We saw more ships than we had ever seen anywhere in any port in the world; there were hundreds of them, so crowded at docks, loading and unloading, that it seemed to us a bomb could hardly fail to hit something. A fleet of trucks moved by, heading toward a huge dock, and stamped on each of these trucks was "Anglo-Egyptian Expedition." A soldier in a pub said to us: "I'm on my way to a country where there's never any fog—nothing but sunshine."

Late that afternoon at the hotel a maid came into my room to adjust the curtains for the blackout. "Night before last," she said, "two air-raid wardens and a priest were killed when a bomb fell just behind the hotel. It was a terrible night and the housekeeper got the wind up. The housekeeper said to me: 'Nothing seems to frighten you, Miss McGillicuddy,' and I said to her: 'What's the use to bother, Miss O'Reilly? Either the bomb has your name on it or it hasn't.'"

Fixing the curtains so that no light could possibly show into the street, Miss McGillicuddy then switched herself into the hall.

There was a string orchestra in the dining-room that evening, and there were waiters, most of them old men, in boiled shirts and tails, who served us a simple rationed dinner with the accustomed elegance of the Adelphi. The dining-room was crowded with lean, weather-beaten Englishmen—the kind of Britishers you see at the polo club in Manila, at the Royal Yacht Club in Bombay, at the Hong Kong Hotel, about the bar at the Cathay in Shanghai. Outside in the lobby there were piles of luggage. We looked at several labels on trunks and read: "Early November Sailing."

England still held open her doorway to the outside world.

We went to lunch next day with the Consul General of the United States, a kindly, friendly man, very lonely without his wife and daughter, who had been sent home in July by the American government. He took us from his office, which had lost twelve hundred dollars' worth of windows, to a little restaurant in a side street, and there we had soup and apple pie and coffee with sugar that he had brought along—granulated sugar from home.

The Consul General said to us: "Do you know what I do sometimes during these long evenings? I peel apples and put up jelly."

Then he told us about Harvey Hiott, a boy from Charleston, South Carolina, who was in Liverpool prison through no fault of his own. In the old days on the San Francisco waterfront, the Consul General said, boys like Harvey got slugged over the head and shanghaied; now shanghaiing was done more subtly, sea captains were more suave.

In August 1939 a Danish ship put into Charleston and, needing an extra sailor, the skipper went ashore and said to a nineteen-year-old fellow: "How would you like to make a three-week trip to Santo Domingo and back to Charleston?" It sounded to Harvey like a wonderful way to round out the summer—he would be back in time for school. The skipper said he needed no papers, so Harvey went home, got some clothes, came back, and sailed away. The ship did not return to Charleston from Santo Domingo, however; it sailed to Jamaica, and it did not return to Charleston from there, either—it went to Spain. Then it touched at French ports and went to Africa and came back to Spain and on to Ireland. Finally a year later it put into Liverpool and Harvey went ashore and asked the Consul General what should he do.

"He seemed a fine boy," said the Consul General. "He had no passport, but there was no doubt about his being American—nobody but a Charlestonian could have that accent—so I told him to jump the ship, no matter what happened."

Harvey jumped and soon afterwards was arrested by the British as a deserter—Danish ships by that time had been commandeered by England. The Consul General went to court with Harvey and got that charge quashed, testifying that Harvey was in Liverpool through no choice of his own, that he had been aboard the ship for a year under duress. Next the British government filed an alien deportation order against Harvey, and it was at that point that Harvey got hopelessly tied up in international red tape. For Harvey was an American, and the American Neutrality Act would not permit Americans under any circumstances to sail from England in anything but an American vessel—and there were no American vessels; the last one had left Galway in July. Under American law he could not leave, and under British law he could not stay. So he was put into Liverpool prison, and the prison had been bombed and six prisoners had been killed. The Consul General asked Helen and me to take up Harvey's case in our papers; he asked us to go and see him, and if we were refused entry, to say we had been sent by the Consul General of the United States.

Helen and I went out and bought long woolen underwear, a woolen shirt and socks and some fruit and candy and went to the prison, a huge damp cold kind of dungeon. Harvey came out and talked to us through a glass window. We were the first people he had seen in three weeks; we brought him the first word he had had from the outside in that length of time. Grinning at us, he said: "I never thought I'd land up in a foreign country in jail."

"We'll get you out," said Helen.

"Do you know who they've got me in here with?" Harvey asked. "They've got me in with a lot of fifth communists."

In London we went to the Embassy and told Joe Kennedy about Harvey. Joe got Herbert Morrison, the Home Secretary, on the telephone, and five hours later, in Liverpool, Harvey was out. The Ambassador brought him to London, and the Lytel family, an American family in the advertising business in London, took him to their farm in Surrey. Harvey was out of jail, but he still was three thousand miles from Charleston.

We drove back to London from Liverpool through rain and fog and sunshine, and on the way we picked up a Canadian airman, hitch-hiking his way to an airdrome from Chester. We passed green English fields and kept asking our way from town to town along the unmarked highways. Once the Canadian said: "England has a lot of scenery to be so small."

In town after town, as we asked directions, we were told by people on the streets: "I don't know the way, I'm a stranger here myself." These were evacuees from London and what they said was true, they no more knew where they were than we did. But we soon found out, if we hesitated a moment, they would begin to tell us about their bombs—about the bombs that had fallen on Limehouse and Stepney and on Bethnal Green.

I remember in one place listening to a group of them talking. "Dearie," said a cockney, "my Aunt Fanny was bombed clear across her flat." "Dear Gawd," responded a second cockney, immediately telling a bomb story of her own, "my uncle that's ninety-two was bombed right out of his bed and his false teeth that was in a water jar on the table fell on the floor and broke." "Blime me," said the first cockney.

Those women, like everyone else in England who had been under bombing, had a sense of having lived up to duty. All of them were heroes, and they knew it; this knowledge gave their very faces a glow.

On that journey we passed through Stratford-on-Avon without stopping —we hadn't the time. In London we found the raids had continued. Kensington Palace had been hit—Kensington, where Queen Mary had been born, where Princess Victoria had been waked up one night to be told she was Queen of England. Bombs had fallen in the Temple, on the north bastion of the Tower of London. There were signs in beauty-shop windows: "Does your face have that shelter look?" On fences there were government notices: "Use coal sparingly. Be glad of any coal. Don't worry about the kind. Your merchant will supply the best he can. Lay one fire. Light it late." In a chemist's shop there was a sign: "Are you worried? All this work at home, all this loss of sleep, all those extra worries—worries about food, worries about separation from HIM, worries about making ends meet. There's a step wise women are taking to repair this damage. They are taking Tonic."

Frank Kent, Jr., of the Baltimore *Sun* had been told by a doctor of a West End hospital about a soldier and a girl who had been brought in dead one night from Hyde Park. The doctor had said to Frank: "Under the circumstances, I didn't know whether to be ashamed or proud of my countrymen."

# THEY COULD TAKE IT

## by W. L. White

I HAVE just been blown up. Not very high—only about half an inch, for the bottom of his bomb's crater was 214 feet from my chair. This evening I had dinner with my Canadian journalist and we knew it was going to be hot.

I can't say that I heard the explosion, which came just after midnight. We were back in the coffee-room. The Canadian wasn't liking it at all, and was working on his third double Scotch. I wasn't liking it either and had just ordered tomato juice. It's got nothing to do with character. Only that if something is likely to happen, I feel very uneasy if my head is fuzzy. Because maybe I would jump too late or in the wrong direction. Tomato juice during raid is my form of cowardice.

Setting down his empty glass and looking around for the waiter, the Canadian remarked how safe this room looked—almost as safe as the shelter. And I was saying that I didn't think so, because it was probably under the central well of the building—that glass skylight above us might be a fake, but it looked real. At this point the huge steel and concrete frame of the hotel gave a sudden, nervous jump, like a ticklish high-school girl. It lifted me about half an inch off my chair. I don't remember much noise, but half a second later glass splinters from the skylight above were tinkling down on our table. It was a very beautiful little Sheraton table with clean graceful lines and, I think, authentic.

"Now there's my point," I said to the Canadian journalist. "It *was* a real skylight." Only then I noticed that the Canadian journalist had disappeared. Or rather most of him had. All I could see was the seat of his pants, stretched rather tautly, while he was down on his knees trying to crawl under our fragile but authentic Sheraton table.

I look around the room. The lights are still on, but they glimmer dully through a curious yellow fog. This is dust which the shock of the explosion has jarred from corners in the plaster ceiling ornaments and the tops of chandeliers. Nothing like a bomb to show up sloppy housekeeping. Only the story is outside. I drag my trench coat and tin hat from under the chair and hustle into them, running to the door, fastening my flashlight onto my belt. It's a sweet little job I bought in Stockholm last year, copied from the German military model, and you can turn it on and let it shine from your stomach while you use both hands.

Only maybe I won't need it, because the street outside is filled with the glow of leaping flames. The bomb hit squarely in the middle of the intersection at one corner of the hotel and must have lit a smashed gas main. Outside there is a great stillness. Not a chip of concrete has been dislodged from our hotel corner nearest the bomb, although every window on that side has been blown in. But on the opposite corner a six-story building with thin brick walls and wooden floors had just dissolved into rubbish. One wall was left, a ragged outline against the sky, the rest of the rubbish trailed like a sand pile out into the middle of the street, spilling over into the bomb crater—a mixture of crumbled bricks and splintered lumber.

This crater was an interesting little inferno. The bomb had shattered both a gas main and a three-foot water main. The water was rippling like a caldron, the gas coming to the surface in huge bubbles, where the white and blue flames, licking the edge of the water-filled crater, made it look like a huge teacup full of molten steel.

Looking down the four streets from this intersection, the pavements seemed covered with heavy hoarfrost which glistened in the light of the quavering fire. It was a coating of pulverized glass from the empty window frames of the houses on either side. It crackled as I walked. Not another sound. Amazing it should be so still—that all this destruction should have been accomplished in a few seconds, the length of time it took for the highest chimney brick to tumble into the deepest part of the cellar—and then this great silence. Only now there are sounds. Cries and muffled shouts. The people in the blown-out buildings are picking themselves up off the glass-covered floors, and starting to get out. They stumble down the dark stairways out into the street. By the leaping light of the flaming gas, I see their faces and their hair are powdered gray with that dust and crumbled plaster which a bomb will shake down for blocks around. Tiny red rivulets of blood, from minor glass cuts, run down their gray faces.

Already the police are there. Two of them are dragging a screaming, bleeding woman away from the house which has collapsed.

"No, I *won't* go!" she cries. "Not without my 'usband and my little boy what was in the same room as I was!"

The A.R.P. wardens begin to arrive from nowhere, and an ambulance— all with steel-helmeted attendants. But now something else arrives—the nasty buz-z-z-z of a Heinkel overhead. Maybe the same one which dropped this bomb. Coming back now to paste us by the leaping light of this gas fire, which makes everything vivid for blocks around. How can the plane help seeing us?

Flames from the edge of that crater are licking the tail end of that pile of splintered lumber which slopes into the hole. It's burning already, but not much—a tubful of water would put it out. Two minutes later a barrel of water would put it out. Ten minutes later, by the time the fire department arrives, it seems as though nothing can stop it. But they unreel the hose and squirt on the blaze. At the other end of the pile a rescue squad is feverishly tugging at the timbers. Word spreads around that a little boy is caught under the wreckage. Here comes the plane, back again, almost over us now—the time before it probably was sliding over in a practice run to take aim. What else can they see but us, by the light of these tall leaping flames—police, rescue squad, ambulances, fire department all busy working and then—look out, here it comes!—s—s—s—s-s-S-S-S-SSSS! Of *course* the firemen drop their nozzle and spring to the shelter of the nearest wall. And who am I to criticize, cowering belly down in the gutter, trying to make myself as flat as possible, my shoulder blades seeming to stick up in the air as high as a pair of angel wings. But the explosion is several blocks away. Quickly the firemen are back, picking up the hose, not more than five precious seconds lost, but it's not nice out here in that leaping light, having to work on with a Heinkel buzzing just above and knowing it's you they're aiming at.

The streets are empty except for the steel-helmeted workers, and the people with bleeding powdery gray faces stumbling down out of nearby buildings, with coats on over their nightgowns and pyjamas, carrying battered suitcases, hastily packed with their most precious things which they will take with them to the deep shelters for the rest of the night.

A girl in her middle twenties suddenly clutches my arm. "You have a torch," she says. "Oh, please come with me—I must go back up."

She leads the way to a darkened entrance, up a flight of creaking stairs—every timber in this building has been loosened by the bomb—another one landing near would surely send it tumbling. Glass splinters under our feet crunch into the stair carpet. There is a smell of gas, probably a fixture snapped by the jar. Hope no one lights a match. What are we after? I hesitate to ask. Maybe a child. Maybe an old woman too sick to walk who must be carried. "It's on the top floor," the girl explains. We climb three more flights, each one more rickety than the last. I am really afraid now. That loose gas on the bottom floors, this whole structure ready to collapse —I want out of here.

She opens the door of her room. There's the bed she was sleeping in, it's rumpled and still warm, its coverlet and the floor are covered with glass from her window and with plaster jarred down from the ceiling. She opens a closet door, fumbles a minute and pulls out—a rabbit fur coat.

She explains she is a stenographer, and this is the only fur coat she ever

246

owned—almost paid for, and all with her own earned money. "I couldn't leave that behind." But won't I stay and have a glass of sherry? No, thanks. Thanks a lot. Not with a Heinkel buzzing over this teetering building and gas escaping in the bottom two floors.

Back down into the street now, where firemen are still dousing the flaming pile of splinters. The rescue men have been driven back. They stand helplessly on the sidewalk, and they tell me about the little boy. "About twelve he was, a little nipper, pinned under a block of concrete. Only the flames came too close before we could get enough men in to lift the block. When the boy saw how close they were, 'e went off 'is little 'ead, clean daffy. Which was God's mercy. 'E probably didn't know it and couldn't feel it when 'e burned."

The faces of all the men were angry under the tin hats, in the light of the flaming gas main. The corner policeman, who had come up, clenched his fist, raised it toward the sky and shook it. "I'd like to get my 'ands on the sods wot done it to the poor little nipper," he said.

\*　　\*　　\*

LONDON, Nov. 15 (Associated Press): ... The city of Coventry was heavily attacked last night, the scale of the raid being comparable with those of the largest night attacks on London.

\*　　\*　　\*

# WHEN THE RAIDS WERE OVER

## by Raymond Daniell

IN THE six months between September 1940 and February 1941 London had more than 500 air raids. If the people of the capital had gone to their shelters every time the warning sounded and stayed there until they heard the all-clear signal they would have spent considerably more than half that time underground. In that time hundreds of tons of bombs of every type were dropped. Yet even at that rate of destruction it probably would take Hitler the rest of his life to make good his threat to raze the British capital.

If there is a formula for describing accurately how much damage has been done to a city by constant raiding I have never discovered it. It is easier to tell what has happened to the soul of a people than it is to portray the physical injuries sustained by a huge, sprawling city like London, which covers an area much greater than New York. Not even photographs tell the story accurately, for they show merely what has been destroyed or left standing in one little sector, whereas the havoc has not been confined to one or two corners of the city but is everywhere.

Probably the best way to visualize what London looks like today is to

247

think of a human body, pock-marked and scarred, but with no mortal wounds and no amputations of arms, legs, fingers, or toes. Not a single bridge across the Thames has been destroyed, although there was hardly a night for six solid months when the bombers did not try to hit them. All the vital public utilities weathered the storm with only temporary and local interruptions of service.

I could take a stranger to the East End of London or to the City back of St. Paul's and let him walk around for hours seeing nothing but ruins. If those were the only parts of London we visited he would go away thinking that things were very bad indeed. Or I might take him on an hour's taxicab ride through the heart of London where here and there he would see a house or a building down among whole blocks without a blemish. He would probably feel that the reports of air-raid damage were exaggerated. It is the old story of the blind men who tried to visualize an elephant by each touching a different part. The one who felt the trunk thought it looked like a snake, but the others each had a different idea.

London has suffered heavily. Many of her historic shrines, her homes, and the loveliest of her churches have been damaged or destroyed. But not enough damage has been done to change the city's physical outlines or even to modify its appearance much. I have read reports written by brief visitors who have come away with an impression of London's wounds as distorted as that of the outlander who, after a brief visit to New York, says to his host, "I just don't see how you stand the pace."

Many arrived long after the *Blitzkrieg* began and saw whole blocks of wreckage in one chunk. They were tremendously impressed. But they weren't there as I was, day after day, night after night. It was a slow, laborious job for the raiders to chip away bit by bit, and piece by piece, the stone and mortar of that ancient and quite durable city. Having lived through six months of Goering's demolition work I am more impressed by its failures than its successes.

Bombs do not always completely destroy the buildings they hit. Sometimes they just knock off a corner, a chimney, or the front steps. Such damage is soon repaired. Many of them land in parks, digging a deep hole in the grass or uprooting a tree but causing no serious damage. Others land in streets, where they are an infernal nuisance, for they not only disrupt traffic but they often tear up water pipes and gas mains and snarl telephone and light cables so badly that it takes days to straighten them out.

I have read several accounts by casual visitors to London about how close to paralysis and collapse London was in mid-September, but I am unimpressed. I was there and I never noticed it. Probably if I had arrived in December or January and heard descriptions at second hand of what life was like I might have thought that what really were temporary dislocations was the beginning of chaos, but having been there all the time I marvel at the smoothness with which the life of the city ran through it all.

There were sections of London that for a few days were without gas for cooking. Here and there there was a block without water. Now and then a street was closed for a block or two because an unexploded time bomb lay buried beneath the pavement. Some telephone exchanges were out of commission for a day or two. Bomb craters in the middle of busy thorough-fares caused traffic jams in several parts of the city, but they weren't much worse than those caused by WPA workers tearing up trolley tracks at home. No section of the capital was isolated, and nobody went hungry or homeless very long. Life went on normally, except for the sleeplessness caused by the early raids, in almost every part of the mammoth city.

One of London's strengths is its great size. It will take an awful lot of bombs to destroy it to the extent that one can say that one-fifth, or one-third, of it is in ruins. It is different with smaller places like Coventry for instance. There the Germans concentrated nearly 1,000 planes—as many as were over London at any one time—and dumped their bombs upon the heart of the city. When I visited this town it was almost impossible to tell where the streets had been, for in the center of the city there was nothing but heaps of broken bricks scattered over what might have been open fields. The shape and contour of the city had been obliterated. Birmingham, which is much larger, looked more like London, with its wounds more scattered and less noticeable.

The nearest the Germans came to matching the havoc they wrought in Coventry was in late December 1940, when the raiders came over London in great numbers and dropped nothing but incendiary bombs upon the City, the financial district, which covers just one square mile. The raid took place at night, when the office buildings were closed and locked. Fires started by incendiaries landing on the roof spread and engulfed whole buildings before the firemen could get inside.

People who were in the East End that night said it was like being trapped in a forest fire. The streets there are narrow and the blaze leaped across from roof to roof. Pedestrians trying to get out of that blazing, doomed part of London found themselves constantly hemmed in and cut off by new fires and toppling buildings. Dynamite had to be used to stop the spread of the flames, and that added to the appearance of devastation afterward. Three weeks later the smell of wet embers still permeated the neighborhood where the Guildhall had stood.

APRIL 16, 1941: *First heavy air raid of year in London.*

MAY 10: *Heaviest raid over London. Westminster Abbey, House of Parliament, and British Museum badly damaged.*

\*     \*     \*

LONDON, May 13 (Associated Press): . . . The Ministry of Information announced early Tuesday that the man who landed from a German fighter plane in Scotland had been identified as Rudolf Hess.

\*     \*     \*

MAY 24: *German battleship* Bismarck *sank British battleship* Hood *off Greenland.*

MAY 27: *British naval units, aided by American-built patrol bombers, sank* Bismarck.

# THE BATTLE OF THE ATLANTIC

## *by Vincent Sheean*

SOON after I arrived in England this time I was permitted, by the Admiralty's courtesy, to go out on Atlantic convoy duty in a destroyer. Mine is not the youngest or smartest destroyer in the navy, but she has a fine record —she sank two submarines in one night last March and brought back the German survivors. Naturally, I cannot tell how she was armed or manned, but after spending a week out there on that vessel, which one officer, with affectionate disrespect, called "an old tin can," I feel certain that no more useful ship of her size or class floats on the sea today.

We left our port in the west of England shortly after eight, one morning, and steamed out toward the rendezvous. We were alone, except for one destroyer of the "town" class, one of the fifty that were once American. The remaining vessels of our escort group, including corvettes and destroyers, were to join us at a certain point. We proceeded with due caution for some miles, following the mine-swept channel. There had been quite an air raid the night before and these winged visitors usually drop some mementos in the sea before they go home. The magnetic mine has more or less ceased to be a puzzle. What with degaussing and mine sweeping, magnetic mines have lost their original importance. But sweeping clean channels for shipping is, of course, one of the most difficult and dangerous jobs the navy does; it is performed chiefly by small trawlers officered from the Royal Naval Volunteer Reserve. This reserve organization was made up of yachtsmen and other amateur seafarers in peacetime. With its corollary, the Royal Navy Reserve—they are known by initials as RNR and RNVR—they have made possible the quick expansion of the navy under stress of war.

The weather was perfect and remained perfect throughout my brief career in the navy. In fact, our captain, who was just completing one of the stormiest years of his life at sea, grew convinced that I had brought the ship luck. This past winter has been terrible on the Atlantic and the task of keeping convoys together and safe in darkness and gales was supremely difficult. All convoy arrangements have greatly improved now, and, as a matter of fact, the convoy we brought in kept its lines as splendidly as any grand fleet. But in the earlier part of war it was a heartbreaking task to keep them together. Whenever one straggles or gets lost in a stormy night, he is easy prey for the Germans, and even, in fact, for the Italians, who prudently reserve their efforts for just such cases. Merchant ships are not always equipped with efficient signaling apparatus and not always blessed by first-class seamanship or navigation. Consequently, during those long nights last winter it was impossible to prevent some straggling. A properly diagrammed convoy, in good weather with sufficient escort, is a very different matter, as it has its guardian warships on all sides.

"We are the shepherds and they are the sheep," our captain told me with a laugh. "And you know how sheep are sometimes. If they get lost, the wolves are on them."

This officer, who must hold the world's record for doing without sleep, is actually called Commander D. G. McIntyre, R. N., D. S. O., but from the first day out I found it difficult to call him anything but Capt. Horatio Hornblower, after the hero of C. S. Forester's celebrated sea story. He had the same modest pertinacity and courage and competence, inspired the same terror in his subordinates, and had the same gift for humorous understatement. On our most dangerous night, when we apparently had submarines all around us and underneath us, Hornblower stood all the watches—as he usually did anyhow—and saw the sun come up in splendor over a convoy ordered and safe.

"Well," he said, with a yawn, "I think I am getting bored with this and had better turn in. As the feller says, when you've seen one wave, you've seen 'em all."

We made our way out to the Atlantic around the Irish coast, on which Hornblower has one particular farm. Everybody on the bridge had binoculars trained on "the captain's farm," which appeared to be a little Irish thatched cottage in a hollow of the green cliff. He has never seen it any closer than this, but whenever he passes it he says, "Now, that's where I want to settle down. Nice, peaceful place." Knowing what I do of Ireland, I wondered if he had chosen well.

Our submarine warnings began as soon as we were well out in the Atlantic. I cannot give the precise numbers, but I can say that ordinary American ideas of how many submarines are operating at any one time are widely exaggerated. The Italians are instantly disregarded by officers, since the Italians have never yet been known to attack convoys or anything except occasional helpless tramps. The Germans are a very different pair of boots, and the positions of their submarines receive careful attention.

Antisubmarine apparatus ranks as a military secret of the first order and there is very little I can say about it. Its principles are well understood in America, where they received parallel but slightly different development. The generic term used for this science in the American Navy is "sound." In the British navy it is called Asdic, a word made from initials of the Antisubmarine Detection Investigation Committee. Apparently only the Americans and British possessed these instruments at the outset of the present war, but as the French navy obtained some such secrets, it is reasonably assumed now that they are in German hands. Even so—as we know also from nightfighting experience—the Germans may know the principles, but they have very little idea of the details. Apparently, when this war began they assumed antisubmarine detection to be about where it was twenty years ago and attacked very boldly, losing a good many submarines before they discovered there was something new going on. They are far more cautious now and try to stay out of the way of destroyers. Their favorite method, when they can do it, is to rise to the surface inside the convoy itself and torpedo merchant ships, making their escape as quickly as possible. With a heavy escort and ample antisubmarine apparatus, this is no longer easy.

We, for example, were shadowed by submarines for a good twenty-four hours and unquestionably had a group—possibly five—all around and perhaps beneath us. But they could not get in.

When you have certain knowledge or the strong suggestion of a submarine's exact position, the system is to drop depth charges all around him and thus force him to rise to the surface or stay down and cave in. When he rises he is then shelled or, in some cases, rammed, and his survivors, who have never saved a single one of their own victims in the entire history of submarine warfare, are always rescued.

Our meeting with the convoy on the second or third day out was a moment of pride to the officers of my destroyer, because it was such a neat piece of navigation. We arrived at our rendezvous on the trackless Atlantic precisely in the middle of the convoy line. The first faint plumes of smoke, which were visible to Hornblower about noon one day, soon thereafter could be seen by lookouts and officers, and finally even by me. There ensued a ceremonial which fascinated my landsman's eyes. The destroyers which had escorted our convoy thus far wheeled about and made off to other duties after a brisk exchange of signals. They were especially gaily camouflaged and, like all destroyers going at full speed, had a sort of bird-like motion over the calm and sunny sea. We then took charge of the convoy, passing the whole thing in review and getting their names and numbers checked. One of our ex-American destroyers had arrived at the rendezvous before us and was flashed the traditional signal: "Well Met!"

Once the review was over, we formed our escort around the convoy according to one of several diagrams determined in advance. During the journey we changed diagrams as the situation demanded. The other escort vessels, including some corvettes and a couple of ex-American destroyers, guarded the convoy on the flanks, with another ex-American rushing furiously back and forth behind it. This seemed an adequate escort to Hornblower, but the next day, when our shadowers apparently grew numerous, the Admiralty dispatched a couple more destroyers posthaste, to stay with us twenty-four hours.

During this period of maximum danger we also had considerable air protection, made up of Sunderland flying boats and Catalinas and, later on, Lockheed Hudsons, Blenheims and a Whitley.

The Sunderland, which looks exactly like a flying whale, has long been the stand-by of the Atlantic patrol. Until the Catalinas went into service, it was almost the only opponent to the Focke-Wulf.

As a matter of fact, we saw no Focke-Wulfs on this journey. For that reason I have formed the opinion that their depredations have been exaggerated. Like all bombers, they are an instrument of terror, and I can well imagine how the mere sight of one strikes a convoy passenger, but in actual fact one torpedo from a submarine does more damage than several ordinary bombing visits. Apparently the Focke-Wulf flies very low, combing a convoy from one end to the other, but takes every precaution to stay out of range of the escort vessels. It seems to be a slow machine with a great range and operates from Norway and France in an arc over the Atlantic. It is vulnerable to almost any type of antiaircraft gunnery at the height at which it ordinarily flies. Escort ships it dodges by every means in its power, but it does not always succeed. From all accounts, this bomber must have been especially made for the Battle of the Atlantic.

A submarine was detected. Hornblower dropped depth charges on it, whereupon as my friend, the lieutenant, put it, "Up popped Otto Kretschmer."

This part of the story reveals the enormous fundamental and instinctive difference between men on opposing sides in this war. Kretschmer, one of the two or three greatest submarine captains Germany has ever had, is a man who has sent literally thousands of men, women and children to their deaths in the sea without lifting a finger to save any of them. Yet when he felt himself in danger of that same fate, he flashed signals in English, demanding to be rescued. And what is more, he was rescued, absolutely instinctively and unthinkingly, because this is the tradition of the Royal Navy.

When he popped up to the surface, my destroyer and another of the same class opened fire. The other one was detached immediately, leaving my ship to deal with Kretschmer. Kretschmer's actual signal, flashed in English, was "I am sunking"; except for one vowel, he got it right. My ship went up to help, but the submarine sunk before a boarding party could get a boat lowered. The survivors leaped out and were picked up by the English boats. They included the captain—Otto Kretschmer himself— and a learning captain, three other officers and thirty ratings.

In all this incredible confusion in the blackest part of the night, the other submarine was lost sight of. My friends think it sank, although the Admiralty does not record it because there is no actual proof.

My destroyer, which is crowded to capacity even at the best of times, now had to accommodate the Germans and the whole crew of Canadians whom they had sunk. Hornblower gave his after cabin—the same one I afterward had—to Kretschmer, and the other officers had stretcher beds on the floor of the adjoining room. All the Englishmen were very curious about their prisoners and talked to them a good deal. The only things they would not permit were the Nazi salute and the words "Heil Hitler." Otherwise they gave the Germans the same food and accommodations as they had themselves. The English sailors taught the Germans the game of darts, apparently new to them.

In the ward room there was an aching need for a fourth at bridge. Eventually the chief engineer, who is a demon for a bridge game and would play with the devil if nobody else could be found, invited Kretschmer to join in. He did so, and when this ship came into quiet waters with its prizes and its laurels, the four at bridge were the chief engineer, Kretschmer and two of the Canadian survivors of the ship Kretschmer had sunk.

All the Germans were astonished to see real butter, sugar and plenty of meat. This happens constantly now with German prisoners, and there must obviously be a widespread belief in Germany that England is starving. Kretschmer also was astonished to see so many ships in perfect order in the convoy next morning. He apparently thought he had done far more damage than he actually did. Operating on the hit-and-run system, as they do, submarines probably have vague and inaccurate ideas of what they actually accomplish.

Kretschmer's worst moment, however, seems to have been when he landed in England as a prisoner. This appears to have depressed him extremely, probably because of the delusion held by practically all German prisoners that they are going to be rescued somehow or somewhere by their colleagues.

Kretschmer asked where he and his fellow prisoners would be sent, and Hornblower said, "I dunno. Maybe Canada."

Kretschmer said, "Good God, not on a tanker, I hope."

Such aces as Kretschmer count more than in any other form of war except possibly solo air fighting. The operation of a submarine involves a whole bag of tricks, devices and expedients, and experience has shown that a very few submarine captains have done the greater part of the damage. German U-boats carry two captains, one of whom is supposed to be learning these tricks from the other. Only one man can possibly command, however, since only one man on a submarine can see out. The really contemptible showing made by Italian submarines during this war is due to the fact that their sub captains are no good. Their submarines are superb and their engines probably better than the Germans', but they have done little or nothing to justify their existence.

When our ship came in, after a singularly prosperous and beautiful trip, Hornblower and two other officers received decorations for their exploit of the 17th of March. Hornblower himself received the D.S.O.

That very night we were subjected to one of the most concentrated air raids I have ever experienced. I was on the quarter-deck of the destroyer throughout that raid and can testify that it is a pretty bad place to be. To my amazement and incomprehension, naval officers all prefer to be on their ships during air raids. I should have thought almost anywhere on shore might be preferable to the deck of a small ship, but this view is not held in the navy. Hornblower told me he hated being caught on shore by a raid. "You feel so helpless," he said.

This particular raid seemed to be intended for our benefit and we took a packet. Next day, when I saw certain holes in a plate a few inches from where my head had been, I realized that it had not all been mere noise and flame. Yet I am glad to report that my destroyer is fit as a fiddle now and has just brought in another enormous convoy safely.

I have personal knowledge of a considerable number of convoys the past few weeks, and in every case known to me, submarines have been unable to attack because the escort was too strong. Of course, we passed lifeboats, wreckage, a well-built but empty raft, and even, once, two corpses, but these were vestiges of earlier misfortunes. Stragglers and strays are almost certain to go down. The enemy is relentless and forever on the prowl for those who cannot defend themselves.

However, it seems clearly proved that properly escorted convoys can be successfully brought in, and on a very large scale. With summer weather and no dark nights, this all-important task can be carried out in relative safety. But—and here's the rub—it imposes an absolutely superhuman task upon the British navy. They no longer have time to make full repairs. They have no leave, and no prospect of getting any. They are literally on duty all the time. My ship had been twenty-seven days at sea during the month before I went aboard. Lines of communication are now so immense all over the world that the navy's resources are stretched to the breaking point. And it has to be borne in mind that the British navy is no longer as enormous as it once was. There were nine hundred destroyers doing this job in the last war, when the job was somewhat less difficult. It is being done now by—well, a smaller number.

If you look at the map, you can easily see how vast the communication lines have become. Since last summer, the bulk of the transport to Egypt and the Red Sea has gone around Africa. Singapore is farther away now than ever before. If the Mediterranean is ever to be freed again to peaceful traffic, it will be at great cost to the navy. In spite of such brilliant successes as the sinking of the *Bismarck* and the imprisonment of the *Scharnhorst* and *Gneisenau* at Brest, the whole burden of maintaining free oceans cannot fall forever on the same shoulders without eventually weakening them. Ships do not improve when they are in constant service, nor do men get any fresher or younger.

And yet, when all is said, there is no armed force I have seen which seems any more certain of ultimate victory than the British navy. They do not consider the possibility of defeat, although they seem well aware that difficulties and dangers are multiplying as never before. The navy is full of radios, on which these men are forever listening, when they get a chance, to hear what is happening to their families at home. The thing that seems to worry them most is the bombing of civilians in cities. About their own job they have no illusions; they know it is bound to be pretty grim, but they propose to get it done. Speaking as a spectator of these men at their job, I can say I believe them.

# CONVOY

## by Harry T. Brundidge

ABOARD a British freighter, in the Irish Sea.—Blinkers flash orders from a destroyer to our ship. We are the flagship of the convoy. Our skipper is commodore. Our blinkers blink signals to other merchantmen and tankers.

The convoy draws far apart. The ships must give the escorting men-o'-war plenty of sea room for maneuvering. Likewise, the ships must avoid the danger of deadly concussions from depth bombs.

Destroyers and corvettes, plainly visible in a sea bathed in golden moonlight, move at high speed. Silhouettes of glorified ash cans—the depth bombs—can be seen as these are projected from the port side of the destroyers. Geysers of water shoot upward. Our ship is rocked by concussions.

The battle is on!

It's the surface ships against the unseen U-boats. We, and all other ships of the convoy are the prey that is being stalked.

I'm on the bridge with the skipper. "Damn the beasts!" he exclaims. "They used to hunt alone and had some concern—some sporting instincts—about survivors. Now they attack in packs like hungry wolves, and shell and machine gun survivors."

The new technique is for a pack to get inside a convoy and when in the middle of it, discharge torpedoes in all directions, then scoot away on the surface. Jerry calls it the Rundel system. We call it "the wolf pack."

"But they're having no good fortune tonight. The men-o'-war are breaking it up. I've no doubt that some have gone down to see Davy Jones about a permanent locker."

Destroyers and corvettes sweep in an ever-widening circle.

"Sparks" comes to the deck with a radio message. Back in London, the admiralty, in Whitehall, advises us there is no danger of an air attack. We are not advised what happened to the enemy planes reported nearby. Whitehall is in constant communication with our ship, but we may not communicate with Whitehall.

Destroyers and corvettes disappear in the horizon. We know the danger is over. We do not know the result of the battle. We probably never will know.

Down in the saloon, Churchill's voice comes over the radio. "Ole Winston" is addressing congress.

Moon over the Irish Sea. Blinkers flash from our ship. Tankers and merchantmen come together in another huddle. It is a starry night. With a moon that belongs over Miami, or Honolulu. It is a night for peace, romance, and love.

But Mars smiles grimly.

Dec. 31, 1941. We are, in effect, prisoners, as we ride at anchor off an Irish town. Mutton for dinner. I wink at Reynolds, the magazine writer, turn to the skipper, who is on my left, and ask: "What? No turkey?" Capt. H—— has a sense of humor. "It hasn't been frozen long enough to get tender. We'll have it later."

Then Edward J. (Ted) O'Leary, partner of former Ambassador Joseph Kennedy in the importation from Scotland and England of two widely known brands of Scotch and gin, waves his Irish hand and produces two bottles of French champagne. Champagne and mutton.

New Year's Day. We are at a third, and next to last, rendezvous. Dawn discloses we picked up many ships in the fog. Here we pick up many more. We move out to sea to get organized. All manner of ships—a whaler, tankers, little tramps and big merchantmen—seem to move helter-skelter about the ocean. All is confusion, or so it seems. Our skipper has relinquished command to an admiral, long since retired, who has been taken from his favorite armchair in his favorite club for convoy duty. He is admiral of the convoy.

The Admiral's flagship—of all things—is an empty, high riding tanker. What a voyage he is going to have.

Signal flags are flown from the tanker. Our ship, other merchantmen, tankers, tramps—ships flying the flags of the Allied nations, men and ships defying mines, icebergs, U-boats and raiders—acting under orders sealed until this very moment, swing into position.

The sea seems full of ships, big and little. Orders keep coming from the flagship. In a matter of minutes there is order where all was confusion.

The ships fall into five lines. We are the first ship in the second line, counting from portside—a ponderous target bobbing like a cork. Destroyers and corvettes sweep in and out. Sunderlands roar overhead. With a zigzagging destroyer in the lead we move on.

From My Notebook. This indeed is a strange New Year's Day. I can think back on many others ... That one when the late August A. Busch phoned to inform me his grandson had been kidnaped ... A lonesome one in Havana, Cuba ... Another on a Danish freighter out in the Pacific Ocean ... Still another and more recent one, coming home from China and Japan aboard the *Asama Maru,* a Japanese N. Y. K. liner ... Thoughts, memories and I am aroused from my reveries by George Shaw, the steward. The captain has sent for me.

From My Notebook, Jan. 2.—It's really getting tough, and I've been in real typhoons in the China Sea and the south Pacific.

Later, Jan. 2—Writers Reynolds, Osborne and myself tried to type a bit and gave it up. We cannot control the bucking of the typewriters. We three induce another passenger to join us at penny ante poker. We give that up. Chips slide from one fellow's stack to another's.

We try writing in long hand. The result looks like a San Francisco laundry ticket. Our ballast consists of 1,000 tons of rubble from bombed English towns—and 1,000 sacks of air mail. We decide there is but one sensible thing to do—crawl into our bunks, trust the guard rails to keep us in them, and try to read. So we do.

4:30 P.M., Jan. 2.—There is a continuous ringing of hand gongs. Life boats. I grab my valuables, jump into a life preserver, and, carrying an extra pair of pants, a sweater, and my great coat, dash out to the boat deck, down the ladder and into Life Boat No. 4.

Anti-aircraft guns are banging away. The lowering sky is full of red tracer bullets. Commands are given. Sailors stand at the davits above us, ready to lower the boats.

Pom-pom-pom-pom-pompom-pompompompom! The pom-pom gun sings its song. Oerlikons chatter. The chief steward raises his eyebrows when I tell him it all looks very much like a swell Fourth of July display.

I learn, for the first time, that Life Boat No. 4 (my boat) also carries the skipper! The last boat off!

Pom-pom, Oerlikon and Lewis guns continue their chant of death for five minutes.

Then the "all clear" sounds.

It's a wild rough day. Seas are mountainous. The temperature is dropping. The wind roars and shrieks. The skipper says frankly, "We're in for it." The barometer is falling. "There's a hurricane ahead," the skipper tells us.

# TEAMWORK

## by William H. Stoneman

LONDON, Jan. 10, 1942—The air forces and navies of the belligerent nations have divided honors during the last two years and they have had really great honors to divide only when they have worked intimately together.

A navy without air force support has been shown to be extremely vulnerable. An air force without naval support to back it up has never been able to achieve strategically decisive results.

Those lessons, hammered home by British experience with the German battleship *Bismarck*, off Crete and, finally, in the Far East where they paid the price of two magnificent battleships for another course of instruction, are likely to guide the strategy of the Allies during the remainder of the war. That the Americans had learned the lesson was indicated by the almost equal value which President Roosevelt gave to ships and planes in his statement to Congress.

The *Bismarck* was knocked out by big guns and was sunk by destroyer torpedoes, but only after she had been crippled by a torpedo from British aircraft. She would never have been sunk, in all probability, had she not been spotted from the air. The British Mediterranean fleet was given a lacing off Greece and Crete when it lost four cruisers and nine destroyers because it did not have air protection. As the whole world knows, the *Repulse* and the *Prince of Wales* were sunk because they ventured to sea without the assurance of air protection.

The same lesson has been repeated a dozen other times: Off Norway where the British were at the mercy of German bombers; at Matapan where the enemy was first spotted by aircraft; again off Sicily when two Italian cruisers were sunk by destroyers after being spotted by aircraft; in the Battle of the Atlantic, where the German success has been due very largely to co-operation between long-range bombers and submarines and, as a matter of fact, just about every other time there has been big-time action at sea or near shore. The Germans have proved, at the same time, in one of the most remarkable and most expensive demonstrations in the history of warfare, that air alone cannot knock out a distant enemy unless it is backed up by great power afloat.

All the figures available show that in actual damage inflicted on enemy ships at sea, the honors are just about even between Allied air forces and Allied surface ships and submarines. The Royal Air Force claims to have sunk or badly damaged 811 ships of all sizes and types since the beginning of the war. The British Navy has perhaps done better than that, but not much.

In action against German and Italian warships, the scores of the two services are also about even, with a slight advantage to the Navy which has been credited with many sinkings after the enemy was first spotted and brought to bay through the use of aircraft. British naval losses also are almost equally attributable to Axis air and sea forces, with a slight margin in favor of the latter.

Two heavy ships of the German Navy were sunk by the British: The *Graf Spee* and the *Bismarck,* both credited to the Navy though the latter was half the R.A.F.'s prey. Of three German cruisers sunk in the present war, two were by a British submarine and one by Norwegian coastal batteries. Only one of the 17 German destroyers sunk was destroyed by a torpedo from a British aircraft, the rest by surface vessels and mines. Yet two of Germany's fanciest heavy ships, the *Scharnhorst* and the *Gneisenau,* and the splendid cruiser *Prinz Eugen* have been bottled up at Brest these many months and the British Navy has been spared the task of chasing them or of protecting convoys against them simply because the R.A.F. has kept them immobilized there by bombing.

The R.A.F. also takes credit for having destroyed most of the armed trawlers, "ack-ack" ships and other armed coastal vessels sent to the bottom.

Against the Italians the R.A.F. has done comparatively better than in the North and its reconnaissance planes have been largely responsible for the great successes in the Mediterranean. True enough, all the nine Italian cruisers destroyed in this war have been credited to surface ships and submarines. But virtually all of them were brought to action because British planes told the Navy where they were. Matapan and the later battle of Sicily both depended largely upon aerial spotting.

Of the 35 Italian destroyers definitely known to be lost the fleet air arm and R.A.F. bombers got at least 10. Of the 35 Italian submarines known to have been sunk, four are credited to combined fleet and air action, four to air, while the cause of several other sinkings is unknown.

The Axis has been comparatively more effective than the Allies, probably because the Axis, having no great fleet, had to concentrate it. The British have officially lost two battleships and two battle cruisers in this war, and one of each such by aerial bombardment. All three British aircraft carriers lost have been sunk by torpedoes. But of the 12 cruisers lost, presumably half were by air; one sunk off Norway, one (the *Southampton*) in the Mediterranean, and four off Crete where, it may be assumed, they were victims of air action.

Armed merchantmen range far off shore and only one of the 14 the British have lost is thought to have been destroyed from the air. But of the 57 destroyers acknowledged lost, at least 24 were by air.

Both arms have been deadly, the lesson is that they are 10 times more deadly when they work together.

FEBRUARY 12, 1942: *German battleships* Scharnhorst *and* Gneisenau *and cruiser,* Prinz Eugen, *eluded British warships in dash from Brest, and arrived safely in home ports.*

MARCH 24: *Dover suffered heaviest raid since 1941.*

MARCH 28: *British commandos raided naval dockyards and U-boat bases at St. Nazaire, France, dropping 3000 tons of bombs.*

APRIL 1: *British raided docks in Boulogne.*

MAY 31: *1000 British planes blasted Cologne, dropping 3000 tons of bombs.*

JUNE 8: *More than 1000 British planes bombed Bremen, the docks at Dieppe and airdromes in France and the Low Countries.*

AUGUST 12: *British planes bombed Mainz, Wiesbaden, and other inland and coastal towns in Germany.*

AUGUST 19: *Nine-hour Allied commando raid over Dieppe carried out under leadership of Canadians.*

# DIEPPE

## by Quentin Reynolds

THE sun had climbed now nearly overhead and it was blood red through the blanket of smoke which lay over Dieppe and the harbor. The greatest raid by sea in modern warfare was now at its height. Even standing there on the deck of a destroyer half a mile from shore, it was hard to believe that this was really happening, that when the men next to you suddenly swayed and gasped, they had actually been hit. It was warfare in Hollywood dress and with Hollywood sound effects. There was only one difference: The bullets were real, the shells and the bombs were real, and the agony on the faces of the wounded was real.

Major General James Roberts in charge of all military affairs on shore sat in a small room on our destroyer getting reports from his men. He directed the entire show from that one small room. He looked worried because he knew that his Canadians were in the forefront of that deadly fire. Four-fifths of the landing force had been Canadians; the rest had been British Commandos in whose ranks were some Americans and Free French. Our destroyer was rapidly filling up with wounded now. They were lying below decks, in gangways, in cabins, on the floor of the wardroom. And still they came. A barge pulled alongside to discharge a dozen Commandos. They looked fierce with their blackened faces and with their thin daggers in their belts. But they were laughing.

It was very funny, a tall Yorkshireman said. "We're the headquarters staff of No. 3 Commandos," he explained. "We're signalers and runners and liaison men. There were twenty of us, and then there were the four hundred who were supposed to do the work. We had orders to put out a gun battery on the west flank. But on the way to shore, an E-boat attacked us and two armed trawlers got after us. In the darkness we all got separated. We twenty found the rendezvous but no one else showed up. They all went, I guess, or landed somewhere else. The young major who was our CO said, 'We have orders to land. What in hell are we waiting for?' So we landed. We only had rifles because we aren't supposed to be the fighting men on the Commandos. We crept near their six-inch gun battery. They were opening up at you chaps out here. We started sniping at them, and the damn' fools turned their six-inch guns on us. We kept moving from tree to tree always under cover. The bloody fools thought they were surrounded. We kept moving and sniping at them and they never did get a chance to give it to you properly. It was a lot of fun."

A lot of fun? Twenty men had done the work that hundreds had been assigned to do. Twenty men had kept a battery of six-inch guns busy, a battery that would otherwise have taken a terrible toll among the vulnerable destroyers and barges and motor launches lying within range. A lot of fun? A brisk breeze came from the east, which was bad because it dispersed the smoke which had to some extent hidden us from the shore batteries. When it cleared we could see the Spitfires overhead darting everywhere, usually in flights of four with each flight being protected by a "Tail-end Charlie" who kept weaving this way and that, acting as the eyes of the flight.

Twice, groups of Dorniers tried to penetrate our umbrella of aircraft; twice, Dorniers went down in flames.

Then an aircraft that was neither a Spitfire nor a Dornier came wobbling toward us. It looked like an Me-109. The ack-ack started to bark angrily, and the approaching plane was framed now by ugly black bursts of smoke. But fortunately not one bullet found its mark. Fortunately, because as it wobbled closer, we saw that it had R.A.F. markings; it was an American Mustang. It seemed out of control and then it glided down to land on the water twenty feet from us. It hit with a great splash and the pilot, as though shot from a cannon, catapulted out of his seat into the water. A motor launch picked him up and brought him to us. He was a tall, good-looking Canadian. His motor had been put out of commission by ack-ack over Dieppe. Instead of bailing out, he had decided to glide into the water as close to our destroyer as he could.

"Only one thing worried me," he said as he stripped off his wet clothes. "Our own ack-ack."

In the control room, General Roberts kept getting reports. The main attacking forces did not penetrate far into the city itself. Suddenly, Roberts, who had gotten older during the past two hours, looked at the plans of the time schedule and said softly, "Bring them home."

His two aides gave orders through the microphones. We knew this would be welcome news to those poor devils on shore.

Roberts said, "Tell Fighter Command to give us cover for the withdrawal."

It was just eleven o'clock and now officially the raid was over. More wounded arrived. Our decks were covered with them now. One bedraggled, soaking-wet figure stumbled aboard. He was a doctor who had been with the landing forces and happily he was unwounded. Our ship's doctor uttered a cry of relief when he saw that help had come. The two went to work. The two doctors had no time to operate or to dig for shrapnel and bullets. They could only clean wounds and give the merciful needle of morphine to deaden the agony.

In the wardroom, there were twenty men lying on the floor. When bombs fell near or our four-inch guns made the whole ship tremble, they never moved. All of them were a little stunned by the tremendous noise and blast that had lasted now for six hours. One man who seemed familiar stumbled into the room. He tried to stand straight but then he collapsed as I grabbed a bottle of brandy and put it to his lips.

"It's a hell of a story, isn't it?" he grinned and then he passed out again.

I was pretty proud of my profession then. This was Wallace Rayburn of the Montreal *Standard,* one of the two correspondents who had managed to reach shore. I helped strip his wet clothes off. He had been hit by shrapnel, not seriously, but he had also been forced to swim for it and he was exhausted.

A tall blond kid looking very Midwestern came into the wardroom in his Ranger uniform. He was Sergeant Kenneth Kenyon of Minneapolis, Minnesota, and he was looking for his Ranger pal Sergeant Matchel Swank, also of Minneapolis, but Swank wasn't with us.

"It was bad on shore," young Kenyon said. "But, my God, how those Canadians can fight!"

Just then Sergeant Swank appeared. He'd been looking for Kenyon. His right arm was bandaged. It was only a small piece of shrapnel. I gave them each a drink of brandy. Neither had ever tasted it before and they didn't like it.

"Does the wound bother you?" I asked him.

"No," he laughed. "I knew nothing could happen to me. My father gave me a small Bible to carry with me. It brought him through the last war and it's going to bring me through this one. Pop's in the Army too."

(Confidential note to Sergeant Major Swank, Camp Dix: That kid of yours is only nineteen but he's a good man. Congratulations!)

I walked on deck for a last look. Dieppe was burning in three places. All of the men had been embarked and it was time to go home. The Destroyer *Berkeley* steamed by us slowly. Once a single Dornier drove through the Spits to drop its bombs. They missed us, but the *Berkeley* wasn't so lucky. She was hit directly, and a thin splinter of flame shot forty feet in the air.

It was a bad hit. The ship listed slowly and you knew she had received her death blow. Motor launches came hurrying, motor torpedo boats came at fifty miles an hour to help. Men tumbled from her sloping sides into the sea to be picked up. We circled the stricken ship looking for survivors. A moment after the last man had been plucked from the water, another British ship blew up the *Berkeley* according to orders. She sank within twenty seconds.

Now there was a movement among the ships all around us. The raid was over. We were on our way home, but our ship remained where she was. One by one the others formed in line and headed away from Dieppe. Our engines finally started to hum and we too moved, but we moved not away from Dieppe but toward it. Roberts was going in again on the chance that we might find a few survivors in the water near the beaches.

The next twenty minutes were not pleasant. All the shore batteries still in action turned on us. The Dorniers and the Focke-Wulfs saw what they thought to be a crippled straggler and they came at us again and again. Shells and bombs threw up huge jets of water close to us, but we steamed steadily on.

I went into the wardroom. If we were hit, the men down there wouldn't have a chance. The wardroom was below the water line. A little Yorkshire steward whose name was Joe Crowther was going from one man to another. Joe is twenty-one. He told reassuring lies.

"We're on our way home now," he said in his slow Yorkshire accents. "It won't be long. Dieppe is far behind us."

Then we were hit. The bomb landed forward and the ship trembled. The noise reverberated from one steel wall to the other, and your head rang with the concussion. Through the noise, the laughter of Joe Crowther came.

"That's our new six-inch gun they're firing," he told the wounded. "If you didn't know better you'd think it was a bomb."

The wounded who had lain tense, their faces drained of color, relaxed. The color came back, and Joe went among them saying, "A nip of brandy; it'll warm you up. Isn't often you can drink free on His Majesty's Royal Navy."

Joe looked at me and winked. We had no six-inch guns on board, but these wounded didn't know that. If I were handing out V. C.'s leading Mess Steward Joe Crowther of Bradford, Yorkshire, would be the first to be given one.

Finally, Roberts was satisfied that no useful purpose could be served by remaining any longer. Reluctantly he gave the order to return. It was nice to hear the throaty roar of the motors sending us along at fifteen knots. They still tried to get us with their bombs, and a Focke-Wulf 190 almost made it. I was on deck when it came from nowhere. It was only a hundred feet above us and it raked us from stem to stern with its cannon and machine guns. It dropped two bombs, one of which hit us. I reeled into the gangway, knocked sideways by the blast. Then it was gone with the discomfited Spits giving chase.

We went on toward England. We caught up with the flotilla just before entering the ten-mile German mine field. Roberts had told his men that he'd be first through the mine field. We slipped ahead of the others for the tortuous one-hour trip. We were all exhausted and a little punch-drunk from the nine hours of constant battering.

I found four U. S. Ranger soldiers sitting together with not a wound among them. They'd been with the No. 4 Commandos. They were Staff Sergeant Kenneth Stemphen of Russell, Minnesota, Corporal William Brady of Grand Forks, North Dakota; Sergeant Alex Szima of Dayton, Ohio; and Corporal Franklin M. Koons of Swea City, Iowa. They were tired but happy. They could talk of nothing but the Commandos.

"I'd like to get hold of that louse back home," husky Corporal Brady said, clenching his big hands, "who told me that the British can't fight. My God, I never saw anything like it!"

"We'd have been dead a dozen times if it hadn't been for our superior officers," Szima added. "They're the greatest fighters in the world. They make us look like sissies."

"How about that sergeant major we carried out?" Koons said. "He had a hole in his belly you could stick your fist through and yet every few minutes he'd yell 'Down!' and we'd drop flat, and sure enough, machine-gun bullets would go over his head."

264

"I fell for that propaganda at home myself," Stemphen said. "Who the hell started it anyhow? Talk about the Russians! If they're half as good as these British they're terrific."

We steamed on, and now the mine field was behind us. The Spitfires flew sedately overhead. They had the sky pretty much to themselves. We relaxed a bit and laughed a little and drank brandy, and even the wounded joked about the blood on their uniforms. We were able to check up a bit. Our crew had been hit badly. Many of them were casualties. All of the "walking wounded" stuck to their posts. It's true what they say about the British navy.

Then ahead we saw a very sweet sight, the shores of England. That shore looked almost as good as the shore of America would have looked. We steamed on and, looking back to the great line of little ships that steamed on so proudly, you couldn't help but choke a little. Nearly all had come back.

Had the raid been a success? Our casualties had been heavy. But quite definitely the raid proved a lot of things and taught us a lot. It had taught us that a large landing force can be transported across the Channel with a reasonable chance of arriving there. It proved that tanks can be landed.

My own view is that the two things lacking were a terrific air bombardment before the landing, and the use of parachute troops. It is true that when you do a preliminary bombing you forfeit the element of surprise. It is also true that only by bombing or dive bombing can gun batteries effectively be silenced and troops allowed to land without having to face a suicidal fire. Parachute troops dropped a few miles inland could have taken the pill boxes which bothered our men so and could have prevented reinforcements from coming up from the rear.

But the greatest lesson of all that we learned at Dieppe was this. Given the opportunity, the British and Canadians fight like Russians. That is nice to know.

SEPTEMBER 14, 1942: *Mass formations of British planes made one hundredth raid on Bremen.*

OCTOBER 12: *German raid on Malta.*

NOVEMBER 11: *After Allied invasion of North Africa, Germans occupied all of France, except a 30-mile semicircle around Toulon, where greater part of French fleet lay at anchor.*

# ON THE WAY TO MURMANSK

## by Robert Carse

THIS is the story of the merchant seamen and how we took the ships to sea through the submarines, the ice, the mines, the planes, and how we brought some of them home again. We were part of the Allied convoy that, off the North Cape of Norway, was repeatedly, savagely attacked by the Nazis in a running six-day-and-night battle. Our losses were severe, there's no sense hiding that, and yet we beat them, won against them, came, most of us, safe into port with our ships and cargoes.

We weren't fighting men when we started out, just a simple bunch of guys that you'd find in any union hall or along any dock in an American port. But we had to fight for our lives and our ships, and we had to take through to our Russian allies the planes, the tanks, the explosives, the ammunition and trucks that had been promised by our President. Out there —out in the Atlantic and up in the Arctic—we learned how to fight, how to knock our enemy out of the sky and from the sea.

It was pretty hard on us at times, for we weren't used to that kind of work, and many of our ships didn't have anything but old-style and light-caliber machine guns, and some ships had nothing at all but luck and the guts of the men handling them. In the Barents Sea, in the Arctic, where there's no night at the season of year when we met our Nazi enemy, they came after us until our eyes closed red and puffed from staring into the sun, and in one day alone we fought 105 planes, with the submarines off behind the icebergs, waiting to slip in and pitch more of it at us. Then it was all we could do to stay on our feet, and we hung onto the guns to keep erect. A couple of days in that battle there was ice on deck and ice coating the breeches and belts and barrels of our machine guns.

We kicked at the ammunition cases to warm our feet and slapped the guns to free the ice and warm our hands, and when they came peeling down out of the sun and the clouds, gray-silver, fast and with the high, sharpening, whining scream, we were ready for them, just as ready as we could get. When they'd dropped their stuff and when they'd gone, and we knew that at least our ship was safe, we thrust the empties aside with our feet and took a smoke and talked about you folks at home, and did you really understand that we were there and what we were doing.

That counted to us, it counted plenty—the States, our folks and our kids, what we called home. It kept our eyes open and our hands on the gun handles. We put an enormous trust in you and how you were fighting your part of the war. Somehow, it saved us, gave us the nervous stamina to take the Nazis' pounding.

My ship, a twenty-year-old, strong, broad-hulled merchantman, had just come in off the Far Eastern run to India and Java and the Spice Islands when I joined her as able seaman in an East Coast port. She was getting the last of her new gear for the voyage to Russia, but there hadn't been time to install the De Gausse anti-mine system or even mount a cannon aboard her. When we cleared from port and put out to sea in early spring, all we had for protection was the skipper's .32-caliber revolver. In our holds, besides the tanks and the planes and the other war supplies for the Russians, were 407 tons of TNT. We were bound on the most difficult and dangerous run in the world, with the *Tirpitz*, the *Scharnhorst* and the rest of them maybe out there waiting for the slow-haul stuff like us.

Nobody quit the ship before we signed articles. Maybe some of them should have, because they weren't much good later on when the Nazis began to heave it at us. Right now, back home here and writing this, I can still see the face of our river pilot going down the ladder just before we reached the open sea. He was so happy to get away from us and into the launch that he was almost laughing aloud and his sunburned face was one big grin.

We had the luck outside, although we saw a couple of vessels that the subs had dumped. They were tankers, one with her bow sticking high and oil still all around her thick. We were on our own, without escort vessels, and up in the crow's-nest on lookout we keenly watched the sea. We were just beginning to feel in our nerves and muscles and bone the shock of that TNT if and when we got it.

It was lovely weather, clear and blue and sunny, and full of stars at night, and some of us who had families missed our folks already, but here was the ship, and we were taking her out, had asked for the job and been glad to get it.

The luck stayed with us. Once we raised a merchant convoy homeward-bound, riding high and light, destroyers with them for escort. Then we made port—glad, too, for the subs lie off there in regular hunting packs, and on each side of the harbor mouth were wrecked tankers which had been pursued by subs until they beached. We went to anchor and waited, then stood out again—this time in convoy formation for the big run across. Outside, it was blowing like hell, a quarterly gale. On the beach, one of the wrecked tankers was still burning, dull red and intense in the black-shaded, white-kicked sea. It was impossible to stand lookout on the foc'sle-head, so it was back up in the crow's-nest again. But the wind came slicing in there, the spindrift with it, enough to make you gasp as you breathed and all but pull the sou'wester off your head. As man relieved man, we talked about what the weather would be like up in the real north and the Arctic. In port, while we'd been loading, the Maritime Commission had issued us all heavy gear, but we didn't want to wear it yet, knowing how much colder it was going to be later on. So we used as little of it as possible and stuck to our own lighter gear.

We were a big convoy. We had a strong escort of destroyers and corvettes, and we felt pretty safe. The gale blew itself out after two days, and we ran into smooth and beautiful spring seas, with small cirrus clouds feathering white around the horizon, and the ships, in great, long gray rows, steadily on station and driving ahead with that slow, slightly perceptible, thrusting motion that has taken so many cargoes around the world. Around and around us went the escort, the gray destroyers and the smaller, lighter corvettes, idling along at convoy speed, then suddenly making a sweep for it and banging off toward the horizon wide open, a great slash of luminous spray along the bows, down the runs and into the foamed cresting of the wake.

Convoy had become routine to us. We were settling down, behind that supple steel line of the escort, into the monotony of a voyage we figured for at least four and a half months. Days were the usual tricks on the wheel, lookout and deck work, but from right abaft the forepeak scuttle on the foredeck to the forward break of the house and all across the main deck to the break of the well deck aft, we were loaded with deck cargo. This, in our ship, was cased trucks, and in our port of departure they had been painted khaki color as camouflage. Shoreside carpenters had built catwalks over the cases for us to use as we moved at our work fore and aft. A narrow gangway spanned the well deck from the break of the main deck to the poop, and often, crossing to our quarters in the poop, we would look down at No. 5 Hatch, left free of deck cargo, and wonder what it would take to detonate the explosives carried there and in No. 4.

As the days went by, though, we got used to that, and we came, in seaman style, to interest ourselves in the very personal affairs of the men with whom we lived and worked. Two of the crew were what in the ships we call "characters," and a third, the steward, was a natural low-life. The characters were a seventeen-year-old Brooklyn boy and a big, thick-lipped, shaggy hulk of a Bronx Irishman who had shipped, the draft board right behind him, as ordinary seaman. The wiper was uniform crazy, had, in fact, been a Western Union boy before he joined the ship, and had come asking for the job with his Western Union cap in his hand. The Bronx character was food-crazy; he gobbled food with both hands and tremendous suction sounds. Between them, the wiper and the Bronx ordinary made the messroom a pretty unsavory place for us for a while.

On a junk pile in our loading port, where some ship's officer had tossed it as worthless, Wipes had found an old khaki-uniform jacket. He wore it at all times, diving bilges in the engine room, off watch and asleep, and in the messroom. It was filthy and he was filthy. Then Juan, our Ecuadorean messman, fixed up Wipes. He told Wipes that the next day was to be the anniversary of the founding of the company, so no work. Wipes slept in the next day, came to mess just in time to get a hearty breakfast long after he should have been below at work. He was lighting a cigarette with a flourish when the first assistant engineer came in the door for him and told him, in explicit language, that there was work for him to do, and plenty of it, and right now.

The baboon-faced steward took care of the Bronx ordinary, who had been complaining constantly, through great gobs of half-masticated food, that in this ship there was no jam. In his other ship—his only other ship—he

268

glubbed at us, there had been jam, and honey too. The steward would trip up the Bronx character with all sorts of questions about his other ship, and what did the character know about the sea and ships, after all? It was he who started calling the character Jammy Boy, and the name stuck.

The only trouble was that the steward, bald-headed and purple-faced, was a belly robber and a penny gripper for the company, and nobody wanted to laugh with him. But in good part he silenced Jammy Boy, and for that we were grateful.

One of the firemen, a gentle and usually quiet-spoken man whom we called Snakebite, and a sturdy, handsome oiler named Nottingham took it on themselves to straighten out the steward. They asked him if he was, as he insisted without cess, the chief steward, who, then, was the second steward? Did he wear his high-pressure officer's cap to show the wholly absent second steward he was chief, or was it just to cover his bald coco from seagull droppings?

With this line of questioning, and other more pungent, forceful verbal attacks, they finally subdued the steward, and the food he gave us was a bit better for it.

Blackout at night, until we got used to it, gave us most of our other laughs during that two weeks at sea.

The chief mate was both nearsighted and jumpy. He tacked from one end of the wheelhouse to the other, cracking solidly into every object he met and anxiously begging pardon. The wheelsmen, silently choking with laughter, would wait until the chief mate at last despaired of staying in the wheelhouse and sought the more simple confines of the bridge wings outside.

Those were good days, looking back on them, out of all the terrible and dangerous days we were to confront afterward. Danger was, of course, always with us there. One night, executing a practice forty-five-degree emergency turn at the orders of our commodore, a big British ship almost cut us down. She was carrying explosives, too, and there were tankers with high-test gasoline close around. It would have been the end of a lot of ships and men, if we had collisioned there. But Charley, the Norwegian lad on the wheel, kept a cool head and brought us clear, and we went on our way, back onto station and column.

Four or five times, far away, we heard depth charges, and for us, just getting our initiation, the sound at first was unrecognizable. It gave a grinding, rasping sort of tremor alongside that we thought must be within the vessel. Then, though, as it was repeated, we knew, and we looked around the messroom into one another's eyes, and the faces and the hands tightened. The voices of the poker players were lower as they went back to their game.

Our course on that run was north and always more north. Then one clear sharp day a lot of hoists broke out from the commodore's ship and the repeating vessels, and a group of Iceland-bound ships stood off by themselves under separate escort, and the hoists for us said to turn east.

We steered a few degrees lower down the card toward south every day, yet we weren't sure. Was it that we were bound for the United Kingdom, after having held so far to the northward? The first signs of nervous dismay and open tension started in the ship. Maybe the *Scharnhorst,* or the *Tirpitz,* or the *Gneisenau* was out there, right over the horizon. Coming down the ladders from the bridge at the end of a trick at the wheel, we were met by a staring group that wanted to know the course, the latest dope as to our position. The steward's face was more baboonlike than ever, and he prowled the deck at night, was up and out, life jacket in hand, at the slightest sound. But we didn't know, the skipper didn't know, and the commodore got his orders from the Admiralty in London. If we met the Nazis, we met them; that was all.

Then one shimmering spring day we reached a port in the United Kingdom. They'd brought us in to the shore here, and for a while we could sleep deeply on our watches below behind the mine gates and with the British antiaircraft searchlights and the scout planes overhead. Scotland, we said. Son of a gun, that meant seeing women again. That meant whisky.

There wasn't much whisky in Scotland, and you could hardly navigate along the streets in the towns and in the cities, for the soldiers. They were everywhere—in the railway stations, in the trains, the public houses, the movies and busses and trams. The racketing crack of their heavy hobbed boots was distinct in the blackout at night, and the steel hobs cast up little blue sparks. Redheaded Allen, my watch partner, and Jersey City Mac, a gay and laughing ordinary, got a big kick out of the talk of the folks in the streets. It was all strictly Harry Lauder to them, and they liked it fine.

We got our guns in that port, eight of them, four double-mount Marlin .30-caliber pieces. They were old American pieces of 1917 issue, given by the States to the British for use in planes and equipped with an automatic trigger on the top of the receiver plate above the breech. But for us they had been refixed with finger triggers and safeties, with steel-tube side and shoulder handles with rubber grips. They were good for 700 rounds a minute out of their khaki web belts, the old Royal Navy armorer told us when he instructed us in them. We were to be our own gunners, the skipper had just made us to understand, and we were a quiet, intent group of men as we watched the armorer handle the piece.

Most of us had never seen a machine gun to put our hands on it before in our lives. It was up to us deck men to use them. The twin pieces, mounted behind a long and heavy steel shield, were placed one on each side of the wheelhouse, topside, the highest place of immediate vantage in the ship, and on each side of the mooring bridge on the poop. That was our armament. With that we were to go out and fight the *Luftwaffe* or anything we met—with .30-caliber tracer bullets fired by a crew whose only actual fire practice was a pair of rounds let go out of the scupper port into the water to get the feel of the guns.

We were eager to go now, eager to get under way and make that run

270

around the North Cape. The nervousness was growing on us. We'd waited long enough, and if we had a nasty job to do let's do it. But there was going to be one week end left before we sailed, we found out, and Mac and Wee Wullie and I took off for Edinburgh. Wee Wullie was a Scot and our deck engineer, came from the town of Mid Calder, had served his apprenticeship in the capital city. He knew Edinburgh well and loved it, and he and Mac and I talked of it on the way.

Edinburgh was slam-bang full of troops. Just that afternoon there had been a great parade, the first of such for Allies' Week. There on Princes Street we met the Free Polish and the Free French soldiers and sailors, Free Norwegians, Free Greeks, and Scots from the crack regiments, of course, Punjabis in their shorts and tall sharp-peaked turbans—every sort of outfit in the British service—and men of the British merchant navy, Hollanders and Norwegians and Greeks and Jugoslavs among them. Those men—the merchant-navy lads—had paraded in ranks with the troops that afternoon, and they'd carried the merchant flag, for they were also fighting men.

Wee Wullie and Mac and I were overtaken by a fit of sadness as we had a little whisky and ale and food in a big restaurant bar on Waterloo Road. We were looking forward to what was ahead of us out to sea, and it wasn't pleasant. But the waitress there made us feel better. She was a middle-aged woman with a husband and a family, yet she was gay with us, and friendly, knew at once that we were merchant seamen. The city was full, what with the parade, and it was doubtful that we'd even get a place to sleep in the Servicemen's Home.

"But I will not have ye sleepin' in the street," she told us, bent over with her hands under her apron, her plain, simple face serious. "No, that I couldn't do, fair ye're wi' us in the war. My own place is full, wi' the family and the lads from the services who're staying wi' us. But there's chairs I've got, and a divan, and my man and I can sit up the night while two of ye take the bed and the third lad the divan."

"No, miss," Wee Wullie said in his slow way. "Me, I can go home to my folks in Mid Calder and these two lads can make a go for it at the servicemen's place. They'll make out all right, the rascals."

"Aye," she said, "but if ye don't, you come back here sure, and ask for me. Mrs. Hughie is the name, and I'll be here till half past ten. Ye've heard me, now?"

Yes, we said, feeling warm and fine inside, we'd heard her.

There was room for us in a school building that the services had taken over as an annex, and as soon as that was set, I skinned back to tell Mrs. Hughie, thank her and shake her hand. Then we lit out down Princes Street past the Walter Scott monument and the smoothly sloping gardens in the high, lavender-shaded Scottish dusk. We roamed the city all that evening and all the next day; then rejoined our ship. She was set to sail; we were to bring up the anchor in a few hours. Here we go, I thought. This is it, and no fooling.

We were eager to go, all of us. Our worst enemies are out there on the sea, we told one another. Meet them, beat them. That's our job, the only one. But in that moment of fierceness, of nervous apprehension of danger and approaching battle, there came to me the clear, full memory of the week end passed in Edinburgh. It was, I knew, the most beautiful and the most friendly city I had ever seen in any country and at any time.

We stood north, out to sea. Once more the tightening of nerves took place as we realized that along this coast the U-boats harried almost every ship and convoy. But danger had become for us a fixed value. Every moment, every second outside port we might get it, so a man could only do his best and wait it out, try to work the ship through.

We came one day into another port. This was no place like our last anchorage, and used only for the purposes of war. More ammunition was brought out to us for our machine guns, and we cleared and inspected our P.A.C. rockets, the ingenious and skillful device by which, through rocket fire, 500 feet of piano wire is suspended above the ship between two small parachutes, to slice the wing right off a diving Nazi plane, or wind and wind snarling around his propeller blades. On our 'midships and after decks also were huge smoke-screen cans, which would help to protect us from the enemy we were very soon to meet.

Now, far to the north, spring was behind us, and the whole spirit of the place where we were, the men we met here, the Free Norwegians who worked as boat crew for the British Naval Control and who the January before had escaped from Norway and been thirty-nine days in a small boat, made us feel the battle spirit. The Norwegians told us, through our own two boxheads, Ole and Charley, of how four of them, one with a pistol, had crept on board a fishing trawler in a Southern Norwegian port, cowed and overcome the German navy crew of eighteen, then taken the boat and put to sea. That was good, we said, and made the gesture of shaking hands with them, passed down cigarettes, chocolate and sugar.

From that port, again in convoy, we ran north. There was talk of the *Tirpitz* again, and of the *Admiral Scheer,* but we held to our course and came in good order up to that island which is one huge, smoky mountain thrusting from the fog swirl and surf rush of the sea.

# LONE WOLVES OF THE RAF

### by Jack Alexander

LATE in 1940, when the Germans were mass-raiding London by night and the British were trying to repay the horror in kind, a new marauding tactic in aerial warfare came quietly into being. It was an intimate, cozy form of homicide in the dark. The Royal Air Force, which originated it, politely called it "intruding." The Luftwaffe, making haste to imitate it, did a fast job of word retooling and wrapped it up in a long, sausagelike package: "*klebeflugzeugfliegen.*" The maneuver capitalized on the attractive vulnerability of bombers after they had returned from the night's mission and were circling over their home airdromes. A squadron of bombers takes a long time to sit down. To avoid collisions, they must circle at different levels while the control tower gives them the signal to descend, one at a time. Their landing lights are on and the airdrome itself is illuminated.

The intruder plane, or *Klebeflugzeug,* usually took off while the raid on its own territory was at its height. Traveling alone, it sped across the Channel, timing its arrival over the enemy airdrome to coincide with that of the homeward-bound bombers. As one RAF pilot describes the final humiliation of the bomber pilot, "He'd dropped his cookies and had slipped safely through the ack-ack barrage. He was mighty glad to get home and he was all hot for his flight supper. Then some dirty cad would sneak in and take a squirt at him."

The man who supplies this salty description of the tactic's climax is Squadron Leader Kendrick H. Salusbury-Hughes, and he delivers it with the hearty relish of one who is in the habit of dining excellently on Huns. Salusbury-Hughes—whose rank corresponds to that of an American major— is one of the leading practitioners of the blood-chilling art of intruding. At this writing he has completed thirty-five sorties and has received the Distinguished Flying Cross. No one could look less like the typical RAF pilot. He is of medium height and has a large nose and a swarthy complexion. He wears broad reddish mustachios which curl up ferociously at the ends. They gave him the appearance of being a successful pirate, and, in a sense, he is.

He hasn't a sign of the traditional British reserve. Once at his ease, he is a voluble talker and he has blue eyes which squint happily when he is telling about a successful piece of intrusion. He smokes a curved pipe and uses it to gesticulate with.

"I am very excitable," he says frankly. "When I am chasing a Hun, I bounce up and down on the seat and bay like a beagle until I can get him in my sights. Then I squirt. If he catches fire or explodes, I cheer and yell *'Sieg heil!'* All this time I am scared to death. I must say that I get a certain thrill out of terror. But the real thrill comes when you get home safely. It is a wonderful feeling. I guess the process is something like beating yourself on the head with a club, so that you can appreciate the contrast when you quit."

Because an intruder plane is a night-roaming lone wolf, its pilot must have unusually good eyesight, a love of poking his nose into trouble and the fighting temperament of a throat-slitting Apache. A sense of malicious mischief helps, too; for, after completing his primary mission, which is well planned in advance, he is expected to go "rhubarbing" until his ammunition is used up.

Rhubarbing, a term of mysterious origin, is slang for being a general nuisance—sweeping the countryside at low level on sheer speculation, bomb-

273

ing and spraying bullets into stray sentries, factories, railway trains, barges and any other unsuspecting target that presents itself. Train busting is one of the most satisfying subordinate phases of intruding. It creates picturesque destruction as locomotive boilers erupt in great clouds of vapor, ammunition cars blast skyward and assorted units of precious rolling stock topple down embankments. The pilot has his mischief, and the enemy's lifeline suffers a hemorrhage. The true intruder scorns heavy bomber work as being too impersonal. He is essentially an individualist who insists upon seeing the damage he is doing.

Salusbury-Hughes, who is thirty-four and about ten years older than the average combat pilot, is one of those rare persons who seem to exult in warfare. He is a Scot, and back in Perthshire he has a wife and two children, a boy of seven and a girl of eight. He prepped at Eton and finished his education at the University of Bonn, where he specialized in languages. Today he speaks five foreign tongues—German, French, Dutch, Italian and Flemish—and can understand several others. His father, a devoted and expert golfer, tried to make a champion of him and actually did get him into the par class. But the grind of practice was irksome to the pupil.

"I gave up golf at the age of eighteen," says Salusbury-Hughes, with the disdainful air of a man who has put away the things of a child.

He has a black contempt for the Nazis, which springs, in part at least, from the Teutonizing of Budapest and Vienna, where he spent his holidays as a college student. After graduation he satisfied a naturally roving instinct by taking up flying and becoming a civil-air-line pilot in England. Later on, he turned to flying instruction and was thus engaged when the war began in 1939.

He was already a member of the RAF Volunteer Reserve and he promptly put in for combat work. Instead of getting it, he was relegated to instructing cadet pilots, on the ground that he was too old for the fierce pace of daylight dogfighting. It was a bitter dose to swallow.

The introduction of intrusion about a year later renewed his hopes of seeing action, and he applied for a transfer. It was still another year before he got it, and meanwhile intruding had been undergoing a process of evolution. The first intruders were clap-trap old Blenheims whose arma-ment consisted of four machine guns, which the pilots called "pea-shooters." The damage a pilot could do with a pea-shooter was limited, and intrusion didn't come into its own until the arrival of DB-7's from America—Douglas Bostons, renamed Havocs by the British. Besides being well gunned, the Havoc carried a bomb load, and a tardy intruder, getting to an enemy air-drome after his prey had already landed, was able to slip in and shower explosives at him on the ground. The Germans soon developed pleasant little antidotes to intrusion. They mocked up decoy planes on the ground, and when the intruder dived to strafe them, he was met with a withering belch of flak. They also used actual planes for decoys, sending them up over airdromes with their wing lights glowing invitingly. As the intruder got within range of a flying decoy, the Nazi pilot would snap off his lights, and a night fighter, which had been stealthily trailing the procession, would pepper the visitor from behind. Many intruders never returned.

Toward the close of 1941, Salusbury-Hughes finally achieved his ambition to be an intruder. His first sortie, or "nursery" trip, was made in an improved version of the Havoc, which carried, besides himself, a navigator and two gunners. Once he got over occupied France, he discovered that he was obsessed with an urgent desire to get back home as soon as possible, but he pushed on. His ports of call were Abbeville, Berck and Le Touquet, and his mission was to destroy any Nazi plane he met. Abbeville proved to be quiet and the Havoc bored on toward its next target. By mistake, it passed low over a blacked-out airdrome. The flak guns opened up.

"We got well and truly plastered," Salusbury-Hughes recalls, "and I was all for getting out of there right away. But the older of my two gunners said, 'You're not going to let him get away with that, are you?' 'What do you mean?' I asked, knowing perfectly well what he meant. 'Bomb the blighter,' said he. I've always had a rule to the effect that if you get into trouble, the best thing to do is to leave it, but I couldn't stand my gunner's disapproval. So we went back to the scene of the crime and dropped four bombs and blew a hangar to hell and gone. It was quite satisfying."

One night Salusbury-Hughes set out specifically to pot Nazi pupils operating out of the night-flying schools which are located along the Loire, south of Paris. What started out to be a pigeon-shooting expedition turned into an exciting evening. Just beyond Chartres, a Dornier 217, with lights on, passed by, flying in the opposite direction.

"We'll have him, won't we?" pleaded Bill Gregory, the navigator.

"So," recalls Salusbury-Hughes, "we nipped smartly back and pursued the wicked enemy. I got excited, as usual, and began bouncing up and down. Then something like a steel vise gripped my knee. It was Bill's fingers. Bill is a North Countryman and he never says anything unless it's to the point. 'Sit still, you fool,' he yelled. The Hun never did see us. We got on his tail and gave him a couple of squirts, and he fell to the ground and burst like an incendiary bomb. Very satisfying.

"We continued down to the Loire and stooged around for a while. It was a filthy night and we didn't see a thing, and the first thing you know, we were lost. 'Bill,' I said, 'do you know where we are?' 'Haven't got the faintest idea,' Bill replied. We took off on a northwesterly course, hoping it would bring us back somewhere in England. Twenty minutes later I saw a lighted airdrome about ten miles off our nose, and as we got closer I could see a plane orbiting up. It had its lights on. I said, 'Bill, do you see what I see?' 'Too true, I do,' said Bill.

"We went hell for leather at him at about seven hundred feet altitude and caught him quite unawares. It was a Heinkel 111. I took a crack at him from close up and he exploded. The concussion threw us over on our back and for a couple of seconds I was a truly frightened man. But after righting the ship, I looked down upon the most marvelous scene it has ever been my pleasure to behold. The Hun had crashed in the middle of the airdrome and burst into a blaze that turned the night into broad daylight. On the ground the Huns were running around like crazy people."

When the Luftwaffe became more and more deeply involved in Russia and North Africa, the mass raids on England ceased and intruding took on more the aspect of a night-blooming rhubarb. Such targets as power stations, railway terminals and illuminating-gas tanks, which the British call gasometers, were pin-pointed on maps and the intruders went out to punch them.

One night, after a thinly rewarded sortie, Salusbury-Hughes came upon a set of searchlights which were revolving horizontally in a geometrical pattern. Recognizing the beams as emanating from the sentry towers of a concentration camp, he let loose his remaining bombs in a near-by field. The lights immediately went out and the intruder flew homeward wondering how many prisoners had been able to escape in the confusion he had created. His favorite spot for unloading spare bombs, however, is a large factory on the Somme below Amiens. He estimates that in about three years he ought to have it put pretty well out of business, unless mass bombing beats him to it.

One night a pilot with an original twist of mind attacked a goods train somewhere in occupied France, and the sport of train busting was born.

"He reported obtaining a most satisfactory explosion," says Salusbury-Hughes. "At first we hesitated to make it a regular practice, for fear of wrecking a passenger train by mistake and killing some Frenchmen. Then we found out that Frenchmen weren't allowed to ride the night trains, so for a while everybody went mad on trains."

It wasn't difficult to find the blacked-out trains in the dark. An intruder, after slapping his plotted targets, would travel homeward "by Bradshaw"— Bradshaw is the name of the British volume which is the equivalent of the American Railway Guide. Picking out a main line, he would follow it at low altitude until he saw sparks from a locomotive. If the night was moonlit, he could locate it through the smoke plume. Then he would make a head-on run at the locomotive and rake the entire train with cannon and pea-shooters, repeating the run in either direction until something happened. It wasn't unusual for a pilot to cripple or destroy two or three trains in an evening, and it still isn't.

One of the first trains Salusbury-Hughes pounced on took refuge in a tunnel. He dropped a bomb at either end of the passage and flew off, hoping that he had at least temporarily trapped the train and upset schedules. He never did find out what actually happened. On another evening he spotted a train standing in a yard at Abbeville. "After a few squirts," he says, "the whole train went up in a very satisfactory explosion. It must have been loaded down with ammunition."

As this is written, Nazi raids on England have been resumed, but are of such small caliber that the chief function of the intruder—destroying enemy bombers over their own bases—is still pretty much in abeyance. In the words of the be-mustached squadron leader, "Night after night we just crack off to see if anything is flying over France. If there isn't, we beat up his airdromes until his flak gets too hot, and then we go around busting trains and gasometers."

The Nazis will no doubt mass-raid England again, as soon as they are able, and rakehelly aerial Commandos like Squadron Leader Salusbury-Hughes will resume their nocturnal rendezvous with the raiders on the other side of the Channel.

They fly lightning-fast Mosquitos now and are more deadly than ever. The Nazis will fly homeward with their wind up. Many will feel the hot blade of gun-fire stabbing them in the back before they have time to shout, *"Achtung, Klebeflugzeug!"* Somehow, this is a comforting thought.

# TARGET: BERLIN

### by James MacDonald

MAY 8, 1943—"Hey, Stinker! Did you have your operational egg?"

"Yes, and I had not only one egg but two."

"You did! How did you manage that?"

"You don't catch me in careless talk."

A third voice; "Old Stinker's shooting a line again. He got just one egg, same as the rest of us."

The scene of this conversation is an overloaded motor truck carrying several dozen young men—most of them barely out of their 'teens—across the field at an R. A. F. bomber station, where their big planes, fueled and "bombed up," are waiting to take off on a raid over Germany. The target tonight happens to be Berlin and the forthcoming raid is one of the biggest ever planned against the capital of the Reich. There is a grueling, many-hour flight ahead, and these youthful veterans of air warfare over Europe know perfectly well what perils they are about to encounter.

But they don't talk about the impending operation. It is much easier to swap jokes about the "operational egg" that has been served to them in their mess as a special treat before boarding their bombers.

Their casual conversation is typical of life aboard an R. A. F. machine during actual flights over enemy territory, which isn't so tense an affair as the majority of civilians probably imagine it to be. On the surface it is curiously informal and everybody appears to be completely at ease. Underneath this surface, however, there is strict attention to business by every member of the plane's crew.

The informality isn't a mere pose. Above all things these R. A. F. young-sters are intolerant of posers and quick to heap acid scorn on any one they catch "shooting a line," as they call it. By the same token they all demand the utmost of each other when they are in the air. "Phoniness" and ineffi-ciency are rigidly taboo.

From the moment of taking off until the moment of returning to the base and alighting from the plane most of the crew of one of Britain's big Lancaster bombers don't see one another. Each has his appointed station aboard the plane and he leaves it only in emergency. The only two who are within touching distance of each other are the pilot and the flight engineer, who sits beside him keeping a close eye on the myriad luminous dials and frequently turning knobs on the big panels in front of him and on his right hand side.

Directly behind the pilot's seat, hooded by a black curtain, sits the aerial navigator, bending over a compact desk, plotting the course with the aid of a tiny electric light. In a cramped and also blacked-out compartment behind the navigator is the plane's wireless operator. Forward, amidships and in the tail are the plane's three gunners. All seven men are within a few steps of each other, but as far as intermingling is concerned during operations, they might just as well be at the far ends of the earth.

What prevents them from feeling utter isolation is the vital system known as "intercom" by which they can talk to each other by telephone. Headsets and mouthpieces are almost as important as the plane's bomb sight, but they aren't always put to serious use.

There's a considerable amount of chit-chat, much of which is couched in very spicy language. Frequently this chatter of voices is broken off abruptly during sudden moments of danger. Thus conversation over the "intercom" is filled with trivial humor and drama.

The take-off, when your plane is loaded with one two-ton high explosive bomb and a heavy load of incendiaries, isn't any time for joking. Over the wireless telephone comes the order from the field's control room telling you to start. Over the "intercom" one hears the pilot's voice saying, "Okay, D for Donald"—the plane's identification letter—and replying that he is taking off.

Then there is a strange silence which is all the stranger because of the deafening roar of the big plane's four powerful motors churning along to get the plane off the ground. The silence arises from the fact that nobody says a word. The pilot has plenty to do to get the plane into the air without cracking up—and to crack up at the start of a raid means that the plane and its cargo explodes, not only blowing every one aboard to bits, but also blasting the field's hangars, barracks, machine shops, and the rest.

Once you have cleared the ground and the plane is struggling with all its strength to gain altitude, the first thing you hear is the impersonal voice of the navigator instructing the pilot, "set course, Ronnie, 115 degrees." Then comes the answer, "Okay, Clay, course 115 degrees." More of that strange silence while the big machine goes steadily upward on a long slow climb to high altitude.

After the plane is well under way, one hears the voice of the flight engineer informing the pilot that the propellers are doing so many "revs" (revolutions per minute). There ensues a technical discussion of whether the plane's speed should be increased or decreased in order to make sure that the correct altitude shall be reached at the exact split second when the plane should be over such and such a place in enemy-occupied territory, where, according to information given the flying crews at the "briefing," trouble can be expected from enemy night fighter planes and ack-ack gunners.

The pilot, flight engineer and navigator, who are so near each other but yet so far apart, are heard exchanging data on the plane's altitude, speed, performance of motors, course and temperature of the air, which by this time is many degrees below zero outside and therefore requires precautions against "icing up" of the wings with resultant destruction of air speed and the possibility of a crash or, as R. A. F. men would say in their own peculiar argot, a "prang."

These problems having been solved, every one settles down to a monotonous flight over the North Sea on the way to Germany. In their respective turrets the plane's gunners are constantly swiveling around and keeping a close lookout against hostile machines. The pilot is still busy climbing. The flight engineer is nursing his beloved motors. The navigator is making swift calculations with a pencil and rulers on a crazy-looking chart. The wireless operator is tuning in on many wave-lengths listening, listening, listening.

But while all this is going on they seem to find time for small talk. One of the interesting aspects of this conversation is that an officer calls a sergeant by his nickname and the sergeant replies to his officer likewise. The conversation begins with the pilot's directing the same question at every one aboard: "How are you doing, Steve?" The flight engineer replies, "Okay, skipper." "And you, Cassie?" to the rear gunner. Back comes answer from the rear gunner who holds the rank of officer to the pilot who is a flight sergeant, "Okay, Ronnie."

So it goes throughout the "kite," with the sergeant pilot, on whom the safety of everybody depends, making sure his crew is comfortable—or as comfortable as it is possible to be. Then one hears somebody say, "Damn it, I had a supper date tonight with a nice girl and no way of telling her I couldn't make it. I bet I catch hell when I see her again." Another voice —this one Canadian—replies, "Don't shoot a line, Johnnie. You aren't the only guy she knows." Another voice, also Canadian, is heard starting to ask a question, "Say, by the way, I meant to ask you today ..."

He never finishes the sentence. The midupper gunner cuts in: "Enemy night fighter half a mile to starboard." Thanks to his training in spotting all types of machines by their silhouettes, he has sighted just in time a Messerschmitt 109 and sounded the warning.

There is no chitchat now. The pilot of the big Lancaster orders every one, "Keep a sharp lookout." That eerie "silence" follows. Suddenly the plane makes an almost perpendicular dive into a cloud far below, wabbles dizzily, regains an even keel and proceeds on its errand. It has successfully won a game of hide and seek.

Over the "intercom" the navigator, having studied his compasses, which are co-ordinated with those on the pilot's instrument board, says calmly,

"Hey, skipper, set the course 91 degrees." There is a slight pause, in which the pilot replies, "Okay, course 91."

By this time the plane is over Germany, making a beeline for Berlin. "We had a bloody good game of darts in the sergeant's mess last night," says the gunner in the forward turret. "That bloke wot's his name in X for X-ray shot a line about how good he was. Taffy took him on—He really was good and . . ."

At that instant the Lancaster dives steeply to the left. Off to the right a British plane has blown up in mid-air as the result of a direct hit by an anti-aircraft shell which has touched off its cargo of high explosive and incendiary bombs. "D for Donald" dives to get out of range of the force of the terrific detonations.

There is a long pause. The pilot's voice comes over the earphones, "That was one of our kites." Another voice: "You know, I thought I smelled its petrol burning." "Funny, I smelled something, too," says a third voice.

By now the plane is only a few minutes' traveling time from the target area. The forward gunner climbs down from his turret into the bomb aimer's compartment in the nose, peers through the bomb sight, and braces himself, his fingers caressing the electric buttons which, when pressed, will release the huge two-ton bomb and hundreds of incendiaries.

This isn't any time for casual conversation. The pilot is very busy weaving his way in and out up and down through the anti-aircraft barrage. Every one is making mental notes of fires far below. The plane streaks across the target area, and leaps like a high-spirited horse when the 4,000-pound bomb is released.

Once again you cross over that blood-red carpet of fire beneath you, and the bomb aimer is busily pressing his buttons, letting go incendiaries. Again the Lancaster runs across from another direction, unloosing more incendiaries. Just once more—all of this in that queer indescribable voiceless "silence." Then the silence is broken as the bomb aimer sings out, "Bombs gone, skipper."

From that instant onward for some time there are only the rapid, cool words of the navigator telling the pilot "Set course" so many degrees and the pilot answering "Okay," so many degrees.

Far from Berlin the plane, which has been flying at various altitudes ranging up to heights where the rarefied air requires the use of oxygen to keep human beings alive, descends to a lower level, a mere few thousand feet where the oxygen supply isn't needed and one can remove the mask from one's face.

Then one hears the flight engineer, who also acts as a sort of plane steward, saying over the "intercom," "Who'll have some tea?" followed by an enthusiastic chorus of all hands, "I will." The flight engineer goes through the ship giving each man a thermos bottle of tea, a couple of oranges, and two or three cakes of chocolate.

Over tea each member of the crew talks about the raid. How big the fires were, what the weather was like over Berlin, and other details of the "show," something after the fashion of members of a football team living over again a big game with an opposing team.

Unexpectedly there is a sudden halt in this conversation as the pilot's voice is heard, saying: "Kite off the port. Keep a sharp lookout." Is it an enemy night fighter—or isn't it? All eyes study the distant plane for a moment or two. Then the mid-upper gunner drawls, "It's one of our kites—a Lank."

Soon the conversation becomes general again. The youngster who had failed to make good on his evening date with a girl brings up the subject again and swears by the deity if he isn't "on ops" (raiding duty) the next night he'll call her up and square himself. Somebody is heard humming the latest tune to reach Britain from the United States, "Praise the Lord and Pass the Ammunition." The pilot interrupts, "How are you doing, Johnnie? you Cassie? Steve?" and so on through all hands. In each case the answer goes back, "Okay."

Finally the plane reaches its base and establishes wireless telephone contact with the airfield control room. "D for Donald" is now directly over the field, but isn't home yet by any means. It must wait its turn to land.

Once again there is that odd silence as the plane makes a wide circle. No time for chitchat now. All communication is limited strictly to the business of landing.

The earphones register the voice of the Waaf in the control room: "D for Donald, take 3,500 feet." The same voice is heard instructing "X for X-ray," "P for Peter," "Zed for Zebra," and so on, to take different altitudes and keep circling until it comes their turn to land. "D for Donald" drops to 2,000 feet and keeps up a monotonous circling; then to 1,500 and circles some more. At last it gets orders to land and down it goes bumping along the "flare path" and the pilot shuts off the hot motors which have been roaring the angry song of war for nine hours.

Every one climbs out of the plane. If they have felt any strain during the trip they certainly don't show it. They open their heavy fur-lined flying jackets, fish in the pockets of their uniforms, produce cigarettes and pass them around.

They have been through hell and come out of it unscathed, and this is how they close one more chapter of their adventurous lives:

"Who's got a match?"

# END OF THE BEGINNING

### by James B. Reston

LONDON, Oct. 22, 1943—A few German planes raided London tonight for the seventh consecutive night; but all these attacks do now is to bring back memories.

Maybe the start of these raids is the same as in 1940. They begin at twilight

281

with that same eerie sound of sirens rising and falling over the million smoky London rooftops. But there similarity ends.

On the eve of this first anniversary of the Battle of El Alamein, great changes have come over this capital. Everything goes up now in the direction of the attacking planes and very little comes down except showers of shrapnel from the anti-aircraft guns.

The theory is that these raids—they hardly come within the scope of "attack"—have a propaganda value for the Germans. The fact is they merely serve to remind the people of the island of their almost miraculous deliverance.

It is true, of course, that before these few Nazis get away they drop some bombs and kill a few persons. But on the whole they perform an important service for the Churchill government, which has been having a little trouble lately in keeping its vast home defense personnel on the alert.

After long months, in which men and women waited at listening posts and lonely anti-aircraft batteries for an enemy that never came and after four winters of unrelieved blackout, the British Government had been faced with repeated demands in the last few weeks to relax the blackout and cut down the civilian defense organization—actions it hesitated very much to take. These seven nights, just before winter comes, have done Prime Minister Winston Churchill a service.

Not all the changes in London since the 1940-41 Blitz are for the better. That remarkable kindness and considerateness among the people, the thankfulness merely to be alive that inspired London and lifted the spirits of every man who lived in the valley of the Thames through those days, are gone.

People have slipped back to the normality of hard work and petty preoccupations. It is only when they get seven straight raids that they think of those terrible ninety nights when 22,837 persons were killed and 28,435 others injured.

But the sharpest contrast with those days lies in the way in which British and Germans have changed positions in the war.

Three years ago the British were yelling about Germany's violating the rights of neutrals. Now one finds the German papers speaking about the Allies' violating the rights of neutrals, and in almost the same phrases.

Indeed, by reading from German papers on the Allied air attacks on Germany it is possible to recapture the feeling one had in 1940 about the destruction in Britain.

Here, for example, are excerpts from German newspapers reaching this office tonight regarding the recent Royal Air Force bombings of Hanover:

"Hanover suffered the heaviest terror raid yet on the night of October 8-9. Considerable damage was caused in residential quarters by innumerable explosive and incendiary bombs, mines and phosphorus cannisters. Large fires inflicted deep wounds on the town. The losses suffered by the population in killed, injured and homeless were very great."

Another German newspaper said of the same RAF blow:

282

"The Anglo-American air pirates struck Hanover with extraordinary force and hardness. Many fires were started and a wave of annihilation and destruction swept through the town.

"Glowing skeletons of houses sheathed in smoke and fire crashed and occasionally threatened to block the exits from burning streets. Thanks to the infinite bravery of the people and the work of all available forces there was no panic."

These confessions of the power of the Allied air offensive illustrate one of the most striking facts of the war, which is that Adolf Hitler made possible his own downfall by resorting to the use of bombing planes against civilian population in the early days.

Nobody who knows the puritanical British people would believe they would sanction the kind of bombing the Allies are now visiting upon Germany unless Hitler had first burned and blasted the cities and villages of Britain.

# Part Six: War in the East

OCTOBER 28, 1940: *The Italians invaded Greece.*

NOVEMBER 20: *The Greeks counterattacked and drove the Italians back to Albania.*

## THE GREEKS MEANT BUSINESS

### by Thomas B. Morgan

TO SHOW to his own people that he was doing something Mussolini projected an invasion of Greece also. He thought it would be no more than a trick in legerdemain. Presto! Change-o! He knew the condition of the Italian army did not permit much of a campaign and decided to buy off the Greek government with large sums of money, which in terms of army expenses would only be a beer ration. Accordingly he chose chunky Emmanuel Grazzi, who had served many years as consul-general in New York and was known in our metropolis only as an excellent bridge player, to act as the go-between. Grazzi was his minister to Greece. The amounts set apart for this clandestine enterprise have been reported variously as from $10,000,000 to $20,000,000. This was big money for Greek government officials. Grazzi decided he had found his men and, what is more, the money was paid over.

Meanwhile Mussolini had called Marshal Badoglio to a conference. He told him that he wanted to take Greece and desired to know the cost. Badoglio replied that it would take ten divisions and there were only seven divisions available. Besides, Badoglio said, it was bound to be a hard campaign. The winter was approaching and the terrain was mountainous and impassable without a large attacking force. Mussolini then told him there would be no resistance as Grazzi had bought off the Greek government. Badoglio said that he would not like to risk it.

Mussolini went ahead. On October 26, a communique issued by the official Italian news agency described an attack "by a band of Greeks armed with rifles and hand grenades on an Albanian outpost." Two Albanian soldiers were killed and three wounded. This was the pretext for invasion. The Greeks had provoked war by attacking Albania, Italian territory, they claimed. On October 28, Grazzi gave a most sumptuous reception in the Italian legation at Athens. The cream of Greek aristocracy was there. Cabinet ministers, bankers, editors and diplomats added greater dignity to the occasion. A while later, the chunky Italian go-between handed a three-hour

284

ultimatum to Prime Minister John Metaxas, in the latter's private apartment. The document demanded the use of Greek naval bases for the Italian fleet and the renunciation of all British guarantees. Before the ultimatum expired, Italian troops were on the march. Six waves of Fascist planes bombed the harbor of Piraeus. The first days of the campaign showed the invincibility of Mussolini's legions. They pierced far into the Pindus mountains on Greek soil. On November 7, they crossed the Kalamas river. Gleefully, Mussolini held a conference with Hitler in Florence and assured him that Grazzi had done a superb job.

Suddenly, the Italians were stopped. The hardy Greek mountaineers had orders to beat them back. The pompous Italian tanks and big rumbling trucks were discourteously halted and thrown into confusion in the recesses of the craggy heights.

"We will throw them into the sea," proclaimed General Alexander Papagos, the Greek commander-in-chief, in his message to his troops. "We will write new and glorious pages in our history. Do not doubt that we shall win our cause."

There was a turn. The Greeks actually began driving the Italians into the sea. The mechanized units were rounded up by the Greek cavalry playing hide-and-seek with them around the rugged hills. It was plain that Grazzi's men who had taken the money would not or could not deliver.

The campaign was fought in the depth of winter with snow eight and ten feet deep. The Italians were ill-clad, some of them even wore their summer uniforms. As the need for greater forces increased, the equipment became less and less efficient. The Italian tanks could not stand up in the rough, mountainous terrain. Their construction was too haphazard to resist a campaign of such severity. They had been made for parade. Not alone were the men poorly clad and improperly fed but there were tragic shortages of munitions. Rifles were faulty. There was a shortage of mules for mountain artillery. What stocks of equipment and munitions remained were always the wrong size or weight.

Besides, very erroneous calculations were made in keeping the army in the field. First, the risk of transport from Italy was not foreseen since the campaign was to be a pushover. Then in the interior of Albania, where the roads were nothing but mere tracks through the passes, there was no place for mechanized units to operate. The only thing which could work with any degree of success was the mule. The Greeks had mules.

Here, too, were evidences of bravery of individual soldiers. Prisoners captured by the Greeks stated that in many battalions only a few survivors could be counted. One battalion entered the line with five hundred and fifty men and only thirty-six survived. With such deplorably poor staff work, it was inevitable that the morale of the soldiers and of the officers of the line should collapse. Here was the answer to the capture of whole regiments of Italians. The only alternative was surrender.

In the spring of 1941, Mussolini made a personal visit to the Greek front. He ordered General Cavallero, who by this time had assumed command, to start an offensive. The attack crumbled when the Italians were thrown back with heavy losses, a habit they had been acquiring all winter. The Greeks claimed that up to that moment they had put 120,000 Italians out of action, had downed a hundred and thirty planes and had captured twelve hundred field guns, fifteen hundred mortars, seven hundred machine-guns and enormous stores. This was the Italian campaign against Greece.

# FASCISM DIED THERE, TOO

### by John T. Whitaker

"DO YOU know about Roosevelt's new note to Athens?" one Italian asks another. "He has told the Greeks that America cannot recognize the conquest of Italy by force."

This is typical of half a dozen stories in Rome and every Italian tells you that a French wit in the Alps put up a sign reading, "Greeks stop here. This is the French frontier."

Mussolini's invasion-in-reverse would be the most ludicrous story in modern history if it had not caused so many thousands of deaths, so much destruction and human misery. The inside story is funnier than Wodehouse and more melodramatic than Oppenheim. It is a gangster story of bribing and double-crossing. Mussolini bribed a half dozen Greek generals to betray their country. They went to Metaxas, and he—the wiliest Greek of them all—said, "Keep the money, be true to your country and keep me informed." They did exactly that and Mussolini, expecting to conquer Greece in 48 hours, has been beaten instead.

Three weeks before Mussolini's "unexpected" ultimatum and his precipitate invasion your correspondent and at least two embassies in Rome knew the exact day and hour of the invasion. I sent four cables setting the zero hour as precisely as I could without risking expulsion. The Italian excuse that the Greeks were providing submarine and air bases for the British was as bald a lie as the trumped-up story some months before of the murder of Daut Hodgia, a bandit described by the Italians as an Albanian patriot. Hodgia had been killed in a drunken brawl two months before the "incident."

Mussolini decided that Greece ought to be his swag after Hitler double-crossed him on the French loot. Mussolini jumped on the back of France, only to be thrown off with bad bruises, because he wanted Savoy, Tunisia, Corsica, Nice and French Somaliland.

But Hitler decided not to give them to Mussolini. Hitler wanted the French colonies and the French Navy for use against the British and he feared that if Mussolini were allowed to despoil France prematurely the navy and the colonies might go to De Gaulle.

Smarting under Hitler's decision, Mussolini looked about for a quick

286

pushover, to which Hitler might agree. Mussolini had always wanted Yugoslavia but he knew that the Serbs would fight him and besides Hitler wanted to drain all the livestock and food out of Yugoslavia before attacking there. Mussolini asked Hitler about Greece and Hitler said: "Okay, but later. You've got to wait until much later in the game."

Mussolini decided to cross Hitler. He called in Ciano and Muti, who had engineered the coup in Albania, and asked them to repeat the performance in Greece. Muti is a 6-foot-2 roughneck who looks like a professional football player. He has the courage of a lion and the brain and education of a 10-year-old child.

Ciano idolized him and told me once in Muti's presence that his friend was "the perfect Fascist" and the most trustworthy lieutenant he had ever found. Ciano made him secretary of the Fascist party but had to remove him later because, with no administrative ability and only a casual knowledge of reading and writing, poor Muti got to chastising inefficient Fascist bosses by beating them up with his bare fists.

Ciano also took Muti to the country club to show him off to his girls and a few foreigners with the kind of obvious pride a man takes in a newly acquired bird dog or mastiff. That ultimately destroyed their friendship. Muti fell in love with one of the girls to whom Ciano introduced him and later when Ciano took the girl away from him simple, forthright Muti did not understand.

Four weeks ago on the airport at Bari, where both are pilots, Muti socked Ciano and Ciano socked back. A man who saw the fight told me it was a thriller. Muti won.

At the time Mussolini ordered them to engineer the conquest of Greece, Ciano and Muti were still friends. They went to work with a will. Ciano began to grind out the press campaign. Muti arranged the Daut Hodgia incident. They dispatched agents to Greece and organized the bombing force. They planned to repeat the Albanian performance verbatim.

Ciano gave the Greeks private intimations that he wanted only Salonika and a few bases and would treat the country well if it merely offered a nominal show of resistance. The invasion was to be a fifth column operation based on treachery by key Greek generals, exploited by methodical bombing that would destroy communications and paralyze Greek resistance. Ciano and Muti promised Mussolini a 48-hour job.

Mussolini was delighted. He decided to confront Hitler with a *fait accompli* and there he set the date of the invasion for the early morning of the day three weeks later when Hitler was to meet him in Florence. In that moment Mussolini's position as an Axis partner was strong enough to permit an independent action. He had the only Axis navy because then there had been no Taranto, he was winning in Africa with British Somaliland for then there had been no Libya, and his air force was going up to give pal Hitler a help on the Channel.

What happened afterwards is now history, as heroic and thrilling as Thermopylae. The Greeks fought. The British rushed in prompt and

287

effective help. Militarily the operation was described to me by one of the highest officers in Italy. Listen to him.

"Militarily the invasion was impossible," he said. "We had seven divisions in Albania. Two of them were necessary to hold the Albanian population from going into revolt. Two others were in reserve. That left us three divisions with which to undertake an offensive. Against us the Greeks disposed of 15 divisions. We might have been able to undertake an offensive had those figures been reversed.

"The Greeks had good staff work and good luck. They got their divisions into position. Better still, knowing that we meant to drive for Salonika they massed their forces into the region of the Kostanza frontier. When impossible weather conditions bogged us down in Epirus our position was strategically untenable. The air force failed to prevent Greek concentrations. The Navy failed to land below Corfu. It was not a military operation. It was a political adventure. No officer in the Italian or any other army would have approved such a military offensive."

Despite this explanation, which is sound, Badoglio as chief of staff came out badly. Why did he not veto the operation, offering his resignation if necessary? Actually Mussolini outmaneuvered him. After the fiasco Badoglio told the King that he meant to resign in protest. The King dissuaded him and sent him to Mussolini. The dictator rose when Badoglio entered his office and said, "Your resignation has been accepted and is effective immediately."

The poor bewildered old general was thus made the butt of the misadventure. Even his fellow officers criticized him for running out when the Italians were beaten and Mussolini informed the public that Badoglio had approved the operation and was responsible for the tragedy—responsible with Ciano.

It is typical of the mood of Italians today that those who know of the bribery and its failure think that the money never reached the Greeks, that it was pocketed by grafting Fascist agents. I don't believe this. I believe the money did reach the Greeks, that Ciano learned shortly before the invasion date that he had been double-crossed but that Mussolini would not abandon his plan. One of Ciano's most trusted agents came back from Athens four days before the invasion date. He said that the Greeks would fight and that the Italian agents had been double-crossed. He said that he reported this to Ciano.

Wherever the responsibility lies it is one of the most brutal and cynical aggressions in history and the long-suffering people of Italy have paid for it as dearly as the Greeks. My dearest Italian friend, the last of a thousand-year line of Roman princes, died in Albania. A fellow officer told me that he bled to death from his wounds—an unnecessary death had there been any organized medical service with the Italian Army.

I have another Italian friend whose hands have been amputated. No gloves were issued to an army sent to fight in snow-filled mountain passes. I have another Italian friend who is probably crippled for life. There were no bandages in the military hospital even when he was brought across the Adriatic to the Italian mainland.

Multiply these cases by several thousand. Add to it the heroism of soldiers and officers who out of shame for their country went on fighting and dying and are doing that even today when they know how cynically and brutally they were betrayed. That is real heroism—to die without faith in order to regain your self-respect as an Italian.

Mussolini has said he will break the back of the Greeks no matter how long it takes, that the Axis hordes will make Greece a second Finland. That may be so but the Greeks have broken his back too. More than princes and peasants lie dead in the mountain passes of Albania. Fascism died there too.

NOVEMBER 23, 1940: *Rumania joined the Axis.*

FEBRUARY 10, 1941: *England severed relations with Rumania.*

MARCH 1: *Bulgaria joined the Axis as German troops entered her territory.*

MARCH 25: *Yugoslavian Government signed a pact with the Axis.*

MARCH 27: *Army coup in Yugoslavia. Peter II assumed power. General Simovich became premier.*

# THE COUP

## by Robert St. John

IT WAS a great day for us newspapermen when Yugoslavia's Prime Minister finally signed the Tri-Partite Pact one cold morning in March. Of course none of us approved this diplomatic defeat of another free country. It was simply that we wanted some sleep, and it looked now as if we could get it. Those of us who had already been through the same sort of thing in other countries like Rumania and Bulgaria were beginning to get worn out by this Hitler technique. I know that we correspondents lost more sleep and more weight than any of the kings or ministers or diplomats during the weeks of pressure politics and uncertainty, the flood of conflicting rumors, the war of nerves.

In every country the story had followed the same old pattern. When we got orders to buy plane tickets for Bucharest or Sofia or Belgrade because a new crisis had developed we knew exactly what it was going to mean. Weeks of "Will they? Won't they?" Weeks of dope stories based on the slimmest of chancellery gossip. Weeks of writing two or three long dispatches a day trying to keep the story alive while we waited for the inevitable to happen.

We had gone through that same sort of thing in Bucharest, waiting for the German troops to march into Rumania. And in Sofia, waiting for Bulgaria to knuckle under to Berlin and let the Nazi army sweep down across the Danube. Now we had gone through it all over again in Belgrade. But at last the jittery days were over. Yugoslavia had given Hitler the green light; sold out—body, soul, and railroad lines. We had written our capitulation stories, packed our bags, and argued over where the next crisis was likely to break out. Turkey was my choice. I was waiting only for an okay from the Associated Press to move on. But then something happened that forced us to unlimber our typewriters in a hurry, dig copy paper out of our suitcases, and get to work in Belgrade again. It was a completely screwball development. It wasn't at all according to the old pattern of Rumania, Bulgaria, and the other capitulation countries. That, of course, made it big news.

Despite public speeches, despite what the controlled radio said and what the weak-livered Yugoslav press told us, we all knew that Prime Minister Cvetkovich had at best only twenty per cent of the population behind him when he joined Yugoslavia to the Axis. But it had been the same in Rumania. There the eighty per cent had remained dumb. And we all expected the same pattern to be followed here in Yugoslavia. There was no reason to believe the eighty per cent would dare speak out in denunciation. But none of us had considered the possibility of a "Diaper Revolution." Yet that is just what it was, a Diaper Revolution. It all started with boys and girls ten, eleven, and twelve years old letting off steam with typical Balkan gusto. Sit-down strikes. Riots. A young revolution in the classrooms of the grammar schools. Hitler pictures torn to shreds. Cvetkovich denounced as a traitor. Slogans deriding the weakness of the government scrawled in childish writing on walls and doors. Thousands of hungry youngsters barricading themselves in their schoolhouses and refusing to obey orders from anyone.

Belgrade was never prouder of its young than that day in March when its young said the things the whole city wanted to say but didn't dare. Crowds of parents gathered around the schoolhouses and smiled silent encouragement up at the kid-packed windows. Police officials scratched their heads and wondered what to do about it. Riots and demonstrations by university students were old stuff to them. For generations they had been putting down outbursts like that with rubber hose and bayonets, but you can't use rubber hose and bayonets on ten-year-old boys and girls, especially if they are your own boys and girls, and more especially if they're saying things you believe yourself and just haven't the nerve to say.

One of the demonstration centers was a school across the street from the Srpski Kralj Hotel, where most of the American press slept, ate, drank, and labored. At one point we watched boys and girls sitting at their desks working away with an eagerness seldom demonstrated before. We could see them through the windows with our field glasses. They were scribbling out inflammatory pamphlets. We watched them during the busy noon hour rush out onto the street and distribute them among the passing crowds. We also saw a furtive fellow in plain clothes slip one of the amateurish handbills in his pocket and duck into our hotel. I followed him to the telephone room, and when he went into a booth I eavesdropped from the next one. He called Secret Police Headquarters, identifying himself merely with a number. Then he read off the words on the leaflet slowly enough for someone at the other end to copy them down.

"Interesting handbills the kids put out," I said casually but with a wink as we bumped into each other coming out of the booths. He looked a bit startled; then he took me off into a corner of the lobby.

"You're an American, aren't you? All right. We're on the same side then. I tell you those kids out there may be making history today. Don't you see what this means?"

"What?" I asked dumbly.

"If this were just a few hundred kids writing a lot of nonsense it wouldn't mean anything, but these kids are only parrots. They're just repeating stuff they heard at home. That's why my office—" he looked around nervously "—that's why my office is watching this thing. This shows how the country feels. This is important. You newspaper boys better keep your pencils sharp. Things are going to happen in Yugoslavia yet!"

It was two-thirty the next morning when things did start happening. I was getting a little sleep, thanks to an arrangement with Ray Brock, of the *New York Times*. He had agreed to keep an eye on the city from midnight until dawn each morning while the post-crisis crisis lasted. I watched things from dawn until noon. We both worked during the afternoon and evening. It was a happy arrangement, because Brock had a weakness for rumba-dancing, which kept him, from midnight until dawn seven mornings a week, traveling from one to another of Belgrade's Serbian cafés, Russian basement dives, and cosmopolitan hot spots. And in those places it was always possible to pick up the latest news, fit to print or not.

At two-thirty on the morning of March twenty-seventh, between rumbas, Brock ran into a hot piece of news in one of his hangouts.

"They tell me," he shouted over the phone, "that fifty to a hundred army tanks are taking up positions around the city. Nobody knows what it all means. I'm going out now through Terrazia."

I agreed to look over the north end of the city and meet Brock in fifteen minutes at the Majestic Hotel.

I found that the streets were not only full of tanks but that thousands of soldiers, all in air force uniform, were taking up some sort of battle formation.

"Move on!" they barked when I tried to approach them. No one would give a hint of what it was all about.

I ordered my Serbian chauffeur to make for the Majestic. We were still two blocks away from the hotel when we were forced to a sudden stop. Soldiers with bayonets held at belly level made a circle around the car. The chauffeur and I were dragged from our seats and marched into a small park. What little Serbian I knew did me no good. We were prisoners, that was clear. Never mind why. Never mind what was happening. Never mind who I was. It made no difference. And never mind what all those soldiers with machine guns hidden in the bushes were there for. Just sit down on a bench and shut up. It was clear that those were the orders and no arguing.

Just then I saw a squad of soldiers bringing in a familiar figure. Milan! Good old Milan, our favorite barman at the Srpski Kralj Hotel. Milan was one of my best sources of information. If anyone knew the answers, he did. We went off into the bushes and had a hooker or two out of a bottle of slivovich Milan always carried in his hip pocket for emergencies, and then he opened up.

Simovich, the commander of the air force, was behind it all. The retired captain was right. We were watching the unfolding of a first-class, full-dress *coup d'état*. On the stroke of two o'clock army units all over the country had been ordered out. At two-thirty they struck, surrounding the royal palace, the regent's palace, the home of every cabinet minister, all the police stations, the gendarmeries, city halls, and other public buildings. They had all their tanks, light artillery, and motorized equipment ready for action in case of opposition. Simovich was pro-British. He was convinced the country would be with him in his attempt to throw out the government that had sold Yugoslavia to Hitler and Mussolini. He was playing a dangerous game and he knew it. Prince Paul, who was ruling as regent for the boy king, Peter, was a "tough old bird," as Milan put it.

At four forty-five the air force lieutenant, in a typically Balkan burst of softheartedness, called me aside, explained he was going to give me a break, and assigned a soldier to escort me through military lines in the direction of the Srpski Kralj. Near the hotel I ran into Kay and Chinigo. We walked along together doing that defensive parrying which rival reporters do so often when each wants to find out what the other knows and yet not disclose his own story. This time we finally agreed to trade information. They had a lot more details than I had about the extent of the military preparations. They knew how many pieces of light artillery had been set up in the streets, how many tanks had rolled into town, what regiments had entrenched themselves behind barbed-wire barricades. But they laughed at my version of what it was all about. Their story was that a peasant revolution had broken out. Mobs of Serbs from the mountain districts were marching on Belgrade to make some kind of demands on Cvetkovich. The army had been called out to defend the capital against the revolters.

I went into the booth and called the American Legation. Maybe they could get word to New York somehow. But the ban on communications had now been extended to diplomats, an unusual procedure even in the Balkans, where we were growing accustomed to having every conceivable obstacle put in the way of sending news whenever there was any news worth sending. Then I studied a map. The Rumanian border was a matter of a hundred miles. It was a hundred and fifty miles to the Bulgarian frontier. It might even be possible to get up to Budapest or down into Greece before the phone lines were opened up again. But if this really was a military putsch, a dash in any direction would be futile. Frontiers would be closed and heavily guarded. And if a man did find some way to get out of the country it might be impossible to get back for days. By that time the story might have assumed even greater proportions: a bloody civil war or a clash with the Nazi troops who were already poised on the frontiers. Belgrade mustn't be left uncovered. Better stay here and take a chance on getting the first call out when the lines open.

While I was changing from the pajamas and overcoat in which I had been tramping the city, two local telephone calls came in. One was from a friend who said he had seen Kay and Chinigo in an automobile, apparently making for the frontier. The other call brought absolute confirmation that it was, after all, a *coup d'état,* which was succeeding beyond the wildest dreams of the plotters. That made the score even. If the two other press association men got out of the country with their stories about the military defending the capital against rebellious peasants, so much the better. They probably never would get back to report the real story.

It was light now, and I made another attempt to get to the Majestic Hotel and keep that two forty-five date with Brock. Traffic was moving freely through the streets. Early morning pedestrians blinked at the tanks, the barbed-wire barricades, the swarms of soldiers, but they kept moving. No one knew then whether to cheer or to curse under his breath. The city still didn't know what it was all about.

A cordon had been thrown around the Majestic. Those inside the circle of soldiers couldn't get out. Those outside, like myself, couldn't get in. On the sidewalk in front of the hotel I suddenly spotted Dave Walker of Reuter's and the London *Daily Mirror.* For two years Dave and I together had covered every major crisis in the Balkans. Of the hundred or more Americans and Englishmen who had worked in these countries since the war began, Walker was without a doubt the best informed, no matter which country he happened to be in. We rushed toward each other. A good-natured soldier in the cordon let us talk a minute over his shoulder. It didn't take Dave long to unload what he knew. The facts were snapped across the soldier's shoulder in quick little sentences.

"Prince Paul has fled. Little King Peter will take over the country. Simovich will be Prime Minister. Cvetkovich, Cinco-Markovitch, and all the rest of the cabinet have been arrested. They caught some of them right here in the Majestic. They're still searching the hotel. That's why all these soldiers are guarding the place."

While we talked, the streets were filling up with people. They were dazed, bewildered people, still wondering what it all meant. Then faintly, far in the distance, we heard a feeble little cheer. It came closer, grew louder. You could sense the news spreading down Mihilova, the main street of Belgrade, and into the little avenues that crisscross Mihilova, like tongues of fire along gasoline-soaked bands of dry grass. The faint cheer became a roar, then an infernal din. No one could talk any more. No one wanted to talk. Everyone just opened his mouth and let out all the noise he could. Here

293

were thousands of people who for months had been throttled, gagged, suppressed.

In the last few weeks they had wanted more than ever before to bellow out denunciation of their own leaders. They had wanted to sing their fiery old Serbian marching songs and carry flags in parades and tell the world how they felt. But they had been gagged. Now the gag was off. Simovich had done that. Simovich was a hero. Long live Simovich! Peter was going to be a king now in something more than name alone. Long live the boy king! Oi, Serbia! Someone started to sing that greatest of national anthems, "Oi, Serbia!" Thousands of lungs filled with air and roared out the words.

A little old shopkeeper ran into his back room and came out with a picture of Peter. Someone nailed it on to a stick, and the parade began. The day had started. A day Serbs will never forget, despite all the tragedy it eventually led to. Street hawkers began selling British emblems for the buttonhole. Where they got the thousands of little metal gadgets no one ever found out, but by night everyone wore one. Paraders carried Union Jacks of all sizes. Big American flags were pulled out of cedar chests and mothballs and hung on buildings.

But the pro-British, pro-Greek, pro-American part was incidental. A lot of people, a lot of sideline observers, missed that point. This riot of emotion was primarily a pro-Serbian party. Yugoslavia's new independence day. A celebration of the end of tyranny and suppression. Freedom had returned. Freedom to yell "Long live the British!" if you wanted to. Freedom to cheer for someone besides Hitler if you wanted to.

"How about the Nazis?" someone yelled. Ah yes, the Nazis. The crowd had almost forgotten the Nazis. A roar went through Terrazia. "Down with the Nazis!" I kept thinking, if Hitler could only hear them now! If Hitler could only hear how they said that word "Nazis" between their teeth, with all the hatred of a people betrayed and then liberated. If Hitler could only see how Yugoslavia really felt about him—Yugoslavia, which he had put down as his new ally—then maybe it would make him realize something about these other countries he had signed up, these other countries that were paying lip service to him. "Down with the Nazis!" The crowd kept roaring out its hatred, and then they started off with a great rush toward the north.

\*    \*    \*

BERLIN, April 6 (Associated Press): The German radio broadcast early today an order by the Fuehrer Adolf Hitler to the German Army to march into Yugoslavia and Greece. . . .

\*    \*    \*

# BOMBS OVER BELGRADE

## by Ray Brock

PERHAPS five minutes had passed and I was trying the international switchboard again, just for luck, when there were rapid footfalls and shouting in the hall and Bob burst into my room.

"*It's on!*" he shouted. "Hitler's on the air, declaring war. Mrzliak is catching him. He's roaring about 'Soldiers of the southeast front!'"

So, I thought, it *has* come. I rang Mr. Lane, MacDonald, and Fortier and passed on the news. Then I rang Natacha Petrovich, who had leased us our new apartment on the Topličin Venac. She had begged me to telephone if it came to war.

"Then it's true," she said softly. "I suppose they will bomb?"

"Assuredly," I said. "If the sirens go again, you must take your mother and your son and find cover. There are Bren guns on the building opposite you, you know. Stukas will unquestionably go for them." She thanked me and rang off. Bob and Leigh White, who had joined him, found a taxi and raced off to the central post in a probably futile effort to get telegrams out of the country. I was alone. The daylight was coming rapidly now. I pushed the button for the waiter and ordered breakfast. The waiter was a youngster who had served me many times in the Srpski Kralj.

"It is war, you know," I told him. "Germany will attack Yugoslavia this morning." His eyes grew wide. He was about fifteen. All the older waiters had been mobilized. "You should get word to your parents," I said. "There may be bombing."

"No telephone," he said and repeated it, "they have no telephone."

"Go home," I told him.

"I cannot do that," he said. "The hotel would discharge me."

"In a few hours," I said, "there may be no hotel. Go home!" Staring at me, he backed out of the room. When my breakfast was served, ten minutes later, another boy I had never seen before brought the tray with orange juice, fried eggs, toast, and double coffee.

Slowly, the pink turned red in the eastern sky and the first bright rays of the sun fanned upward. From up the street toward the Spomenik sounded the noise of an automobile at high speed and I turned, drinking my coffee, and watched a large taxi speeding toward the hotel. It halted immediately below, with a squealing of brakes and tires, and Bob and Leigh tumbled out. Leigh's face looked up whitely.

"*Germans!*" he yelled. "Thirty Germans—planes—on their way to Belgrade! Officer at the post—" The rest of it faded out as Leigh dashed into the hotel below, following Bob. Through the open door of my room I heard the two Americans pounding up the stairs and then I heard what I was listening for. It was a steadily growing vibration from the east, a swiftly increasing throb that, in a few seconds, grew to a mounting, uneven drone that echoed everywhere and seemed to fill the air all about. My binoculars were ready and I leveled them into the now blinding glare of the rising sun. I moved them right, then left. Then I saw the bombers. They were coming on in perfect formation, flanked by fighters, and in a sudden glint of sunlight I spotted more fighters high above them. Bob and Leigh were on the balcony now, pointing and shouting.

"There they *come!*" exclaimed Leigh. I was counting rapidly, excluding the fighters. There were not just thirty bombers, but nearer sixty. They must have made rendezvous with a second bombardment unit, I thought automatically. The mighty roaring of the oncoming war planes was becoming deafening, beating the sky apart.

"Come on!" Leigh shouted. Bob formed with his mouth the word *"Where?"* "To the park!" shouted Leigh, pointing due left to the Kalemegdan gardens. They rushed from the balcony and Hill, who had just entered, turned and followed them. I remained on the balcony, seeing White, St. John, Cecil Brown, and Mike Tckinigo sprinting for the park. Suddenly it was very lonely. The bombers were just beyond the city now, and I knew they had begun to unload. From about ten thousand feet, I made it. Suddenly the entire right bank of the formation began to peel off and I recognized Stukas—about thirty of them.

Down they dived across the Sava toward Zemun airdrome, their high whine amplifying into a series of nerve-racking roars, and then the bombs began to fall. The Heinkels and Dorniers, gliding in, had begun laying their sticks across the upper end of the capital. They whistled down, and whole quarters of the city erupted in streaks of flame and smoke. The incessant eeeeeEEEEEAAAAAH! whine of the diving Stukas and the detonations of their bombs blended with the ground-shaking blasts of the sticks of bombs landing across the upper Kralja Milana and the Terazia. The first wave had flashed over, and in the brief interval I heard the faraway, high stutter of machine guns. Ack-ack bursts, which had passed unnoticed as the Stukas began diving, resumed now and became heavier. Puffballs dotted the sky about the second wave of gliding bombers. This wave, of about thirty bombers, swept farther northward, and I ducked instinctively as bombs whistled down near by, exploding in the familiar, marching *boom-Boom-*BOOM-BOOM-BAM! Up the street two blocks away a blinding flash ripped outward and the blast blotted out the street in smoke and flame. Far out and up through the swiftly gathering haze, I saw another bomber wave coming, headed directly over our end of the city. I ran out onto the landing and downstairs and into the street. The next sticks started coming down like a clattering of tin trays. I made the last ten yards at a sprint and dived for the ground. I felt, rather than heard, the thudding of the bombs beyond the hotel, and the atmosphere about me seemed to explode in a series of deafening roars. Ahead, about fifteen yards as I remembered, was a shallow air-raid shelter which would stop bomb splinters. I ran for it.

"Welcome, stranger!" grinned Cecil Brown. He was huddled in the sunken entrance with Leigh White and Russ Hill. I ducked inside and

296

ran through to the farther end to see if there was a second emergency exit. There wasn't. I returned to the entrance, crowding through a small group of Serbs, some of them taxi-drivers from the hotel stand opposite.

There was a lull. We emerged from the entranceway into the sunlit haze of smoke and dust. Above we heard the whine and drone of diving and zooming war planes, but only scattering ack-ack bursts of aerial machine-gunning indicated there were no more big waves of bombers overhead.

"What now?" said Bob. He was making a note in his loose-leaf book, timing the last wave of bombers.

"I'd like some breakfast," said Leigh. "Bombing's easier on a full tummy."

"Might as well," I said. "There'll be no transport for all that stuff." I indicated the massed luggage, about seventeen or nineteen pieces in all. "And we might get another ten or fifteen minutes' respite." We entered the dining-room. The woman, I saw her now, still huddled, whimpering, beneath a table. Her husband or escort was trying to persuade her to get back on her feet. We found a table well inside away from the big plate-glass windows overlooking the Kalemegdan. One of the waiters, a neat-looking little Bosnian, I remembered, took our orders. He served us quickly and efficiently, hardly looking up when a salvo of incendiaries, dropped probably from a high-flying squadron—for we heard no low-flying bombers—plopped into the street just outside and burned luridly along the tram tracks.

As I had my second double coffee, the small elevator boy brought me a sheaf of papers. It was the hotel bill, a big one, including telephone slips of Sulzberger's totaling about nine thousand dinars. I paid the bill and left the youngster two hundred dinars and some odd change. I had plenty of dinars and, I reflected, he probably would need money to get away on, if he could manage it. All of us assumed that a German flying column probably had crossed the Hungarian frontier at daybreak and was advancing upon Belgrade.

"Remember Barcelona?" Leigh was saying. "They never gave us anything like this—not even in the middle of March '38. And I've got a hunch it's not—"

Leigh stopped, looking through the big windows. We followed his glance and saw two men running, looking back and upward. Simultaneously we heard more bombers. Immediately sticks of big bombs began crashing nearby, marching nearer. Brown and White went under the table. Tckinigo followed. Bob and I slid under the piano, still clutching our coffees, and kicked a heavy instrument case, probably a trombone's, across our flank. It might stop splinters. This wave sounded like bad news. Bombs were falling all about, and suddenly I heard a salvo coming that I knew was bound our way.

"—boom-Boom-BOOM-BAM-WHA-AAM! They landed and the hotel shivered, plaster falling, glass crashing. The lights went out. I looked upward, quivering, waiting for that rushing roar that meant the building was coming down. Another stick began to fall across the street. Bob's coffee cup was trembling but he hadn't spilled a drop. In a few seconds' quiet between bombs, I fumbled a cigarette out of my pocket. My palms were sweating. I couldn't find a match. Then I discovered the small elevator boy kneeling beside the piano. Coolly, calmly, he was extracting a match and lighting it.

"*Chibitza?*" he asked. I nodded wordlessly and he touched the flame to my moist cigarette. He smiled reassuringly. Flushing with shame, I slid from under the piano. Bob was already getting up and dusting his knees. Leigh was swallowing a last mouthful of hot coffee. Tckinigo and Cecil Brown emptied the croissant plate and munched hungrily. The bombs were falling blocks away now.

For the first time I noticed that the dumpy little woman down the room had fainted. The man with her was fanning her face with a menu and dabbing water upon her face with his handkerchief. Our Bosnian waiter was standing respectfully at the man's elbow, holding a glass of water.

"Do you smell something?" said Bob curiously. We sniffed. Then we coughed. The air in the restaurant was acrid with fumes, and as I looked toward the lobby door, a puff of gray smoke wafted inward. At that instant, we heard hysterical shouting from the lobby and a man's voice crying out in French.

"Get out!" he cried. "The hotel's been hit. The top floor is in flames!" We dashed for the lobby.

# GREEK TRAGEDY

## *by Leland Stowe*

THE paralyzing Nazi defeat of Yugoslavia was due to numerous factors, all of which are not yet clear. Nevertheless it is unquestionable that Belgrade's straddle-the-fence, appeasement-minded Cvetkovitch government was in great measure to blame; by refusing to co-ordinate secret plans for defense with the British and Greek high commands, by maintaining friendly relations with the Berlin-Rome dictatorships against the overwhelming opposition of the Yugoslav people's instincts and desires; by neglecting, especially, to build deep tank traps which would block every road of invasion from Bulgaria. Had these defenses been prepared adequately Nazi divisions, regardless of their terrific superiority in aviation support, would never have been able to break swiftly through into southern Yugoslavia and cut off the Yugoslav forces from the Greeks and British. In this respect the Nazis' blitzkrieg through Yugoslavia registered much swifter and more stunning progress than it had any right to make. Thus the true fighting caliber of Yugoslav troops never had a chance to show itself at anything like its full value.

Far sooner than they had a right to expect, Nazi motorized divisions were sweeping down to Salonika and engaging the Greek and British forces which were anchored on Mount Olympus. For reasons which defy all logic and remain unexplained, the main Greek army in Albania failed to withdraw swiftly into northern Greece. The towering six-thousand-foot pass, north of Metsovo and Jannina, was apparently left open to the Germans, even after they had broken through and captured Larissa. Even one Greek division on that pass could have held up the Germans for a very long time. Having driven from Kalabaka up over that single winding narrow road to the crest of the mountain range, I know what an impregnable line could have been formed there. At this writing it remains a mystery why Greek forces in strong numbers were not stationed there. Elsewhere, in central Greece and along the eastern coast, perhaps no more than a hundred thousand Greeks, Australians, New Zealanders, and British fought a remarkably tenacious and skillful withdrawing action for more than two weeks. Anzacs and Britishers held Thermopylae for days, fighting magnificently and only falling back when they were threatened with being cut off from the rear. Throughout the entire battle for Greece the Anglo-Greek allies were outnumbered at least three to one on the ground and fifty or seventy to one in the air. Below Thermopylae stood no natural barrier to keep the Germans out of Athens, yet the invaders had to spend days of severe fighting before at last they broke through to the capital. For the Nazis it was still a brilliantly successful campaign and a fabulous victory. Nevertheless the initial resistance of the Yugoslavs and the achievement of the British and Greek troops was vastly underestimated by most casual readers of newspaper headlines in America.

I talked with Premier-General Metaxas only three weeks before his sudden death. His face did not reveal the strain of leadership which those first desperately uncertain weeks of the Italian invasion had imposed. He was calm and perfectly at ease, but his eyes kindled with pride when he spoke of the Greek people. He had never doubted for a moment, he said, how the Greeks would respond or how they would fight. Then he said something which I shall never forget as long as I live.

"After all, for us—who are Greek Orthodox—death is only an episode."

For all those who love freedom or hope to preserve freedom in our time *death is only an episode*. I thought of the Norwegian regulars and volunteers who battled for two months against enormous Nazi odds. I thought of the magnificent Poles who held Warsaw for three weeks or more and who still fight, without a country, on land and on the sea and in the air. I thought of the British people in Coventry and in scores of cities and towns; of the RAF boys flying over those damnable Albanian mountains day after day. I thought of the little Greek soldiers in front of Tepeleni and up in the freezing snows of the Nemeroka range and of the Greeks with mud-slimed hands piling rocks into the ruts beside the pontoon bridge below Leskovik. I thought of all the great and noble people I have met and seen and known during these months of war—the only nobility and the sole aristocracy of the world in which we live. All of these humble people, unknown and unsung, had repudiated forever the damning, corroding, rotting philosophy of defeatism and "practicability." All were and are infinitely bigger than themselves. How could they do it? Where did they attain this spiritual grandeur? Why?

"Death is only an episode."

When I reached home, people came to hear me lecture and often people said: "Well, you certainly have had some wonderful experiences." Perhaps they were meaning to ask what it was that I, personally, had got out of covering the war. In any case, I have had ample time to ask myself that question and I know the answer. I knew it even as General Metaxas was speaking. I have had many things—comradeship, a certain amount of danger and hardship, adventure, high laughter and deep sorrow, despair and unexpected joy, disillusionment and a quietly deepened faith. I have had very many things which will be part of me for the rest of my days. But of them all nothing is richer and more heart-warmingly real than this: I have had the inestimable privilege of working and living and sometimes sharing a small portion of their dangers with people for whom freedom is the breath of life itself, and death—just an episode. I have been with little people who were very great. I have seen what makes man more than man, and woman more than woman. I have seen the tawdry, shameful abdication of frightened or greedy persons who would save their skins or their fortunes at all cost—at any cost. But I have seen, far more often and again and again, the sublime grandeur of a great legion of little people who would make no compromise with falsehoods, murder, slavery, and dishonor. I have seen men and women die and, dying, live forever.

\* \* \*

ATHENS, April 27, 1941 (Associated Press): The first detachment of German motorcyclists entered the center of Athens at 9:30 A.M. today....

\* \* \*

# CONQUEST OF CRETE

### by Frank Gervasi

GEOFF is an old reporter friend of mine. We covered Europe together for years and every few months we'd meet in Paris, Budapest, Rome or Berlin in the old days. I hadn't seen Geoff for nearly two years, not since one day in London just before the war when he told me he was joining up. He said he was sick of reporting. He said he hated diplomats and politicians. War was coming, he said, and they were doing nothing either to prepare for it or avoid it. Geoff said he wanted to fight. He was tired of talk and newsprint and of men of little faith and little knowledge.

When I arrived in Cairo the gang told me Geoff was in Greece. He'd joined the army as he said he'd do and he was an officer in the New Zealand forces. Geoff was an Anzac even before he was a Britisher. I remembered him as a slight, sharp-featured little man with burning blue eyes and an inexhaustible vitality, and I could see him fighting Germans with the same grim look on his face he wore that night he pounded a typewriter in the hotel in Munich. They evacuated Greece and Geoff didn't come to Cairo, and we all worried about Geoff. Greece, you'll remember, was just more of the same—one Englishman against five Germans, one British tank against fifteen German tanks, one Hurricane against twenty Messerschmitts. The British fought for nearly six weeks in Greece, bone and muscle against fire and steel, and then there was Navplion. The boys fought their way to the beach at Navplion as they'd fought free of France to embark at Dunkirk. In Cairo we wondered what next.

Yesterday I was sitting in the main salon in Shepheard's and thinking how like the movie conception of a harem the place looked, with its Byzantine columns and mosquelike high dome and the brightly striped silk coverings on the low couches with their mounds of pillows. It was cool in the salon. The doors and windows of the hotel had been shut to seal out the heat hurled from pavements and masonry by the relentless sun. I hoped vaguely that it would rain. I wished fervently that all the rich refugees who clutter Cairo and Cairo's better hotels would suddenly go away because they reminded me of Paris, Amsterdam and Athens. The light was uncertain, so I didn't recognize Geoff at first.

He'd grown square and sturdy with a face chiseled in bronze and his eyes held a level look of fierce contempt. Geoff's mouth cracked in a smile when he saw me, and that look left his eyes and he said, "Hello, guy." And I said "Hello, Geoff." And he dropped onto the couch. He said he'd just returned from Crete. His legs were sunburned where his khaki shorts ended and his long woolen socks began. His hands looked as though he'd been grubbing in nail kegs and tanning fluid and they had been cut and scratched a thousand times and were healing. Otherwise there wasn't a mark on him that you could see.

He said he was on the wagon. He said he was saving it up until later in the day. At six o'clock, he said, his leave would begin and he would be getting drunk, and would I join him? I said I would, and then I asked him how it had been in Crete. He just looked at me and said nothing and I was trying to think of something else to say when he said, "It was awful. It was just bloody awful."

They didn't mind the bombs. Except where bombs hit groups of men squarely, they didn't do much damage. A bomb that explodes fifty yards away is harmless if you're in a slit trench. It was the strafing that was bad. The Germans have developed the technique of strafing into a fine, cruel art. They strafe and scatter small fragmentation bombs that spread over a wide area and there is nothing you can do about it but stand there and keep firing your Bren gun at the Messerschmitts, and there's small percentage in that because as you fire you give away where you are and if the bombs don't get you, then the next Heinie will. "They hosed us with bullets," Geoff said.

The men lay in zigzag trenches. They'd lie for three or four hours at a time trying to shield themselves from the bullets. The German planes held the British in their trenches with the strafing while near by they dropped paratroops by the hundred. One day they dropped 5,000 in a few hours, the Germans falling out of the big Junkers planes thirty at a time, three planes at a time, three planes every seventy seconds.

"After a while," Geoff said, "you get used to strafing. You're not afraid. You just lie there, your guts tied up inside you into one cold, painful lump. I remember finding an old newspaper lying in the dirt in the bottom of my trench. I pulled it out and started reading an article on agriculture. I read it all through and got drowsy and looked at the chap next to me and he was sound asleep and the Jerries were blasting us with bullets. Funny, isn't it?"

But the boys couldn't sleep long. Once the strafing ceased the enemy would come, Tommy guns blazing, mortars throwing five- and six-inch shells or mortar bombs from 5,000 yards. Some mortars! After a heavy strafing and mortar bombing the boys would lift themselves up out of the trenches to face the enemy. They'd stumble out, bayonets agleam, and go for them.

"I can't figure it out," Geoff said. "I always thought the German was pretty brave. But he isn't, Frank. He's no better than the Italian. The Jerry isn't for steel. They'd turn and run and squeal like frightened pigs. Either he isn't for steel or he had orders not to mix with us. When the German mixed with us we gave him hell. The enemy's losses must have been terrific. We butchered them, Frank. Still I think the German had orders not to mix it because when he did he lost the support of the mortars and it made it harder for the Messerschmitts to strafe and dive-bomb."

Bit by bit he put together for me the pieces of the Cretan puzzle. And when he'd finished he'd proved again what had already been proved. Courage alone can't win battles and so far in their ventures in Norway, France and Greece courage has been the Briton's principal weapon. What Geoff had to say proved once again what every correspondent who has covered this war and the war in Spain already knew. It is that planes and tanks and rapid-fire arms will win every time over high faith and morale and rifles. More specifically, the battle of Crete showed the futility of any major military operation undertaken without superiority in the air and co-ordinated with at least equality in numbers of tanks and artillery and men in the field below. And Crete proved too that with aerial and armored equipment there must also be perfect ground organization insuring supplies of food, ammunition, water, fuel, medical attention and replacements of every description.

But there's a long distance sometimes between things as generals would like to have them and conditions as they are. When you jolly well haven't got air superiority or tank superiority you've got to fight anyhow. Geoff

302

reminded me of that and the son of a certain important British politician reminded me of that too while we had a drink on the terrace at Shepheard's. "We've just bloody well got to fight," he said, "and hold the enemy, no matter what the odds. And we're fighting for you Americans, old boy, fighting so that you'll have time to get ready."

APRIL 5, 1941: *Russia signed pact with Yugoslavia.*

APRIL 13: *Russia signed non-aggression pact with Japan.*

# RUSSIA AND JAPAN

## by John Scott

STALIN hastened to draw up and sign a pact with the Jugoslavs, knowing that it would stiffen Serb resistance, while, if concluded before German-Jugoslav hostilities actually broke out, it would not involve the Russians too seriously.

Gabrilovich and Molotov affixed their signatures just in time, however, as within a few hours of the signature of the pact, on the evening of April fifth, Belgrade was bombed and Jugoslavia invaded at a number of points.

The Moscow papers on April sixth featured the text of the pact and a large photograph of Stalin smiling on as Molotov and Gabrilovich signed. These newspapers did not, however, inform the Soviet public of the German attack on Jugoslavia until the next day.

On April thirteenth all Moscow papers published the text of a note delivered by Vice-Commissar of Foreign Affairs Vyshinsky to the Hungarian Minister in Moscow. The note reminded the Hungarians that only four months previously they had concluded a treaty of eternal friendship with Jugoslavia; it further pointed out to the gentlemen of Budapest that Hungary itself had a large national-minority population and pertinently asked the question:

"How would you feel if someone attempted to 'liberate' them from your domination?"

This was a menacing question, as one of the largest national minorities in Hungary was the "Carpatho-Ukrainians," a Slavic people with openly-expressed pro-Russian sentiments, inhabiting the Carpathian Mountains in what was until 1939 eastern Czechoslovakia.

While this extremely blunt statement of Russian sympathies was being delivered, Stalin was in earnest conversation with the Japanese Foreign Minister, Matsuoko, about the possibility of the conclusion of a non-aggression or neutrality pact.

On the night of April twelfth, my Japanese colleagues had been glum and pessimistic. No pact would be signed, they said. Matsuoko was leaving the next day for his ten-day Trans-Siberian trip homeward.

However, at eleven A.M. on the next day Stalin called Matsuoko to the Kremlin. At two P.M. on April thirteenth, after a three-hour conversation, a five-year neutrality pact was signed by Matsuoko and Molotov. It provided that both signatories maintain neutrality in case either became the object of military action by a third power. The first political agreement to be concluded between the two countries since the Russian Revolution, it strengthened Japan's hand in the Far East as well as improving considerably Russia's position *vis-à-vis* Germany.

The obvious explanation was that Stalin wanted his eastern frontier secure in case of a German attack from the west, which he felt was possible, if not imminent.

The departure of Matsuoko from Moscow involved one of the most astonishing performances I saw during eight years in Russia. Both Russians and Japanese were delighted with their pact and went out to celebrate after signing it.

The train was to leave the Yaroslavsky Station at four-fifty-five. We journalists arrived at four-thirty, and found the station roped off and patrolled by squads of uniformed and plain-clothes policemen, as is customary in Moscow when important personages appear in public places. Half an hour passed and no one appeared on the platform except the diplomatic representatives of the lesser Axis powers, the German military and naval attachés in full dress uniform, and the chief of the Protocol Department of the Soviet Foreign Office. We still had not sent full stories on the pact itself, and were anxious to get back to the Press Department and have our cables censored and sent. We called the residence of the Japanese Ambassador and were told that Matsuoko was engaged and would arrive at the station shortly.

Soviet railroad officials walked up and down the platform looking at their watches. Soviet trains sometimes arrived late, but serious attempts were being made to have them at least depart on time. At about five-fifteen a high railroad official appeared and stated that the departure of the train had been postponed until five-fifty-five. It was the regular Trans-Siberian express, but the last four cars were reserved for Matsuoko and his suite. The passengers in the rest of the train had long ago taken their places, and were looking out of the windows to see what the trouble was, while police looked on vigilantly. We pushed through the police lines and the crowd of open-mouthed Moscovites and had vodkas at the station bar.

At five-fifty the limousines began to arrive, first the German Ambassador, Count von der Schulenberg, then Italian Ambassador Rosso, then numerous Japanese with important-looking briefcases. The number of plain-clothes men on the platform increased with each diplomatic arrival; there were about fifty diplomats and at least twice as many "Y.M.C.A. men," as the plain-clothes men were called by flippant foreigners. Matsuoko arrived at five-fifty-five, and walked down the platform flanked by Solomon Lozovsky, Vice-Commissar of Foreign Affairs.

They shook hands in a rather dazed fashion with Schulenberg and Rosso. I had met Matsuoko and everyone else there before. So after exchanging a few words with the Japanese correspondents, who were noticeably tight and smiling from ear to ear, I turned to go. I went about five steps and nearly bumped into Stalin, who was cruising down the platform under his own steam, dressed in his long military coat, leather boots with overshoes over them, and his brown visored cap. Molotov was just behind him.

We did not often have opportunities to see Stalin close up. He was very retiring and extremely well guarded. Furthermore, he had never seen any foreign dignitary off at a railroad station. Two years before when Ribbentrop came to Moscow he was met by a vice-commissar. I therefore got out my Leica, and stayed to see what would happen.

The Japanese came to life with a bang when Stalin and Molotov made their unexpected appearance. The Soviet leaders were surrounded by Japanese diplomats and attachés who began shaking their hands, slapping their backs, and talking in several languages, and in very raucous voices. Then we realized why they had appeared dazed. They were all very definitely in their cups, as were some of the Russians. While the foreign diplomats and newspapermen gathered around craning their necks, Stalin and Molotov began embracing the Japanese, patting them on the shoulders and exchanging expressions of intimate friendship.

As few of the Japanese or Russians could speak each other's language, the remark most frequently heard was "ah ... ha" very loud, with the accent on the "ha," punctuated by a slap on the back or a playful punch in the ribs. Stalin went up to the aged and diminutive Japanese Ambassador General, punched him rather hard on the shoulder with an "ah ... ha," so that the four-foot-ten, bald-pated general staggered back three or four steps, which caused Matsuoko to laugh in glee.

I was wedged in between half a dozen towering German military men dressed up like Christmas trees, trying my best to get some pictures without being too conspicuous. Everyone pushed and shoved trying to see what was going on. Stalin's plain-clothes guards looked very worried because they could not keep their eye on Russia's bull-necked and gray-haired leader. The Japanese Military Attaché staggered up to the dapper and fastidious Barkov, Soviet Chief of Protocol, and began slapping him on the back. Just then Stalin detached himself from the crowd of Japanese and came over toward me.

Stalin is a smallish man, five feet five or six in height, and has a very distinctive bearlike walk. He swings his arms very low and puts his right arm forward at the same time as his right foot, instead of vice versa like most people. The "vozhd" was sixty-one and looked his age. He swung up to Colonel Krebs, assistant to the German Military Attaché, who was standing right in front of me, tapped him on the chest, and looked up into his face searchingly for a few seconds. "German?" he said, not sure of the uniform. The six-foot German stood at attention and mumbled out an embarrassed affirmative in bad Russian. "Ah ... ha," said Stalin, slapping him on the back and shaking his hand. "Budyem s vami druzyami." ("We will be friends with you.") The colonel said nothing and Stalin laughed and shook for a dozen seconds.

This incident impressed me tremendously. He made this declaration of friendship for a German soldier he did not know with sincerity. Stalin wanted very much to be friends with Germany. But he feared hostilities would develop nevertheless. The Soviet-Japanese Pact just signed strengthened Russia's hand considerably in her game with Germany.

The crowd surged along the platform. Everyone craned his neck trying to hear what Stalin was saying. Molotov exchanged an "ah...ha" with Tatekawa. For about the third time Stalin shook Matsuoko's hand, and they embraced.

Finally Stalin and Matsuoko got into the special car which was to take the Japanese Foreign Minister across Siberia. Inside the car Stalin said to Matsuoko, "You are an Asiatic. I am an Asiatic. Out there" and he waved his hand toward the platform where the diplomats were standing "are all those Europeans." Again raucous laughter from both Asiatics.

Finally, after Stalin and Molotov had spent nearly twenty minutes on the platform, the train whistled and pulled out, an hour and twenty-five minutes late. Stalin ambled down the platform, and climbed into his huge armor-plated Packard with its three-inch-thick machine-gun bullet-proof windows, and his squad of guards, and drove off.

We went back to the Press Department and spent the evening trying to get the story through the censorship. We did not succeed. Stalin and Molotov had come to the station, and the atmosphere had been friendly, that was all we could say.

The Embassies, however, did send out full reports. The whole performance was staged to impress the Germans, in my opinion. And the egocentric and dull-witted Matsuoko thought it was a genuine expression of Soviet friendship to Japan, coupled with the hit he personally had made with the Soviet leaders.

JUNE 22, 1941: *German armies attacked Russia on 2500-mile front from the Baltic to the Black Sea.*

# RUSSIA INVADED

## *by Margaret Bourke-White*

THE next day was the twenty-second of June, and it brought an event of such magnitude that the whole course of our work was changed.

It was Sunday, and there was a peculiar tension in the atmosphere. Crowds of peasants gathered in knots around the loudspeaker in the public square. An important announcement from the government was expected, no one knew just when. (All over the Soviet Union, dance music, news, and government proclamations come over the government-controlled radio through a loudspeaker which blares out constantly in the center of each small town.)

We drove from one village to another, through the tropical vegetation that bordered the Black Sea, and in each public square stood knots of people, restlessly grouped about the loudspeakers, waiting uneasily for they knew not what.

We went back to our hotel and had tea, and at four o'clock Petrov went out to the square again to see if the news had come through. When he came back, Elisaveta ran down to meet him. For a long time we could see them from our balcony, walking back and forth in the garden below.

"I think the war has caught up with us," remarked Erskine.

"If it really has, I wish they'd come up and tell us something," I said.

"It's their war," said Erskine. "Let them talk it over first."

When they came into our room they were smiling, not with joy but with relief.

Molotov had spoken from the Kremlin. Before daybreak, German planes had flown over the Soviet border and dropped bombs on Kharkov, Kiev, and other Soviet cities. Troops were being rushed to the border, and the indications were that the most intense warfare in history had begun.

We drove from one collective farm to another that afternoon, and everywhere there were scenes of the most enthusiastic patriotism. Collective farmers were pledging their support, their work, their lives, to victory of their country. But everywhere there was one question on everyone's lips: where did Great Britain stand?

How could they, as Soviet citizens, guess what would be the policy of capitalistic nations? Could all this be a frame-up between England and Germany? Financial interests are powerful, the collective farmers kept reminding one another, and might swing the tide against the will of the people. The Russian people admired the brave citizens of England, who had showed so much courage during the bombings, and if they were to be together in the struggle it could mean much.

It was almost dusk when we reached a large citrus-fruit collective farm on a hill overlooking the Black Sea. The collective farmers had gathered in a clearing in an orange grove, where a loudspeaker had been mounted. Just as we arrived, the amplifier blared out a second announcement from the government: Churchill had made a speech, and the translation was being read from the Kremlin. Churchill had stated that Great Britain would stand with the Soviet Union to meet their common enemy.

I saw tears of joy stream down the cheeks of those farmers. "With Great Britain and the Soviet Union together against the invader," they began to shout, "the bloody Fascists will be crushed."

We packed our bags and drove from Sukhumi to Sochi, where we hoped to get a train back to Moscow. We were fortunate that the head of the district Party Committee had been able to lend us a car. All along the way, whenever we paused for petrol or water, dozens of people pressed up to us, wishing to engage our car if we could spare it. They were all trying to find transportation from their vacation spots so they could get back to enlist.

In the jewel-like resort of Sochi, steeply banked above the sea, the rest homes were emptying rapidly. Its principal street, twisting through flowering groves and over cliffs, was lined with resthouses: the sanatoria of the Arctic workers, of the Donbas coal miners, of the *Pravda* newspaper staff; the Red Army House, and the rest home for locomotive workers. This last, where we stayed, was a Pompeian, pillared structure, run according to the plan we had found in Mineralnye Vody—giving reduced rates or free vacations to *otlichniki,* the most efficient workers. But the *otlichnik* locomotive workers were leaving as fast as they could get room on the trains.

The Red Army House had been emptied before we arrived. It is a colossal glass and concrete structure, startlingly modern, and with a private funicular to shuttle vacationing soldiers down the dizzy grade to the beach. Now its pair of little cars stood idle on their sloping tracks.

Reaching the station, we found a crowd that pressed about it for blocks. Petrov forced his way into the throng, and the fact that he was able to return with tickets was evidence of the influential place which writers are accorded in the Soviet Union.

Our two-day train trip back to Moscow was an hour-by-hour struggle to get news. During each stop, we tried to listen to the station radio, but troop trains roaring in the opposite direction drowned out the loudspeakers. In the larger stations, Petrov would be out on the platform before the train stopped, trying to get a newspaper. But the papers vanished, the instant they appeared, into hundreds of outstretched hands.

# LUFTWAFFE OVER MOSCOW

## *by Erskine Caldwell*

THE bombing of Moscow began exactly one month after war started. The four million citizens of the city had been prepared for its coming by a series of practice air-raid alarms, and half an hour before the first explosive, a one-thousand-pounder, dropped in front of the Kremlin gates, practically everyone in the city was sitting in a shelter.

Everyone who was not in some way connected with air-raid defense was compelled to go to a shelter. The penalty for violating the order was fine and imprisonment. Few attempted to evade the law, thousands stood in line on the streets nightly waiting for shelters to open.

I went down into one of the subway shelters that first night and, along with several thousand others, was herded along the tracks deep into the tubes. Militiamen paced up and down along the catwalks ordering the people to sit down. No one was allowed to stand up or to move to another position once he had sat down. After an hour I decided to go up to see what was happening. I walked up the tracks to the station platform. A militiaman ordered me back. I protested, and said that I wanted to leave. He was as firm as a Soviet militiaman can be until I took out my night pass and showed it to him, saying something about being an American and having duties to perform even during air raids. The night pass was of no value during raids, a special raid pass being necessary for such times, but by talking fast and waving the night pass as though it were something that could not be ignored, I succeeded in getting past him. The next day I secured a raid pass, and I was never held in a shelter as long as I remained in Moscow.

The Germans dropped everything they could unload from two hundred planes that night, coming over the city in waves at half-hour intervals for five and a half hours. Thousands of fire bombs about the size and shape of prizewinning cucumbers were showered on buildings and streets. Weeks of training in fire-fighting had its results when city fire-fighting brigades and citizens posted on every roof of the city prevented Moscow from burning to the ground. As fast as the incendiaries fell they were snuffed out with sand or by dunking them into barrels of water which had been placed on top floors and rooftops. Occasionally a fire would get started, and its fiery red glow would flare up for a short time and then die down as it was brought under control.

During all this time explosive bombs were whistling downward, blasting into buildings and tearing craters in streets. The raid was directed at the entire city, the Kremlin not excepted, and for miles in all directions the sound of exploding bombs rocked and jarred the night. The hailstorm of fire bombs came down without letup for three hours, and the only times bombs were not falling were when the raiders, their racks empty, streaked back towards the west. There was only a short interval of time before a new wave of fully loaded planes came in from the northwest to dump their loads.

The air defense was in action continuously for those five and a half hours. Searchlights by the hundreds stabbed their beams into the sky, most of them being concentrated in a ring around the city. Anti-aircraft guns cracked and boomed all night long from another circle, filling the night with dazzling star-bursts. This city defense formed a complete circle around Moscow. The ring was about three miles deep, with alternating sections of searchlights and anti-aircraft artillery. The defense was concentrated five miles from the center of the city, and had a circumference of about fifty miles.

Inside the ring, which meant the greater portion of Moscow, machineguns and lighter artillery were mounted on rooftops. These shot a continuous stream of fire at the low-flying Luftwaffe during its first raid. Tracer bullets that left streaks of red, yellow, or green in their wake crisscrossed the sky. A rapid-firing cannon that shot five shells in five seconds was used for close-range action. These big cannon rattled windows and made an ear-splitting noise that sounded as if the world were being blown to smithereens. The most dazzling sight of all was the shower of flaming onions, tracer shells that were fired from artillery. These flaming onions went up in strings of six, each one being a different color. The object of using this type of ground-fire was to enable gunners to trace the course of the large caliber shell aimed at the low-flying craft. It had twice the range of machine-gun tracer fire. In addition, the shells burst upon contact, whereas machine-gun bullets could merely penetrate.

For the first and only time, the Luftwaffe flew low over Moscow. The planes, when caught in searchlight beams, were usually at heights of about 1,000 feet, although I saw one plane, which looked like a huge silver moth, at five hundred feet. At the peak of the raid I saw a plane, caught in the web of five searchlight beams, suddenly nose-up and apparently come to a dead stop in the air. It had been hit by fire from one of the quick-shooting rooftop cannon. There was an explosion, the plane shook like a leaf in a storm, and a moment later it nosed down and plummeted to earth like a dead duck. Halfway down it burst into flame. A moment later a parachute fluttered open and drifted slowly downward with a figure of a man dangling like a puppet from its harness. Just after the first parachute, a second one streaked downward, unopened. It fell like a stone in the street.

After the first two hours, the Germans apparently changed their tactics. Later waves of planes began dropping flares over the city, long strings of brilliant glows that lighted up the streets until newspaper print could be read on the bulletin boards on the sides of buildings. As the flares drifted slowly downward like feathers in still air, demolition bombs rained on the city. Not far from where I stood an oil bomb plowed into an apartment house, its liquid spraying the entire block. A yellowish glow sprang up instantly, and while the smoke and flame shot upward a cloud of debris peppered buildings several hundred feet away. The Germans overhead concentrated on the glow, releasing tons of explosives at the target they had made.

In the midst of all this there were no human sounds, except for the clatter of feet on tin roofs as fire brigades scampered over the buildings to get at incendiary fires. There were killed and wounded, but there was no sound of their voices. There were no shouts and yells, no excited cries. The people who were at work went about their duties with silent determination. Down in the streets only the militia and civilian fire defense workers were about. Red Army soldiers sat in shelters alongside civilians. The people in the shelters could hear the thuds and earth-rumbling explosions of five-hundred-, thousand-, and two-thousand-pound bombs, but they knew nothing of the fiery display above that turned Moscow's night as light as day.

Several times there were intervals of absolute calm when not a single sound could be heard anywhere. Once during one of these moments, the chimes on the Kremlin clock struck a quarter-hour. It sounded as if it were coming from another world.

But there were few such momentary lulls. The crashing of demolition bombs into buildings, the whine of machine-gun bullets, and the deafening bang-bang of rapid-fire cannon on the rooftops went on and on hour after hour. More parachute flares were dropped, most of them in the vicinity of the Kremlin, which evidently was one of the major targets of the Luftwaffe. Once in a while a plane dived down to within a few hundred feet of the rooftops as though seeking an objective. But they climbed back or ducked into clouds as soon as possible when ground-fire began ripping into them.

# SCORCHED EARTH

## by Alice-Leone Moats

STALIN made a speech at six o'clock on the morning of July third. It was his first talk to the Russian people since 1938. No announcement was made beforehand that he would be speaking; the population was merely advised to expect an important broadcast on that day, and loud-speakers must be left on to await it.

It was the famous "scorched earth" speech. The front pages of the newspapers carried the text in full, with a photograph of Stalin. For weeks afterwards reprints could be seen stuck on all the walls of the city.

The next day, opening his press conference Lozovsky said that the American government's declaration of its attitude toward the U.S.S.R. had caused great satisfaction in the Soviet Union; that the Soviet Union's policy toward Japan remained the same as it had been when Matsuoka signed the neutrality pact in Moscow; that he couldn't comment upon the Japanese government's declaration of neutrality and vigilance until he had time to study the text; that no problems serious enough to bring on war had existed between the U.S.S.R. and Hungary; the reasons for hostilities had been provided by German and Italian planes, represented as Russian, dropping bombs on Hungary. He devoted the major part of the conference to refuting claims that the Soviet government had fled to the Urals, that Moscow had been destroyed, and that the Red army was in full retreat.

Referring to German announcements of the taking of Riga and Minsk, he said that in such a great war the loss of this or that city was unimportant. If it was found necessary to give up a city, it would be done. Although as yet the seizure of Minsk and Riga was just a Nazi dream, he saw nothing impossible in the abandonment of those cities. He repeated, as he was to do very often, "In a country the size of the Soviet Union, cities are merely geographical points and their loss is not as serious as it sounds. It is the army that counts, and it must be kept intact at all costs."

"Napoleon once said," he observed, " 'One cannot sit on bayonets.' That is precisely what the Germans are trying to do. The capture of each town weakens rather than strengthens them."

He went on: "If necessary, we can mobilize another ten million men without any ill effect on our man power or production. That is why we remain so calm in the face of adversity. Hitler says that he wants to break up the British Empire, and he seems to think that the shortest way to

London is by way of Moscow. According to the English song, 'It's a Long Way to Tipperary.' Gospodin Gitler will find that it's an even longer one to Moscow. The war has only begun. Unfortunately it will bring tremendous suffering, but people who want to keep their liberty must be willing to defend it. The Nazis can win a hundred battles, but we can guarantee that they will never win the war."

That evening I heard the first rumor that the United States would soon send an economic mission to Moscow. There were many who wondered if it would arrive in time. There were reports that some high-placed members of certain commissariats had already left town. The street in front of the Foreign Office was black with charred paper which had drifted down from the chimneys of the Foreign Office and the Lubianka across the way. That aroused conjectures as to whether the Narkomindel and the G.P.U. were burning records preparatory to moving their offices elsewhere. Some commissariats, I learned on good authority, had already been moved out of Moscow. However, not as forerunners of a mass evacuation. They had merely been sent away from the capital in an effort to decentralize a very overcentralized government. Some of the factories were already being transferred to safer localities.

The American Ambassador told a correspondent that day that, in view of all these signs, he foresaw that Moscow would soon be evacuated. He was making all the necessary preparations to move the embassay to Sverdlovsk at a moment's notice. Convinced that the authorities wouldn't give him much time in which to get ready, he had placed his packed suitcases in rows; the first to be grabbed up if there were only fifteen minutes, the first and second if there were half an hour, and so on.

One afternoon he took Walter Thurston with him in the car and drove for miles along the roads leading out of Moscow, trying to figure which would be the best one to follow if he were caught in Spaso, which would be the best if he were at the dacha. His car aroused suspicions in a village, and it was only through the intercession of the G.P.U. escort that he wasn't arrested. He had also ordered the rowboat at the dacha repaired, with the idea of using it if the roads were impassable. His plan was that he and Walter Thurston should row down the Kliasma to the Volga.

The embassy doctor told us that he had spent several days selecting the provisions that were to be carried along in case of a hurried evacuation. "I have worked out a balanced diet," he announced. On questioning him we found that the "balanced diet" consisted almost exclusively of baked beans. A few days later he returned to America, and when we finally did evacuate Moscow the food packed by the embassy staff provided more variety.

At about one o'clock in the morning there was an air-raid alarm. I legged it over to Spaso and, not knowing how to find the cellar entrance, rang the front doorbell. Charlie Thayer soon appeared, looking very sleepy, and directed me to the back of the house.

I found the cook, a maid, and the night watchman sitting on a bench in the back yard and joined them. There was no sound of airplanes, so we remained there until the all clear. The cook, a large lady wearing not only a coat and gloves but also a hat with a draped taffeta crown, kept me entertained with accounts of her former splendor. She said she had once been the leading hostess of Moscow and the owner of the house that later became the German Embassy.

JULY 13, 1941: *Great Britain and Soviet Russia signed mutual aid pact.*

JULY 15: *Germans reached Stalin line.*

\* \* \*

LONDON, August 16 (United Press): The Soviet High Command admitted Thursday that Smolensk had been taken by the Germans....

BERLIN, September 19 (Associated Press): The Germans' Ukrainian offensive... occupied Kiev... the German High Command announced... today. ... Kiev... fell during the morning....

\* \* \*

# HITLER'S "VICTORY"

## *by Howard K. Smith*

ON October 8, the Fuehrer issued a High Command communiqué, the first news, telling of progress. And on the morning of October 9, after poring over his maps and pronouncing what he saw on them good, he called in his lipless little press chief, Dr. Otto Dietrich, from an adjoining hut in the headquarters. Removing his horn-rimmed glasses which he wears in private but sedulously guards from the range of court photographers, the Fuehrer became expansive before the Doctor, bidding him to go to town and reveal all. The period of "strategic silence" had ended. Dietrich caught the bright, "historical" mood of his Leader and returned to his hut to order an underling to contact Dr. Goebbels in Berlin on the telephone, and instruct him to gather the world press; there was history to be made. Then Dr. Dietrich put on his gray great-coat, kicked the first light eastern snow off his polished boots, and enplaned for Berlin, important as the good horse Roland who carried the joyous news from Ghent to Aix.

When the telephone rang, I was lying in bed with a miserable cold and a skull-splitting headache. It was the secretary of Dr. Froelich, the Propaganda Ministry's liaison officer for the American press and radio. She was excited, and told me I should come to an important special press conference at noon sharp; something of extremely great importance. No, she did not know what it was about, but be there on time, for at five minutes after twelve the doors would be barred and guarded.

I had no broadcast that afternoon. And besides, after two years packed with repetitions of Nazi full-dress shows, I was inured to "history" and indifferent, anyway, to the further progress of a world which had never discovered an effective remedy for the common head-cold. So I turned over and tried to go to sleep. The telephone rang again. It was Guido Enderis, the chief of the *New York Times'* Berlin office, for whom I had been writing on occasion. His man, Brooks Peters, had gone home to escape the Berlin blues, so, would I cover the special conference for the *Times*? He had been assured of its historic import. Reluctantly, I yielded.

I put on my clothes, stuffed two handkerchiefs in my pocket, and took the underground to the Wilhelmstrasse. The red-plush Theater Hall of the Propaganda Ministry was filled with reporters from everywhere, guessing in a dozen different languages what it was all about. My head throbbed. Before the audience was a long conference table, and around the table in little clots stood a bevy of gorgeous uniforms—green, brown, gray and two shades of blue, well stuffed with Prussian officers, party officials and just bureaucrats of the Ministry, beaming with joy at an opportunity to appear before their daily *Publikum* in costumes which lent glamour to waistlines and limbs made for mufti.

As on all Nazi "historic" occasions—except those in which Hitler is the leading man, for he can afford to risk non-conformity—the central show-piece was impressively and precisely late. At 12.30 on the dot, a few officers rushed through the door into the room, indicating the coming of the Leader's emissary. The clots dissolved into one fine phalanx and in walked little Dr. Dietrich, flapping his right palm back over his shoulder in imitation of his Fuehrer's salute and grinning as if fair to bursting with the tidings he bore. There was profuse handshaking, sandwiched each time between stiff-armed salutes. Cameras snapped and flashlight bulbs flashed. On the great stage behind the central figure, Dietrich, the red velvet curtains were drawn apart to reveal a monstrous map of European Russia thrice as high as the speaker. The effect was impressive.

Dietrich was introduced briefly and oilily by Dr. Brauweiler, a musty old Nazi party wheel-horse who had been appointed leader of the foreign press section of the Ministry after the arrest of Boehmer, and given a natty blue uniform for having kept his mouth and head shut for eight years. Then the little doctor rose and held forth. I regret I cannot quote him directly. But it is a strange, strange feature of this grand occasion that the text of what Dietrich said has never been published. Unlike most other important utterances of Nazi leaders, his words were never rebroadcast to the German people—a feature which caused inquisitive whispering in German and foreign circles alike. It is just possible that somewhere among the roses of enthusiasm which blossomed out in uniform that happy day, there was a little, inconspicuous thorn of prudence, some little bureaucrat, who cast the vaguest shadow of a doubt over the mind of Dr. Goebbels, the producer of the show, with dampening references to the uncertain space between the cup and the lip, and with that hateful phrase which is anathema to the best laid plans of mice and men: "But, suppose it doesn't turn out that way?" If there was such a bureaucrat, you may be sure that, however much he may have been considered an unwelcome cold douche on that merry day, he has since been promoted and given a new uniform for his counsel.

For Dietrich said bold words and cast moderating and conditional phrases to the four winds. In the vernacular of the diplomatic correspondent, Dietrich put himself away, away out on a mighty high limb. With an air of finality, Dietrich announced the very *last remnants* of the Red Army were locked in two steel German pockets before Moscow and were undergoing swift, merciless annihilation. This was sensational. To understand how big the story was one must remember the circumstances. This was the first substantial news about the mighty, new offensive. It came directly from Adolf Hitler himself, and could not be doubted. Dietrich continued: behind the two pockets there stood between the German armies and Moscow just so much space and nothing more. As one correspondent later put it, Dietrich indicated that between Germany and the complete conquest of the untold riches of Russia there remained only "the time it takes man and machine to cover the given distance." After seven short days, the Fuehrer's offensive had smashed the Red Army to splinters, the decision was reached and the eastern continent lay, like a limp virgin, in the mighty arms of the lustful, hungry German Mars. ". . . And on that, Gentlemen, I stake my whole journalistic reputation!" Dietrich shouted, swinging his fist high in the air in a dramatic gesture.

Now nobody will contest the contention that the Nazis tell lies, and great big ones. But it is true that Hitler himself has never told a lie about a specific military fact which can be checked. There are two good reasons for this. First, he does not have to lie about them; you don't have to tell a fib when you're winning. Second, a specific military fact can be so easily checked, and if it were found out that the "Almighty" had told a blunt untruth, especially about something so big as this particular event, it would be disastrous to his position. So we of the fourth estate had no choice but to believe these dramatic assertions were gospel truth. Behind his unrecorded words there arose, in the minds of his listeners, inevitable images. Russia, with her rich resources in Hitler's hands: an increment of almost 200,000,000 units of slave labor to make implements of war, bringing the total of manpower at Germany's disposal to a figure greater than that of England, and North and South America combined. Hitler's armies, ten million men, flushed with victory, eager for more of the easy, national sport, were in the main free to return west and flood England, at long last, with blood and Nazis. The American news agency men, in the first row, were sitting on the edges of their seats, tensely eyeing the door behind which were telephones, leading to more telephones to America and the world. My headache receded in my consciousness and in its place settled the more painful conviction—common to all there—that the eastern war was over; and, perhaps, the decision in the entire conflict already lay in Hitler's hands.

315

When Dietrich finished tense excitement prevailed. The uniforms gathered round him and pumped his hand as a sort of mutual congratulation on the German victory. The agency men had burst through the doorway and were giving short, hot bulletins over the phones to their offices. Axis and Balkan correspondents applauded and cheered, then stood and raised their arms in salute to Dietrich, who sped out of the room to return to the Fuehrer's headquarters and be on hand for the last terrible blows, the *coups de grâce,* the Grand Finale.

I walked down the marble stairs from the Theater Hall and talked briefly to Oechsner, who had just returned from his breather in America, and Lochner. The mood was grim all around. I went alone, then, up the Wilhelmstrasse to the Adlon bar for alcoholic reinforcement against my cold. The bar radio announced a special communiqué could be expected from the Fuehrer's headquarters in a few minutes; when it came the barman turned up the volume and the specifically military report Dietrich had made in his speech, minus the trimmings and predictions, was announced. I scanned my notes and began writing a tentative lead on the back of an envelope; but it was one of those insidious stories whose implications grow on you as you think more about it. I left the hotel, took a taxi to the *Times* office to get that accessory which is indispensable to clear thinking on my part, a typewriter; although my deadline was still hours away.

My insidious "growing" reaction was apparently universal. Several American bureau chiefs had been invited the day before to leave on October 10 on a trip to the eastern front—the juiciest journalistic plum the German High Command could offer. But so strong was the conviction among us that the end was perhaps a matter of only hours away that Louis Lochner, of the Associated Press, telephoned the Propaganda Ministry, after studying his notes, and informed the proper official that he had decided to relinquish his place on the trip and remain in Berlin. It was too hazardous leaving his base of communications at a moment like this. Then Pierre Huss, of I.N.S., phoned and delivered, with regret, the same message. Oechsner, of U.P., wavered but ultimately decided to take a chance on going to the East. That afternoon powerful pieces, "situationers" reeking with historic implications, went over the wires from Berlin.

But what escaped almost every correspondent was the reaction of the German people themselves. At this time, in the atmosphere of triumph, that feature was, after all, secondary to considerations such as the new strategic and economic advantages the total conquest of Russia offered Hitler. But when that atmosphere dissolved, when the true consequences became clear, the main, and, for Hitler, disastrous feature was: the People.

The little thorn of prudence kept the full strength of Dietrich's predictions from them. The papers published no direct quotations. But they did publish condensed, expurgated, indirect summaries of the "epochal" conference which were strong enough to make German hearts beat faster. Headlines shouted: "The Veil over the New Offensive is lifted!"; "Dietrich:

316

'Campaign in East Decided!' " The *Voelkischer Beobachter* headline read: "The Great Hour has Struck! Army groups of Timoshenko, Voroshilov encircled—Budenny Army-group in dissolution." Quoting the Fuehrer's order of the day to the army at the beginning of the offensive, to "strike the last mighty blow, which will crush this enemy before the beginning of winter," and to complete "the last great battle of decision of this year," the official Nazi newspaper commented in bold language, only a few degrees less perilously committal than Dietrich's own words: "That order has already essentially been carried out. In the sense of the Fuehrer's order, the strategic decision has already been gained. If ever the concept 'Blitzkrieg' was realized, it is here!—Seven short days have sufficed to deal a deathblow to the largest war machine in the world, a blow from which Russia can never, never recover."

The response was electric. There was visible alleviation in faces that for weeks had been dismally drawn. In Baarz' beer-restaurant behind Unter den Linden, people stood and saluted when the radio, after repeating the High Command communiqué, played *Horst Wessel* and *Deutschland ueber Alles*. Rumors, which are the dangerous daily diet of people in any totalitarian country where news is twisted or kept from them, spread over Berlin like wildfire. In Baarz', a waiter whispered to me, had I heard, Stalin had requested an armistice. At home, the janitor in my apartment house stopped me in the hall to tell me he had it from reliable sources who had good friends high up in the party that Moscow had fallen this noon. The civil population were hanging wreaths of roses on German tanks in joy at being liberated. It would be announced in a special communiqué tonight or tomorrow. In the days that followed, bookshops got in new sets of Russian grammars and simple readers for beginners in the tongue, and displayed shop windows full of them; the eagerness to get a job in the rich, new colony was everywhere. The economic minister of the Reich, Dr. Walter Funk, sat himself down and wrote a fine speech about Germany's colonial mission in Russia, entitled "The contribution of the East to the New Europe," and next day the papers published it under the heading: "Europe's Economic Future Secured."

The horrible slaughter of Germany's best sons was nearing an end. The boys were being taken out of the Panzers by Christmas. To parched desert-dwellers, the rains had come. Even as God had promised, and his apostles confirmed. And grateful worshipers were wallowing joyously in the coolness of it.

It is hard to realize what this meant to the German people, unless you have lived through those two years of war with them, and watched them suffer. As the core of strong, steel-willed leadership, they have been remarkably timid and sensitive to trends. They have detested this war from the moment it broke out, and they, the People, have been willing to end it at any juncture. Before it came, they feared it far more than the peoples their leaders and their army threatened with annihilation. On the few occasions on which the end appeared to be in sight, they have been gleeful as children. Dr. Goebbels had not distinguished himself on the score of telling the truth. But when he said, "The German People did not want this war," he knew, for once, what he was talking about.

OCTOBER 11, 1941: *Evacuation of Moscow ordered.*

# FROM MOSCOW TO KUIBYSHEV

### by *Wallace Carroll*

A PLANE dived out of the gray clouds and roared down low over the train. Quentin Reynolds of *Collier's* leaned out of an upper berth and asked in a loud and innocent voice:

"What does that black cross mean on the wings of that plane?"

A dozen faces popped out of other compartments.

"What cross? Where?"

The Russian soldier leaning on his rifle at the end of the corridor grinned and pointed to the plane, which had dived so low that the red star on its wings could be seen for a moment.

"It's ours," he said.

Reynolds, looking very much pleased with the success of his little joke, drew in his head and went back to sleep.

After a night in the unheated hard car, Shapiro and I had been promoted to comfortable quarters in the soft car. We were luckier than we realized at the moment, because we were to spend four and a half days on the six-hundred-and-eighty-eight-mile trip to Kuibyshev, which normally took a little over a day. This startling average speed of seven miles an hour earned for our train the name of the "Kuibyshev Komet."

At noon we halted at Ryazan, only a hundred miles southeast of Moscow. Here we were not much farther from the front than in the capital, as the Germans had swung south of Moscow and were threatening Tula, about eighty-five miles southwest of Ryazan. The German Air Force had already been paying its respects to this stretch of the railroad. Earlier in the morning we had passed a heavily bombed village and now, on a siding, we saw a line of passenger cars which had been blasted by aerial bombs and riddled by shrapnel and machine-gun bullets.

We waited in the station for several hours. A trainload of field guns, army trucks, and timber came in from the southeast and went on toward Moscow. Late in the afternoon, we moved forward again, but halted after an hour on a siding at a small village. In a little while a trainload of heavy machinery from Moscow factories pulled into the station and went on ahead of us. In another hour a train of flatcars and boxcars filled with men and women followed the first. They were presumably the workers who manned the machines; it was a principle of the evacuation that workers should not be separated from the machinery they operated.

This went on for four days. We waited on sidings while trainloads of tanks and guns went toward the front and while trains loaded with machinery and workers went ahead of us to the new factories in the Urals. There were some on our train who damned "Russian inefficiency" which kept important people like us waiting while other trains were given priority. The bitter truth was that our train carrying diplomats and newspapermen of twenty nations and a hundred Russian officials as well was the least important train on the line. Some governments might have pushed us through in record time as a matter of prestige—Fascist countries had won plenty of prestige before the war by making tourist trains run on time. The realistic Russians, however, did not care whether we reached Kuibyshev in one day or ten. What they wanted was to get those arms to the front and get the new factories operating as soon as possible.

On Sunday we waited eight hours on a siding near the Volga. In a train of boxcars next to ours were several hundred peasants of German descent from the Mariupol district of the southern Ukraine. They had been ordered to go to Siberia and had been on the road sixteen days, living in these boxcars without conveniences of any kind. Men, women, and children slept on the straw-covered floor. They cooked their meals on fires which they built next to the tracks at wayside stops.

At four o'clock in the afternoon we moved on and sighted the Volga, a winding gray stream with broad mudflats. In the twilight, peasant women were going down to the river, each carrying two water buckets on a stick across her shoulders. We crossed the river on a bridge which was at least half a mile long. At the next village we bought watermelons from the peasants and found them refreshing after four days on almost nothing but canned food.

At nine o'clock on Monday morning we arrived at Kuibyshev, by far the largest and most modern community we had seen along the way. Ambassador Steinhardt and his staff went immediately to a modern apartment building where they were to live and work, the British contingent to the headquarters of the Pioneers, or Communist Boy Scouts, and the correspondents to the Grand Hotel on the main street.

All in all, everyone settled down to life in Kuibyshev with a minimum of fuss. A day or two after our arrival, Lozovsky, Paglunov, and the censors turned up at the big school building which had been taken over by the Foreign Office, and we resumed our daily battles with them. Although the Grand Hotel was not-so-grand, it had its compensations. Through the lobby and dining-room moved people whom we would rarely, if ever, have seen in Moscow. Maxim Litvinov was there, looking in better health than when I had last seen him in Geneva three years before. From besieged Leningrad came Dmitri Shostakovitch, a nervous ascetic-looking man, absorbed in the creation of his seventh symphony which would celebrate the heroism and sacrifice of the Soviet workers and peasants. Out of the half-forgotten past came Mikhail Borodin, whom Sun Yat-sen had called "the Lafayette of the Chinese Revolution." He was now the editor of the *Moscow News,* the only English-language newspaper in the Soviet Union. Alexander Troyanovsky, the first Soviet Ambassador to the United States, turned up. So did Jacob Suritz, the former Soviet Ambassador to Paris and a delegate to the League of Nations.

One night in the lobby I ran into Alexander Afinogenov, the popular dramatist, whose play, *Distant Point,* was then being performed in London. He was a tall, handsome man with a boyish face, and he was wearing the uniform of a Soviet war correspondent.

"When are we going to play poker?" he asked me. "It's been years since I've played with Americans. We must have a game soon."

"Yes," I said, "it will have to be soon. I'm leaving in a few days."

The game never was held. Afinogenov returned to Moscow, went on duty as an air-raid warden, and was killed by a German bomb a week after I last spoke to him.

One afternoon a group of familiar faces appeared in the lobby—Nina, Oscar Emma, John Evans, Sergei, Alexei, their wives and children—thirteen persons in all. They had left Moscow the day after our departure, driven to the Volga, and then come down by river steamer. Kuibyshev was already bulging with foreigners and Soviet government employees. There were no rooms in the hotels and no vacant apartments. Once again the indomitable Shapiro set to work and found places for his retainers in the rooms of friends, in the public rooms of the hotel, and wherever space could be had.

They were not the only refugees from Moscow. I used to wander down the terraced hills to the Volga docks to see the women from the capital lugging their bundles and their children off the paddle-wheel steamers which came down the river from Kazan. They used to sit on their bundles for hours in the pale autumn sunlight, waiting with characteristic Russian patience for someone to tell them where they could sleep. From the opposite direction the steamers brought soldiers from the Ukrainian front, men bearded and unkempt, their elbows out, and with holes in their shoes and trousers. These were the remnants of some of Budenny's divisions which obviously had taken a heavy pounding. Some of the men limped from wounds which had not yet completely healed, but others still marched with spirit. They were being reorganized and re-equipped and would be sent back to Timoshenko, who had taken command of the southern front.

\*  \*  \*

BERLIN, Oct. 27, 1941 (Associated Press): ... The Nazis announced that German forces had captured the Ukrainian center of Kharkov and Belgorod and were smashing on toward Rostov on the Don....

\*  \*  \*

NOVEMBER 29: *Russian Army retook Rostov.*

DECEMBER 4: *The Russians began a counteroffensive along the entire front.*

\* \* \*

Moscow, Dec. 12 (Associated Press): Russia announced tonight the utter defeat of a crumbling German army of 750,000 men on the Moscow front, with 85,000 Germans killed and twenty-three of an original fifty-one divisions either smashed, routed, surrounded or retreating.

LONDON, May 8, 1942 (United Press): The Moscow radio today reported the recapture of 345 villages and settlements by guerrillas in the Orel sector of the Bryansk front, 225 miles southwest of Moscow.

Moscow, May 21 (Associated Press): The strongly fortified Nazi defense line guarding Kharkov ... has been breached at one point. ... *Red Star,* the Russian Army newspaper asserted tonight.

Moscow, May 24 (Associated Press): The Russians announced officially today that their forces have abandoned the Kerch peninsula, eastern Crimean gateway to the Caucasus.

\* \* \*

# SEVASTOPOL

### by Larry Lesueur

*July 3*

AT midnight tonight Moscow announced that Sevastopol had fallen. In two hundred fifty days of heroic resistance the defenders had cost the Germans and Rumanians 300,000 casualties. Said Moscow: "In the past twenty-five days the Germans threw 300,000 soldiers, 400 tanks, and 900 planes into the attack and lost 150,000 men, including 60,000 killed." The defenders acknowledged the loss of 40,775 casualties, not counting the deaths among the civilian population. The Germans got "nothing but ruins," the communiqué added.

Until the last moment the Germans never knew how thin the line of defenders really was, after the pulverizing effects of their siege guns and incessant mass bombardments, the heaviest yet known in this war. They finally charged through lines held only by the dead to meet the last obstinate defenders in bloody hand-to-hand combats on the streets, while rifles still spoke from the gaping windows of the defiant city. The Germans claimed angrily that they were forced to asphyxiate with smoke bombs the Red Army men who defended their city to the last from its underground passageways.

The defense of Sevastopol has held up the ultimate German drive on the oil of Baku for an entire month. Now Hitler can be expected to switch his troops against the forces of Timoshenko defending Rostov, the "Gateway to the Caucasus."

321

*July 4*

THE Russians are the same in victory as in defeat. The Red Army acknowledges that it has fallen back on the Kursk front, where a great tank battle has been raging for seven days. The Berlin radio says that the Axis troops are driving forward along a 120-mile front between Kursk and Kharkov, and advanced forces are plunging toward the River Don, 130 miles eastward.

This is such a large country that the war seems to be taking place a long way from Moscow. I can see no change in the expression or the attitude of the people. They maintain their look of stolid resignation and unshakable determination. The domestic propaganda in the Moscow papers blazes with fiery words encouraging those far from the front to do their utmost for the men in battle.

This is the most nationalistic country I have ever lived in. I remembered United Nations Day in May, when every Moscow public building flew the State flag of the Soviet Union, the red banner with the gold hammer and sickle. There wasn't an American, British, or Chinese flag to be seen in the city except over their respective embassies. Nothing is allowed to distract the public from the fact that they are standing off the main forces of the German Army alone in Europe.

When I first came to Soviet Russia I was alert for any sign that the people were in disagreement with the Communist system, but I have now almost forgotten about a possible fifth column. The impact of the war, with its tidal wave of nationalism, has cemented the public spirit so firmly that any ideas of fissures in the social structure would be far-fetched.

The people are fully conscious of the inexorable nature of the Soviet Government and the Kremlin, however. Sometimes when I have discussed the iron regimentation of the Soviet system, I have heard Russians murmur: "Perhaps it would not be like this if Lenin had lived." But I've rarely heard complaints about the ideals of the party. The few Russians with whom I have an opportunity to talk readily agree that there is no true Communism in Russia, but only State socialism or State capitalism. Then they get a faraway look in their eyes and give me the pat phrase that under Stalin the slogan is. "From each according to his capacities, to each according to his *work*." They add that when they achieve true Communism, this will be changed to: "From each according to his capacities, to each according to his *needs*." No one will venture to say when this ideal of equality for all will be reached.

*July 6*

A RARE treat today. I was given a few old copies of the *Saturday Evening Post* and *Life* at the American Embassy. English reading matter is extremely scarce in Moscow, and even the most ancient magazines are highly prized by us.

Katya came to the hotel after dinner and we pored over the magazines

322

side by side, looking at the pictures. She was an unusual subject, for she had never seen an advertisement before. The Soviet magazines are devoted entirely to reading matter and the only forms of advertising in the newspapers are theater notices and the classified ads referring to apartment exchanges or factories looking for persons with specialized skills.

Pointing with her red nails at an advertisement for Listerine, she drew back in horror. It was a picture of a handsome, care-free young man unconscious of the fact that there was dandruff on his shoulders. The tiny specks on his dark suit were illustrated under a magnifying glass and revealed a mass of what seemed to be white, ugsome worms. In a frightened voice she demanded: "Does every man in America have those on his shoulder?" Nonplussed, I made a half-hearted effort to explain and then gave up.

I turned the page. We looked at a family of cartoon camels talking up their product by means of blurbs issuing from their mouths. Katya was delighted. "Ah!" she exclaimed with pleasure. "The circus! What are the animals saying about it?" Weakly, I attempted to translate the words of the camels into Russian, but went down in defeat.

I turned the page again. Here was something she could appreciate. A dozen styles of women's shoes were displayed. Bending her dark head over the page, Katya gloated over the shoes. She had never seen so many styles before. She finally selected a pair of extremely high-heeled pumps as her favorite.

We both pondered the rich color prints of strawberry shortcake and thick, sizzling steaks with mouth-watering interest. I was hypnotized by the automobile ads, showing the absolute perfection of human existence, a happy group of extremely good-looking young men and women, all in bathing suits, admiring a shining new car. Although I couldn't really remember having ever seen such a sight, it made me homesick for America.

The waiter brought in our supper of bread and cheese, salami, and two glasses of tea. I took two lumps of sugar out of my secret hoard on top of the wardrobe.

## July 7

THE news is getting worse. The Germans are hurling the full weight of their huge mechanized army against the south of Russia. The hope is disappearing that the Red Army, stiffened by experienced young officers and thousands of new weapons, can hold the German tanks within confined areas to deny them broad fields of maneuver.

The Germans, who defended themselves behind "hedgehogs" of fortified villages all winter, are now using a "hedgehog" system for their offensive. The march of the panzer columns is guarded on the flanks by field guns mounted on a tank chassis. These self-propelled cannon crawl along at the same pace as the tanks and defend the panzers from sudden flank attacks like a porcupine sticking out its quills.

The Germans have also come up with a new weapon. Light artillery has been mounted on the sides of motorcycles. The German riders wait in ambush in the forest until Soviet tanks appear. Then they roar out in company, attacking the big Soviet armored machines in their vulnerable sides and rears like wolves attacking a bear. After delivering a few violent blows the motorcyclists speed away out of danger. Another Nazi device is the "portable mine field." The Germans have ingeniously rigged mines on wires and pulleys which they set out in clearings where Russian tanks are likely to make an attack. When the Red Army tanks approach, the German infantry hastily pulls the wires and tries to drag the mines into the path of the Soviet machines. Still another Nazi tactic is the digging of "anti-tank cells." These are extremely narrow pits in the ground, just large enough for two men to hide in. When Soviet tanks draw near, the Germans cower below the surface and allow the iron monsters to pass over their heads or alongside them. Then the German "tank-exterminators" throw off the camouflaged cover of their pit and jump out to hurl grenades and fire-bottles at the rear of the Russian war machines.

The Russians are countering the German "tank-exterminators" by building their big forty-six ton Voroshilov tank with a limited number of open apertures and covering these with overhanging metal guards so that the liquid from the fire-bottles won't penetrate the interior.

Soviet tankmen have the highest praise for their Red Army women, who play a big role in the radio vans that accompany the Red tank columns. In the heat of a mass tank battle, when the wave-lengths are crowded with shouts by the tankmen of both sides, it is the acuteness of women's hearing that enables them to distinguish between the voices. The Germans often shout misleading orders in Russian over the open circuits, but the Russians say that their radio women can tell the difference instantly between a phony order and one radioed by their own men.

But despite the Soviet's preparations over the winter, the German tank army, paced by the dive-bombers of the Luftwaffe, is rolling relentlessly south, heading for Marshal Timoshenko's headquarters at Voronezh and for Rostov.

JULY 7, 1942: *The German Army captured Voronezh.*

JULY 27: *The Red Army evacuated Rostov.*

AUGUST 12: *Prime Minister Churchill arrived at Moscow.*

# MR. CHURCHILL GOES TO MOSCOW

## by Henry C. Cassidy

WHEN Germany forced the Soviet Union and Great Britain into alliance, Churchill and Stalin made the best they could of it, with as much good grace as they could command. Churchill, particularly, made several mentions of letting bygones be bygones, as in his telegram to Stalin, after Molotov's visit to London, in which he asserted, "We have done a great deal toward beating down the barrier between our two countries."

Their meeting in Moscow, from August 12 to 15, 1942, therefore, ranked with the great encounters of strong men of all times.

The issue was the second front. The situation, as it was generally understood in Moscow, was this: the British and Americans agreed, during Molotov's visit to London and Washington, on the "urgent tasks of creating a second front in Europe in 1942." President Roosevelt was willing. Churchill, however, turned against it. The President was placed in the position of not being able to go ahead alone with a plan which was definitely opposed by the leader of his main associated power. The second front was off for 1942.

I was sitting in my living room at 4:30 P.M., August 12, talking with Robert Magidoff, when a roar penetrated the thin roof. We looked into the pale blue sky, where a light breeze was chasing white clouds illuminated by a bright sun, and saw three great, four-motored, fan-tailed American B-24 bombers pass overhead and coast to a landing at the central airport. Above them, so high they could hardly be seen, dipped an escort of Soviet fighters. It was Churchill, arriving with his party.

His coming had been kept generally secret. The correspondents, however, had known of it for days. Clark Kerr had locked himself in his embassy, declining to see anyone. Travelers from Teheran reported hectic preparations among the British there for an important reception. Others said a Soviet guard of honor had been sent out to the Kuibyshev airport, only to be told to return another day. In Moscow, special guards were detailed to the airport. The National Hotel was roped off and the sidewalk in front of it carpeted. The wall of the foreign office guest-house was given a fresh coat of black paint and supplies were carried into its yard. All that, for us, added up to a visit by Churchill.

Some of the correspondents saw the Prime Minister riding away from the airport. Even if they had not recognized him, his cigar, a rarity in Moscow, was enough to identify him. Others telephoned the British embassy and asked whether they could see Churchill's secretary. A slow-witted clerk said, "Just a moment, please, I'll ask him," and then returned, chastened, to say, "I don't know anything about him." We handed telegrams in to the press department, saying Churchill had arrived, and received the same answer: "Nothing is known about it." So the battle was on, and we could not describe it. Churchill, officially, was not in Moscow.

325

At the airport the visitors were met by a delegation of Soviet officials, with Molotov at their head. The flags of the Soviet Union, Great Britain, and the United States snapped from the flagpoles. A military band played the three national anthems. A guard of honor, composed of men chosen specially for their height, not to be outdone by the Buckingham Palace guards, stood at attention.

Churchill inspected the guard, and then spoke into a microphone for the newsreels. "We are determined that we will continue hand in hand, whatever our suffering, whatever our toils," he said. "We will continue hand in hand, like comrades and brothers, until every vestige of the Nazi regime has been beaten into the ground, until the memory only of it remains as an example and a warning for future times."

Averell Harriman, who came with Churchill as President Roosevelt's personal representative, also spoke briefly: "The President of the United States charged me to accompany the British Prime Minister on his eventful journey to Moscow at this crucial moment of the war. The President of the United States stands back of everything that Mr. Churchill has come to do here, and America will be fighting with the Russians hand in hand at the front."

Churchill gave his famous "V" for victory sign and turned away to his automobile. Behind him there was excited speculation over two subjects. One was Harriman's reference to America fighting with the Russians at the front. The other was Churchill's V sign. Most Russians who saw it thought the two fingers meant there would be two fronts. The word for victory, in Russian, is *pobeda*. He should have given the P sign in Moscow.

Churchill talked with Stalin for three hours and forty minutes at the Kremlin the evening of August 12. He conferred with Molotov the next afternoon and again with Stalin the next evening. What was said behind the closed doors, those on the inside would not say, those on the outside could not pretend to know.

It was natural to assume, however, that the principal subjects were those the whole world was then discussing: the German surge across the Don, east toward Stalingrad, south toward the Caucasus; and Russian anxiety over the second front. It was easy, also, to see the way the talks were going, from such indications as a conversation between two Englishmen which took place in my presence. "It's really too bad they brought the old gentleman out here," said one who was no youth himself. "It's not going so well, is it?" said the other. "The old boy's in a foul temper."

On the third evening, there was a Kremlin dinner, the most animated ever held in this series of traditional endings to official visits. Nearly one hundred guests, members of the British and United States missions in Moscow and highest Soviet leaders, trooped into the Catherine Hall of the Great Palace at 9 P.M. for the spectacle.

Stalin sat in the center of the long main table with Churchill on his right and Harriman on his left. Beside each of the guests of honor sat an interterpreter. Across the table was Molotov, with Clark Kerr on his right and Admiral Standley on his left.

326

There was a sensation at the very start when Churchill entered, wearing blue overalls with a zipper front, open at the neck and with no tie. It was the first time he had appeared in Moscow in this costume. It may have been the same costume which was admired in Washington, but not in Moscow; it was no success, particularly at a Kremlin dinner which the Russians, so informal on some occasions but so formal on others, consider as a great state occasion. No one asked the Primie Minister for an explanation of his attire, and he offered none. One Russian guest, who could not contain his curiosity, however, leaned over and asked a British general confidentially whether that was the kind of suit worn by British parachutists during commando raids on France.

Mixed with the meal were countless toasts. The first was by Stalin, the usual salutation to his guests. Molotov proposed a toast to President Roosevelt, to which Churchill responded with a booming "To the President," which could be heard all over the hall. Admiral Standley offered a libation to the union of Great Britain, the United States, and Russia. General Wavell made a brief speech in fluent, precise Russian. As the party warmed up, Stalin appeared to be growing higher, Churchill lower, in spirits.

There was a difficult moment when Clark Kerr proposed a toast to Stalin. Everyone rose to drink—except Churchill. Squatting heavily in his chair, he muttered across to his envoy, something to this effect: "Haven't you been in the diplomatic service long enough to know an ambassador addresses his words to the foreign minister of the country to which he is accredited?" An interpreter, meanwhile, was translating Clark Kerr's words. The ambassador's usually ruddy face flushed an even deeper red. When the translation was finished, he turned quickly to Molotov and spoke a few more polite words. Those were translated, and everyone—including Churchill, who then rose—drank the toast.

Stalin, by now, was in peak form. He stood, with a smile, and said something like this:

"I should like to propose a toast that no one can answer. It is to intelligence officers. They cannot answer, because no one knows who they are, but their work is important."

He went on to say he had been reading up on this subject, and recalled an incident which occurred during what he called the "Gibraltar" campaign of the last war. He evidently meant the "Gallipoli" campaign, a sore spot for Churchill, who then was first lord of the admiralty when the Allies failed to take the Dardanelles. Stalin pointed out the campaign was virtually won, but because of flaws in their intelligence work, the British did not realize or follow up their advantage, and so failed.

That was the most awkward moment of the meal. Stalin's toast could be taken to mean all sorts of things—that Allied intelligence officers were now working, unknown, virtually as spies, in the Soviet Union; that, as they had in the last war, they were again making mistakes. It was a direct gibe at Churchill.

327

Captain Jack Duncan, the United States naval attaché, a swashbuckling sailor from Springfield, Missouri, who was never fazed by any little thing like a toast, saved the situation. He rose and said:

"I can answer that toast to intelligence officers, because I'm one of them. If we make mistakes, it is because we know only what you tell us—and that's not much."

Stalin roared with laughter, and called down the table, "If there's anything you want to know, ask me. I'll be your intelligence officer."

Stalin left his seat, walked to Duncan's and drank a personal toast to him. And when the dinner broke up about 1 A.M., Stalin and Duncan walked out of the room together, arm in arm.

*　*　*

Moscow, Aug. 26, 1942 (United Press): The Battle of Stalingrad has begun, the Soviet High Command indicated today, in announcing that large German tank and infantry forces were beating strongly against Red Army defenses "northwest of Stalingrad."

*　*　*

SEPTEMBER 20: *Mr. Willkie landed at the Moscow airport.*

# WENDELL WILLKIE IN THE KREMLIN

## *by Walter Graebner*

WHEN the hope of the Russian people for a Second Front in Europe in 1942 began to vanish, relations between the Soviet Union and America and England cooled almost as fast and to the same degree as the weather. From a comfortable seventy, they dropped in one month to a chilly forty. The simple fact was that the Russians didn't think America and Britain were fighting the war with anything like the same amount of sweat and blood that the Russians were giving. And geographical or strategical reasons didn't convince them that America and Britain could not fight this way.

This was the backdrop for the interesting week's drama that began to unfold when Wendell Willkie landed in Moscow at twenty minutes after two on a Sunday afternoon in a pouring rain. He smiled broadly as he stepped briskly out of a Liberator (the Russians called them Monsters) and pumped the hands of dark-overcoated Foreign Office officials. He said: "Delighted to meet you" to everyone, but when Associated Press' bald Eddie Gilmore walked up, Willkie said: "Well hello, Eddie, God bless you." He stood bareheaded for five minutes while cameras ground and clicked, then remarked about the cold and put his old gray hat back on his head.

After Willkie conferred with Stalin he told me in odd moments all that he could about the interview and several days later gave me the following account for publication in *Life:*

"Stalin's invitation to me to come to the Kremlin for a conference reached the Foreign Office Guest House where I am staying on my third evening in Moscow.

"The time set for the meeting was 7:30 on the evening of September 23d.

"The moment I entered his office Mr. Stalin rose from his chair at the end of the long birch conference table and strode toward me. He was dressed in pink whipcord trousers, a gray military blouse and black boots. Though stockily built he was shorter than I expected him to be, despite reports I had read to that effect. Actually he would have to stand on tiptoes to look over my shoulder. As we shook hands his first words were: 'Glad to see you, Mr. Willkie.' I replied: 'Delighted to see you, Mr. Stalin.' After this exchange I greeted Mr. Molotov who remained throughout the interview. Besides the interpreter, no one else was present.

"We felt completely at ease with one another throughout the conference. It was clear from the outset that Mr. Stalin did not look upon my visit as a courtesy call (which it wasn't), but as an opportunity for a frank heart-to-heart discussion about the war and the problems which always beset united nations in war and peace. Realizing that the greatest battle of the war—the battle for Stalingrad—was drawing to a climax every minute that we were sitting there, I thought it only proper after an hour that I should make a move to leave—although there was really much more that I wished to take up with him. But when I made this move he urged me to remain longer. We talked for another hour with only one break: when Mr. Stalin left for a few minutes to wash his hands.

"First, Mr. Stalin inquired about my journey. I told him that the military position in Egypt was much better than I had expected to find it, that the British had recently dealt Rommel's forces a stunning blow and that throughout the entire Middle East in general the military and political situation for the Allies had become much firmer. Turning to lighter aspects of the trip, I said that I had enjoyed my air journey immensely, adding that one had to ride in airplanes really to understand how small are man and his works. 'Aha, so there's something of the philosopher in you,' Mr. Stalin said, with a twinkle in his brown eyes.

"Most of our conversation concerned military matters of a highly secret nature which, needless to say, cannot be disclosed. I can, however, state that Mr. Stalin gave frank, comprehensive and satisfactory replies to all of the many questions I raised. Furthermore, he said that Hitler, by rolling across South Russia to the Volga, had struck a terrible blow at the Soviet Union. But he left no doubt in my mind about Russia's power and determination to resist Germany at every tree, hillock, bridge and street until the United Nations destroy Hitler's war machine.

"At one stage of our conference, Stalin made a convincing appeal for the United Nations to put every ounce of energy into the war effort with the greatest possible speed. If the will was present, he said that seemingly im-

329

possible obstacles could be overcome. In the simple eloquence and sincerity with which he spoke these words he showed a tremendous power of persuasiveness. Certainly one of the keys to his greatness lies in this ability.

"I told Mr. Stalin that I was eager to get back to America to tell everyone what I had seen of the great fight Russia was putting up, both at the front and behind it. The work that women were doing in factories, hospitals, on farms and on the transportation system was particularly impressive to me, I explained.

"Thereupon Mr. Stalin looked at me like an old friend and said: 'Mr. Willkie, do you mind if I make a suggestion?' I said: 'Of course not.' Stalin then said: 'Yes, tell America all that you've seen here. Tell Americans if you like that we need all the products they can send from their great workshops. We will be most grateful. But I would suggest that you understate the case rather than give anyone the impression that you are encouraging Americans to assume a patronizing attitude toward us.' These I thought were wise words from a sagacious and alert man.

"With every minute that passed my appreciation of Stalin's gift for clear, straight thinking increased. He never talked around a subject, but always stuck right to the point until there was nothing more to say. When he spoke —and of course it was always through an interpreter—he looked me straight in the eye and when I talked he listened attentively to every word, though he doesn't understand English.

"Stalin appeared to be in excellent health and spirits, though he probably works as hard and shoulders as great a responsibility as any man in the world. The war has turned some of his jet-black hairs gray, but it has also steeled his heart more than ever against Fascist tyranny."

The final proof of Willkie's success in Russia was Stalin's dinner in the Kremlin. The invitation came during his conference at the Kremlin, Stalin saying, "I'd like to have you over to dinner one night before you go." Willkie said, "I'd be honored." Stalin said, "How would Thursday be?" Willkie said, "Not so good because I am going to the Front." Stalin then said, "Let's make it Saturday." So Saturday it was—at 7:30 on a warm, hazy, moonlit evening. It was a smallish affair with only twenty-five present, including Generals Faymonville and Bradley, American Military Attaché Joseph Michela, Admiral Standley and Sir Archibald Clark Kerr (the only Briton present). The conversation flowed freely and gaily as dozens of toasts were drunk to Roosevelt, Churchill, Willkie, Stalin and the United Nations. Once, after something Stalin had said, Willkie remarked, "Mr. Stalin, you certainly have your eye on the ball." Stalin wanted to know exactly what this American slang meant and Willkie explained fully using golf as an illustration. At this compliment Stalin chuckled for a long time. After dinner Stalin put on a movie about the defenses of Moscow.

Willkie departed, as he had come, in a giant Liberator.

# THE NAZIS ENTER STALINGRAD

## by Ralph Parker

SEPTEMBER 27, 1942—Within the city the opposing forces are split into small groups of desperate men armed to the teeth. Every man uses an automatic weapon, enemies jostle one another on a staircase or in a corridor. Perhaps never before in military history has so much firepower and weight of material clashed in so small a space. In effect hundreds of planes and tanks and thousands of shock troops are grappling for mastery on a five-kopek piece.

It is a war *à l'outrance*. You may lose the hall of a building and from the staircase see the enemy pour across the threshold. But there cannot be surrender. From the first-floor windows your machine gun tries to keep more from entering, while tommy-gunners wait for the enemy to climb higher. And if you lose the first floor, there is one above and then there is the roof above that.

Only stone houses remain in Stalingrad. The German pattern of bombing has reduced many of these to ruins. Although only a few buildings are fit to live in, they still provide cover in the violent fighting. The fiercest engagements occur at street crossings and in adjacent blocks between small groups of tanks and shock troops and grenadiers. Powerful barricades are built. Heavy furniture and even safes from offices are placed across the streets, while by the Volga thousands are filling sandbags with which labyrinthine fortifications are hastily built.

Stalingrad is being converted into a honeycomb of defenses for battles for every house and every street. Each house must become a fortress and each group of Red Army men a garrison. Water, food and ammunition must be stored in every building and tunnels dug to connect them.

NOVEMBER 19: *The Russians opened a counter-offensive. Rzhev and Stalingrad were relieved.*

DECEMBER 16: *The Russians launched an offensive across the Don.*

\* \* \*

Moscow, December 31 (Associated Press): A special Soviet communiqué said tonight that the German Army in Stalingrad "is liquidated completely."

\* \* \*

331

# COUNTERATTACK!

### by James E. Brown

MARSHAL SHAPOSHNIKOFF launched the Red Army counterattack early in November, 1942. It was primarily intended to relieve Stalingrad, but it resulted in an unbroken series of Russian victories as the Soviets swept across the Don steppes beyond Rostov and Kharkov. The winter of 1942-43 will long be remembered in the U.S.S.R. for glorious successes on the battlefield and untold suffering at home.

Stalin altered his long-standing policy of requesting only war material under the Lease-Lend agreement, and several shiploads of American food arrived for the army early in 1943.

Shaposhnikoff's plans, although hampered by many complications, were finally implemented by young Gen. Konstantin Rokossovsky with clockwork precision. Faulty railroad communications had delayed the offensive for many weeks as the relief army waited at Saratov for supplies from the interior.

The Soviets were undecided in October whether to attempt to relieve Lieutenant-General Chuikov's hard-pressed Stalingrad garrison, but Shaposhnikoff wanted to wait for more equipment. The initial engagements northeast of Kleitskaya quickly convinced the Germans of the overwhelming Red Army strength, and they began to retreat, leaving Marshal von Paulus with 300,000 men to continue the siege of Stalingrad. It was clear that von Paulus would be cut off, but it was reasoned that his army could prevent the Soviets using either the Stalingrad railway or the Volga River, both transport arteries urgently needed by the Russians, and his troops could engage large Soviet forces while the main German armies were carrying out their retreat.

Hitler rewarded von Paulus for maintaining his suicidal position by promoting him from general to field-marshal, but the Rumanian and Hungarian generals with him were simply ordered to continue the siege. They were not given medals. The Italians apparently were still treated with more consideration by the Germans than were their Balkan allies because the Italian Eighth Army was allowed to retreat from the hopeless Stalingrad position. It did not save them, however, for in the second half of December, during the Russian Middle Don offensive, the Italians suffered a crushing defeat at Meshkov. The Thirty-Fifth Army Corps and the Second Army Corps were routed, and, within a few days, many thousands were captured, 22,000 killed and 12,000 wounded.

While Lieutenant-General Chuikov was hammering von Paulus' isolated army on the steppes in front of Stalingrad, Rokossovsky's fresh troops were driving across the snow-swept Middle Don towards Rostov. The retreating German divisions fought a rear-guard action to enable their troops in the Caucasus to effect a junction with them at Rostov. Most of the Nazi divisions between Salk and Kropotkin were able to reach Rostov before their escape was cut off, but the Germans at Maikop and Georgievsk fled to Novorossisk and from there marched north and were ferried across to the Kerch Peninsula. The Russians had lost Rostov once, recaptured it and lost it once more, and they entered the ruins of that once-beautiful city vowing never to surrender again. Von Paulus' troops, starving and frozen, capitulated to the Red Army, freeing the Soviets from menace on their rear and their southern flank as they pressed forward from Rossosh and Millerovo towards Kharkov. Meanwhile, at Stalingrad, Russian engineers were picking their way through mines and corpses that littered the ruined city. The tractor plant, one of the biggest in the world, had been completely destroyed; 14,000 houses had been razed by shells or by fire. Only the foundations were left on which to rebuild the city.

Joy in the Stalingrad victory was soon increased by the national elation which followed the Red Army relief of Leningrad. The former Czarist capital city had been under terrible siege for over a year; the story of the people's privation has not yet been adequately written and may not be until after the war. Yet the saga of Leningrad has already been expressed in music, Shostakovitch's unforgettable symphony, composed by the near-sighted artist between air raids while he was serving as an auxiliary fireman. Torn with self-doubts concerning his ability before the war, Shostakovitch drew inspiration from the sublime courage and self-sacrifice of his fellow defenders and composed a symphony that must rank with the best work of Prokofief. The Soviets claim it as outstanding among the music that has come out of Russia since the revolution. But, if the artistic triumph of Leningrad goes to Shostakovitch, the military award must be given to General Zhukoff for breaking the blockade.

General Zhukoff, promoted by Stalin to position of first assistant to Marshal Shaposhnikoff, was virtually second in command of the Red Army. A brilliant military tactician, tough and ruthless, he was trusted implicitly by the Kremlin. For this reason, he was given the task closest to Stalin's heart: breaking the siege of Leningrad, and was granted all the war material and troops he requested for the job. It was a nut-cracking assignment, and, although Zhukoff suffered heavy casualties, he drove through the Nazi lines to the city. Stalin's judgment of men was again justified.

The story of Leningrad, however, has one other postscript which may be remembered long after the military records have been forgotten: the rise of a new Soviet leader. It established Andre Zhdanoff, the mayor of the city, as the second most important political figure in the U.S.S.R. and the likely successor to Joseph Stalin. Zhdanoff, a member of the 12-man inner cabinet, or Politburo, as it is called, succeeded Kiroff as head of the People's Commissariat after the latter was assassinated in 1934. He is a nationalist like Stalin and has taken little interest in the work of the Third International.

Victories in the field stimulated Red Army morale during the winter of 1942-43, but the population at home could only gain comfort by reading of these successes. Reality for them represented long hours of work, poor food, worn-out clothing, and numbing cold. Women came home from factories facing cheerless evenings thinking of dead or missing husbands and sons. There was little laughter on the streets; the faces of men and women seemed pinched and somber, and many showed signs of malnutrition.

For these reasons the Anglo-American invasion of North Africa meant little to them; it was a remote event that seemed to have little bearing on their problems. Stalin wrote a reply to a letter from Henry Cassidy in which the correspondent had asked him his opinion of the invasion: Stalin indicated he approved of it, but his praise was lukewarm. The North African landing was a constructive Allied move, a necessary preliminary to an attack on the European continent, but it had small effect on the Soviet-German war. The Russians said it had no effect; the Allies, on the other hand, claimed it forced the Nazis to withdraw certain divisions from the Soviet Union and transfer them to Western Europe. The Roosevelt-Churchill invitation for Stalin to confer with them at Casablanca or Cairo was unwise and betrayed a fundamental misunderstanding of the Soviet position. The refusal was bound to come, and it did come: Stalin was too busy "fighting the war" (sic). He had no time for words, he wanted action. It was obvious, of course, that if he were really too busy he could have sent Molotov.

There were three reasons for his refusal, and Churchill, after his unpleasant Moscow trip, must have been aware of them. First, the intense Soviet bitterness because they were fighting alone in Europe; second, their single-mindedness about the conflict: their one aim was to drive the Germans out of Russia, and they had no desire for discussion of the global aspects which interested Britain and America; third, Stalin's inherent distaste for such dramatic gestures. But there was much, after all, that could not be discussed through the medium of the ordinary diplomatic channels. Churchill may have hoped that the presence of President Roosevelt would cause Stalin to accept the invitation. The President cannot be blamed for trying for a personal meeting with Stalin to learn his views on the war and post-war problems; the United States has a legitimate right to know these things. But it is regrettable that Roosevelt did not wait until the Americans had a foothold in Europe; Stalin might then be more willing for discussion.

\* \* \*

LONDON, Jan. 31, 1943 (Associated Press): Almost complete destruction of the 330,000-man German force at Stalingrad.... Taken prisoner were Field Marshal General Friedrich Paulus, commander of the crushed German 6th Army and 4th Tank Army, and 16 of his generals.

\* \* \*

# REBIRTH OF STALINGRAD

## by Henry Shapiro

MOSCOW, Feb. 3.—New life surged through the charnel house of Stalingrad today after a night of eerie quiet which followed the surrender or death of the last of 330,000 German and satellite troops whom Adolf Hitler sacrificed in his vain attempt to make good his boast that the Red bastion of the Volga would fall.

The battle which started late last August when the Germans broke across the Don ended at 4 P.M. yesterday.

In the final hours, resistance had been carried on by groups of German officers in pillboxes, dugouts and fortified buildings.

German soldiers had shot many officers who refused to yield.

Russian troops, entering the last of the enemy strongholds, found 3,000 Germans lying in rags on the floor of one great underground hospital. Many were dead. Many more were dying of wounds, hunger and cold.

Today the women and children and the scattering of aged men of the civilian population who had survived the siege, many of them in caves in the high Volga bank, a few in deep dugouts emerged to seek the ruins of their homes, some carrying a few rags of clothing, one a chair, nucleus of a new collection of furniture, determined to lose no time in starting life anew in confidence that the Germans would not be back.

The Russians liberated 12,000 men and women whom the Germans had intended, when the Red Army broke across the Don last Nov. 19, and encircled the city four days later, to deport to slavery.

Thousands of frozen German bodies still littered the streets, thousands more lay where they had fallen in fortified buildings or in the many underground field hospitals where they had died of wounds, disease or the cold.

Red Army first-aid men sought in these deep refuges those of the enemy wounded who still lived.

Salvage squads collected more and more spoils to add to the enormous quantities already gathered; sanitary squads started to clean up the streets; burial squads tried to collect the innumerable enemy dead; those soldiers native of Stalingrad who had the time to spare wandered the streets they had freed in what a special communiqué issued last night called one of the greatest battles in the history of wars.

Three special announcements told of the end of the battle—an order of the day by Premier Josef Stalin, supreme commander in chief who himself conceived and directed the Red Army offensive and selected the site for the break-through which freed the great city named for him; a proud report to "Comrade" Stalin—"Battle report No. 0079 O/P"—in which Marshal of Artillery N. N. Voronov, representing the general staff of the supreme command; Col. Gen. R. K. Rokossovsky, commanding the troops on the Don front; Major General Telegin, of the Don front military council; and

Lieutenant General Valinin, chief of staff of the Don front, announced the victory, and the special communiqué reviewing the final operations.

Stalin's order of the day addressed to Rokossovsky and Voronov said:

"I congratulate you and the troops of the Don front on the successful liquidation of the German Fascist troops encircled at Stalingrad. I express my gratitude to all men, commanders and political instructors of the Don front for the successful battle operations."

Forty-five thousand of the Germans who, the Germans insisted, were fighting to the death, had surrendered in the two past days, including most of the generals—unwounded, like Paulus, who, according to the Germans, only survived because he was unconscious and could not kill himself. The generals walked out.

\* \* \*

LONDON, Feb. 16 (United Press): The capture of Kharkov was announced by the Red Army in a special communiqué broadcast from Moscow.

\* \* \*

# SHAKEUP IN THE GENERAL STAFF

## by George Axelsson

STOCKHOLM, Sweden, Sept. 22, 1943—General Marshal Fedor von Bock, German commander in chief of the Stalingrad and southeastern fronts, appears to have been recalled. Five days ago a Swedish journalist now in Stockholm saw him walking through the streets of Berlin in mufti.

The newspaper man, in a conversation today, drew the conclusion that if the Marshal had not been dismissed he could not have spared the time from the Stalingrad front, where the fate of the German Army in Russia now seems to be at stake.

The correspondent, who claims to know Marshal von Bock by sight from personal contacts stretching over the last eighteen months, declared emphatically that he recognized the German commander in a Berlin residential district and said he was wearing an ordinary lounge suit and a soft hat. As he approached the Marshal, the latter refused to talk with him, but acknowledged his identity, the correspondent reported.

Rumors of Marshal von Bock's dismissal first reached here ten days ago, emanating from many sources. But this appears to be the first definite confirmation of his recall.

Marshal von Bock, long regarded as one of the sternest of disciplinarians and most brilliant commanders of the German Army, is known to have sided with General Field Marshal von Brauchitsch, former Commander in Chief, who was dismissed last December after a breach had developed between the German High Command and the Nazi party.

As a member of an old Junker family, Marshal von Bock said firmly at the time, according to reports available here, that he was not prepared to countenance dual command of the Army by generals and Nazi or Elite Guard commissars.

Later he was removed from his command on the Moscow front and returned to Germany, where he spent the Winter in the country recovering from "diplomatic" illness.

Adolf Hitler eventually swallowed his pride rather than let the Army perish in Russian snows on his "intuition" and brought back Marshal von Bock as well as Marshal von Brauchitsch, the latter only in a consultative capacity. The General Staff is reported to have told Herr Hitler that Marshal von Bock was the only man capable of carrying out the gigantic project of smashing the Russian southeastern sector in the Caucasus and toward the Volga.

Two reasons are now believed to have led to Marshal von Bock's second dismissal, if dismissal it be. The first is that he has reportedly protested the steady withdrawal of the Elite Black Guard divisions from the Stalingrad and Caucasus fighting lines to positions in the rear. It is recalled that no High Command communiqué of the last month has mentioned the participation of the Elite Guard in the fighting on Stalingrad or Caucasian fronts as formerly, paying tribute only to the regular infantry, the Panzer groups and the Alpine troops, as well as the Italian, Hungarian and Rumanian "stage extras."

The second reason advanced is that Marshal von Bock is reported to have told Herr Hitler in no uncertain terms that too much was being demanded of the divisions engaged at Stalingrad, warning that unless fresh divisions, and particularly Elite Guard units, were brought up to reinforce the battle front, he would run the risk not only of failing to take the city but also of breaking the morale of the army.

# ANNIVERSARY 1943

*by W. H. Lawrence*

MOSCOW, Nov. 6.—Whatever may be history's verdict with respect to the internationalist or isolationist record of various countries, it is sufficient to say that the four largest global powers—Russia, China, the United States and Britain—are determined to work together to win this war and prevent, so far as is humanly possible, the outbreak of another.

It is this good news that sets the stage for Moscow's celebration tomorrow of the Soviet revolution's twenty-sixth anniversary. The Soviet people are confident as they never have been before of an early victory over Germany. Were the facts of war not so close, with the casualty lists still mounting as the Red Army drives the Germans west, it is likely that Moscow would be a gay town for this anniversary.

Moscow's mood has undergone a great change in the last year. It is most natural because this summer for the first time they drove the Germans back in good weather after stopping cold the mighty German offensive in July.

A few statistics give the reason for Moscow's satisfaction this Nov. 7. On the revolution's anniversary in 1941 the Germans were only nineteen miles from Moscow. In 1942 they were ninety miles from Moscow, but this year they are approximately 200 miles away. On what is now the Kiev front the Germans have been driven back 315 miles in a year and on the Dniepropetrovsk front they have retreated 278 miles.

In the last year, moreover, the Soviets have received evidence that Anglo-American military forces meant business, although the second front for which the Russians have long been asking still has not been established. When the anniversary was celebrated last year, it was just one day before the Allied landings in North Africa and the man in the street did not know that was about to happen. In his anniversary eve speech last year Stalin said the Germans were able to carry on a great 1942 summer offensive without risk to themselves because there was no second front in Europe.

Now the picture is changed and a four-power pact for post-war collaboration has been signed. This marks a great milestone in Soviet relations with the rest of the world and those of the rest of the world with the Soviet Union.

There have been times when it seemed the Soviet Union wanted co-operation for peace with the rest of the world but there was no reciprocity. Especially was this true during 1939, when Soviet delegates to the League of Nations, notably Maxim M. Litvinoff, fought long, hard and losing battles for collective security against the aggression inherent in the Axis.

The Russians always have looked on themselves as internationalists. They have asserted time and again their willingness to co-operate with the rest of the world, and they have asserted that whatever isolation they have followed has resulted because other powers "isolated" them.

In democratic countries, especially Britain and the United States, there have been times when they thought Russia did not want co-operation with them, notably in 1939, when the Soviet-German pact signature preceded Adolf Hitler's march into Poland by only a few weeks. One undoubted factor in Russia's decision at that time was the attitude of Poland itself, whose conduct in foreign relations convinced Soviet leaders that Poland preferred the risk of defeat at Hitler's hands to acceptance of Soviet help.

When Foreign Secretaries Cordell Hull, Anthony Eden and Vyacheslaff M. Molotoff sat down around the large table in the white marble-walled Spiridonovka Palace, they adopted at once a general attitude of let-bygones-be-bygones. The result was that last Saturday these three men, together with Chinese Ambassador Foo Ping-sheung, could affix their names to a declaration pledging concerted action against common enemies to win the war and preserve future peace. They agreed to act together in establishing an international organization open to membership of all peace-loving states, large and small, which the whole world hopes will be a better League of Nations.

# THE HANGING OF ZOYA

## by Maurice Hindus

TOGETHER with a group of young guerrillas Zoya went off deep into the German rear. Nights they scouted for guerrillas and for the Red Army. They cut telephone wires, blew up bridges, harassed German transportation. By day they remained in the forest, built a fire, warmed themselves, and slept with their backs against tree trunks. Always they had to be on the alert lest they be ambushed. They felt hungry but didn't complain; the work was too important, too exciting, and they didn't bother about personal well-being.

The time came to return to headquarters. But Zoya remembered Petrisht-shevo and decided to go there and "disturb" the rest of the German vaca-tionists.

"I may perish there," she told her companions, "but I'll take the lives of ten Germans."

Together with ten other guerrillas Zoya started for Petrishtshevo. In the dead of night they drew close to the village. Zoya's companions remained behind as guards and scouts, and she proceeded alone to her destination. Soon afterward flames rose from several buildings, the ones her com-mander had ordered her to set afire. Quickly she got away and joined her companions. As they were retreating from the village they could see the burning buildings. Zoya had done more—she had cut the telephone lines so that the Germans in Petrishtshevo could not at once communicate with other German units.

In the evening of the following day guerrilla scouts brought back the report that the fires which Zoya had started had caused little damage: only a few houses had burned down before the flames were put out. Whether any of the Germans who lived in these houses had perished the scouts were unable to establish. Zoya regarded her mission a failure. Disgusted with her-self, she said:

"I shall go again."

"Yes," said the guerrilla commander, "but wait until they calm down—they have guards at every house now."

"I shall wait a day," said Zoya; "then I'll go."

She wouldn't let anyone talk her into waiting any longer. She had failed in her purpose and she had no right to fail. That was the way she reasoned, the same self-willed, resolute girl she had always been, impatient to perform well and promptly the assignment at hand, whether a problem in geometry, teaching a housemaid to read and to write, or setting fire to homes in which German soldiers were living.

In her diary she wrote down the line from *Hamlet*:

"Adieu, adieu, adieu! remember me!"

The next evening she made herself ready for another trip to Petrishtshevo. She dressed like a man in cotton quilted trousers, knee-high felt boots, a fur jacket, a fur cap. Over her back she slung her case in which she carried several bottles of benzine, matches, ammunition, a few personal effects. Around her waist she wore her regulation leather belt and a revolver in a leather holster. Before leaving the dugout she said to a friend named Klava:

"If anything happens to me, you must promise to write my mother."

Klava seized her hand and said:

"How can I write your mother when I don't even know your real name?"

"That's not important. Write to the Komsomol committee in the Timiryazev district in Moscow. They'll deliver the letter."

Not even in this crucial moment would she disclose her identity to a fellow guerrilla who had become her closest friend but whom she had known only a short time. Together the two girls went out of the dugout. They bade each other farewell and Zoya left. Soon she was swallowed by the woods and the darkness.

She followed the road she had followed two days earlier on her first trip to Petrishtshevo. Finally she came in sight of the village, the cottages looming out of the snow like dark spots on the horizon. She walked nearer and nearer. No sounds anywhere. No sight of guards. No lights. The village seemed fast asleep. Zoya's objective was the stable which, according to the information scouts had imparted to the commander, was sheltering two hundred horses. Whipping the gun out of her holster and holding it in her hand, she proceeded to the designated objective. Still no sound of anything, no sight of anybody. Slipping the gun inside her bosom, she knelt down. Without wasting a second she drew a bottle of benzine out of her little case, poured it over a bunch of kindling wood she had gathered, and struck a match. The match broke. She struck a second, and suddenly someone seized her from behind.

Pushing away her assailant, she drew her gun out of her bosom. But she had no time to pull the trigger. The gun was knocked out of her hand. Her shoulders were firmly held, and her hands were tied behind her back by a rope. The German guard sounded the alarm. Other soldiers swiftly came along and led Zoya to a house in which lived a peasant named Sedov. On the top of the oven lay Sedov's wife and his young daughter. Awakened by the sudden noise, they looked down and saw the Germans snatch the fur cap off "the boy" they had brought in, then the felt boots. Then they took out of the case two bottles of benzine and a box of matches. The Germans were slow in stripping the fur jacket and the sweater off their captive. They had to untie the prisoner's hands first and presently they discovered not a boy but a girl!

Barefooted, her warm clothes removed, her hands tied behind her back, Zoya was led at the point of a gun to another house, that of a peasant named Voronin. There the Germans had their local headquarters. Zoya had studied German in school. She not only read but spoke the language and therefore understood everything that was said by her captors. But she never intimated to them that she knew German.

A German officer pointed to a long bench and she sat down. Facing her was a table with a telephone, a typewriter, a radio, sets of papers. More and more German officers were arriving, among them Lieutenant Colonel Ruderer, commander of the 332d Regiment. He questioned Zoya.

"Who are you?"

"I won't tell you."

"Was it you who set fire to the stable night before last?"

"Yes."

"What was your purpose in doing this?"

"I wanted to destroy you."

"When did you cross the border?"

"Friday."

"You were quick in getting here."

"Why did you suppose I wouldn't be?"

He tried to find out who had sent her, who were her associates, where they were hiding. To all these questions the eighteen-year-old girl replied: "No, I don't know, I won't tell," or she remained silent.

Exasperated, the colonel exclaimed:

"You don't know? Soon you'll find out."

He ordered her flogged. Aften ten strokes he stopped the flogging and started to question her again.

"Will you tell now where the guerrillas are?"

"I will not."

"Ten more strokes!"

The woman of the house saw it, counted the strokes, then later, when the Germans were driven from Petrishtshevo, she told the story to the investigators. She wept with pity and, being a religious woman, made the sign of the cross over her body. But Zoya remained obdurate. Again and again she was asked the question that was uppermost in the mind of the German officer:

"Will you tell now where the guerrillas are?"

"I will not," Zoya said.

So she was flogged and flogged. Her clothes were soaked in blood. But she neither wept nor complained. She only bit her lips, bit them so hard they bled and swelled. Not a word of information could the Germans extract from her except on unimportant subjects, and then she did not always tell the truth. To the question where she was from she once said, "From Saratov," which is on the middle Volga and hundreds of miles away from Petrishtshevo. She would not tell what her name was or anything about her family.

After two hours of this inquisition she was led barefooted and thinly clad to still another house—to the home of a peasant named Vasily Kulik. He and his wife Praskovya were asleep on the oven. They wakened instantly. By the light of the lamp, Vasily took a good look at her. Her lips were swollen and bleeding. Her forehead was cut and full of black lumps. Her arms and legs were also swollen. She breathed hard and her hair was disheveled. Her hands were tied behind her back. Her clothes, the few she was permitted to wear, were red with blood. The guard ordered her to sit down on a bench and stationed himself at the door.

Vasily took a dipper of water to Zoya, but the guard stopped him. Seizing the lamp, he held it out to Zoya, shouting that kerosene was the drink for people like herself. Finally the guard relented, and Zoya drank two dippers of cool water.

The German soldier taunted her, shook his fists at her. Vasily begged him to leave the girl alone, if only for the sake of his little children, but the guard went on abusing the helpless girl. Zoya endured it all in silence.

The guard remained with her from ten in the evening until two in the morning. Every hour, at the point of his gun, he ordered Zoya into the street. Though barefooted and in scarcely more than her underwear, she obeyed without a murmur of protest. Following her with a gun at her back, the guard made her walk the street from fifteen to twenty minutes.

Another guard came. Finding an opportune moment the peasant woman Praskovya went over and talked to Zoya, gave her water which she drank. "She ought to lie down," said Praskovya, glancing at the German. He shrugged, and the woman said to the girl, "Lie down." Zoya's feet were numb and her hands were still tied.

"Untie my hands," she said to the soldier in German.

The soldier surveyed her. She looked helpless enough, and he granted her request. Zoya lay down, and Praskovya covered her with a blanket.

"Who are you?" asked Praskovya.

"Why do you want to know?" Vigilant and distrustful, Zoya was on her guard even against Russians she didn't know.

"Have you a mother?" the peasant woman asked.

No answer.

"Was it you who were here two days ago? Speak. Don't be afraid. He"—pointing at the German with her eyes—"doesn't understand our language."

Zoya answered: "It was I."

"You set the houses on fire?"

"Yes."

"Why?"

"Those were my instructions. To burn Germans, destroy their military supplies. How many houses have I burned?"

"Three."

Zoya sighed: "So few. What else burned?"

"Twenty of their horses and—what do you call it?—the telephone cable."

"Have any Germans been burned?"

"Only one."

"Only one. What a pity."

Through the few remaining hours of the night Zoya slept.

342

In the morning the German lieutenant colonel and other officers came again and started to question her. She remained as mute and stubborn as the night before. Not one word of information could they wring from her. She complained that the soldiers had stripped her almost naked, and the colonel said, "Give her back her clothes." A soldier brought only a part of her things—the waistcoat, the trousers, the stockings, her bag in which she had kept matches, sugar, salt. The fur cap, the fur jacket, the felt boots, the knitted sweater were missing, presumably appropriated by a soldier or officer. Her gloves were given to the redheaded cook in the officers' messroom.

Zoya was permitted to dress, but her spine wouldn't bend and her fingers refused to obey her will. Praskovya helped her. The Germans made one more effort to question her. It was useless. They gave up.

The gallows in the public square was ready. From the crosspole on the top dangled a rope. Beneath were two boxes laid on top of each other. Zoya was led to the place of execution. Over her breast the Germans had hung one of her bottles of benzine and a little board with the inscription "Incendiary of homes."

Several hundred German soldiers gathered on the square. Ten German cavalrymen with drawn swords were stationed round the gallows as if to fight off a sudden raid of guerrillas in an attempt to rescue their Tanya. The peasants in the village were ordered to attend the hanging. Not many came and some of these quietly slipped away. Zoya was lifted by German soldiers to the top box. The noose was thrown over her neck.

One officer brought out his camera to make a photographic record of the execution. It took him some time before he obtained all the views he wanted. Zoya was waiting quietly, and the peasants who remained on the square turned their eyes and sobbed. . . . Then, taking advantage of the waiting, Zoya turned to her people and said:

"Here, comrades! Why do you look so gloomy? Be brave, fight on, kill Germans, burn them, poison them!"

The executioner pulled the rope. The knot started to choke Zoya and with a superhuman effort she loosened it with her hands and shouted:

"Farewell, people! Fight on, fight on! Stalin is with us!"

These were her last words.

With his heavy boot the executioner kicked the box from under Zoya's feet, and she remained suspended in the air.

That was on the fifth day of December. For three weeks, or until December 25, frozen and blown about by wind and snow, the body remained swinging on the gallows. With a view to terrorizing Russians into submissiveness the Germans wouldn't permit the peasantry of the village to take it down. Then they relented. The peasants carried the body not to the village cemetery but to the rear of the schoolhouse. There, under the shadow of outspread willows, they chopped out a grave in the frozen earth and without speeches or songs, without any mark of solemnity or public demonstration, with the noose frozen to her neck, they laid Zoya to rest.

On December 1, 1942, all Russia was cheered by the following announcement which appeared in *Izvestia:*

"In the course of the first few days (of the Rzhev offensive) the soldiers of General Povetkin smashed several units of German troops. Among them, and now completely devastated, was the regiment whose soldiers had executed Zoya Kosmodemyanskaya."

# Part Seven: The Far East

*       *       *

PEIPING, Sept. 19, 1931 (Associated Press): After a three-hour artillery bombardment Japanese troops today occupied Mukden, capital of Manchuria, according to dispatches received here by Marshal Chang Hsueh-Liang, Governor of Manchuria.

*       *       *

# THE MANCHURIAN INCIDENT

## by Wilfrid Fleisher

JAPAN started on her conquest of Manchuria on September 18, 1931, which must be reckoned the most important date in Japan's modern history, not because of the Manchurian invasion itself, but because it marked the beginning of a decade during which Japan has retraced her way to a military barbarism rooted in feudal days while at the same time divorcing herself from her associations with the Western democracies which had contributed so much to her progress and advancement in the preceding sixty years.

On the night of September 18, 1931, a section of the track of the South Manchuria Railway line, north of Mukden, was mysteriously blown up, an incident which led to the rapid Japanese military occupation of the whole of Manchuria. The most conflicting reports have been made of that incident, the Japanese claiming that Chinese soldiers sabotaged the railway and attacked the Japanese railway guards as a prelude to a "general assault" against Japanese forces in Manchuria, whereas the Chinese contended that Japanese had set off the explosion to gain a pretext for a conquest of Manchuria.

I have in my possession a piece of evidence that shows clearly the Japanese move was premeditated and indicating that a secret Japanese mobilization had been carried out in advance. It is nothing more than the issue of the *China Press* of September 17, 1931, published at Shanghai, which reported from Nanking—almost two days in advance of the railway explosion—that "the Japanese authorities are secretly mobilizing preparatory to moving against Manchuria in connection with the Nakamura incident."

The Nakamura incident refers to the killing of Captain Shintaro Nakamura, a Japanese officer who was on a secret mission in northern Manchuria for the Japanese army and was traveling in the guise of an agricultural expert. The Chinese contended they shot him as a spy. There was great

345

indignation among Japanese army officers, and the Manchurian outbreak has been ascribed, in part at least, to this affair.

From what I was able to learn in Japan, the Japanese plan for conquest of Manchuria had been carefully prepared and was put into effect by a group of so-called "junior officers" without the knowledge of the commander-in-chief of the Japanese forces in Manchuria, Lieutenant General Shigeru Honjo, who was compelled to act. This group comprised Major General Miyake, a little-known officer then or since; Colonel Doihara, frequently referred to as Japan's "Lawrence," actually one of her most astute plotters and long since a lieutenant general; Colonel Itagaki, who later became a lieutenant general and Minister of War; and Colonel Ishihara. Their coup amounted virtually to an army revolt and marked the seizure of power in the army by the so-called younger-officer element.

Colonel Ishihara, then a staff officer in Manchuria, who testified before the Lytton Commission, told of receiving the report of the railway explosion on the night of September 18 and then going into conference with other Japanese officers. "By that time," he related, "Lieutenant General Honjo, our commander, had arrived, and we expressed the opinion that all troops should be concentrated in Mukden. Quite difficult discussions continued among the officers, but a final decision was reached at 1:20 A.M." The "quite difficult discussions" no doubt refer to the successful efforts of the younger-officer group to force General Honjo to act.

On the morning of September 19, when vendors were rushing about the streets of Tokyo with full-page extras telling of the outbreak in Manchuria and the Japanese attack on Mukden, I hurried around to Toshio Shiratori, the Foreign Office spokesman, and was told by him that had Baron Shidehara, then Foreign Minister, known of the initial clash, he never would have permitted it to assume the proportions it did. The cabinet meeting held that day decided to localize the conflict in Manchuria as much as possible, but the cabinet's instructions, telegraphed to Japanese Consul General Hayashi in Mukden, to be passed on to General Honjo, could not be delivered because Hayashi could not get in to see Honjo.

The Japanese occupation of Manchuria was completed by the end of the year, and Henry Pu-yi, the former boy emperor of China, who was led by Colonel Doihara from his refuge in the Japanese concession in Tientsin to Changchun—renamed Hsinking by the Japanese—was established as emperor of the puppet State. All this went on in complete defiance of repeated resolutions of the League of Nations and a series of protests from Henry L. Stimson, then American Secretary of State, culminating in a note on January 7, 1932, enunciating the doctrine of non-recognition as applicable to the Japanese-created state of Manchukuo.

Japan flatly rejected the recommendations of the Lytton Commission, which envisaged an autonomous Manchuria under nominal Chinese sovereignty, and the withdrawal of Japanese troops from Manchuria as "too refined and intricate, and not adapted to the realities of the Far East" and withdrew in protest from the League of Nations.

The effect of Japanese defiance of the League and the world Powers cannot be overestimated and must be looked upon as constituting the first blow which finally wrecked the peace structure erected after the first World War. Japan's action demonstrated the League's inability to compel a major Power to accept its verdict and set an example, which Italy was quick to emulate at the time of her Ethiopian campaign and which was the forerunner of now well-known Axis technique.

The Sino-Japanese hostilities in Manchuria were extended to Shanghai in January 1932, when a force of 2,500 Japanese marines launched a surprise attack on Chapei, a populous Chinese-administered district north of the International Settlement, after the mayor of Shanghai had accepted a set of Japanese demands, contained in an ultimatum, for suppression of all anti-Japanese activities growing out of the Japanese occupation of Manchuria. The Japanese dispatched a large expeditionary force to Shanghai and met with severe resistance on the part of the Chinese Nineteenth Route Army. Hostilities continued for three months, and an armistice was not actually reached until May.

Perhaps few persons in this country realize how strained American-Japanese relations became during the Japanese invasion of Manchuria. The climax was reached when Stimson's non-recognition note was received in Tokyo. It was reported that the American ambassador, Cameron Forbes, then sent word to Secretary Stimson saying: "If you want to send any more notes, you had better send battleships to deliver them." I have never been able to confirm whether such a message was actually sent by Ambassador Forbes, but the story aptly illustrates the state of mind then prevailing in Japan.

SEPTEMBER 22, 1931: *Japan accepted China's informal offer of arbitration. In both Nanking and Canton opposing political and military leaders put aside their differences to unite against the common danger.*

SEPTEMBER 25: *Japan proclaimed a policy of protection for the South Manchurian Railway. She continued to occupy more territory in Manchuria.*

JANUARY 29, 1932: *China appealed to the League of Nations in regard to the Japanese invasion of Manchuria and Shanghai, but this appeal was opposed by the Japanese.*

FEBRUARY 9: *Japanese attacked Woosung forts 15 miles from Shanghai.*

FEBRUARY 12: *Henry Pu-Yi, last Emperor of China, was installed as puppet ruler of Manchukuo by the Japanese.*

\* \* \*

SHANGHAI, February 13, 1932 (Associated Press): The Chapei section of Shanghai was blasted and torn today by howitzer shells and air bombs.... The Japanese command announced they had succeeded in breaking up a threatening Chinese counterattack before it got started.

* * *

# ASSASSINATION OF A PRIME MINISTER

### by Hugh Byas

THE date was May 15, 1932. It went into Japanese history as the May Fifteenth incident.

At five o'clock that Sunday evening nine naval and military officers of ages between twenty-four and twenty-eight alighted from two taxicabs at the side entrance of the Yasukuni Shrine in Tokyo. The shrine is dedicated to all members of the fighting services who have died in Japan's wars. There is no holier place in Tokyo.

If anyone gave a passing glance to the young officers it was only to think that they had probably been ordered to Manchuria, where the Imperial army was then extending the Imperial Way. They worshipped at the shrine. They piled into their taxis, five in one, four in the other. In five minutes they had passed the British Embassy with its Sunday Union Jack flying and were entering the front and back gates of the Prime Minister's official residence. The group who dismounted at the front gate carried revolvers and hand grenades, expecting that the police guards would oppose them, but no challenge was offered to officers wearing the Emperor's uniform.

One of the officers asked a police sergeant to show them the Prime Minister's private apartments. They pointed revolvers at him but he refused. Lost among passages and staircases, the officers wandered about, not knowing where to go. Some went upstairs and found the cabinet room empty. A "large man" appeared and they asked to be taken to the Prime Minister, saying they had come from the Naval Academy. Before the "large man" had done anything a group of three or four men appeared from somewhere and ran away when a shot was fired in their direction. Then someone heard a key turning in a lock and an officer shouted: "That must be the way to the private apartments." They knocked. A voice called: "Who is there?" A naval lieutenant burst open the flimsy door with his shoulder and they rushed in.

They found the Prime Minister, Mr. Inukai, a diminutive alert man of seventy-five. His first name was Tsuyoshi but his friends knew him as "Ki." He had been in politics all his life and had at one time led a party of his own called the Kokuminto or Nationalist Party. It did not grow big enough to compete with the major parties, and Inukai finally disbanded it and led his followers into the ranks of the Seiyukai, the more conservative of the

348

two parties which at that time were the alternative ins and outs of Japanese politics. The Seiyukai was looking for a leader; Inukai's age and standing and the "dowry" of voting power that he brought with him got him the post and in due time the Prime Ministership. He was a very small man, quick and fearless. His goatee beard was of a vague gray color which somehow suggested, quite erroneously, that it had once been blond. Late in life he had attained the goal of his ambition and he was intensely proud of being the Emperor's first Minister.

He led the officers into a Japanese room. His daughter-in-law, carrying her baby, was with him, and one of the officers, "knowing what would happen in a few minutes," as he said at the trial, told her to go away, but she stayed. The young men were rather confused and some were impressed by the old man's calm demeanor as he asked them to take off their shoes and sit down and talk it over. He had a cigarette in his hand and he lit it. "As I observed," said one of the officers in his testimony, "our leader was willing to talk with the Prime Minister." The group that had gone to the back door burst in, headed by Lieutenant Masayoshi Yamagishi, a man of action, carrying a dagger.

"No use talking," said Yamagishi. "Fire!" The word was shouted like an order and they all began firing. One shot the Prime Minister in the neck and another, deliberately, in the stomach. The Prime Minister sank on the matted floor and never spoke again. "Believing the whole affair was over," the officers walked out. A policeman armed with a stick challenged them and they shot him. No one else interfered.

They drove on to the Bank of Japan, hurled a grenade at the door, and went to the gendarmerie building, where they surrendered.

A third group of officers had been detailed to destroy the offices of the Seiyukai, the Prime Minister's party. They threw two bombs which did not explode. They went to the Metropolitan Police office and threw three bombs, one of which struck an electric-light pole and shattered a window. Duty done, they proceeded to the gendarmerie headquarters and surrendered. The student who had accompanied the officers to Tsuchiura went to the Mitsubishi Bank and threw a bomb which exploded in the yard. Another conspirator went to the house of Count Makino, Lord Keeper of the Imperial Seals, and flung a grenade at a man who happened to be standing at the front door. It missed him.

That evening the official residence of the War Minister was the scene of an incident which was rigidly censored. The War Minister, General Sadao Araki, was out of town. His colleague, General Jinsaburo Mazaki, Vice-Chief of the General Staff, who, like Araki, sympathized with the young officers, hurried to the War Minister's headquarters when he heard of the murder and the attacks on the police headquarters and the Bank of Japan. Many senior officers had already assembled; talk was excited and confused. Some thought the incident merely an escapade by headstrong young men; others saw it as the prelude to revolt.

Several young officers in uniform came from their barracks in Tokyo demanding audience with the War Minister. Mazaki received them. They said they had come to ask the War Minister to rise. "Our comrades are ready all over the country. They expect action. We must rise today."

General Mazaki replied: "The War Minister will not rise. We should not rise. That is General Araki's opinion and mine too."

Mazaki told them to keep cool heads. He reminded them that in the Satsuma revolt of 1877 the nation had been expected to support the rebels, but did not.

Messages sent to newspapers abroad that night said the Prime Minister had been shot by "men wearing officers' uniform." The correspondents and the public were unwilling to believe that officers of the army and navy had taken to political murder. The affair looked like a murderous prank by bloody-minded boy scouts carrying pistols and grenades instead of clasp knives and whistles. Its amateurishness seemed to prove that the movement was confined to a few young fanatics. The public soon recovered its confidence in the discipline and loyalty of the army. Actually the army was honeycombed with political agitation.

The murder of Prime Minister Inukai was the third political crime committed that spring. On the evening of February 9, as the Finance Minister, Junnosuke Inouye, was entering a hall in the suburbs of Tokyo to address a political meeting, he was shot dead by a country youth of twenty-two. Four weeks later Baron Takuma Dan, managing director of the holding company which controls the enterprises of the immense Mitsui corporation, was killed at his office door by another country youth aged twenty-one.

A significant trinity had fallen—banker, capitalist, politician—each victim the highest representative of a class. The killings of Finance Minister Inouye and Baron Takuma Dan were isolated events, complete in themselves. The murder of the Prime Minister was accompanied by actions which constituted a "token" revolution. The attacks on banks, party offices, and police headquarters have already been described. In the evening, after the officers had surrendered, a band of civilians from the country bombed the powerhouses of Tokyo and its suburbs in an effort to throw the capital into darkness. The attack was badly planned, feebly executed, and completely futile. The raiders were the principal and some students of the Native-Land-Loving School, already referred to. Some of them had drunk blood with the brotherhood which killed Inouye and Takuma Dan.

All the crimes were part of a single plan. The murders were intended to strike terror into the governing and possessing classes, and the raids on powerhouses and banks and police headquarters were to create such confusion that martial law would be proclaimed. Some of the young officers thought martial law the same thing as military government. They believed that if they created an opportunity the army would use it to bring about what they called a second restoration, taking power from the politicians and the capitalists and returning it to the Emperor, who would thereupon

350

entrust it to faithful soldiers and patriots. But all this did not come out until the public trials were held a year later.

MAY 4, 1932: *A truce was signed between China and Japan, and the Japanese evacuated Shanghai.*

AUGUST 21: *Hostilities were renewed when the Japanese invaded Jehol.*

OCTOBER 10: *The Chinese failed in their attempts to overthrow the Japanese hold in Manchukuo.*

MARCH 27, 1933: *Japan withdrew from the League of Nations.*

JUNE 2: *North China was declared an independent state by the Japanese, after it had been a neutral state through the treason of a few Chinese generals.*

MARCH 1, 1934: *Henry Pu-Yi, last Manchu Emperor of China, and newly appointed puppet ruler of Manchukuo, was made Emperor of Manchukuo by the Japanese, with the title Kang-Teh.*

NOVEMBER 27, 1935: *Japan invaded the region of Peiping warning Great Britain not to interfere. The Chinese Government moved to Nanking.*

DECEMBER 1: *A pro-Tokyo state was formed in China, with the alleged aid of the Nanking Government.*

\* \* \*

TOKYO, Dec. 13, 1936 (Associated Press): Generalissimo Chiang Kai-shek, hitherto all-powerful military and administrative head of the Chinese state, was a prisoner today at Sian-Fu, capital of Shensi province, of mutinous troops commanded by Marshal Chang Hsiao-Liang, one-time warlord of Manchuria....

\* \* \*

JULY 7, 1937: *Initial clashes took place between Japanese and Chinese at the Lukoukaio road.*

# HELL IN SHANGHAI

## *by Carroll Alcott*

HELL broke loose in Shanghai on the second afternoon of war, August 14, 1937. It started when Chinese pilots from Nanking attempted to bomb the flagship of the Japanese China Seas Fleet, the *Idzumo*, a ten-thousand-ton cruiser tied up in the Whangpoo River directly opposite the Japanese

351

Consulate. Anti-aircraft fire from the ship not only drove the Chinese away but hit the bomb racks on one of the planes. Four 250-pound demolition bombs were loosened. Unaware of the damage to his bomb racks, and apparently frightened, the pilot turned his plane at an altitude of about fifteen hundred feet and flew over the International Settlement.

Two bombs, jarred completely loose from their fastenings, dropped on Nanking Road. One hit the Palace Hotel, the other the street. Nanking Road was packed with thousands of Chinese refugees from the nearby hinterlands, and so unexpected was the bombing that none of them had time to scatter into the shelter of nearby sidestreets and buildings. When the smoke had cleared away, almost three thousand dead and wounded were piled in heaps on the pavement.

It was a bloody tangle of bodies that had been blown to bits. Heads, torsos, legs, and arms were scattered about. Men and women were blown from the street through the windows of the fifth and six floors of the Cathay Hotel. The lobby of the Palace Hotel across the street was filled with wounded and dying people. Just by luck, my wife and daughter were in the part of the hotel that faced the waterfront, and rooms there were not damaged.

Less than a minute later, one mile away in front of the Great World Amusement Resort on Avenue Edward VII, the thoroughfare separating the French Concession from the International Settlement, the other two bombs on the broken rack came loose and dropped. Approximately two thousand more dead and wounded were piled in the streets.

The exact number of casualties resulting from both bombings may never be known. There were too many mangled bodies to allow for an accurate count. But when the police had completed their job of checking those killed instantly and those who subsequently died of their wounds, it was found that the four bombs had accounted for about four thousand lives.

Even after five years I still have nightmares resulting from what I saw on Nanking Road and Avenue Edward VII. Though death in its most violent forms is nothing new to me, I sometimes wake from my sleep in a cold sweat, with the moans of hundreds of dying Chinese men and women ringing in my head. Photographed on my mind are the bleeding bodies and limbs of the dead being tossed into police vans and trucks as though they had just come out of an abattoir.

Especially vivid is the recollection of picking my rickshaw coolie out of a shop window into which he had been thrown as the bombs hit the hotel district. He was pulling me across Nanking Road on Szechuen Road, less than a block from the scene of death. Concussion tossed me from my seat and hurled me a good twenty feet through the air to the pavement. We were both badly shaken, but no more by our fall than by the devastation that lay before us.

\* \* \*

SHANGHAI, Dec. 13, 1937 (International News Service): . . . Most of the 54 known survivors of the United States gunboat *Panay* and three Standard-

Vacuum oil tankers, destroyed by Japanese bombs, were safe aboard the British patrol boat H. M. S. *Bee* tonight.

SHANGHAI, Dec. 14 (International News Service): ... Covered by small "dare-to-die" bands of suicidal troops, General Tang Shen-Si today led his defeated army of 300,000 out of Nanking.

* * *

# FALL OF NANKING

## by A. T. Steele

NANKING (via the U. S. S. *Oahu*), Dec. 15.—"Four days in hell" would be the most fitting way to describe the siege and capture of Nanking.

I have just boarded the gunboat *Oahu* with the first group of foreigners to leave the capital since the attack began. The last thing we saw as we left the city was a band of 300 Chinese being methodically executed before the wall near the waterfront, where already corpses were piled knee deep.

It was a characteristic picture of the mad Nanking scene of the last few days.

The story of Nanking's fall is a story of indescribable panic and confusion among the entrapped Chinese defenders, followed by a reign of terror by the conquering army which cost thousands of lives, many of them innocent ones.

While the behavior of the Chinese before the city's abandonment was deplorable in many ways, it was mild compared to the excesses of the invading force.

All foreigners in Nanking are safe.

Japanese brutality at Nanking is costing them a golden opportunity to win the sympathy of the Chinese population, whose friendship they claim to be seeking.

After the complete collapse of Chinese morale and the blind panic which followed, Nanking experienced a distant sense of release when the Japanese entered, feeling that the behavior of the Japanese could not possibly be worse than that of their own defeated army. They were quickly disillusioned.

The Japanese could have completed the occupation of the remainder of the city almost without firing a shot, by offering mercy to the trapped Chinese soldiers, most of whom had discarded their arms and would surrender. However, they chose the course of systematic extermination.

It was like killing sheep. How many troops were trapped and killed it is difficult to estimate, but it may be anywhere between 5,000 and 20,000.

With the overland routes cut off, the Chinese swarmed to the river through the Ksiakwan gate, which became quickly choked. Emerging via this gate today I found it necessary to drive my car over heaps of bodies

353

five feet high, over which hundreds of Japanese trucks and guns had already passed.

Streets throughout the city were littered with the bodies of civilians and abandoned Chinese equipment and uniforms. Many troops who were unable to obtain boats across the river leaped into the river to almost certain death.

Japanese looting made the Chinese looting, which had preceded it, look like a Sunday school picnic. They invaded foreign properties, among them the residence of the American ambassador, Nelson T. Johnson.

In the American-operated University Hospital they relieved the nurses of watches and money. They stole at least two American-owned cars, ripping off the flags. They even invaded the camps of refugees, stripping many poor of the few dollars they owned.

This account is based on the observations of myself and other foreigners remaining in Nanking throughout the siege.

JAN. 11, 1938: *Japanese sailors took Tsingtao, a Shantung seaport in North China.*

JANUARY 12: *Japan refused to divulge her battleship building plans, in response to a note from the United States and France.*

OCTOBER 21: *Canton fell.*

OCTOBER 25: *Hankow fell.*

# THE GREAT MIGRATION

## *by Jerome Beatty*

DECEMBER, 1938—China's non-military population has turned about face and in an extraordinary migration is marching Southwest carrying tools, typewriters and textbooks past troops and munitions on their way to the front—to build with American culture and industrial methods a new, streamlined nation in hinterlands inhabited by people often as backward as the blacks Livingstone found in the heart of Africa.

The provinces of Yunnan, Szechuan, Hunan, Sikang, Kwangsi and Kweichow, one-sixth of old China, are just funny names to you and me, but to the Chinese and their mostly American-educated leaders, they make up a promised land with an area about equal to the British Isles, Belgium, the Netherlands, France, Germany, Switzerland and Italy combined. The Japanese are in only a very small part of it.

China has lost the best of its country. Under Japanese control are its Northern and Eastern provinces, its largest cities, all its seaports, its best public buildings, businesses, railroads, waterways and highways, 90 per cent of its industrial plants, much of its minerals and productive land. For two years it has been moving out as the Japanese shells came tearing in.

Unlike America's movement west, it is not agricultural. It is an orderly and directed migration of millions of city folks—bankers, stenographers, coolies, teachers, street sweepers, dentists, storekeepers, mechanics, lawyers. They go in boats, on trains, on foot, in rickshas, in motor cars, trucks and buses, struggling over mountain trails, sometimes dodging bombs and bullets from Japanese planes, carrying a crushing load of all they own, to set up shop in a new land. The government, which has spent more than a million dollars for such transport, moved 3,853,682 in the last six months of 1938. That's a small part of the total.

They've shipped more than 350 factories, 75,000 tons of machinery and office appliances, piece by piece, by boat, by truck and in rickshas. Universities and libraries have been moved, books, test tubes, microscopes and blackboards—when any were left after Japanese attack—sometimes carried by hand. They believe a university is its faculty, not its buildings or its athletic teams, and teachers and students, bombed out, have traveled hundreds of miles and are carrying on effectively in any buildings they can find. When one university moved from Changsha to Kunming, in Yunnan, 304 students and 11 members of the faculty hadn't money enough to ride. So they walked, more than a thousand weary miles over mountains, through sand and slush. There was some grumbling—not because they were hungry and their feet were blistered, but because they were losing seventy days of study.

The Chinese government had hoped to move the farmers, too, and when a survey showed that in the back of supposedly terribly over-populated China lay 63,000,000 uncultivated acres, it set aside 4,000,000 acres of good land as a starter and offered to lend money to 300,000 families, if they would move out of the areas occupied by the Japanese, and produce food for China. It turned out that the Chinese farmer won't leave his land, no matter how it is torn by shells, no matter whose flag flies over him.

The migration is jamming Chungking, the present capital, Chengtu and other centers of the Southwest, but the most important feature of the exodus has been the discovery and development of Yunnan and its little antique, walled capital, Kunming, once known as Yunnanfu, the city farthest from China's former seat of government, Peiping.

Yunnan is that country over near Mandalay that the dawn comes up like thunder out of. It touches Tibet, Burma and French Indo-China and except for the long road to Russia is now the only door to China not in Japanese hands. It is a hidden paradise whose 12,000,000 primitive people, until a year or so ago, had advanced little since Marco Polo visited them in 1283. Its governor is a war lord who elected himself ten years ago with machine guns and an army of mercenaries and who can read and write pretty well.

Until war came to China, Rudyard Kipling, intrepid explorers in search of the giant panda and a few Frenchmen from French Indo-China were about the only folks who paid any attention to Yunnan. The French built a not-bad little hotel in Kunming and traded with the Chinese, but the natives of Yunnan have no use for foreigners and instead of the Chinese adopting French ways, the French became Chinese-like and many learned to use opium.

Kunming's only connections with foreign lands were the old Ambassador's Road, a narrow, dangerous mountain trail, forty days by pack horse, west to Mandalay, and a slow French railroad south to Indo-China, that ran a sleeping car once a week, each way. Kunming is 6,500 feet high, surrounded by mountains and the railroad goes through 155 tunnels in the 296 miles to the border. More than 12,000 Chinese and several hundred Frenchmen died on the eight-year job of getting the railroad through those mountains. Although it has been bombed by Japanese planes, Kunming is about the safest city in Chinese territory.

Today Kunming is a boom town. Its population, once less than 50,000, has increased from 100,000 to 250,000 in the last year. In mobs that remind you of Coney Island on a boiling Sunday, day and night folks from the East pour in. Hundreds sleep in alleys and sheds. Back along the way, millions have settled, almost always under government orders.

Kunming's rough, stone-block streets are full of trucks and passenger cars, still so strange that when a driver stops to change a tire, traffic is blocked by a mass of rickshas, pack horses and dilapidated Chinese who fight to get a look. There are new traffic police and stop lights. Neither does much good, for the coolies don't get the idea and the police, unaccustomed to gasoline fumes, are so busy holding handkerchiefs to their noses they can't always make the proper signs.

The smoke of new factories rises toward swarms of airplanes from the Government training school. The cost of living is soaring. New residents can't get a house and if they could they'd have to pay $15 a month (American) for a good one, instead of $5, which was the price a year ago. Modern stores are being opened, a movie theater and hotels with rooms with bath are planned. They may even get running water in the American Consulate. It is as though a fragment of modern New York suddenly had dropped into the ancient camp of Sitting Bull. Most of the Chinese residents, who were perfectly happy in their lazy, backward existence, are thoroughly disgusted with the whole nerve-wracking business and wish that civilization never had been invented.

In Kunming are the Americans who are helping China in aviation. There is China's airplane factory, bombed out of a hideout near Canton, directed by Charles Day, a veteran in aviation engineering. Major Claire Chennault, retired U. S. A. aviation officer, heads China's flying school, now at Kunming. He is assisted by 12 American flyers and turns out 150 Chinese aviators, ready for war, every six months. Hidden near Burma, headed by Americans, a Curtiss-Wright factory is building, to make war planes for China. The aviators who fly the Generalissimo and Madame Chiang are

Americans, as are the pilots on one of the two regular airlines, which is partly owned by Pan-American Airways. The other line is partly German owned. No American is in any combat unit, but they all constantly are in danger from Japanese attack. They went over in a gay spirit of adventure and signed long-term contracts at excellent salaries. Most of them are gay no longer and wish they could go home. One recently announced he was through risking his life, and quit. Two weeks after he arrived in America he was killed near Seattle while testing a plane that fell apart in the air.

Kunming is destined to be one of the great cities of the Far East, China's front door, playing the part of an inland Shanghai and Canton—at least until the war ends. Outside the city, thousands of men, women and children are working on new railroads to the West and Northeast. One of these days, travelers from Europe will disembark at Rangoon and go chugety-chug over mountains on a railroad, built by a Purdue man, to Kunming and on to the Yangtze and Shanghai. Today, if you don't mind being blocked in mountain passes by American-made trucks carrying war supplies, panting in the high altitudes, backing and filling to go around the turns, you can drive in five days from Burma to Kunming over an amazing road, just completed, following generally the Old Ambassador's Road. More than 300,000 conscripted men, women and children who never had seen a motor car until the road was opened, built 700 miles of highway in less than twelve months without the aid of one piece of mechanical equipment—not even a wheelbarrow.

The highway to Chungking and the roundabout road to Haiphong, the Indo-China seaport through which come most of the goods, have been improved and are packed with motor cars, horses and pedestrians. The French railroad has pepped up its service and brings trainloads of freight each day, and the sleeping car, filled to overflowing, runs twice a week, each way. Airlines connect Kunming with Indo-China and with Chungking, meeting planes to Hong Kong. An airline direct to Rangoon and to Hong Kong soon will be operating. The Japanese now and then shoot down a passenger plane but nobody except me seemed to worry about that.

Amid this surge of modern transport Old China still operates effectively. Over the ancient 400-mile opium trail from Kunming to Suifu on the Yangtze, directed by a former graduate of the University of Pennsylvania, 50,000 coolies and 15,000 of those little Chinese horses constantly are on the march, going 30 miles a day. A man carries the same load as a horse—a case of munitions or five five-gallon cans of gasoline—from Kunming toward the war areas, returning with tung oil, used in making paint, to be shipped to America to pay for them.

Kunming is the only city in the Southwest in which investors are risking much money in new buildings. They fear neither Japanese invasion nor a collapse of the boom. Some predict the city will replace Chungking as China's capital. A University of Michigan man is promoting a typically American real estate development, with club house, playgrounds, school and hospital, outside the city.

357

Long lines of trucks bring through Kunming goods from other factories, probably even more important, that the Chinese won't tell you about. They're secluded all over the Southwest, some in huge caves. The Chinese, rightfully, are very spy-conscious. They won't tell much. Picture-taking is forbidden.

Yunnan's governor has a right-hand man—Y. T. Miao, graduate of the University of Minnesota, 1917. He is head of the provincial bank, one of the owners of vast tin mines in Yunnan, and the most powerful man in the province. Mr. Miao, whose ancestors were wild tribesmen in the hills, is president of the newly-organized Rotary Club of Kunming of which 26 of its 32 members are graduates of American universities. They're not entirely Americanized yet. They eat solemnly with chopsticks and wear no badges and sing no songs. Mr. Miao also is president of the American Returned Students Club. There were eleven in Kunming a year ago. Today there are 400. When you find yourself lost in Kunming, unable to tell your ricksha man where to go, you sit and wait. In a few minutes along will come a Chinese in Western dress, probably wearing a Phi Beta Kappa key, and carrying a slide rule, who not only will help you out but probably will insist upon taking you down to the Kunming Café where you'll eat a hamburger and lemon pie and discuss your mutual friends in America. They're very proud of their American education, these Chinese. On their calling cards, under their names, often is the name of their university and their degrees— in Chinese on one side, in English on the other.

Kunming has taken more refugee universities than it can comfortably house. More than 5,000 students, men and women, and hundreds of faculty members—80 per cent American-educated—have moved there. Southwest Associated University, the largest and most important in China, made up of three great universities that fled from Peiping, is in Kunming. The National Sun Yat-sen University, with 2,000 students, driven out of Canton and looking for a home, hopes to settle there. National Tung Chi University, its $10,000,000 plant completely destroyed in Shanghai, moved twice before finally going to Kunming with nearly 2,000 students who are studying medicine, engineering and science. A medical school from Shanghai and one from Nanchang, with 600 students, are there turning out doctors for war work. Five missionary colleges, bombed out, have combined in Central China College, established in Yunnan, 370 miles out on the Burma road.

The National Library of Peiping, when it moved to Kunming, with thirty of its staff, was forced to abandon most of its books, but brought more than 10,000 that would be needed by the universities and scholars. The librarian is a Columbia graduate. The library has all the important foreign scientific and technical journals and files of popular newspapers and magazines, which usually arrive about two months after publication. For historians it is gathering everything written about the war, including Japanese propaganda. For those who will direct China's rehabilitation it has a collection of literature telling how other nations rebuilt, after their wars. As soon as arrangements can be made properly to house them, the treasures from the Palace Museum at Peiping, now hidden throughout China, will be collected in Kunming.

The Chinese say the movement Southwest is primarily a temporary expedient, that they will win the war some day and many of the folks will move back. Maybe they are right, for it's going to be difficult to conquer a nation of shifty bulldogs. But even if China loses, the war has had great compensations—it has united China and advanced by hundreds of years its vast, unexplored back country.

# BURMA ROAD

## by Vanya Oakes

THE Chinese have a traditional phrase, "There is a thing to be done." Machinery must be moved from Hankow; dugouts blasted in Chungking; new industries started; the Burma Road built. And so—the thing which was to be done, was done.

The major activity in West China centered, of course, around the Burma Road—getting it built and under operation, then keeping it open. It was done in the typical Chinese manner. A vast clamor of chaos, out of which you would swear nothing as utilitarian as a major highway could emerge in a hundred years. As late as the autumn of 1938 I would have sworn that the Burma Road would always be as much of a myth as Shangri-La. Yet, along about Christmas, people began straggling in over it. By the time I myself went over it in May, 1939, there was regular traffic and, until the Japanese closed it up from the Burma end, the estimate of its regular flow was four hundred trucks a day. "There is a thing to be done" had certainly taken tangible form. There was a road to be hewn out of mountains. And so—it had been done. Panegyrics have been written about that seven-hundred-dred-mile stretch, over mountains averaging seven thousand feet high, some even two or three thousand feet higher. But the fact is that the Road will always be one of the wonders of the world. At the much fought-over Salween River it drops forty-five hundred feet, rising immediately forty-five hundred feet on the other side. Nature is extravagant in China; when the plains stretch, they stretch endlessly; the green of the rice fields is the greenest green in the whole world; when the mountains rise, they do not rise gradually, but rocket skyward, five, eight, ten thousand feet in a few miles.

The Burma Road brought into being a new breed—the Burma Road truck-drivers. From the beginning they have suffered from a very bad reputation—undeservedly, it seems to me. Thieves, ruffians, devils, maniacs —versed, it was said, in sins too devious to be comprehended by the average human being. On the contrary, they are actually the unsung heroes of China.

Certainly they were reckless, tough. But here was road so savage that only the savage could understand it. Like all savages their vulnerability had a certain ludicrousness. I went over the road twice, and I constantly observed the drivers as a group, around the terminus which was Kunming. I saw them under conditions calculated to test the iron in men's souls, and the only time I ever saw the Burma Road drivers completely out of self-control was over—the theft of their shoes.

They had not the slightest objection to driving steadily from 6 A.M. to 10 P.M. in the pouring rain along a road from which at any second they might easily tumble three or four thousand feet over a side.

The crime oftenest cited against the truck-drivers was "squeeze." It was certainly no secret that the drivers did indulge in squeeze. Nor was it any secret to fair-minded observers that they were justified. There was, indeed, a very simple reason, an economic reason purely, for which, in the West, we have the high-sounding name Inflation. All over China prices were going up, owing to the war, and the truck-drivers, who risked their necks every day for something between ten and twenty dollars a month, simply resorted to squeeze as a means of bringing their income more into proportion to what it cost them to stay alive so they could drive the trucks at all! If it had not been for the Burma Road and its drivers, after the Indo-China Railway was closed in June, 1940, there simply would not have been equipment sufficient to keep the Chinese troops in there pitching. Squeeze seemed, thus, a pretty niggardly price to pay.

My first trip over the road in May, 1939, just after it had been opened to traffic, was what might be termed an erratic expedition. Several cars consigned to government officials up in Chungking were being dispatched in convoy from Rangoon, and I hooked a ride, so to speak. In the crowd was a contingent of volunteer drivers from Singapore, on their way to the training school established by T. L. Soong. They were apportioned among the convoy, a pair to a car.

As had the Great Wall of China, the Burma Road had been built solely by the hands of millions of Chinese, using implements no more modern than the pickaxe. All along the way the Government had simply conscripted the villagers wholesale—men, women, and children. The younger, able-bodied men scurried up and sliced hunks out of the mountains while the women and older men hammered out the boulders down below. The really old folk and the children would then break the boulders into small chips and pound them into the surface of the road. This was the basic technique by which the Road had been wrenched from the mountains. Naturally there was room for improvement; the sort of improvement a steam roller, for instance, could provide.

A steam roller had been brought in sections to the yard of the Southwestern Transportation Company. It had finally been assembled and there it stood, all bright red and green and shining. I arrived on the spot just when it was due for its trial run.

360

The gates of the yard were opened. Outside the entire village had collected. The driver got things going and the contraption began groaning and chugging, giving off clouds of steam. The villagers gaped anxiously. Snorting and growling, the steam roller lumbered toward the gate.

Panic seized the villagers. "Mogui! Mogui!" they began screeching. Evil spirits! Evil spirits! The red-and-green thing was a new species of evil dragon, come to destroy the village. Everyone knew that dragons were always red and green.

In mere seconds the crowd vanished into thin air, leaving not a soul in sight to witness the triumph of mechanical ingenuity of the West. The doors and windows of every house in the village were slapped shut, and every villager was indoors, absolutely quiet, so the evil spirits would not get at them to steal away the children.

After a few hours things quieted down and surreptitiously life reassumed its round. We all thought that the incident of the red-and-green dragon was closed.

But a few days later genuine disaster descended on the village. Probably paid by Japanese agents, tribesmen from the hills suddenly swooped down in the night and killed about twenty or so of the Chinese customs employees. The villagers were up in arms at once. Making a great to-do they threatened to kill the entire staff of the Southwestern Transportation Company immediately if the cause of all this woe—the steam roller, the red-and-green dragon—were not disposed of at once.

The swaba of the district took a hand. . . . A swaba is not quite as elevated as a feudal princeling, yet he is something more than a tribal chieftain. This swaba had been to Peking to school for a few years and had brought back with him—in addition to an amazing collection of chromium furniture and a liking for cocktails and American coffee—the realization that there was a bigger unit than merely his own small preserves, a vague conception of China as a nation. . . . He came and personally guaranteed that the steam roller had no evil intentions.

This swaba of Mangshih was the Number 1 fixer in many a difficult situation during the months of adjustment. He made his two Western-style houses not only a hostel for itinerants like myself but a center for many constructive activities. His methods were curiously similar to those of the Beetle, and some of us took to referring to him as Beetle Number 2. To the swaba of Mangshih a debt is owed for his service in the actual building of the Burma Road and for helping to maintain a working order afterward; and, as a result, for the maintenance of Chinese resistance.

* * *

SHANGHAI, Sept. 16, 1939 (United Press): A Japanese army spokesman announced today that hostilities between Soviet and Japanese forces on the Manchu-Mongol border ceased at 1 P.M. today. A Japanese-Russian truce was agreed on yesterday.

# RUSSO-JAPANESE CLASH

## by Relman Morin

IT could happen at any moment. Just the year before [1939] I had gone into Mongolia because of a clash between the Far Eastern Red Army and the Japanese. Officially it was just another "border incident." Japanese and Russian army patrols were forever exchanging shots along the ephemeral boundary between Siberia and the adjacent Japanese territories. Usually they passed off with a few volleys. But this one in 1939 had contained some political inferences that made it more important. Some Mongol sheepmen, nomads, had driven their flocks across from the Soviet side into grazing land that presumably belonged to other Mongols under Japanese protection. Both Japan and Russia were bidding for Mongol sympathy then, and still are, cozening, edulcorating, and posing as protectors. So the Japanese had detailed units of the crack Kyantung army to help their Mongols expel the Soviet Mongols, and in a few days a full-scale war had developed.

The Russians were magnificent. They gave the Japanese one of the most thorough and complete defeats any army has ever suffered. In one operation they tricked the Japanese into chasing them into a horseshoe-shaped bit of terrain, surrounded on three sides by foothills. Concealed in the hills, their artillery waited. As the Japanese came howling down in pursuit, the Russians pumped shells in from three sides. In the whole incident the Japanese lost around 50,000 killed and wounded. They also lost face, terribly, in the eyes of the Mongols, and that, for an Oriental, was even more serious than the 50,000 casualties.

Having been behind the Japanese lines, I had not seen much of the Far Eastern Red Army. I saw its handiwork, masses of Japanese dead, piled up for burning and destined for those little white boxes that they present to the families, and the smashed artillery and the ugly, gutted skeletons of trucks and supply trains. But I never was close enough to see the Red Army, itself.

These battles, however, tended to confirm a story we all had heard: namely, that Moscow, for years, had been developing a Far Eastern army to be used against Japan alone. It had been built to fight as a separate unit, independently of European Russia. It had its own bases in Siberia, its own arsenals of supply, almost as though it was the army of another country, four thousand miles from Moscow. Presumably it would be held intact, no matter what happened in European Russia; no units would be withdrawn. Two of the greatest Red soldiers, Voroshilov and Tukachevsky, had had a hand in organizing it.

That was the story. There was no opportunity to verify it from where I sat during those lovely bloody autumn days in Mongolia. Only one thing was certain: Japan's best army had received a thorough and terrible beating.

On my last day at the front—the last day they let me stay—I had come back to Hailar, a desolate village on the railroad. I had left my bags in a geisha house there. A Japanese secretary from the Embassy in Hsingking, assigned to "help" me at the front, had led the way to the geisha house when we first arrived in Hailar. There was no other place to stay. We returned now and I went to take a bath. A Japanese bath is a two-act routine. First you sluice off with buckets of hot water, cover yourself with soap, and then wash off the soap. Then you go into the next room to a large pool, almost big enough for swimming, and sit there and soak.

I was up to my chin in the big pool when one of the geisha entered. She was nude, having just finished the first half of the bath. Having seen me with the Japanese secretary several days before, she was not surprised, and she certainly was not embarrassed. (Japanese saying: "In Japan nakedness is seen but not looked at.") We greeted each other and she stepped into the pool with a luxurious sigh. Very soon two more of the girls came in, and finally all seventeen were there. It was their afternoon bath hour. We talked about the war and the weather and it was a very nice bath indeed. I still think the shower is an institution of the uncivilized.

And then, in that same month, Russia and Germany had entered into a non-aggression pact. Ostensibly, it removed all threat to Russia's western border and left her free for whatever might come in the Far East. Japan had to consider that. Likewise, she would have to take into account the terrible efficiency of the Siberian army. That one defeat, of course, would not necessarily deter the Japanese from trying again. They do not give up easily.

# CHINESE GUERRILLAS

## by Agnes Smedley

BY November 9, 1939 I had entered the fringe of the guerrilla region along the southern shores of the lower Yangtze. A party of some twenty of us, including many students from Shanghai and printers and students from Hankow, floated on bamboo rafts down a river approaching the Yangtze.

Narrow paths wound along the mountain sides, and a platoon of New Fourth Army guerrillas, our bodyguards, marched jauntily along them, shouting across the river to one another or to the soldiers who sat on the prow of each raft with rifles ready. No one in our party understood the guerrillas, for they spoke the Fukien dialect. Once I asked a man sitting on the raft behind me what they were singing. He told me it was the *Guerrilla Marching Song,* celebrating their comrades, the flying troops who "feared neither towering mountains nor deep waters."

Instead of the dark, dreary institutions which I had expected, the New Fourth Army had the beginnings of the first modern medical service of any Chinese army. The Rear Base Hospital for the severely wounded, like the field hospital near general headquarters some twenty-five miles nearer the Yangtze, had a system modeled on the best Western hospitals. Whenever medical workers and supplies permitted, the system was being extended to the fighting detachments in the field.

This medical service was the achievement of General Yeh Ting, commander of the New Fourth Army. He, along with Dr. Sheng, had first induced eleven qualified doctors and twenty trained nurses to join the Army. Finding it increasingly difficult to get more, they hoped to found a medical training school to train hundreds of educated youth as sanitary workers for the companies in the field.

This Rear Base Hospital, located in the village of Hsiao Hokuo, was also the supply center for the entire Army, some of whose fighting units were two or three weeks' marching distance down the Yangtze. The hospital wards and living-quarters of the staff were in great stone ancestral temples. Their exterior walls were painted to match the earth, the interiors whitewashed, and the earthen or stone floors sprinkled with lime. Carpenters and tinsmiths had modeled and constructed every conceivable kind of equipment for the wards, laboratory, dispensary, and operating-theater. They had constructed wooden boxes, each capable of carrying thirty pounds of medical supplies; a man could carry two, one slung at each end of a bamboo pole. Army trucks gathered empty gasoline tins along the highways of the rear, and from these the tinsmiths manufactured equipment, including containers for salves. For medicine which could not be transported in metal containers, carpenters had even manufactured bottles from bamboo.

Organically connected with the civilian population as it was, the New Fourth Army, like the Eighth Route, opened its medical service to civilians without charge. By December 1938 the two rear base hospitals had given treatment to 35,000 civilians. There was no other public medical service in the war zones of the lower Yangtze and most of its supplies had been donated by Chinese people's organizations, the Red Cross Medical Corps, and individuals.

The Political Department of the New Fourth Army permeated all branches of the Army and anti-Japanese people's organizations and constituted a kind of revolutionary educational system. This work extended to the Army hospitals; neither the Eighth Route nor the New Fourth Army surrendered any of their wounded to the hospitals of the Army Medical Administration of the Ministry of War. The chief reason was that they wished to prevent the disintegration of the Army's man-power and hoped to continue their revolutionary training.

It was this system, and the Marxian political theory in which it was rooted, that bred charges against these armies and, in later years, again brought the country to the brink of civil war. Charges that the armies did not fight were simply untrue; they fought the Japanese bravely, but rejected the Kuomintang political system. . . .

We had walked since dawn—up jagged mountains, across the floor of valleys, along narrow paths where no animal could go. We rested in villages whose streets were bordered by open gutters filled with the green scum that bred disease, and where people came in crowds, pleading for medicine. Their bodies were a mass of scabies scores and the hair of the women was matted and wild. The heads of the children were covered with boils or the creeping ringworm that destroys even the roots of the hair. In the summer there had been cholera, and in the winter smallpox would come. And everywhere there was trachoma, malaria, dysentery.

Once we crossed a motor highway along which Japanese trucks dared to venture from time to time. In the afternoon we stood on the crest of a high mountain range and looked down on glory. Below us lay a natural basin of gold with a long azure lake reflecting the azure sky. Fields of ripe grain gleamed like liquid gold. A few small white villages, set in green foliage, sparkled like jewels, and above and about this vision towered black volcanic peaks.

"Our hospital is in that temple," one of our guards said, pointing.

An hour later we were walking through the basin toward the temple. It had roofs of colored tile and upturned corners and it was shadowed by ancient gnarled trees. On the paths in front of the temple stood lines of men in faded blue uniforms. Each man was waving a small triangular paper banner of welcome, and as we came in sight they began singing the guerrilla marching song. One of them came down the path to salute us. He saluted with his left hand, his right arm held rigidly against his breast, the fingers stiff and bent like the claws of a bird. His features were finely chiseled and sensitive, his black eyes eager, and the whole expression of his face had a strangely spiritual quality.

He led us up to the rows of men awaiting us, and as we came near I saw that most of them were crippled. Some were on crutches, some were without an arm or a leg, some had stiff legs or arms, and the bones of one man's leg had knit together at an angle. Almost all were maimed for life, yet almost all of them were in their early twenties. A good doctor could have prevented their deformities. Looking into their faces, I saw that they were anemic—obviously from undernourishment and suffering.

That evening I sat around a table with some of these men. Facing me was the man with the strangely beautiful face. In answer to my questions he told me that he was Chen Fang-chuen; he was twenty-six years old and had been in this Army since the fall of Nanking. Before joining the Army he had been a poor peasant, unable to read or write. Once in the Army, he had always been at the front and had been wounded three times. In the hospital he had found only other wounded men like himself and had been unable to learn. Now the wounded had some textbooks and were asking one another about the words. They had tried to learn a few each day, but never knew whether they were right because there was no educated man among them.

"How did you get that stiff arm, and that hand?" I asked.

365

"One night in a drizzling rain," he began, "our commander said we were to attack the enemy coming from Hweiyuan. The news passed into our hearts and the hearts of the people so that we all forgot the bad weather. It was the 10th of August. Our commander said: 'Wherever we go, victory will follow. The enemy from Hweiyuan city has sent a column against us. With them they have a hundred puppet troops led by a traitor. They will have one heavy machine-gun and three light machine-guns, rifles, hand-grenades. They think they can surround us before daybreak and attack us at dawn. But their movements are always slow. They will have to start marching at two or three in the morning. We must keep them marching all day in the heat before we give them a welcome. Now, tonight we and all the *lao pei hsing* (people) in Chungchuan will move to Sunyingtze. The Imperial Army will have to pardon us for not being here to receive them. They may feel poorly about that.'

"We all laughed.

"When the enemy came to Chungchuan next morning, there was not a shadow to greet them besides one very old man. They asked him about us, but he said he had never seen us and was so old that he couldn't remember if he had even heard of us. Then they marched on to Sunchaochuang, thinking they might surprise and exterminate us there. We were not there either, so they fired off their guns to make a big noise. They think that scares people. Some of the people then said that we were in another village farther on. It was noon and very hot before the devils reached that village. Sweat was running down their faces and they were tired, but they were ashamed to lose face by going back to Hweiyuan. So they marched on to another village, where they ordered everybody out to a meeting to hear one of them explain how the great Imperial Army had come to protect them from Communist bandits—that means us—and the party Army—that means the Kuomintang. As soon as they had protected the people, they said, they would withdraw.

"Well, the people made them welcome and some of them whispered, as if in secret, that we were at Neuwangmiao. Of course we were not, but when we were told that they were going there, we decided to give them a welcome.

"Our commander picked three of the best platoons, and I was in one of them. We took our three light machine-guns and found good positions along the path leading to Neuwangmiao. Many *lao pei hsing* came to carry away our wounded, and some had spears and big swords.

"The enemy soon came along. By that time they had been marching for about twelve hours. Our machine-guns went rat-a-tat-tat and many of the enemy fell. Some began to run, but some fought, and before long everybody was fighting except the devils who were carrying away the dead and wounded. They all began to retreat and we followed, and soon they began to leave their dead and wounded behind, though they try never to do that. We 'escorted' them for hours, right up to Hweiyuan, and by then there were not many of them left. I did not go so far, for I was wounded;

366

but I heard all about it afterwards. Our Commander had said we ought to escort the devils right up to their barracks."

"That was a warm welcome and a very polite farewell," I remarked with admiration, and the men laughed.

"Now the lessons of this battle were many," the story-teller added, as if quoting from a textbook. "First, a guerrilla unit in a certain place should continue moving to new locations, particularly if close to the enemy. We did that. But our intelligence service was too slow; our reserves could not come up quickly enough to help us exterminate the enemy completely. That was a weakness. Third, after opening fire we did not charge quickly, and many of the enemy escaped. That was also a weakness. Those were the lessons we learned."

# THE DRAGON LICKS HIS WOUNDS

### by Edgar Snow

APRIL, 1940—After thirty-three months of uneven contest, without a real ally in the world, China stubbornly fights on, refusing to admit defeat.

Those months have seen other men and other nations, once thought to be made of far sterner stuff than the amiable Chinaman, disappear from the map. Proud Austria gave up its independence at a wave of Hitler's sword, and Albania succumbed to a squadron of Il Duce's airmen. The Spanish Republic went down at last before the Italo-German guns of Franco. Czechoslovakia, credited with one of Europe's best armies, an impregnable defense line, splendid arsenals, and a well-organized people, lost its birthright by an umbrella at Munich, and in the end did not strike a blow for its freedom. And Poland, formerly considered a military power of some consequence, became another historical memory within a month after Nazi-Soviet invasion. Even Finland, after making her valiant stand, was forced to succumb.

But here is China—ragged, backward, miserably armed, the China which was "not a state but only a geographical expression" according to Tokyo, the China which experts predicted could not last six months against the mechanized forces of Japan—still taking it, nearly three years later! The Dragon has gone down for the count several times since 1937, but always has painfully got to his feet and come back for more. And each licking of his wounds leaves him feeling more certain that the Nips just haven't got what it takes for the knockout blow.

How much longer can China keep it up? Is she nearing the end? Is the undeclared war about to enter a stage of undeclared peace?

I'll tell you a story about a young Chinese engineer I met recently while traveling far in the west. He had just flown to Hong Kong and back, for his first visit "outside" since the war began. He had forgotten, he said, that

367

stores anywhere held so much merchandise. Fascinated, he had spent two days shopping.

"What did you buy?" I asked him.

He took a box from his pocket and opened it before me. "This is the best thing I bought," he grinned. The box contained—of all things—a set of false teeth.

"Not for yourself, surely?"

"Yes," he explained quite seriously. "I don't need them now, but I will in a few years, and I won't be able to get back to Hong Kong till the war is over."

I got the same kind of shock in Shensi, where I found Wu Ch'u-fei, an old friend, at the northwestern headquarters of Chinese Industrial Co-operatives. Mr. Wu, also an engineer, educated in America and trained at a Ford plant, was making plans for a new house. His wife and children were on the coast, and would stay there. But meanwhile Wu was building himself a little house, which he hoped would "last till the war is over," when he could rejoin his family in the south.

That is significant of the spirit of men who are just discovering a new empire in their country, over there beyond the eastern plains now occupied by Japan. During a journey of more than 3,000 miles by plane, truck, ricksha and pony, I interviewed dozens of officials, politicians and generals, and they talked about as you would expect such people at war to talk. But it was the little fellow with a job of work to do, the man with a field to hoe, a machine to run, a school to teach, or a gun to shoot, whose attitude interested me. And I did not find "peace" an obsession with any of them.

With their wonderful genius at adaptation and improvisation, the Chinese appear to have reached a point where war now seems to be the only reality, and the quite-to-be-expected state of affairs. "Living between heaven and earth," the famous Ah Q, of Chinese fiction, always argued, "the superior man cannot avoid a certain amount of unpleasantness." Living between heaven and earth, the Chinese have decided, men cannot avoid a certain amount of war. A dozen years of civil strife merely served as a dress rehearsal to condition many for present hardships, which, except among some wealthy and high officials, are taken as routine.

Once I was a passenger for a weird fortnight on the back of an army truck loaded beyond capacity, as usual, with freight and humanity. Many a Chinese who formerly traveled only in private compartments is now glad to anchor himself to anything propelled by a combustion engine, when the alternative is muleback or foot. On my truck was the demure lily-footed wife of a guerrilla general. Day after day she clung to a mountain of cargo, amidst soldiers and students, like a queen bee lost in a tornado. A hundred times she painfully scaled down the side of the truck on her bound feet, when the driver negotiated a bad stretch, or we had to scatter for an air raid. At night her bed was a couple of boards or the floor of a lousy inn. Yet she never once complained. She gave the impression of having been bouncing on and off trucks all her life.

Chinese morale is all the more remarkable when one realizes the true weakness of the material basis on which it rests. Whether in the end this morale will be enough to sustain China indefinitely remains to be seen. The odds are desperate, as a brief clinical examination will show.

I suggested transport difficulties, and it is here, in X-ray, that one sees China's inner wounds most clearly. Think what it would mean if, in an attack on America, we lost all our railways but the Western Pacific, all our factories east of the Mississippi, all our Navy, merchant shipping and seaports, 70 per cent of our highways and most of our vehicles, and were dependent for oil and supplies mainly on two highways connecting our Western States with Mexico and Canada. Even so, we would still be better off than the Chinese. In a single city like St. Louis we should still have more modern industry than the combined plants in the some 2,000,000 square miles that comprise Free China today.

Across that immense territory there are only about 25,000 kilometers of passable motor roads, but thousands of workmen are adding to them at the rate of seven miles a day. There is but one railway connection with the outer world, the vulnerable line down from mountainous Yunnan to French Indo-China. Over this and the 400-mile trans-Yunnan highway to Burma come well over half of China's necessities, and over them go, in exchange, the tung oil, wolframite, tungsten, tin, tea, hides, bristles and other commodities which China still exports to America and Europe.

A new railway system is being built deep in the interior to connect the Yangtze Valley with the Irrawaddy and the Indian Ocean. But Chiang Chia-ngau, Minister of Communications, told me that even under ideal conditions he cannot hope to realize this ancient dream before 1943.

Airplanes continue to carry passengers in from Burma and Hong Kong, thank heaven and the intrepid American pilots of the China National Aviation Corporation. Forced to resort to blind flying after the Japanese shot down one of their planes near Canton, killing nearly all aboard by machine-gunning, the C. N. A. C. not only maintained its old lines but recently took on new routes when the German Eurasia Company had to discontinue. Airplanes add little, however, to the mobility of the Chinese without position or the price of a ticket.

The ordinary man has another possibility, a ride by truck. There are probably not more than 15,000 navigable trucks and cars on the roads of Free China. Nearly all are American—including Soviet trucks made in American factories in Moscow—and nearly all are recent models. Recent, but not new; for a truck is old in this China after one trip in the interior, and the mortality among yearlings is something fierce. For every truck there are at least five imperative official claims for transport—munitions, troops, medical supplies and wounded, government-trade-monopolies shipments, and industrial demands. After these the list is endless. Last of all come the needs of civilian passengers. Seats in the few real commercial busses are sold out days in advance, while the private car virtually does not exist.

China needs ten times more trucks operating on ten times more roads, but cannot import gasoline fast enough to turn the motors she has. Close to the southern border it is sometimes possible, without convening a plenary session of the Kuomintang and the army, to buy gasoline for ten or twelve Chinese dollars a gallon. Far up in the interior, where fuel is more precious than life, you cannot get it for anything less than a government mandate, and often not for that. On one occasion I pleaded with a couple of generals nearly half a night for ten gallons of gas to fill our empty tank, and only because they were profound gentlemen did I finally get three.

Supplementing inadequate motorization are thousands of mule carts, running on old American automobile wheels and used tires. Even a mule cart costs $1100 Chinese—$1000 for the pair of tires and the wheels, and $100 for the body. But it is cheap compared with the $18,000 for a two-ton truck at Chungking. Horses and mules are insufficient, however, many having been appropriated by the military, and an army of rickshas has been mobilized. I have seen long caravans of them, each man pulling an eighth of a ton of cotton, on a 500-mile trip. Still slower are the thousands of camels, donkeys and human burden-bearers whose calloused backs carry an incredible amount of freight of all kinds.

In the face of transport difficulties alone, it is less remarkable that there is such industrial weakness in independent China than that there is any industry at all. In most towns and cities where the government is now developing new bases, the progress made since the "migration to the west" represents a first introduction to modern industry.

More than 90 per cent of all China's prewar industry was immobilized by the loss of the northern cities and Shanghai, Wusih, Nanking, Hankow and Canton. In Shanghai alone, 5,525 factories and 16,851 workshops were destroyed, seized or immobilized by Japanese occupation. Even before the fall of Canton and Hankow, Japan had already deprived China of 70 per cent of her electrical plants. China's infant iron and steel industry was almost totally obliterated when Japan took over Chinese mines and furnaces in the north and in the Yangtze Valley. Most of the existing chemical industry was lost, featured by Japan's capture, intact, of the government's newly completed 10,000,000-yuan-dollar nitrogen-fixation plant near Nanking. The Chinese could not bear to destroy it!

Production in the cotton-textile industry was reduced by more than 90 per cent. Of fifty-four Chinese silk filatures in Shanghai, only four survived, and 75 per cent of the silk-weaving factories were totally destroyed. Before the war it was estimated that there were some 15,000 machine shops in all China. An industrial expert who recently made a tour through the new government bases told me that there are certainly fewer than 500 machine shops in Free China today.

So it isn't just a question of mending an old fabric but of creating an almost completely new one out of the chaos of war. What a task for even a well-organized state, rich in technique. Naturally enough, the Chinese do not like to stress the magnitude of the problem themselves, but prefer to talk about future plans, so that the casual observer tends to mistake promise for performance. Though many experts have minutely examined Japan's industrial malaise, I don't recall having seen anywhere a true estimate of the profound industrial poverty of what remains of fighting China.

The basic inadequacy is steel. In provinces now under Chungking's control, no high-test steel is produced, not even structural or machine steel of good quality. There is very little steel scrap in the southwest, adjacent to foreign sources, and in Szechwan, the center of China's new industrialization, it can scarcely be bought at all. Lack of it is one reason why Chungking's largest electric blast furnace, with 100-ton capacity, is not yet producing. Local pig-iron output is only slightly more than 100 tons a day. Chungking's only good steel is at present produced by an electric blast furnace with a daily output of four tons.

Other small furnaces scattered in the west produced less than six tons per day in 1939, so that China's total daily production of steel, which could normally be considered suitable for munitions, was probably not much more than 10 tons. Compare this with the 300-ton capacity of China's Lung Yun plant, which the Japanese seized, near Pciping. For a larger headache, compare it with Japan's own steel production—more than 15,000 tons daily.

An American-born Chinese engineer is building a sponge-iron plant in Szechwan, which should soon be producing. It would provide China with her cheapest and most reliable source of good steel, but its capacity is small. Once it is completed, however, the government will duplicate it in many other small works, spread over the country to avoid offering obvious bombing targets.

About the long march of Chinese industry from the coast into the far west much has been written—too much. The government did have schemes for the compulsory removal of plants, but like other "comprehensive plans" —of which much was said prior to 1937—they remained chiefly on paper. Partly due to bureaucratic incompetence, corruption and stupidity, but due also to the peculiar comprador character of Chinese capital, only a handful of industrialists proved willing to move voluntarily or to make large-scale investments in the wild west. On the contrary, millions in capital fled abroad or to the foreign concessions "for the duration."

Credit for what transfer of industry did occur belongs mainly to wee, soft-voiced Weng Wen-hao, world-famous geologist, who alone seemed to have the foresight, integrity and determination to demand that heroic efforts be made to push the stuff inland before it was too late. One of the living forces in a government still cluttered with useless timber, Doctor Weng, now Minister of Economy, has achieved minor miracles, considering the obstacles in his path. By his persistence he has won more battles than most generals.

I shall not forget dropping in on Weng one morning after the Japanese had delivered an enormous parcel of scrap iron—probably American—which wrecked part of his ministry. Still shaken by the event myself—I happened to be knocked down in a dugout fifty yards away—I found this amazing little man at his desk, dressed in pale-lavender-silk pajama pants, quite unperturbed. He did not even mention the ruin around him until I drew attention to the holes in his office walls.

But with all Weng's energy he was able to get only 354 private factories moved to the interior. Quite small plants by western measurement, their total of 63,000 tons of machinery could be lost in a great American steel plant. They included machine shops, electrical-goods and chemical factories, and the majority were miscellaneous light industries. Many are waiting for new power plants to be completed; only about 200 were actually in production early in 1940, and about half of those were in one province—Szechwan.

The remaining industry, with the exception of Chinese Industrial Co-operatives, is largely monopolized by the government, not so much out of choice as because wealthy Chinese, despite huge profits to be made, are only beginning to be lured inland. The government directly owns newly built lead, zinc, tin-smelting, machine-manufacturing, radio-supplies, electrical-goods, alcohol, and cracking plants. It owns, jointly with the bankers and private capital a paper mill, a caustic-soda works, and a few odds and ends. They are unassuming ventures, the largest and most important being the government cracking plant, with a capacity of 3,000 gallons of gasoline and fuel oil per day—made from vegetables.

Many other light and heavy industries are planned or under construction, but impediments must be overcome in every direction before anything like self-sufficient industry can be developed. Exaggerated claims of what can or is being done get no support from modest Doctor Weng. He admits that even if his schedule is fulfilled 100 per cent, it cannot fundamentally alter the general picture for many months. With rare but characteristic honesty, Weng told me the transport tie-up alone might prevent him from realizing more than 10 per cent of his immediate program.

Quite separate in administration and personnel from any of those efforts are the co-operative industries, which have attracted much attention abroad. Right after the Shanghai war a New Zealander named Rewi Alley and two Americans worked out a plan which they called the Chinese Industrial Co-operatives. They argued that it was pointless to attempt to feed nonproducing refugees for a few months, after which they would starve or be used as slave labor or rice soldiers by the Japanese. They advocated "productive relief" by mobilizing China's refugees and unemployed to start thousands of small "semimobile" co-operative industries, located in the hinterland close to unexploited raw materials, using salvaged tools and machinery to begin with. Financed by relief funds and government loans, and assisted by a staff of organizers and technicians, the refugees could buy over their own plants while learning how to operate them democratically.

Probably the "Indusco plan," as it is now called, would have been interred along with other amateur advice, had it not been ardently sponsored by the dynamic British ambassador, Sir Archibald Clark Kerr. First principle of most career diplomats is actively to avoid action; Clark Kerr succeeds by breaking the tradition at least once a day. He broke it, for example, when he personally presented the Indusco scheme to Generalissimo and Mme.

Chiang Kai-shek, and Dr. H. H. Kung. They agreed to try it out. Clark Kerr also secured the release of Rewi Alley by the Shanghai Municipal Council—where he was on contract as chief of the settlement's industrial section—and sent him to the Generalissimo. Chiang appointed him to carry out the plan.

Alley proceeded to break quite a few precedents himself. Organization is the most difficult of all tasks in China; in wartime the handicaps seemed insuperable for a foreigner. But Alley, in many ways the most extraordinary man I know, had the right personality combination. He knew written and spoken Chinese, and had wide technical knowledge as well as broad experience in China. In a few months the organization had, by its direct non-political methods and a unique absence of bureaucracy, attracted an excellent staff of skilled young men, predominantly Christian. Among them were graduates of American engineering schools, half a dozen of whom once worked together at the Ford Motor plant, where an American missionary named Bailie for years sent promising Chinese boys to be trained.

No doubt, in a country with a stabilized industrial economy—if you can suggest one!—such a method would prove impracticable, but in a nation just amputated of its industry it has worked. Indusco set up a record in China for the shortest distance between planning and action. In six months there were more than 200 co-op factories, in a year and a half more than 1,600. Today there are more than 500 technicians and organizers directing an Indusco line some 2,000 miles long, stretching from northern guerrilla districts behind Japanese lines—where industries are so mobile they move with the troops—clear down to Yunnan and Kwangsi. With more than 50,000 worker members, monthly production at this writing is estimated at 6,000,000 yuan dollars, embracing more than 300 articles, including everything from pens to printing presses. Largest production is for civilian markets, but last January these small factories also produced more than 100,000 woolen blankets to warm freezing troops on the northern front, besides making tens of thousands of gloves, caps, greatcoats, uniforms, gauze bandages, tents, cots and stretchers.

Such figures probably mean little unless one is familiar with the dramatic character of their physical setting. But every one of those pathetic little factories has behind it a moving story of human personality, of amazing fortitude and courage, as I discovered on visits to many of them. Here the tale of the Acadians has been re-enacted countless times, and the little triangle of Indusco has meant life and a future for thousands of derelicts, the scrap material of war, who had about reached the end of hope.

The loan method is unique because no security is required other than the co-op's word. To the amazement of skeptics, who predicted that refugees would scamper off with both tools and money, there has been but one case of outright embezzlement. By their labor the members pay loans in installments. Experience has shown that seven dollars (U. S.) will provide permanent relief in the form of one co-op job.

Indusco also brought new hope to Christian missionaries in China, giving them something to hand out besides Bibles and rice bowls. Many are now raising funds to supplement meager government aid, and lending valuable technical help. The day of soup-kitchen relief seems about over, except in Japanese-held points, where industrial co-operatives are naturally a "dangerous thought." Americans have made large contributions; more than $600,000 (Chinese) has been raised in the Philippines alone, where Mrs. Francis B. Sayre, wife of the United States High Commissioner, and Mrs. Paul V. McNutt are both honorary chairmen of a big committee to promote the movement. Overseas Chinese are among its stanchest backers.

Industrial co-operatives are becoming quite important as a factor in maintaining civilian morale. By producing cheap commodity goods they not only oppose Japanese economic conquest but help keep down the cost of living, which is rising on manufactured articles out of all proportion to food staples. Coffee is twenty dollars (Chinese) a pound, whisky seventy dollars a quart, American cigarettes four dollars a package—when you can get them—but except for such imported luxuries, prices on local staple foods are still astonishingly low. Indices show that, outside two or three big cities, the war increase is only about 80 per cent in interior provinces. In occupied Shanghai, the index is more than 350 per cent against 1937, and rice riots have occurred, while in the west there is no real food shortage for either troops or civilians.

Despite its string-and-bamboo industrial framework, China is not beaten in the military field, but shows steady, if slow, progress. One of our American observers, who has followed every phase of Chinese war performance, told me that China's troops are better trained, better led and better equipped than they were at the opening of hostilities. Accustomed to war in western terms of seeking a decision, however, he confessed his inability to envisage the end of a strategy which, he felt, nowhere indicated a decision in a formal military sense at all.

The fact is that Chinese military leaders divide decision into parts, and in the mere denial of total victory to Japan see for themselves a limited victory. "Originally," Generalissimo Chiang told me, "the Japanese expected to conquer China and beat us to our knees in three months. Japan's objective, the achievement of quick victory, was frustrated long ago, and this in itself constitutes a partial victory for us." And he sees another phase of decision on the moral front. "Spiritually," he said to me, "Japan has already lost the war, and because of this cannot finally win militarily."

Chinese seem to retain unshaken faith in the main pattern of their strategy —which, like the ambiguous lines of a Chinese brush painting, gains strength by its omission of detail—but there is much disagreement in interpretation. The theory of this strategy, the "three-stage prolonged war," was originally formulated by Mao Tse-tung, the Communist leader, and won pretty general acceptance. Briefly, the three periods are: (1) Japanese offensive, Chinese retreat in space but "advance in time"; (2) Japanese offensive attains its climax at the foothills of Western China, Japanese war energy diminishes, China continues to mobilize; (3) Japan's internal and international contradictions reach a breaking point, coinciding with China's maximum mobilization, followed by large-scale counteroffensive and victory.

The theory is more specific in terms of space than in time, however, and few agree concerning the particular stage of war at a given moment. With the outbreak of the European war many Chinese believed the period of "large-scale counteroffensive" had arrived, but I happened to be in Yenan then, and the view of Mao Tse-tung was quite different. He considered that the war was just on the threshold of the second stage—"stalemate."

"It is still possible," Mao said, "that the enemy may attempt a comparatively big strategic offensive, a drive on Pakhoi [later consummated], or on Changsha [later attempted, but repulsed with Japan's heaviest losses of the war], or on Sian [evidently now about to begin]. But the main character of the period is that great offensive on the part of Japan, and strategic retreat on our part, are over. The substantial requirements are present for a stage of stalemate, the central meaning of which for us is preparation for eventual counterattack. During this period China must bring her national strength to the highest point of mobilization, for counterattack to be launched under favorable conditions."

Japanese describe such statements as highly "insolent," and it is just because of such Chinese "unreasonableness," they say, that they cannot deal with "the outrageous Chiang Kai-shek regime." The Japanese general who recently took Nanning actually wrote a letter to Gen. Pai Chung-hsi and, pleading with him to be "sincere," bitterly upbraided him for not bringing out his main forces to be annihilated like a samurai. Indeed, to a person making a first visit to Yenan, the curious capital of a big guerrilla empire which stretches from the grasslands of Ningsia to the Yellow Sea—and is mostly back of Japanese lines—it might seem that Mao Tse-tung's words are somewhat presumptuous.

Men back there seem, oddly, to have forgotten that there was ever comfort or peace, and where there is no deep nostalgia there is no profound war weariness. You get the most curious impression that people actually dread the thought of peace as men dread anything unknown, until you find yourself feeling that it would probably have highly disturbing effects on the present normalcy of things as they are.

A Chinese professor, when I commented on this, said that it was because war is at present the best peace China can get. "To abandon war today means to sacrifice what peace we still have. Our people in Manchuria and Eastern China do not have peace; what they have got is slavery. To submit to Japan now would not mean peace but only an extension of war—with all the weapons in the hands of the enemy."

And perhaps that paradox is the best explanation of why China has fought on, in what to many must seem a hopeless struggle; why, despite bitter internal antagonisms between rival armies and parties and provinces, they have stood together, if not as one man, at least as one nation; why wave after wave of China's youth has gone stoically into battle knowing that, if wounded, the chances are five to one against their receiving proper medical care; why thousands of Chinese farmers in the guerrilla districts have joined self-defense corps and, realizing that the Japanese will, in revenge, burn their homes and torture and kill their families, if caught, have given from their tiny stores with a generosity that puts to shame the wealthy Chinese hoarding their treasure in Hong Kong and Shanghai; and why farmers, engineers, merchants, laborers, doctors, thousands of young men and women, but thousands of elders, too, have trekked hundreds of miles overland, often on foot—and many on bound feet—to find new homes and work in what they now call "Free China."

Here, indeed, the world must salute a fighting heart where many least expected to find it. I believe that out of the valley of slaughter a greater nation than the one which entered it will emerge—and greater than the one which is seeking its extinction.

# CHUNGKING

## by Brooks Atkinson

CROSS the hump of the Himalayas, from Assam in India to Yunnan in China, and you leave an unsmiling people for a good-humored one. The Chinese laugh sociably and easily. A good deal of their laughing just now in this part of Free China is at the long-nosed Americans who clatter down the bumpy roads in ferret-like jeeps, going much too fast, making much too much noise and looking much too scrambled to be mature human beings.

Chinese soldiers drive jeeps too, but they are businesslike drivers who go from one place to another on a definite mission. Owing to the shortage of fuel in Free China, the American drivers are also likely to be on a definite errand, but they dart through the street crowds with startling ingenuity as if they were riding a drunken mosquito.

An occasional ricksha coolie who has felt the hot breath of a jeep singe his legs bursts into a tirade of shrill anger. But most of the Chinese grin with tolerant amusement at the wild men from the West who belong to the race that produced the dashing A. V. G.'s. Obviously the American boys are crazy, but their craziness knocked down an incredible number of Jap planes in the Burma campaign last Spring and has steadily gone on knocking them down in Canton, Hong Kong and other cities that live under the tyranny of Tokyo. "Ting hao," the boys in the street shout, meaning O. K. in the Chinese language. They give the victory sign with their fingers.

If you stop in the crowded streets, they surround you, look you over with candid curiosity, discuss your shoes which are masterpieces, stare at your cap which is insanely comic or consider the jaunty cut of your flamboyantly warm overcoat. Very likely the examination is not so flattering as you assume. The extravagance of the Americans must seem a little indecent to people who have tasted the long bitterness of warfare.

But the bustle that the Americans have introduced into the cantonments where they are living and working is a source of unending astonishment and amusement to the neighborhood Chinese, and on the whole they are inclined to think that it is a good thing at this particular moment.

Not that the Chinese are lacking in bustle. They are workers too. The first impression a traveler receives is of physical energy in action. Probably this initial impression comes from the nature of their transport industry, which is largely by manpower.

But the number of coolies trotting along the margin of the road with heavy baskets of vegetables is the thing that impresses an American most, for it is primitive labor. By 8 o'clock in the morning the coolies are already five miles out of town with a return load of goods, running in short steps, breathing rapidly, concentrating on what they are doing. In town a coolie will carry a full-size desk on his back. Four coolies will carry an office safe on poles suspended from their shoulders.

By and large, a lot of work is done in China by a race of individualists with a respect for labor equivalent to the austere attitude of the Old Testament. No physical energy is wasted. No land is wasted either, for the country buildings are closely surrounded with neatly planted and scrupulously cultivated squares of growing stuffs and the hills are terraced with gardens.

Although the temperature does not drop low in the parts of China visited by this correspondent, the cold is damp and it nips the bones. The snow that fell in Yunnan Province the other day was said to be the first in ten years, but it was no warmer on that account. In blockaded China a heated room is unusual; a warm room is rare. What heating there is comes from small charcoal braziers or sheet metal stoves that burn anthracite. Even the government officials in Chungking, the wartime capital, share the common lot and sit in cold rooms wrapped up in overcoats and mufflers, drinking an occasional glass of hot water. The formal press conference with Dr. K. C. Wu, Vice Minister of Foreign Affairs, and the anonymous military spokesman is held in a stone-cold room with the doors wide open.

Not that Chinese people are impervious to the cold. The peasants in their blue cotton garb and sandals shiver before the sun is well up, and the sentry walks his beat smartly and handles his rifle briskly to keep his blood running warm. But physical discomfort is regarded less seriously in China than it is in America; and after five and a half years of war and a long ordeal of destructive bombing, Chungking cannot afford the luxury of stoves or central heating.

To Americans accustomed to physical comforts all this may sound dismal. Many people find it so, but to a newcomer still impervious to the minor vexations of life it seems a good deal less vital than the spirit of the Chinese people. They had, they say, a low point last May when it appeared that the dam had broken and the Americans and British were less effective against the Japanese than the Chinese had been alone. But even when the Burma

Road was cut, China did not fall as it should have according to logic. By making the most of the least they have no doubt of their endurance now. They are industrious and cheerful. It is stimulating to be in their company.

In the Chinese written language the ideograph for "tomorrow" is "bright day." After five and a half years of strangling warfare they are optimistic. Harried by an efficiently organized enemy, they have lost nearly everything except Free China and confidence in victory. Perhaps that is one of the reasons why they laugh so readily on the streets.

# "MADE IN JAPAN"

## by Joseph Newman

PUPPETS originally were introduced into Japan from China. After inverting the art, Japan, in return, introduced it into China. With some understanding of human nature and the importance which Orientals attach to "face," the Japanese saw the value of giving conquered peoples the illusion of self-rule and independence. This was done by recruiting from among them puppets which the Japanese could manipulate to their advantage without themselves appearing too much in the public eye. The operators in the new art of handling human puppets were the Japanese militarists, who developed it originally with great success in their own country.

Perhaps it was first used on the Asiatic continent in Korea, where the Japanese succeeded in organizing Korean gangs to assist them in the murder of the Korean Queen in 1895. After the country was thoroughly undermined by the use of terror and corruption, Japan annexed Korea but did not destroy the royal family, which was used by the militarists in an attempt to placate the outraged nationalism of the Koreans. The Royal House of Korea became the first appendage to the Imperial House of Japan. To draw the Korean family closer to the Japanese, the head of the Korean house, Prince Gin Ri, was given a Japanese wife so that the future royal family would be half Korean and half Japanese. If this process is continued, as the Japanese undoubtedly plan, all that will be left of the Korean family will be the name. The blood will be almost all Japanese, which is the material the militarists prefer for their puppets. To make Ri feel even more like one of the family, they gave him a home not far from Hirohito's palace and a commission in the army so that he could learn to strut and bow like other chosen subjects of the god-emperor.

From Korea the practice of puppetry spread with the Japanese like a plague in China. All types and kinds of agents were hired by the Japanese in Manchuria, where finally Henry Pu Yi, former emperor of China who was being kept in stock for just such an occasion, was made chief of all puppets and crowned Emperor Kangte. The Japanese militarists also tried

378

to sell Henry the idea of taking a Japanese wife, but the common rumor in Tokyo was that he resisted vigorously, holding out for his most attractive Chinese sweetheart, Yueh Hua, daughter of a Manchurian businessman. Although she was a commoner, they were married in 1934.

But that appears to have been the only serious difference between the Manchurian puppet and the militarists. When he was asked to visit Tokyo in 1940 to pay respects to his superior puppet, Hirohito, on the mythical twenty-sixth centennial anniversary of the founding of the empire, Henry agreed. His imperial stature of about six feet created a rather embarrassing scene at the Tokyo railway station, where Hirohito was taken to meet him. It is bad manners in Japan to look down upon the god-emperor, and most Japanese do not even dare look up at him when he passes in the street. It was understood that buildings more than eight stories high were not permitted in Tokyo so as to make it impossible to look down upon the palace grounds, an offensive act. Airplanes fly around but not over the palace.

But when Henry met Hirohito at the Tokyo station he either had to look down at him, because the superior puppet was of inferior height, or look over him. Nervous smiles on all faces present concealed Henry's bad manners as he smiled down at Hirohito from his lofty position. It may have been one of Henry's brief moments of pleasure in Tokyo. Few Japanese failed to observe the difference in height between the senior and junior gods when photographs of the meeting at the station appeared in evening newspapers.

Henry, nevertheless, was given the same reverence by the god-loving Japanese as Hirohito receives from his subjects and was treated as one of the members of the divine family. Whenever the chief emperor passes on the streets, residents of apartment houses along the imperial route are ordered by police to pull down their blinds so as not to look down. The same consideration was shown Henry. Residents of the Bunka Apartment, where a number of foreigners lived, found the following typewritten note in English under their doors shortly after Henry's arrival in Tokyo:

NOTICE

His Majesty, the Emperor of Manchukuo, who is now visiting Japan, is expected to pass through the front of the Bunka on Sunday, the 30th. You are requested to pull down all blinds of your windows facing down, east, west and south during the following hours:

2:00 P.M.—2:50 P.M.
3:30 P.M.—4:10 P.M.

You are also requested not to look down the party from your rooms.

THE MANAGEMENT

The first period was to take care of Henry's trip from the palace to some function to which he was being taken, while the second period was to cover his return to the palace. About an hour before his car was scheduled to pass the apartment, policemen knocked on my door and asked to be admitted.

They are the civilian rulers of Japan and exercise more direct control than the emperor. They need no warrants to break into a room, so that when they ask for admission it never is denied. Two of them had called to see whether the foreigner had complied with the instructions of the management's notice. The window shades had been drawn full length. The police, however, were not quite satisfied. They asked why the windows had not been shut, apparently suspecting that a wayward breeze might touch off the spring so that the blind would recoil just at the strategic moment when Henry was passing beneath. The windows therefore were closed and the blinds drawn again. The officers grunted approval and moved on to inspect another room. To the disappointment of foreign residents, Henry did not pass through the front of the apartment, as the notice promised, but only by it.

When Henry returned to Manchukuo, the army had a surprise for him: a brand new imperial sanctuary just like the one he had just seen in Hirohito's garden. Enshrined in the sanctuary was the spirit of the Japanese Sun Goddess. It was understood that Henry was not as pleased with the gift as he might have been, but he already had been taught to bow low in front of Shinto shrines just as Hirohito did, so that he was expected to overcome his prejudices against the Japanese gods more easily than those against Japanese girls. This shrine was to be for Manchukuo what the Ise Grand Shrine was for Japan, and Henry was to play Hirohito's role as the living deity in charge of the dead gods.

A third leading puppet manipulated by the Japanese on the Asiatic stage is Wang Ching-wei, slick, sleeky, revolutionary renegade who deserted Chiang Kai-shek for the pleasure of a prison at Nanking. Chester Holcombe, a young newspaperman from Rochester, New York, who worked for a short time in Tokyo and then drifted on to Shanghai, wheedled a permit from the Japanese army to go up to Nanking to interview Wang, who is closely guarded by his rulers. In the course of the interview, Wang was said to have told Holcombe that he was not very happy with his job as "president" of the Japanese-controlled government and that he was virtually a prisoner. Holcombe wrote the story of his interview, which was published by that singularly courageous American-owned weekly in Shanghai, *The China Weekly Review,* under the caption, "The Prisoner of Nanking." The story incensed the militarists in Shanghai, and Holcombe was promptly put down on their blacklist together with other Americans who were bold enough to speak up under the bayonets of the Japanese.

It is not unlikely that Wang deliberately "planted" the story on Holcombe in the hope that it would cause some loss of face for the Japanese militarists and result in relaxation of their hold on him and his gang. The general dissatisfaction of Wang and his clique and their fear that they might be sold out by the Japanese in a deal with Chungking led to an effort by the Japanese to placate them the following year, in the summer of 1941, when the leading Nanking puppets were taken to Tokyo for reconditioning. An elaborate reception was given Wang, who was personally entertained at the

380

palace by Hirohito himself. The admission of Wang to the holy precincts of the palace marked a new low in the visitors which the militarists selected for Hirohito, but it also served to fix the seal of sanctity upon Wang and to guarantee him that he would not be sold short in a possible peace with Chiang Kai-shek.

APRIL 2, 1941: *Japanese seized Lashio, terminus of the Burma road.*

JUNE 1, 1941: *The British closed the Burma road.*

JULY 31: *Japan occupied Indo-China.*

# INDO-CHINA

## *by Hallett Abend*

FRENCHMEN, in their days of opulence and power, were in the habit of referring to their great colonial possession of Indo-China as France's "balcony on the Pacific." A strange phrase, that, to describe a treasure house which might have become of inestimable value to the French Empire. Instead, for lack of attention, the props of the balcony rotted, and at the first strong push the whole structure crashed.

France today has neither balcony nor window on the Pacific. Indo-China is in the hands of the Japanese, and so are the French concession areas in Shanghai, Canton, Hankow, and Tientsin; and her groups of Pacific islands are nominally controlled by adherents of General De Gaulle, but are actually under the domination of the American naval, military, and air forces.

The French concessions in China will not be handed back to France. That is a certainty. They were profitable, but they were no credit to the French. In Shanghai, for instance, the French Concession was the center of gambling, prostitution, and the opium trade when China was trying to eradicate the drug evil. The police graft was colossal, and it was well known that most of the high French officials of the concession could, within a few years, retire to France with sizable fortunes which were certainly not saved from their salaries.

Both the Vichy and De Gaulle factions are in the habit of declaring with typical Gallic emphasis that after the war the French Empire must be restored in its entirety. But why? Just because France has suffered? That would be a fatuous excuse. Take the case of French Indo-China: the people there have suffered too. Suffered under rapacious French misgovernment. To hand them back to French domination after their Japanese oppressors have been driven out would be a criminal folly.

The term "colony," to most American readers, usually seems to imply

381

a smallish scrap of territory. But the French colony of Indo China is actually much larger than France. Here are the figures: Indo-China, 286,422 square miles; France, 212,659 square miles. And the population of Indo-China is about 24,000,000, or more than half the population of France itself.

The acquisition of Indo-China was managed piecemeal. It began about 1860, with pressure being put upon the native kingdoms of Cambodia and Annam, but actual consolidation was not completed until 1907. When France and Germany went to war in 1939 the Union of Indo-China was made up of the colony of Cochin China, ruled by a French governor, the four protectorates of Cambodia, Annam, Laos, and Tonkin, and the port of Kwangchowan, leased from China. The administration of all these areas was centralized under a governor general. Laos, in theory, was ruled by a native prince, and Cambodia by a king, but these dignitaries, like the native heads of the protectorates of Tonkin and Annam, were actually subject to the dictation of French officials responsible only to the French governor general.

Although there was maintained a pretense of "indirect rule," and mandarins or local officials usually enforced the laws, the entire area was really ruled by the French and administered in the interests of France and French investors. Native elements were permitted to play only an ineffective and humiliating part in the real administration.

There is no real racial unity or nationalistic feeling in Indo-China. For many years the princes and kings of the region paid tribute to the Chinese emperors at Peking, but the Chinese Government of today has no wish to revive any ancient claims for suzerainty. The Annamites are the most up-and-doing group of the natives and almost outnumber all the other groups put together. Their culture is strongly related to that of China, whereas the culture of the Cambodians has been more largely influenced by India. In the interior there are primitive tribesmen, the Maos and the Laotians, who are almost untouched by life in the outside world.

The French put thousands of Annamites into uniform and tried to use them in Europe and elsewhere during the first World War. Although these peoples had for centuries been accustomed to the petty strife of tribes and principalities, they did not make good soldiers for the type of modern warfare of 1914-18 and could not stand up under heavy artillery or machine-gun fire, even with one French non-commissioned officer to every ten natives. After a while the Annamites were used principally for supply trains, to clean up the battlefields, and to bury the dead. Indo-China probably offers no reserve of military man power for the United Nations, even after they reconquer the area and have weapons enough to supply new native armies.

The rich, red alluvial soil of the deltas of the great Mekong and Red rivers supports most of the population with bountiful crops of rice. This grain has been made the staple food and principal export of Indo-China, with the result that the rice-growing regions are densely overpopulated, and the mountains and plateau districts have been neglected and are still mainly covered with jungle. The country has rich tin mines and considerable coal and zinc. Beginnings had been made in the cultivation of rubber groves, but the output did not bulk large in world trade, and most of the colony's exports, besides the rice, were pepper, maize, tea, hides, and dried fish. Imports were largely confined to cotton and silk fabrics, kerosene, and machinery.

French manufacturers, joining in the general plan of milking the country dry, managed to secure the enactment of high import tariffs against all goods not of French origin, but even so Japanese cotton goods were largely replacing cotton goods from France even before the Japanese took military possession. Indo-China was deliberately kept in the status of an agricultural colony, exporting raw materials and importing such quantities of French manufactured goods as the low standard of living of the millions of natives would permit them to purchase.

Even after the Japanese began their career of expansion in 1931 and talked openly of the necessity of moving southward, France did little to strengthen the defenses of this rich and vulnerable area and did nothing at all to build up an efficient and honest corps of colonial administrators. In spite of the near-by example of the United States in the Philippine Islands, the French made almost no attempt to cut down the high percentage of illiteracy and suppressed with heavy hand any incipient movements for autonomy or eventual independence.

French Indo-China was easily the worst example of the white man's imperialism to be found in all of East Asia and the southern seas. French policy was selfish and greedy, and was not offset by the fact that the French did not enforce a social color line against the natives and half-castes as did the British in most of their Empire, and as many of the Americans did in the Philippines.

The Filipinos, when the invasion came, fought shoulder to shoulder beside American soldiers and Marines because they felt they were fighting for their own future and eventual freedom. But the natives of French Indo-China had no reason to oppose the Japanese, except that they had heard of the atrocious manner in which Japanese soldiers treated the people of the occupied areas of China.

# FROM SAIGON TO SINGAPORE

### by Carl Randau

## I

AUGUST 1, 1941—On the third morning out from Manila, the *D'Artagnan's* passengers huddled forward on the rail to watch anxiously for the first glimpse of Cap St. Jacques. Most of the passengers were French, and now with France almost cut off from the world, they regarded Indo-China as their home. They were returning to it on the first ship to approach Saigon since the Japanese occupation. They were nervous, uncertain and angry.

They wondered which they would see first—the point of Cap St. Jacques which guards the mouth of the Saigon River, or warships. It was a warship. A Japanese cruiser, dull gray, and top-heavy forward, could be seen through the mist, riding at anchor in the roads off the river's mouth.

Riding far out from the river, well at sea, was a whole fleet of vessels. It was now possible to distinguish a second cruiser, several destroyers and gunboats, and beyond them, bunched so closely that it was impossible to make a precise count, a group of transports and freighters. Soon it was apparent that there were at least 30 ships of various kinds all riding at anchor—a grim welcome to the home-coming Frenchmen.

The D'Artagnan plowed along steadily toward the river's mouth, remaining at a considerable distance from the nearest Japanese ships. There was no apparent exchange of recognition. At first the French passengers and the crew—officers as well as deckhands—seemed unable to believe that they were actually seeing foreign warships in their own coastal waters.

"They will pay dearly for this, they will pay double, yes, even more," one officer mumbled. "The outrage. Yes, it is horrible to be defeated in war. There is then no insult from which you are saved. But they will pay. You will see. Another day it will be another story."

Soon the low banks of the Saigon River began to close in upon us, and we left the warships and transports behind. Our vessel was almost a ghost ship. Formerly a great liner on the run from Marseille to Yokohama, it had been reduced almost to the status of a freighter. With accommodations for 175 in first class, it had 14 passengers, and instead of the former list of 400 or 500 passengers in all classes, it now carried exactly 35. Its crew, too, was reduced, partly because fewer were needed with so few passengers, and partly because on every stop at Manila men from the engine room and from the decks disappeared to join the Free French forces.

About half way up the river to Saigon is the tidy, neat quarantine and immigration station. French officers came aboard with the first real news about Japanese activities in Saigon and in the surrounding areas. To the French passengers it was disquieting news. Houses were being pre-empted right and left; many persons were homeless, and even the hotels had been forced to turn out their French residents. There were so many Japanese ships along the docks of the city that it would not be possible for the D'Artagnan to tie up at her home pier. This was indeed a welcome: a French ship coming back to its home port to find that newly arrived "protectors" had usurped its dock!

Arrangements were made to send out a tender to meet the incoming ship, but soon word was received by radio from Saigon that the Japanese had reconsidered. They would remove the transport that was now at the D'Artagnan's pier and permit her to dock.

On the decks of a number of the transports were high piles of flat-bottom boats, indicating that the Japanese had arrived ready for landings along the shore if trouble should be encountered in getting to the docks. But there was no trouble, no resistance of any kind. The French authorities, acting under unwelcome orders from Vichy, had been coldly polite and permitted the Japanese to land where and when they wanted. They couldn't do otherwise. The French were still permitted to keep control of the customs and immigration, and so we encountered no Japanese officialdom at all in getting ashore. The customs officials were so dispirited by the arrival of their new Japanese masters that they made only a pretense of inspecting baggage and papers and wryly wished travelers *bon chance*.

It was already dark before our rickshas reached the Hotel Continental, our baggage preceding us in a little pony cart. Taxicabs are a rarity because of gasoline restrictions, and most of the motor traffic is now Japanese. We were lucky to get a room out of which two Japanese officers had that day moved to a French merchant's home.

On the terrace of the Continental, the gathering place of the French community—the Café de la Paix of Saigon—we sat a little later with companions from the *D'Artagnan* and some of their Saigon friends.

"It is the fault of England and the United States that we now have the Japanese on our hands," said a sad-eyed, sweating importer with nothing to import. "If America had sent us 100 airplanes when we wanted to buy them, we should have stopped the Japanese last year. And England! England should have helped save Paris and then the Japanese would never have dared bother us here."

He had started the argument. His view was not unpopular, but neither was it accepted by all. There was too much disgust with some of Vichy's recent activities to permit of a concentration of ill will against the U. S. A. or England. In fact, it is now to America and England that the French of Indo-China are looking to restore to them their lost colony.

Up to recently, until the Vichy Government completely capitulated to the Japanese, there seems still to have been a strong pro-Vichy feeling among the French of Indo-China. Pétain had remained the complete hero, but his popularity has begun to wane. Some of the irreverent are now calling the Japanese in Saigon *les enfants de Pétain*. Most of the anti-Vichy expressions, however, are directed against Darlan. He is blamed for misleading Pétain, and the blame that is not heaped on Darlan is reserved for Vice-Adm. Jean Decoux, the Governor General of Indo-China.

Decoux now is absent in Hanoi, the political capital is the North, but his fellow Frenchmen of Saigon regard his acceptance of the Japanese terms as a personal affront.

"I knew he was going to sell us out," said a young Frenchman from the customs service, speaking most indiscreetly. "I knew he was lying when he said he would hold out against any demands. He knew he was going up there to turn the country over to the Japs. We'll never get it back now unless America comes in and helps England defeat the Nazis. They are leaving the big job to the Russians. It is too much to expect the Russians to do the job alone, though I must say they are doing much better than we did."

There were nods of approval, and then more talk of how hard it would be ever to get the Japanese out of the country. Several Japanese officers passed by almost brushing the table at which we sat, but no one lowered his voice. Other Japanese were sitting farther along the terrace, but they were intent on their drinking—of which there is much by the invading troops. It was agreed the Japanese would try to make Indo-China a permanent Japanese colony. One man said he had heard the Japanese were already preparing a postage cancellation stamp reading "Saigon, Japan." (The Japanese deny this.) It is true that last year soon after the Japanese seized Hainan Island, cancellation stamps appeared: "Hainan, Japan," and that France registered an ineffective protest in Tokyo.

But ever since the fall of France there have been serious uprisings of natives against French rule in Indo-China. Throughout Saigon there are trenches, now frequently covered with weeds, where the French officialdom prepared to resist any uprising should it reach the city. The uprisings are seldom discussed. The French like to forget the brutality with which they put them down. They offer two stereotyped explanations for the troubles: they were Japanese-financed and they were Communist-inspired. The conflict between these reasons doesn't seem to bother anyone. But there are now many graves in Indo-China of leaders of a popular nationalist movement, and many natives are in prison for political activities.

All in all, the French of Indo-China are an embittered lot. Their chief thoughts are of revenge and of a return to the *status quo ante*. And chiefly they think it is the duty of the U. S. A. to get them back their colony.

II

*August 7, 1941*

Singapore (By Air Mail).—There were not many Americans or British left in Saigon when the Japanese troops arrived. To these few the most important subject soon became: "How can we get out?"

Japan's seizure of Indo-China put an end to nearly all foreign business except Japanese. Exporters and importers received daily lists of new restrictions and additions to the items that could no longer be imported. Banks were subjected to regulations that made it doubtful if they could survive. British rice millers, oil distributors and rubber growers faced the unpleasant prospect of internment in Japanese camps if war should extend to Thailand.

One of these Britishers who had made up his mind to leave Saigon told me of the remarks of his Annamite houseboy who was helping him pack.

"Master, what I do when eggs begin fall?" the boy asked.

"What eggs?" the employer asked.

"English eggs—from sky."

An exporter, until recently one of the biggest rice dealers in the Orient, explained why he was closing his business.

"The Japanese not only took over most of my office and warehouse, but insisted that I employ a number of Jap clerks," he said. "Only if I followed these instructions, could I continue to do any business with Japanese buyers, I was notified. If I stayed under such circumstances, I would soon be working for the Japanese. I'm through."

By the time it had become clear that there was no sound reason for American and British business men to linger in Saigon, it was difficult to get away. There had formerly been many ships to Hongkong, to Manila, to Singapore, to Bangkok, to Batavia. Abruptly nearly all shipping ceased. There had been regular air lines to Singapore and to Bangkok. Now there were no air lines. The Japanese army had taken over all air fields, civil as well as military.

Almost overnight Saigon had become an isolated community after having for many years been only 3½ hours from Singapore by commercial airline.

To Manila there now remained only the infrequent and uncertain sailings of the *Messageries Maritime* line. Most of the Americans in Saigon took the first boat out on this route after the Japanese arrived.

The British wanted to get away to Singapore and on to Australia. They had only one possible way: the *Pasquier,* a little, 33-year-old ship of less than 3000 tons which the Dutch Line discarded 12 years ago as unworthy of passenger service. This boat is now operated by a small Indo-China company, used chiefly to ship hogs, cattle, rice and duck eggs to Singapore, once or twice a month.

For many days after the British resolved to evacuate, it remained doubtful if even this tub of a ship would be permitted to sail. The company, suddenly overwhelmed with demands for space, would sell no tickets pending word from the Japanese officials. Then suddenly on a Monday morning applicants were told they could buy tickets at once on a tentative basis. Maybe the ship would sail the next day; if it didn't sail then, there was no telling when it would go, and money would at once be refunded.

Though we had been told on Saturday that we could not hope to book passage, a cabin was miraculously available on Monday. Advised to be on board Tuesday by 11 A.M., we punctually carted our baggage to the muddy banks of the Saigon river, loaded it onto a sampan, and were rowed out in the rain toward what looked like a half-sunken and abandoned ship.

On the after deck, under a sheet-iron covering, most of the 70 passengers were already gathered. The rubber planter, a somber-faced, white-haired man who had lived 25 years in Indo-China, was being seen off by several French friends. They shared a water glass into which he poured whisky from a Black Label Johnnie Walker bottle. The manager of the British-owned Chartered Bank was playing with his 3-year-old son while his wife sought to shield their 6-month-old baby girl from the rain by pulling a canvas over her carriage. The father was remaining in Saigon awaiting orders from Hongkong or London. He was sending his wife and children to Australia. He shared a drink from the rubber planter's glass, and passed it along to his wife, who was trying hard to smile.

Probably because of the heavy passenger list, deckhands were struggling with a life boat. The ropes were tangled, the pulleys wouldn't work, and even as they sought to lower it for a test they almost stove in its side.

The afternoon dragged on. At 2 o'clock the ship was still surrounded by the sampans from which cattle, hogs and assorted freights were being loaded. The cattle were hauled up by ropes around their horns, and hung perilously in mid-air, kicking out wildly as the incompetent handlers lowered them into the hold. The hogs were less trouble. They were chloroformed and rolled up in bamboo crates. Piled high on the deck were bamboo baskets of duck eggs, each egg lined with a thick coating of chemically treated mud that was intended both to protect it from breakage and to preserve it. It was the covering of the eggs and not the hogs and cattle that gave off that stench that penetrated the ship.

There were 4000 cases of eggs. For more than four days we were not to be rid of that dreadful odor, a stench that made all the other odors of the Orient, even the authoritative smells of Shanghai seem like *Chanel No. 5* by comparison.

# A TOPIC OF CONVERSATION

## by Leane Zugsmith

TOKYO, August 17, 1941—At first, I thought the heart of Tokyo could be New York with lower buildings and leafy trees; or Philadelphia with wider streets and better buildings. The resemblance faded abruptly and forever. Even in the center of the great stretchy capital, the modern street blocks are pierced with curved lanes, lined with matchbox houses, two stories high, one room wide, their tindery shingles the color of damp earth.

Traffic moves British style: keep to the left. Again comparisons fail, for traffic is sparse and composed mostly of bicycles. The new taxis look, inside and out, like anybody's overworked 1935 model of a cheap sedan. They can be distinguished by a label, inscribed with Japanese characters and pasted on the windshield; they can less easily be commandeered. Usually, they're occupied and racing convulsively, hampered only by occasional traffic lights. The paved streets, like the cement or brick sidewalks, are pitted and bumpy. There is neither time nor labor nor materials to employ for repairs in a country at war. And the theory behind the cab drivers' speed is that they can presently let out the clutch and coast, husbanding their rationed gas.

Trolley cars, with baby-sized Imperial flags like ears sticking out in front; buses, subway and elevated trains are packed every hour of the day. In nearly every station in the city, it's a Times Square rush-hour contest to board a car. Inside, men and children take precedence over women. A stooped grandmother, with a child strapped on her back, packages in her arms, kimono and high wooden clogs obstructing her movements, is the customary strap-hanger.

I was prepared to see most Japanese women hatless, wearing the kimono, looking a little hunchbacked with the short outer kimono coat shrouding the lump made by the bow of the sash, moving like quick pigeons. It was a little unexpected to find silk stockings worn only by the few women who wear western dress. Everyone else wears a short cottony white sock, like a foot mitten.

But it's definitely startling to see one of the many men wearing a copy of a sporty American felt hat, a wrist-watch, horn-rimmed spectacles, carrying a stick, smoking a cigarette and otherwise clothed in a kimono, feet in cottony two-toed socks and perched on wooden clogs.

Schoolgirls wear a kind of old-fashioned western uniform: navy blue middy blouse and pleated skirt, ill-fitting and a little dusty-looking. Occasionally, they put small round navy blue felt hats over their straight black bobbed hair; usually, they wear dark cotton-like stockings and western shoes. Schoolboys wear navy blue suits and most of them look younger as well as bigger than their clothes.

The weather isn't a topic of conversation for the elevator man and you; not here. The earthquake is. After our fourth day in Tokyo, we were entitled to discuss earthquakes, too. At noon that day we were eating in a tremendous restaurant, a Nipponese Schrafft's on the top floor of a block-square steel and concrete building. The top floor of the highest buildings here is always the eighth. Because of earthquakes, there are regulations limiting the height of buildings.

We were carried to the top story in an Otis elevator and for a moment we couldn't hear the clogs on the street that, all day long, sound like a rapid pingpong game. The restaurant was foreign style; we didn't have to leave our shoes outside, could sit on chairs and eat with familiar cutlery. The menu was foreign-style, printed in English as well as in Japanese, and cooked foreign style.

Like all restaurants of this order, there is a selection of an A or a B table d'hote. Although I knew by then that the flavor would be the same, I think I chose an A lunch at the moment the window panes began to shiver. The building—think of Altman's and you'll see it—swayed from side to side, staggered and, in less than a minute, was tranquil.

The other guests, all Japanese, laughed. We followed with some fake guffaws. At that moment, I was remembering not only my first earthquake, I was learning something more valuable than the meager store of Japanese phrases I had acquired. *I had discovered that Japanese laugh because they're uneasy, because they're abashed, because they're in despair.*

Yosuke Matsuoka laughs before answering an awkward question posed by an American or an Englishman. Ko Ichii, spokesman for the Cabinet Information Board, giggles before he tells the press that a certain power is being unfriendly. The Japanese acquaintance with whom you dine, drink and spend an entire evening, laughs before he answers or skirts the questions that dart too near.

We went to the Shrine for the War Dead during the five solemn days of the ceremonies. Bereaved relatives were stumbling around the city. Families with no one at the front reverently visited the Shrine; and the stalls around it were stacked with crates of food and drink contributed by Japanese so that the dead should neither hunger nor thirst. With us was an elderly seedy Japanese who had attended an American university so many years before that his English was as rusty as his dress. Before he joined the bareheaded throng at the steps of the Shrine, he turned to us and uttered a gurgly laugh, low in his throat and prolonged.

"I had a relative killed in China," he said when he'd finished laughing.

# BEFORE THE DELUGE

### by Otto D. Tolischus

*August 18, 1941*

GREW conferred with Foreign Minister Toyoda for two hours today. When I called on him, he would not say a word about what, except to suggest that it ranged over a wide field. As far as I knew, it was the first extensive American-Japanese conference since the freezing decrees, and the "wide field" obviously involved the fundamentals of American-Japanese relations. So America and Japan were still discussing them, which was encouraging.

The one thing I learned was that Grew had protested against the difficulties put in the way of Americans wishing to leave Japan or Japanese-controlled territories. The *President Coolidge* had been scheduled to call at Yokohama, but the Japanese had made so many difficulties that the call was canceled—much to the disappointment of some 200 Americans who had been waiting for such an opportunity for weeks.

According to reports from the outside, the American press was accusing Japan of holding the Americans as hostages.

*August 19*

Questioned about Grew's protest and the cancellation of the *President Coolidge*, Spokesman Ishii gave today an involved and not very reassuring explanation. He denied that Americans were being kept as hostages, and said they were free to leave "if the Japanese Government consents." According to new regulations, he said, issued a few days ago to permit the Government to keep closer track of every individual, anybody wishing to

390

leave Japan must obtain a permit from the governor of his prefecture and must file his application for it at least three days in advance. But, he added, the question of Americans leaving Japan stood not by itself alone, but had to be considered in connection with other inconveniences resulting from the freezing regulations and the consequent cessation of shipping. Moreover, he insisted that in asking permission for the *President Coolidge* to call, the American Embassy had "promised" that only 22 American officials would sail on it, which was agreeable to the Foreign Office, but that the American Embassy had "broken its promise" by extending the original request to include an unspecified number of Americans.

"We wished to keep our promise as a matter of virtue," he declared, "but the American authorities did not keep their promise. We are very sorry."

Asked why no more Americans could be allowed to sail, Ishii replied that there were several considerations. Asked what these considerations were, he said: "There is no need to explain."

As a matter of fact, not only Americans but most foreigners in Japan were already under severe restrictions. The prohibition of any language other than Japanese on the long-distance telephone had prevented all foreigners depending on the telephone from leaving their home cities, and there were many amusing anecdotes about diplomats retaliating by having their cooks or chauffeurs call up the Foreign Minister from summer residences outside Tokyo to make appointments. Travel had become virtually impossible. Even short trips within Japan required special permits. And Japanese ships to Shanghai were "sold out." One reason was that the Japanese Government had ordered all Jewish and Polish refugees stranded in Japan for lack of entry visas to other countries to leave by September 15, and they had priority on shipping accommodations. But the Government did not dare to make the exit prohibition complete, and a few individual Americans were still permitted to leave via Shanghai.

The press continued its campaign—against America, against Britain, and against Russia. "If Britain and the United States mean to block Japan's progress, Japan will have no alternative but to brush aside their obstacles by force," said the *Nichi Nichi*. Other organs charged that America and Great Britain were attempting to break down the Russo-Japanese neutrality pact and had demanded air bases in Kamchatka and the Maritime Provinces, which threatened to convert Vladivostok into another Singapore. The *Yomiuri* denounced Roosevelt as an "imperialistic bloodsucker" and assailed British "sweatshop imperialism." And Sadao Araki, former War Minister and one-time Army idol, demanded that Japan eliminate the Russian menace once and for all.

*August 20*

As part of Japan's total mobilization, the Cabinet decided today to put the entire shipping industry, including ship crews and shipyards, under state control. A special war shipping corporation was to be organized to supervise transportation at fixed rates, requisition ships, draft crews, fix wages, and supervise compulsory shipbuilding at fixed prices. But, in line with the Government's present economic policy, operation was to be left to owners' organizations, for which the Government was to provide subsidies and to make up all losses.

Likewise, eleven of the biggest banks in Japan agreed at a conference to form a joint financial syndicate to supply funds for expanding industrial production, meaning armament production. The syndicate was put under the Finance Ministry and the Bank of Japan. Ogura urged the banks to judge industrial loans not by the standards of their own liquidity, but "from the higher standpoint of enterprise, without making the safety of their funds the primary consideration."

## August 21

After trying to ignore the Atlantic Charter proclaimed by Roosevelt and Churchill August 14, or attempting to brush it aside as "nothing new," the press finally began to discuss it in a serious vein. The *Asahi* saw its greatest significance in the open proclamation to the world of America's and Great Britain's common war aims, which meant a solid common front. But the very fact that it made no specific mention of the Far East appeared to some organs "very suspicious," and Japan was cautioned to be on her guard. For, they argued, the Charter aimed at resuscitating in both Europe and the Far East all the forces in favor of the status quo, and refused to recognize the New Order. Therefore, these organs concluded, "Japan's determination to fight for her righteous cause can be only strengthened by it."

Another indication of the drift of events was the appointment of Eiji Amau, former Ambassador to Italy, as Vice-Foreign Minister. Amau was famed abroad as the author of the Amau statement in 1934 declaring that Japan would assume sole responsibility for maintaining peace and order in East Asia.

My American colleagues were getting queries from New York today about a dispatch I had sent the previous day regarding Japanese annexation not only of the Spratly Islands, but of the whole group of islands adjacent to them, which brought prospective Japanese bases to within seventy miles of the Philippines. I had discovered this annexation on new Japanese maps sold publicly in the bookstores, and had consulted my colleagues about whether this was new or not sometime ago. They had sent the story then, but as I heard no more about it, I took a chance on sending it a week late, and found I had still scored a scoop.

## August 22

Twenty-two Americans of the Tokyo and Moscow Embassies obtained permission and accommodations to sail on a Japanese ship for Shanghai.

392

Grew's protests had apparently obtained results. Ishii declared at today's press conference: "Our civilization is too proud to take hostages."

However, prodded by German correspondents, Ishii also declared that American shipments to Vladivostok were "an intentional provocation" of Japan, which Japan viewed "with grave concern." The Soya and Tsugaru straits, he said, were still open legally, but emphasized that this was not a matter of legality alone. "The Japanese have very strong feelings about this," he warned.

## August 25

The Japanese public learned for the first time today that active negotiations were proceeding between Japan and the United States when the press reported Churchill's Empire broadcast of the previous day, saying: "The United States is laboring with infinite patience to arrive at a fair and amicable settlement which will give Japan the utmost reassurance of her legitimate interests," adding: "We earnestly hope these negotiations will succeed."

This was supplemented with reports about a new conference between Hull and Nomura, following which Nomura told the Japanese press:

"I believe it possible to alleviate the estrangement between Japan and the United States and it is foolish not to make an effort to that end. Secretary of State Hull and myself discussed various questions as friends rather than as diplomats. We did not arrive at any conclusion today, but I believe it can be done some day."

Ishii said: "The Government would welcome negotiations with the United States if they would lead to a reasonable conclusion."

For a moment, this looked like a break in the clouds. The *Japan Times Advertiser,* as the Foreign Office organ, carried Churchill's speech under the banner headline: "England Urges Japan Agree to Solution. Both America and Britain Will Respect Japan's Legitimate Interests." But to the rest of the press, acting presumably under guidance of the militant elements in the Government, Churchill's announcement of negotiations looked like weakness, and his warning that "if these hopes fail, we shall, of course, range ourselves unhesitatingly at the side of the United States," was their cue for new outbursts of rage. The *Mainichi,* English-language publication of the *Nichi Nichi,* opined that as a result of Japan's "resolute attitude and her occupation of French Indo-China, Britain has come to show a certain understanding of Japan's peaceful southward policy and is seeking a diplomatic settlement." But other organs thought the declaration merely implemented the Roosevelt-Churchill agreement and saw in it the materialization of ABCD co-operation with Russia to "destroy the work of the reorganization of East Asia, of which Japan is the central sponsor." The Churchill declaration was therefore denounced as "lies, fraud, bluff, gibberish, and ridiculous," and the press reiterated Japan's "firm determination." The only way to secure peace in the Pacific, it declared, was for America and Great Britain "to reflect, and abandon the maneuvers to check Japan, recognize Japan's Greater Asia Coprosperity Sphere, and remove themselves from East Asia."

Teiichi Muto urged the immediate declaration of the Soya and Tsugaru straits as Japanese territorial waters, to bar American shipments to Vladivostok.

## November 5

Hope of maintaining peace in the Pacific rose with a bound today when the Japanese Government announced that it had dispatched Saburo Kurusu, one of Japan's most experienced diplomats, to Washington to assist Nomura. Official quarters said Kurusu was being dispatched in an effort to facilitate amicable American-Japanese negotiations based on Konoye's "peace message" to Roosevelt. The Embassy was elated, and there was an inclination to hail the dispatch of the new envoy as the "silver lining" that had suddenly rimmed the war clouds over the Pacific at the moment when they had begun to look darkest.

Kurusu left Tokyo by plane for Hong Kong, where the American Clipper plane was being held for him through the good offices of Grew, who had called Hull by telephone during the night for that purpose.

Kurusu was the Japanese Ambassador to Berlin who had signed the Axis alliance pact. But he had told the Japanese press some time ago that this alliance aimed fundamentally at peace, and only secondarily at establishment of a new world order, and that therefore the talks between Roosevelt and Nomura were in harmony with it.

Yet it was difficult to be hopeful. Even while Kurusu was en route, Tojo reiterated before the Privy Council his Government's inflexible determination to carry out Japan's immutable policies, aiming at "successful conclusion of the China Incident and the establishment of a Greater East Asia Coprosperity Sphere."

## November 6

The Government lodged "a most solemn protest" with Russia today against the sinking of the *Kehi Maru,* demanding that the Soviets reply with "sincerity." Ishii said that Japan could no longer rely on Soviet sincerity. Russian mines, he said, were dangerous to all shipping, and he added: "Japan stands for freedom of the seas."

The press today interpreted the dispatch of Kurusu as "proof of Japan's sincerity" in wishing to avoid conflict with the United States, but the *Miyako* said: "Evidently, Tojo wishes to get a quick decision on Japanese-American talks." The *Japan Times Advertiser* warned: "This country is able to move in a number of directions, which requires its potential enemies to be prepared at many places, distributing and decentralizing their strength."

394

## November 7

Ishii declared at the press conference today that Kurusu's trip was a token of Japan's "honest desire to come to a conclusion in the Washington negotiations," but he denied Domei's hint that there was a time limit to the negotiations.

Domei declared the outcome of the visit would depend on "whether the United States shows any sincerity toward Japan." That word "sincerity" had ominous connotations.

## December 5

Tomokazu Hori, successor to Ishii as government spokesman, announced at the press conference today that the Washington negotiations would continue.

"Both sides will continue to negotiate to find a common formula to ease the situation in the Pacific," he said.

"With sincerity?" I asked.

"If there were no sincerity, there would be no need to continue the negotiations," he replied.

Hori came from Shanghai, where he was known as a heavy drinker and—an excellent poker-player, good at bluffing.

Replying to queries about the Japanese troops in French Indo-China, he said their number was within the agreed limit, as reported in news dispatches from Vichy. "There cannot be any complaint from any other quarters," he said with a grin. A question as to whether the limit he referred to was the original limit or a new one remained without reply.

The vernacular press was scouring the dictionary today for epithets to hurl at Hull and the United States. The *Japan Times Advertiser* said that Hull's revelation was an unstatesmanlike attempt to seize the propagandist initiative and put the responsibility for a breakdown of the negotiations on Japan.

Admiral Hisao Matsunaga, chief of the Oceanic Department of the Japanese Airways, again assured the Japanese they need not fear the encirclement front, because it was lacking in suitable air bases, effective planes, and trained personnel. He put the whole air strength of America, Britain, China, and the Netherlands in the Far East at 1,000 planes—250 American, 400 British, and the rest mostly trainers. This contrasted with the 4,000 naval planes announced by Hiraide. Moreover, said the Admiral, most of the planes of the other side were old or short-range planes that could not possibly bomb Japan and get back to their bases, except about 20 Consolidated PBY-28 bombers that had appeared in the Philippines, Singapore, and Surabaya. There were only about 200 air bases along the whole ABCD line, he said, including Singapore, Java, and the Philippines, and the gravest deficiency on the other side was the shortage of trained pilots. For all these reasons, he declared: "We can place full confidence in our preparations."

# Part Eight: United States at War

* * *

Washington, December 8, 1941 (Associated Press): Japan's formal declaration of war . . . came two hours and 55 minutes after Japanese planes spread death and terrific destruction in Honolulu and Pearl Harbor at 7:35 A.M. Hawaiian time . . . Sunday.

* * *

# FROM THE WHITE HOUSE

## by Forrest Davis and Ernest K. Lindley

THE blow that was about to fall cast no shadow into the unseasonably warm sunshine of December 7, 1941. At midday Washington was the capital of a people technically at peace, psychologically at war: a "white" war against overseas aggressors and, at home, among themselves on the question of how far to pursue the war abroad. The first note of menace reached the capital almost inadvertently at 1:45 P.M. It came by way of an alert, intercepted at Mare Island and relayed to the Navy Department, which read:

> From CINCPAC (Commander in chief Pacific fleet) to all ships present Hawaiian area: Air raid on Pearl Harbor. This is no drill.

In the final sentence, Admiral Husband E. Kimmel was correcting the incredulous reaction of Hawaii, which had accepted the first Japanese bombs as evidence of a particularly realistic maneuver.

At the Navy Department, Secretary Frank Knox, about to depart on a routine visit to the Washington Navy Yard, received the message from one of his companions, Admiral Harold R. Stark, Chief of Naval Operations, who had it from a panting Communications officer. By a rueful irony, the Secretary's annual report, attesting the Navy's fitness, had appeared in that morning's Sunday newspapers, which now lay strewn through millions of American living rooms. Handing the message to Knox, Stark failed to comment.

"What," demanded the Secretary, "does this mean?"

"It's the beginning," replied Stark, somewhat vaguely, whereupon Rear Admiral R. K. Turner, of War Plans, standing alongside the Secretary, broke in with the definitive: "By God, sir, they've attacked us!"

Back into his private office hurried the Secretary. In private life a Chicago newspaper publisher, he nevertheless keeps his office as nautical as a man-of-war's wardroom. Behind his desk stands a bank of telephones, one a direct wire to the White House. He lifted that receiver and jiggled the hook. The color had drained from Knox's loyal, good-humored, and eupeptic features. Forty-two hours later, at 8:00 A.M. on Tuesday, the Secretary, conscious of his share in the blame for the surprise at Pearl Harbor, was flying to Hawaii to see for himself the extent of the disaster. On Monday he had notified the President he thought it was his duty to go, overcoming mild objections from Mr. Roosevelt, who privately applauded the decision. The Secretary of the Navy regarded his mission as an expiation.

At the moment when Knox lifted the White House phone, half of Washington was lingering over Sunday midday dinners. Such was the case with the President, who was eating from a tray on his desk in the oval study, a large, littered, intensely personal chamber on the second floor of the White House. With him were his friend, Harry L. Hopkins, lounging on a couch in a V-necked sweater and slacks, and the President's Scottie, Falla, expertly pouching morsels from the tray. After an exhausting week with the Far Eastern crisis, aggravated by clogged sinuses, Mr. Roosevelt had dedicated this day to rest. Saturday he had worked late, clearing his desk while the White House staff took a half day for Christmas shopping. Today, tieless and in shirt sleeves, he hoped to catch up with his neglected stamp collection. After a late breakfast, Hopkins, whose health is poor, had strolled in from his bedroom down the book-lined corridor for some relaxed talk. The President might have been any one of a million Americans putting in a loafing Sunday afternoon with a crony and a hobby.

There was this difference: the imminence of war could not be banished wholly from the President's study. Mr. Roosevelt expected war—but not this week end. Only yesterday he had cabled Emperor Hirohito, immured behind his moat in Tokyo, to solicit his help in "dispelling the dark clouds." The overnight cables had reported a large movement of Japanese transports toward the Gulf of Siam, but the President held on to a faint hope that even yet the Emperor might restrain the war party. In any case, there had been no warning. The Japanese had not even answered Cordell Hull's comprehensive note of November 26, and the President did not anticipate that afternoon a thrust to the heart of United States sea power. If war did come, he assumed, along with 132,000,000 other Americans, it would break first in Siam, the East Indies, or the Malay Peninsula.

The White House, therefore, was, like the country, at peace. Elsewhere in the great Regency-Georgian mansion, Mrs. Roosevelt was giving a luncheon for an American radio commentator recently home from London, but the President's calendar was bare and the executive staff scattered. A "do not disturb" order had been confidently placed with the switchboard. Mr. Roosevelt was topping his dinner with an apple when his desk telephone jangled disobediently.

The President lifted his receiver on an apologetic operator agitatedly

397

saying that Secretary Knox had insisted on being put through . . . the call was most urgent. The President cut the operator short: "Put him on," and then, "Hello, Frank."

In a tone and at a pace the President still regards as a model of casualness on the brink of crisis, Knox began: "Mr. President, it looks like the Japanese have attacked Pearl Harbor. . . ."

"NO!" the President interrupted.

"It's true," said the Secretary. "I'll read you the message," which he did. The hands of the brass ship's clock on the President's desk stood at 1:47. The message, which was, as we have seen, a service alert to the fleet and not an official report to Washington, did lack explicitness, and its terse language gave no insight into how the attack was being met, no hint as to the extent, weight, or gravity of the air raid. Yet its meaning was plain to the President: the flag had been fired upon, Hawaii, not Siam, had been subjected to the overt act, and the war, so long dreaded, so exhaustively debated, had come to America. Directing that Knox see at once to safeguarding the Panama Canal and the Alaskan bases, and to doubling the guards at all Naval establishments against sabotage, the President rang off, bidding the operator get him Secretary Hull. Thrice that afternoon he lodged anxious inquiries about the Canal with the Navy Department.

Just before Hull lifted his receiver at the State Department, Hopkins said: "This is it." For a long while the President's *fidus Achates* had predicted that World War II would overtake America in the Pacific rather than in the Atlantic.

By coincidence the Japanese Ambassador, Admiral Kichisaburo Nomura, and Saburo Kurusu, the last-minute "peace envoy," were due at that moment at the State Department with Tokyo's answer to the note of the 26th, an answer rendered superfluous by the happenings in Hawaii a half-hour earlier. (The first bombs fell on Pearl Harbor at 1:20 P.M., Washington time.) At 1:10, the Japanese Embassy had telephoned for an appointment to deliver the answer: 1:45 was the hour set, but the diplomats were not yet at the State Department when the President telephoned.

To Mr. Hull the President said: "Frank Knox has just telephoned a report of an air raid over Pearl Harbor. We haven't confirmed it yet." The Secretary, a man of fire and storm under a gently benign manner, uttered a profane comment. In his graphic phraseology, the Japanese war party had, for some time, been succinctly characterized as "Dillinger."

Of all the ranking officials in Washington, Mr. Hull should have been the least surprised. Five weeks earlier, before the arrival of Kurusu, he had warned the Army and Navy that the Far Eastern crisis, having passed outside the bounds of diplomacy, was now in their lap. A fortnight before he had been more precise. Reminding his War Cabinet colleagues of Japan's proclivity for beginning wars by stealth, he had suggested that all hands in the Pacific be on watchful guard lest a shock attack on a wide front "stampede the hell out of our scattered forces."

But with Mr. Hull foresight never lapses into imprudence. He is not, by nature, a jumper at conclusions. The President had said the report was unconfirmed. So little did the Secretary relax his customary caution that he withheld from his associates the news that the country constructively was at war and the next day, at a press conference, recalled only that an "unconfirmed report" had reached him from "an official source" before the arrival of the Japanese envoys. Because the report lacked corroboration, he had elected to see them.

In turn the President telephoned Henry L. Stimson, Secretary of War; General George C. Marshall, Chief of Staff; Viscount Halifax, the British Ambassador; and Sumner Welles, the Under Secretary of State. Ten years earlier, Stimson, as Hoover's Secretary of State and Hull's immediate predecessor, had labored to arouse the Western World against the explosive implications of Japan's "Manchuria incident." Today he observed the cycle of aggression begun at Mukden conclude its march around the globe.

General Marshall and some of his staff had been at his office all morning. Shortly before one o'clock he went to his quarters at Fort Myer and was at dinner when he was called to the telephone by Lieutenant Colonel (now Colonel) John R. Deane, then assistant secretary of the War Department General Staff. A messenger from the Navy Department had just handed Deane a penciled note, apparently a brief bulletin from the Navy radio operator at Pearl Harbor, stating that an attack was in progress. General Marshall directed that all the key officers of the War Department be informed. He immediately returned to his office. Soon afterward, a second message came from the Navy Department. This one was typed and of a more formal character than the first, although it contained little additional information.

Halifax, the stooped, bony, melancholy, and conscientiously useful British Ambassador, was reading in the library of the huge Georgian Embassy building on Massachusetts Avenue. With the Ambassador were William Hayter, first secretary of legation, and Angus Malcolm, His Lordship's private secretary. After talking sympathetically with the President, Halifax directed Hayter to put in a call for London and himself began telephoning ranking officers of the Embassy and other leading Britons in Washington that America, at long last, was in the war. In an admirable demonstration of British composure, Malcolm continued at the stint he had set himself for that afternoon, addressing Christmas cards to catch a pouch for London.

The London connection could not be had until about three o'clock (9:00 P.M., London wartime). It being Sunday night, a lone duty clerk at the Foreign Office received the news and at once telephoned it to Winston Churchill, the Prime Minister, and Anthony Eden, the Foreign Secretary. Meanwhile, the radio had carried the news to America, and a pickup by the British Broadcasting Corporation had beaten the telephone report to the Prime Minister.

# TOKYO: DECEMBER 7TH

### by Otto D. Tolischus

*December 7.*

IT was a bright, warm, and pleasant December Sunday. But under the circumstances, ominously quiet. The press seemed to have exhausted itself and for lack of any new developments was devoid of any interest. Even the diatribes against America and Great Britain had ceased. The only news that caught my eye was a small item that Thai troops were at last marching toward the south, and I made a note of it for my next story. All Japan seemed to be waiting for something. Tojo was scheduled to make a pronouncement Monday morning, and I arranged with Ofusa, my assistant, to be on hand early to telephone it to New York. Ruth Kelley, of the American Embassy's clerical staff, stopped in at noon to discuss the possibility of writing something about Japan for a newspaper or a magazine. She said there was so little to do at the Embassy at the moment that time was heavy on her hands. Diplomatic work was also at a standstill. She said she was going to an afternoon party at Max Hill's, Associated Press correspondent.

I spent the whole day finishing a personality sketch about Grew for the *New York Times Magazine.* It started out:

> Four score and seven years ago, the "black ships" of Commodore Matthew Calbraith Perry came knocking at the barred doors of the little-known and self-isolated Japanese islands and, giving the coup de grâce to the tottering feudal regime of the "Taikun," opened the country up to modern ideas and world commerce, and thereby started Japan off on her sky-rocketing career under the restored rule of the Tenno-Emperor. It meant the overthrow of the proud Samurai, whose rule had imperiled the country, and they did not like it. But before long, the Japanese people recognized Perry as their benefactor, and have regarded him as such ever since.

> Today, having absorbed all they think they can learn from the Occident in the line of warfare, the descendants of the Samurai are reviving the old cry against the "foreign barbarians" and propose to return to a new kind of isolation not only of Japan, but of the entire Orient, in the name of a "Greater East Asia Coprosperity Sphere" put under Japanese control and dedicated to the exclusion of all Occidental influence. In this effort, they have, in their own words, "drawn the sword against the leaders of certain East-Asiatic races who have not awakened to the new situation," and now threaten to draw the sword against any and all Occidental powers should these dare to stand in their way.

> As a result, the long-predicted war between the white and yellow races in general, and war between Japan and the United States in

particular, has become an imminent possibility. And whether it shall become a grim reality is now the great issue being decided in Tokyo and Washington.

After looking at it, I thought it sounded a little strong. But I decided to let it stand. That was the situation!

After finishing it, I sent Ofusa with the sketch to Grew to get it approved. Shortly afterward, Grew telephoned to say that he was delighted with it. Having an eerie feeling, I tried to call his attention to the opening paragraphs and said: "Well, that's how I see the situation." About 10 P.M., he and Mrs. Grew called up to make a slight correction regarding a personal detail. There was nothing in their voices to indicate apprehension.

(I didn't know then that President Roosevelt had sent a personal message to the Emperor with a last appeal for peace. It had been delayed in transmission, presumably purposely, and it was not till midnight that Grew was able to present it to Togo. As Grew later told me, he was convinced that Togo himself did not know then that war was at hand. Togo asked: "Why the hurry?" My own dispatches of that Sunday never reached New York.)

## December 8.

Loud pounding on my locked bedroom door routed me out of bed at seven o'clock this morning. When I opened, four plainclothes men stalked in and surrounded me.

"We are from the Metropolitan Police," said the leader. "Put on your coat. The procurator wants to see you."

My first thought was: The Grew story! I took what little comfort there was in the fact that I was being arrested by the police, and not by the supposedly tougher gendarmes. I was permitted to dress, even shave, and to eat a substantial breakfast. The policemen advised me to dress warmly, as it was "very cold outside." They seemed to be elated about something and joked while drinking precious coffee served by Kyo-san.

"I bet you don't know the big news," said one of them.

I was in no pleasant mood and showed it. The leader spoke up warningly: "We are treating you like a gentleman."

"I don't see why you shouldn't," I said.

I was marched out through the kitchen door to a waiting taxi, and that was the last I saw of my home. On the way to the local police station, the police finally began to enlighten me.

"There is war between Japan and America, Britain, and the Dutch," one of them said. "There has been a battle. Manila, Singapore, and Hong Kong have been bombed." There was no mention of Pearl Harbor.

# MANILA

## by Clark Lee

AT noon on Wednesday, December 10, Manila got its first close up of the Japanese Air Force.

The planes were almost overhead when we saw them from our office on the third floor of the TVT building. We looked out the window and there they were, flying high and straight in, from the north. We counted them. There were fifty-four in three tight "V's," the whole formation making one big "V." Their wings were silver in the noonday sun and they were barely distinguishable against the white wisps of clouds far up in the blue sky. Seeing how high the planes were flying we realized the Japs knew all about the use of oxygen for the crews of high-altitude bombers.

I jumped over the city editor's desk and onto the fire escape which led to the roof. I got up a few rungs on the iron ladder and suddenly found it difficult to hold on. My knees were doing a combination jitterbug-rumba. We didn't know whether the Japs were going to bomb the whole city or concentrate on definite targets, and in either case the TVT newspapers, which had been extremely antagonistic to Japan, were a legitimate target.

I finally made the top and looked down on the surrounding wooden buildings, each of them a firetrap. From the roof of a near-by building a .50-caliber machine gun started chattering. Rifles crackled from the streets, although the planes were far above the range of any ordinary anti-aircraft gun, to say nothing of rifles. Then black puffs blossomed high in the sky and I looked down toward the bay front where my new friends of the previous night, Sergeant Smith and Corporal Davis and the others, were firing their 37-mm. guns. But their shells were bursting at 10,000 feet, only halfway up to the planes.

Most of the people in the TVT editorial and press rooms had run down to the first floor when we shouted that the planes were in sight. Down in an alley alongside the building a bunch of newsboys were unconcernedly pitching pennies against a wall. The police were having difficulty keeping the crowds off the streets. After the first raids, when the people saw the Japs weren't bombing the center of the city, it became even more difficult, and in the TVT and other offices the workers kept on with their jobs during attacks.

The planes went right on past, out of sight, into the sun. There were distant, fairly loud, explosions. I got down from the roof and went to the rear of the building. From a window I saw fires in the direction of Nichols Field and Fort McKinley. The smoke was black and fierce, and the flames were high, and it looked as if the gasoline dumps had been hit.

The planes turned out over the bay and were lost to view. Fifteen minutes later from the direction of Cavite, we saw smoke, and knew that the naval base was being attacked.

Inside the TVT people asked, "Where are our fighters, sir? Why do they not attack the Japs?" We couldn't see any fighters in the air.

Jack Percival, the Australian reporter, and I climbed into a car and sped through the center of the city and out Dewey Boulevard along the bay.

Two tremendous fires were burning in Cavite, punctuated by explosions. But from the distance of nine miles across the water it was impossible to distinguish individual buildings or tell whether the naval base itself or the town had been hit. We saw one mine sweeper speeding in toward Cavite. It seemed to be running right into the flame and smoke.

We went on out to Nichols Field and drove through back roads to the nearest fire. Nipa shacks were burning hotly, while their occupants aided the firemen in trying to put out the flames. Nipa, which is coconut fiber, throws up a dense black smoke when it burns and very much resembles an oil fire, and this fact caused frequent reports and rumors that oil dumps around Manila had been hit by bombs when actually the bombs had missed their targets and landed in Filipino villages.

In the large grounds of an American-owned estate there was a deep crater thirty feet wide behind the servants' quarters. On the lawn a five-year-old Filipino girl was lying, her abdomen ripped open by bomb fragments. Her father was bandaging a wound in his leg. "Those damn Japs, sir, have killed my baby," he said. Nobody was crying or showing signs of grief.

The homes of Americans on Harrison Boulevard had also been hit. Bombs seemed to do more damage to buildings of concrete and steel than to the nipa shacks on stilts. Frequently, part of a shack would be torn away by a direct hit and half of it would still be standing. There were bomb craters in the Elizaldes' polo field, across from Nichols Field.

At Nichols Field no damage had been done to our planes or hangars or barracks. We saw several planes that had been ruined the night before by a direct hit on a hangar, but most of them were old Martin B-18's, twin-engined bombers which had been on their last wings even before the war started.

Neither the Army nor Navy would give us any details about the bombing of Cavite, except to intimate that it had been "very bad." Russell Brines, who lived on Dewey Boulevard near Nichols Field and facing the bay, had seen two dogfights in which Jap planes were shot down. They belonged to a fighter escort accompanying the bombers and they dived on the airfields and strafed our fighters in an attempt to pin them to the ground. Despite those excellent tactics, a few of our fighters got into the air and fought successfully. Brines, his wife, and daughter had spent an hour crouched behind the seawall in front of their home, sheltered from machine-gun bullets fired by the planes zooming above their heads, and from shell fragments from the anti-aircraft guns at Cavite.

# MACARTHUR

## by Henry C. Wolfe

WHEN General Douglas MacArthur commanded the Rainbow Division on the Western Front, he was warned that a certain projected military operation might entail 3,000 casualties. "Very well," replied the General, "if we lose three thousand men, we lose three thousand and one!" He emphasized the *one*.

That answer sums up the military philosophy of the soldier who has been named head of the Far East Command. A daring but practical strategist, he insists on sharing action with his men. At du Feys he attacked a German machine-gun nest with a bayonet.

As commander of the famous Rainbow, he had a way of locating his headquarters between assault battalions, though that was hardly the safest and most comfortable place for his officers to get to. "It shortens my lines of communications," he explained.

Like his father, Arthur MacArthur, "Boy Colonel of the West," the General has shattered one Army precedent after another in the interests of improved military service. Recognition of the superiority of the Garand rifle, defense orientation of the CCC program, institution of the four-army system—these are but a few of the dashing MacArthur's contributions to the modernization of Uncle Sam's military establishment. A list of the changes that he has sponsored would make one of the most impressive pages in the annals of the United States Army.

Tall, dark-haired, handsome Douglas MacArthur is the storybook hero to end storybook heroes. No fiction writer would dare invent so fabulous a character. But in the hard-boiled realities of a hard-boiled, warring world, the "Kid General" keeps right on adding to his record of achievement.

Most recent of his honors is the Philippine appointment, which gives him the full title of Commander-in-Chief of the United States Army of the Far East. It was not just another routine military appointment. There was drama —drama on a worldwide stage—in the naming of General MacArthur to this post in the far-off, tropical islands of the Philippine archipelago. In July, 1941, Herr Hitler's Axis partner, Japan, moved into Indo-China and threatened to strike at Thailand, Singapore and the Netherlands East Indies. A general war in the Pacific appeared imminent. But the United States matched Nippon's moves with several blitz moves of her own. We clapped an oil embargo on Japan and froze her credits in America. We incorporated the armed forces of the Philippines into the Army of the United States. And we made Lieutenant General Douglas MacArthur commander of the combined Filipino-American defense establishment.

Just as soon as the appointment was made, things began to hum. General MacArthur immediately asked President Quezon to call to active duty 10 regiments of the Philippine Army. Then he summoned virtually all the reserve officers to take command of the growing number of men under arms. He set in motion plans to muster into service other reserve military units just as fast as conditions would permit. He conducted blackouts and air-raid drills and began the construction of shelters for the civilian population.

To the War Department he emphasized the necessity of rushing additional troops and equipment to him. As a result, Army transports from the United States soon were unloading more soldiers, trucks, guns, munitions, airplanes, and food. He named seven American officers to supervise the training, transportation, housing, and equipment of the expanding forces. Everything worked smoothly, quickly and efficiently. The Commander-in-Chief had long ago laid plans for the defense emergency.

Always a great executive, MacArthur increased his own time on the job to 12 hours a day. He passed the word right down the line from his Chief of Staff to his sergeants and corporals that the Filipino-American force must become a crack military organization, the equal of any fighting force in the world.

But the Commander-in-Chief's most important work lies in a far broader field. He is the American representative who works with the military leaders of the other democracies—Britain, the Netherlands, and China—out in the Far East. It is his responsibility to act for the United States in the councils of the democratic front. In ability and experience he is the man of men for this work. General Marshall in Washington and General MacArthur in Manila make a combination that is no less than providential for us at this critical point in the world's history.

The significance of MacArthur's appointment was not lost on Tokyo and Berlin. Together the new army and the new commander constituted a warning that the United States means to hold the Philippines. More than that, it signified that we intend to play a major role in the Far East, that Pacific affairs are our affairs. In short, the veteran who once carried the ball against the Reich's 1917 line is on the job today to call the plays against the Reich's Far Eastern line.

The athletic, six-foot Commander-in-Chief is no stranger to America's far-Pacific outpost. As a 23-year-old lieutenant of Engineers he was sent there in 1903 and found himself welcome in the palm-shaded Spanish setting because of his father's fine pioneer work when he was military governor of the islands. From 1922 to 1925 he commanded the post of Manila, the 23rd Infantry Brigade and the Philippine Division. In 1928 he was made Commanding General of the Philippine Department of the United States Army.

In 1930 he was made Chief of Staff of the United States Army, but he had not seen the last of the islands by any means. After his pyrotechnic five-year period as head of our whole land force, he received an invitation from President Quezon of the newly formed Commonwealth of the Philippines: would the General act as military adviser to the Commonwealth? It was characteristic that it took a conference of less than five minutes for him to reach his decision. Yes, he would take over the job. The new adviser—soon to be made a field marshal—would supplement the corps of native Philippine Scouts with a ten-year potential 400,000 reserves trained at the rate of 40,000 soldiers a year. Despite the meagerness of the military appropriations allotted him, he embarked on a program that included modern defense works, an efficient little air force and a fleet of speedy coast-defense boats. At Baguio he established the Philippine Military Academy that turns out a body of cadets smart enough to please even as tough a drillmaster as himself—and he is a former superintendent of West Point.

But civil life beckoned to the 57-year-old general, promising him time for many cultural pursuits that soldiering had denied him. For one thing he wanted to write. Gifted with a flair for memorable phrasing, he had long looked forward to getting his words on paper. Moreover, in April, 1937, he had married, and was anxious to settle down to the enjoyment of a regular family life. At the close of 1937, therefore, in his thirty-fourth year of service, he retired from active duty.

In accepting the request for retirement, President Roosevelt wrote him: "Your record in war and peace is a brilliant chapter in American history."

The record glitters with "firsts," "onlys," and superlatives. He was born at Little Rock Barracks, Arkansas, January 26, 1880, the son of Lieutenant General Arthur MacArthur, Civil War hero and later an outstanding officer of the Spanish-American and Philippine wars. Graduating from West Point in 1903, young Douglas was first in a class of 93, having hung up the Academy's best scholastic record for 25 years.

He was the youngest of American division commanders when he went to France with the famous Rainbow Division. And his promotions were as rapid as his exploits were spectacular. He had a hot head in valorous deeds and a cool one in strategy. After six days of hard fighting near the Forêt de Nesle, for instance, he noticed that the Germans were evacuating their positions. Tired though his men were, he unexpectedly reformed his columns, personally instructed each regiment in the details of his plan and struck in a surprise attack on the Germans' exposed flanks. Not only did he capture the sector but provided the relief division with a more advantageous position for a heavier attack.

Wherever the thick of battle was, there was MacArthur. Or was it the other way around? Secretary of War Newton D. Baker called him the greatest fighting front-line general of the war. He led the 84th Infantry Brigade in the first entirely American offensive, St. Mihiel. His outfit broke the strong German Kremhilde Line and his men were deep in the Meuse-Argonne drive. Within sight of Sedan when the Armistice was declared, he took his division to the Rhineland as part of the army of occupation. In one battle he was burned with gas but refused hospitalization. In another he was wounded. He talked with his men, ate with them, kept their morale high. It is surprising that the romance of the Rainbow commander has not been made a cinema play.

Back in the United States after the war he became superintendent at

West Point, the youngest on record. At that, he looked younger than his 39 years. In modernizing the United States Military Academy he aimed to change its spirit from "conservative narrowness to liberal progressiveness," a change of far-reaching importance to today's defense program.

Another "youngest" in the General's career was his designation as Chief of Staff of the United States Army. He was 51 years old at the time of his appointment in 1930, and he is the only Chief of Staff to serve longer than four years. And what a ghost army he inherited. The depression and the cult of pacifism in the United States had resulted in wide-scale reductions in our defense forces. Obsolescence was the order of the day, and—most discouraging of all for the progressive Chief of Staff—indifference. How to modernize and built up from such a peacetime low?

It is hard to imagine it, but the tall, aristocratic general almost licked the boots of various gentlemen to get a hearing for his Army reforms and the money for his program of military expansion. He was desperate. He visited Europe, inspecting the growing military machines on the war-brooding continent and contrasting them with his own outmoded Army. He begged for 46,250 privates. Congress and the brass hats called him a radical. Supposing the persuasive military man did get his fantastic number of privates, where would he house them? But the long-range planning of the Chief of Staff had anticipated that objection. PWA funds had been earmarked for repairs and new buildings. And he continued to warn, wheedle and push the plan for the mechanization and aviation expansion of his revitalized Army. Douglas MacArthur was not only the spark plug of our national-defense program but the father of the country's defense-mindedness.

It is an ironic sort of tribute that the war which the military experts saw coming in Europe should have put an abrupt end to his retirement from Army service. But the hero of St. Mihiel and the Meuse-Argonne belonged where the danger seemed greatest. In July, 1941, that was not far from Manila Bay. In Manila the General has his headquarters in the ancient Walled City district. Built on top of the costly old walls erected by Philip II, they once were the headquarters of the Philippine Constabulary, which, in 1901, was the sole armed force the Filipino people had. General MacArthur calls his offices "the cradle of Philippine defense," and says that he feels "like an old dog glad to be back in the harness again." He and his wife and small son live in a suite at the Manila Hotel on the palm fringed shore of historic Manila Bay.

During the years which preceded the present war there was much public and private discussion about the advisability of our attempting to defend the Philippines. A considerable body of professional and public opinion accepted the theory that the islands were a military and naval liability to us. Those who held this view urged that the United States retire from the archipelago and let it fall into the lap of the first aggressor who came along. General MacArthur sharply challenged this defeatist attitude. He maintained that the Philippines could be defended—must be defended. He pointed out that when the islands reached a certain stage of military evolution no aggressor would dare to make the attempt to invade them.

Shortly after General MacArthur's appointment to his new office, a delegation of Filipino veterans of the Spanish War called on him. They had served under his father, General Arthur MacArthur. Might they have permission to form a regiment that would be taken into the American Army? They wanted to serve under their old leader's son. These men were followed by a delegation of Filipino labor leaders who pledged the support of their unions. They wished "to reiterate the unswerving loyalty of Filipino labor to the Government of the United States because of its efforts to help the Philippines in defending itself against aggression."

His affection for the Filipinos is wholehearted. Talking about them to the writer, he said: "There exists no traditional enmity between the Filipino and any other race. To the contrary, there dwells here a peace-loving, democratic and hard-working people, isolated by hundreds of miles from irritating contacts with others, and whose sole ambition is to develop the resources of the country to the betterment of its own educational, cultural, and economic levels."

From President Quezon down, the Filipinos idolize their Field Marshal. His democratic ways, his culture, his ability as a speaker and his memory for names and faces appeal to them. It was said of him in 1929 that he knew the name of every noncommissioned officer in the Philippine Scouts. They are proud to be led by a hero who has received numerous decorations for bravery and distinguished service both from the United States and foreign countries.

Above all, they like him because he is a MacArthur. The history of the Philippines in the twentieth century is inseparable from the history of the MacArthurs. It was the kindly, far-sighted, brilliant Arthur MacArthur who, as military governor of the islands, started the Filipinos on the path to self-government. When he turned the Philippines over to the civil authorities he left them with the foundation for their present laws, schools, and defenses.

In the interests of defense, his son must carry on: he must perfect the military organization of the Philppines. There is more at stake now than the defense of the islands. The tropical archipelago in the western Pacific is the Far Eastern keystone of our security and of all that our security symbolizes. In fusing the Filipino-American Army into a powerful fighting unit MacArthur is deeply conscious of the fact that he is manning the ramparts of democracy.

But he puts the matter much more simply when you ask him about his work. Leaning earnestly across his desk, he says in a quiet voice:

"The United States has directed me to defend these islands. I propose to do so."

# THE LAST OF THE *REPULSE*

*by Cecil Brown*

WE were looking for trouble and we were ready for it. "Looking for trouble," was the way Admiral Phillips put it when we sailed out of Singapore on that unforgettable Monday, December 8th, at dusk, for a sweep northward to intercept the convoys reinforcing the Japanese bridgeheads on the north coast of Malaya. We were looking for trouble. We found it.

It's Wednesday now, and my watch says it's 11 A.M. The *Repulse* and the *Prince of Wales* are still hunting, but they're also being hunted. Yesterday, at 5:20 P.M., during a one-hour break in the gray, rain-filled clouds, the Jap Nakajima Naka 93 spotted us. The Nakajima Naka 93 is a twin-float reconnaissance plane. The plane shadowed us constantly and we expected an attack all last night, convinced it would come, inevitably, at any moment.

I wasn't worried, particularly, for the very good reason that under me there were 32,000 tons of armor-clad ship—H.M.S. *Repulse*. And around me were 1,260 stanch sailormen. Half a mile ahead H.M.S. *Prince of Wales* steamed at 26 knots through the South China Sea, 55 miles from the Malay Coast, 150 miles north of Singapore. The beautiful ship moved with what seemed a prideful invulnerability and accentuated our sense of security.

The clouds have gone now, and the sky is a robin's-egg blue and the sun is bright yellow. Our ships move through pea-green water, white where the hulls cleave it. Ahead, the *Wales'* fifteen-inch guns jut from port and starboard from turrets that bulge like muscles. They seem to quiver, eagerly. A few destroyers flank us. They are pygmy ships and seem ridiculous and impertinent in such powerful company.

The crews, their battle bowlers on, are sitting beside their guns, waiting for attack alarm. Standing on the flag deck, I look down over the decks of the *Repulse*. The pom-poms, multiple high-altitude ack-acks, are pointed skyward. The guns seem no less eager for combat than the crews themselves.

The flag deck is a good spot from which to watch most phases of any action. Of course it has its disadvantages too. Yesterday one of the deck officers said to me, quietly, "You know, old boy, in every action there are usually casualties on the flag deck." I said, "Thanks."

I wear a white antiflash hood, something like the snow helmets the boys wear skiing. It covers the head over an ordinary steel helmet and comes down over the shoulders. It's to protect against burns from exploding shells or bombs. Jumpers cover my shorts and bush jacket. I've got a camera hanging around my neck. Wonder if I'll get a chance to use it?

At 11 A.M., to the second, the ship's communications system bellows: "Enemy aircraft approaching—Action Stations!" I see them coming, 10,000 feet high, like a lengthened star-sapphire necklace, grayish against the blue sky.

Flame tongues flash from the guns of the *Wales* up ahead and just as the

409

blasts reach us the guns of the *Repulse* let go. I've never been so close to so many big guns before. The roar is deafening. The flash of flame from their barrel mouths is blinding.

I'm standing on the flag deck, in the lee of a funnel, eight feet from a battery of pom-poms. I'm getting my tonsils sunburned by gaping open-mouthed at the planes overhead, at the bombs coming down, materializing suddenly out of nothingness and streaming toward us like ever-enlarging teardrops. There's a magnetic, hypnotic, limb-freezing fascination in that sight.

Nine Jap planes are now directly overhead. Their formation is undisturbed. The sky is filled with black puffs and they seem a discordant profanation of that beautiful sky. Suddenly, fifteen feet off the side of the ship, directly opposite where I'm standing, a geyser of water rises and drenches us and simultaneously we feel the crash of a bomb on the catapult deck.

All around us the water rises in white pyramids. I hear the cry, "Fire in marines' mess and hangar!" I run back to see the damage but the bomb penetrated and exploded, and only smoke is coming up. Our aircraft is knocked off its track and a red-bearded New Zealand fleet air-arm pilot is atop the crane attempting to lift the plane to drop it overside, since its gasoline constitutes a menace. As I pass the gun crews they seem extraordinarily calm, replenishing ammunition, laughing. "Let's get them all next time." I hear somebody say, "Bloody good bombing for those blokes." When I return to the flag deck I note a three-inch hole in the funnel from a bomb-splinter eighteen inches above the spot where I'd been standing. It's obvious my number isn't up yet. Just as I reach the flag deck again I see a splash three miles distant off the port beam and a roar goes up: "We got him!"

Smoke is still coming up from the catapult deck and strenuous efforts are under way to control the fire. Four stokers come up to the flag deck to get first aid. They're blackened and scorched, and their clothes are water-soaked.

They are very calm but wild-eyed and stunned, and their hands are shaking. It isn't a pleasant sight, and someone says, "Make way for these men. They need first aid."

A stoker says, "Water. I want some water." A glass is placed to his lips.

It's 11:40. The *Prince of Wales* seems to be hit. She's reduced her speed and signals, "We've a man overboard." A destroyer pushes up to her side. Standing less than 100 feet away, it's as incongruous as a baby running to protect its mamma. The flag-deck lieutenant says: "Those Japs were good, weren't they?"

I say, "Too good to suit me. How badly is the *Wales* hit?" The lieutenant says, "I don't know. They haven't told us yet."

We are all lighting cigarettes, sucking deeply, and our exhalations are more like sighs. The pause is too brief. At 11:45 distant specks appear. Now they are identifiable. They are nine torpedo-carrying bombers, circling a mile away at one thousand feet. They are now like moths around our flaming guns.

410

They swoop lower. A bugle blows to stand by. The communications pipes roar to stand by for a barrage, and instantly every gun aboard the *Repulse* is stuttering and roaring and the whole ship vibrates and the pom-poms are tossing empties furiously. But their clatter is unheard in the bigger roar of the guns. A voice beside me says, "Look at those yellow ———— come!" The *Repulse* is twisting and snaking violently to avoid torpedoes. My only weapon is a fountain pen and a notebook, so I sidle beside a multiple Vickers gun spewing 2,000 half-inch bullets every minute.

A few feet to my right an eight-barreled pom-pom is spitting, and half a dozen feet away a four-inch high-altitude ack-ack is crashing, its barrel nearly horizontal instead of skyward, to meet the onrushing torpedo bombers, which are coming down gracefully 100 yards above the water.

A cooling liquid is gushing over the guns and the paint blisters on them are as big as tennis balls. Gunners are moving like a movie running too fast. Some are very young and eager and breathless with excitement; their faces streaked with sweat. The white cloth antiflash helmets covering their heads, cheeks and shoulders are now soaked and discolored. Some are wearing life belts and Mae Wests.

A whole pom-pom swings this way and that, with its seated trigger man, feet braced, riding with it. That is a dizzy job.

I've already seen three torpedoes drop. One plane just dropped a torpedo 300 yards distant. The whole side of the plane is exposed. Shells and tracers are ripping into it. It's fascinating to watch.

The tracers are cross-stitching the sky, at eye level, with long, thin white lines, slightly curved. For me this whole picture—orange flame belching from the four-inchers, white tracers from pom-poms and Vickers guns, and gray airplanes so close I can see the pilots' profiles; astonishingly close, like butterflies pinned on blue cardboard—is a confusing, macabre kind of fun.

But this, I realize, is deadly business too. Three gunners ten feet from me slump over with Japanese machine-gun bullets in them. It's difficult to comprehend sudden death. But they aren't the only casualties in this terrible moment. A torpedo bomber has just dropped a tin fish and banked without gaining altitude. It glides beautifully, parallel with the *Repulse* at a ten-degree angle and still tracers are plowing into it. It doesn't seem to me the plane is going to crash until an instant later I see that it isn't going to pull out and is still gliding toward the sea. It strikes the water and immediately bursts into flame.

I run to the starboard side of the flag deck, where another torpedo bomber is coming in. It is difficult to judge distance but I guess it's no more than 200 yards away when it swerves. I don't see the torpedo. And with good reason. There's a huge hole in the side of the plane. It's aflame, and instantly it seems to buckle. As though it's got a cramp it dives, shapeless, flaming, seaward. It's just a pillar of fire until it hits the water and spreads out into nothingness.

There are nine bombers in that attack which ends at 11:51.

A flag-deck sailor runs past to transmit a message to the bridge deck directly above: *"Prince of Wales,* steering gear is gone." The decks of the *Repulse* are littered with empty shell cases. Upon the faces of the sailors there's a mixture of incredulity and a sort of sensuous pleasure, but I don't detect fear. There's an ecstatic happiness, but strangely, I don't see anything approaching hate for the attackers. For the British this is a contest. This facial expression is interpreted by an officer who turns to me and says: "Plucky blokes, those Japs. That was as beautiful an attack as ever I expect to see." He'll never see another action. He's at the bottom of the South China Sea.

Our great concern is that the Japs are going to crash-dive the ship. I know enough about naval warfare to know that the flag deck is a good spot on which to crash-dive. Suddenly it occurs to me how wonderful it would be to be back in Ohio. A voice says: "Here they come again."

At 12:01 ten torpedo bombers launch an attack at all angles. One even launches a torpedo directly astern, which seems silly since we are twisting rapidly. Planes coming from port and starboard are headed directly at the bow. I see the *Prince of Wales* being subjected to an attack also and a bomber is coming toward us from a thousand yards, directly ahead.

I think, "Here comes a crash-dive." No, this certainly isn't fun. The smell of cordite is suffocating. My eyes ache with the blows of shell blasts.

It's the same as before—amazingly daring torpedo bombers are targets for mere moments and are seemingly unaffected by the almost solid wall of shells and bullets. The water is streaked with the tracks of torpedoes. A sudden roar goes up on one side of the ship. It's another bomber down, but I didn't see it.

If it wasn't so awe-inspiring it would be routine; the way planes rush in, drop a tin fish, machine-gun the decks of the *Repulse* and roar away. Now they're all gone. Those who are able to light cigarettes do so, and I take off my steel helmet and notice the sailors blowing up their life belts.

At 12:20 I see ten bombers approaching. It's impossible to tell whether this will be a high-level or a torpedo attack. They come closer, lower, and it's definitely a torpedo attack. The communications pipes again, "Stand by for barrage," and hell breaks loose. A plane is diving straight for the middle of the ship off the port side, 500 yards away, and tracers are rushing to meet it, but it comes on and now seems suspended in the air 100 yards above the water and the torpedo drops.

It is streaking for us. There is a deadly fascination in watching it. The watcher shouts, "Stand by for a torpedo." The torpedo strikes the ship about twenty yards astern of my position. It feels as though the ship has crashed a dock. I am thrown four feet across the deck but I keep my feet. Almost immediately, it seems, the ship lists and the communications pipes bellow: "Blow up your life belts." I take down mine from the shelf and start putting it on, having blown two or three puffs into the tube when communications says: "All possible men to starboard."

But a Japanese plane invalidated that command. Instantly there's another crash to starboard. Incredibly quickly, the *Repulse* is listing to port, and I haven't finished blowing up my life belt. Captain William Tennant's cool voice is piped over the communications system: "All hands on deck. Abandon ship. God be with you!"

Those last words came out of the ship's loud-speakers. We all start streaming down the ladders to reach the quarter-deck. The coolness of everyone is incredible. There is no pushing, but no pausing either. One youngster seems in a great hurry and an officer quietly says to him: "Now, now, we are all going along that way, too."

Beside a pom-pom two men are dead. I see four sailors, two of them midshipmen, just eighteen, carry a comrade with a machine-gunned leg to the edge of the ship and throw him seaward to give him a chance to be rescued. I see a lifeboat jammed with ratings (British for seamen) and a half a dozen officers.

I climb a cable hand over hand and finally I swing myself into a tiny, precarious corner. Someone shouts, "This boat will never get off."

As a matter of fact, no boats of the *Repulse* take away. We all pile out. I drop ten feet to the slippery, slanting deck and crash into a bulkhead. I'm dizzy when I pick myself up and scramble away on my hands and knees, grabbing cables and deck protuberances to reach the edge of the ship. The ship is almost on her side and in a swell position to capsize and there are at least 500 heads bobbing in the water.

The tide is sweeping them swiftly astern. From masts fore and aft men jump 70, 80, 90 feet into the sea. One doesn't jump far enough and hits the slanting hull and crumples and flops into the water like a sack of wet cement. Another misses his direction and dives straight down a funnel, but most appear to leap clear. Standing on the edge of the ship, which is now like the ridge of an Army tent, I hate to leave the *Repulse*.

The whole thing has become suddenly unbelievable, and now I see the *Prince of Wales* sinking, shrouded in smoke. Men beside me are sliding down the side of the ship, bouncing their rumps over rivets, hitting bulges and shooting off into space. An officer who last evening said to me, "I find *Alice in Wonderland* the best book to read during wartime," stands up and dives. He dives back inside the ship, into the torpedo hole under the water line.

Sailors are throwing into the sea anything floatable. I turn back. On deck there's a padre, who is administering to a dying gunner. Men are running along the hull of the ship to dive from a point nearer the water. As though a hammer had crashed down on my head, it suddenly came to me. "Cecil, old boy, you aren't going to get out of this."

You do queer things at such moments. I take off my shoes and carefully lay them down together as I would at the foot of a bed. I see the admiralty photographer engaged in similar idiocy. He opens a lifeboat locker and places his expensive camera inside and carefully closes the lid.

I am most unwilling to leave behind my new portable typewriter, which is in my cabin and now under water. I slide down four feet along the side of the ship and brace my feet in a porthole and remove my steel helmet and lay it inside the port. Ten feet away the whole hull is torn as wide and jagged as a slashed tin can.

I still hate to leave the crazy-angled ship and my false security for that oily mess below. A sailor at my side stands up and dives with outstretched arms. Beautiful. That decides me.

I jump twenty feet. My ignorance of shipwreck technique is profound. It doesn't occur to me to swim away from the ship to avoid the suction until I see others striking out vigorously. It doesn't occur to me that the ship might explode or the oil catch fire.

But now I'm swimming away and I grab a small piece of wood, and when I'm 50 feet from the *Repulse* I slide under water. The stern is vertical and almost immediately I feel the powerful suction, and oil sweeps over my head and I swallow much of that unpleasant stuff. The wood I'd grabbed was a small bench and I hang onto it and manage to lie atop it and take off my socks.

But the effort required is excessive and I drink oil again, and someone calls across the water, "You all right, old boy?" I say, "Yes," and gulp more oil.

I'm not giving up, but I have suddenly a pessimistic view of my chances of floating a half mile to the destroyers. The tide and oil make swimming difficult. Every face in the water around me is black with oil.

One ten yards distant yells, "I've a cramp," and disappears. I see four or five others just give up and slide under water without a sound. One officer is blowing up the life belts of half a dozen seamen in the water. The stronger are constantly swimming to the side of men who are getting glassy-eyed, some supporting others and hanging onto planks.

Many faces are blood-streaked and oil-soaked. After 55 minutes in the water I manage to reach a Carley float which is jam-packed. A Royal marine pulls me up and supports me to keep me from falling off. Jap planes are still overhead. Someone says, "Watch out for those yellow ————, they're going to machine-gun us," and another says, "Best thing to do is dive under water." A marine rasps out, "Shut up with that guff!" I thought, "After all this we gotta get machine-gunned."

I knew that if I dived under water I'd never come up. But the Japs don't molest us, although if one bomb drops anywhere near, it will kill us all with its concussion. After an hour and a half the raft gains a destroyer, and a line is tossed to us. The marine loops it around me and yells, "Heave up," and I'm dragged through foot-thick oil and hauled on deck. Admiral Phillips and Captain Leach have gone down with the *Prince of Wales,* and Captain Tennant of the *Repulse* is saved. I am suddenly very tired, but I am not too tired to inquire about the officer I'd seen pumping life belts for the glassy-eyed sailors.

It seems that while in the water he took off his belt and gave it to a sailor who was unable to swim. The officer isn't among the survivors.

Some of those men running alongside ship to dive jumped off the stern

414

and, since the screws were still turning, they were caught in the blades. At least twelve marines died thus. Highest dive made was by a midshipman. He leaped from atop the mainmast, the highest point on the ship. He dived 170 feet and was saved.

On the Carley float I managed to reach, one sailor lay back and died from exhaustion and from swallowing oil. We were forced to push him off to make room for others still in the water and hanging precariously onto the float. I'm glad I knew how to swim.

\* \* \*

WASHINGTON, Dec. 24, 1941 (Associated Press): Fewer than 400 Marines with 12 fighter planes and a small quantity of weapons held Wake Island for 14 days against heavy Japanese attacks.

LONDON, Dec. 25 (International News Service): Hong Kong, Britain's eastermost Asiatic bastion, fell to the Japanese today after its vastly outnumbered garrison waged a magnificent defense for seven days ...

WASHINGTON, Jan. 2, 1942 (International News Service): Manila, capital of the Philippines, fell to the Japanese on this, the 27th day of the war. Cavite, naval base ten miles from Manila on Manila Bay, was evacuated shortly before the Japanese entered the city, the Navy Department announced.

SINGAPORE, Jan. 31 (Associated Press): Jungle-weary British Imperials gave up the fight in Malaya today, withdrew into the ... little island of Singapore ...

LONDON, Feb. 15 (Associated Press): Prime Minister Churchill announced ... tonight the fall of Singapore.

# UNCONDITIONAL SURRENDER

## by George Weller

THE interview on February 5, 1942, in the Ford Motor assembly plant between Yamashita and Percival (as the Japanese represented it) was hard and peremptory on Yamashita's part, without any trace of that grace and respectful address which the Japanese customarily use on formal occasions. Although such Allied humiliations, when offered to the Japanese people, are frequently exaggerated to set an example of ruthlessness—it is hard to say, for example, whether the captive crew of the U.S.S. *Houston* was actually beaten with whips, as the Japanese people were told—the *Domei* version of the conversation is worth giving, if only to indicate what the Japanese believe such a submission should sound like:

415

*Yamashita*. I am not asking whether you wish to surrender or not, and, if you wish to do so, I insist it be unconditionally. What is your answer, yes or no?

*Percival*. Will you give me until tomorrow?

*Yamashita*. Tomorrow? I cannot wait. It is understood, then, that Japanese forces will have to attack tonight.

*Percival*. How about waiting until 11:30 P.M. Tokyo time?

*Yamashita*. If that is to be the case, Japanese forces will have to resume the attack until then. Will you say yes or no?

Percival was silent.

*Yamashita*. I want to hear a decisive answer, and I insist upon unconditional surrender. What do you say?

*Percival*. Yes.

The Japanese even had songs ready for Tokyo children to sing in honor of the taking of Singapore. Yamashita said that he would "consider a triumphal entry into London" but he had "no plans to hold one for the fall of Singapore." Actually he had little time to dawdle; the unspoken fact was that Singapore's glorious conqueror was badly needed on Bataan to handle the stubborn Americans.... The Japanese said they would put 1,000 armed "British" soldiers at work policing Singapore. The "British" were of course Indians; the Japanese rarely miss a trick of propaganda.

One or two nurses, jockeys, and old men stayed behind in Kuala Lumpur and elsewhere above Singapore. In Singapore itself there were about 3,000 women and children and perhaps as many as 3,500 male civilians left behind.

Gordon Bennett escaped two hours after the surrender of Singapore. His aide, Captain Gordon Walker, swam out from the water front to a sampan, rowed it ashore, and with several other officers started down the strait. They got aboard a junk crowded with British officers and loaded with antiaircraft shells, slipped past the silent guns of Blakang Mati, and so southward for five days. Walker has said: "All of us were in a bad state of nerves and everyone wanted to run the boat. It was hell. After twenty-four hours we began to eat, and took a cup of water a day, a handful of rice and some carefully divided cubes of pineapple and bully beef." From the junk the Bennett party transferred to the *Tern,* one of those 30-foot police launches formerly in the Singapore harbor service, and went through Sumatra by way of Jambi, Muaratebo, and Padang to Java and safety.

A large number of refugees leaving Singapore Friday the thirteenth were bombed and machine-gunned off Pombong in the Lingga archipelago north of "bomb alley," and were rescued from Singkep after swimming ashore, through the uncommon (and never recognized) heroism of L. A. Canty, a captain in the Royal Army Supply Corps.

Among the marooned on Singkep, who had made their way thither from Pombong, but who had escaped by crossing the strait and going up the

Indragiri River, were Nunn of the MVAF and his wife, and David Millar, director of the Chartered Bank, who had been wounded in the head when the strafing Zeros machine-gunned the water after the ships were sunk. All three had been aboard the *Kuala* or a ship accompanying her, both of which went to the bottom south of Singapore like many others, including probably the *Vyner Brooke* and the *Gi-ang Seng,* which the *Daisy* had loaded with passengers a week before. (Millar reached India only to die of nephritis and typhoid; the Nunns were lost en route.)

On his improvised hospital ship under the quaking gray tarpaulin, flying a Red Cross made of four white tablecloths sewed together with two crossed red Malay sarongs in the middle, Canty brought all his castaways back to the mouth of the Jambi River, and then 200 miles up again to the burned-out town. He was back at Jambi at 2:30 A.M. on February 26, eleven days after the simultaneous fall of Singapore and Palembang, only two days before the invasion of Java itself. Canty loaded all except thirteen severely wounded and four volunteer nurses aboard trucks, produced by the patient and unfailingly helpful Dutch, sent the movable wounded through Muara-tebo to the hospital at Sawahlunto—where they were treated by an Australian doctor from Rengat to the east, likewise a Singapore escapee, who sacrificed his freedom to stay with them. Canty by a margin of twenty minutes caught a destroyer leaving Padang, was transferred to an Australian cruiser at sea, and reached India.

Two noteworthy comments on Singapore appeared. The first was that of Harold Guard of the United Press, an Englishman who wrote from Batavia a week later:

> Singapore was lost in 70 days by bureaucracy, complacency and a legion of fifth columnists. . . . Chinese volunteers were organized only a week before the invasion of Singapore Island and were sent out to fight with only shotguns against Japanese dive bombers and tanks. There were no plans to use native man power and no effort to mobilize and encourage the natives to defend Malaya. The Imperials fought bravely and skillfully and might have held it if only part of the promised allied aerial reinforcements had arrived. The complacent refusal of the colonial bureaucrats to recognize the obvious was appalling. On April 18, 1941, almost eight months before the attack, I wrote a dispatch that the defense of the Malayan peninsula did not in the opinion of military men offer sufficient protection against an attack on Singapore from the rear. The military censor at Singapore approved the dispatch only because, as he told me, it was so absurd that I would appear ridiculous. . . .

The other summary is an American one and was made a week before the island fell by Major T. H. Thomas in the *Christian Science Monitor*. To General Percival's valedictory, "Today we stand beleaguered in our island fortress," Thomas had this to say:

417

Singapore is an island, and it was then beleaguered but it was not a fortress in any possible sense of the word. At no time was it intended to serve as one—nothing in the position itself or its elaborate development as a naval base in the postwar years prepared it in any way to stand out against an attack from the mainland. Never, in all that time, was it ever conceived that such a contingency might arise.... There was, in short, no idea of Singapore ever having to stand as an isolated position.

It is not conceivable that this was a mere oversight; that the engineers and naval officers who laid out the whole position were stupid enough to plan it inside out. Their plan was sound and the tragic fiasco now under way is due in no way to blunders or failings of the troops on the spot. It is the inevitable consequence of the course pursued in the general conduct of the war by the British and American Governments.

The Japanese spent a week, beginning February 15, sweeping up the mines. Then their first naval vessels came down the South China Sea and entered Keppel Harbor. They claimed to have taken in all 26 transports and warships, including a "white-painted British patrol boat seized at a certain port while it was evacuating British women and children."

Singapore to the end was never taken by sea.

Two rooms of charts were the centers of Singapore's operations. One map room was in the long green-camouflaged building in the hollow cut by the Japanese golf course. Here Chicagonews had seen General Percival himself produce his identity card before entering. (If the Japs had substituted another Percival in his place, they would have been foiled.)

Five hundred miles away to the south, at Lembang in Java, by the great volcano Bandung, were the master charts of the whole vast South Pacific, Wavell's overwhelming responsibility. Here, among others, was a map of Singapore Island. For security's sake, when the maps were not in use and at night, a white curtain was drawn down over each one, to be raised again each morning when staff conferences began.

Then came the day when the Japanese crossed the island, their tank column finally bisecting Singapore from the causeway to Pasir Panyang.

The next morning, when the faces of the maps of Sumatra, the Philippines, Borneo, Java, Celebes, New Guinea, and northern Australia stood revealed in vast array, their isinglass covered with crayoned lines and scribbled numbers of units—American, British, Dutch—over one chart the white shroud had been drawn down covering the line in orange pencil from the causeway of Johore to Pasir Panyang. And the blank face of the map, white and empty, looked out upon the last staff conference, asking an unspoken question.

When would the deliverers of Singapore come?

# JAPANESE GENERALS

## by John Hersey

BY the end of the first week in January the Japanese were recovered from their surprise at having Manila given them and had regrouped their forces above Bataan. They were ready to strike.

In a month of successes they had grown very confident. Here at the gate of Bataan they thought they had the possum up a tree. On the 10th Japanese planes dropped leaflets over MacArthur's lines bearing this polite, almost affectionate message to the General:

"You are well aware that you are doomed. The end is near. The question is how long you will be able to resist. You have already cut rations by half. I appreciate the fighting spirit of yourself and your troops who have been fighting with courage. Your prestige and honor have been upheld.

"However, in order to avoid needless bloodshed and to save your 1st, 31st Divisions, and the remnants of other divisions, together with your auxiliary troops, you are advised to surrender...."

General MacArthur declined the invitation. He was ready—far readier than the Japanese imagined—to take the blow.

The battle began that same day with the first of a series of attacks, each of which was intended to end MacArthur's resistance. After each one failed in the face of General MacArthur's anticipatory tactics, the Japanese tried a new type of assault.

First they tried frontal attack. For obvious reasons, this is the most expensive kind of attack, but having done a lot of pushing, the Japanese thought they could push MacArthur and his men right off Bataan into the sea. Their first frontal attack, in which they used artillery ranging up to 105-mm. mortars, plenty of machine guns, automatic rifles, tommy guns, grenades, and, along the roads, tanks, struck hard at General MacArthur's right flank. His communiqué called it "tremendous." But after a quick concentration of his own artillery, General MacArthur reported the enemy thrown back "with heavy casualties and at relatively slight cost to the defenders." The attack subsided into an artillery duel in which the defenders' artillerymen, groping out with explosive fingers for enemy guns, silenced eleven batteries.

Next the Japanese tried infiltration, the tactic which won the Malayan campaign. Specially trained men slipped through the American-Filipino lines under cover of night and vegetation, met at previously appointed rendezvous, and tried to cut off sections of the defending units. Some of the infiltrated men acted as solo snipers, gunning especially for American officers. Infiltration failed on Bataan.

On March 8 General MacArthur reported home that he had heard "from various sources hitherto regarded as reliable"—evidently Filipinos sneaking through the Japanese lines—that General Homma had committed suicide.

Before the war General Masuhara Homma was generally thought to be for democracy. As a young man he had studied at Oxford, and he had revisited England several times as attaché and aide. He was a jovial-looking soldier, and the English thought him a good fellow. He accentuated his cheerful plumpness by shaving his head; his eyes were bright; and he always seemed polite and eager to please.

He got his fighting experience in North China, where he was for some time commander of the important garrison at Tientsin. I met him there, in the summer of 1939, under circumstances which made him seem anything but suicide-bent.

Tientsin was my birthplace and my home as a child, and I returned there that summer with considerable excitement. Much of the town I found unchanged at first: Victoria Park was still just as Victorian, there were still bikes in front of the swimming club, and the canal smelled the same. There were minor changes—the little American school had moved and there was a hairdresser in the dark second-floor room front where my desk had been; the part of town out toward the racecourse had spread and grown ugly, the little pond near the 15th Infantry barracks where we had so often sailed the good rowboat *Enyap* was filled in, and the Pavilion in the Rec, with as many spires as Xanadu, had been torn down and an ugly, sanitary clubhouse put up. It was not until many hours had passed that I suddenly realized the real change: Tientsin had become a prison.

The British and French concessions were blockaded, allegedly to stop a flow of smuggled arms, but actually to put pressure on the British. A barbed-wire fence stretched all the way around, and the day after I arrived a coolie was found dead on the fence—for it was charged with electricity. The only openings were at certain streets. At the openings there were inspection sheds, where every British man, woman, and child who passed through was inspected; many were undressed and some were rather unpleasantly insulted. A diplomatic fuss was made, and it fell to Masuhara Homma to clear the air.

General Yamashita, the conqueror of Singapore, who succeeded Homma, was considered to be one of the leaders of the pro-German faction in the Japanese Army. He first went to Germany just before the first World War, and although Kaiser Wilhelm had ballyhooed the then fashionable Yellow Peril, there were many Germans who saw at least a spiritual kinship in the Japanese—such men as Karl Haushofer, who is now Hitler's theorist on geopolitics. Haushofer had met Yamashita in Japan in 1908, and he now befriended the visitor, filled him with admiration for German puissance, and flattered him and his people by publicly referring to the Japanese as "the Prussians of the East."

Two of Yamashita's classmates in the Staff College in Tokyo were Hideki Tojo, Japan's Premier at the time of Pearl Harbor, and Hoshira Oshima, Japan's Ambassador to Berlin. Yamashita and Oshima were sent to Europe after the first World War, Oshima to Berlin and Yamashita first to Germany and then to Poland, where he learned to hate Communism. Later, from 1927 to 1930, Yamashita was military attaché in Vienna, where he paid repeated visits to aircraft factories and where he struck up a friendship with Alexander Lohr, who, at the time of Bataan, was a Colonel General in command of the Fourth German Air Fleet.

Pretty soon, as Japan began to march, Yamashita began talking just like a Nazi. He spoke of Japan as a have-not, and he once said: "War is the mother of creation." In China he fought under another Germanophile, General Count Juichi Terauchi. When he was given the job of reorganizing the Japanese Air Force in 1940, he went straight to Germany to see how to do it. He was taken in hand by German officers who had seen action in the Far East, notably Vice Admiral Grassman of the Navy and Colonel General Otto Keller of the Luftwaffe, who was later to command the First German Air Fleet against Russia. For over six months these men took Yamashita to see planes being made and pilots being trained; to inspect the broken Maginot Line and German forts on the Channel coast; and even, it is said, to fly in an air raid over Britain.

His big thrill was an interview with Hitler. "I felt," he said afterward, "that in the mind of Hitler there was much of spiritual matters, transcending material plans. When I met the Führer, he said that since boyhood he had been attracted by Japan. He read carefully reports of Japan's victory over Russia when he was only seventeen years old and was impressed by Japan's astonishing strength." He said that the Führer promised to remember Japan in his will, with a protocol instructing the German people "to bind themselves eternally to the Japanese spirit."

Japan, said Yamashita after this experience, would surprise the world. "In a short time," he said, "something great will happen. You just watch, and wait."

The world watched and waited to see what Yamashita would do on Bataan. For several weeks he planned his attacks, waited for reinforcements, grouped his forces, and pounded Corregidor and Bataan with artillery and bombs. His reinforcements were numerous. The General now had Japan's first team, and good Japanese troops are good.

MARCH 8, 1942: *Japanese cut Burma Road.*

# THE FATE OF THE DUTCH EAST INDIES

## by John McCutcheon Raleigh

JAVA was as much of an armed fortress as every resource of the Dutch could make it. It was the portcullis protecting the Indian Ocean and Australia. Properly reinforced, it could have been a bastion still unconquered today. The papers now are quoting alarming shortages of rubber and oil. That need not have been.

421

Military experts have testified in private, and otherwise, that Java could have been held, if sufficient aircraft had arrived, and if what was present had been used as it should have been.

The Hollanders were ready to fight to the death, and did, neither evacuating their loved ones nor giving up an unnecessary inch. Still, long before Java faced the menace of invasion fleets, the Allied command was adjudging Java as "untenable"!

Significant, too, is the fact that, until very late in the game, no Dutchman was a member of the Allied High Command. The insult alone, is startling. Swallowing a justified anger, the Dutch continued to co-operate. Parts of Borneo were occupied. Then came the first great Jap invasion fleet bound for Java. It came with a hundred ships through the Straits of Macassar. Dutch and Allied bombers went out to meet it. Forty-three transports were sunk. The Japs had no other recourse than to go ahead, for the fifty hidden airfields in Borneo's interior meant destruction. Thereafter, no more vessels were sunk. Where were Allied bombers?

General ter Poorten, Dutch Commander in Chief of the army, had brought the press to Bandoeng, N.E.I. military headquarters, for a conference similar to Helfrich's appeal. There he had stated that twenty-five per cent of the first line of the Dutch air force had been destroyed. This occurred between December 8 and the end of the year.

This may account for the nearly unobstructed landings made by the Japanese on Bali and Java itself. Another source believes that bombs were not to be had. A more dreary theory is that Wavell, at the crux of the Macassar Straits Battle, sent seventy-three bombers to Malaya on a mission, which was said to have been unsuccessful.

There is little doubt that Java might have been, at this moment, an Allied strong point, if the powers had possessed the vision to read the writing on the wall.

It would not have taken myriads of planes. A squadron, or two, of up-to-date American fighters, and fifty bombers might have saved the N.E.I. This I was told by an American officer who was present in Java during the battles off the coast and while the Japs were infiltrating inland. The United States sent one fighter squadron and a handful of Flying Fortresses, rescued from the Philippines.

The aircraft carrier *Langley* appeared, with eighty or more modern fighter planes aboard, at Freemantle, Australia. She was bound for Java. Stubborn stevedores delayed port facilities. The *Langley* waited three long days and then set out for Tjilatchap, on the west coast of Java, in disgust. She was sunk with her precious cargo. If all had gone according to plan, a high ranking officer told me, the planes were to have been unloaded at Freemantle, assembled and flown to the battle lines, as were those of another squadron. Timor was then unoccupied and was being used as the intermediate refueling point.

Aussie stevedores, too, share part of the blame for Java's loss. It is probable that the eighty planes, if rushed to conflict areas, would have delayed the

Japanese long enough to enable stronger forces to come to the rescue of the beleaguered Dutch.

The Dutch surrendered on March 8, 1942. Conditions just after the Japanese occupation of Bandoeng, in Java, were outlined to me by a Dutch naval flying officer, who left the Indies a day after the Dutch garrison in Bandoeng surrendered.

This lieutenant, when he saw the situation to be hopeless, flew his PBY seaplane to Lake Tjitjalenka, some miles from Bandoeng, and then returned on foot to the city for orders. Meanwhile the Japanese had marched in, at midnight on March 8, and were issuing instructions to the populace. Certain parts of the city were set aside by the enemy. All Dutchmen and their families were told to proceed to these districts, and remain there. To the lieutenant's knowledge, there were no scenes of either torture or humiliation for the Hollanders.

However, three days later, when Nirom, the Dutch State Radio in the N.E.I., was taken over by the Japs, an announcement was made which predicted the temper of enemy soldiery engaged. A Japanese broadcast ordered that all liquor supplies Dutchmen might have on hand be destroyed, and, under no circumstances, be allowed to fall into the hands of Tokyo's invading troops. Apparently the Jap High Command could not trust the discipline of its charges.

All guns were to be turned over to the Japanese, the broadcast continued. This gave the Dutch lieutenant an idea. He returned to Lake Tjitjalenka and calmly took off in the daytime. Enemy fighter patrols must have been resting, according to my informant, for he saw no Jap ships in the air all the way to Australia. If he was spotted, the Japanese must have thought him one of their own men flying a captured plane.

General ter Poorten surrendered to the Japanese commander, said my Dutch friend, shortly after occupation of Bandoeng.

Typical of the Hollanders' attitude was the General's eloquent silence when the Japanese military chief took his sword.

"How many divisions have you?" asked the Jap.

"One, here," replied ter Poorten.

"But I have nine," exclaimed the Japanese. "I don't understand. Why do you fight?"

General ter Poorten turned away.

All of the Dutch army did not lay down its arms on March 8, in Bandoeng, when General ter Poorten, Commander in Chief of the Netherlands East Indian land forces, had his sword snatched from his hand by an arrogant Jap, flanked by a grinning Nazi major general.

Two Dutchmen, who, by their military experience and ability, were ideally suited for the task, retreated into convenient, friendly mountains with several thousands of troops. In the east of Java, General Pesman remains—at this writing—a threat to Jap occupation troops in and around Surabaya.

Southwest of Bandoeng, General W. Schilling harries Japs all the way from Batavia to the Sunda Straits.

It is not the war of massed tank divisions, of hundreds of dive bombers, and whole corps of infiltrating infantry. Sapped of morale, and filled with terror, Jap troops and police stay close to campfires when the swift eastern end of day changes roads, paths, and city suburbs from well-guarded sectors to places of ambush—where sudden death from razor sharp *klewangs,* and tossed chunks of raw explosives are nightly occurrences.

The saga of these tiny Dutch forces will not be written in full until the war is over. Their bravery and determination, cut off almost hopelessly from any help, is yet a song unsung.

# FAREWELL TO BATAAN

## by Melville Jacoby

WE sit by the side of a Bataan roadway waiting. We're leaving Bataan, we're leaving MacArthur, the Bulkeleys, Wermuths, the men on the firing lines whose exploits are yet untold.

The past months are dreamlike. Only the people we've known make reality—our friends whom we left behind that New Year's Eve in Manila, knowing they would awaken in an occupied defenseless city; the doctors in Bataan we had seen working night and day at base hospitals, unflinching while planes were overhead; the quiet, lanky boy, an ex-bank clerk from California, who walked through Jap lines with a tank rivet in his throat and found himself a hero; the Filipino Scout who, awakening from his operation, found he had lost his leg and would be unable to fight the Japs any more, turned his hurt eyes to the young blonde nurse staring down at him and said, "I do not want to live now, Mum." Our thoughts rove to the first Manila bombing when people stood on the street just watching squadron after squadron of Jap bombers plaster the old Walled City, sending the Santo Domingo church up in flames.

Then our surroundings bring our thoughts back to the present—the big banyan trees, the incessant dust screen, the sloping saddle of Mariveles mountain that we always watch when the cry, "Tojo's coming," is heard. But Tojo does not bother us today as we feel impregnable for the first time in this war. An overloaded jeep bounces by to a skidding halt, throwing up a barrage of dust. The men jump down asking for cigarettes. There's a lieutenant we know and we pass out almost our last Camels, which they light one from each other. I look closely at these men and notice the deep lines war makes on their faces, the whitish tinge the dust gives their hair and beards, the lack of starch in their uniforms. Only their rifles and 45's, which have gained new value to them, show military polish. We swap the usual chit-chat in Bataan—rumors of convoys, the fall of Singapore and what the American planes lost there could have done in Bataan. Then it is time for them to climb back in the jeep and head for the front line.

Finally, it is time for us to move toward the shore where a boat soon will be waiting. Each tree and trail we pass en route seems to hold a particular memory for us and we visit for a few minutes at an ack-ack battery, exchanging news again. The men are out of humor. There have been no Japs over them for nearly a week. They like action now. We pass the Quartermaster's motor pool and wonder how they keep cars and trucks running under these conditions. A soldier drives a car in for air, which he gets from a hose hanging from a banyan tree. We keep passing these vital behind-the-lines organizations—the bakery in the jungle turning out the Army's supply of bread, a cleared space where caribau mules are slaughtered by the Vet Corps for meat, one of General Harold George's airfields which looks like a trail through the woods. We drive through a civilian refugee camp where 7,500 homeless Filipinos live in the open and line up this time every afternoon for rice. They are there again, mothers, children, some men, all preferring Bataan's bombings and hardships to life under the Nips' new order.

We then reach the shoreline which breaks openly and evenly from clusters of coconut palms. An M. P. passes us with a nod, says no planes up now and asks for our last Camel. Our boat is not yet in, so we stand talking to an officer with field glasses, which we borrow to look across the bay toward Manila.

The glasses show clearly the jagged white line of Manila's buildings. We can pick out the Manila Hotel with glasses and imagine the scene inside— Jap officers with long curved swords at their sides strutting around the lobby, and curt sentries with sharp bayonets in front symbolizing the New Order. Every Filipino escaping from Manila tells us that it is a common sight to see one of his countrymen tied for three days and nights on a lamppost on the streets, fed only bread and water. This is the punishment for those who "misbehave"—i.e., walk behind a Jap sentry, cross forbidden areas in the city or touch the ropes marking forbidden zones, which are difficult to recognize because the warning signs are all in Japanese. The story of a young Filipino boy who touched a Jap tank and was then tied to it, bayoneted and slowly beaten, is a story half-a-dozen witnesses report.

Manila has changed much, our Filipino informants tell us. The streets are empty at night except for the Japanese. American stores are all nailed shut, their shelves emptied. Steady streams of Jap-run trucks head north from Manila towards Lingayen Gulf where ships wait to carry the loot back to Japan—the same as in Manchuria, Occupied China, Indo-China. Jap civilians already have begun to prosper, being the only ones allowed access to wholesale houses and privileges—making as much as 500 per cent profit on goods. Little wonder they were willing to set off flares, signals, lights and operate radio stations near our airfields to help get Jap forces in.

Manila is a strange city now, they say—quiet, frightened, and filling with refugees from the countryside where Jap troops loot, rape, kill. An officer standing beside us hears us talk about Manila and says his wife and two kids are there. He asks if we have any news of Americans, aside from the fact that 3,000 of them are confined in Santo Tomas University campus. We tell this officer what the last Filipinos from Manila told us—that Americans in concentration camps are no longer allowed to receive food from friendly Filipinos outside but are now tossed meals by Jap sentries like dogs. We know about three British businessmen shot by a Jap firing squad for "trying to escape" from a concentration camp and we've heard rumors about two Manila newsmen who reportedly committed suicide, jumping from a roof at Santo Tomas.

The same rumors tell of the death of a noted Manila radio commentator known throughout the Far East as Don Bell, who was on the Jap blacklist. The details of Don Bell's death that have circulated suggest he was tortured by the Japs who used cigarette butts on his skin and then finished him off with the bayonet. Bell's funeral procession reportedly went through Manila but no one was allowed on the streets. Bell had been telling the truth too long for the Japanese.

Then our boat comes and we go aboard, carrying light packs and slightly embarrassed at taking anything from Bataan. The sun is already down as we head toward our next mode of transportation. Manila is behind, Bataan is to our right, Corregidor and its string of satellite fortresses to our left. The occasional flashes of shells falling on the "Rock" of Corregidor fade into tiny dots behind. Suddenly it is now all one scene to us—the entire Philippines, the Far East—not just Bataan and Corregidor fighting their own battle but the millions of people of Asia. We have seen MacArthur's men fighting. We carry a last picture of the General himself, tall, determined, neat, leaping from his desk like a man of 30, clapping a fellow officer on the back who has done well, pacing incessantly, sending his men from him inspired by his rolling flow of words spoken in a low emotional voice.

# WE HAVE DONE OUR BEST

## by Carlos P. Romulo

I WAS the last man out of Bataan.

I escaped from that bloody trap because the Japanese had set a price upon my head and because General Douglas MacArthur was able to arrange my last-minute rescue in a makeshift amphibian nicknamed "the Duck." The obsolete crate could not rise seventy feet above Manila Bay, while Japanese ack-ack shells and machine-gun bullets brightened the night around us—the night of April 8-9, 1942, that saw the fall of Bataan.

I lived through the fall of the Philippines.

Before my escape from Bataan I spent four months in hell. This may sound overdramatic, but I know no other word to describe Manila, Corregidor, and Bataan—three tight little components of hell. I had spent four months in the stinking fox holes of Bataan and the filthy stone tunnel of Corregidor. I had seen the battle of the Philippines, first by the side of MacArthur and then with Lieutenant General Jonathan M. "Skinny" Wainwright, who took his place on Corregidor when MacArthur left to assume the supreme Southwest Pacific command.

This is the story of seventeen million Filipinos who cast their lot with America when the hour of danger struck for the American flag. It is the story of seven thousand American soldiers and seventy-five thousand Filipinos against two hundred and fifty thousand Japanese—a hopeless fight by men who gradually lost hope as their numbers shrank and more Japanese poured down the hills and scaled the cliffs of Bataan. I saw Filipino boys I knew and loved blown to shreds before my eyes—as one American soldier put it, "trapped like rats but dying like men."

April first marked our fourth month of war—my third month on Corregidor.

We have looked forward to April.

"Hang on until then," I had urged the boys on the front lines. "Help is sure to come in April."

From the first day of April I began sensing that all was not right on Bataan. As I read the intelligence and operations reports I realized that the front lines were not holding. I had not been to Bataan for a week, and during that time I knew that the battleground had shifted.

I wanted to see for myself if these reports tallied with the actual situation.

Also I wanted to get back to the peninsula and talk with the boys. If things were as bad as they seemed, I did not want them to think the Voice of Freedom was deserting them. I was a man with a price on my head. I had as much reason as any of them to keep on defying the Japanese.

On April fourth I set out for Bataan.

This day that was to mark the turning point in the Battle of the Philippines began for me with an incident that seemed of the greatest importance. In fact, so vital did it seem at the time that that night, upon my return to the tunnel after one of the most terrible days a man could ever experience, I wrote a detailed account of that day on my typewriter with a ribbon that could hardly make itself legible, and with trembling hands I added the important notation:

"I had a Coca-Cola."

There is no use attempting to explain how important that seemed to me. That day I had seen men blown to shreds; I had seen white-faced nurses drag themselves from the bloody debris of a bombed hospital; I had escaped death many times. All this paled and was forgotten before the miracle of a five-cent drink any American can buy at his corner store.

That morning an American corporal whom I knew came furtively into headquarters.

427

"I got sumpin' for you, Colonel," he whispered mysteriously.

I became terribly excited. I thought word of my family had arrived by one of our information carriers. Surprises were rare on the Rock.

"I'll tell you this afternoon," he kept repeating stubbornly. He didn't want to spoil his surprise.

I protested that I would be on Bataan all day. After much persuasion I finally wormed out of him the fact that his "surprise" was a bottle of Coca-Cola.

He explained that a provision barge had been sunk off the Rock and he and his buddies had been daring reprisal from the sharks by diving into the waters and coming up with luxuries long forgotten on Corregidor. For some reason the cargo seemed to have consisted mainly of raisins. Most of them had been spoiled by the salt water, and almost everyone who ate the raisins got dysentery. But they ate them anyway.

My friend had fished up eleven bottles of Coca-Cola. He promised to secrete his gift in my bed sometime during the day.

With this treat in mind I left for Bataan, and throughout that day of death and despair my mind kept darting anxiously back to the bottled treasure hidden in my bed. What if somebody found it?

I considered the friends I would invite to share this debauch.

When I returned to the tunnel late that night of April fourth on Bataan my body was twitching with nervous exhaustion. I went straight to my cot in the lateral and peeled under the covers. They were there—three bottles, sticky with salt from the sea. The corporal had not forgotten!

An awful thought struck me. Were they spoiled? Had salt water seeped under the tin caps?

Like a man broaching a Nihilist plot I whispered to two of my best friends in headquarters, Colonel Pilet and Colonel Galdbraith. I led them to the darkest corner I could find in the officers' mess off the tunnel. I had planned a little ritual with these bottles—drinking a toast to victory from them, out in the moonlight on the hillside. But bombs were falling on the Rock. They had fallen all day over Corregidor and Bataan. There was no leaving the tunnel that night.

Drop by drop, smacking our lips loudly, we finished the last bottles of coke we would see on Corregidor. As I tilted mine for the final sip I was again shocked by the trembling of my hands. I did not like that nervous tremor. Once, after an automobile accident, it had come upon me as a prelude to a paralytic attack. I could not bear the thought of being sick on Corregidor. But nothing more had been said about getting me off the Rock. I had a morbid fear of that stifling underground hospital. My mind went back to Base Hospital No. 1 on Bataan. I had been in it that morning, when it had been bombed and completely destroyed.

No wonder my hands twitched, clutching that bottle. Between the time of my leaving the tunnel that day and re-entering it again I had traveled through every stratum of suffering that could be known outside of hell.

That morning of April fourth I drove to the eastern front in an army

428

command car. I found that the Bagac and Morong lines were finished. The entire front position of Bataan had moved back since my last visit the week before.

I left my car, as always, at one of the command posts and began my trek over the fields, zigzagging from fox hole to fox hole behind the barbed-wire barricades.

I talked to boy after boy. Still after four months, they asked the same question: "When is help coming?"

And still I assured them, "Soon!"

I told them of General MacArthur's plans in Australia. I read them President Quezon's message from Melbourne. And I found that although their lines had been pushed back and their ranks depleted, the men on Bataan felt they were holding their own.

The morale was high.

How could they do it? I found myself wondering. How could they live like that, starve, sicken, undergo the wretchedness of animals trapped in their lairs, and still continue to hold faith?

I was between fox holes when I saw an echelon of Japanese planes dropping their eggs up ahead. By the position of the ships I knew I was in line to be bombed. I had to choose a fox hole quickly. I ran toward one and saw that it already held four boys crouched together and that there was not room for me. I jumped into the next. As I fell a volcano seemed to erupt under my feet and I was half buried under a shower of gravel. I pulled myself out of the rock pile and stood up. The fox hole I had tried to enter first was an empty crater. The four boys had completely vanished, as if they had never existed.

I ran back to the command post over the field that was still being bombed systematically by the visiting planes. At the post I heard a report being telephoned in:

"Base Hospital No. 1 has just been hit."

The hospital was near by. I jumped into my car and rushed there. It was a typical field hospital, made up of canvas tents and bamboo sidings. As I entered the main ward a great detonation shook the place and the bamboo walls crashed in.

This hospital had been bombed by the Japanese only three days before. At the time General Wainwright said that he could not believe the Japanese had intentionally blasted the hospital.

"It must have been a mistake," he said. "Surely the Japanese did not intend to bomb a hospital where the big red cross was so plainly displayed!"

We had quoted his statement over the Voice of Freedom, and a reply came whizzing back from the Japanese station KZRH in Manila. The Japanese commentator agreed that the hospital bombing had indeed been a mistake and the Japanese High Command wished to apologize!

This time the Japanese had made a complete job of it.

I stood in the main tent between the beds and saw the walls and roof collapse and the air thicken with swirling dust. Patients and their beds were buried under debris. The doctors and nurses—those who were able to move—were dragging themselves out of the rubbish heaps on the dirt floor. With dazed expressions they brushed themselves off and staggered about trying to attend to the wounded, while bombs continued to roar ground-ward and the earth rocked under our feet.

Men in splints and bandages heaved themselves off the beds and tried to roll under them for safety. Wounded men screamed their agony, and others lay in broken positions without moving.

Then I saw Father William Thomas Cummings standing on a chair over this scene of bedlam and death. The tall, thin figure of this Maryknoll Mission priest, in the uniform that bore the Cross collar ornaments, was a familiar one on the battlefields. It was he who had said in one of his field sermons on Bataan:

"There are no atheists in the fox holes."

Now, in calm and even tones, Father Cummings began his recital of the Lord's Prayer.

He was hit by shrapnel. Blood poured down his face.

Again and again his [General Lim's] 41st Division had been able to throw back the Japanese offensive and had levied a terrible price from the enemy before withdrawing their lines. They were the heroes who had launched MacArthur's first attack against Homma's men, when they mowed them down in Abucay. Those thousands of Japanese dead still lay unburied, piled one upon another, as they had died under the mouths of our guns at Abucay.

To me this division of Filipinos are the greatest heroes of the Battle of the Philippines. Someday a book will be written of the deeds of Lim's 41st Division.

There was the time Colonel George S. Clark of Spokane had telephoned the front to ask for help in closing a breach. Japanese troops had infiltrated the lines of his 57th Infantry and were pouring in in great numbers. Clark had called another command post to ask for help, but by mistake he had got General Lim on the telephone. Each recognized the voice of the other. Clark had no time to waste.

"General Lim! There's a breach of my left flank. Can you send me some men to close it?"

Lim spoke as quickly. "All my men are busy. All I can send you are some engineers."

"Send anybody!" begged Clark.

Lim went immediately to his engineers. They were bridge builders, pontoon constructors, road makers. He didn't have to tell them how dangerous was the task ahead.

"I want thirty men to close a breach," Lim told them.

One hundred volunteered.

The engineers of Lim moved into that dangerous breach, armed with rifles, and pushed back the Japanese. They closed the line for Colonel Clark.

430

Colonel Clark was picked up unconscious in a fox hole after this battle ended. He had beriberi, which affects the heart, and the strain of continuous battle broke him. I used to see him in the hospital lateral on Corregidor tossing in delirium, crying over and over the roll call of his dead soldiers. They had fought in delaying action from Pampanga to Bataan. They had kept on fighting.

That afternoon at sunset I met General Lim on the front lines. He was haggard and his eyes were sunken, and his hair, once so black, had turned gray. He was smoking a cigar made of rolled guava leaves tied together with a piece of string. As we shook hands I noticed that his was unnaturally warm.

"Malaria?" I asked.

He nodded, and I saw that he could hardly stand on his feet.

"Why don't you go to the hospital?"

He looked at me dull-eyed. "What use?" he asked. "There are no medicines there."

He pointed over the field to his boys in the fox holes.

"Look at them," he said starkly. "A third of them are dying from malaria and dysentery, and we have no medicines to give them."

He added in a low voice, "And, you know, we have not been eating."

I looked. Those boys were to Lim like his own sons. I looked out over the fox holes and saw many faces that I had known in happier days in Manila. Only, were they familiar? At times I could not be sure. I would have to look at a face several times to be sure it was that of a man I knew. Hunger changes the brain and body of a man.

In one of the fox holes I saw Major Jacobo Zobel, who was one of our wealthy Manila playboys and whose palatial home on Dewey Boulevard had been one of the social centers of Manila. I had seen him last at a formal party standing beside the President in the white-and-gold uniform of an aide, introducing guests to Quezon. I had cheered his smashing plays in the polo games at the Manila Club.

Now I saw him there, in rags, with sunken eyes and shaggy, matted hair. He must have lost nearly half his weight. He looked like an old man.

He called over to me in a voice shaking with malarial fever, "When are we going to get help?"

I answered mechanically, "Pronto!"

I saw Ernesto Rufino, who had owned all the movie houses in Manila and who once had been roly-poly and now was thin as a broomstick.

Lieutenant Santos, aide to Lim, whom I remembered in the amusement and luxury of a wealthy and playful Manila, looked at me from a skeleton face gray as paper.

They were men I had known in another luxurious world, and I did not recognize them. I knew them only when General Lim pointed them out to me in the fox holes, saying, "There is Jake, and that is Rufino."

For two months they had kept fighting on that handful of rice a day.

431

Through tropical heat and disease and bombing and gunfire they had held on—when they could not possibly hold on—because help was coming from America and they couldn't let America down!

I can still hear Lim's voice: "...we have not been eating."

I can still see him, that brave Filipino general, his scarecrow body outlined against the sunset of that terrible day of April 4, 1942.

He seemed to me the embodiment of the Philippine Army on Bataan: ragged, starved, sick unto death, beaten back hour after hour—but invincible!

He said in a tired voice, "We have done our best."

Up to that moment I had not lost hope.

\* \* \*

WASHINGTON, April 9, 1942 (International News Service): ...An extraordinary War Department communiqué... quoted Lt. Gen. Jonathan Wainwright from his...headquarters on powerful Corregidor Island as stating that the Bataan defenses probably have been overcome.

\* \* \*

TOKYO, April 18 (United Press): (From Japanese broadcast recorded by the United Press in San Francisco)—Enemy bombers appeared over Tokyo today. The bombing inflicted telling damage on schools and hospitals.

\* \* \*

# RETREAT WITH STILWELL

### by Jack Belden

MAY, 1942—"I'm radioing the British to get police, guides, food, and water on this road. If they don't, there's going to be a catastrophe. Everyone trying to get out and everyone out of hand. Thousands will die."

Stilwell was right. Thousands did die.

The retreat from Burma was one of the bitterest retreats in modern times, ranking only below the Long March of the Chinese Communists in point of physical hardship and duration of march. Even as late as October 1942, as I wrote these lines, it was still going on. Remnants of the Allied armies, six months after the finish of the Burma campaign, were still lost in the jungles, wandering at the base of the Tibet fastnesses, fed by airplane drops, but slowly dying of malaria, exhaustion, and starvation, still unable to escape.

For this catastrophe history will find the people responsible. I can only indicate that such a disaster occurred.

General Stilwell, with the concurrence of General Lo Cho-ying, the Chinese commander-in-chief, made a plan to bring the Chinese Army out of Burma into India. But orders from Chungking later countermanded this plan. When that order came, General Stilwell was out of radio contact with Chungking, General Lo had disappeared to the north, and the new movement of the Chinese Army was already under way.

The change in the plan created the utmost confusion, made supply almost impossible, held thousands of troops for weeks in a malignant malaria district—and doomed many Chinese soldiers to death. Had the original plan been carried out, there is little doubt that between five and six thousand lives would have been saved. But the plan was not carried out—thousands died—thousands were murdered by incompetence.

At half past three on the morning of the 7th of May, while sleep still gripped our tired camp like a disease, I rose from a blanket on the ground, turned my jeep headlights across the yard where weary men lay, and shouted: "Rise and shine!"

Men blinked, shoved their heads under the blankets, and growled when I shook them, saying: "You'd make a good sergeant, you've got a nasty voice."

We lined up for breakfast. Not having a mess kit, I borrowed a flat tin cover from someone and shoved down all the rice I could get. Plates were washed in a gasoline tin of water; canteens were filled with boiled water. Those who didn't get any used cold well-water, placing a few iodine drops in it to decontaminate it. The lights from the bonfires died. The lanterns of the muleteers shone on the horsehair covering of their mule packs. To these they strapped baggage, the larger of the bedding rolls, and the heavier boxes of food. The carriers put bamboo ropes around boxes and lifted them up on poles. There were not enough carriers, and some baggage was left over, so that Frank Merrill had to shoulder his own large pack. Many of the others were carrying two water bottles, two pistols, rucksacks. I had made my pack purposely light, thrown away a heavy blanket, put the rest of my stuff on a mule pack, and carried only a canteen, which I slung around my neck by a cord, as I had no regulation army belt to which it could be fastened.

General Stilwell shoved a carrier guide out in front of him on the path and called to General Sibert: "Okay, Si! Let her go."

Sibert held a police whistle to his lips and blew a sharp blast. "Fall in," he shouted.

Dorn and I fell in behind Stilwell with the rest of the American group behind us; then the British; then the Seagraves, and at the end the Chinese and the carriers.

Stilwell slung a tommy gun over his shoulder, called: "Forward march," and started down the path at a slow pace.

We were off to India. The column went with agonizing slowness; after half an hour Sibert blew his whistle; Stilwell halted and called a ten-minute rest.

The sun beating down with a naked flame on that open beach drove

433

us to seek refuge among the trees, brambles, and bushes on an embankment hanging over the other side of the stream. Here, on top of a coarse prickly undergrowth, beneath trees from which great lianas hung down like braided ropes, Stilwell, Dorn, and I lay on a blanket together, shifting our position every fifteen minutes as the sun found a hole in the overhead shade and mercilessly burned us, and a regiment of ants and bugs crawled into our clothing and prevented us from getting any sleep.

A meal of rice, bully beef, and tea was served on the sands about four o'clock. Men and women lined up before black iron pans, looked at the white grain mixture spotted with red bits of meat, and then gobbled it down greedily. Then we started marching once again.

Although the hot fire had gone out of the air, the accumulative effects of the morning's march plus the abrasive action on our feet of the sand and gravel in our shoes made the evening hike for most of us a grueling affair; and in the end we went even slower than we had in the morning. The general sloshed with the same steady pace through the water, the tommy gun still on his back, but the main group could not keep up with him. Stragglers began to fall behind so that we had to form a stragglers' detachment to pick them up. At one of the halts the general put his gun down for a moment, leaning it against a rock, and at a nodded signal from Pinky Dorn I picked it up and wandered toward the rear; for both of us knew that if the general saw me, he would not let me carry his gun. In this manner I fell in with the Seagrave group on the march, and thereby discovered the pleasantest and ablest companions in the whole column.

At the start of the trip it had been generally feared that our rate of march would be dictated by the comparative slowness of the girls, but here on the first day, at any rate, they not only were marching as fast as anyone else, but were doing so in high spirits, bouncing, splashing and playing in the water, kicking up their legs, holding their skirts high, and singing like chorus girls. Yet they were not at all like Follies beauties—save in age, as all of them fell between seventeen and twenty-three—for the faces of most of them, while attractive and full of expression, were on the whole quite plain and were hidden by sun helmets which came down over their ears and under which many of them had placed towels to absorb the sweat from their foreheads. Yet in that atmosphere and environment they were the perfect companions. And their high-pitched, girlish voices, raised in song and echoing through the cliffs enclosing the stream, provided in moments of drooping morale and excessive fatigue marching rhythms, varying in mood and effect from the soothing to the stirring, that no military band could have equaled. Their own native Karen songs, war songs they had learned from Chinese soldiers, Christian hymns, and ancient American jazz were, save for General Stilwell's dogged, cool perseverance, the one invigorating influence we had on the march. With a feeling of nostalgia I can still hear them sloshing through the river, stumbling through the jungle, and streaming down steep mountain sides, singing in their childish, abandoned way,

434

We'll follow General Stilwell when he comes,
We'll follow General Stilwell when he comes;
Singing Ky Yi Yeepi Yeepi Yi,
Singing Ky Yi Yeepi Yeepi Yi,
Singing . . .

Of all the high officials who came out of Burma, there was only one who had the guts and honesty to tell the world the simple truth.

For five days more, General Stilwell led us across the mountains, increasing his daily rate of march from fourteen to twenty-one miles, until finally he burst out of the jungle and gave his report on the Burma War.

"The Japs ran us out of Burma," he said.

"We were licked."

# NEW GUINEA

## by John Lardner

MAY, 1942—The pilot sitting beside me showed his teeth exultantly as we rode home from the blistering of Lae.

"I'm impartial," he lied at the top of his voice. "But that's the best plane in the world."

Whether it was or not, it was the plane he was learning and loving his job in, the job in this war that Americans and Britons are developing with fullest genius: the smiting of the enemy from the air.

I met the crew in front of the plane, a heavy shadow lined up with other shadows on the field in the early morning darkness. The men were standing in a knot, chewing cheese and crackers. They offered me some. Then the pilot, full of good will, dug me a piece of fruit cake out of a box. He wore a white mosquito head-net cocked rakishly over his nose, and he was taut and boisterous and strictly business all at the same time.

A gunner from another plane walked over and traded limericks with our bombardier. The pilot stood and listened detachedly, gnawing fruit cake.

He was Lieutenant Robert R. Hatch, from Goldsboro, North Carolina, with a wide puckish face and a shrewd eye. He was the captain of this team. . . .

"Let's go!" said Hatch, catching the signal.

I crawled into the belly of the plane, to find the navigator busy at work. The men took their places. We had rushed down the runway in our turn, and were rocketing toward our goal on the north coast of New Guinea before I observed the extra passenger. A small frog jumped across the radio operator's table and vanished under the navigator's desk. I didn't see him again, but for better or worse he was with us when Lae was bombed.

We were past Papua and past the mountains when the sun came up. Shaped like the profile of a turtle headed west in a hurry, the island of New

Guinea presented the hump of its shell to us as we moved high over the coastline, hung briefly over the fifth degree of south latitude, and then swung back toward the target.

The plane was on top of Lae before I discovered it firsthand, tucked in a cleft of coastline, behind a round little harbor. We swept down in a clean angle, as though we were riding a shaft of the rising sun. I saw Hatch's left arm go up in a fierce, triumphant gesture, and looking over his shoulder I saw planes, fat planes, lined up on the square-cut field below.

It came fast then. We hit them from 1,200 feet.

Turning back quickly, I peered down the well of the bomb bay, with Bevan. The shutters flew open beneath us, and we watched the long, sleek yellow pineapples fall clear and hurtle down on the field. They smashed cleanly on the target, all of them, with a concussion that shook the plane in the air and made us flinch away from the hole. We saw fires breaking out before the shutters closed. Then we were climbing.

Say what you will about the Zero, this Jap pursuit plane with the red ball on its dingy green fuselage is ubiquitous, and when it finds you it fawns upon you like a puppy with machine guns for a tongue. Anti-aircraft burst around us, and rocked us, but the airman seldom worries about those long-shot gamblers on the ground. More sinister were the red lines that cut across our nose: tracer bullets. A Zero was alongside.

He wasn't with us long. Shemberger threw a burst back at him from the turret, and then we went away from him as though he were anchored—which is the way it seems when you have an advantage of more than sixty miles an hour in speed, as we did. No Zero lived at that time that could catch the ship we rode.

Exhilaration filled the ship all the way south across the mountains and over the green Coral Sea, where the atolls made yellow blisters on the surface below us and Hatch let me take the controls for a minute and shook with laughter when we promptly lost altitude.

"Say," yelled the pilot presently, "did you notice you got no parachute on? We didn't have an extra one. But it don't make any difference."

"It don't?"

"No. Our policy is to all go down with the ship. That way, we land together and we all got a chance together."

We stopped to gas up at a barren little base on the way home. There was bread and marmalade at the mess shack there, and oranges. Waiting on the field, Hatch and Seffern played catch with an orange, and Seffern, as he wound up elaborately, told of the only home run he ever hit in his life. Young Robbie spoke to me tolerantly of the fourth estate—"Good, clean work," he pronounced. Bevan, the Boston athlete, wanted to know how the Bruins had made out in the last Stanley Cup hockey playoffs. They hadn't made out so good.

We got our last thrill of the day then, thrown in for good measure and absolutely unsolicited. Doggedly the Zeros had trailed us south, and with them came bombers. The alarm sounded, and the crews on the ground

436

beelined for their planes, for there is nothing more humiliating, useless, and downright impractical than to be caught on the ground, in the open, with your aeronautical pants down.

There is nothing more scary, I should add, because something always goes a little wrong when you try to take off under the condition known as "or else." One of the engines missed. Then the door failed to shut tight, and Ware had to leap down to the ground again to adjust it from the outside. But we did get off, after sitting there for what seemed like a couple of minutes longer than forever. For one of the ships in our flight, it was closer than a barbershop shave—the first of the Mitsubishis to arrive, dropped a bomb near by that damaged our neighbor's fuselage.

But we all got home. All the teams that went north to plaster Lae that day in behalf of democracy came safely to roost at their base. It was there that Hatch proudly showed me his ship's bullet scars from her last mission —"We got a square hit on an aircraft carrier"—and it was there, as we waited for the truck to take us to mess, that the northerners in the crew considered ways and means to mutiny against Hatch; he had painted the name "Dixie" on her nose over her trade mark of the Jap carrier going down.

# PANAMA PATROL

## by Walter Davenport

MAY, 1942—We're flying high and wide. The Pacific's so calm in the white of the moon, it looks frozen. Our ship's a light bomber—a swift murdering swooper that has us thinking of the beautiful Harpies that snatched to hell and gone whom the gods condemned. This is war but it doesn't seem like war. Too quiet. You have to remind yourself.

We make notes as we soar, bank, dive, and we hope we'll be able to read them later. Gilky's at the controls—relaxed, nonchalant, his elbow on the shelf of the instrument panel, his chin in his hand. If it weren't for the long, lancing search of his eyes you'd say he was bored. We make a note of that and he senses that we're studying him. He grins at us as, suddenly, almost joyously obeying the touch of his hand, the plane peels off to the side, slips laterally, dives at the sea. Whatever we were writing then became halfway a sluthering pencil line. Gilky thinks that's fun.

"Why don't you just hand in your notes?" he shouts. "Fool 'em. Look wise. Let the editor try to figure it out. Fool the Japs too. Some Jap will shortwave it to Tokyo figuring maybe it's code. Jap High Command will lock themselves up in a room trying to make something out of it. Fool 'em. Maybe they'll come over personally to see what we're pulling. I wish they'd come. Hell, I wish they'd come! What's that down there? Pull yourself together, you! We're going look-see!"

Brigadier General Adlai Gilkeson of Lansdale, Pennsylvania, and the United States Army Air Forces, boss of the Caribbean Interceptor Command, beloved from the White House down to the last Central American jungle airfield as "Gilk" or "Gilky," throws the ship over as you'd cut at a bush with a switch. We dive at an unnamed ripple in the black and silver swell of the misnamed ocean. It's only a smuggler's craft—one of the long, low motorboats that crawl back and forth between matted Colombia's Solano Bay, past the Canal and on to Parita Bay in the Gulf of Panama. Perhaps he's our friend, at least a friend of Captain Leo McIntire, chief of Civilian Intelligence in the ten-mile-wide Canal Zone, leased in perpetuity by the Republic of Panama to the United States. Anyway, he waves to us, doffs his hat with a great sweeping gesture that may be salute but more likely derision.

McIntire knows them all—all contraband runners from dour Colombia to storybook Costa Rica. They hail him in the streets, they crowd his office, they write him hundreds of impassioned letters to tell him who's who and what's what and what's new in the ten thousand coves and inlets that the Navy knows only by hearsay and which a thousand planes could do no more than skim over. Leo McIntire's an incredible book all by himself if he cared and dared to write it.

Gilky's sore. If ever there's been a man spoiling for fight, it's Gilk. This Panama Canal assignment is purely defensive. Land, sea and air forces, such as they are today and such as they'll be tomorrow, walk and fly the Isthmus and skitter up and down its shores, waiting, waiting, waiting for the attack. They're sure it will come. Waiting makes them thin and sharp and short of temper. They sit beside the huge detectors, their long-distance ears, mounted and cocked on the hills and mountains. Hour follows hour; days and nights pass by. No Japs. Gilk grows picturesquely profane. He'd rather get licked in a fight than loaf around waiting for one.

"D'ya see that fighter?" says Gilk, before we leave Albrook Field to make our patrol. "D'ya see it?" He points to a long sleek beauty whiskered with machine guns and engined to pace the wind. His voice is wistful.

"Come the Japs to blast the locks," says Gilk, "and I'll wait until I've got all my boys in the air. When the last interceptors are up I'll turn control over to someone and take off in that one myself and get me my ration of little yella fellas. Oh, why don't they come?"

So we're out over the Pacific with Gilk, hoping tonight's the night. This is the place to be if you want to get the Panama picture. Before we strike south we see things that make us laugh, that make us hope, that make us calculate. The Canal, except where they're hacking down and around hills to make the new locks, is blacked out—in a manner of speaking. From the Zone, no lights stab up at you but there's a sultry glow upon the ground from hooded lamps, and millions of stars mock the futile gloom. Ancon, Balboa, and Quarry Heights, whereon sits the quiet, hewn-faced commander of the Canal Defense, Lieutenant General Frank Andrews, are shadowy but wholly visible. Gilky and the rest of us, streaking across the

438

star-spangled skies, could blast Ancon, Balboa, and Quarry Heights to blood and dust (and die happy) if we were the enemy.

We could smash the Pedro Miguel Locks if we could get this far. However, this is no secret. The Japs know it. The Nazis know it. For years we've been giving away thousands of maps and cross-section charts, photographs and engineers' tables, until the Canal itself hasn't a ghost of a secret left. All the enemy would have to do is get this far in and this far down. That's all. That's the enemy's problem.

But even if he gets by Gilk and the interceptors, his troubles will have just begun. We can go no further along this line. Use your imagination and don't boggle at improbabilities. The Canal Zone is tropically rich and riotous with defense surprises. We've heard the Albrook organ play its *Danse Macabre*. Have you seen and heard Walt Disney's Fantasia? That gives you a thin hint, as the Old Mill Stream gives you a hint of Niagara Falls. Gilk built the Albrook organ. You should hear him play it. We've climbed the mountains where former•bellhops, divinity students, milkmen, soda jerkers, college sophomores and ticket scalpers have become jungle troops, anti-aircraft artillerymen, bomb and bolo fighters swinging from tree to tree, screaming back at howler monkeys. The temptation is strong to tell you more of what we've seen below there, from Mexico to South America—and beyond. But that's for the speedy Jap to find out and we predict no joy for him when he tries it. These lads, shackled to defense, eager to take the offensive, are too hungry for a fight.

This is the place to be, looking down upon the scramble of peoples, the clustered communities, the clean fifty-two-mile gash of free and impounded water that is the all-important Canal. Down below there, afoot or in the last-gasp taxis driven by brown men who make the chauffeurs of prewar Paris seem like scary old ladies, you're permanently confused. The only thing you're sure of is that those Panamanian taxi drivers ought to be in the tank corps, they and their brothers who drive those chivas or public busses. Incidentally, they drive on the left side of the street like the British. We asked one of them why. He said that there'd be too many accidents if he drove on the right, and that's as good a reason as anyone will give you for anything down there.

From up here, flying with Gilk or with young Lieutenant Colonel Tom Darcy, aide to General Andrews, or with Lieutenant Red Woolsey, a big, shy, clean kid from Oklahoma, the garble of town and tongue, position and politics, greed and glory unlaces itself. We have a quick look and write it down as we go. We have a night of hopeful patrol before us. We shall cover many miles of sea and sky before we get back.

We see the shine of the Canal, the sweep of Albrook Field, the winding roads of Balboa Heights and the broad, smug, termite-gnawed government houses. Yonder, similarly gloomed down but not blacked out are the United States Naval Reservation, Fort Amador, Ancon and Sosa Hills, Diablo Heights and Corozal; and beyond, the new locks. These districts "dark down" at six when the hot daylight ceases and suddenly it's night. There is no evening, no twilight. Suddenly it's night. But blackout—lights out—doesn't happen until eleven and you wonder why they wait almost until midnight. You wonder until you see it from the skies. Actually you can't blackout the Canal any more than Londoners could blackout the beckoning, guiding Thames, any more than New York can blackout the East and Hudson rivers.

Up here, our plane roaring defiance, we get our land bearings and sort out what was a garble below. In the skies we begin to understand why the Canal and its environs make such a complex problem of defense, why the Canal's defense means diplomacy as well as guns and guts. The skein unravels, the jigsaw puzzle sorts itself out. Yonder, where the City of Panama ends in a crooked finger in the sea, is the American Embassy. There is Ambassador Wilson, a clever gentleman, knowing his Latin Americans, hugely respected by them. He got this delicate post because he is those things. He is the skillful balance between the Panamanian government and the United States Army, a man of infinite tact and patience. The big fellow on Quarry Heights, General Andrews (Andy to his men) is lucky to have Wilson here. The State Department, thinking and acting often timorously in terms of the Good Neighbor Policy, is frequently more appeasive than aggressive, and Andrews, a soldier to his last fiber, must think of everything. But in Wilson's deft hands, the State Department side is never a blockade.

A step up Central Avenue on the flank of Cathedral Plaza is the Presidencia—Panama's White House. Therein sits Señor Ricardo Adolfo de la Guardia, Panama's president. De la Guardia became president as the result of last October's *coup d'état* which sent the Huey Longish Arnulfo Arias into exile. In Washington's eyes, Arias was tricky if not treacherous, a little too prone to listen indulgently to the cause of our enemies. Perhaps however he was merely a shrewd politician eager to drive a harder, more profitable bargain with the Canal's owner, the United States.

We haven't time to go into that but he surely got the works when the time came; and de la Guardia, a less spectacular statesman whose heart is in Panama not Havana, has taken over, co-operating completely with Washington. If we had time, we'd tell you how it happened—a grand tale of how to get rid of a political boss. Too bad the United States hasn't studied the Latin-American procedure. She could use it occasionally and be the better for it.

Looking down through the clear, dark blue we can see the Canal Administration Building, the seat of the civil government of the Canal Zone. From that headquarters, Major General Glen E. Edgerton, governor, and Colonel Joe Mehaffey, engineer of maintenance, rule the affairs of seventy-five thousand civil employees among whom the caste system is more than somewhat prevalent. It is just as impossible for the low-paid worker (the silver set) to break into the social circles of the upper brackets (the gold crowd) as it would be for the guy who mows your lawn to ride Mrs. Astor's plush horse. But neither Edgerton nor Mehaffey, both tough-minded United States Army engineers, are much concerned with anything but running the Canal.

One last look before we strike out above the jungle, over the Pacific, to the far-flung airfields, the battered mountaintops. High above all these groups on Quarry Heights is the commander—General Andrews. Andy's a flier too. He's pushing toward sixty, was built for offensive warfare. He's an old cavalryman, turned airman. We didn't fly with him but saw him bring in his huge Army transport plane as neatly as you'd wheel a pram the length of a suburban block. He gives you a feeling of deep security. He smiles infrequently. Even a professional grinner would find little to smile about in Andy's job.

At last we're off to see what lies beyond the man-made jungle of politics, administration, government, and rumor. The jungle that nature grew, with its cats and apes, snakes and birds, rotting vegetation and infested swamp —that will be peace. We swarm over the fortified islands in Panama Bay. The huge guns crouch in their pits, great clumsy beasts ready to rear and hurl tons of steel beyond the horizon. Somehow they don't impress us.

Perhaps we remember what so many airmen, so many new-school soldiers have said about them—that they are all right if the enemy is fool enough to get within their brief lateral sweep. But that's not the way the game is played today. The new order tells you that they'd be more use melted down and recast into five-inch antiaircraft guns. But there they are, as everybody from here to Tokyo knows, monsters of the wars of yesterday! However, we'd advise nobody to try bombing them into silence. They're stoutly protected from attack from the air. We wouldn't tell you how, even if we hadn't been warned away from the subject by Major Bob Bruskin and his boss, Colonel Robert G. Kirkwood, G-2.

We fly to the east, down the Darien country toward Colombia. Presently two huge slim birds pass us, turn, circle high above us. They dive at us, turning themselves almost inside out. They know who we are but they take no chances these days and nights over Panama. They verify us and go back to their stunting, showing us what P-39 and P-40 fighters splitting the clouds at hundreds of miles an hour could do to a bomber. They circle us, deftly maneuvering us into a new airfield cut out of the raw jungle on the Pacific side.

Gilky knows all about it of course, because this field is one of the cunningly contrived and hidden bases of his Interceptor Command. All we saw when we swooped suddenly into the clearing was a field. Then out of the palms, the thick curtains of vines, came the kids who fly the fighters. We saw no planes until we got behind those curtains. All of them can be off the ground in much less than four minutes. They can be back in their cover before the roar of their descent dies, and there is no order or rote to their cover. There is no solid-phalanx stuff about the disposition of Gilky's planes —as there was at Pearl Harbor. (Trouble with this story is that we always have to pipe down the moment we get warmed up.)

We had a beer at the Stork Club. If you'd been there you could have read the sign on the barracks door for yourself. The shack near by was 10 Downing Street. Next to that was 1600 Pennsylvania Avenue. Next, The Brown

Derby, Twenty-one, The Mark Hopkins and Ye Olde Bucket of Bloode.

One of the lads told us that all aviators have to be more or less crazy. He was studying medicine when he got into the Army Air Force, said he was going in for surgery but had changed his mind. But eventually he's going to make it psychiatry. He thinks it would be a sin not to, after being in a laboratory like the Air Force. He has the various psychoses stages catalogued but admits that changes may have to be made. For example, if you have a persecution complex you'll be best in a scout plane, observing. He says that the heavy bombers—the flying fortresses—are ideal ships for homicidal maniacs.

"It's like musicians and artists," he said. "If they're any good at all they're crazy. There's one guy here who wouldn't have a mattress. When he goes to bed he takes everything off but his boots. Wraps a blanket around his head. Yale man."

They are a talented mob. You could dig up a small professional dance band. In Ye Olde Bucket of Bloode we were about to be entertained by a magician when the alert sounded, and just as mysteriously as they had appeared, the airmen vanished. Seconds later the jungle roared as ship after ship took off. So did we. Gilky swinging east again. He's a veteran but if he lives to be a hundred he'll never be an old-timer. Not old-timer stuff. They say he could fly a rocking-chair if you gave him a couple of palm-leaf fans. Back in the first World War he flew Martin biplanes which made sixty miles an hour and inspired the old Army brass hats to predict that they had no place in combat because they were too fast and would overshoot their target. Some of these men are still in the Army, still shaking their heads.

Gilk was getting bored. No Japs. The best we could do was a buzzard. It made a three-inch dent in one of our wings, but the buzzard was all through in a lovely explosion of feathers. Buzzards fly by the hundreds over the Isthmus. They got used to the slower planes, diving out of their way. But the new fast fighters have caught them unprepared for real speed. The pilots don't go for them intentionally because they're oversize buzzards and can do a lot of damage if they smack you square. Anyway we had to be content with a large buzzard before landing in our next jungle hideaway.

# HONG KONG 1942

### by Gwen Dew

THE Japanese general at headquarters shot questions at the guests.

"Where are your soldiers?"

Major Manners and Mr. Shields acted as spokesmen. "They went away during the night."

"Where?"

442

"We don't know."

Then the general would point to this man or that one. "Who are you?"

"I'm a banker."

"Who are you?"

"I'm a businessman."

"Why aren't you fighting? Don't you know your country is at war with Japan?"

The men tried to explain that in Britain and America certain men fight, others stay home to carry on the national business.

The Jap rolled his words out like warning thunder. "In Japan *every* man fights. It makes no difference what his position is in peace-time. This is *war*."

The group was stretched out in a long line, their arms still above their heads. The soldiers searched them, taking jewelry from some, smashing things they took from others. Finally the general seemed satisfied with his questioning. But he took a last parting shot that nearly broke the spirit of the prisoners.

"If *your* soldiers have gone away, leaving women and children unprotected, *our* soldiers will protect you."

It was a humiliating statement which everyone had to take. It was impossible to explain that our soldiers had gone away, under the most dangerous conditions, so that the women, children, and civilian men might have a chance to live.

It was a curious day of restless quiet. There was no more movement of the British soldiers, no more firing, no more sense of activity. Everything was finished. We were prisoners, and the Japanese intended us to know that. This was what I would have dreaded most in all the world if I had thought it could happen to me. In choosing to go into a war zone I knew that I might be injured or killed, but that didn't seem important. But if I had been told in advance that I was to be captured by the Japs, I might not have faced it.

While we were sweeping and cleaning the dining-room, putting the tables back in their usual places, the Jap soldiers stood guard in the doorway, with their guns dropped loosely over their arms, but always pointing at us. One little soldier in a baggy uniform stomped over to the piano and began playing. It gave a last crazy touch to the morning—British and Americans taking orders from monkey men, and one of them, who had just finished ferocious fighting, attracted to the piano on the orchestra stand!

We had luncheon at two o'clock, and some tea at five. That luncheon was the last full meal we were to have for forty-four hours; in fact, the last one with our kind of food for six months.

The following story was told to me by one of the nurses who went through the worst of all experiences at St. Stephen's. She told it undramatically and methodically, but there were black circles under her eyes, and her thin, nervous hands, which kept knitting the air, give hints of the

443

inner turmoil that retelling it occasioned. I hesitated a long time to ask her to live through the hours again with me, but I felt that I must have the story direct from one who knew every damnable second of it. And obviously she felt that it must be told, exactly and correctly, so that those who do not come close to the Japanese can know what sort of men they are.

No woman on earth is going to tell of being gang-raped by enemy soldiers unless it is imperative, and only the bravest would be willing to tell her story to the world. I marveled at the inner strength which made her able to answer my most searching questions, and yet I sensed all through it the perspective which she had taken of the blackening experience: she was a soldier at her post; she had suffered grievous wounds which would leave scars on her soul forever, but she had gone through this in line of duty, and she had done her part without fear, just as would any brave soldier.

I checked and rechecked every detail of this story; it has been attested to by soldiers who were present and by those who lived through it. This is no vague "atrocity story"; this is stark truth. I give it to you as one of the most dastardly and blackest pages of Japanese history—ranking with the rape of Nanking.

"It was six A.M. of Christmas morning that the Japs came to St. Stephen's," the nurse said. "We had established an emergency hospital here in the auditorium and the balcony. There were cots, but many of the wounded lay on the floor. A big Red Cross flag was over the doorway. Some Canadian soldiers, exhausted, stopped for a minute to warn us the Japs were coming with their Bren and Lower guns, and stumbled on.

"Colonel Dr. Black, who was in charge, went to meet the Japs. He stepped to the door, put his arms across it, and said, pointing to the Red Cross: 'This is a hospital, and only wounded are here.'

"The Japanese, without hesitation or further examination, bayoneted Dr. Black." The girl stopped a minute as her memory unwound the ghastly picture. "Then they stepped over him, entered, and bayoneted Dr. Whitney, the doctor next in charge.

"We had converted the auditorium into an emergency ward, where hundreds of British and Canadian wounded soldiers were lying. Those blood-mad Japs stormed in and, despite the efforts of all the nurses to stop them, ripped the bandages from the wounded. Then they bayoneted and killed fifty-two of these helpless men while we could only watch."

Silence dripped into time as we faced the pictures she was painting.

"Then—then—" the nurse's hands worked quicker and quicker—"they lined up all of the nurses, all of us Volunteers from Hong Kong. They took away the first three, and they never came back. We kept asking for them, but they never came back. Then they took the rest of us, one by one, and raped us time and time again.

"They kept us in a small room, and whenever a Jap wanted us he came and took us away. All Christmas Day. All Christmas night. I lost track of the times they used each one of us. Twenty-four hours of it—can I ever, ever forget it?"

444

She couldn't say more. I couldn't ask more.

When the bodies of the other nurses were found, it was evident they had been attacked and then killed.

At dawn the day after Christmas a daring British doctor from Fort Stanley, at the risk of his life, drove an ambulance up to the door of the building, and the nurses ran for it. They were taken to the fort, where the husbands of some of them had been fighting, and were given medical attention and rest, although some insisted on going to work almost at once because there were wounded who needed their care.

In our concentration camp was the husband of one of the women involved. He had been at Repulse Bay, and I remembered him. He was nearly heartbroken in actuality, and mentally tortured, for his wife was one of the women who were first violated and then bayoneted. We used to see him sitting silently by the hour near a bush, looking far out at space. We wondered why "Trudy" Begg didn't go to the little cemetery with the token graves near by, and whether he hadn't become a little unbalanced by his torturous thoughts. Finally we were to find that it was under this bush that the remnants of his wife's body had been found, and to him this was her burial place.

There is a hillside cemetery at Stanley, where pine trees stand eternal guard, and the sighing of soft winds gives music to those who lie beneath the ground. Row after row of lovely hibiscus embroider the stone path which leads through the cemetery, and the pines stand sentinel along the gray wall. The cemetery is a record of years of British work on this stony island, with many of the graves bearing the mark of 1846, when a malaria epidemic nearly wiped out the fort. There are graves of babies who could not stand this transplanted life, and of small children who succumbed to strange Chinese illnesses. There are records of soldiers who defended the fort, and of their wives who fought beside them.

But there is no record of any who died more valiantly in the defense of the honor of their country and of democratic principles than that on the bare wooden crosses which stand above the two empty graves. There are no bodies here because the Japanese soldiers took possession of the hospital, of all of Stanley, and refused burial to those who did not die in vain.

On one of the crosses are the words:

> COLONEL BLACK
> CAPTAIN WHITNEY

And on the other:

> MRS. BEGG
> MRS. BUXTON
> MRS. WHITE

They will stand forever in our memories as monuments of honor to these valiant men and women of Great Britain, and as fingers of shame pointing at the country which has no standards of humanity, decency, or traditions, the Empire of Japan.

445

# CITY IN PRISON

## by Joseph Alsop, Jr.

IT was a warm winter morning, lit by a pale sunlight that grimly illuminated the wounds of the city, when the Japanese ordered all British, Dutch, and American nationals in Hong Kong to report at the Murray Parade Ground with such personal effects as they could carry. Along with nearly 3,500 others—men, women and children, old and young, sick and healthy—I began that day the experience of internment.

It endured for me until the Americans were exchanged six months later, and still endures for the 3,000-odd British and Dutch who remain behind the barbed wire in Stanley Camp. It was a singular experience, different from military internment—we were all civilians or pretended civilians—and perhaps more interesting, for we were the bits and pieces of a complete, highly organized peacetime society which had been blown sky high and come down together again at haphazard. And for this very reason it was a most curious commentary on people and their relations to one another and to their surroundings, and seems worth writing about even now in America, where the war is so incredibly distant despite the gaps in families and the uniforms in the streets, where respectable people who began scrabbling in garbage cans would be hastily bundled off to the psychiatrists.

The society I speak of was the former ruling caste of the British crown colony of Hong Kong. I was, of course, an interloper, only there at all because the Pan American shuttle clipper had brought me to Hong Kong the night before Pearl Harbor, on my way back from a mission to Manila for Gen. C. L. Chennault and the American Volunteer Group. Being an island, the place was a trap and I could not return to my post on General Chennault's staff.

They wanted no last-minute volunteers. So, while the days of fighting passed with dreadful swiftness, I picked up wounded until the surrender came on Christmas Day. That afternoon, before the first files of Japanese troops—little, animal-looking men—marched into the deathly still center of the city, I burned my passport and papers and obtained from the American consulate officials roosting gloomily in their big office a new "certificate of identification" as a newspaperman. So, barring the accidents of investigation, since I was not in uniform, I was ready for what was to come.

Between the surrender on Christmas Day and the Japanese order that settled our fate, there was more than a week of suspense—of crowding together, day after day, in the odd places where the abrupt end of fighting had left us; of anxious discussion of Japanese intentions, and of occasional sallies into the streets to buy food and supplies from the Chinese hawkers, who soon swarmed everywhere with the miscellaneous loot of the city in little boxes and baskets. The Hong Kong garrison was interned at once, but civilians and ostensible civilians were let alone.

446

Everyone tried vaguely to prepare for an unforeseeable future. My efforts, which turned out better than the average, were the purchase of a small canned-food reserve and the manufacture of emergency bedding out of a borrowed blackout curtain and two chair cushions from the American Club. On the night before internment I removed to the Gloucester to stay with the local A.P. correspondent, Vaughn Meisling, who had, with great generosity and courage, offered to support my self-identification as a newspaperman.

Next morning the Queens Road, the broad street which runs past the Murray Parade Ground, was filled with English and Americans of all sorts, alone and in groups, all lugging suitcases and bundles. Huge crowds of Chinese, unaccustomed to seeing the city's privileged caste carrying anything heavier than the morning newspaper, looked on from the sidewalks in pleased astonishment. The parade ground, a big, square, railed-in space at the heart of the city, next to the barracks, was filled with more people, all milling about aimlessly, or sitting limply on little heaps of battered-looking luggage. Shortly before noon a detachment of Japanese gendarmes and interpreters drove up, and after a good many misunderstandings everyone was lined up in a column of fours. After a short inspection, the 200 people at the head of the column were marched off by a couple of gendarmes. The column moved forward, and the inspection and marching off were repeated several times, until my section of the column was reached. We fell to the lot of a squat captain of *gendarmerie* with a face like a dog and an unshakable belief that any command in Japanese, if only shouted loudly, would be understood by all. He had a way of kicking people in the stomach if they did not grasp his wishes soon enough, but, luckily, he generally gestured when he bellowed. We moved off docilely behind him, between the walls of Chinese spectators, down Queens Road into the poorer district of the city.

After trudging a mile and a half, we turned abruptly into a narrow alley and were halted before the grilled door of an ancient, dilapidated and very dirty building. Painted on the peeling plaster was an announcement in Chinese that it was the Stag Hotel, offering comfortable rooms at cheap rates. In reality, it was a Chinese brothel of the third class.

The Stag must, I think, have been built as a private house by a rich early China trader. The original rooms were very large, and there were still traces of good workmanship here and there. But now the rooms had been partitioned off into innumerable little cells, and the partitions, which were of chicken wire after the first eight feet, had been put in without regard to light or ventilation.

For furniture the cells had only large, very hard Chinese beds, a broken-down chair or so and a grimy washstand. Each cell which had once housed a single Chinese prostitute was now marked in chalk on the door as accommodation for a minimum of three and commonly four or five people.

But there was no time to complain. We all scrambled for rooms, while the gendarme captain and his staff tramped up and down the corridors,

447

hustling the elderly and bewildered, and constantly making the queer barking sounds habitual in irritated Japanese. The brothel proprietor and his seedy runners stood about in obvious enjoyment of our discomfiture. They resented us, since our arrival had deprived them of their customary means of livelihood.

On paper the ensuing seventeen days look pretty macabre. There were about 140 of us in the Stag—seven other brothels held the balance of the civilian internees in Hong Kong. There was no heat, no light, no bedding except what the internees had brought or the prostitutes left behind. There were only three toilets in the entire establishment, and all three worked only intermittently. It was bitterly cold a good part of the time, with the damp, penetrating chilliness which Hong Kong in winter shares with Boston.

The effect of the cold was vastly increased by the shortage of food. The Japanese occasionally delivered a little rice and the scrag end of an animal, but the deliveries were made to the brothel proprietor, and, except in the last few days, the cooking was in the hands of the brothel runners.

On our seventeenth morning in the brothel, the expectation of transfer to a permanent internment camp was actually fulfilled.

After our suitcases and bundles had been searched for weapons, a big old harbor boat took us around Hong Kong Island to Stanley Peninsula. Stanley Peninsula, which was to be our home until our release, is a narrow, hilly, infertile neck of land running out to a bigger hill on which stands Stanley Fort.

Billeting was the first great problem. It was done at haphazard, on the principle of first come, first served, except that large blocks had been set aside for special groups. The American bachelors' quarters were in the former warders' club.

The community in Stanley created a sort of *ersatz* life for itself, choosing its own leaders, inventing its own political issues, furnishing its rooms with the refuse of a battlefield, substituting barter and the black market for the normal processes of commerce, and even sometimes holding its own parties.

They were something, those Stanley parties. I used sometimes to be invited by a couple formerly celebrated for the sinister lavishness of their hospitality, from whose house it had once been difficult to escape sober and without indigestion. Four or five people, most of them dressed in rags and tatters, would gather solemnly in the couple's room and seat themselves on the remnant of a chair and the couch made of boards supported on concrete bombproofing blocks, which were the furniture. The host and hostess, still using the old lavish gestures and intonations, would produce a brew of tea leaves stewed for the third time and a little plate of cakes made of part of their luncheon rice sweetened with black-market sugar and roasted on the top of a biscuit tin over a fire of carefully collected twigs. The guests would compliment the hostess on the fare as though it had been the cocktails and rich sandwiches of the old days, and the meal would be consumed

448

with immense attention to an exact division, down to the very last drop and crumb of the tea and cakes.

At every point in the life of the camp, there was the same singular substitution of values. A sweetened rice cake was a rich sandwich; a tin of baked beans became the equivalent of lunch at the Colony, and a cell which would have aroused the fury of any housing authority in the United States had the status of a penthouse apartment.

With new values, but old patterns, the life of the camp went on. Mothers tended their children and taught them. Housewives cleaned their apartments—with little or no soap. Fathers of families did their best to be breadwinners—when there was no bread. The community exchanged the day's small news every morning and evening in the roadways between blocks of buildings. Politicians busied themselves with issues and policies. Occasionally, the Japanese, who stood in the same relationship to us as providence to nations in the outer world, brusquely and surprisingly intervened.

MAY 8, 1942: *Battle of Coral Sea and American victory.*

# THE *LEXINGTON* GOES TO GLORY

## *by Stanley Johnston*

MAY, 1942—As we again passed the *Lexington's* stern on our way back to the cruiser there was a heavy explosion aboard her that sent the amidships portion of the flight deck hurtling into the air. Flames burst through. Almost immediately there came another blinding flash, a tremendous shock and a billowing cloud of black smoke soaring skyward as the 1,000-pound bombs exploded. Bits of the steel deck and side plates showered the sea for hundreds of yards around, endangering all in the water and boats.

I later learned that Commander Seligman and Capt. Sherman were still on ropes, just making their way off the *Lexington* when this blast shook them loose and threw them into the sea.

Only a few minutes later the after tip of the flight deck was blasted away. Planes were tossed into the water when the torpedo war-heads let go. Captain Sherman and Commander Seligman were swimming to a cutter when this happened, from where they were transferred to a cruiser already crowded with more than 800 *Lex* survivors. They were the last men off and had just made one more final inspection to see that everyone else was clear.

Seligman told me of this later:

"We were walking back to the stern and I was urging the skipper to hurry because I knew those bombs were overdue. He seemed to be thinking and suddenly stopped, asked me to wait a minute and trotted over to the island. I saw him go into his emergency cabin for a minute and as he came

449

out a minute later he was firmly adjusting his No. 1 cap to his head—the one with the newest and heaviest gold braid.

"He grinned as we walked over to the side and said: 'I hear there's not to be any more gold braid till after the war, and I wouldn't like to have to use that yellow cotton substitute. Thought I'd better save my best one.' "

Seligman tells that when they reached the stern the skipper ordered him to "lower away." He selected a rope and started down, but Capt. Sherman stood above him, musing as he looked back over the smoking ship.

"Come on, skipper, don't wait any longer," Seligman urged him. Capt. Sherman looked down at him and slowly replied: "I was just thinking . . . wouldn't I look silly if I left this ship and the fires went out?"

From the *Lex* our lookouts who suspected each curling whitecap as the periscope wake of a submarine and whose vigilant gaze ranged the surface of the waters day and night, had seen thousands of sharks in the few days just preceding our final battles. So every man on the ship rather expected that if the time ever came when he would have to abandon ship those sharks would be a menace.

"If we ever had to swim in this ocean the sharks would get us," the deck crews used to assure one another in their leisure-moment huddles—the Navy calls this "shooting the breeze."

But when the time really came, and we were abandoning the *Lex* by the thousands, not a shark was to be seen. Neither we watching from the flight deck nor the sharp eyes of lookouts on the rescue vessels ever saw a fin or the betraying flicker of a tail.

Several explanations were offered. One group held that it was pure luck —the luck of a Lady, as the *Lexington* was often referred to.

The more analytical however, attributed the total absence of sharks to the fact that they were frightened off by the repeated heavy explosions in the great hull. These blasts, which shook the whole 46,000 tons of her several times a minute toward the end, traveled for great distances through the water. Any heavy underwater explosion kills fish for hundreds of feet around because fluid transmits shock over long distances. Air is compressible so explosions soon lose their force, but water is incompressible and spreads explosive shocks further. To this fact we probably have to attribute the disappearance of "the denizens of the deeps."

It was into this clear warm water that Capt. Sherman and his Executive Officer plunged when the bomb blast amidships shook them off their hemp ropes. Both men spluttered a bit and then began swimming toward a whale-boat searching for the last few men still in the water. Both were unceremoniously hauled aboard, the Skipper still wearing his gold-braid-loaded No. 1 cap.

Reminiscing about this a few weeks later, after he had been made a Rear Admiral and was called to Washington from San Diego, he told me:

"The boys picked me up by one arm and the seat of my britches and hauled me over the gunnel to drop me flat on my face."

"That's about the only way you can pull a man out of the water."

450

"Yes, that's true," he drawled, smiling. "But I thought they might have a more elegant way of bringing a captain aboard."

It was 6:30 P.M. now and almost dark, as night descends quickly in the tropics. The sun had dropped into the sea and the rescue work was nearly over. Our whaleboat was filled with weary swimmers, some of whom were very ill after having swallowed seawater on top of ice cream, and was disembarking its cargo. All the men except Ensign George Markham and myself had climbed the boarding netting dropped from the cruiser's deck when there was another terrific explosion, one of the heaviest of all, aboard the *Lex*. The 16,000 to 20,000 pounds of torpedo war-head guncotton finally had detonated.

"Everybody take cover," came the shout from the deck officers.

George and I stole one look at the poor old *Lexington* and saw bits and particles, airplanes, plates, planks, pieces large and small all going up into the air in the midst of a blinding white flame and smoke. We pressed lovingly against the heaving steel sides of that cruiser, hugging her for seconds while the debris splashed into the sea for hundreds of feet around.

But even then the apparently indestructible old *Lex* didn't sink. Instead she began to burn harder than ever. The flight deck was now ripped wide open from stem to stern. Apparently this last blast had ruptured great holes in the oil and fuel tanks, for the flames now were shooting hundreds of feet high up into the air where they were crowned by thick black smoke.

Night had fallen. It might have been a starry night—but none of us could tell. The leaping, towering flames from the *Lexington* hid all feebler light from the skies. Every bit of flotsam and every outline of the great ship showed up in a blinding glare. Around her the velvety tropic night was the deeper for the contrast. Two destroyers were easing slowly around her burning bulk, nosing in here and there to be sure no one was left in the water.

At 7:15 P.M. Admiral Fletcher aboard Carrier II gave a signal for the fleet to re-form and move away. We had been lying there immobile for at least three hours—the best way of asking for trouble in submarine-infested waters. It was time for us to go but the ships moved off slowly as though reluctant to leave their gallant comrade.

We didn't leave her entirely alone. One destroyer stayed behind, circling around her now cherry-red hull and the maelstrom of fire within her bosom. It was evident that she might burn for hours before sinking. What a signal beacon in the darkness she made! Japanese subs or snooper planes could see her for 100 miles or more and pinprick our position on their charts without any difficulty.

So the Admiral gave orders to sink her.

That lone, remaining destroyer did the job. Standing off 1,500 yards her crew sent four torpedoes coursing—this time into the starboard side. Their explosions were almost lost in the terrific updrafts created by her fires. But their effect was not.

451

She had been settling slowly through the hours, almost on an even keel. Now she shook herself as the torpedoes pierced her last internal ramparts.

Clouds of steam began to hiss upward with the flames. Her white-hot plates groaned and screamed as the water caused them to shrink and buckle. Inside her there were new blasts, rumblings, concussions—as pressures caved in bulkheads, as gasoline vapors exploded. And now the settling was more rapid.

Still she remained upright, dipping neither bow nor stern. Gradually the waves folded over her. One of her officers standing beside me, watching this final act, murmured: "There she goes. She didn't turn over. She is going down with her head up. Dear old *Lex*. A lady to the last!"

# BATTLE OF MIDWAY

## *by Robert J. Casey*

JUNE 4, *Thursday*. North of Midway Islands.

*1:00.* Just learned that the Army planes from Midway located another part of the Jap invasion force late Wednesday afternoon.

*6:00.* I got up for reveille and looked out at a clotted sky, a black sea and odd gray moonlight.

*8:45.* I'm beginning to have a great deal of respect for Admiral Spruance who is conducting this expedition. It is getting more and more apparent as we steam toward the west that we haven't been detected. . . . It's a miracle but that seems to be the way of it.

We have an inferior force. It's probably one of the largest the United States ever sent anywhere in a gesture of anger but what of it. About half the Jap navy—and not the worst end of it—is out there ahead.

*9:10.* We make a right-angle turn. The wind stiffens, if that were possible, and the SBD's and STB's go off.

It's much too windy for me to hear what's being said in sky control so I don't know whether or not any contact has been made with the Japs. Anyway the haul isn't too far for these planes if they have to go all the way to Midway. It's comforting to see them up and something of a relief, too. It won't be long now one way or the other and if anything's coming to us we'll soon know it. If we don't get the Jap he'll certainly get us.

From the signal yards the flags come down and the flags go up—red, yellow, blue, white, crossed, striped, checkered. Lads are running up and down the ladders of the foremast with dispatch blanks in their hands. It's all spectacular and beginning to be thrilling.

*10:30.* We go into a terrific lateral-pass maneuver and the ships start running across each other's bows. Donald Duck raises his voice: "Antiaircraft stations stand by to repel attack."

I go back to my place on the foremast. Then comes the usual wait and study of the sky. You can't help but think that this fine day which you were finding so useful to our bombers is going to be just as helpful to Hirohito's bombers.

*10:35.* Usual reports of approaching aircraft. . . . "Unidentified plane, bearing three-three-eight—forty-eight thousand." "Unidentified plane bearing two-seven-oh—fifty-two thousand. . . ." Everybody is tense of course because sometimes these hysterical shouts turn out to make sense.

We are now leading the procession abreast of the cans. A cruiser—a floating arsenal of ack-ack—has come over alongside our old carrier.

*10:45.* Ten planes show up off the starboard bow. They may be the *Yorktown's* SBD's. As we glower at them we get the answer—the step pyramid of the *Yorktown's* bridge structure comes up over the horizon. More planes are reported but the *Yorktown* claims them for her own and we withdraw from the contest.

We are still plowing along at top speed. On the lower decks the roar of the engines is so great that you have to shout to be heard a few feet. The cans, if we keep on at this rate, will have to refuel tonight. One lone gooney is sailing along with us easily and hopefully.

At the moment the carrier nearest us has sent out fighters, dive bombers, and torpedo planes. If the *Yorktown* has contributed as many as our old carrier, there ought to be about 180 planes on the way to the attack, 105 of them bombers or torpedo carriers.

*11:15.* A report has come in that one of our fortresses has attacked and damaged a carrier, presumably in the reserve group. The attack on Midway has been driven off—eight planes shot down over the island, the Marines claiming a bag of thirty off shore.

It's odd how the battle is shaping up to fit the specifications of the story the medical colonel told me when we went into Honolulu after the Coral Sea. The colonel said that the fight had already occurred. I said it hadn't. Nature as usual is imitating art.

*11:35.* We head now into the wind and it's very chilly. Some fighter planes are coming in, presumably part of our protective patrol. Against the sky they tumble along like a cloud of May flies. We're making crochet patterns all over the sea again.

*11:40.* There is some contact off the starboard quarter. Maybe that's why the fighters came in. They shoot over the rim of the sea and we continue our cotillion.

I'm getting sleepy. A gray half-moon hanging belatedly in the thin blue sky reminds me so much of myself.

*11:45.* Fighters come back to land on our carrier. Apparently a false alarm.

*12:00.* Mickey Reeves signaled me to come down to the bridge for a sandwich. So I was right at headquarters when first reports began to come in from our planes. The first message was brief. The Jap carriers had been located, a little belatedly, and they were virtually without air cover. . . . Apparently all their planes had been sent out to make the conquest of

Midway quick and easy. However, the squadron commander of the TBD unit reporting, said that his planes were virtually out of fuel.

"Request permission," he called, "to withdraw from action and refuel." The admiral's answer was terse.

"Attack at once."

So as I sat down in the chartroom to bite into a ham sandwich, the planes had begun to move in on the carriers. Whatever might be the result, we'd never be able to criticize the quality of our opportunity....

I sat there thinking. The Jap air admiral undoubtedly had figured us as permanent fixtures in the southwest Pacific where last he had had word of us. So just about now he'd be looking up at the sky suddenly clouded with SBD's and asking himself the Japanese equivalent of "Where the hell did those things come from?"

*12:45.* Enemy planes reported off port at twelve miles. New alert sounds. The kids drop their food and sidle off to their guns. The Grummans once more leap off our carrier.

*1:00.* Still no sign of the visitors. I guess the contact was another of those phonies that breed so rapidly in times like this.

*1:15.* Fifteen of the ————'s bombers come over. The squadron is intact and in tight formation, its work, whatever it was, finished.

*1:20.* The carriers swing around, apparently getting ready to take on returning planes which are now showing up in two's and three's. Everything is set to repel an attack, and with good reason. If these planes have failed in their mission or fought a draw or left the Jap carriers usable we may expect a quick and vicious attack in return. If by some remote juju we have put all four carriers out of commission we have just about gained mastery of the Pacific including the Japanese side of the international date line, or so the more educated of my spies tell me.

I went back to the wardroom and contemplated this phenomenon. Presently the word filtered back to us that the attack had been a complete success. All the carriers had been hit and severely damaged. At least three of them were burning. One, apparently, had been sunk in the first two or three minutes of the engagement.

One battleship of the north group of the force that we had attacked was afire. A second battleship had been hit. Reports from the Army told of hits on two more battleships and another carrier. Discounting these messages to the fullest extent and recognizing how easy it is for one observer to duplicate the report of another, it was still obvious that we had had something of a field day, still obvious that the bulk of Japan's attacking planes must presently be going into the drink for want of any other place to land.

*June 6, Saturday.* At sea west of Midway. Sunny. Calm. Warmer.

It is estimated on the basis of today's reports that between 18,000 and 20,000 men were killed in this brief battle. While we aren't wasting too much sympathy on our enemy at the moment, we are awed by the catastrophe that overtook him. There is chill in the thought that there, but for the Grace of God, go we. Had we been seen ... Had the Japs attacked us before making the try for Midway ...

*September 30, Wednesday.* Army Maneuver Area, Desert Center, California. Hot....

... so the world knows now that Midway was one of the great battles of history, as significant as Trafalgar or Jutland or Tsushima and already promising more far-reaching results.

The communiqué writers were coy about it at first. We got off the transport in San Francisco—the survivors of the *Yorktown, Hamman,* and *Simms* and I—to find the West Coast jittery about a supposed threat to the westernmost Aleutian Island, newspapers filled with reports of bush-league bombings in the Mediterranean, radio commentators still patronizing the Navy by new assertion of the faith that it would probably turn out all right. Nobody seemed to have heard about Midway—or if they had they classed it as a nice bit of work like the raids of the Marshalls and Marcus or as a brilliant but inconclusive business like that of the Coral Sea. A lot of the wounded men who came down the planks of the transports in our convoy probably were puzzled by the silence that greeted them where they had expected bunting and brass bands. They still didn't know that so far as the nation was aware of it, they hadn't been anywhere.

When I got time I called a managing editor about this matter. He assured me that the people of the United States weren't minimizing the importance of the "engagement in the North Pacific" (sic). "But," he said, "we've got to be realistic about the Navy. We can't let wishful thinking dictate our news policies. I think the Navy will come through but we're not going to do public morale any good if we exaggerate the significance of a lot of minor battles. Nobody'll be more willing than I'll be to break out the Crack-of-Doom type when the turning point comes."

"Good God! Man," I asked him, "don't you know that the turning point has come and passed you by?"

"No," he said, "I hadn't heard of it."

JUNE 4, 1942: *Japanese landed in Aleutians.*

# MISSION OVER KISKA

### by Corey Ford

THERE was a large relief-map of Kiska in the Pilot's Alert Quonset Hut, down near the line. It was made of plaster-of-paris, painted bright green and brown and blue, and it rested horizontally across two sawhorses. It was very popular with the combat-crews, because Kiska Harbor was just the right size and shape to accommodate the average pilot's rear-end. If you sat with your back to Kiska Volcano, the base of your spine rested exactly on the Jap camp-area at Salmon Lagoon, the heavily fortified ridges of North and South Head furnished an admirable support for either buttock, and you straddled Little Kiska in the harbor's mouth like the pummel of a saddle....

It was on North and South Heads, guarding the harbor, that the anti-aircraft was most severe. You forgot instantly those stories you'd read of a few beleaguered Nips clinging by their fingertips to a rock, when you flew over Kiska for the first time on a routine bombing-mission. Here was no easy rock to take, you realized. Here was a veritable Bering Sea Malta, its sheltered harbor protected by the enfolding hills, its base honey-combed by underground passages, its approaches guarded by ack-ack as powerful as that of a full-size task-force.

You came in low beneath the overcast, flying in elements of two, the rest of the medium bombers strung out on either side of you, the slim nervous fighter-planes following in an intent echelon on your tail. You were surprised by two things, as you first gazed down on Kiska through the bomber's glass nose: how small it looked—the total Jap installations, including the sub-base, covered only a couple of square miles, and the congested camp-area itself was not much more than a city-block—and how quiet and deserted it seemed. The snow was melting along the volcano's sides, the lowlands were dotted with patches of green, as pleasant as a New Hampshire meadow in the early spring.

Everything was ominously quiet as you came over the ridge. There were no excited Japs running to man the guns, no troops stampeding up the streets, no sign of human life anywhere. You wondered for a disappointed moment if everyone had pulled out and gone home. Small but distinct below you were the solidly built structures of the camp-area, the buildings well revetted and thatched with straw, the orderly streets lined with telephone-poles. You could see the two big hangars at the water's edge, and the ramp leading up to them. You saw piles of fresh lumber, trucks and tractors, even a row of 'rickshas with their empty shafts resting parallel on the ground. It gave you a funny feeling to see Jap 'rickshas on American soil.

You were starting your bombing-run over the silent camp, and now you could see the foxholes and zigzag trenches and the neat deserted roads leading towards the adjoining sub-base, towards the radio station on the hill behind the camp, towards the gun-emplacements on the ridges. A couple of transports squatted in the harbor like fat hens, their barges huddled around them like a brood of chicks. And still there was no movement, no sign of life: nothing but the stabbing orange-yellow tracers fanning the sky, the regular scarlet flashes of the heavier artillery like a signal-light in a control tower, the ever-increasing puffs of black smoke that materialized silently, leisurely in the air around you and behind you

456

as the bombardier tripped the switch and a string of fat blunt bombs waddled downward towards the target....

Each morning, after breakfast, the combat-crews would gather in the Alert Hut to hear the day's mission briefed. They would pile out of the mess-hall hurriedly, zipping up their fleece-lined leather flying-suits, clamber into a waiting recon car, and jolt down to the hut through the inky blackness of an Alaska winter morning, hoping against hope that today's weather would be okay to make the run. They would pack in the car ten-deep, sitting on one another's laps, draping themselves along the fenders, straddling the radiator, singing *"It's* a grand old flag, da da *da* da da da...."* "I bet I've logged more hours in this recon that I have in the airplane." "I thought I'd wait till I found out if we were going on a mission this morning before I took a laxative." "If we go on a mission, pal, you won't need a laxative." "Da da *da* da da da...." "Anybody checked the weather yet?"

The briefing was usually informal. The squadron commander would stand beside a chart at one end of the room, and the pilots and navigators and bombardiers would gather around him, lounging against the wall, straddling a bench backward, resting an arm on a neighbor's padded leather shoulder, smoking, listening. He would talk in a low pleasant voice, quite casually, as though he were outlining a play in football.

"We're going to climb to about nine or ten thousand on the way out. We'll go north of the chain, come around the Volcano to Pillar Rock, turn in towards the island here—" indicating the spot on the chart "—and make a ninety-degree diving turn. All flights javelin right. First element will use a 6,500 base altitude; second element 5,500. Start your bombing run about here." He points to the chart again. "First element will take the hangars, the second the sub-base. Use a loose formation except against fighter opposition, in which case we'll close up as in regular tactics. Shipping in the harbor gets first priorities, of course. Remember, on your bombing-run the co-pilot will maintain airspeed, the pilot flies the ship. Rendezvous five miles north of here," putting his finger on a dot on the chart. "We'll have fighter coverage. In case a peashooter has any trouble, you, Jim—" he jabs his thumb towards a pilot beside you, who nods silently "—will lead it back to the base. Maintain radio silence on the way out. Standard frequency. Any questions?

"Will we have much Zero opposition?"

"I think so, yes."

"Anti-aircraft?"

"The Navy communiqué will state as usual that there was no anti-aircraft fire," dryly, "but look out for those gremlins." He takes out his watch. "Everybody synchronize their watches. We ought to hear about the weather in an hour or so."

The group relaxes; now there is nothing to do but wait. And wait, and wait. A cribbage game starts up, someone goes to work on a jigsaw puzzle, the men light cigarettes, loosen their flying-suits, sprawl in chairs and

457

bury themselves in six-months-old magazines, fling their leather jackets on the floor and stretch out on them and talk. They talk a language all their own, a jargon peculiar to pilots. "I had to goose it coming in...." "Boy, did I sweat it out...." "Then I shoveled the coal to it and gunned it around again...." Strange vivid phrases strike your ear: flying language. Bend back the throttles. Hang it on the props. Plunk the tail in first. Balloon over the runway. Milk up the flaps. Someone recalls the last mission: "When that Zero came alongside you, Dave, did the Jap look like that one you always see in the movies, the one that grabs his stomach and bends over and goes 'Ugh'?" "Six no trump." "Say, I wonder why we can't drop a bomb right down inside the crater of Kiska Volcano and touch it off." "Da da *da* da...." "Shut up," from the cribbage game, "we're trying to add." "Shouldn't it be almost time to hear about the weather?"

They tell you the hard-luck story of Sammy, little bombardier from New York's lower East Side. It seems that after Sammy won his bombardier's wings he got engaged to a girl, and he went down town to buy her a ring. "It costs five hundred smackers," Sammy himself interrupts eagerly, "but when I tell the jeweler I'm a bombardier, he claps me on the back and says, 'My boy, I'll knock off a hundred bucks for every bomb you drop on Germany.'" Sammy sighs. "So what happens? So I get sent to Alaska."

Or they tell you about the Colonel's dog. The Colonel's dog is a big Siberian husky named Skook, and whenever the Colonel leads a mission, he takes Skook in the bomber with him. Nobody is quite sure how many times Skook has made the run over the target, but the Colonel never leaves him back at the base. Claims a dog isn't safe back at the base, with all those trucks going by....

Or they tell you about the B-17 pilot, returning from a photographic mission over Attu, whose fuel-transfer pump went out of commission and his gas supply began to run low. An enlisted man investigated the fuse-box, discovered that a short had blown them out. The pilot met the emergency by unpinning the gold Second Lieutenant's bar from his shoulder and using it as an emergency fuse, so they could work the pump to get home. "Maybe a Second Lieutenant's bar is only worth $150 a month," laconically, "but it saved a third of a million dollars' worth of airplane."

Or one of the cribbage-players, laying down his hand, recalls plaintively the only time he ever got hurt in a raid. A 30-caliber armor-piercing shell hit the radio set, ricocheted off the structural frame at the rear of his armored seat, bounced off the windshield support, and landed in his lap. He picked it up with his glove, and absently dropped it into his rear pants-pocket; and the still-hot shell gave him a bad burn on his rump. "Had to go to the doc and get it treated," he adds. "That Kiska anti-aircraft is dangerous."

You wait and wait, and finally the phone rings; and the room is suddenly very quiet while the squadron commander picks up the phone. They know the answer by the look on his face. If his face falls, that means the mission is off again, and someone swears softly, and they go back to their cribbage and magazines and more waiting. But if his face gets very bright and tough-looking, then chairs scrape back hurriedly, zippers are yanked up, they grab briefcases and charts and pile through the door, jostling, shouting over a shoulder: "Keep dinner hot for me." "If anybody has to bail out, remember to fill out your Form One first." *"It's* a grand old flag, da da *da* da...." "Nobody touch that jigsaw puzzle, I'm going to finish it when I get back."

But he never finishes it; he never gets back. It was a tough mission today. Usually they buzz the field when they get back from a mission; but today they come in quietly, one by one. The squadron commander lands his airplane first and taxies to a halt; the ground-crew swarm over the ship eagerly to count the holes. There are sixty-four holes. He murmurs apologetically to his crew-chief: "I'm afraid I didn't do your airplane much good, Sergeant."

"No, sir," with a reproachful look, "you sure didn't."

Jim's plane is late landing; they had a little trouble on the way. It seems one of the bombs jumped its shackles and hung suspended halfway through the bomb-bay doors. The other bombs spilled out over it, but the first bomb still dangled there, its fuse cocked, and they couldn't get their bomb-bay doors shut again. The bomb-bay opening on a medium is so small you can't get down there with your 'chute on; so the tail-gunner—he was the smallest member of the crew—took off his 'chute and lowered himself down through the bottom of the plane by his hands. There he dangled in space over the Bering Sea until his groping feet found support. Somehow he balanced himself, bent down and released the bomb.

Russ shoots a landing with one punctured tire. A slug from a Jap machine gun had driven up through the left engine nacelle and made a two-inch gash in the rubber; but Russ wobbles the hot little ship to a safe halt, flat tire and all, and sticks his head out of the cockpit. "Bombardier's dead," he announces briefly. Russ's bombardier was Sammy. You wonder fleetingly whether Sammy's girl will ever know about that five hundred dollar ring....

AUGUST 7, 1942: *United States Marines landed in the Solomons.*

# FIRST GUADALCANAL NOTES

*by Richard Tregaskis*

GUADALCANAL, Solomon Islands, Sept. 8.—With surprising success—as much of a surprise to the American forces as to the enemy—U. S. Marine raiders today effected a landing on the island beach near Tasimboko.

Privileged to accompany the raiders, well-trained American counterparts of British Commandos, I had sailed from Guadalcanal yesterday with the attacking forces.

The Marines landed and pushed on towards Tasimboko as supporting aircraft bombed the village with high explosives.

Our first contact with the enemy came with dramatic suddenness.

There was an outburst of running in all directions among our troops and I rushed out to the beach to see six Jap boats lying on the sand and 10 or 12 Japs moving among them, tiny in the distance.

Colonel Merritt A. Edson, of Chester, Vt., nicknamed "Red Mike" by his admiring troops, ordered Major Floyd W. Nickerson, of Spokane, Wash., leader of the most advanced company of Marines, to open fire.

I burrowed deeper into the wet jungle foliage when bullets whirred in the leaves behind me.

A man was hit about 75 feet to my left. "Pass the word back for a corpsman," came the usual sickening request for the first aid.

Now there came a terrific blast ahead, so close and loud that the concussion shook one from head to foot. We suspected that it was a Jap field piece firing.

We knew the field was very close because the concussion of the gun's firing shook dirt and twigs on us. But now the fire was answered by our own mortars and by quick, loud, close firing from our automatic weapons.

More machine-gun firing, more heavy crashing of shell-firing follows: and then again, silence.

In the "breather," Col. Edson came up to the advanced position occupied by Maj. Nickerson under the very muzzle of the big Jap gun or guns. Modern warfare demands that officers, like men, must be on the spot, exposed to fire.

I heard "Nick" and "Red Mike" talking in whispers as they crouched in a clump of thick bush.

"We're trying to locate that firing up ahead," said Nick.

A runner came with the news that the Japs were moving along our left flank, trying to get to our rear. Col. Edson sent out a few squads of men to stop that.

Then we heard the planes. They were ours, set to bomb and strafe the village. Col. Edson called a runner.

"Go up and tell Maj. Nickerson to move his troops forward as rapidly as possible while the planes are strafing and bombing Tasimboko," he said.

There was a long silence after the planes came over and dropped bombs. There was the sound of movement in the bush ahead and to our left.

"There are troops going through there," said Col. Edson. "Find out who they are."

Seven minutes later, there was a terrific bang and clatter as firing opened again. One bullet came very close to me. I burrowed again.

We could hear machine guns, Browning automatic rifles, and the Jap artillery banging. The firing came from the left, this time.

460

"The boys got on the other side of us," said Col. Edson.

Now there was another explosion, the loudest we had heard. It seemed to come from a distance of only a few yards ahead. It shook a shower of palm leaves on our heads. And we could hear the shell whiz over our heads and explode a couple of hundred yards to our rear.

A runner came up, seeking Col. Edson.

"The Japs were sneaking along our flank," he said.

I could see Col. Edson was worried, but he brightened a little when Maj. Nickerson came in a few minutes later to say that one of the 75's had been knocked out, the gunners killed by rifle fire.

I went ahead with the Major when he returned to his foremost troops. In a jungle grove, a thick tangle of vines and leaves, we halted while firing cracked around us.

It was raining hard. We squatted in the wet leaves.

"Keep those squads spread out," said the Major, making a sweeping gesture towards the men who clustered around us in the brake.

"Davis lost one squad of the second platoon with one shell."

I heard a runner reporting that a second Jap 75 had been put out of action and the gunner killed.

Meanwhile, the surface craft had swung in close to shore and were shelling Tasimboko. We saw the yellow flashes of flame at the gun muzzles, saw the puffs of dirty smoke on shore, then heard the explosions.

A raider from the company led by Capt. John J. Antonelli of Lawrence, Mass., came into the command post with the happy word:

"We secured the problem and took the village."

We had lost contact, before that, with Antonelli's company and were worried about them.

Just then Maj. Nickerson passed the word that his forward elements had reached Tasimboko, and that Jap resistance was at an end. The Japs had folded.

Nickerson's troops had knocked out two 75's, and there were no more ahead. Four others, which were not manned, had been captured, said "Nick." Nick's troops had knocked out and taken four machine guns.

The raiders spent the afternoon burning the village and destroying the guns and ammunition they had found. There were .303 shells, .25 caliber shells, American-made .45 caliber shells bearing a Dutch stamp (evidently from Java), and Danish and American automatic rifles.

There were 80 mm. mortar shells evidently taken from the Philippines. And plenty of big 75mm. shells. It was a good haul. There must have been half a million shells, altogether.

We found a radio station in the village. That, too, was destroyed.

It was estimated that we had killed 27 Japs, besides destroying the great stores of food and ammunition we had found.

The men were well provided with British cigarettes bearing a Netherlands East Indies tax stamp.

# HEROES

### *by John Hersey*

OCTOBER, 1942—The group to which I attached myself were wounded in a dreadful way. They had no open wounds; they shed no blood; they seemed merely to have been attacked by some mysterious germ of war that made them groan, hold their sides, limp and stagger. They were shock and blast victims.

There were not enough corpsmen attached to Rigaud's company to assist more than the unconscious and leg-wounded men, so they set these men to helping each other. It was like the blind leading the blind, except that they were also halt.

Some of them were in no condition to walk themselves, to say nothing of helping other men to walk. The group careened along the trail, making hurt noises and not much headway. It was clear that alone they would never reach the advance dressing station.

At times a wounded man and the two helping him would all go crashing to the ground, the hurt man groaning and the helpers apologizing bitterly. Sometimes such a three would cut down three others, and the injured and apologetic men would be piled up like cordwood. Now and then a man would faint for a few seconds, and it would be necessary for the whole sickly caravan to wait while someone doused muddy water over his forehead and brought him to.

The walking wounded were magnificent. None of them complained about their own hurts, but inquired politely of each other. There were no whimpers or complaints, only deep-seated groans which expressed real pain.

Our order of march was something like this: First there was a man who kept striking the sides of his befuddled skull with his fists. The second kept his hands over his ears. Then there came two or three men whose legs were badly battered, who behaved like football players with excruciating charley horses; they were able to walk alone, just, but they walked with one leg free and the other stiff, as if it were wooden. The middle of the safari was taken up with the worst wounded and their helpers, and then there were two or three more who could walk—men who generally ached and wished to vomit. In the rear there was a character who shook his head, as if puzzled rather than hurt.

They were a strange-looking band, but they were certainly courageous. I got to like some of them very much in a short time.

OCTOBER 26, 1942: *Japanese defeated in Battle of Solomons.*

# THE FIFTH BATTLE OF THE SOLOMONS

## by Ira Wolfert

THE fifth battle of the Solomons, which in many ways proved a Japanese disaster unprecedented in the history of the world's great navies, began with a dispute over reinforcements of men and supplies for our embattled land forces on Guadalcanal.

Reconnaissance had revealed that the Japanese were building up an extensive force to retake the Solomons, but we threw the first punch, landing the initial wave of our reinforcements on November 11. We held the initiative that day and on November 12 when the second wave landed.

As night fell, the planes departed from the stage, and the ships with their big guns entered. Search planes had been watching the Japs all day long and their next move was expected. Admiral Callaghan's force shepherded transports to safety. The Japs apparently watched them, but lost them in the darkness, for during the night they came stepping breezily to deliver what might have been the decisive blow of the battle.

The land forces had girded themselves for a repetition of the October 13 bombardment. Men huddled in foxholes, and asked each other silently with their embittered faces, "Where's our Navy?" and wondered what would be left to stop the Jap transports.

Those seven hours of darkness, with each moment as silent as held breath, were the blackest our troops have faced since Bataan, but at the end of them our Navy was there, incredibly, like a Tom Mix of old, like the hero of some antique melodrama. It turned the tide of the whole battle by throwing its steel and flesh into the breach against what may be the heaviest Jap force yet engaged by surface ships in this war.

Again the beach had a front-row seat for the devastating action. Admiral Callaghan's force steaming in line dove headlong into a vastly more powerful Jap fleet which was swinging around tiny Savo Island with guns set for point-blank blasting of Guadalcanal, and loaded with high-explosive shells instead of armor-piercing shells. Matching cruisers and destroyers against battleships is like putting a good bantamweight against a good heavyweight, but the Japs unquestionably were caught with their kimonos down around their ankles. They could have stayed out of range and knocked out our ships with impunity, and then finished us on the ground at their leisure.

We opened fire first. The Jap ships, steaming full speed, were on us, over us, and all around us in the first minute. Torpedoes need several hundred feet in order to arm themselves with their propellers. Our destroyers discharged torpedoes from such close range that they could not wind up enough to explode. The range was so close that the Japs could not depress their guns enough to fire at the waterline, which is why so many hits landed on the bridge and two of our admirals were killed.

The action was illuminated in brief, blinding flashes by Jap searchlights which were shot out as soon as they were turned on, by muzzle flashes from big guns, by fantastic streams of tracers, and by huge orange-colored explosions as two Jap destroyers and one of our destroyers blew up within seconds of one another. Two Jap planes, which were overhead intending to drop flares on the target, were caught and blown to bits.

After thirty minutes the Japs crawled out of the harbor without having dropped a single shell on Guadalcanal, but in the morning twenty new Jap landing boats were seen on their portion of the beach, so a landing must have been made under the cover of the battle.

Admiral Norman Scott was killed a minute and ten seconds after the battle started, standing with his glasses glued on the enemy. Admiral Callaghan and Captain Cassin Young, commanding his ship, were killed about twenty seconds later, leaving Lieutenant Commander Bruce McCandless senior officer aboard the cruiser flagship. Lieutenant Commander McCandless was unable to inform the remainder of the force of Admiral Callaghan's death, so he took command of the flagship. In the next few moments five high-explosive shells landed, one at a time, exactly where he had been standing only seconds before. His valor earned for him promotion and recommendation for the Medal of Honor.

Four of our destroyers and at least two Jap destroyers and this "whatzit," which most of us call a battleship, but which the Navy called "heavy cruiser or battleship," sank within thirty minutes. One of our mortally hit light cruisers remained on the scene with a crippled heavy cruiser fumbling and floundering for such Jap ships as were unable to withdraw. They found one cruiser at dawn, and the heavy cruiser shot it to its death, turning it bottom-side up with the first salvo.

In the midst of this basin which crackled with the fire of small guns, schools of sharks threaded their way, hacking at corpses and the wounded. Over it roared steadily an all-day-long shuttle service of airplanes, running to sink the Jap "unsinkable battleship."

The battleship, making about five knots, was screened by five destroyers which were left behind from the battle, while the rest of the Jap force, if any, scuttled off. Captain George Dooley, of Hopland, California, led Marine torpedo planes in the first attack, and made another an hour later, scoring direct hits in each attack.

Then Lieutenant Albert D. Coffin, of Indianapolis, leading a squadron of Navy torpedo planes to reinforce Guadalcanal against the Jap transports which then were moving out of range to the northwest, tripped over the spectacle of the battleship. Lieutenant Coffin paused, fascinated, and dropped three torpedoes into the ship before continuing on his way.

Then Omaha-born Lieutenant Harold "Swede" Larsen joined the fray with his friend, Major Joe Sailer, of Philadelphia, who led dive-bombers. Major Sailer, thousands of feet above Lieutenant Larsen, synchronized watches with his friend and ticked off the second by radio, saying, "Mark one, Mark two, Mark three, Mark four, and... and... and go!"

Major Sailer dropped as Lieutenant Larsen launched Torpedo Squadron Eight out of a bordering squall. The Navy observer reported seeing Lieutenant Larsen's torpedoes hit the side of the battleship directly under Major Sailer's bomb. This was pool-shark shooting, to say the least.

The assaults continued interminably and so frequently that the battleship, although able to go from four to six knots, could make only ten miles in the entire day.

Lieutenant Coffin's men, fresh from Navy luxury, arrived all spruced up —freshly bathed, shaved, and combed, in neatly pressed flying suits. As tht endless day wore on, they gradually assumed a grimy look like the rest of us here.

Bullet-holes sprouted in ever-increasing numbers in their fuselages as the same planes returned again and again for attack. But still the battleship remained unsunk.

"We've got to sink it," said Lieutenant Coffin, "or else the admirals will stop building carriers and start building battleships over again."

When night shielded the battleship from further attack, the ship's whole stern was cherry-red from internal fires. It lay bloodstained on the darkening waters, but one battery just forward of midships kept their guns firing.

The Jap destroyers and battleship had shot all day long without getting a single one of our planes and wounded only one man. In the end the "unsinkable battleship" had eleven torpedoes in it and four heavy bombs and three medium bombs on it from above.

At 11:20 on Saturday night, the fourteenth, the Emperor's divisions, still flowing toward us monstrously, like some amputated torso gushing blood from almost every inch, made a last desperate effort to take Guadalcanal. Their warships returned to help them, but once again our Navy outwitted the Jap and anticipated his every move.

This time we also outgunned him, and the Jap's last effort was his costliest.

The Japs came sweeping down from the west. Our battleship force tailed them, but let them go around the north side of Savo Island while we, lagging a little behind, came around the south side, and caught them in that dream maneuver of all naval warriors—"crossing the T."

This battle was also visible from the beach. It is believed here to be the first naval battle in history in which sixteen-inch guns were used against vessels. It was even more spectacular and terrible than Friday morning's battle, and again lasted about thirty minutes.

In that time I counted eleven ships burning and exploding and sinking, two of them ours, but the Navy believes in erring on the side of caution.

At 11:50 the surviving Jap ships began steaming westward, firing over their shoulders. Our force gave chase, but the Japs were lost in the darkness shortly after one o'clock. But at five o'clock on Sunday morning flashes from explosions could be seen from Russell Island, forty miles away, which may have been the jittery Japs tumbling over one another and firing away

465

at each other. The glares were so vast that they lit up the tired faces of the beach spectators even from that distance.

The morning's first light found the remains of the Jap sea train beached less than seven miles from where this is being written—four cargo vessels. Destroyers have been shelling them, and our fliers, still calling themselves the "buzzard brigade," have been over them without intermission, strafing and bombing.

All four ships were gutted before noon. The ship nearest us, beached by the Poha River, had no superstructure or deck, and the fliers could see into the bowels of it, which were as red as an excavated heart. But the relentless Japs still had gunners—standing in the water on the stern, throwing rocks.

The Japs managed to throw off what stores they could onto the beach, but they could not drag them toward the trees. Our fliers keep pounding the Jap corpse, cremating it with Molotov cocktails. The Jap stores are now making a fire a thousand yards long and two hundred yards wide on the beach, and we intend to keep that fire burning until there's nothing left to burn. It warms our hearts.

# FLIGHT TO GUADALCANAL

## by Hanson W. Baldwin

NOVEMBER 1, 1942—The inspector examines the baggage. "Any cameras, explosives, firearms? Any matches?"

The great plane is stripped down, many of the seats are gone and freight and mail are in their place. The passengers are few—a naval officer, a marine officer, airline employees, a Hawaiian business man whose firm is doing priority work for the Navy. The curtains are drawn tight until the Clipper is well offshore and high above the carpet of the clouds....

The business man tells about Dec. 7 and what it was like to be in Honolulu during the Battle of Midway. The marine officer tells about the Makin raid. An OWI representative, bound for Australia, asks questions about the Pacific.

Dinner is good and plentiful. The stewards wear white jackets—white jackets in the midst of a Pacific war! Afterward, the seats are turned into bunks; we bed down for the night 8,000 feet above the sea. In the morning we shall be in Hawaii, shall be in a different world, a different environment, a world of war....

\* \* \*

The leaves of the hao tree are green beneath the hotel window; the curling surf of Waikiki breaks in lazy rollers against the reef. The hibiscus is in bloom and the poinsettias—but they were blooming, too, on Dec. 7, when the oil smoke and the flame towered above Pearl Harbor in a funeral pyre that marked the end of an era. And threaded through the surf and edging the seawall in front of the hotel is barbed wire. The soft green leaves and tiny half flowers of the naupaka—the "flower with the legend"—are laced with wire; the flame trees and the sandy beaches and the coral outcroppings are hedged with it; around the base of Diamond Head it is coiled; Oahu is girdled with it.... "Paradise of the Pacific" no longer, but citadel and fortress, strategic focus of the Pacific, the Hawaiian Islands at war are grim in the midst of beauty.

The face of "The Islands" has forever changed. New airfields, new barracks, new gun positions sear its surface; today there are many more air fields on Oahu than there were on Dec. 7. Pearl Harbor has sprawled out far beyond the lochs where once Japanese fishermen idled; its machine shops work in through the nights. Here is the main base of the Pacific Fleet; here are the men and here the machines that must send out our fighting ships refreshed and repaired. There is little sign of damage—only the rusty bottom of the old *Utah,* like some giant embayed whale, breaks the surface off Ford Island; only the rusty bottom of the old *Oklahoma,* and the shattered top hamper of the *Arizona* are monuments to the "date that will live in infamy."...

But at Hickam Field, where a grinning young Air Corps officer—cocky, confident—takes us on what he calls "the $3 tour," some of the hangars still gaze with blank eyes at the sun, windows still shattered, roofs partly repaired....

Honolulu at night is a city of the dead. The blackout is complete. Automobile headlamps are painted blue or red and the ghostly glare creeps slowly down the deserted streets, halts frequently as auxiliary police inspect passes, and moves on. There is curfew; the living habits of hundreds of thousands have been changed by war. No longer do the ukuleles strum and the beachboys sing in the courtyards of the Moana or the Royal Hawaiian; it is early to bed in the darkness, and early to rise in the dawn.

In the morning you swim at Waikiki, avoiding the sharp coral outcroppings and sidestepping the barbed wire on the beach, but you can't avoid the war. Your companion is a commander from a carrier and for a long time he floats silently. You accuse him of being lazy.

"I might have to do this some day," he says quietly. "I'm practicing."

*   *   *

This time it's a Navy Martin twin-engined patrol bomber—and you're heading south. We were late in starting, and above the clouds the day seems gray. The fuselage is stacked high with mail bags; the passengers are naval enlisted pilots, square-cut, clean-looking, assertive youngsters—a paymaster commander, a lieutenant commander.

There is much that is monotonous about flight above miles of water. You rarely see the ocean—and then only as a streak of wind-rippled blue-green, through a cloud rift. The engines make too much noise for talk, unless one shouts; you read or you sleep—hour after hour—as the leagues of distance melt away beneath you.

You read and you sleep and you think—think about what the destroyer skipper told you at Pearl:

"What's it like to be dive-bombed? I guess you don't realize much; you're too tense; you're too keyed up, trying to estimate the exact moment to give her rudder to avoid 'em. No, you're so tense you're not scared. You're too scared, I guess, to be scared. But you can't relax afterward; you can't un-tense. I didn't sleep for two nights afterward. I kept going over and over in my mind every detail of the action, every second we lived that day. Then the third night I slept."

\* \* \*

As the sun is westering, the pilot sets her down, cutting a clean white furrow in the green waters of the lagoon. Here is romance, here enchantment—a coral atoll fronded with palms. Suddenly your throat tightens and you gulp; you had not seen it before—the Flag flying over the white sand and the coral and the blue-green water, the Flag flying deep in the heart of the Pacific.

Palmyra is a tiny atoll, but it bristles with guns. A marine colonel takes you around. He wears shorts and shirt and sun helmet and is bronzed with the sun. The fiddler crabs scuttle, claws waving. "There used to be a lot of big tree-climbing coconut crabs here, but the marines have scared 'em away."

Over there just off the beach is a deep pool, where sea turtles used to swim; "but the boys have got most of them, too." We climb an observation tower in the moonlight; it is hidden with morning glory and air plants. Beneath us lies the tiny atoll—the lagoon in the center, the ocean around us. The island is a narrow strip of beach, but thickly grown with palms and pandanus and pisonia, with dwarf magnolia clustering in hummocks beneath the trees. The moon glistens over the immensity of the Pacific—the Pacific stretching away to the westward to the Japanese shores. Beneath us in the rough trail an armed patrol, rifles at the ready, moves silently upon its rounds.

In the morning at sun-up the noise of the engines sends boobies and frigate birds circling in clouds above the green lagoon.

\* \* \*

We cross the Equator and cruise on through sunny skies to the next dot in the Pacific. It is a tiny outpost, bigger than Palmyra, but bare and barren —a strip of sand crowned by a few low windblown bushes. Soldiers greet us. We spend the night there. The island is "alerted"; Jap submarines and a Jap task force are somewhere about lost in the immensity of the water to the west. The soldiers stand by their guns; forever and forever there are men scanning each sector of the sea and sky.

The war comes to you, as you fly across the Pacific, in a thousand incongruous ways. You are never far from it; you never can be; the talk is all of men at arms. In Suva in the Fijis Americanisms have already made their indelible impression. The Fijis are British islands, but here, too, as in other areas of the Pacific, fighting Americans have established headquarters and defense bases. They are in strange contrast—these soldiers of ours—to the black-skinned, picturesque natives, with their huge crowns of kinky hair. Native policemen, with blue military tunics, white scalloped skirts, crowned with the great head of hair distinctive of the Fijis, direct the traffic in Suva, and American "jeep" drivers have learned to distinguish the arm signals that are so different from those of Times Square.

In the Fijis kava is the native drink and song is the native language. There is probably no more melodious rhythm in the world than a sonorous chorus of Fiji islanders.

The native greeting—a carry-over from jungle days—is "Bula," which means almost everything from "Hello" or "Good morning" to "Peace" and "How are you?" It is uttered everywhere. A jeep full of American soldiers may pass a fine-looking native on the road and suddenly a loud "Bula!" and a wave of the hand accompanied by a flashing smile will speed them on their way. "Bula" has become a part of the American language in the Fijis, but the Americans have paid back the debt in full.

For one evening at a sing-song when the natives had entertained, a chorus of officers reciprocated the star number—the song that brought roars of approval and boisterous applause from the native audience was "Boola, boola, Eli Yale." Now all over the Fijis you may hear the natives humming "Eli Yale." But barbed wire is strung on the Fiji beaches, too.

* * *

New Caledonia is French—Fighting French. It is also American—fighting American, for here, too, in another outpost of the Pacific are quartered our men-at-arms.

New Caledonia is a land of mountains and metal. Iron oxide reddens the soil; nickel smelters in Noumea work day and night.

We find the American commander at his headquarters, French tiles beneath his feet, Parisian wallpaper blossoming behind his desk. Out in the hills and mountains of New Caledonia—an island shaped somewhat like a cigar—are his men, the men of America in bivouacs and camps among the hills. New Caledonia offers an interesting problem in defense; it is 270 miles long, 20 to 25 miles wide, rugged, wild and with few communications. The mountains are rugged and precipitous—studded with niaouli trees; from the rocky crags hawks prey upon the Army's homing pigeons.

We call upon the Fighting French commander—a colonel who had escaped from a French prison camp. He is expressive in his gestures:

"We want only to meet the enemy," he says.

* * *

It is an easy flight in a marine transport plane—a DC-3 cargo ship—from New Caledonia, via our bases in the New Hebrides, to the embattled airfield on Guadalcanal.

The fuselage is jammed with extra gas tanks, a load of surgical gauze, oil cans and drugs and eight passengers. We take off, skip over a low range of hills, hurdle the high mountains of New Caledonia and cruise out over blue waters. We fly for hundreds of miles past islands and mountains little known to man—past volcanoes smoking and quiescent—Mount Bendow, 3,720 feet; Mount Marum, 4,380 feet. These islands of the South Seas —fabled in song and story—are no pin pricks on a map; some of them are much larger than Long Island. Some are unexplored wilderness virtually unknown save to the native.

\* \* \*

It is getting lighter outside—and we are drawing closer and closer to Guadalcanal. The co-pilot stands up in the navigator's hatch and with a pair of binoculars slowly searches the heavens. The Congressman is sleeping on a pile of packages of surgical gauze. By 5:45 the day is at hand, but the clouds more frequent, the cover good. These planes are familiarly dubbed by their pilots "the flying box cars." Because they are transports and therefore virtually unarmed, the pilots' motto is "In clouds we trust."

At 6:40 we sight many ships—convoy steaming south. We strain our eyes. "Thank God, they're ours," someone says.

It's 7:05 now. The marine crew sergeant has replaced the co-pilot in the navigator's hatch and is keeping a close watch for Zeros. The admiral's aide puts on his yellow "Mae West" life jacket with its carbon dioxide containers which inflate it when you're in the water; we follow suit. We buckle on our parachute harness and deal out the parachutes. There's a moment of tension when there appears to be one too few to go around, but it's found. We put on the steel helmets and have the gas masks at hand—and settle back in the bucket-shaped aluminum seats which line the fuselage to wait.

The crew sergeant is still searching—searching. We're to be met by an escort of Grummans off Guadalcanal.

"There's Guadalcanal."

A high tumbled mass of heavily forested mountains breaks the horizon. We come on it fast; quickly it assumes shape and form—the world's newest battlefield. Our fighters should be somewhere here now—but we're ahead of time; we circle and wait.

Someone laughs.

"I know what a quail feels like now."

(We think of the sub skippers back at Pearl, how they said, "You feel naked and defenseless when your sub is on the surface in a bright moonlight night." That's how you feel now—you feel naked.)

\* \* \*

The crew sergeant never stops his searching for an instant now; always, without ceasing, he looks skyward, scanning 360 degrees of arc. You can't see anything from the windows save the rugged contour of the island as you flash past it above Sealark Channel, and occasionally a white strip of beach fringed by green jungle, so you watch the crew sergeant.

By and by he stops his searching, reaches down and taps the pilot on the shoulder and points up and to the left. The DC-3 is opened wide now. She'll go no faster; she's practically skidding along the water; she'll go no lower; she's got no guns; she can do no more. The pilot looks up and nods. We strain our eyes through the window.

There are three fighters up there—far away and headed on an opposite course. Are they Zeros or Grummans? They are too distant to distinguish. There is a moment's suspense; then they're gone into a cloud bank—probably our fighter escort....

The pilot takes her on in. He banks above Lunga Bay, skims over the tips of the coconut palms, blasted by shellfire and bombs, and eases her down on the strip between the bomb craters. It is 8:15.

As she taxis to a stop near "the pagoda" and the engines cease their everlasting roar, we take off our parachute harness and the Mae Wests; the door opens and we step out onto Henderson Field, Guadalcanal.

There are grins and wide smiles, and someone says again, heartily: "Well, I know what a quail feels like now."

The marines around the plane are grinning. The sounds of the motors dies....

Guadalcanal. It looks peaceful. There are some bomb craters in the grass near the air strip, but most of them have been filled in; in the center of a slight rise in the field is a wooden building peculiar to Japanese architecture.

"Let's go up to 'The Pagoda,'" the marine says.

We pile into the jeep and roll up to "The Pagoda."

The marines are grinning, but they are dirty and unkempt. Their uniforms are creaseless and soiled, their hands and nails black with field dirt. And when you look at them closely you see the tired creases around their eyes....

But they're grinning. There's hand-shaking, and the Congressman slaps several backs. Later, at breakfast, you eat oatmeal and swallow great mugs of scalding coffee.

"It's the first time we've had the officers' mess set up," the captain explains happily. "Help yourself."

\* \* \*

After breakfast, you cruise around the American beachhead on Guadalcanal in a jeep. There's not much to see and you don't have time to see it before the DC-3 is to leave again. But you go down to the prisoners' stockade and see some dejected-looking "termites"—the marines' name for the Japanese labor battalion—and half a dozen military prisoners, the crew of a bomber shot down over Tulagi. They all look at you with dumb eyes and you stare back. There's nothing to say. You go up to the bivouac area.

There are some tents scattered around beneath the palms. Slit branches or fox holes near everyone. A marine gives money and a package of Japanese cigarettes. He points up to some trees and down to a slit branch. You notice that the fronded tops on some of the palms have been clipped sharply as though by a knife.

"A marine was killed there a coupla nights ago," the private remarks, motioning toward a slit trench. "The shell hit the palm top and exploded right over the trench. One o' them damn submarines again, I guess." . . .

You go over to Headquarters deep in some jungle growth. You hear statistics, look at maps. . . . Always there are stories—stories of death and danger set against the background of the jungle and danger yet to come.

\* \* \*

ALLIED HEADQUARTERS IN AUSTRALIA, Dec. 15, 1942 (Associated Press): Allied infantrymen swept over Japanese troops at Buna village on the eastern New Guinea coast yesterday. . . .

\* \* \*

# BUNA VICTORY

### *by Pat Robinson*

JANUARY, 1943—You have read, perhaps, of how our boys drove the Japs out of Buna, Gona, Cape Endaiadere, and Sanananda Point. But I wonder if you realize the hardships our boys underwent or the fierce fighting that took place before that task was finished.

To get a clear picture of what happened, you must first realize the nature of the terrain and how the Japs controlled it.

Buna, for instance, is hardly more than a name on a map. Before the Japs took it last June, there were exactly six European houses and a few native huts there. But its strategic value is immense, because with that region in our hands we can build and use airfields there and step up our bombing of other Jap strongholds a thousandfold.

Between Port Moresby on the western side of the peninsula, which forms the tail of New Guinea, and the Buna region on the east, lies the Owen Stanley Range which contains some of the densest jungle on earth and which rises 13,000 feet into skies of cobalt blue.

It is a gorgeously beautiful land but it is a poisonous brooding beauty that always seems to hold the promise of death.

Before we took Buna we had to fly across that range from Moresby to get a crack at any Jap stronghold. That requires only 20 minutes of flying time and you might suppose it would be easy. Actually, there are days when neither the Japs nor ourselves can get across the range.

472

Dense clouds close down over the mountains every afternoon and any pilot would have to fly blind to get across and perhaps crash into a mountain side. Many a plane has been lost in just that way.

The weather "builds up," as the pilots say, on the Buna side of the range to make it the worst flying weather to be found anywhere on earth. Thick clouds rise from sea level to more than 50,000 feet and that "front" is usually at least 100 miles wide and 1,000 miles long. It is almost impossible to go through it, around it, under it or over it.

It is always dangerous to fly over there but it is far more so at night when a pilot may run into a thunderhead at any time. These thunderheads have both a downdraft and an updraft and they are strong enough to tear the wings off even our biggest bombers.

Captain Dick Robinson, a red-headed pilot of a B-26, once ran into a thunderhead at 10,000 feet and in a flash his plane dropped to 1,500 feet before he came out of it. Fortunately, he was over the sea at the time. Had he been over the mountains—well, he would not have been able to tell me about it.

Those mountains have been both a blessing and a curse to us. They were a blessing before the Japs started their drive over them toward Port Moresby because our listening posts stationed in the mountains could give us warning of an impending Jap air raid.

As the Japs drove on over the Kokoda Trail toward Moresby we lost our "eyes" and "ears" and there came a time when we had no warning at all of a raid and the Japs would be over us bombing and strafing before we had a chance to get a plane off the ground. When we drove the Japs back over the range and took Buna we recovered all our listening posts and now the Japs dare not come over raiding except at night.

The mountains were a curse to us when we had to cross them ourselves, driving the Japs before us. But cross them we did. And the way our own troops crossed them made aviation history.

Lieut. General George Kenney, head of the air corps over there, proposed to transport thousands of troops from Australia to New Guinea and thence over the Owen Stanley Range by air. The Australians thought he was crazy and I have an idea some of our own military men also thought so.

The troops were needed in a hurry and Kenney knew it would take too long to transport them to New Guinea by water. He convinced MacArthur the job could be done and MacArthur, having explicit faith in Kenney, told him to go ahead.

Kenney at once commandeered every old transport plane he could find, stuck a lot of daring young pilots in them, and told them to go ahead. Believe it or not, they transported thousands of troops, most of whom had never flown in their lives, without loss of a single man.

I saw them land in New Guinea and I saw them take off again to fly over the mountains. Again the job was completed without loss. Not only

473

did they fly all the troops, but they also flew ammunition, clothing, food, jeeps, and even large dismantled guns.

It was a job surpassing even that accomplished by the Germans at Crete.

But the job had only begun. For many weeks thereafter the transport boys had to keep those troops fed and to do it they carried 600,000 pounds of stuff a day, shuttling back and forth as many as seven times a day. They'd take over supplies, land on fields where no civilian plane would dream of landing, and bring back wounded men.

They gave one of the grandest examples of American initiative, pluck, skill, and daring the world has ever seen and when the story of this war is written no little credit must go to the boys of the transport command.

# PT'S TO THE FRONT

## by Charles A. Rawlings

SOMEWHERE IN THE SOUTH PACIFIC—January, 1943

THOSE black night waters where the motor torpedo boats, the PT's, fought for Guadalcanal in the dark of the moon are sinister seas. Getting ready for night, they brood away the hot afternoons, with the green-plush island mountains reflected in their dirty mirror surfaces.

Their names have an evil witches' ring. The Lengo Channel leads in from the eastward between Florida Island and Guadalcanal. The Slot leads in westward between Savo Island and Guadalcanal's western tip, grim Cape Esperance. The Japanese destroyers named that channel, wearing a groove in the sea coming down from Buin. They went back, scattered and frightened, through the Sandfly, north of Savo. Iron-bottomed Bay! That deep, still pool, the open water about Savo Island, is floored with more cruisers and destroyers and crews' shark-picked bones than the Japanese navy likes to think about, or our Navy either, for that matter.

The little PT's, the expendables, haunted those eerie channels from mid-October until the Guadalcanal campaign was over, early in February. They were the Navy on guard there. The big fighting ships, the task forces, came steaming up when the word was out that the big Japanese fighting ships were coming down, and the fleets met and fought the four thunderous battles of Savo Island in Iron-bottomed Bay. Then they withdrew—those that were still afloat—and licked their wounds. But the PT's lived up there on station, working desperately on repairs and sleeping when they could up in the creeks amid the mangroves—waking the great Solomon Islands' bats with the sudden cranking-up roar of their motors at dusk as they slid out on nightly patrol.

Their task was hard. When the enemy came down with surface contingents too small to risk bringing up our real fighting forces, it was the motor torpedo boats' job to turn him back. He came down in the dark of the moon with his Tokyo Express. Splendid destroyers made up that train —2,000-ton, sleek, bristling sea terriers with forty knots in their throttles and each with enough 4.7 metal in a broadside to blow PT boats into the air like lightning hitting a plywood stack in a lumberyard.

From October's dark nights to the waning moon in early February, the PT war heads cleared the rail and sped toward dark enemy shadows in the Slot and the Lengo and the Sandfly—in seventeen engagements. Their toll included one cruiser, twelve destroyers, one submarine and one big cargo transport, sunk. Five PT's with half their crews were lost too.

The first sound of enemy guns came at 0200. The Japs were in Lengo Channel, shelling Henderson Field. The commander of the squadron at that time, a two and a half striper who later was invalided out with malaria, sent his quartermaster on the double up the wharf to NOB—naval operating base.

"Just tell somebody up there," he instructed the youngster, "that we're going in. I don't need any orders. We'll go over there and give those Japs a lesson."

We were at the PT table in officers' mess in the wardroom, and a big blond lieutenant was telling the yarn. Most of the other PT boat commanders and seconds in command were there. Big Robbie, a full lieutenant, the present squadron leader and the patriarch of the fleet, sat at the head of the table.

He is twenty-seven, and because he is so old and wise he will probably get another stripe and go on the staff when he comes north after the holiday. He will not quite know what to do in a shore job, he says, when it comes time to go out on night patrol. He had sixty of them in the 110 days the show lasted, and routine adventure is a strong drug.

Down the table were the rest—ensigns and junior grades—all combat-seasoned, all fine small-boat fighters. All jungle-seasoned men, too, who had slept with anopheles mosquitoes and licked their bout of fever, and who had learned to keep their heads and tempers week after week in the sweat-soaked never-ending heat and tension. They were twenty-two and twenty-three and twenty-one years old. They were just the same blond, dark, good-looking, homely, cynical, jolly, ironical, wisecracking college kids anybody can see anywhere. The same ones everybody knew couldn't be any good along about 1940 and early '41.

They all listened and let the big blond lieutenant named Bill tell the yarn, for he had been second in command in the lead boat that night—the "No. 1 Boat," they called her, after the PT fashion, which frowns on naming boats after cute girls and whimseys as something too jivey and air-forcey. And the No. 1 Boat, she killed—well, as Bill said:

" 'We'll go over there and give those Japs a lesson,' said the C.O. And that's how we all felt too. Just like Bulkeley and Kelly did it in the Philippines, we'd do it in Guadalcanal. Boy, were we green then!"

The four boats slid away from Government Wharf and in column crept across Tulagi Harbor. They threaded the narrow channel through the coral reef that later was to become famous as the cornerstone of the Hard-Rock Club, restricted to men who have put boats aground. Outside was the darkest night they had ever seen. Not a star, not a rift in the sky, not a breath of air. Across the water, they but dimly knew how far away—for they were very new—were the flashes of the Jap guns.

Over the little intership-radio phones the command came, "Deploy!" Then, very soon afterward, "Attack!" The four boats fanned out, and they attacked and attacked and attacked.

"I suppose," said Bill, "you could have heard us twenty miles and seen us fifteen that night. We were throwing white water all over the bay. *When are we goin' to get to these Japs?* I said to myself. *How far away is this funny place?* All at once the Japs knocked off firing. They had heard us over the roar of their own guns. And the next thing I knew, there was the Guadalcanal beach."

They all slowed down then. All was silence and blackness for a long, long moment. Then quickly, all at once, the Japanese searchlights went on. They were frightened searchlights. They were looking for mysterious dragons that had come roaring over the black waters at them.

The No. 1 Boat, realizing that she must be inside the Jap fleet, between it and the shore, came slowly about and headed out again.

To the westward then pandemonium broke out in the Japanese fleet. Something they did not understand was harrying them—mad dragons. Their tactics centered about one big idea—to get out of the Lengo Channel. A destroyer found one of the PT boats with her searchlight at 200 yards, and the PT answered the destroyer's fire with her machine gun, shooting out the searchlight. The third PT found another destroyer flying at full speed west, and tried to get set for a shot, but could not. The fourth boat saw the last Jap, also a destroyer, trying to escape north to Savo Island, and had enough time to close on a collision course and fired two torpedoes. They hit, and at the sound a sister Japanese destroyer just ahead turned and came back, shooting 4.7 salvos at the PT running full speed in a cloud of smoke. Their courses were converging, and the PT—it was commanded by the older Princeton brother—fired in the destroyer's face just in time and scared her off. Then silence and darkness closed down over Guadalcanal and her black waters, and the marines heaved a weary sigh and settled down to their first sleep for many nights.

There was a good breakfast for the PT crews the next morning. The Jap force had been estimated by NOB by that time at one battleship, four light cruisers, and eight destroyers. It had been thrown into confusion and driven off. There was convincing evidence that one cruiser and one destroyer had been sunk. The PT men were heroes.

But, explained Bill, "The C.O. was a fine leader. He knew we had just been lucky. 'We've got to study,' he said, 'some different tactics. We stampeded the Japs last night because they thought were were dragons, but we very near stampeded ourselves as well. This high-speed deploying in the dark is not so hot.' "

JANUARY, 1943: *Brazil pledged closest co-operation with the United Nations. It was decided to send an expeditionary force to Europe. President Roosevelt conferred with Brazil's president at Natal.*

# TOUR OF DUTY

## *by Walter Winchell*

JANUARY, 1943—Aboard a Navy patrol plane over the South Atlantic: Some men are more fortunate than others. Some men are richer than many. Some men stay in love longer than most—and most men never experience the wallop that goes with being at the bow-gun of a Navy patrol plane (a PBY) a few feet over the submarine-infested South Atlantic.

\* \* \*

How even a veteran bombardier can keep his eyes open or focused on a target out there in the open bow—with the fierce wind blinding and bayoneting him—is something I do not savvy.... The powerful gun kicks the way Joe Louis punches and shakes you violently the way Lew Fields shook Joe Weber.... At any rate, there you are out there under the huge propellers —several feet ahead of the pilot—alone.... Except for the hurricane-tempo'd wind and perhaps a Nazi sub hiding below.

\* \* \*

I was reminded of the time Senator Holman of Oregon and Senator Chandler of Kentucky flew to the Aleutians through heavy fog and storm most of the way. And picked up a soldier at some Alaskan base, who immediately took his battle station and trained his gun on the skies.

"Son," said Senator Holman, "whatcha fussin' with that there weapon fer that-a-way?" ... "I'm being ready," replied the gunner, "in case we meet some Jap planes." ... The white-as-a-sheet Holman turned to the whiterthan-that Chandler and intoned: "Ain't it silly what some of us Senators will do to get into trouble—when we don't have to?"

\* \* \*

My good break came from missing connections with the plane that was to take me to the next port on the tour.... Had I made that plane I would have missed one of the biggest thrills of them all.... That thrill was not my first flight in a PBY—a huge and comfortable Catalina (one of which

477

helped sink the Bismarck); or firing the bow-gun—or circling low over oil specks that stained the beautiful aquamarine below.... The big wallop came several hours later when he reached the base.

\* \* \*

I am not permitted to divulge the excitement I witnessed at this place.... The four paragraphs about it were blue-penciled even before I had the chance to correct the spelling.... It was my first experience with an official gremlin, too.... For the first time in 22 years of newspapering I realized how tame the toughest editors are.

\* \* \*

All I was trying to jot down was that some fellows were luckier than other fellows.... That some pilots had reasons for being happier than others and that the U. S. now has fewer enemies than it had.

\* \* \*

And so I cannot reveal at this time what all that excitement was about.... I cannot even elaborate that the excitement was enjoyed by a lot of very happy men, and that the reason they were so excited and happy was that certain other men, with dialects, were unhappy or dead.

\* \* \*

The PBY on which I hitch-hiked was manned by the most youthful fellows I encountered down there.... Most were only 21. Some were 23 or 25, and some were a little more seasoned.... But all featured beards that must have been months in blooming.... All the other fliers I met at various places were clean-shaven.... "Why the whiskers?" I asked.

"They haven't been as lucky as other chaps," explained an officer, "and so they agreed not to shave until they got a sub."

I kept wishing that on this routine flight I would not prove a jinx to them —and that they could get—a shave.

\* \* \*

The Atlantic seemed as tame as any Florida lake.... I was instructed to occupy one of the co-pilot's pews—handed a helmet containing earphones— and some dark specks....I just sat there wishing hard that they'd all get lucky.... Now and then the Captain brought the plane down to a few feet over the water—to circle over oil specks.... They are really huge gobs of scum from tankers and ships, they said.... Sometimes it might be from an ill-fated merchantman, but not always.

\* \* \*

At the Admiral's morning conference I was shown a dispatch that told of a merchant ship sunk the night before, and that a PBY patrolling the area had radio'd seeing two lifeboats with survivors.... But when he returned to the scene later he saw only one.... We were instructed to keep our eyes open for those survivors.... That saving them would be even better than sinking an enemy sub.... But there was no trace of them.... I never learned whether they had been rescued or not.... I kept thinking of them throughout the flight—knowing that brave men somewhere were suffering—not only from the suffocating humidity and heat—but from the blinding sun. Even with dark specs my eyes ached from the glare.

\* \* \*

About 100 miles from our destination the earphones crackled.... The plane was ordered in.... Enemy subs were reported—and a squadron of PBY's were on the way for the attack.... Ours was too far from the scene to join the killer-group and still have enough fuel to get back.... The disappointment on the faces of the crew was painful to see.... I was their jinx, after all.... They were "out of the money" again.... Other fellows had all the luck.

\* \* \*

As the PBY came down gracefully the crew was greeted with more sour news.... They were to get their chow while their ship was being readied—to relieve one of the "killer-group." ... But by the time they were ready to climb like homesick angels—a flash radio'd that the "show" was over.

JANUARY 12, 1943: *Beginning of the Aleutian campaign. Constantine Harbor and Amchitka Island were retaken by United States forces.*

# ALEUTIAN CAMPAIGN

## *by Keith Wheeler*

ACCORDING to several of the nation's more vocal military thinkers, the Aleutian campaign began as and deserved only such heed as was due a Japanese sideshow of the three-ring circus which foozled at Midway. When the Midway show laid an egg, the thinkers said, the Japs hung on to Kiska only to save face. Perhaps they were right.

Certainly in the first months we treated Kiska as a sideshow. From the time the Japs appeared over Dutch Harbor until our cruisers bombarded Kiska in early August 1942, our measures to evict the invaders consisted only of the brave but feeble efforts of two dozen Catalina flying boats and half as many heavy Army bombers working from makeshift bases at the extreme limit of their range—plus certain laudable contributions by a few submarines. Our High Command's attitude toward the Aleutians appeared to be that we ought to keep the Japs away if we could, but we shouldn't use more than a fly swatter to do it.

After their initial stabs at Dutch Harbor and Umnak in June 1942, the

Japs made no further move eastward along the undefended chain. Instead they went to work on Kiska with such earnest industry as to indicate an intention to remain.

Their accomplishments in the following eight months were many, varied, and wonderful to behold. Late in December 1942 aerial photographs taken under fire showed nearly one hundred and fifty permanent buildings of various types, plus numerous conical tents. The buildings included hangars, vehicle repair and storage shops, warehouses, machine shops, and housing for personnel. They looked to be solidly constructed, laid out with an eye for order and permanence, and well protected with deep earth and sandbag revetments.

There were also such useful gimcracks as a marine railway and submarine repair base with auxiliary cranes, shops, and handling gear; fuel storage depots, radio stations, deeply emplaced three-gun coast-defense batteries, two large seaplane hangars to which a ramp climbed from the beach, power houses, radio installations, a narrow-gauge railway, small-boat landings, supply dumps, several miles of well-graded roadway, a network of telephone lines, dozens of antiaircraft emplacements, including both heavy guns and light automatic pom-poms and machine guns, and a half-built fighter runway.

Fresh evidence of the Aleutians' new place in the plans of war was confided to us a couple of days after Christmas. A new advance westward was imminent. The troops and transports were already loaded and awaiting favorable weather. The cruiser's job, with sundry other ships, would be to protect the new landing, or to pave the way for it if it turned out that Japs were already in possession of the place.

This new venture, we learned, was aimed at Amchitka, a low-lying forty-mile snake of tundra stretching southeast-northwest between the Bering and the Pacific. Its tail was within sight of Kiska and its open-jawed head embracing Constantine Harbor, where the troops were to land, was only seventy-three miles from Kiska Harbor.

The plans called for establishment of an Army base and initial construction of a fighter field to protect it and to provide for a shuttle service of strafers to Kiska.

Again, however, it did not look as though Kiska was the chief concern. Constantine Harbor lay twenty-two hundred miles from Tokyo and only eight hundred miles from Paramushiri, the Japanese naval and air base at the head of the Kurile chain. The bombers of 1942, with straining, were capable of reaching Paramushiri with a load and getting home again. And there was much talk of next year's bombers, outsize behemoths that would be able to tote bomb loads from Amchitka to Tokyo and come back.

We met Brigadier General Lloyd E. Jones, a wire-thin smiling officer, who had learned his Aleutian soldiering as commanding officer of the Army post at Cold Bay far to the eastward. Colonel Marc Logie, the expedition's executive officer, was a burly, barrel-chested veteran of Alaskan operations. He had fought in three wars, served in half a dozen armies.

The fourteen-thousand-ton transport was jam-packed with troops. They ate in relays, slept even in the passageways for lack of bunks. This transport would carry the entire initial landing force of combat troops, some two thousand men together with food, ammunition, tentage, guns, fuel—all the simple but bulky necessities of existence and battle in the winter-whipped treeless tundra.

Most of the troops were Alaskan veterans, toughened by two years of drudgery in the toughest, bleakest, most unsettled terrain in the world. They knew how to get along without such pleasurable adjuncts of civilizations as houses, chairs, food served at tables, and baths. They had been getting along without them for two years. They were a hard and competent lot, and one got the idea that they would be an unpleasant bunch to assault.

The occupation plan called first for combat troops and a fighting landing. So far as we knew the Japs had not yet occupied Amchitka, but we had no guarantee. In any case, the place was only fifteen minutes' flying time from the Jap base and some sort of interruption seemed certain.

We got out of the harbor on January 11 into the teeth of a roaring northeaster. There were destroyers snuffing ahead and on our flanks, and out there somewhere in the wild gale we knew our cruiser and its consorts kept vigil over us.

In the evening General Jones spoke over the ship's loudspeaker system, competing for attention with an epidemic of seasickness among the land-bred troops.

"Tomorrow, when we land, you as a soldier or sailor will be closer to the heart of the Japanese Empire than any soldier, sailor, or Marine. When you reach the beach, do not stop. Each step you take forward will take you that much closer to our final objective."

"Hallelujah!" snarled a seasick private retching in the passageway.

Dawn comes late in the Aleutians in midwinter. At 9:30 A.M. the transport with her escorts was probing carefully into Constantine Harbor. The island lay before us, low, barren, and streaked with snow. Unlike most of the Aleutians, Amchitka is low and boggy for almost the whole of its forty-mile length.

We edged by the rock-fanged reef in the upper half of the harbor entrance and slid into its questionable shelter. The gale had faded to a breeze and the silver-gray morning was calm, though icy cold. The high-sided transport coasted slowly into the quiet water. If the Japs were here and intended to do anything about this, now was the time for it to begin.

Nothing happened. There was no move on the island; it was as flat and dead as a corpse.

The upper decks seethed into life as we drew into the harbor. Engines roared and blue gasoline smoke hung in a cloud about the ship as the crews of landing barges started their motors with the boats still hanging in the davits. The troops, each man carrying a full hundred pounds in addition to his own weight, milled on the deck, pushing toward debarkation points at the rail. Orders bellowed out of the loudspeakers. The ship's cranes came ponderously alive and reached for the Higgins tank-and-jeep lighters chocked on forecastle and quarterdeck.

Chain roared in the hawse pipes and the ship stopped and swung to her anchor. Landing barges, already loaded with soldiers, descended to the water with their motors snarling. The cranes lifted the heavier boats and set them in the water one after another.

The first wave was already in the boats and on the water. As fast as other boats reached the surface, they were jockeyed under rope cargo nets draped from the rails. The troops scrambled over the side and crawled laboriously down the sagging nets. From the rail they looked like an army of hump-backed ants scrambling down a wall.

These were assault troops, each man a miniature army. Each carried his weapon—rifle, tommy gun, or pistol—ammunition, sleeping bag, emergency rations for three days, shelter half, bayonet, mess kit, plus whatever odd personal gear his fancy or the available space in his krupsack had urged him to pack.

The first boats had hit the beach, and the men, black and antlike as seen from the ship, were scrambling through the shallow breakers and up the low tundra headland.

A square-nosed gray-painted jeep lighter drew up to the cargo net draped under our place on the rail.

"Over you go, soldiers," the sergeant said. He swung a leg over the rail, grabbed the upper cross rope of the net, and began to descend. I struggled down after him, much engaged in trying to avoid breaking a leg in the treacherously unstable net.

I tumbled into the alternately soaring and swooping boat and looked up. The ship's high side crawled with descending brown-clad figures struggling painfully with their burdens. As each man reached the boat, he grabbed the net and hung on, stiffening the loose rope network to make the descent easier for those still to come. The heavy assemblies of a machine gun came down to us on lines, and the last man tumbled into the landing barge. We had thirty-six men aboard together with their gear.

A fine spot, I thought. With a concentration of Zeros only fifteen minutes away a man would have to be a chump to want to spend much time in one of these sardine cans. What a target we'd present to a strafer.

Our boat swung away from the ship and milled in the bay, joining other boats of its wave. When all were assembled, they raced toward the beach a quarter of a mile away—a ragged assault line.

This was no pleasure cruise. I was resigned to a wetting. The boat slowed and nosed in toward the beach. She grounded a hundred yards from shore. The coxswain waited for an incoming swell to slap her stern, then gunned the motor. The jeep lighter, designed for this business, crawled closer to the black-sand beach. Twice she scrambled over sandbars and finally stopped a hundred feet from land. The square bow flopped down and formed a ramp. We charged out of the boat.

We lit in knee-deep water. It poured into my boots, and it was ice cold.

The laden soldier beside me stumbled and fell on his face. He struggled to his feet again and sloshed on toward shore. A curling comber refrigerated by the polar icecap swirled around the boat and slapped us in the seats.

I staggered out of the water, across a narrow strip of hard black sand, and up a steep short slope matted with tangled grass. I crawled over the crest and found myself in a cemetery. There were six graves, two fenced with wrought-iron pickets and one with a stone cross at the head. There were the blackened foundations of two burned buildings, one tiny hut fashioned of driftwood and nearly covered with tundra sod and one unadorned barabara. The barabara is the native Aleut hut, a habitation as closely approaching a badger den as man can contrive.

Across the tundra plain ahead were hunched figures swiftly fanning out toward dozens of prearranged objectives. Whether any enemy appeared or not, this operation was to be carried out on the assumption that a Jap lurked behind every tundra hummock.

The arctic brine in my boots already had changed my feet to aching clubs, and I headed for the hut. Its doorway was two feet by three and I went through on hands and knees, not even pausing to admire the elegant glass doorknob which dangled from it on a bit of wire.

I tugged off my boots, twisted a quart of brine out of each sock and inspected my blue feet. There didn't seem to be anything to do about it, so I put the socks back on, poured out a quart of ice water remaining in the boots, and put them on.

Half an hour later I wandered along the beach and climbed to a low tundra headland, where I found three men crouched over an infinitesimal fire in the bottom of a natural trench. They had an empty tin can and were brewing hot cocoa from a D-ration chocolate bar. They were hospitable, and the cocoa was delicious notwithstanding the sand and tundra root with which it was mixed.

The cocoa makers had a second guest, Sergeant Daniel Clawson, of the Infantry. Barefooted, barelegged, and with his bare and blue backside turned to the arctic breeze, Sergeant Clawson was searching through his knapsack for a suit of dry underwear. The clothes he had just peeled off lay over a tundra hummock dripping merrily.

"I have never been so damned c-c-c-cold in my whole d-d-d-damned life," the sergeant chattered. He looked it.

MAY 18, 1943: *United States forces landed on Attu Island.*

AUGUST 15: *American and Canadian troops invaded the island of Kiska.*

NOVEMBER 20: *At dawn, United States Army troops and Marines began landing operations on the islands of Makin and Tarawa in the Gilberts.*

# TARAWA

### by Robert Sherrod

NOVEMBER 20, 1943—As darkness began to settle over Tarawa, we could see more Americans heading for shore through the dimming light. "Couple of companies of reinforcements,". said an officer. These men were being unloaded at the end of the pier. They could not yet walk along the pier, but they could crawl beneath it and alongside it. The Japs kept trying to peppei them with machine guns and rifles, but their aim generally was not good. Some men would land at the end of the five-hundred-yard pier, and try to walk down it, but the Japs would increase their fire until the Americans usually had to jump into the water or get hit. Even the artillery which was being brought in, 37-mm. anti-tank guns and 75-mm. pack howitzers, were pushed and pulled through the water—they could have been rolled down the pier in one-tenth the time, if it had been possible.

Bill Hipple and I borrowed a shovel—correspondents rarely carry shovels —walked up the beach about twenty yards, and began looking for a spot to dig a foxhole. We stopped at a coconut-log pillbox and cautiously mounted the seawall to look in it. Inside were four Japs lying beside their machine gun. They were dead.

We jumped off the seawall, back onto the sand. This seemed as good a place as any to dig a foxhole, even if it were only ten feet from four dead Japs who were already beginning to smell. We dug the foxhole wide enough for the two of us, and deep enough so that we would be below the surface of the ground when the Jap bombers came over. We agreed that one would try to sleep while the other stood watch. I knew I was not going to sleep, though I hadn't slept the night before aboard ship—how long ago that seemed, aboard ship! And Bill knew he wasn't going to sleep. For one thing, the Japs would fire their mortars and rifles all night, if only to keep the Marines awake.

I was quite certain that this was my last night on earth. We had twenty feet along perhaps one-sixteenth of one-half of one side of the island, plus a few men in shellholes on either side of the airstrip. The Japs had nearly all the rest. Although we had landed a lot of troops—perhaps three thousand —by this time, most were crowded into such a small space that we did not have room for foxholes to hold them all. And if the Japs counterattacked, what could we do except shoot at them from behind our seawall until they finally overwhelmed us?

For the first time since morning, I was really scared—this was worse than wading into the machine-gun fire, because the unknown was going to happen under cover of darkness. I tried to joke about it. "Well, Bill," I said, "it hasn't been such a bad life." "Yeah," he said, "but I'm so damned young to die."

My knees shook. My whole body trembled like jelly. I peered into the darkness over the seawall, seeing nothing, hearing nothing except an occasional shot from a Jap sniper's rifle. But, I reasoned, it hasn't been a bad life at that. Suppose I don't live until morning? I have already lived fully and quite satisfactorily. Why should I be afraid to die? My family will be well provided for, with my own insurance and the insurance my company carries on its war correspondents. It will be tough on my children, growing up without a father, but at least they will have a very capable mother and the satisfaction of knowing that their father died in line of duty. And why should any war correspondent assume that he can claim exemption from the death that had already come to Colonel Amey and Doc Welte? If I were not here as a war correspondent I would be here as a Marine, anyway. These people made me sick who were always saying, "Oh, what dangers you war correspondents must go through!" I say: war is dangerous, period. And what right has any American to feel that he should not be in it as fully as any other American? This is, I reflected, the United States' war, not the sailors' war or the Marines' war or the soldiers' war. What the hell?

During the night word was passed down the line: the Japs have broken through to the end of the pier. Now we were cut off, even from Major Crowe's battalion. I had not yet heard any word from the other assault battalion which had landed up on the western tip of Betio.

About an hour before dawn we heard the unmistakable purring of a Jap flying-boat's engines. "Old Washing Machine Charley," commented one of the Marines in a nearby foxhole. "I haven't seen him since we were at Guadalcanal. He doesn't do much harm but he keeps you awake." The bomber circled back and forth across the island, evidently trying to find out what was going on down there.

During the night I did not see a single Marine fire his rifle. Such firing might have given away our positions. Whatever else, I decided, these Marines were not trigger-happy. They were not forever firing at some figment of their imagination.

NOVEMBER 28, 1943—Just eight days after the first Marines hit the beach at Betio, I was again in Honolulu. Already there were rumblings about Tarawa. People on the U. S. mainland had gasped when they heard the dread phrase, "heavy casualties." They gasped again when it was announced that 1,026 Marines had been killed, 2,600 wounded: "This must not happen again," thundered an editorial. "Our intelligence must have been faulty," guessed a member of Congress.

This attitude, following the finest victory U. S. troops had won in this war, was amazing. It was the clearest indication that the peacetime United States (i.e., the United States as of December, 1943) simply found it impossible to bridge the great chasm that separates the pleasures of peace from the horrors of war. Like the generation they educated, the people had not thought of war in terms of men being killed—war seemed so far away.

Tarawa, it seemed to me, marked the beginning of offensive thrusts in the Pacific. Tarawa appeared to be the opening key to offensive operations throughout the whole Pacific—as important in its way as Guadalcanal was important to the defense of the U. S.-Australian supply line. Tarawa required four days; Guadalcanal, six months. Total casualties among Marines alone, not even including malaria cases, were about twenty per cent higher on Guadalcanal.

Tarawa was not perfectly planned or perfectly executed. Few military operations are, particularly when the enemy is alert. Said Julian Smith: "We made mistakes, but you can't know it all the first time. We learned a lot which will benefit us in the future. And we made fewer mistakes than the Japs did." Tarawa was the first frontal assault on a heavily defended atoll. By all the rules concerning amphibious assaults, the Marines should have suffered far heavier casualties than the defenders. Yet, for every Marine who was killed more than four Japs died—four of the best troops the Emperor had. Looking at the defenses of Betio, it was no wonder our colonels could say: "With two battalions of Marines I could have held this island until hell froze over."

Tarawa must have given the Japanese General Staff something to think about.

The lessons of Tarawa were many. It is a shame that some very fine Americans had to pay for those lessons with their lives, but they gave their lives that others on other enemy beaches might live. On Tarawa we learned what our best weapons were, what weapons needed improving, what tactics could best be applied to other operations. We learned a great deal about the most effective methods of applying Naval gunfire and bombs to atolls. Our capacity to learn, after two years of war, had improved beyond measure. The same blind refusal to learn, which had characterized many of our operations early in the war, had almost disappeared. We were learning, and learning how to learn faster.

The facts were cruel, but inescapable: Probably no amount of shelling and bombing could obviate the necessity of sending in foot soldiers to finish the job. The corollary was this: there is no easy way to win the war; there is no panacea which will prevent men from getting killed. To me it seemed that to deprecate the Tarawa victory was almost to defame the memory of the gallant men who lost their lives achieving it.

Why, then, did so many Americans throw up their hands at the heavy losses on Tarawa? Why did they not realize that there would be many other bigger and bloodier Tarawas in the three or four years of Japanese war following the first Tarawa? After two years of observing the Japanese I had become convinced that they had only one strategy: to burrow into the ground as far and as securely as possible, waiting for the Americans to dig them out; then to hope that the Americans would grow sick of their own losses before completing the job. Result: a Japanese victory through negotiated peace. It seemed to me that those Americans who were horrified by Tarawa were playing into Japanese hands. It also seemed that there was no way to defeat the Japanese except by extermination.

Then I reasoned that many Americans had never been led to expect anything but an easy war. Through their own wishful thinking, bolstered by comfort-inspiring yarns from the war theaters, they had really believed that this place or that place could be "bombed out of the war." It seemed to many that machines alone would win the war for us, perhaps with the loss of only a few pilots, and close combat would not be necessary. As a matter of fact, by the end of 1943 our airplanes, after a poor start, had far outdistanced anything the Japanese could put in the air. We really did not worry particularly about Japanese airpower. If we could get close enough, we could gain air supremacy wherever we chose. But did that mean we could win the war by getting only a few pilots killed? It did not. Certainly, air supremacy was necessary. But airpower could not win the war alone. Despite airplanes and the best machines we could produce, the road to Tokyo would be lined with the grave of many a foot soldier. This came as a surprise to many people.

Our information services had failed to impress the people with the hard facts of war. Early in the war our communiqués gave the impression that we were bowling over the enemy every time our handful of bombers dropped a few pitiful tons from 30,000 feet. The stories accompanying the communiqués gave the impression that any American could lick any twenty Japs. Later, the communiqués became more matter-of-fact. But the communiqués, which made fairly dry reading, were rewritten by press association reporters who waited for them back at rear headquarters. The stories almost invariably came out liberally sprinkled with "smash" and "pound" and other "vivid" verbs. These "vivid" verbs impressed the headline writers back in the home office. They impressed the reading public which saw them in tall type. But they sometimes did not impress the miserable, bloody soldiers in the front lines where the action had taken place. Gloomily observed a sergeant: "The war that is being written in the newspapers must be a different war from the one we see." Sometimes I thought I could see a whole generation losing its faith in the press. One night a censor showed me four different letters saying, in effect: "I wish we could give you the story of this battle without the sugar-coating you see in the newspapers."

Whose fault was this? Surely, there must have been some reason for tens of millions of people getting false impressions about the war. Mostly, it was not the correspondents' fault. The stories which gave false impressions were not usually the front-line stories. But the front-line stories had to be sent back from the front. They were printed somewhat later, usually on an inside page. The stories which the soldiers thought deceived their people back home were the "flashes" of rewritten communiqués, sent by reporters who were nowhere near the battle. These communiqué stories carrying "vivid" verbs were the stories that got the big headlines. And the press association system willy-nilly prevented these reporters from making any evaluation of the news, from saying: "Does this actually mean anything, and if it does, what does it mean in relation to the whole picture?" The speed with which the competing press associations had to send their dispatches did not contribute to the coolness of evaluation. By the time the radio announcers had read an additional lilt into the press association dispatches—it was no wonder that our soldiers spat in disgust.

Said a bomber pilot, after returning from the Pacific: "When I told my mother what the war was really like, and how long it was going to take, she sat down and cried. She didn't know we were just beginning to fight the Japs."

My third trip back to the United States since the war began was a letdown. I had imagined that everybody, after two years, would realize the seriousness of the war and the necessity of working as hard as possible toward ending it. But I found a nation wallowing in unprecedented prosperity. There was a steel strike going on, and a railroad strike was threatened. Men lobbying for special privilege swarmed around a Congress which appeared afraid to tax the people's new-found, inflationary wealth. Justice Byrnes cautioned a group of newsmen that we might expect a half million casualties within a few months—and got an editorial spanking for it. A "high military spokesman" generally identified as General Marshall said bitterly that labor strikes played into the hands of enemy propagandists. Labor leaders got furious at that. The truth was that many Americans were not prepared psychologically to accept the cruel facts of war.

The men on Tarawa would have known what the general and the justice meant. On Tarawa, late in 1943, there was a more realistic approach to the war than there was in the United States.

DECEMBER 5, 1943: *United States forces began their all-out attack on the Marshall Islands.*

# AUGURY OF DEATH

## *by Raymond Clapper*

JANUARY, 1944—Aboard an aircraft carrier somewhere in the Pacific—To the men aboard a warship in a combat zone, religion becomes a far more important thing than you might suppose if you judged by civilian standards at home. You can get some idea of the reason why from the story of a flier who became afraid. I have his name, but I shall not use it now.

One of the chaplains was telling about it because it was a strange and puzzling experience. Chaplains have many unusual experiences with the men, because, as this one said, bluejackets are not as irreligious as they seem or want to appear.

This particular chaplain, a young man, has been with the navy seven years. Before that he was pastor of a Lutheran church at a West Coast port. There is also a priest aboard. And the gunnery officer, who once studied to be a rabbi, conducts Jewish services each Friday night with a usual attendance of about 30. The several Mormons aboard attend the Protestant services.

Sixty per cent of the crew are Catholic. Mass is held daily. Protestants and Catholics each have a devotional service every evening. There are two masses on Sundays. Christian Science readings are given by a lay reader for a group of about 15.

That suggests the religious activity and interest among the 3,000 men aboard this carrier out here in the Pacific, where they are facing some pretty serious business for men of their years, or for men of any years for that matter. They want communion service before they go into combat. Before each action prayers are always said over the loudspeaker system.

It was on Christmas Eve that the young man who was afraid, a radio gunner, came to the Protestant chaplain after communion and asked to see him privately. They were going to strike at Kavieng on Christmas morning, and this was the communion service the night before the dangerous mission.

We will just call this young man the unknown flier, for I suppose he was something like all of these men and like all the rest of us. Formerly he had been doing quiet patrol work in the Caribbean, and he asked for more active duty aboard a carrier. He was transferred to Norfolk for carrier training. There he met a girl and they were married, and some months later he came out here. Their baby is to be born this month, or it may have come into the world by now.

The young airman had been on five attacks during the softening up of Tarawa, on two against Nauru, and on the first very tough blow at Rabaul. So he had been through some of it.

On Christmas Eve the chaplain sat down with him. The boy said his baby was to be born soon and he was afraid to go up the next day. The chaplain asked if he had ever been scared before. He said he had, but never like this.

"I have been sick to my stomach," he said, "I am so scared."

The chaplain said he thought he could get the boy excused from the Christmas Day raid. The boy wouldn't hear of that.

"I am not yellow," he said. "I have to fly tomorrow. If I don't I will never fly again. I want you to help me."

The chaplain was silent for a moment before he went on.

"I tried to assure him of the Lord's care and that He would watch over him," he told me.

He said the boy was more afraid of being afraid than he was afraid of flying.

Early Christmas morning the planes went out. When they came back the young airman was dead in the rear cockpit. He was the only one hit among those who came back. There were only two small machine-gun bullet holes on the underside of the plane. Both these bullets hit him.

Because this carrier was operating under battle conditions no regular services could be held Christmas Day. All hands were at battle stations all day. But a few minutes were taken out to hold services for burial at sea.

Three of us were in the room talking, and it was a long time before we looked up at each other.

"I have heard of such things," said the chaplain at last. "But that was my first contact with it. It is one of those mysteries for which I can find no explanation. I don't suppose anyone has found an explanation."

I don't know exactly why I should feel the story of this young man so far down in my throat even now as I write it.

# *Part Nine:* Africa

\* \* \*

Cairo, Sept. 14, 1940 (Associated Press): Italy's legions swept across the Egyptian frontier tonight, tanks and armored cars rolling into the ruined villages of Sollum and Musaid under heavy attacks by the British Royal Air Force.

\* \* \*

DECEMBER 9: *British opened offensive against Italians in Egypt.*

DECEMBER 11: *British took Sidi Barani.*

DECEMBER 15: *The British drove the Italians out of Egypt and invaded Libya.*

JANUARY 5, 1941: *Bardia fell to the British.*

JANUARY 20: *Eritrea was invaded by British Army.*

\* \* \*

Cairo, Jan. 22 (Associated Press): The fall of the Italian Libyan base of Tobruk to the British Army in North Africa was announced officially tonight.

Cairo, March 20 (United Press): Cairo headquarters said that . . . the British reoccupied Berbera, capital of British Somaliland.

Cairo, April 2 (Associated Press): British forces were said today to have cornered nearly 100,000 Italian troops still fighting in East Africa and to be driving in for knockout blows.

London, April 15 (Associated Press): Thousands of British Imperial troops from the East African front were reported hastening to the defense of Egypt.

\* \* \*

# BRITISH VICTORY AND DEFEAT

## *by Allan A. Michie*

WAVELL had prepared his attack long and carefully. He confessed that he studied the layout of Graziani's defenses for weeks until one day he suddenly decided that they could be broken. Wavell is a cautious commander. Pressed time and again to begin his offensive by British Cabinet

491

Ministers who were trying to divert the attention of the British public from air raids at home, Wavell refused to attack until his preparations were completed, and twice postponed his drive on the grounds that his men needed more practice under desert conditions. I was in London then and I heard at a dinner party from a reliable source that Anthony Eden had been sent out to Cairo to inform Wavell that if he did not attack immediately Churchill would be compelled to remove him as Middle East commander-in-chief.

On December 9th [1940] when enough reinforcements of men and material had arrived to reduce his inferiority to only one to three against the Italians, Wavell attacked.

Supported by less than one armored division, Wavell was never able to use more than 30,000 men at one time. The success of his lightning strokes depended on the employment of a small but highly mobile force. The use of a larger army in the desert, even if the troops had been available, would have involved problems of transport and supplies which Wavell was not then equipped to handle.

Moving up at night from Mersa Matruh and concealing themselves in the daytime, Wavell's forces launched a surprise attack on Sidi Barrani. The Italian defenses were well laid out and strongly held. One Italian division was entrenched in positions to the east of the town; a second to the south at Tummar; a third to the southwest at Sofafi. The Maletti mechanized column was stationed in the south, at Nibeiwa. Utilizing surprise to the utmost, Wavell drove a wedge between the Italian outside defenses, captured them by the evening of the first day's attack, and two days afterward entered Sidi Barrani itself.

When I arrived in Egypt later I learned that Wavell's tactical plan had cautiously left the door open for a British retreat if the attack proved unsuccessful. His men carried supplies and water for five days' fighting. At the end of that time, if Sidi Barrani still held out, they were to withdraw and the British action would have been explained as a successful, large-scale raid.

General Wavell is a believer in unlimited pursuit. "In pursuit you must always stretch the possibilities to the limit," he says. "The troops, having beaten the enemy, will want to rest. They must be given as objectives not those you think they will reach, but the farthest they can possibly reach."

Wavell applied this philosophy in the extreme. Using captured Italian food, fuel, transport, and ammunition, his men pressed on to Bardia, Tobruk, Derna, and Bengasi. In eight weeks they had pushed the Italians back almost 600 miles. The harried Italians were given no time to recover before the British were on top of them. Wavell's Middle East RAF, outnumbered though it was at the outset of the campaign, blasted the Italian planes on the ground and gained undisputed command of the air.

On the 16th, eight days after the attack began, the important Egyptian-Libyan border fortifications of Salum, Fort Capuzzo, and Sidi Omar fell to the British. In London at that time the Nazi bombers were giving us

492

some pretty uncomfortable nights, but as we emerged from our shelters in the mornings we would have the headline announcements of more and more Wavell victories to cheer us on.

Two days after the fall of Sidi Omar, the British reached the outer perimeter of Bardia's defenses.

Bardia was even better protected than Sidi Barrani. Its strong natural position had been improved with four years of work by the Italians and the fortifications included an outer ring of defenses circled by a 10-foot tank trap, which was protected by a strong shoulder-high barrier of barbed wire, inside which was a network of blockhouses and machine-gun emplacements. The garrison of more than 40,000 Italians, well-supplied with artillery, believed the town was impregnable.

For more than two weeks the British carefully reconnoitered the defenses, meticulously recording every detail of the fortifications, tank-traps, land-mines, and gun positions. On January 3rd, under cover of a severe bombardment from land, sea, and air, the Australians charged the outer defenses, while sappers cut the wire and infantry poured through to level the ditch and make a passage for the tanks. The Italian artillerymen fought doggedly, but once the tanks broke through the outer ring of forts the Italian infantry quickly surrendered, and on the afternoon of January 5th, Bardia was in British hands.

In this action alone Wavell's army captured 40,000 prisoners, 130 light and medium tanks, and nearly 500 guns of all calibers. British losses were fewer than 600 casualties. From the opening day of the attack until then, the British had destroyed or captured seven Italian divisions, plus the mechanized unit commanded by General Maletti.

The fall of Bardia gave the British a port of supply for the attack on Tobruk, seventy miles to the west. At the time of the attack on Bardia, British light mechanized forces had swept around to Tobruk and occupied the airfield of El Adem, fifteen miles south of the town, and then pushed on to straddle the coast road at the rear of Tobruk, blocking reinforcements from arriving and the defenders from retreating.

The British made the same careful study of Tobruk's defenses before their attack that they had made at Bardia. Then, while British and Free French troops engaged the Italians along the whole outer perimeter of defenses, the Australians followed the British tanks through a weak spot in the defenses, and on January 22nd, Tobruk fell. At the cost of fewer than 500 British casualties, another 25,000 Italians were taken prisoners. This brought to eleven the number of Italian divisions put out of action since the opening of Wavell's campaign.

About four divisions of Graziani's original fifteen were left in the remainder of Cyrenaica, Libya's eastern province. Wavell's army pressed on behind them, and eight days after the fall of Tobruk, Derna, nearly 100 miles to the west, was captured. The remnants of Graziani's once-vaunted army retreated rapidly along the coastal road through Bengasi toward Tripoli.

Lieutenant General Sir H. Maitland Wilson, Wavell's field commander, who I believe is one of the most competent generals in any army, then decided on a brilliant and unexpected stroke. He sent a British armored unit across the interior of the Cyrenaican hump, a country of forbidding wastelands which no army had ever crossed, to trap the retreating Italians south of Bengasi. Traveling by compass and the stars, the British tanks and Bren gun carriers made a forced drive of 150 miles in thirty-six hours to reach the Mediterranean coast near Soluch.

They reached their objective with little time to spare. In another two hours the Italian columns would have been beyond Soluch and out of the trap. British forces were outnumbered five to one in both tanks and men, and the Italians fought fiercely for two days in a desperate effort to break through, but on February 7th, with the Australians pressing down from Bengasi in the rear, the Italians completely collapsed.

Wavell's victory was remarkable. In two months his army had advanced almost 600 miles, and as Mussolini himself was forced to admit, had destroyed the 10th Italian Army Corps with all its equipment. The British had taken close to 140,000 prisoners, including nineteen generals and an admiral, at the amazing cost of 1,774 casualties, of whom only 438 were killed.

If the Italian prisoners alone had fought as a single body, they could have slowed up and perhaps stopped the British advance, but the Italians, with few exceptions, didn't want to fight. Some units, particularly the artillerymen and the anti-aircraft gunners, fought well. If their officers had stayed with them, the Italians might have put up a much better show, but many of their officers threw down their arms at the first sound of firing. The first to run were invariably the Fascist party Blackshirts. At most places the Italians resisted only until it became unhealthy and then surrendered in droves. They came in so fast that wisecracking British Tommies used to tell us that more Italians were injured trying to become prisoners of war than in the actual fighting.

Wavell intended to pursue the battered remnants of Graziani's army to Tripoli, but Britain's obligation to assist the Greeks interfered. Wavell was requested to send half of his desert fighters and 150 tanks, more than half of his armored force, to Greece.

A light British mechanized force was left to hold the British advance posts in Cyrenaica, while a division garrisoned Bengasi. These forces were thought to be strong enough to hold Cyrenaica until the successful British campaign in Italian East Africa released additional troops, but the Nazis, although they enjoyed the spectacle of their weak-sister Axis comrades in retreat, were strategically compelled to take a part in the North African campaign. In order to pin down Wavell's forces to prevent large-scale British intervention in the Balkans and to keep alive the Axis threat to Suez, it was necessary for the Germans to take over from Graziani's army.

The British had demonstrated that success in the desert depended on tanks and motorized equipment. Early in February, while the British were mopping up Graziani's forces around Bengasi, German armored units began arriving in Tripoli and by the end of March the Nazis had one panzer division and most of a second division in Libya.

Late in February I was in Lisbon, on my way home for a vacation, when I heard that the Germans had made their first appearance in a reconnaissance raid against the British forward position at El Agheila. On March 24th [1941] the British were forced to evacuate it. While the world's attention was concentrated on the battle of Greece, heavy German panzer units then attacked and almost wiped out the light British armored brigade in Cyrenaica and when this British protection was removed, swiftly pushed up the coast to attack the British infantry division at Bengasi. The British rapidly withdrew, but the Germans, reversing the exploit of General Wilson's armored columns which had crossed Cyrenaica by interior desert roads, encircled the retreating Britishers and captured 2,000 prisoners, including four generals: Lieutenant General Sir Richard O'Connor, one of the best in the British Army, Lieutenant General Sir Philip Neame, Major General Gambier-Parry, and Major General Carton de Wiart.

On April 9th, the retreating British established themselves inside the fortifications of Tobruk, where they were to remain for seven and a half months. By-passing Tobruk, the German tank units, followed by Italian infantrymen who were tasting sweet revenge, seized Bardia on April 12th, and two weeks later crossed the Egyptian frontier. The British made a stand at Salum, were driven out, and fell back on Mersa Matruh where Wavell's offensive had started.

# HELLFIRE

## by Frank Gervasi

IN fact, to stall as long as possible while tanks and planes arrive from the United States and England seemed to be the principal objective of the British during May [1941], when the entire Middle Eastern and Mediterranean situation looked black indeed.

Everywhere in the western desert I heard the same old refrain, from generals down to Tommies. We want tanks, tanks and more tanks, they said. And we want planes, planes and more planes. And don't forget the trucks. They were polite about it and they were firm. The Tommies were polite, too, and very blunt. From passing trucks, they yelled, "Hey there, Yank, how about those tanks?"

Some planes arrived from America. Martin bombers went into action against the Germans in the western desert. I saw them bomb Fort Capuzzo at sunset one evening. I saw ten tall columns of black smoke and dust rise against the flat orange sky and then I saw the planes return looking very cocky about it all. Tomahawks ground strafed and bombed German planes which had "accidentally" landed on airports in Vichy-controlled Syria.

The obvious lack of material with which to outshoot the superiorly armed German tanks galled the British command. With adequate material, the British could inflict upon the enemy its first major defeat since the war started. The results of such a blow would be of enormous importance. Combined with large-scale air bombing of Germany from England, a crushing defeat of the Germans in the desert would begin the breaking up of German morale and military organization. Moreover, the British Middle Eastern command was charged with the responsibility of maintaining military prestige in the Arab kingdom. This was essential to prevent German inroads into Arabia. But the British command here has been treated as a sort of military stepchild.

London knew Sir Archibald Wavell to be a magician, so they decided to let him work his magic—without a wand. I found it puzzling that so much attention should have been paid to pouring planes, tanks, and guns into Britain while a few were so obviously needed here. I asked the general about it. The general was boss of operations on the western-desert front. I asked him why planes and other weapons weren't being diverted in greater numbers to the Middle East, and he replied, "We can't lose the war here. We can always give the Jerry hell with very little. But let's assume the worst. Let's assume that we are obliged to withdraw completely from the southern Mediterranean. That doesn't lose the war with the Germans. It prolongs it. We fight on from Aden, from India, from the interior of Africa. I'm not saying this will happen, mind you. I'm merely pointing out the possibility which might arise if we are suddenly overwhelmed by unpredictable superiority in materials, machines, and men.

"But England must stand. We couldn't lose the war here in years, but in England it could be technically lost in five minutes. We must make the island safe."

But it also occurred to the general that, although England couldn't lose the war here in Egypt, she could go a long way toward winning it. And in doing so she would retain a hold on one of the few battlefields left on which the war to free the world of Hitler and destroy German imperialistic ambitions can continue.

The British don't believe Hitler's propaganda that he doesn't want Egypt. They know very well he wants Egypt, for Egypt is the Nile, and in that river's valley that winds like a green vine northward through the Sudan and the Egyptian desert to flower in many tendrils at the Delta, there is cotton and tobacco and grain. Egypt is the breadbasket of northeast Africa, and Hitler wants it. All but some two hundred thousand of Egypt's seventeen million people are born, live, and die in that valley.

We left the general and pushed on along the scabby road toward El Sollum. We found the colonel who commands a battery of 25-pounders just this side of the escarpment under Hellfire Pass relaxing after a tough day. He sat on a folding chair in front of some planks set on sawhorses in his "drawing room." This was a flat space dug out of the ruins of what might have been an ancient Roman villa buried in the sand in the dunes at the sea's edge. Over the cleared space between two crumbling walls was stretched a camouflage net from which fluttered strips of canvas and green rag.

The net was hung from two poles, and the whole gave the effect of the loggia of a Mediterranean summer villa. Beyond the terrace-like arrangement where the colonel smoked and sipped tea was the startlingly blue Mediterranean.

The colonel hadn't shaved for at least three days. Nobody shaves or washes up front. There isn't time during operations. Field glasses hung from a strap about his neck. His shirt front was unbuttoned most of the way down, and he was strictly a utilitarian colonel. He rose and was as glad to see us as any man would be who hadn't talked to anybody but his junior officers for days and hadn't talked or thought about anything but killing Germans for months.

He was as cordial and correct as though he were playing host in a Mayfair club. He gave us tea and American cigarettes and he asked a thousand questions about America. He wanted to know how the American electoral college operated, and I had one awful time explaining, and I guess I didn't do a very good job, because he said at the end he thought perhaps the British parliamentary system was simpler.

While we talked, two planes came. The colonel squinted up at them and said, "Wrong ones." And a few seconds later I knew what he meant. They dropped six bombs in a line between us and Hellfire Pass. The first was less than two hundred yards from where we stood, and the last one in the white gash on the escarpment a mile and a half away, where the road passed.

I looked down over the desert, where I knew there were men and guns, but I couldn't see anything. The men were in the slit trenches near the camouflaged guns.

"I suppose he couldn't see us very well from up there," the colonel said. "He knows we're here in this region, because we've been firing on positions up there over the edge of the escarpment all day, but he can't find us. Well, are you ready for a drink?"

We had one and then we turned back. We'd come up to see whether the British were still holding Hellfire. Apparently they were.

NOVEMBER 19, 1941: *The British Imperial Army began an offensive in Libya.*

DECEMBER 2: *German and Italian forces cut the corridor between Rezegh and Tobruk.*

DECEMBER 14: *Axis forces withdrew in Libya.*

# PRISONER OF THE AXIS

### by Harold Denny

NOVEMBER 1941.—Coming into Benghazi that evening was a little like a home-coming.

I had a special feeling toward Benghazi. Only a few weeks earlier, I had flown over this once-flourishing and urbane capital of Cyrenaica in a British bombing raid. Before the raid I had studied Intelligence maps and descriptions until I knew the city by heart. I shall never forget the raid itself and my merged feelings of fear and awe at the deadly beauty of white tracer bullets converging on us, the frightening searchlights catching us, the rainbow fountains where batteries were pumping steel and variegated tracers at us, the anti-aircraft shells rolling lazily up and unfolding in orange, red, and white blossoms, and the blazing buildings and the parachute flares lighting the ground below.

On each of my three nights as a prisoner in Benghazi my British bomber friends came over and knocked the stuffing out of the quays and warehouses on the waterfront. Since I knew there was no possibility of their dropping any bombs on our place of imprisonment, these were the most enjoyable air-raids I ever experienced. The Italian sentries would let no one out of the buildings except to obey a summons of nature. Forthwith our camp was swept by an epidemic of psychogenic polyuria, by which malady several dozen of us wangled our way outside for a few minutes' view of the dazzling anti-aircraft show before the outraged sentries drove us back indoors. We cheered each salvo of bombs and laughed at the patter of anti-aircraft fragments on our iron roof.

Benghazi was faintly homelike too, after my brief period alone, because I found already there the British with whom I had been captured and others whom I had known on earlier battle-fields. Some were of Jock Campbell's original command who had given me my first introduction to Libyan warfare. Others were old messmates of Brigadier Gatehouse's tank outfit. There seemed to be representatives of every branch and unit in the desert. There were even a few naval officers and ratings captured when their vessel's engine had broken down just under the enemy's guns.

The British correspondents and Colonel Buckley, and the bulk of the South African prisoners, had arrived there a day ahead of me.

At Benghazi the prisoners were quartered in unfinished Italian army barracks some distance from the city proper. We had two long, large barn-like buildings on either side of a small parade ground. The officer prisoners lived in one, enlisted men in the other. Here again the Italians had meant well, but again the influx of prisoners had swamped them. There were cots for only a few dozen out of a thousand or more prisoners, and straw mattresses and blankets for a few score more. Most of us had to sleep in inadequate clothing on the concrete floor.

Officers found their men in the building opposite even worse off. Many officers gave their blankets to their men, pretending that they had others, and then slept coverless themselves. Our rations were thin, which encouraged us to believe that the R.A.F. and the British navy were wrecking Axis communications.

But hardship did not down the prisoners. As prison guards showed me into the officers' barracks where I was to sleep, the British were singing, of all things, "Swanee River." When they had done with that they swung into a roaring soldier chorus, "Singing yip-eye-yip-eye-addy-yip-ayea!"

Buckley saw me enter and beckoned to me. It happened to be Thanksgiving night, so we two Americans feasted on Buckley's little tin of bully-beef and his one bread-roll, the size of a fist.

Next morning Eddie Ward, Anderson, and I found our two drivers and Ward's radio technician, a corporal whom we had greatly liked. We were relieved that they had come through unhurt, but we regretted deeply having led them into captivity. When we apologized to them, though, they turned it off with a generous "Oh, that's all right."

The Italians were rushing officer prisoners to Italy ahead of enlisted men, for fear the officers, who presumably were more valuable, would be rescued by the advancing British. On about November 28, as nearly as I can calculate it, we were taken in trucks from our prison camps to Benghazi's smashed waterfront. In a harbor littered with sunken ships, we were embarked on an Italian light cruiser. Rations for the voyage were issued to us on the quay—one small tin of bully-beef and two fist-sized bread-rolls per man per day.

About sixty of us were put in the wardroom, which had been cleared of furniture. The others were lodged in the crew's quarters forward. On this ship I again met Brigadier Sterling. An officer's cabin had been allotted him. Two or three colonels had others. We of lesser rank filled every inch of the wardroom. The space was too small for all to lie down at once, so at night some officers dozed standing, like horses in a stable. At first we blamed the Italians for our discomfort, but presently we realized that the Italian naval officers had accepted considerable hardship in giving up their wardroom and some of their cabins. We even found Italian officers sleeping on the floor in the corridors.

Evidently fearing the British fleet, our cruiser crowded on all speed in crossing the Mediterranean. So we raced to Suda Bay in Crete, a place of terrible memory for some of our party, and stayed there until dusk. We were allowed on deck. A few cargo ships were unloading supplies for the German forces. The hulks of other ships, sunk in the Battle of Crete, stuck up above the water. Half on shore and half in the water was the rusted and fire-blackened corpse of the cruiser *York,* lost in that costly battle. On the shore at one point we could see a prisoner-of-war camp, canvas tents sitting in the mud inside a barbed-wire stockade, and we wondered who were the inmates and how they fared.

After a week of short rations we were ravenously hungry. And few had any cigarettes. Eddie Ward, however, had got five hundred cigarettes from an Italian soldier in Africa in exchange for his watch, and was making them go as far as possible for all of us. After a long interval Eddie would light a cigarette and we would form a circle of five or six men. Eddie would take one long drag, then pass the cigarette to the man on his right, who would take his drag, and so it would go on, around and around the circle, until the cigarette was too short to hold.

Two ill-dressed Cretans rowed out in a dinghy and circled the cruiser, watching for a chance to throw us tangerines. But always Italian soldiers were waiting at the rail, and the Cretans did not like Italians. The boatmen retired, but returned later, loaded to the gunwales with fruit. They tossed up a few tangerines to draw the Italians to one part of the deck, then hurried to the other side, to which we rushed, and tied their baskets of fruit to cords which we let down. One British officer tried to give the Cretans bread in return, but they refused it, looking injured at the suggestion.

We sailed at dusk into a disagreeable night. A hatch in the wardroom roof was open for ventilation. The sea was rough, and repeatedly huge waves poured through in solid floods. No one slept much. By morning the wardroom deck was awash and we were drenched and shivering. The British officers quartered forward with the crew fared better. They were able to keep dry, and the Italian sailors entertained them with songs and accordion music.

After daylight many of us stood on the afterdeck while the cruiser raced along the coast of the Peloponnesus, skirting the fabled islands of Greece. Before dark we were scudding across the Adriatic. Later on our third night we steamed through a long narrow passage into the harbor and naval base of Taranto.

We felt by then that we could not face another night on that cold, soggy ship, and we cheered up when we were disembarked on the blacked-out waterfront in a cluster of Italian warships. There was a considerable crowd, and many people, including Italian naval officers, pushed forward to give us cigarettes. We were marched along the waterside for a quarter-mile, then up a ladder into a great ship. It turned out to be the queenly Italian liner *Vittoria,* seeming hardly real after what we had just come through. The ship was brilliantly lighted inside, and the crew stood at attention in the passages. We were shown into the glittering first-class dining room. Wet, dirty, bearded, and tattered, we were ushered to snowy tables, decorated with flowers and bottles of good wine. Italian waiters served us as attentively as if we had been de luxe passengers bulging with tips. We had a rich minestrone, liberal cuts of cold meats, vegetables, salad, and fruit. A spokesman for the ship apologized that conditions did not permit the serving of a better meal.

Our cruiser's captain had felt badly over our miserable voyage, we learned, and had wirelessed ahead asking this service. Brigadier Sterling, senior British officer present, made a little speech of thanks in behalf of all of us.

Brigadier Sterling was taken off to some undisclosed destination that night. The rest of us were taken in a special train of first-class carriages to Brindisi and thence by truck, toward dawn of December 2, to the transit prison camp at Tutarano, a few miles outside the city.

This again was a new, half-organized camp and we were its first inmates. To the Italian sentries, who were either raw recruits or old men, we were the first experience of the enemy. This to them was the front line, and they prepared to sell their lives dearly. They were very jittery, menacing us with bayonets at the drop of a tin hat, but they soon calmed down.

\* \* \*

CAIRO, December 26, 1941 (United Press): British Imperials were officially reported today driving broken Axis armies into the Agedabia sector, 90 miles beyond Benghazi, after counting more than 13,000 prisoners.... The city of Benghazi, which was taken without opposition as the enemy fled west and south, was virtually destroyed, according to official dispatches.

\* \* \*

# TOBRUK LIBERATED

## by Russell Hill

DEC. 1942.—The Tobruk garrison had succeeded in establishing contact with New Zealanders of the 8th Army at the beginning of the campaign's second week. But it was only in the most formal sense that the fortress was thereby "relieved." By the time the New Zealand Division had reached Bel Hamed and El Duda, it was exhausted from the battles it had fought. The commander of the army corps of which the New Zealand Division formed a part is reported to have wired, when the first contact was made:

"Tobruk is relieved, but not half so much as I am!"

We continued up the road as far as Sidi Barrani and got some information from the town major there about the position of the enemy pockets of resistance in the frontier area. We left the road and followed a rough track up the escarpment to a point near Sofafi. By nightfall we had arrived near Conference Cairn, about halfway between Sofafi and the Wire. We didn't make very good time driving on these desert tracks. While Silk prepared some supper, Noble and I borrowed two spades from some South Africans and enlarged three shallow slit-trenches so that we could put our bedding into them and be protected from the wind.

In the morning we set out once more, crossing the Wire between Sidi Omar and Sherferzen. To the northeast we could hear the sound of shellfire from the British guns that were pounding the enemy pockets along the Wire, and at Halfaya and Sollum. We set our compasses for Tobruk and

501

started driving in a beeline across the desert. In the afternoon we came to Sidi Rezegh. For over two weeks it had been the main battlefield of the campaign. It had been taken and retaken half a dozen times. Finally, only a few days before we reached there, the battle had passed on to other fields. We had before our eyes an appalling sight of destruction. For miles in every direction, on the flat, scrub-covered desert, were the wrecks of tanks, armored cars, staff cars, ambulances, trucks, and motorcycles—thousands upon thousands of lifeless vehicles. Not one of them moved or could move.

Around a curve in the road we came out above the town and harbor of Tobruk. It felt good to see it again, and even the wrecked ships in the harbor looked friendly and reassuring. Overhead a large formation of Tomahawks was flying. That was also a reassuring, though not a familiar sight in Tobruk. As the sun sank over the western horizon, rimming the white clouds with gold, I went down into the town of Tobruk, to the harbor, to see if I could find any of the friends I had made on my first visit, six months earlier.

I was not disappointed. In a house along the waterfront the Movement Control office was still open. There was a sign on the door: "Business as usual!"

Major O'Shaughnessy, the man who was in charge of getting supplies into Tobruk and who had supervised the evacuation of the old garrison and the disembarkation of the new one, was carrying on in high spirts. He was decorated for his services. He deserved it if anyone did. We got to talking about old times. He reminded me of the "Bardia Bill" guns that used to interrupt his work in the port, and told me he had just come back from inspecting six of them that the Germans had abandoned in their retreat. They had turned out to be French 155-millimeter field-pieces. On the wall of his office the major had penciled a comparison of the First World War with the Second World War, listing in each case the Allied nations and the enemy nations side by side. Those countries occupied by the enemy had been crossed out, and underneath them he had written in the latest recruits to the Allied cause, the United States and those Latin-American nations which had declared war on the Axis.

O'Shaughnessy had evacuated a whole garrison, but he himself had refused to leave. He had become genuinely fond of Tobruk and, after living through so many hard days there, could not bear to leave before the happy day of liberation came. Now he was enjoying his triumph. It was a personal victory. I got the impression that he himself, by willing it, had pushed the enemy away from the gates of Tobruk. And that was in a way a true impression, for his indomitable spirit typified the spirit of Tobruk, and it was that spirit which had won through. There was one battalion of Australians which, like O'Shaughnessy, had lived through the entire eight months of the siege. It was planned to evacuate them, but the relief of the fort came before it was their turn to leave; so they joined with the others and went forth to fight in the Battle of El Duda. Apart from this battalion, all of General Morshead's men had left, to be replaced by Poles, Indians, and Englishmen.

*　*　*

BERLIN (from German Broadcasts), Jan. 29, 1942 (United Press): German and Italian troops have occupied Benghazi, the German radio said today. The occupation was said to have occurred at dawn.

LONDON, June 20 (United Press): The British radio said tonight, on the basis of advices from the North African front, that Axis troops probably have entered Bardia....

*　*　*

# ROMMEL IN TOBRUK

## *by Alan Moorehead*

TOBRUK itself was not the business end of the garrison. These guns and mines and men scattered across the plain above were the town's defenses and most of the garrison was stationed up here on the escarpment. Most of the telegraph poles had been cut off as they acted as ranging points for enemy artillery, and so again there was nothing much to see on this eastern half of the perimeter. The cross-roads where the vehicles turned off to El Adem airport was still busy when I passed. We were checked by the sentries at the eastern exit on the coast road and drove on smartly towards Gambut. It was always a relief to get out of Tobruk. I think we knew then that the place was doomed.

In command of the garrison was a South African, H. B. Klopper. He had proved himself an able chief-of-staff to Major-General deVilliers and a few weeks before the battle of Tobruk he was promoted to major-general and given this all-important post. Throughout the campaign he had under his command two full South African brigades with their artillery. At no time were they employed in the fighting and now on June 19th these fresh troops were disposed mainly on the western and southwestern sectors of the perimeter. To them was added the composite brigade which Pienaar dropped off in his passage through the perimeter, various units of the Guards, including the Coldstreams, and about a brigade of Indians who had retired into the southeastern sector of the perimeter after taking part in the fighting outside. In tanks the garrison was weak. About fifty of all classes were collected out of the workshops and put together as a scratch force. There were in addition the administrative personnel, non-combatants who were employed in the workshops, storage dumps, and in the port. In all it was reckoned that Klopper had under his command more than twenty thousand men of whom at least half were fresh. In fire power and actual numbers they were slightly less than the garrison which had held Tobruk through the past year.

503

There was no doubt at all in the mind of the High Command that the garrison should be held once again at all costs. The question was whether this firm decision had been communicated to the men who had to defend the place. For days beforehand I heard doubts expressed among the troops. Everyone wanted to know, "If the Gazala line falls are we going to try and hold Tobruk?" It was the major question in the desert and as one disaster succeeded another the men felt they were being left in the dark. Few of them would have gladly chosen to go into Tobruk in these circumstances.

In the old days there had been no doubt in the minds of the men defending Tobruk. They had turned the earth with their own hands, had dug the original trenches, embedded the guns, seen their friends killed and wounded in sorties and raids, had faced impending disaster several times, and at the last moment driven it off. They had the habit of defense. They were organized and keyed to it. Tobruk meant a great deal to them. They believed that they were defending London and their own homes across its scarred sulphur-colored plains, and the perimeter was as real to them as the cliffs of Dover.

Now it was altogether different. The new defenders had come as tenants into a strange house and moreover a house that had fallen somewhat into disrepair. Thousands of them had bundled pell-mell into the fortress at the last moment and they were tired and hungry and embittered from their set-backs in the past five days. Many came in without their equipment and their guns had been scuttled in the retreat from the line. Communications got into an appalling state and units were badly mixed up. A brigade would find its signalers or its engineers missing. Valuable hours were lost while men waited idly for orders. Ambulances got themselves in the wrong places and the roads were jammed with traffic. Things had gone so badly and so quickly. One defeat had followed another with bewildering rapidity and as is usual in such cases rumors far outstripped the actual facts. The anxiety in men's minds was expressed and passed on from mouth to mouth until it was quoted as a fact. Meanwhile the real urgent business of digging in and getting organized was badly delayed. And it was hours, not days, that counted now.

Moreover it can scarcely have contributed to the morale of the defenders to see hundreds of lorries filled with troops passing straight through the garrison and on to the east. Inevitably as these men passed through they spoke of the enemy on their heels. Just as inevitably it suggested to the defenders that they were being left in the lurch, that they were being used as a rear-guard in an action that was already doomed. And one must remember that all around them was the confusion of men seeking orders, of convoys not knowing where to go, of intense congestion round the petrol and water points, of mounting rumors helped on by the actual air-raids on the garrison.

The British High Command was all through this last day making frantic efforts to get the garrison ready. Before the perimeter was sealed, General

Gort had conferred with Klopper and issued a rousing order of the day. Ritchie could still communicate by radio with Klopper from the outside and he sent across a number of instructions. Auchinleck had visited the front and when he returned to Cairo he sent an urgent instruction to Ritchie that he was to expect immediate attack on Tobruk and that it would most likely come from El Duda in the southeast. El Duda was the permanent weak spot in the perimeter. In 1941 the Australians had taken Tobruk from the Italians by attacking through El Duda. Rommel had planned to assault the garrison from that point in the previous winter. And it was to that point that the defenders had sallied out in November. Tobruk like Bardia had originally fallen to us in a day. All the recent history of the desert showed that these tight-skinned perimeter fortresses fell very quickly once they were penetrated. Klopper, however, maintained his fresh South Africans on the west and southwest (possibly he had no time to move them), and the defense of the vital southeast fell to tired troops who had fought fairly steadily through the previous week, who were partly disorganized, and who had lost quantities of their equipment.

Ritchie also was urged to collect and send out the meager remnants of our armor from Egypt so that they could create a diversion on Sidi Rezegh and soften the blow on Tobruk when it came. The RAF meanwhile had been forced right out of Libya and for the moment found themselves out of range. Given a few more days to organize landing fields something could have been done to get a fighter screen over Tobruk, but there was no question now of there being a few more days. Tobruk was going to its fate much in the same way as Crete did—without air protection.

Klopper had his headquarters well inside the perimeter against the cliffs. But at the very earliest moment of the attack he was bombed out and forced to go to another place. Then again the Stukas got onto him. Through these critical hours he was hounded from one place to another, and inevitably his communications broke down. It was not yet midday and his messages to the outside world became fewer and fewer. Back in Egypt, Ritchie could do nothing more. As in the Crete action the Senior generals had simply to sit and wait for news and were unable to act upon it when they got it.

In his extremity Klopper radioed Ritchie that the position was hopeless. He said, "I will try to fight my way out to the west." Ritchie had no choice but to accept this advice and he agreed. There was a long silence on the radio. Tensely and helplessly, the rest of the Eighth Army waited for the news— news that could only now be had. Then Klopper's last message came in saying tersely, "It is too late. Most of my vehicles have been destroyed and it is no longer possible to move. I will continue resistance only long enough to carry out essential demolition."

This was the last word out of Tobruk that day. As when a ship sinks at sea and the radio splutters and falls silent, so now the town plunged into its disaster and was isolated from all the outside world at the end.

All this time the bulk of the South African troops in the west and south-west had not been seriously drawn into the battle. They were now astonished and bewildered to receive from Klopper the order "surrender." Bitter and confused dispute broke out. The officers who brought the orders were surrounded by angry men saying, "It's a lie. You've got it wrong. What the hell is happening." Some declared they would not obey, others urged delay, others again said they had to obey orders. All this time the Germans were creeping closer.

In defiance of orders or in their absence, these soldiers simply went on shooting at anything they could see because they felt there was nothing else to do. When British officers were sent to them by the Germans to demand their surrender a few refused and shot it out to the last. There were many bitter skirmishes.

Some lucky few, including the Coldstreams, simply took matters into their own hands and under the cover of night fought their way out and escaped to the east. A few more came out in dribbles of fours and fives for days afterwards. But these totaled only a few hundreds. All the rest of that garrison of more than twenty thousand were killed or captured. It was defeat as complete as may be. In equipment alone the enemy had won the richest treasure the desert had ever yielded. Rommel had here enough British vehicles, enough tanks and guns, enough petrol and fuel, and enough ammunition to re-equip at once and drive straight on to Egypt. The road lay open before him. He left four Italian battalions behind to handle the prisoners and reopen the port. Then he set out. The smashing of Tobruk had taken just one day [June 21, 1942].

# FEAR COMES TO CAIRO

### by Frank Gervasi

JUNE, 1942—Upwards of four hundred Americans fled from Cairo during the crucial three days preceding Auchinleck's stand at El Alamein, where the Egyptian desert narrows to a bottleneck between the sea and the edge of the Qattara salt marsh fifty miles to the south.

Those weird days during which Cairo lived from rumor to rumor, oscillating violently between profound pessimism and the heights of optimism, demonstrated again the power of propaganda. The enemy bombarded Egypt with broadcasts.

"The Axis isn't making war on the Egyptian people," shouted Radio Roma. "It means merely to liberate Egypt from the domination of the British. Don't worry! Lay in a week's supplies and remain indoors—no harm will come to you. But see that the Jews and Greeks don't get away."

The Jewish and Greek refugees were disturbed. On the first day, the Ministry of the Interior ran out of stamps for exit visas; banks couldn't cope with the withdrawals and were obliged to reissue pound notes previously recalled from circulation for replacement.

Automobiles which had become scarcer than new ones at home and sold at fantastic prices—such as $3,000 for a second-hand, low-priced make—suddenly swamped the market. I could have bought a year-old car in excellent condition for $500, and I almost did, for the tires—only I couldn't figure out a way of putting the transaction into my expense account.

Hysteria spreads in an endangered city much as a disease must spread throughout the circulatory system of a human body. The virus of fear enters the streets and buildings of a city, and gradually the city's heartbeat quickens. People's voices grow louder. The volume of traffic and the noise it makes increase in the streets. People's movements quicken and their gregarious instincts assert themselves strangely. They want to be together, to find out what others know about the "situation," but they make their plans for escape alone. Self-preservation dominates love and hate and the primary rules of friendship. The instinct for self-preservation asserts itself so strongly that it enables acquisitive, property-loving people to abandon all they own.

The first symptoms of fear in Cairo—that had seemed so safe, so remote from war—were felt upon the fall of Mersa Matruh. It had been the popular notion that the British armies would make a major stand there instead of drawing the enemy as far eastward as El Alamein. Nobody had told the people that, but everyone believed Egypt would live or die on the defense position that reached southward from Mersa Matruh.

When that town fell, refugees and évacués began arriving from Alexandria, the obvious target of Rommel's advance. Well-dressed women held onto the leashes of spaniels and terriers with one hand and clutched jewel boxes with the other. Jewel boxes are always a dead giveaway.

For Americans, the most significant straw in the wind was word from the legation that it might be wise to evacuate. They had been warned repeatedly for the past two years that unless they had substantial reasons for remaining in Cairo it would be a good idea to go home while ships were still available and while America was still neutral. But nobody paid any attention to the admonitions from tall, imperturbable Alexander Kirk, the American Minister.

Finally, on the day when fear drove scores to the legation to learn what would be the best way of getting home—in some cases to demand immediate air transport to Brazil and home, as though such accommodation was the inalienable right of Americans—callers found scraps of charred paper whirling about in a lazy breeze in the vicinity of the legation building. Documents were being burned.

Somehow there's something final and irrevocable about the fact that an embassy or a legation burns its documents. For nearly three years correspondents had cabled such news from capitals of Europe, the Balkans, the Far East, as the first paragraphs of obituaries on diplomatic relations between

Axis nations and those in the Democratic camp, or as death notices of at least a score of countries. It was a familiar sight at the American legation.

In the mild and largely unnecessary chaos of the crisis the PAA officials kept their heads. They anticipated the legation's last-minute demands for transportation for legation staffs, civilians, and members of the large military missions. They had planes ready, and trucks were waiting to carry passengers to the airport; they had worked out every detail of where the people should be distributed. They hadn't anticipated the Army's insistence on priority for military people over diplomats and civilians. Neither had the civilians.

In contrast to Americans and other foreigners who became affected by the prevailing "flap," which is British for panicky withdrawals, the English, at least outwardly, retained their poise. The British Ambassador's wife, pretty, petite Lady Lampson, visited native sooks and bought trinkets just to show people that everything was quite all right. Her husband, Sir Miles, attended the races in Alexandria, and the back pages of English-language local newspapers carried their usual dull accounts of cricket, tennis, swimming, and horse-racing events.

At Heliopolis, the morning the first of the American évacués were en route to the airport, boys rolled out the cricket pitch. Reuter's bulletin in the morning edition comforted the refugees with word that the Dodgers and Yanks led their leagues.

Cairo's night life remained unaffected throughout the critical days. What panic there was seemed to recede each evening with sunset. People dined, wined, danced, and only occasional air-raid alerts reminded them of war. They danced on the Continental Roof while men died less than a hundred miles away, and it was shocking until you rationalized it all by admitting there was nothing else these people could do.

One "crisis night" I dined well with friends at the Mohamed Ali Club. There was consommé gelé, sole meunière, poulet en casserole. We had strawberries and cream, black coffee, and fragile little cakes. The moselle was well chilled, the burgundy blood-warm, and the champagne cold enough to split stone.

The Americans took their flight from Cairo seriously. It did some of them lots of good. It made them aware there was a war, an enormous and important war, going on. Until they had been tagged, weighed, and ordered about, they hadn't realized it. They were quiet and serious as they strained for a last look at the irregular splotch of buildings that the city made beside the Nile. By the time they landed at Luxor they had relaxed considerably.

After being mauled about in the rough air over sands which had begun to warm up under the morning sun they began feeling that perhaps the whole business had been unnecessary. The same people who had clamored for seats on a plane were saying they had been stampeded, but when you asked them who had stampeded them they didn't know. Then they became refugees again, slightly bewildered and definitely unhappy people. Hitler had acquired several hundred positive enemies—those he chased out of Cairo.

I hope that I shall never again know the humiliation of retreat. I know many Britons who feel as I do. When Tobruk fell—why it fell was not clear to us at the moment—we knew the life of Egypt, the western approach to India, and the oil of the Middle East lay within Germany's reach. We prayed for a miracle and bounced along eastward toward Alexandria, the dust of the desert swirling into our trucks, raising an almost impenetrable, lung-stinging fog in which figures and guns and tanks and vehicles moved as though in a nightmare that would never end.

As is common in such military tragedies, men and officers cast about for someone to blame. Surprising as it might seem, the blameworthy one was not felt to be General Auchinleck, for whom all had great sympathy and respect. But men and officers were brutally frank in their excoriations of some of Auchinleck's officers and of Churchill himself. I am personally convinced that Churchill, despite his great genius, could not have survived total defeat in Egypt. The political and strategic courage which caused Auchinleck, the Middle East commander at the time, to take the field, retreat for some hundreds of miles, and make a stand at El Alamein, saved Churchill as much as those qualities saved Egypt. Auchinleck, as we shall see, was materially aided by American airplanes, but he was principally supported by his own unquestionable integrity as an officer and as a man. This is probably why the Auk was not broken but relieved of his command to fight again another day elsewhere. I would not be surprised to see him turn up on a new front in command of a new and even greater enterprise than the Egyptian one. He is a young man, young enough to learn by experience, and as he stood in the path of the British retreat from Gazala, a rock in a swift, back-flowing stream, he must have learned much. Nonetheless, Churchill needed a goat, and the Auk was it, as Wavell had been, following the debacles in Greece and Crete the year before.

Rancor against Churchill was rife in the Middle East by the end of June. Churchill responded quickly.

Three British generals figuratively lost their heads for their responsibility in the military debacle which preceded Auchinleck's stand at the gate to Egypt. They were General Neil Ritchie, commander of the battered Eighth Army; Lieutenant General Willoughby Norrie, commander of the Thirtieth Corps, and Major General William Messervy, commander of the Seventh Armored Division.

Other military heads fell, for the story of ineptitude and all-around bungling of the defense of Egypt was one certain to arouse the white-hot anger of Englishmen at home. It was such a story of laziness and incompetence and of misuse of weapons superior both in quantity and quality to those of the enemy that not even the defeat of General Rommel's Afrika Korps could expunge the guilt of certain men.

Brigadier generals and other high-ranking British officers with whom I talked in Cairo blamed Churchill. They said he named the generals, ordered the movements of troops, and otherwise commanded the British armies. They were outspoken in their criticism of Churchill as a man who considers himself "God's gift to tacticians," and, they added, "he's nothing of the sort." Their loyalty to the Prime Minister was as unquestionable as their recognition of his great talents as a writer, an author, a statesman, and a politician. But they prefaced their opinions of Churchill the tactician with the remark, "Remember Gallipoli." He has the laugh on these critics now. Winston's fabulous luck held. Egypt was saved. But the Prime Minister came close to political disaster in June 1942.

JUNE 25, 1942: *Rommel's troops began the drive towards Alexandria.*

JULY 21: *The British Eighth Army stemmed Rommel's advance at El Alamein.*

# MEDITERRANEAN FLEET

## by Larry Allen

SEPTEMBER, 1942—With the British Mediterranean fleet—If you want action and adventure, travel with Britain's Mediterranean fleet!

This is what 28 months' riding aboard British battleships, aircraft carriers, cruisers, destroyers, gunboats, torpedo boats, and supply transports has brought this correspondent:

Four torpedoes, 1,000,000 pounds of bombs, dive-bombing attacks on 90 out of 100 trips to sea, and a birdseye view of nearly every island in the Mediterranean and countries bordering its waters during cruises aggregating 110,000 miles.

That's more than four times around the world, just hunting trouble, and usually the fleet has found it.

So has this correspondent. The escapes from death have been numerous and frequent. Some people in Alexandria say I have a charmed life. But Admiral Sir Henry Harwood, commander-in-chief of the Mediterranean fleet, says I am becoming a "Jonah," because every time I go to sea "there's hell to pay."

And so it has been, but not necessarily of my own choosing.

There was a time—before the Luftwaffe and Nazi submarines flocked to the Mediterranean—when the fleet could splash about in "Mare Nostrum" as it pleased, with little to worry about except occasional high-level bombing attacks by Italian aircraft.

But those days are gone. It's "action stations" from the moment a warship leaves port until it anchors safely again.

The personal reactions of a correspondent when undergoing an intense dive-bombing attack, or being shelled by enemy warships or shore batteries, are varied and strange.

510

I try to keep my mind on just one thing: "This will make a swell story if it gets through okay—and the censor lets it go." But I frankly admit there are many times when I have prayed and made my peace with God because I just couldn't see a chance in the world of ever getting back to port alive—and neither could the officers and sailors of the ship I was aboard.

The year 1940 was my most pleasant with the British fleet, then a powerful fighting combination of four battleships, two aircraft carriers, nearly a score of cruisers and dozens of destroyers.

The Italian warships seldom left port. So rarely, in fact, that the British coined this expression: "The British Navy likes rum, the Americans drink whisky, but the Italians stick to port."

When they ventured forth within gun-range of British warships they usually hit the bottom in record time. I saw half a dozen Italian destroyers and cruisers go down under the withering blasts of British guns in that year.

The daring raid on Taranto, chief base of the Italian battle fleet, on Nov. 11, 1940, will always remain one of my most thrilling trips to sea.

The fleet had splashed about for a week, almost within sight of the Italian coastline, trying to draw Mussolini's much-vaunted warships out for a showdown fight. But they refused to budge. So Admiral Sir Andrew Browne Cunningham, then commander-in-chief, said, "If they won't come out, we'll go in and blast them out."

The world knows the rest of the story. Aboard the aircraft carrier *Illustrious,* I saw nine torpedo bombers skim off her broad flight deck in the moonlight, swoop into Taranto's land-locked harbor, shove their "tinfish" into three battleships and two cruisers, and safely return to the *Illustrious*. That, for the time being, broke the backbone of Mussolini's battlefleet.

In December of that year, Cunningham took his battlefleet into the mine-dotted waters of the Adriatic and 15-inch guns poured more than 100 tons of high explosive shells into Il Duce's Albanian base of Valona.

The year 1941 brought a new phase in warfare in the Mediterranean. It marked the advent of the Luftwaffe in force in this sea for the first time.

After Cunningham's fleet had thrown hundreds of tons of shells into Bardia and other Libyan positions, clearing the way for the British Army's advance and the capture of 100,000 Axis prisoners, the men-o-war were sent westward to just off Pantelleria to pick up a convoy coming through from the western Mediterranean.

I saw an Italian destroyer which attempted to interfere with the convoy blasted to bits on the morning of Jan. 10, and two others put to flight by British destroyers and cruisers.

By noon 100 Nazi Stukas were over the fleet, concentrating their attention upon the aircraft-carrier *Illustrious*.

That was one of the most terrifying experiences of my life. For seven solid hours Nazi divebombers droned over the *Illustrious,* dropping more than 100,000 pounds of bombs. The carrier received seven direct hits of 1,250-pound bombs.

Lashing about like a wounded tiger, the *Illustrious* flung tens of thousands of pom-pom and 4.5-inch shells at the diving Stukas. Burning furiously and listing badly, the carrier finally made the port of Valletta, Malta, where for another week she was kept busy firing her guns at Stukas determined to sink her at all costs.

Blown by bomb blast from the Admiral's bridge to the Air Intelligence quarters nearly 30 feet below, I prayed that afternoon. But I got out of it with a few cuts and bruises and considerable shock.

I was off to sea again on the next big trip and so on to April 23, 1941. That night Cunningham boldly sailed into the mine-laden waters of Tripoli Harbor and plastered that Barbary Coast nest of Nazis and Italians with 1,000 tons of high-explosive and armor-piercing shells. Tripoli's waterfront was ablaze when we sailed away.

Then the battle of Crete, when the Nazis hurled millions of pounds of bombs upon the fleet, trying to destroy every warship and prevent the evacuation of 17,000 British troops from the island in May, 1941. The whole sea around Crete was turned into a great mass of geysers with hundreds of bombs crashing into the water. The Navy evacuated the soldiers, but lost four cruisers and eight destroyers under air attack.

If I needed anything after the *Illustrious* to convince me that a fleet must have air protection to carry out a successful operation, all doubts were dispelled after seeing warships, having exhausted their ammunition, picked off like sitting ducks by droning Stukas making their kill. There were heated demands that adequate air protection be provided to stop this slaughter of warships and personnel.

All through the Summer of 1941, the fleet was busy bombarding along the Libyan coast or taking a crack at knots of Vichy French resistance along the Syrian coast. We were bombed and shelled, but for me, the worst was yet to come.

In November, 1941, a U-boat fired torpedoes at the battleship *Queen Elizabeth* off Libya. They missed. The U-boat reversed position, came within incredibly short range and launched four torpedoes at the battleship *Barham*.

From the quarter-deck of the *Queen Elizabeth,* I saw the great man-o-war list heavily, suddenly, and then the fourth torpedo touched off her magazine, blowing her to bits. So terrific was the explosion and at such close range were the torpedoes fired that the U-boat was forced to surface, but quickly dived and got away. The death of that battleship was one of the most spectacular things I have ever seen.

Came December. We bombarded Axis gun positions east of Tobruk. Then, another trip to sea, apparently to apprehend an Axis Libya-bound convoy, but after two days at sea we turned eastward.

I was aboard the cruiser *Galatea*. For seven hours, we were dive-bombed by Stukas before darkness on Dec. 15. Just after midnight, a U-boat fired three torpedoes into the *Galatea*. She hurled over immediately, and disappeared in two minutes.

I went through the most agonizing moments of my life. I couldn't swim and knew that I was going to die. I mumbled a prayer to God, rushed to the starboard side of the cruiser and tried to blow a bit of air into my life-belt. The cruiser turned over and I slid feet first down her starboard side into the water, now covered with a thick scum of fuel oil.

I went under, time and again. I swallowed gallons of oil and water. I screamed, I prayed, I fought my way to the surface time after time. Forty-five minutes of this hell and finally rescue by a destroyer. I was literally "a dead fish." Sailors pumped oil and water out of my lungs, whispered to each other, "It's no use. He's finished."

But I kept thinking, "what a swell story. I've got to live." It took months to get all the oily scum off my body and out of my lungs. But I wrote my story as soon as I landed—and I was as naked as the day I was born. Then I went to bed for a week.

Since then, there have been long cruises to sea with the British warships, hunting and finding trouble, bombarding the Axis' main bases, and I've just had my fourth torpedo in six months.

A correspondent often feels so helpless when in the midst of action, because for him there is no "action station." You just stand on the bridge, watch the guns fire, the bombs drop, and feel the shells whiz over you.

But there's usually a good story. So I like it!

SEPTEMBER 6, 1942: *The British put a definite halt to Rommel's break through to the Nile.*

\* \* \*

BRITISH EIGHTH ARMY FIELD HEADQUARTERS IN THE EGYPTIAN DESERT, NOV. 5 (Associated Press): Lieutenant-General Bernard L. Montgomery, commander of the 8th Army, announced this morning that his forces battling the Axis had achieved complete and absolute victory.

ALLIED HEADQUARTERS IN NORTH AFRICA, Nov. 8 (Associated Press): American soldiers, Marines, and sailors from one of the greatest naval armadas ever put into a single military operation swarmed ashore today on the Vichy-controlled North Africa shore before dawn.

\* \* \*

# ALGIERS

*by John A. Parris, Jr.*

NOVEMBER 8, 1942—Algiers was a white, triangular wound against the dun hills behind the harbor.

A British destroyer nosed past the barges across the entrance to the harbor and darted up to one of the docks. A small force of American Rangers dropped over the side and scurried toward the big, white French Admiralty Building on the waterfront.

The crisp crackle of machine-gun and rifle fire shattered the silence of the early dawn.

The Allied bombers came in low over Algiers.

The French and Arabs and Berbers poured out of their houses and filled the streets. Their eyes lifted to the skies. They saw something drop from the planes, thousands of little somethings that floated and drifted and fluttered and spun toward the earth. The sky was white with these little white objects.

Then the French and the Arabs and the Berbers who gazed into the sky realized what they were. They were leaflets.

The leaflets fell in the square and along the boulevard and on the roof tops.

The wind blew one at the feet of a middle-aged Frenchman. He stooped down and picked it up. An American flag was imprinted on the front. The text was in French.

A dozen persons crowded around the Frenchman. He began reading aloud. These were the words:

"The President of the United States has asked me, as commanding officer of the American Expeditionary Forces, to convey to all the people in Morocco and North Africa the following message:

"No nation is more closely bound by historic ties and deep affection to the people of France and their friends than the United States of America.

"Americans are striving not only for their safe future, but also for the restoration of the ideals, the liberties and the democracy of all those who have lived under the Tricolor.

"We come among you to save you from conquerors who would remove forever your rights of self-government, your right to religious freedom, and your rights to live your own lives in peace.

"We come among you solely to destroy your enemies and not to harm you.

"We come among you with the assurance that we will leave just as soon as the menace of Germany and Italy is removed from you.

"I am appealing to your sense of realism, self-interest, and ideals. Do not obstruct this great purpose.

"Help us, and the day of world peace will be hastened."

A little old French woman pulled the shawl closer about her shoulders. There was a faraway look in her old eyes.

"I remember the Americans in the last war," she said. "They used to buy wine from me. Now," her voice was low and the words came slowly, "now maybe we can all go back to France one day soon."

"Allo Maroc, allo Maroc..."

Moroccans turned up the volume on their radios.

"...this is the transmitter of American armed forces..."

The announcer began broadcasting President Roosevelt's proclamation to the French people.

"...the enemy must go..."

The tall, monocled German paced the floor of the German Armistice Commission headquarters in Casablanca. He was angry and he was shouting. A French officer stood in a corner of the room watching the German pace back and forth, shouting in French, sometimes in German.

"Find that station," the German shouted, "and destroy it. I tell you it has got to be destroyed."

"But," the Frenchman tried to explain, "it seems to be broadcasting from Rabat. That means the city is in American hands."

The radio voice was now warning the French armies on land, sea, and in the air in North Africa to refrain from hostile action and follow certain orders.

"... to all naval and merchant marine units: first, stay where you are. Second, make no attempt to scuttle your vessels ..."

The French captain of the *Jean Bart* ordered his gun crews to keep firing.

"... to coast-guard units: withdraw from the neighborhood of your cannon and your stations ..."

The coastal batteries growled and hurled shot and shell toward the sea, toward the oncoming Allied ships.

"... to aviation units: do not take off. All airplanes must remain in their usual places ..."

A squadron of Dewoitines lifted from La Senia airdrome and winged away toward the coast. But the pilots at the Rabat airdrome were having trouble. Something was the matter with their planes. The motors wouldn't start.

"... general orders: in general you must obey all orders given to you by my officers."

The voice said that General Eisenhower had given formal orders that no offensive actions should be taken against the French forces "on condition that for your part you take the same attitude.

"To avoid any possible misunderstanding," continued the American radio voice, "the French forces should identify themselves in daylight by flying the French Tricolor and the American flag one above the other, and at night by turning on a searchlight and directing it vertically toward the sky."

On this golden autumn Sabbath morning of November eighth the war seems to have moved on from the beaches here at Arzu to the hills and beyond where the desert stretches its white wastes in endless miles.

There in the billowing field of broom-sage, just under the brow of the hill, lies the still form of a boy in khaki for whom the war is over. The blood that has spattered and soaked into the crushed yellow-flowered shrubs is dry and turning rusty.

The little dome-shaped pillbox there at the entrance to the seaplane base is shattered and torn and gaping with shell holes. A French soldier lies in a grotesque heap. He has no face. Bits of skull and brains are scattered on the floor, mixed with plaster and bits of concrete.

But the sound of war has moved on.

The ship sways at anchor. Two British sailors stand at the stern fastening a piece of silk to a rope that dangles from a mast. Slowly they raise the piece of silk—the Stars and Stripes.

As Old Glory ripples up there above our heads, a broad-shouldered young giant from Illinois, Captain Clinton E. Frank of Evanston who made football history at Yale, lowers his arm. But his eyes are still fastened on that bit of patch-work silk.

"When I see her flying like that," he says, "I sort of get a lump in my throat. Until you've seen her break folds a long way from home you really don't realize how much she means to you."

The shore batteries here at Arzu are silent now and only the intermittent ping and whine of a sniper's bullet breaks the silence of the immediate shore. But from down Oran way comes the muffled roll of heavy guns. When the wind freshens from the southwest it carries an acrid smell of gunpowder.

To the east, on beyond where the pink, little champagne-manufacturing town of Monstaganem juts out into the Mediterranean along the coast to Algiers, there is still the sound of heavy cannonading. The boom of six-inch guns breaks and rolls like claps of big thunder. There are nine thunderous rolls within a matter of seconds. The British naval captain says it sounds as if a sea battle might be going on. From the sea behind Monstaganem smoke boils toward the horizon.

Two destroyers break through the smoke screen on our starboard side. Between them is the French troop transport *J'Amique,* her decks crowded with soldiers in khaki uniforms. They wear red fezzes. She's been caught trying to escape to the high seas.

The morning wears on, heavy and expectant, and the French are still resisting. We had expected the fighting, if any, to be short and only a sort of token resistance. Our State Department agents had reported only twenty-four hours before that there probably wouldn't be any shooting at all, certainly not any organized resistance to speak of. They had warned, however, if there was any resistance it would probably come from the French navy and the Foreign Legion, that band of mercenary fighters of every land and every creed who fought for the pure joy of fighting and the little gold and glory that went with it.

The wireless room whistles and chatters in rattling cipher, bringing news of the landings, the progress of our lightning offensive.

"...Green forces landed west of Oran...sweeping objectives with little opposition..."

That is good news.

"...fighting is heavy in Oran harbor...our forces are meeting stiff resistance..."

This isn't according to plan.

"...red forces moving from east of Oran have met little opposition and are making rapid progress toward Tafaraoui...expect to reach airdrome by three o'clock...our paratroops have captured Tafaraoui but are being threatened by a strong Foreign Legion armored column moving up from

Sidi Bel Abbes...reinforcements are needed...La Senia airdrome is still in enemy hands...some of our paratroops have been captured...."

There is no news of our progress at Algiers and Casablanca, but rumor is running rampant on the transport. Our forces have suffered heavy losses at Casablanca...Algiers has fallen without a shot. So the rumors go. The Germans have invaded Spain...Spanish Moroccans have joined the French and are crossing into Algeria and French Morocco...heavy fighting is going on...the Spanish have wiped the Gibraltar air field clean with machine-gun and artillery fire...dozens of American and British fighters and bombers have been destroyed on the ground....

The ship is a floating rumor mill.

The continuous roll of heavy guns doesn't help to allay our fears.

# THE WOUNDED ARE WAITING

## by Leo Disher

AT ten o'clock I slumped into a chair in the wardroom and picked up my typewriter and began writing a story to send to United Press—a story about men going into battle, what they said in those last minutes, what they did, how they felt. I wrote...

ABOARD A BRITISH SLOOP OF WAR APPROACHING ORAN, Nov. 7—(UP)—This might be a fashionable club room back in New York or London. It has that kind of atmosphere tonight. The war seems a long way off. The men are deep in the easy chairs, their legs hooked over the sides, reading and smoking.

In a few hours these men are going to be fighting—killing and fighting for their lives. But right now they are calm. And if they are thinking about the minutes ahead you can't tell it.

There are no jitters aboard the ship.

Along the lounge to the left of me are three big chairs lashed together. In them are two American infantry lieutenants and a British commando captain. Other officers are moving about the wardroom, waiting idly.

Lieutenant-Colonel George Marshall, commander of the Americans, just came down the broad stairway in the center, and after talking a moment with Lieutenant Victor Wales, Jr., of Washington, D. C., he went out again.

Directly opposite me, on the other side of the lounge, the ship's doctor, a slight, baldish fellow, is spreading a white cover on the mess-table. That's where he will do his operating.

On the deck above, next to the top deck, the American soldiers are trying to sleep. They are stretched head to foot in every available space in the passageways. To get by, officers first must rouse the men. It's amazing that they can sleep now.

Marshall's adjutant, Lieutenant John Cole, 23, R. F. D. No. 1, Lexington,

517

Kentucky, has just brought in a can of grease paint. The officers are spreading it on their faces and hands.

Cole eyed my leg judiciously and said, "It looks heavy." I told him it was heavy. "It needs some camouflage," he drawled and picked up the black grease paint. He daubed it on the cast. Then he said, "We'll have to float it." Stepping over to a pile of equipment, he picked up a life-tube and came back. He wrapped the tube around the cast. "One more tube," he said, "and it's certain to float."

"One more tube," I said, "and they can shoot me for a barrage balloon. Cousin, enough is enough."

It is now eleven o'clock. The heavy-set lieutenant who is acting as chief of staff to the task force commander has come into the wardroom. He's wearing American battle-coveralls. Two six-guns are strapped low on his hips in western-style holsters. Under his arm is a tommy gun.

The lieutenant will stand on the ship's bridge as we go into the harbor and broadcast to the French over a loudspeaker. He will say: "Don't fire ... we are Americans ... don't fire."

I asked Duncan if he would be talking in French.

"Yes," he replied. "French ... with an American accent. I've been training, you know ... you'd be surprised how good I am."

Midnight.

Mike came down a moment ago, blacked so that he looked like the end man in a minstrel show. He has explosives strapped to his waist and his legs. He is wearing British battle-dress. He just told the doctor: "If they get me in the legs, Doc, shoot me. No, don't. But shoot me if they get me in the eyes—and for God's sake give me a drink first!"

The commando captain got out of his chair abruptly and stalked from the room. He had been sitting for some minutes staring at the wall. As he got up he said to no one in particular: "I've got it all figured out: I've got one chance in ten."

Most of the other officers have finished their preparations and have gone to their battle stations. Just before midnight, Colonel Marshall returned to the lounge and called his officers for a conference. He said a report had been received that there are now eight French warships in the harbor. A cruiser-type destroyer has tied up at the end of the harbor where we intend to dock.

Marshall said the plans had been changed slightly. He said we would go alongside the cruiser and board her with grappling irons.

As this is being written the ship is turning away from her convoy remnant. Two launches are following us with the cutter *Hartland*.

We are heading due south and have begun our final run for Oran. ...

I looked back at the *Walney*, expecting to hear the final explosion any moment. She was dying, fearfully, shuddering with explosions. I thought that in one red flash I could see the Stars and Stripes still flying from her stern. She went down that way. She never struck her colors.

With infinite weariness I swam into the blackness between a lurching merchant ship and the pier. My eyes closed. My fingers clawed water. I touched a rope and discovered I was again determined to live. I hauled myself up until I got my elbows over the pier rim. Then the full weight of the cast on my leg caught me and I knew I couldn't make it. Slowly and painfully I began losing my grip. Then a single hand groped down and braced me. I swung my good leg up and it caught. Then the hand from above began to pull, and I rolled over the edge with open, gasping mouth pressed against the stone surface of the pier. I could see the man who had pulled me up as a hazy, unreal figure swaying near me. But I saw enough. He had used only one hand because the other had been shot away. I never knew his name, never even knew his nationality, because just then a bullet struck my injured foot. Another bullet later hit the wall and bounced into my temple. I was crawling, sprawling into the dirt, crawling again.

A French patrol eventually passed. I called out: "Wounded ... here." There were seven or eight of us huddled wet and wounded in the dirt against the wall. One man was groaning, half gurgling.

The Frenchmen stopped, looked toward us, and there was a rattle of weapons. One of them flashed on a light.

"Wounded," I repeated. I thought they didn't understand me. I thought they were going to fire on us.

The French came over and, behind the light, peered down at us. Some of the men struggled to their feet. The Frenchmen searched them for weapons. Then they began moving us away.

I swung along on my right foot, with one arm over the shoulders of a French soldier and the other around a man from the ships. We stopped every fifteen or twenty feet so I could rest. In this fashion we crossed a hundred yards of open space with explosions sounding in the night around us.

Finally, a French soldier took me over his back like a sack of meal and carried me into a hole in the cliffs. The hole led on, became a corridor, then a system of corridors. French soldiers, some of them wounded, stared silently. The tunnel, at the end, led to a space where doctors worked in bright, glaring lights.

I saw then that the man from the ships who had helped carry me had a bullet wound in his shoulder.

They put me on a stretcher. They carried me back to the tunnel mouth again and placed me on the ground and waited for an ambulance. It was just getting light—the first light of dawn. A light rain had begun to fall. Below me, there in the half-light, I saw ships flaming, burning in the harbor.

Groaning, wet and bloody men were placed in the ambulance. We rode through the streets of Oran and came to a winding road on a hill where we were transferred from the ambulance to an open-bed truck. Natives gathered around us, staring curiously, shaking their heads as they saw the gaping wounds, blood and tatters. A British seaman with his leg almost shot off cursed them in a fine Yorkshire accent.

In a long hospital ward, a French nurse stuck a cigarette between my lips and a doctor found a total of twenty-six assorted holes in me. I tried to sleep but the hospital shuddered to the roar of big guns.

In the next bed the American soldier who had helped carry me woke up and grinned. "Ain't it," he asked, "a helluva day?"

Our first meal came in buckets carried by an orderly who left hunks of dark brown bread at each table. Soup and mashed beans were served in tin plates. Black wine came in tin cups.

Sometime next day, a man across the aisle died, shouting deliriously.

A retired French naval officer came into the ward, listened to the sound of guns coming nearer. "Very soon we will be your prisoners," he said.

Sometime in that interval doctors came, leading the soldier who had jumped out of the frying pan into the fire. He didn't have a scratch on him, but wouldn't or couldn't talk.

Word of the number of casualties was passing around, and survivors learned that the young lieutenant who had worried about his wife having a baby was lost, and that the kid from Kentucky had been machine-gunned to death in the water.

Later we could hear machine guns firing beneath the window and tanks rumbling into the streets. Then there was a sudden flurry among the French in the ward.

An American Army sergeant came through the doorway and paused. His head was bandaged, his battle-dress covered with mud. He walked unsteadily, but his ugly mug was sweetened by a smile of triumph.

All over the ward Americans began sitting up excitedly, but one fellow with a busted shoulder was the first to realize what had happened—that it was all over at Oran.

"Hey, Sarge!" he shouted. "Great God, Sarge! Come here!"

# AMERICAN PARATROOPS

## by Lowell Bennett

SO it was that on November 15, 1942, seven days after the original landings, a battalion of American parachutists flew from Algiers to seize an airdrome on the Tunisian frontier in the first Allied move east to squeeze Rommel. British parachutists were scheduled to fly east that day, too, but en route they encountered bad weather and were forced to turn back. It was a spectacular move, one that proved the Germans no longer had a monopoly in three-dimension operations.

Enemy planes were flying into Tunisia every day. Junkers transports were bringing in infantry and artillery troops; ships were sneaking across the Sicily-Bizerte straits nightly with their equipment. If the Allies were to capture Tunisia without a major battle developing, they would have to move fast. It was first decided to seize forward airdromes along the frontier and inside Tunisia, to prevent the Germans from taking them over. This would afford the First Army sufficient air cover for its advance.

Tebessa was one such airdrome; although small, it was ideally located for fighter planes to cover the central area. Three reporters went along with the American parachutists, which was also a record—for the first time the press was represented in battle-jumping operations. They had planned, as already told, to jump with the paratroopers, but only one extra parachute had been found, and Thompson had gotten that. Kluckhohn and I would fly with the troops, watch them jump, then come back to write the story.

We left before dawn, while it was still so dark the planes could not be seen on the field. There were C-47 and C-53 transports; and parachutists

The troops had spent the night in a giant hangar on Maison Blanche airdrome; a few of them had slept, but mostly they had been busy checking their equipment and writing letters home. In a near-by hangar British paratroops also waited.

Colonel Raff, Major Yarborough and Major Yardley, heads of the American battalion, spent the night working over their maps and putting the final touches to their plan.

"Yarborough, there's a railroad running near the airdrome," announced Raff. "Maybe we'll be able to steal a train and load it up with guns. Then we can drive right into Tunisia and knock hell out of the Germans, all by ourselves."

Raff was like that. He's the kind of commander men either desert or will die for. His battalion had long ago voted to die for him. He is only about five foot seven or eight inches tall. But he's hard and wiry, knows a lot about airplanes and more about parachuting. He had gone to West Point, came out to join the Air Corps, but was turned down because he wasn't big enough! Disappointed, he learned to fly anyway, then managed to join the Parachute Corps when it was inaugurated only two years before the war. Now, at thirty-five, he was a lieutenant colonel, commanding a battalion of some of America's best fighters. His was to be the job of leading off our offensive to the east.

The parachutists were all volunteers. They had trained at Fort Benning in Georgia for at least a year before going to Britain, where they had spent more months in hard practicing for this day. At Oran they had had a baptism, but this time they were starting to operate against the Germans. Everyone of them had jumped at least fourteen times, many of them more. They were a little nervous, but perhaps it was more excitement than anything else. In long lines they filed out to the planes, stowed their equipment, then climbed in to sit crowded in a plane.

Two other planes were loaded with hampers of food, blankets, extra munitions and medical supplies. Unlike their British counterparts, our 'chutists carry almost everything they need with them when they drop from the planes. The British trooper travels lightly, and some of his equipment is dropped to him afterward. Ours are loaded down, and are certainly formidable with their assortment of weapons.

The planes filled rapidly and taxied into line to follow each other up. For escort this time we had plenty of fighters, Spitfires and Lightnings. We bumped down the runway, and roared up to begin a slow climbing circle of the 'drome, as the other planes took off to complete the formation. This was accomplished in only a few moments, and as the sun began to appear behind us, the air fleet swung east.

Out over the coast, where the air would be smoother, we roared at about three miles a minute. For safety the planes all came down to just fifty or sixty feet above the water, with the fighters hovering above, like humming birds beside eagles.

As the sun came up the weather warmed; the sky turned to a real Mediterranean blue; the water below us was as unruffled as a summer resort lake in New Jersey. Off to the right, though, the Algerian coastline resembled that of northern Scotland, mountainous, barren.

Inside the plane the men didn't sleep on this trip. There was a tenseness, a subdued excitement. They were veterans, but after all they were still boys, most of them not much over twenty. Reports before we had left had said the Germans were flying fighter patrols along the coast to intercept any attempt to move troops eastward. Despite our strong fighter escort, the transport planes would be sitting ducks for enemy interceptors.

Lieutenant Ralph Miller from Youngstown, Ohio, tried to relieve the tenseness.

"What the hell. When you jump you've only got two things to worry about: whether your 'chute opens or whether it doesn't. If it doesn't open you've got nothing to worry about. If it does you've only got to worry about landing."

But that only made all of them check their harnesses again. Wires attached to a release clip on each man's 'chute led back to a main cord along the fuselage. When the men stepped out of the plane the wires would tighten, releasing the 'chute, which would open almost as soon as the jumper left the aircraft.

Marcus Kuhec, young private from Milwaukee, leaned over to say:

"I hope my 'chute rigger isn't still sore at me because I owe him ten bucks," and patted his parachute.

For over an hour we roared along just off the coast; the ride was smooth but the noise was terrific. It was like riding an express train. On the next air ride, we promised ourselves, there would be cotton for the ears and chewing gum for dry mouths.

At the easternmost corner of Algeria, the formation banked right and swung in over the mountains. We climbed to avoid the peaks, reaching up thousands of feet. The air became very bumpy; the transport bucked and jerked as it hit air pockets and currents. The parachutists took an active interest in everything. They peered out of the little windows at the other planes, at the ground, at the fighters which had closed in about us.

522

These were dangerous airs. German fighters could reach us here from their bases near Tunis. Our escort increased its activity, sweeping around and above us. The transports had little or no armament; all would be lost unless the fighters could keep off any interceptors. The paratroopers could poke their machine guns through the slots in the windows, but their range wouldn't be very effective against six-hundred-yard cannon and machine-gun fire.

A bell sounded in the plane above the engine's roar. That meant we were within a few minutes of the target. The men hitched up their harness, hastily rechecked their equipment and looked around at each other.

I climbed forward to the navigator's seat, just behind the pilots. In the roof of the plane was a glass bowl, sticking up about two feet above the fuselage. Through that it was possible to see the whole formation, and by craning one's neck the ground could be seen. Suddenly, below, Tebessa air-drome appeared. It was hardly more than an oversized flat field. There were a few huts, probably native homes, scattered around its edge. As we came closer, slit-trenches pockmarking the edge of the field were observed. Then men appeared in the trenches, Frenchmen. Would they fight, or would they be on the Allies' side? They were looking up at us, tiny, almost indistinguishable as humans at that distance.

The formation circled the field, losing height. We were at low altitude. The transport's crew unscrewed and pulled away the escape hatch from the side of the plane. The 'chutists lined up facing the doorway, the release wires stretching from their bulky backs like long thin tails, it seemed.

This was it. Suddenly someone dived out of the leading plane, then every plane disgorged leaping, falling, tumbling humans. And just as suddenly, just as automatically, the sky filled with graceful white blossoms, as the parachutes opened and men began to float down to earth. Jack Thompson had jumped among the first, just after Colonel Raff in the leading plane. It was stirring to hear the noise of the plane, to mark the speed, to see the number of men suspended by enormous silken umbrellas, close to the ground.

In a few seconds, while we banked and started to circle the field again, the men had landed. They were in a small area, maybe a hundred square yards, and from each stretched out shroud cords with a white sheet at the end. Everyone of them lay absolutely still. For a moment we were horror-stricken; it seemed as if the parachutists were all dead. Then memory helped out. That was the system; the troops lay flat on the ground for a few moments, to get back their breath, unhitch the harness and present as poor targets to the enemy as possible.

As we were circling back, they began to get up and move across the field, in open formation, just like infantrymen, with their guns at high port. But there was no fight. The French had seen the white stars on the transports' wings. They climbed out of their trenches and waved the Americans on.

We were over the field again, even lower. The plane's crew pushed hampers and bags out the hatch; these were filled with the supplies the

523

paratroops would need. They were attacked to wires for automatic release just as the men had been, and through the glass bowl I saw them blowing away from the plane to land near the men. From below someone signaled with a Very gun.

\* \* \*

LONDON, Nov. 27, 1942 (Associated Press): Vichy announced the suicide of the French home fleet of sixty or more warships at Toulon today.

\* \* \*

# BRITISH FIRST ARMY

## by Ned Russell

NOVEMBER saw the British First Army scramble wildly for Tunis and almost win it, but December and January were months of maddening frustration, the hardest sort of slogging and living, and some of the most disheartening disappointments. But with all that, those two months saw the First Army begin to develop and grow into one of the best the Allies possessed. The process began in that period, but actually wasn't completed until April. Many thousands of British and American soldiers died or were badly wounded in that gruesome, but necessary, transition of inexperienced boys into an army of tough, shrewd veterans. The men of the First Army, and the Americans who were gradually withdrawn from the organization of the First Army itself, learned that fighting is the only way to learn to fight.

At the same time, the vast mechanical organization of the British and American forces began to take a shape that simply never existed in the early days. The trucks and guns and tanks and airplanes and ammunition, and even the items that the layman rarely imagines as part of a military expedition—telephone wires, bulldozers, soap, spare parts for all the vehicles and weapons, toothbrushes, razors, water cans and gasoline cans and boots and socks—began to flow on a colossal scale. The Allied forces were growing into a single machine which could be wielded without fear of something going wrong simply because some seemingly unimportant item wasn't within easy reach. I remember a moment in November when a tank attack had to be postponed because someone had neglected or forgotten to supply grease for the tanks. It had to be flown to the front from Algiers.

The first heroes of the campaign were the men of the Hampshire regiment. Their feat, which I think was never matched in the North African campaign, did not become known until the end of the first week in December. They had relieved my friends of the Northamptonshire regiment in the fighting for Djedeida and they took the brunt of the German counterattack all the way back to Medjez-el-Bab. They went into the line in front of Djedeida on November 29. Before they were relieved, near Medjez-el-

Bab, they had only a few left. But against that, they had the first Victoria Cross decoration in the North African campaign. The V.C., the highest award for gallantry in the British forces, was given posthumously to Major "Pat" LePatourel. He had led repeated infantry charges against impossible odds and had disappeared. Everyone was convinced that he was dead, but soon after his award had been approved, his family in England received a letter from him in a hospital in Italy where he was recovering from wounds. I believe it was the only posthumous V.C. ever given to a living soldier.

When they were fighting their way back from Djedeida and Tebourba, the Hampshires were cut off from their supplies almost from the start. They were hit repeatedly by German tanks—the Hampshires had no tanks—and by numerically superior German infantry. Once, they were attacked by sixty-five tanks. On December 3, they went into Tebourba, hoping to get more precise orders from brigade headquarters, but they found the town had been abandoned and they were on their own. Behind them, the road was cut by German machine-gunners and tanks lying in the hills overlooking the road. Their casualties already had been very severe and they were no longer an effective fighting force. But their commander was determined that they should escape to reorganize, re-equip, and get reinforcements to fight again. He ordered all the survivors to arm themselves with rifles, automatic weapons, grenades and ammunition taken from the supplies of their wounded comrades and from the bodies of their dead. It was a question of fighting their way through the Germans with nothing more than they could carry on their backs or stuff into the big pockets of their uniforms. Their commander told them to split up into groups of two or three men each, grab what food and water they could find in stranded vehicles and head for Medjez-el-Bab.

On December 4, the battalion's medical officer, quartermaster officer and chaplain, who had left the front earlier, started to gather the last survivors together in a wood five miles northeast of Medjez-el-Bab. For two days, the little parties appeared, one by one, out of the hills through which they had crawled and walked and fought. I don't suppose anyone knows yet how many were killed and how many were wounded during those eight days and nights, but the important thing, as far as all the Allied forces were concerned, was that the battalion never lagged in its spirit and never faltered in its determination to get back to fight again.

The Americans of C.C.B., a combat command from the First Armored Division, were moved into the battle to stiffen the Allied defenses. The brigade had been cut viciously, and if it had not been for the Americans, the line in front of Medjez-el-Bab might never have been held. However, on December 5, intelligence information showed that the Germans were reinforcing in the Tebourba area. The next day, they attacked toward Medjez-el-Bab with a fury and a violence which matched anything they had displayed before. They hit out against the weak, tired remnants of the brigade and C.C.B. men with tanks, heavy machine-guns and mortars. It was decided that the Allies could not hold their line and would be compelled to withdraw behind Medjez-el-Bab. The British engineers laid mines all around and in the town until one of their officers described the whole area as "one bloody great mine."

Plans were made for a general withdrawal to regroup the forces which had been in the fighting for most of the past month and to find suitable places for the new units which were beginning to arrive. However, on December 8, British patrols, thrusting into the German positions in the hills at night and snatching prisoners out of the darkness, reported indications that the Germans also were planning to pull back. The British and Americans apparently had fought them to a standstill without realizing it. At the same time, as those patrols came back to their headquarters early that morning, they were drenched with rain. The rain storms which were to become so famous to the world for the way in which they soaked the north Tunisian mountains and valleys, had begun. After the first few hours of this opening storm, the whole battle area and everything for miles behind it became a mass of thick, glue-like mud. Movement was impossible except on the slippery paved roads. It was impossible to get heavy vehicles and tanks from the muddy fields onto the roads, or, if they were on the roads, to get them far enough off them for safety, in dispersal, from air attack.

The Germans obviously were in much the same predicament, although their superiority in the air made the weather less of a determining factor. However, they made no immediate effort to exploit their advantage and on December 9, General Anderson decided to abandon his plans for withdrawal behind Medjez-el-Bab. The town, he ordered, was to be held "at all costs." Just as this order went out, the Germans took advantage of a sunny day and sent thirty-eight tanks rolling along the two roads from Tebourba and Tunis to attack the town.

It was a crucial day in the campaign. Light American tanks went out into the rolling Tunis plain to fight the heavily armed German Mark Fours and Mark Threes. Most of the American tanks were knocked out by the Germans, who plowed forward. A French crew of a French seventy-five-millimeter gun, World War I vintage, guarding one of the approaches to the town, knocked out four or five tanks and ended its role in the battle with one officer loading and firing the gun alone while his dozen comrades lay dead or wounded around him. Late in the afternoon, the Germans simply turned around and went back to their bases. I think everyone was bewildered by the German withdrawal. It just didn't make sense, because the town's defenses were being slowly beaten down and they never had been strong enough to withstand an assault of such proportions. Apparently the Germans thought the defenses were stronger than they were. They called the operation a "reconnaissance in force," a term often used to minimize disappointment over the failure of an attack.

# AND NOT A TEAR WAS SHED

## by Wes Gallagher

DECEMBER 24, 1942—Stocky, poker-faced Admiral Darlan, dressed in his inevitable dark suit, strode rapidly from his car through the honor guard of red-caped Spahis into the cool shadows of the luxurious summer palace overlooking Algiers Harbor.

It was the day before Christmas, and the admiral was riding high. He had played one losing horse during the war when he had jumped on Hitler's band wagon with the fall of France, but now he was installed more firmly with each passing day as North Africa's high commissioner. It was true that the Americans and British did not like him, but what did that matter? Offhand he could not think of anyone who liked him, but still he was in power, and that was all that was necessary.

As he approached his offices neither he nor his aide gave more than a passing glance to the slight figure standing in the anteroom. There was usually some caller there waiting to ask a favor—a political job, perhaps.

But twenty-two-year-old Fernand Bonnier de la Chapelle, dreamy young university student, wanted no favors. He stepped closer to the door, raised a small pistol, and fired several times. One bullet struck the admiral in the jaw, another in the neck.

As Darlan sagged against the door, blood pouring down his clothes, his aide leaped at Chapelle but went down with a bullet in his groin.

Rushing into the room, Darlan's chauffeur, Adjutant André Vuichard, grappled with Chapelle and yanked the pistol away from him. The young student offered no resistance and showed no fear when Spahis running into the room had to be physically restrained by officials from hacking him down with their swords.

Barely conscious and unable to speak, Darlan was carried to his car and taken to a hospital, where the last sacraments of the Catholic Church were administered. He died within forty-five minutes of the shooting.

Thus ended one of the most complicated political careers in French history.

Doctors said he could not have suffered much, because his features were composed and peaceful. But Darlan's poker face was his stock in trade, and it is doubtful if he would have lost it even in death.

I had last seen that inscrutable countenance in operation eight days before in his home some distance from the palace. Then he had greeted the American and British newspapermen at his first "press conference." He had blandly declared, "I seek no assistance nor support for any personal ambitions."

Two weeks before that he had assumed dictatorial powers over the North African Empire in an official proclamation modestly describing himself as "Chief of State and Commander in Chief of the Army, Air Force, and

Navy." His "Imperial Council," composed of the governors general of the provinces and military chiefs, did not have the power to order him out of the rain. It was purely advisory, and Darlan was not the type of man to take advice unless it was backed with military force.

Indicative of the admiral's character was the trouble I had in framing a list of questions I had submitted to him some ten days before the press conference. It had taken hours to frame the list, because every question I thought of could have been construed as a personal insult. Finally I gave it up and asked a blunderbuss question which read: "Would you like to give any explanation of your change in views as expressed a few weeks ago [while in Vichy] with your present position on the side of the Allies?"

It was like asking a man if he had stopped beating his wife.

At the press conference Darlan pulled out the questions and a neat set of typewritten answers and turned them over to me, thus giving me a nice beat on the rest of the newspapermen.

The admiral replied that he had played hand in glove with the Germans to "save all that could be saved in my unfortunate country and its Empire."

It was a pat answer that any Quisling might give.

As Pétain's assistant, Darlan had joined the Germans in imposing Axis sponsored laws in North Africa and imprisoned thousands who did not support the Vichy regime. As high commissioner under the American occupation he agreed to free those whom he had helped imprison and to repeal the Vichy laws.

He was all things to all men—if they had the power. The wonder of it was that he lived as long as he did.

He died because the Allies landed in North Africa on November 8 instead of November 9. If they had come twenty-four hours later Darlan might have lived indefinitely, because young Chapelle would have been attending the university at Lyon. The French youth had booked passage on a steamer for Vichy, France, and the ship was ready to sail when the Allies landed.

There have been many stories about Darlan's death and not a few "official" red herrings tossed about. Darlan had so many enemies that it is little wonder numerous "plots" were uncovered. Immediately after the shooting, Darlan's henchmen seized upon the fact that Chapelle's mother was Italian to issue a communiqué, inferring that the youth was linked with the Axis. A communiqué issued by General Jean Bergeret, adjutant to Darlan who later resigned in Giraud's house cleaning of Vichyites, said: "Admiral Darlan has just become a victim of an assassin, inspired by those who did not pardon him for having taken up arms on the side of the Allies against Germany."

There never was any support for this statement, and it was not believed by Darlan's henchmen themselves, for they shortly took twelve persons into "protective custody," presumably in connection with the slaying. Most of the twelve were Jews, practically all were De Gaullists, and several had supported the American landings. When the initial hysteria subsided they were released.

528

The Count of Paris, weak-chinned pig farmer by vocation and politician by desire, was in Algiers at the time of Darlan's murder. From his presence grew another theory which was given rapid circulation in ill-informed circles. This was to the effect that Darlan had been murdered in a Royalist putsch engineered by French army officers to place the Count of Paris in power as "King of North Africa."

At least one glib-tongued American radio broadcaster, who cared little for the facts if the story was good, expounded this solution at some length. The Count of Paris, with the usual pretender's illusions of grandeur, probably thought this would be an ideal solution and before Darlan's death had approached Murphy with the idea of stepping into power. He was given a chilly and somewhat amused reception.

Even the Count of Paris' most ardent followers were not stupid enough to believe that America and Britain would accept a Spanish Moroccan pig farmer as a "king" in North Africa.

To find the solution to Darlan's murder one must go back to the youth who fired the shots—Fernand Bonnier de la Chapelle. He was twenty-two years old six days before the Allied landings. He was an unstable youth given to violent enthusiasms, which were short-lived. His father was an Algiers newspaperman and his mother an Italian now living in Italy. At the age of eight he went to live with an uncle in Paris. When the Germans overran France he was in the French equivalent of the Boy Scouts and helping with ambulance work. He joined a youthful underground group working against the Nazis and finally had to leave the German-occupied section of France in December 1940.

At Marseille he fell in with De Gaullists and tried to get to London, but upon more conservative advice he returned to Algiers to finish high school. In a few months he was dissatisfied with his studies and joined the French Flying Corps at near-by Blida airfield, but his enthusiasm for flying was short-lived and his father obtained his release. He then joined the Chantiers de la Jeunesse to serve the required period of military training. His stay in the youth group was also brief, and he returned to school to study law and make speeches against the Axis at student gatherings.

At this point, shortly before the Allied landings, he fell under the influence of a group of older men and left his home in order to "be free to act," as he told his father. Then, in late October he decided to go to Lyon to school and arranged passage on November 8. He was wild with joy when the Allies landed and immediately joined the French Commandos for training in order to fight the Germans. He appeared seldom at home and was seen often in the company of older men—mostly experienced and grasping politicians, not above using youthful zest to their own ends. He was an ardent and outspoken De Gaullist, and there appears to be little doubt that a group of self-seeking older men "used" Chapelle's idealism. After shooting Darlan, he made no attempt to get away, a feat which might easily have been accomplished in the confusion. There is reason to believe that he had been told he would be "protected" and would never come to trial.

The belief that the fanaticism of Chapelle had been exploited was voiced by Giraud. "I would like to believe that the murder was the work of a lunatic, but such men must not be led by those with other ideas and perhaps other plans," Giraud declared in announcing that police officers had been arrested who "knew Darlan was going to be murdered and did not warn their superiors."

It was shortly after this statement that two figures were taken into custody, although there are indications that the Giraud administration is inclined to let the Darlan matter gather cobwebs and never bring anyone to trial. One of those arrested was Henri d'Astier de la Vigerie, chief of the State Police under Darlan. He was a brother of General d'Astier de la Vigerie, the De Gaulle supporter, but also paid allegiance to the Royalists. On the side, he had accepted a Vichy appointment as captain of a boys' camp eight months before the Allied landings and took a post under Darlan, who acted in the "name of Pétain." Almost the only thing certain about D'Astier de la Vigerie was his interest in D'Astier de la Vigerie. The second man arrested was a priest named Cordier.

There were motives for Darlan's death by the basketful. He had double-crossed the Axis and Vichy. He was an unsurmountable stumbling block to negotiations with De Gaulle. He was ready to sacrifice any man in his administration to further his own ends, and many were slated for political axes.

These are the facts. It is unlikely that the men behind the young Frenchman who pumped the bullets into Darlan ever will be brought to trial.

Chapelle shed no light on the slaying. He was sentenced to be shot Christmas Day and was executed the next morning. An ugly story, not beyond the realms of possibility, seeped about that the youth, to be silenced, was told the bullets in the firing squad's rifles were blanks, that he was to fall as though killed and would later be spirited away. Chapelle's identity was never revealed in the government-controlled French papers, nor were any details of the court-martial.

Thus the official curtain hurriedly closed over the death of the admiral.

Nearly 8,000 persons walked passed Darlan's casket as the body lay in state. They were children, many women, long lines of sober political figures, French soldiers and sailors, and a few curious American soldiers.

And not a tear was shed.

# CASABLANCA CONFERENCE

### by John A. Parris, Jr.

JANUARY, 1943—One moment the garden was empty. Then Colonel Elliott Roosevelt appeared at the back door of the villa carrying two more chairs.

The President walked out onto the terrace. He was dressed in a gray business suit and black tie. As usual, he was smoking a cigarette in a long holder. And he was smiling.

A minute later, Prime Minister Churchill stepped from the villa into the garden. He was wearing a gray pin-stripe suit and black shoes with zippers. He wore a gray hat and had a big black cigar in his mouth.

Then General Henri Honoré Giraud, administrator of North Africa, tall and immaculate, and General Charles DeGaulle, leader of the Fighting French, joined the conference. Giraud sat at the end seat on the President's right. On the President's left was DeGaulle and to the latter's left sat Churchill.

The fifteen correspondents made their entrance. The President recognized some of them who had covered his press conferences back in Washington and greeted them personally. The cameramen moved up their cameras and began taking pictures.

Roosevelt turned to the Prime Minister and asked him if he wished to take off his hat.

"I wear a hat to keep the sun from my eyes," Churchill said. "You know, you should wear one."

The President smiled. "I was born without a hat," he said. "I don't see any reason for wearing one now."

They both laughed.

This was probably the most informal press conference ever held. And probably the most important meeting of leaders of two great nations in history. Roosevelt suggested that the correspondents move closer and said it was all right for them to sit on the ground. The boys gathered closer, sprawling on the grass at the feet of Roosevelt and Churchill.

The President did most of the talking, but Churchill interjected to say that the discussions of the past ten days had been the most successful war talks of his career. The results of the conference, he said, would give the Allied armies their best chance of victory.

In Berlin, the "Little Corporal" stormed at Himmler and wanted to know why the Gestapo couldn't find out where Roosevelt and Churchill were meeting. Was the Gestapo slipping? Was Himmler paying attention to business? These were things Hitler asked his ruthless police chief. Der Fuehrer was in no mood for the answers Himmler gave him. In a few hours the world would know what Hitler wanted to know then. He would have to wait along with John Smith and Billy Brown.

531

If Adolf Hitler could have heard what Roosevelt was telling the fifteen correspondents he would have realized that his number was up. For there was something deeply prophetic in the President's words, a warning and a promise—a warning to Hitler and a promise to the silent little peoples of the world who prayed for deliverance from the Axis monsters.

The President said that the United Nations had made plans to dig down to the bottom of their resources—if necessary—in order to carry out the extermination of Axis war power as quickly as possible. America, Britain and Russia were determined to end the reign of Hitler and Mussolini and Hirohito.

By a strange coincidence, Churchill and Roosevelt laid the plans for Hitler's extermination just a week before the tenth anniversary of Der Fuehrer's rise to power in Germany. Just ten years after Hitler received the post of chancellor from a man who probably depised him—tired, old President von Hindenburg. Where there had been great celebrations before honoring the "Little Corporal" there would be silence, and a rising fear in the hearts of Germans at home and on the battlefields of Russia and Africa, in the hearts of Nazi fliers and sailors and U-boat crewmen. Whether Hitler would live another year or be in power to celebrate his position seemed problematical. Especially in view of the decisions made by Roosevelt and Churchill.

A shadow was falling across Hitler and his philosophy. Roosevelt and Churchill, speaking to correspondents, left no doubt that the United Nations would relax in any way in holding and pushing the initiative until the enemy had been overwhelmed. There was every indication that the Allied war effort would be progressively integrated.

North Africa had to be freed and that would be done just as speedily as possible. The move was already under way. It didn't seem likely that any new fronts would be opened until the enemy had been cleared from Tunisia.

The pattern was forming. It started with the invasion of North Africa. It took further shape as the Eighth Army rocked Mussolini back on his heels. The fall of North Africa was only a matter of time, time that was fast running out like sand in an hour glass. Then to greater things.

Roosevelt and Churchill were confident of the future as they sat there in the garden talking.

They explained that originally they had not intended to meet in Casablanca. They had hoped to meet farther east, possibly Cairo, for a United Nations conference, not an Anglo-American one. Premier Joseph Stalin had been invited but was unable to leave Russia at the time because of the great offensive which he himself as commander in chief was directing. If Stalin could have found time to leave Russia the conference would have been held elsewhere. Stalin, however, was kept informed minutely of what went on, and so was Generalissimo Chiang Kai-shek.

In another respect the Casablanca conference must have held disappointment for Roosevelt and Churchill. They had hoped to bring about unity between Giraud and DeGalle and clear up a smelly political mess in North Africa.

Giraud and DeGaulle met and talked there at Casablanca but they were still as far apart as the two poles. For the time being, at least, there seemed to be two French empires. General Giraud said he saw no immediate prospect of a single, united French movement.

During the ten-day conference the President went on a tour of the area.

One day American troops, who had landed at Casablanca, lined up for what they thought was just another dreary review. Down the line came a jeep and in it, to their utter astonishment, was the President, their Commander in Chief. Standing rigidly at attention and unable to look in the direction from which the President was coming, each was surprised in turn as Roosevelt's jeep drew opposite him.

Their eyes literally popped when they saw the President pass only six feet away with a big smile on his face. Few soldiers were able to wipe off their own smiles of pleasure when the presidential car had passed.

The President spoke to some of the men. He lunched with them in the field and said it was a darn good lunch.

After he reviewed the troops he went to Port Lyautey, where heavy fighting had occurred when the Americans had landed in November. He saw the graves at the joint French and American military cemetery and placed wreaths on the American and French graves. He said the French were brave fighters.

"I saw the equipment of our soldiers," he explained to the war correspondents. "They are ready for action at any time. They wish the people back home could see them, for they have the finest weapons any nation can give them. They are eager to fight again, and I think they will like to have me say a word for the fineness and bravery of the French we fought."

When the press conference ended President Roosevelt left the garden and went to his villa while Churchill chatted with Ward Price of the London *Daily Mail*. When the British Prime Minister left, he was chewing a no-longer lighted cigar and pointing to his V-for-Victory lapel button.

While the correspondents were in Casablanca they were kept herded together with G-men watching their movements.

Walter Logan of the United Press, who had been on a trip to Dakar, wandered into Casablanca a couple of days after Roosevelt and Churchill arrived. The other correspondents selected to cover the press conference were still in Algiers and were only to be flown down at the conclusion of the war council. When Logan arrived he sensed that something momentous was stirring and began asking questions. He didn't pass on any of the rumors he heard, but his probing aroused the ire of G-2, which is U. S. Army Intelligence and they called him in.

"If you go near a certain villa," a G-2 officer told Logan, "you will be shot."

After that Logan tried not to notice the many Army and Navy photographers, the influx of R.A.F. pilots and American pilots with recent news from the United States, civilians and consuls with Finnish and other baggage labels.

One of the most popular rumors was that the airport defenses had been instructed not to fire on any planes at certain hours despite the circumstances—which, if true, meant that certain unfriendly planes were expected to land as well as certain neutrals.

So well kept was the secret of the meeting of Churchill and Roosevelt that Hitler didn't know about it until it was announced by American and British radios.

There were reports from Switzerland that Himmler had recalled Gestapo agents from Tangier and Madrid because they had failed to discover the meeting.

\* \* \*

CAIRO, Jan. 22 1943 (International News Service): All important defense posts in Tripoli were reported tonight in possession of the British 8th Army.

\* \* \*

# GERMAN COUNTERATTACK

### by Phil Ault

TWO months in southern Tunisia, from mid-February until mid-April, changed the American army in North Africa from a "test tube baby" into a tried, competent body of fighting men. The doughboys didn't reach their peak until the final attack at Bizerte. But during those days on the semi-arid plains and raw brown mountains in the south, they turned the corner.

From there the road leads to Europe.

They had confidence, determination and most precious of all, experience. They had learned how.

That is what lies behind the splendid American performance that drove the Germans from Mateur, and finally Bizerte.

The real turning point came in the great natural amphitheater of the Kasserine plain, there in late February. On this sixteen-mile valley floor between Kasserine Pass and Djebel Hamra Pass to the northwest, surrounded by a circle of jagged mountains, the Americans rallied from a bad defeat and halted a critical enemy drive.

Never after that did the Germans win another inch of ground from them.

After months of sparring in southern Tunisia, Rommel sent the weight of his freshly equipped Twenty-first Panzer Division streaming from Faid Pass on Sunday morning, February 14.

The British Eighth Army was nearing the Mareth Line, further south. Rommel thought it essential to widen his coastal corridor.

534

The Americans were spread too thin, with too little. They had taken over the area from the French only a short time before. As events proved, what strength they had was not too well placed, not too well used. Whose fault that was it is difficult to determine. Not one man's, certainly.

Defeated in detail by large forces which overwhelmed their scattered, smaller detachments, the Americans reeled back on their heels. In quick succession they lost Sidi-bou-Zid, Sbeitla and Kasserine Village.

Further southwest, they were forced to abandon Gafsa and Feriana, forty-five miles up the Constantine road, because the garrisons faced isolation.

About a hundred American tanks were lost, hundreds of American men captured and hundreds killed. The airfields at Thelepte were abandoned.

The Americans fell back to a mountainous line north of Kasserine and Feriana, defending their key supply point at Tebessa. Quickly the German infantry and tanks penetrated the American minefields and artillery at Kasserine Pass, some four miles north of the village, and poured into the great two-pronged amphitheater.

They were headed for Tebessa and ultimately for a great encirclement operation by which Rommel hoped to get behind the British First Army facing Tunis. That would change the whole North African battle picture.

He thought he had the Americans in rout.

Then came Kasserine.

Washington's Birthday broke raw and rainy over the Kasserine valley floor.

Masses of sodden clouds clung to the rocky sawtooth hills that made the huge U-shaped valley a vast amphitheater. The aerial ceiling lifted barely two hundred feet above the bunchgrass and clay.

Drab, dripping mist spread a blinding filter over the battlefield where the American army, aided by the British, was fighting grimly to halt a defeat that had assumed critical proportions.

Groups of American tank men in greasy green coveralls rolled up their blankets from under the treads of their General Grant and Sherman tanks deployed in "hull down" positions in the *wadis*—dry stream beds—that criss-crossed the plain.

They wondered what the day would produce. They knew the German guns, tanks and infantry had advanced some eleven miles across the plains the previous day despite stiffening American resistance.

Private Pressley Hornsby, who used to dig coal at Harlan, Kentucky, drawled wistfully as he climbed into his Grant, "Wish I had me only a nice mining feud to worry about. They sure play rougher here."

They knew the day probably would answer whether they could keep their toe-hold on the plain, whether Combat Command B could hold Djebel Hamra Pass, or whether the Germans would open the gateway to Tebessa, twenty-two miles away.

They knew also they might get killed.

In the ridges protecting the pass, artillerymen arranged the piles of ammunition that had been brought forward during the night. Over on the west side of the valley, and around the fringes, infantrymen looked to their rifles.

North of Kasserine Pass the valley formed a rough U-shape, with the pass itself as the base. The left prong ran up northwest to Hamra, the right prong north to Thala. Single mud tracks ran through each prong. A forbidding hill *massif* separated the prongs and prevented men in one from seeing what men in the other were doing.

The roads joined at the pass itself.

Boxlike white adobe Arab huts speckled the plain. Beds of neatly planted cactus provided food for the camels and slight cover for the soldiers. All around in the mist rose the mountains.

Early on the twenty-second it became apparent that Rommel had found American resistance in the Hamra prong very tough the previous afternoon and had decided to commit the bulk of his armor in a thrust up the Thala prong. A column of some seventy tanks churned toward Thala, gleaming in the slight cold rain. They hoped to break through the British armor and American artillery that had been gathered hastily at the head of the prong and circle around behind the Hamra position to Tebessa.

They ran into the thump-thump-thump of heavy artillery and made little progress. Once they were less than two miles from Thala. They never got there.

Toward Hamra, Rommel threw the rest of his striking forces, including Italian infantry. He was fully committed.

They found dozens of American 75-, 105- and 155-millimeter guns waiting for them on the plain before the pass. Hundreds of shells rained down on the attackers.

Over on the west edge of the valley, Italian and American infantry clashed in the *wadis* with machine guns, rifles and grenades. Their private little war was invisible through the mist to observers in the hills.

The Grants and Shermans hidden in the *wadis* used their 75-millimeter guns as fixed artillery, adding to the flashing curtain of fire.

Mobile tank destroyers, guns mounted on tank and half-track chassis, darted about the field in the gloom. One would stop, fire two or three quick shells, then dash two or three hundred yards away. A few seconds later came the pumph-pumph-pumph of the deadly German 88-millimeter guns in reply, right on the spot where the American gun had been.

Withal, there was a minimum of personal contact. It was an armor and artillery fight. Before the day was out, it was an air fight, too.

Crews of the tanks went twelve hours without crawling outside the steel hulls. One tank man suggested plaintively that designers of future tanks had better install toilet facilities.

Typical of the tank fight that day was the Grant tank commanded by Sergeant William Williams, a twenty-five-year-old native of Nashville, Tennessee. From 9 A.M. until after dark the five men lived and fought in the confines of their steel castle.

536

Williams as commander stood with his head sticking out the turret, directing fire. He was bundled up against the cold in a wool knit cap and scarf beneath his steel helmet. Grime smeared his unshaven face.

The Grant was firing at anything it saw moving, working at about a 1500-yard range. German shells burst all around it, pitting neat holes in the light brown earth and chewing the road into a wretched, upheaved path.

What they did to the American position was nothing compared to the havoc wrought by the American barrage, as the doughboys were to see later.

"Those 88 shells were whizzing past so low that I ducked and stuck my head up again like I was doing setting up exercises," Williams said. "Shells were banging all around. Fragments hitting the tank sounded like rain on a tin roof. But the Jerries didn't hit my tank."

All the tank crew ate that day was canned meat and vegetable hash, mixed with canned meat and beans, that they took from a case of C-rations each tank carried. There wasn't much time for eating, anyway.

At night kitchen trucks carrying hot food dashed onto the battlefield, dodging shells as they dashed from tank to tank. The KP crews ladled a mass of hot food into each man's messkit.

"That was one time the mess gang really showed speed," Williams said.

Men watching the battle from hilltop observation posts could see little of the fighting in the gloom. They heard echoing salvos of shells, and they saw spurts of flame as a vehicle was hit.

They were intensely surprised during the morning when they saw a few pairs of American Boston light bombers scudding beneath the low ceiling right above the enemy positions.

Low-altitude bombing that morning was almost a suicide mission, but the situation was critical. The fight was at its crisis, and every ounce of hitting power was needed. Crews of the swift light bombers back on their field at Youks-les-Bains, just north of Tebessa, were told the situation and the risks they faced. They went.

The planes came in pairs, wing to wing, screaming along the ground at three hundred miles an hour as their bellies almost touched the grass. Fires blossomed in their wake. At one time during the day twenty-five columns of smoke and fire were leaping into the low gray sky from burning pyres of equipment. Part was the work of bombers, part of artillery.

Noon came and went, and there was little change.

In mid afternoon the sky broke. Patches of blue appeared. With them came the American air force in its most sensational display of striking power to date. It was a display that was to be greatly outdone later in the closing phases of the campaign, but at that time it was the finest air show in Tunisia.

Swarms of bombers and fighters that literally filled the sky swept through the mountain passes and over the plain. They struck with bombs, machine guns and cannon at the Axis troops and vehicles.

Particularly they concentrated their wrath in the Kasserine Pass itself—

the bottleneck through which all Axis forces must pass if they were forced to withdraw.

Days later when the Allies once more held the pass, we were able to see what damage those planes had wrought. White gashes on the brownish rock showed where bombs had exploded. Traffic had to snake around great craters in the road.

Burned-out Axis tanks, guns and vehicles lay like charred dead on the slopes.

By 5 P.M. the crisis was past. Allied gunpowder had proved superior.

Before the American position at Hamra the enemy began to withdraw, still firing heavily in retort to the endless American barrage. In the other prong, Thala still was in Allied hands.

As the Hamra column drew back, the Thala column became increasingly exposed on its left flank. The backbone of the attack was broken.

Fighting continued on the plain before Hamra until about 9 P.M. The moon was rising, and through its shadowy light came more Allied bombers to press home the attack against the faltering enemy. For three hours they dropped bombs in relays on the pass, the road and gun positions.

\* \* \*

ALLIED HEADQUARTERS IN NORTH AFRICA, Feb. 18, 1943 (Associated Press): German tank formations stood almost at the Algerian border today after capturing 4,000 square miles of central Tunisia from American forces.

ALLIED NORTH AFRICAN HEADQUARTERS, March 18 (Associated Press): American armored troops, commanded by the leading U. S. Army tank specialist, Lt. Gen. George S. Patton, Jr., advanced 30 miles to capture Gafsa.

ALLIED HEADQUARTERS, NORTH AFRICA, March 22 (United Press): The British 8th Army has torn big holes in Mareth Line positions, established a toe hold inside the enemy lines and seized all primary objectives, in a mighty drive timed with a swift American push from the northwest to trap Rommel's Africa Corps, front reports said tonight.

\* \* \*

# THE PLAINS BEYOND GAFSA

## by Ralph Ingersoll

TO defend these plains beyond Gafsa, the first week we were there, the division could do no more than move a combat team out to the center of each. The men dug into the hard sand as best they could. Beyond the farthest machine-gun posts we chose sites each day for as many mines as we could lay that night. At night, the working parties would at least be free from observation from the air.

While we worked, the infantrymen and the artillerymen worked too, bringing up ammunition and rations. The Signal Corps men got the wire down between the command posts and the observations posts and ran wire back to division headquarters. The ambulances came up and the medical officers checked sites for their clearing stations. The men cleaned their guns first and then dug their foxholes. Finally, here and there, pup tents went up. The men who had been sleeping in the open were now under cover again.

Company A's men moved in before the rain stopped the first evening. All that first day we had been inspecting the chaos the rain and mud had wrought. Where we thought we could be helpful, we sent one of the bulldozers up to pull vehicles out of the mud.

No one who has not seen it can believe the immobility of a mobile column when the mud is more than axle-deep. It doesn't matter that the main roads are hard. Motorized columns can use a road only to move from one place to another. They cannot halt on a road for even a few hours. Whenever they stop their vehicles must take off to either side, disperse. When the ground is wet they barely grind their way out, and when they try to start again, their wheels begin to sing and spin and down they go.

Not one or two or three of the vehicles stick; they all stick. And the men get out and try to lift them and throw raincoats and tarpaulins under the wheels but these only disappear into the mud. Then the vehicles hitch themselves to one another, with the cables from their winches, but by now they are dug in to above the floorboards. There is nothing for it but to wait. The only comfort is that the enemy must wait too. While it is really stormy his planes will be grounded as well. The war is called on account of rain.

While it was still raining, as I said, we found billets for company A under cover. First we drove around the outskirts of Gafsa, getting out to inspect each building that looked habitable. We looked at the hinges of the doors for wires that might lead to booby traps. Then we inspected the floors to see if they had been disturbed, and the shutters on the windows before we opened them.

The company commanders of other outfits were also out hunting for a place to dry their men. The few buildings there were rapidly filling up. The law of squatters' rights was in effect. A building or a group of buildings belonged to the man who saw it first—and left a sentry to guard his rights while he went back to bring up his outfit.

Finally, after an hour's hunt, we came to a pleasant little sidestreet with a row of stuccoed houses, each with its own flower garden between it and the sidewalk. The windows of the first houses we came to were smashed in and the doors hung empty and the gardens were mostly trampled weeds. We chose one and began to explore.

It had been a photographer's house. There were only two rooms in it, but the floor in one was piled high with photographic paraphernalia and stacks of pictures of Italian belles in their wedding dresses and boys dressed up in evening clothes or in uniforms. There were some pictures of Arabs. While we were looking at them, a very old little lady in black came in and began talking Italian at us. Piecing together the expressions and gestures, we could follow her. She lived next door. This had been her brother's house. Her brother was now in prison in Algiers—the French had arrested him. She wanted us to be sure she was very happy we had come and we were quite welcome to the house and she would help us clean it out. And how long, please, before the war would be over? She was very old—at least ninety.

The photographer's house was all right and we could use three houses across the street from which all the furniture had been taken. They would be all right after the filth and the water had been swept from the floor. The water had come in through the broken windows and made desolate pools on the tiled floor.

We sent back to the grove for the company and just before it turned dark our column rolled up the street, the big 2½-ton trucks and the kitchen truck, followed by the peeps. The first sergeant came over to confer with us. His platoon sergeants went into the empty buildings at once to stake their respective claims. The kitchen truck rolled past and circled a row of empty buildings to rest under a big tree behind them. We had had supper several hours before, standing in the rain in the other grove, handing up our mess kits and getting them filled in the truck, and then eating quickly before the rainwater diluted and cooled the stew. But now at dusk the rain was stopping and soon we would have a roof over our heads. The C.O. said to the first sergeant, "Just get them under cover tonight and tomorrow we'll sort things out."

From somewhere in the bottom of one of the trucks came the officers' cots. The men carried them in and stood the bundles in the corners. While they were unpacking the rest of the stuff, we set them up in the midst of the trash. From the trash we fished odd pieces of cloth and cardboard and stuffed the windows so that the light would not shine out. Then we lit two candles and unrolled our bedding rolls on the cots.

We were well inside the limits of the village and there were troops all around us. The sergeant thought one sentry was all we needed and the skipper agreed. He told the sergeant to let the men sleep until seven. Everyone was in except one second lieutenant and his platoon. They would be out all night scratching in mines. The rest of us took off our outer, or wettest, clothing and our shoes, and climbed in between damp blankets. We were asleep without conversation that first night. Other nights we would sit in the candlelight and talk and talk and then go on talking after we were in bed, like kids in a boarding school with no monitor around to hush us up.

The skipper of company A, Lieutenant Cobb—the young man who'd been getting his hair cut the day I met him—had been an aircraft designer. He wasn't quite sure how he had gotten to where he was. He'd had a reserve

540

commission from his ROTC in college, and when the war started there was a lot of talk and correspondence about his getting commissioned in the Air Corps. He was also an essential employee in an essential industry. But one day in the middle of the correspondence, orders had come for him to report to an engineers' camp. He said he was tired of waiting so he had gone. He had a wife and a baby. He showed me their pictures and the other lieutenants kidded him about showing them to me. Then one second lieutenant said, "To hell with it, I want to show him my girl's picture," and presently we all showed each other all the snapshots we had with us and talked about the different parts of the country we came from.

Cobb was about twenty-six or twenty-seven. His four second lieutenants were younger than he. Only one other had been any kind of an engineer in civil life. Cobb and he were very interested in mines and how they worked and had all kinds of ideas for their improvement.

The five of them had become so close that they were like brothers. Cobb was, of course, the eldest brother. But the others seemed to have arranged themselves until each, according to his temperament and how bright he was, had a fixed place at the family table. The youngster who was figuratively at the foot of the table was the baby of the family. The others seemed fond of him but were inclined to leave him out of conversations. He would venture remarks from time to time, but nobody would let him finish saying what he started.

By the second day out, the family had adopted me. The colonel had said something about my reporting back to battalion, but the brothers would have none of it. "Battalion doesn't care, forget it," they said. "You'll see a lot more with us. Besides we need company."

To hear the brothers speak of battalion headquarters and what went on there, you would think it was in Algiers and its officers remote and protected from the realities of war. The officers of A company respected the officers of the other three companies of engineers. These were equals. But the officers at battalion were old fogies and could not possibly understand what life was really like.

The brothers were very proud of their men and told fabulous lies about them. The company clerk who moved in with us the next day was, they said, the foremost scholar in the army. He had been, they assured me, the dramatic critic on a big New York paper. He had read everything in the world and there wasn't any question he couldn't answer. Besides, he was a writer and would write the history of the company one day and all of them would be famous. So-and-so—in hushed voices—was a killer; the finest soldier in the outfit, but you had to watch him to be sure he was killing enemies. The killer was an old army man who had been first sergeant until the brothers concluded that he did not understand soldiers who had been in the army only eighteen months. How good company A's cook was, was a military secret which I must guard with my life. If the battalion ever found out what he could make Spam taste like, he would be transferred and then the war would not be worth going on with.

The brothers had written a song about the First Engineer Battalion with twenty or thirty stanzas to it. It was a narrative and traced the history of the battalion from training camp to training camp, from maneuver to maneuver in America, and then across by convoy to England. It mourned over the Scottish weather and grew excited over the impending departure for no one knew where until the southbound convoy was three days at sea. It told of the landing on the Mediterranean coast and the trip up to the front—wherever the First Battalion goes, there goes rain—and of the first battle of Medjez-el-Bab and of holding the Pass at Kasserine and of the move into Feriana. While I was with them, they wrote the first verse about Gafsa. They were always going to find pencil and paper and write this ballad down for me, but there never was time.

It's hard to say why there never was time because we spent so much just talking. While we were waiting for details to come back between trips out into the field, in the early morning after mess, and at night when there was shelter in which we could light candles, we sat around and told stories. I had a lot of stories to trade because I had been traveling from one end of Africa to the other and I had stories of landings in Morocco and Algeria.

* * *

ALLIED HEADQUARTERS, NORTH AFRICA, March 10, 1943 (International News Service): ... The British Army swept into Sfax at 8:15 o'clock this morning after an advance of some forty miles within twenty-four hours, in which the smaller port of Mahares was taken.

* * *

# HILL 609

### by Drew Middleton

WITH the Second United States Corps, in Tunisia, May 4.—On the slopes of Hill 609 poppies blow as red as any in Flanders and among them lie Americans who died as bravely and as grandly as any who fell in the Argonne, at Gettysburg or at Bunker Hill.

For here, almost 2,000 feet high and topped by an ugly, jagged cliff, is a monument to Americans for all Americans to revere—Hill 609.

You know that the Germans held Bizerte by a chain of mountain fortresses. Because it was the highest, Djebel Tahent, which the staff called Hill 609, was the most important—the key to Mateur and the approaches to Bizerte.

From its summits you look out onto the flat roofs of Mateur, thirteen miles away, and beyond to two lakes, Achkel and Bizerte. Beyond them, shimmering in the heat haze, you see faintly, through glasses, a white smear on the horizon. That is Bizerte.

542

The Germans made of this hill an incredibly strong fortress. Every approach—an Arab village of stone huts, fields of wheat on the slopes, the twisting, rutted tracks—was swept by machine-gun and cannon fire. The garrison holding it was Germans of the line infantry, seasoned fighters. They had been told to hold it fourteen days. They held it less than fourteen hours after the attack had started.

History books will say, as history books do: "American infantry advancing through the mountains captured the German positions and opened the road to Mateur."

It was a little more difficult than that. First there came the guns—"Long Toms," or 155-mm. rifles; 105s and 75s—starting the echoes rumbling through the valley. For two days they hammered away, scooping vast chunks of earth out of the side of the hill and sending the enemy into the caves that he had blasted into its sides. They fired on and on, despite the sharp counter-battery fire of the Germans and the fighter-bombers that threaded their way through the valleys at zero altitude to attack the gun positions.

Early Saturday, when the barrage had reached its height, infantry, supported on the flank by a few tanks, moved forward. You can follow the path of those soldiers through the wheat just as you would follow the path of Pickett's charge through the Summer wheat at Gettysburg.

When the barrage had lifted there was only the steady drumfire of the German machine guns. But the American soldiers—khaki-clad, their rifles held at the ready, their figures curiously foreshortened by their bucket helmets—dashed forward. Through the cornfield along the road, dodging through the Arab village, pausing to fire, waiting for their own machine guns to open up—they went ahead.

The Arab village was heavily held. Our attack was checked briefly there. But American ingenuity and American courage had the answer. Tracer bullets from machine guns marked the village and, from behind, there came the bark of guns. The German positions dissolved into a dusty ruin. The infantry advanced.

Sweating wearily, the troops reached the summit and saw before them the last small wedge of Tunisia that the Germans have kept. They were subjected to heavy mortar and machine-gun fire there from the enemy on the reverse side of the mountain. So they went forward—down this time—and cleaned him out with the bayonet. There were still a few knots of resistance on the hill, so the big men with their shirts open at the collar—the men who, the prisoners say, do not sing like the English or shout like the French—went over the hill again, routing them out.

You can go there, as I did, three days after the battle and find it quiet. There are no monuments, as at Little Round Top or in the Argonne. Just the green grass, the slightly yellow wheat, the dirty white of the Arab village. There is a little graveyard being dug, with black German crosses. Down at the bottom there is an American one. The crosses there are white and they are interspersed with the Star of David for the Jewish dead.

543

They are dead—and, you hope, resting lightly. The Arabs—poor, meek people—are coming back to their hill. An old white horse roams the field where the machine guns chattered. Little boys play in the streets of the Arab hamlet, oblivious of unexploded mines. Perhaps in time the American cemetery, with its white crosses, will be forgotten and the winds will blow poppies over the graves.

You go up the summit again, past the caves that the Germans had blasted in the rock to shield them from our artillery fire and bombing; past the caverns that held at least twenty men, where they ate and slept as our forces massed in the valley below them; past the gun pits and the ruined guns that the Germans fought so well; past bits of uniform.

On the summit, looking toward Mateur and Bizerte, you can see dust clouds along the roads as the Second United States Corps moves forward. It moves because Hill 609 fell, and many a good man with it. The wind brings you the dull boom of gunfire, the brisk note of machine guns in the distance, where the enemy holds the road to Ferryville. But, despite the signs of battle, from concrete gun emplacements to bits of equipment, this hill is quiet. History was made here only yesterday, but today only the wind blows over the rich grass and ruffles the wheat. And there is silence in the graveyards so far from home.

# WE TAKE TUNIS AND BIZERTE

### by Frank L. Kluckhohn

ALLIED Headquarters in North Africa, May 7.—Tunis and Bizerte, last main Axis strongholds in Africa, were captured today by British and American forces just 181 days after the Allied landing in North Africa.

Amid the crash of artillery and the crackle of small arms, German and Italian forces—once within sixty miles of Alexandria—faced surrender or annihilation without a Dunkerque. And Southern Europe lies open to invasion by the Allies, who now control the southern shore of the Mediterranean.

The Germans with their backs to the sea fought frantically to hold Tunis, but the avenging dust-streaked, bare-waisted Tommies of Britain's First Army, who were forced by the Germans to evacuate France in 1940, stormed into the city at 4:20 P.M. Five minutes earlier American armed reconnaissance units and light tanks had pushed into Bizerte, key naval base of this part of the Mediterranean.

The remnants of Field Marshal General Erwin Rommel's once victorious and highly touted Africa Corps, their leader apparently fled to Europe, and Col. Gen. Dietloff von Arnim's crack tank and infantry units, also perhaps without their leader, broke under the mighty force of Allied tanks, big guns, thousands of planes and divisions of veteran fighting men that General Sir Harold R. L. G. Alexander hurled against them yesterday morning.

Now the fleeing, broken Axis remnants are being mercilessly strafed along roads jammed by their retreat. The Allied air forces are lashing with machine gun and cannon at the fleeing men and vehicles that are madly racing toward the Cape Bon peninsula. Other enemy forces, cut off, are being mopped up. Only in the hills lying between the Enfidaville area and the plain of Tunis are Axis forces holding out strongly, and their future is regarded as hopeless.

Tonight, as word of the long-awaited triumph spread, there were demonstrations of joy all over North Africa. But up forward the Americans and the British were still grimly battling, determined to crush the enemy completely and to keep as many as possible from reaching Cape Bon. This hilly ground is the last place left for the Axis forces to make a stand, but they have lost guns, tanks and ammunition. They may not last long.

Today as yesterday, yellow clouds of dust, turned up by tanks and moving vehicles, as well as cordite smoke from explosives, hung over the battlefields along a sixty-mile area that could no longer be called a front.

Lumbering lethal American tanks ground into Ferryville in the Bizerte naval base ring at noon. Reconnaissance units including many New Yorkers were quickly thrust between Bizerte's twin lakes and were the first to reach the Bizerte outskirts. United States infantry on the north shore of Lake Achkel drove toward the red brick houses of the city that they saw yesterday from nine miles away.

From a point four miles beyond the village of Massicault, British armor followed by massed infantry thrust twelve miles to the white city of Tunis, whose many mosques had come into their view last night. It was bitter, bloody fighting all the way but early in the forenoon tanks captured suburban Le Bardo, center of much of the arterial system of Tunis, and placed the city under their guns.

Last night guns of American tanks cast shells into Ferryville, throwing plumes of fire into pitch black darkness. Simultaneously, British guns were flashing in the Tunis area.

The Germans, hard-pressed, their morale weakening, had no rest as the two-pronged American drive reached toward Bizerte and the British slashed toward Tunis.

In the far-reaching events of today sight had been lost of the exact position of American units, including New Yorkers, fighting their way toward Tebourba Junction northwest of Tunis, and of the British battling northward to join them. The Americans were known this morning to be not more than four miles west of Chouigui Pass. An Anglo-American junction would cut off and make easier the capture of many Axis troops between Tunis and Bizerte.

In late November, 1942, a light, combined Anglo-American striking force came to within twelve miles of Tunis near the village of Djedeida. It lost, however, what amounted to a race to get to Tunis before the Germans established themselves.

Today, as General Alexander noted in his order of the day, read to troops before the final victorious onslaught, the Allies struck with "two victorious armies"—armies that would not be denied.

The British drive to Tunis was begun at 3 A.M. yesterday morning on a ten-mile front from north of Medjez-el-Bab near Djebel-bou-Aoukaz, captured the previous day. It followed the lines of the shortest road to Tunis.

Infantry divisions took hill positions, thus eliminating danger to British armor from anti-tank artillery fire on the flanks.

Then the armored divisions were hurled forward as a spearhead.

The armored force on the right or southern flank of the drive toward Massicault, the pivot of the whole Axis Tunis position, encountered thirty-five enemy tanks at a point six miles south-southwest of Massicault.

The enemy tanks were being employed as a stationary strong point of defense. A number of them were destroyed by the British tanks and the others were forced to withdraw.

An infantry brigade equipped with large anti-tank guns was then placed in a position four miles south of Massicault to protect against a counter-attack by German tanks.

Another strong British armored force on the left or north flank passed in the direction of St. Cyprien, seven miles beyond Massicault and just north of the Tunis road, by-passing Furna and forcing twenty-five enemy tanks to withdraw and cutting the road north of Massicault.

By 3 P.M. Massicault had been occupied, leading armored elements moving on the line running obliquely north and south four miles east from this town. The enemy suffered heavy losses despite his hasty withdrawal. By dusk Tunis, only twelve miles from St. Cyprien, was brought under artillery fire.

Second United States Corps forces yesterday ran into stubborn resistance all along their front from the sea to a point just north and west of the Tebourba.

In the north, near the seacoast, an American force advanced to within nine miles of Bizerte, an advance of three miles from their starting point. They took 250 prisoners, mostly Italians.

Other Americans, after bloody fighting, completely cleared Djebel Achkel, which previously had been mistakenly reported taken, and Djebel Zarour. Their tanks charged right into anti-tank guns, destroying six in one case by over-running their position. Three hundred prisoners were picked up by this unit.

Still another large American infantry force captured high ground between Chouigui Pass and Tebourba at a point only four miles from the latter. While the pass was not completely cleared at the time the last word was received, the Germans in the Tebourba area were in a precarious position, with the Americans coming from the northwest and the British from the south.

546

In the center of the line yesterday divisions of the Nineteenth French Corps made slow but steady progress toward Zaghouan, threading through extensive mine fields in stiff fighting. The Eighth Army advanced somewhat in an area nine miles northeast of Djebibina. It also went through bloody fighting and some of the worst mine fields yet encountered in Tunisia.

\* \* \*

ALLIED HEADQUARTERS, NORTH AFRICA, May 10, 1943 (International News Service): Three mighty Allied columns hammered ceaselessly tonight at the cracking door to Cape Bon peninsula, where Axis troops now officially estimated at 80,000 were caught in a giant death pocket from which all escape was blocked.

\* \* \*

# TWO WORLDS

### by Erika Mann

THE Arab town of X is one of the oldest and finest in Morocco. Separated from the new French settlement by several miles, its thirteenth century walls, its narrow shopping streets, its magnificent palace, its sacred mosques and its bewitching smells—sweet, heavy, and indefinable—used to attract tourists from all over the world. Yet, in contrast to other renowned "curiosities," it has retained in full its genuineness and integrity, and its dark inhabitants keep living their exotic lives, undisturbed by the ever changing "white" influences about them.

Near the old city, the swanky hotel Y opens its wide halls and stylish apartments to the sightseer. It was strangely fascinating to come back to the gorgeous old place now that it was run by the American military. Gone was the lazy international crowd I'd known there. Instead, British and American soldiers, Red Cross personnel, girls in the uniforms of the Wrens or Waafs, and some few determined looking civilians, lacking utterly in the flawless elegance displayed by their predecessors, went about their business. And it had to be a vital one, at that, if it was to secure them a room at the Y.

Like most commodities, matches proved to be scarce in X. So I gratefully accepted the light offered me in the Y's lobby by a fair-haired lad in the uniform of the U. S. Transport Command. Twenty-year-old Lieutenant G. comes from Spokane, Washington. He isn't actually stationed in X; but then, he told me, it doesn't really matter much just where he is stationed. He is on the run most of the time, and the distances he covered during this past year are prodigious. Once he'd made 5600 miles in thirty-six hours: flying from somewhere in India to somewhere in Africa. And dozens of times he had crossed the Sahara, and throughout the whole Middle Eastern Theater of Operations he felt quite at home.

"Not at home, really!" he informed me, "I just know it all pretty well by now. But you wouldn't believe what a difference it makes to get back to one's own station once in a while, to sleep in one's own barracks with one's own photos on the walls, and to see one's own friends, makes all the difference in the world—even though it's still Africa one is coming 'home' to!"

He didn't care much for Africa, it appeared. What he cared for—and deeply so—was Spokane and the State of Washington. And it was indeed fortunate that his companion and superior, twenty-two-year-old Captain C., also originated from there.

"No matter where we are," said Lieutenant G., "we keep talking of home; and nobody dare stick his head into our cockpit who won't admit that our State happens to be the best and finest on earth."

I wondered how long he had been over here.

About a year and a half. But he'd seen and learned more in that period of time than in the whole decade preceding it. "To begin with," he said, shaking his head as if in bewilderment, "I'd never known, even faintly, just how fortunate we are over there. Gee, I wouldn't want to live anywhere but in the U. S.! And once back, I'll sure stay for good and for keeps. Why, I don't even want my family ever to go and visit any of these odd places around here! Funny isn't it? Usually, I'm pretty eager to have them share all my experiences. But not this time. I don't think they'd like it, either. It's all much too strange!"

And strange it was indeed, listening to this kid from Spokane, as he talked about Cairo and Jerusalem, Tripoli and Dakar, Irak and Syria, as if those far-away places were nothing but bus-stations on his daily way to school.

"Bethlehem!" he said, again shaking his head. "We've been circling over that one, recently, for fifteen minutes solid; yet, there wasn't a thing to explain just why on earth Our Lord chose that particular spot. Was there anything extraordinary about it at the time? Was it pretty or anything?"

Clearly, Our Lord couldn't well have chosen nonexistent Spokane; but in his, Lieutenant G.'s opinion, there must have been some places somewhere in the world, even then, which would at least have somehow resembled the real thing and would thus have been infinitely more suitable than dusty old Bethlehem.

"It's the dust that gets me!" he declared. "Even where it's green around here, it's still dusty and olive colored. The desert, of course, is the worst of all. If I'd ever be forced down in the desert, first thing I'd do would be to bury my gun and walk away from it just as fast as I could. I don't want to shoot myself, and I'm afraid that's exactly what might happen if I didn't get rid of the thing in time. I'm quite ready to die for my country, but if at all possible I want to live, see? I want to get home to my girl. I've been going with her ever since I entered high school, and we never even needed to get formally engaged. We always knew that we belonged to each other. You don't happen to have any small Portuguese banknotes, do you?"

Slightly startled, I produced a ten escudo note. Would I, please sign it for him? I did; whereupon I was shown the little treasure to which my modest contribution was to be added; a long flag composed of all sorts of paper money, from dollars and shillings to francs, liras, pesetas, dinars, and piasters, neatly fastened to each other with paste and covered with the signatures of all who had been the lieutenant's passengers at one time or another. Many a proud name could be found among the autographs.

"It's supposed to be my good luck charm," he announced, "but actually, it's for her. Think she's going to like it?"

Of this I was firmly convinced; all the more so, since no less a person than a captured Italian General figured among the signatories.

"He was a funny old dog, too!" giggled Lieutenant G. "Didn't seem to mind captivity a bit. And did he like those green life savers I offered him! Enjoyed them like a baby. So, I had him sign my lira note. But I wouldn't have that Nazi lieutenant scribble his name for me for anything. He was a real bad egg, just as sneering and arrogant and repulsive as they show them in the movies. We've sure got to get rid of that type once and for all!"

"When shall we?" I asked. "Come on now, let's have some careless talk, *as well as* some idle speculation: when do you think the European show will be over?"

On this my friend had very definite ideas. "I've set up a little time-table of my own," he reported, "and so far, it's proved quite correct. Around Christmas last, I decided that we'd have Africa cleaned up by the end of May. Now, that wasn't so bad, was it? I also predicted that Italy would collapse sometime in October, and that Germany would follow suit early next year."

He had it all worked out and explained to me, eagerly, why, to his mind, things would develop thus and not otherwise. Again I felt how strange it was, that I should be sitting here in this transfigured Moroccan town with this American youngster, who had never cared for world affairs, who had wanted nothing but to work in peace and in Spokane, Washington, and to set up house with the girl he'd been fond of since childhood. He looked exceedingly young, very neat, and very honest. His mother, I thought, must be rather proud of him. Then I wondered if his life had ever been acutely endangered.

He smiled. "Sure!" he said, "and not just once! Toughest time we had, though, was when one of our ships had been forced down by engine trouble on hostile territory. Since there didn't seem to be much hostile life anywhere near the spot, we decided to land, rescue the crew, and destroy their machine. The place wasn't really fit for a landing and we had to set her down on a mountain top which was flat all right, but didn't give us much of a runway. You can look far and wide for a bird that could have made it. Yet ours did, and everything seemed to go smoothly until those natives appeared in our rear, suddenly, and as if from nowhere. There they were, standing quite close to our plane, while we were burning the damaged one. Silly fools they were! Instead of getting busy on our ship, they opened fire on us. Even so, matters didn't look too rosy, for we couldn't afford a great deal of shooting for fear of hurting our plane. My captain managed to get behind them and shoot two of them before they knew what was what. The other three were so good as to turn around to see what the trouble was, and the battle was all over. Still, I don't think I'd like to go through that one again. It was a bit too narrow for comfort."

* * *

At ten o'clock sharp the Lieutenant bade me good night. We were to depart at seven A.M. which meant that he'd have to be out there at six.

I walked out into the warm night and toward the old city. No sooner had I passed the market place and entered the Soukes district, than I saw myself accompanied by an Arab boy who disclosed that he was a guide, that his name was Mohammed Number Two, and that he would be delighted to show me around.

In his own way he was quite handsome, Mohammed, slender, graceful, and melancholy—his fine eyes several shades darker than his fawn colored skin, and his childlike face marked by the pensive fatigue of his ancient race. Despite the vague sadness of his gestures and looks, however, Mohammed was extremely talkative. He spoke French fluently and knew quite a bit of English. He'd been to Chicago, he informed me casually, as well as to Brussels, Paris, and Amsterdam,—oh, not so long ago, perhaps two years, or four. I didn't believe a word of it all. Mohammed, I decided, must be smoking hashish, that intoxicating herb to which Arabs are sometimes addicted, and which makes them happy, unreliable, peaceable, and also makes them inventive.

Would I care for some mint tea? Mohammed wanted to know. If so, we could go to a small terrace near here, from where one overlooked the town, and where we wouldn't be disturbed by either peddlers, beggars, or dragomen.

Presently I found myself up there, sipping the sweet and sharp liquid Mohammed had ordered, and listening to his pleasantly veiled voice. He was twenty, he told me; and I thought of Lieutenant G. who was just as old, just as exceedingly young. But how unlike they were, those two, how utterly incomparable! Fair, neat, and honest Flight Lieutenant G. knew this world to be small. Yet its children still differed from each other in a way both bewildering and enchanting!

Mohammed—fragile, deerlike, and iridescent—spoke of his wife to be, and I inquired when he expected to get married.

In three years from now, he said, adding that I might have known, since he'd told me his age. "We all marry when we are twenty-three."

My question as to whether he had already found himself a girl he answered firmly in the negative. Nor would he ever do anything of the kind. It was his parents who would present to him the bride and he wouldn't lay eyes on her until the day of their marriage.

"Do you think the war will be over by then?" I asked him, remembering the Lieutenant's time-table and schedule. Did Mohammend indulge in similar speculations? But Mohammed merely shrugged.

"Patience!" he demanded gently. "We'll have to be very patient, and one day it will be over. For a long time there was three of us—three peoples in our town—Arabs, Frenchmen, and Jews. Now there are four of us, for now there are also Americans. We don't mind. They give us soap, and to those who work for them they give money. They are friendly, I believe— quite friendly and homesick. They, too, will have to be patient."

There was something very sweet and very wise in his words and in the way he said them.

Beneath us, a pair of American M.P.'s raced across the square on their motorcycles. The air was hazy and heavy with smells. As Mohammed paused for a moment to sip his tea, the murmuring of voices could be heard in some distance. Arabs—hundreds of them—had gathered in three wide circles around three men who were standing, while their listeners sat crouched on the ground.

"Our story-tellers!" said Mohammed. "They are very good. But one of them—the old one with the biggest crowd at his feet—is truly excellent. He's been telling the same story for sixteen years now, spinning it on and on, and inventing a new chapter every evening. And there won't be an end to it before he dies. Then, one of his pupils will take over and the story will never die. It's a religious story—they all are—based on some tiny anecdote out of the Koran. But to make such a small incident into a story that lasts for generations takes great talent and knowledge. Also, it takes great patience."

He saw me "home," Mohammed. Walking noiselessly in the shadow of the trees that fringed the street, he seemed to avoid the moonlight. Did he mean to spare me the "embarrassment" of being seen with him? When I prepared to remunerate him for his services he silently shook his head. And when I insisted, he grew very earnest.

"Please," he said, "*please* do not now offend me! I've so much enjoyed this evening. And I shall never forget it!"

I yielded, and Mohammed, having bowed deeply, but with great dignity and grace, disappeared in the darkness.

His brother in age, Flight Lieutenant G. from Spokane, Washington, awaited us at the airdrome at seven A.M. Even then, the day was glaringly hot. The desert sent out its dry and sulky winds. Cloaked in a cloud of dust, we ascended.

# THE NAZIS CRACK

## by Pierre J. Huss

*Allied Headquarters in North Africa*—June, 1943

TUNISIA was the proving ground which certified the Allied invasion of the Continent. In the acid test, our assault armies, air forces and generals emerged with flying colors. By the same token, the Axis—from Hitler's ablest generals and most elite troops down to the dispirited Italians— revealed inherent weak spots which are bound to become bleeding wounds, once the conflict for the "European Fortress" develops cyclonic violence.

Current events will record that the Axis signed its own death warrant at the historic moment when the German Commander in Chief in North Africa, General Jurgen von Arnim, raised the white flag in defeat south of Tunis. We know Hitler still has millions of battle-seasoned men behind formidable fortifications. In North Africa we didn't wipe out his main armies or fortification systems—not even a fraction of them—but we did wipe out the flaming Nazi myth, upset traditional Prussian military creeds and demonstrated as a necessary prelude to the recapture of the Continent that the proud Wehrmacht can be pummeled into dust—can even be made to cry for mercy.

I saw it happen, step for step, from St. Patrick's Day to the spectacular collapse early in May. I covered decisive battles and examined at first hand the underlying causes of this turn in the tide. I know the Wehrmacht like my own pocket from long years in Berlin for International News Service and was thus able to evaluate straws in the wind. That's why I put so much stock in an incident experienced by the Americans in the latter part of March.

It was a spring night over El Guettar and the African sky was studded with diamond-bright stars and lighted by a Turkish moon. The highway to Gabès curved like a dark macadam carpet through a mile-wide valley which, drenched with the hot sun by day, cools to freezing after sunset. Across the valley thousands of American soldiers slept in uneasy silence under a couple of blankets, sometimes awakening to listen to Luftwaffers sneaking overhead.

Djebel Berda—that bullheaded sweeping ridge flanking the right edge of El Guettar Valley—sat in gloomy silence. A whole nest of stinging Nazi 88-mm. guns infested the tree-bearded slopes and ravines. On the left a pale dust road streaked off from the main highway into the jagged ridges of horseshoe-shaped Djebel Mcheltat.

During the day Gumtree Road was the favorite target of Nazi artillery and dive bombers; at night anything was apt to happen, especially while Rommel's hard-pressed Afrika Korps slowly passed northwards from Gabès on the sea. Djebel Berda and Djebel Mcheltat were Axis steel gates barring the United States Second Corps thrust to the Mediterranean; any break-through in that sector would have cut off the doomed retreating German troops. Djebel Mcheltat stretched deeper toward the sea and was more strongly held, for which reason Gumtree Road became an American lance prodding into Rommel's flank. In turn, he snapped back viciously and repeatedly feinted dangerously toward El Guettar.

Consequently, the Americans' ears stayed sharply alert on this starry night. Outposts on the far edge of Gumtree Road heard suspicious movements on the slopes held by Nazi grenadiers. A dark smoke cloud came drifting over the valley. Suddenly it lighted with blood-red flashes mixed with rocket bursts. Deafening explosions, machine gunning, hysterical howling, even demoniacal laughter turned the broken silence into a nightmare. Through the whole sector sleepy-eyed Yanks stumbled into slit trenches, grabbing for rifles and machine-gun belts. Seconds seemed hours; everything was in an uproar like a panic-stricken mob. Amid the eerie din came the roar of racing motors and gun flashes—presumably Nazi armored cars and Panzers under way in waves. Above all sounded the strange metallic shouting: *"HITLER KOMMT! SURRENDER!"*

Random shots rattled from the American side. Then from somewhere out of a foxhole came an angry Brooklyn voice:

"Jeeze, fellers, them Heinies have gone nuts. They're trying to scare us. Them bastards ain't got nothing back of 'em. Give 'em hell."

That broke the spell. Within seconds, hundreds of Yanks turned loose every gun and hand grenade they could lay their hands on and stopped the German panic tactics dead.

Three years ago I heard laughter in Berlin cafés when fighters on leave from the front recounted these tricks. I had seen those Nazi motor trucks equipped with loudspeakers with magnified phonograph voices. All of it was part of the German psychological warfare, but so far as I know the Yanks never fell for Hitler hokum.

Many times during those hot dusty days, I looked across valleys foaming with richly colored spring flowers and pictured Nazi gun crews loading and firing their guns with the practiced precision so familiar to me. I could hear the cryptic German commands, constant heiling and heel-snapping I had endured for many years when covering the Reich for INS. To all out-ward appearances, the Wehrmacht in Tunisia was as powerful as in the days when it swept over Poland and France. It required careful probing to ferret out the truth and reach the conclusion that Hitler's forces in North Africa were like a porcelain egg, with a hard exterior and a hollow inside, ready to collapse once the outside shell was crushed.

Looking back, I am convinced Allied leaders like Eisenhower and Alexander divined that truth and incorporated it in their final battle plans. The 2,000-mile trek across Egypt and Libya had taken the heart out of the Afrika Korps, a fact which the wily Rommel realized early enough to return to Berlin on sick leave and pass the buck to von Arnim.

On smoking firing fronts, I recognized forerunners of inevitable disaster.

The failure of Nazi terror tactics against the Yanks on Gumtree Road was prophetic.

The German mentality simply couldn't or wouldn't grasp the fact that the Allied Armies had become full-grown under a unified command and were ready to assert their mastery of Tunisia. Nazi ground troops gained false courage from misleading Berlin propaganda in which the Yanks were depicted as easy marks. The Axis shock of surprise was all the more effective, therefore, when the Second Corps uncorked a stunning offensive and knocked the stuffing out of picked German troops.

In the same way, the Germans misjudged the stolid, pipe-sucking British soldier. Daily on British fronts, I heard glib-tongued Goebbels mouthpieces harp over Axis waves that aristocratic British officers, too indolent to fight the war, paused in the middle of the afternoon to enjoy a leisurely tea instead of attending to the battle. Perhaps so, but I saw those British officers get in their full day's fighting without missing tea. There's a knack to it as natural as the American's knack of chewing gum.

The stolid Tommy with his 1918 soup-plate helmet is never flustered, not even under the heaviest fire. That's what the Germans ran up against. I have General Eisenhower's word that General Alexander anticipated the German mind perfectly. He outsmarted them by planning with Montgomery to take over the rôle of "holding army" above Enfidaville while the task of capturing Bizerte and Tunis was assigned to the United States Second Corps and the British First Army respectively. The Germans fell for that ruse and concentrated their whole defense reserves down south against the Eighth Army. They realized their error too late.

To my mind, another weak link in the Axis armor was the monotony of the Berlin-Rome propaganda. It hasn't changed since I was in Berlin. Either Goebbels was stumped, or else he was kept in blissful ignorance of the African situation.

The Yanks and Tommies have it over the ironclad Nazi military mentality. Whenever the going gets tough they find refuge in an innate sense of humor, which serves to blow off steam.

The Luftwaffe was simply wiped out of the skies by improved Anglo-American planes and synchronized air-land operations. The Allied Air Forces did something else which left the Nazis gasping, when Allied technical laboratories converted fast Hurricane planes into flying artillery by attaching cannon firing armor-piercing shells beneath each wing. Panzers and field positions never knew what hit them. The deadly effect of this flying artillery contributed extensively to our African victory and is a tribute to Allied inventive genius.

The drain on Hitler's manpower in the Reich was increasingly evident in Tunisia, where for the first time I saw companies made up of political unreliables who had been given the choice of fighting or rotting in concentration camps.

Tunisia demonstrated that the Nazis, if arrogant in victory, are servile in defeat. Even the crack Hitler regiments couldn't take it. They cringed

554

when shells from Allied tanks and planes swept over them like hail. They recoiled in terror before naked American, British and French bayonets. In capitulating, every Nazi from von Arnim down disobeyed Hitler's personal orders, "Stand and die."

From the military viewpoint, the Axis end in Tunisia was ignominy without gallantry. For Allied purposes, we proved to our own conclusive satisfaction that Hitler's Wehrmacht is vulnerable and can be defeated behind the strongest fortifications. That is a big fact. The Wehrmacht can be cracked rapidly under combined attacks planned and executed on mass-scale principles.

It was Hitler who used to shout, at officer assemblies in secret Berlin Chancellery meetings on the eve of an invasion, that victory in his eyes is incomplete unless the opposing armies are totally wiped out. In Tunisia, Allied arms applied that principle successfully against the Wehrmacht and gave Hitler a prophetic sample of the pattern and ability with which we are now ready to enact the Casablanca verdict that the Axis' unconditional surrender alone will terminate the war.

# THIS MAN ROMMEL

## by Richard D. McMillan

IS Rommel a general of genius or an average soldier who, helped by both his luck and the superboosting he received as a No. 1 Nazi and intimate friend of Hitler, has muddled through against inferior British leaders in the various battles he fought with us in the desert?

Not until we know the full history of the war from both sides shall we be able to assess the qualities of the "Killer of Coburg" as a leader and strategist in battle.

This much we do know: Rommel is a fearless man, an opportunist who yet fails to seize opportunities, and in defeat a champion "escaper."

We have had many examples of his courage in battle. He led his Panzers and Panzer troops to battle in an armored car, braving our shells with complete indifference.

His opportunism was demonstrated once again, after many instances in Libya, in the fighting in Tunisia, where with an inferior force he turned and smashed at the Anglo-Americans on three sides, in the center, in the southwest, at El Hamma, and to the southeast, along the Mareth line.

When we broke through at El Alamein he succeeded in snatching his crack 21st Panzer Division (the Afrika Korps's veteran fighters) from the clutches of Montgomery and his men.

In September he attacked in a Panzer rush that was scheduled to crack through the British lines to the south of the main Alamein positions. He drove through the wilderness of wadis and strange conical-shaped hills

555

and slaty-grey, sun-baked tablelands between Deir el Munassib (one of the strong points in the southern tip of the Alamein line) and marshy wastes of the Qattara Depression.

Here he revealed the cardinal weakness of his military training and mental make-up. He might be daring, quick in action, ready to take risks, ruthless and tireless, but one thing he lacked—real originality. He has the fatal German weakness of doing the same thing once too often. Hitler has it. He seized the Sudetenland. He smashed Czechoslovakia. He went on and on believing that the day of reckoning would never come.

Rommel showed lightning speed in his escape. Seizing every available vehicle, he gave orders to the two Panzer units and the Panzer grenadiers of the 90th Light to make for the frontier. "Out of Egypt at once," he ordered.

In eight days he had reached the border. By a miracle of organization he managed to obtain sufficient supplies of oil to keep his Panzers moving— this although he was under constant day and night bombing from the RAF. All along the line of his retreat, petrol bousers blazed night and day. Trucks burned, guns, tanks, armored cars, shell, and other dumps were charred embers.

I had personal experience of the lightning movement of the Afrika Korps in the advance around the southern end of the Gazala front, which isolated the Fighting French in their hastily improvised desert fort of Bir Hacheim. In the twilight of late May the Panzers, with the 90th Light, clanked southeast, wheeled around Hacheim, and, force-marching through the night, halted at dawn. They were ten miles from Tobruk, straddling the Axis Strasse—the road the Axis built to by-pass Tobruk during the siege. In the night they had covered seventy miles. Incidentally, they had submerged at least 10,000 British troops in their march—including a general—but such was their haste to keep the rendezvous at Tobruk that they did not take much trouble with their prisoners. Many hundreds of them—including the general—escaped in the dark and tramped back to our lines.

A Royal Army Service Corps driver, captured by the enemy in their sweep north behind the Gazala line, drove with the Panzers to the Axis Strasse. In the uncertain light just before dawn, they took up positions. The British began shelling on both flanks. The enemy withdrew. The British driver drove off through the smoke of the barrage. I met him as he staggered along the road into our lines.

"They caught me in my truck last night," he said. "It is a very strong flying column."

"Flying column!" I exclaimed. "Why, it's the main weight of the Afrika Korps. You have been with the spearhead of their drive to capture Tobruk!"

"Blimy!" he ejaculated, a surprised smile lighting his tired eyes and grubby face. "You don't tell me!"

He said the speed and timing of the advance was so minutely scheduled that the Germans did not stop for food or drink. They swallowed pep tablets and had an occasional sip of water from their water bottles. The

556

Panzers marched in V formation, with strong mobile anti-aircraft elements, armored cars, and mobile artillery on both flanks and to the rear protecting the Panzer shock troops and supplies. They had their food and water slung on the armor of their tanks.

"I have never seen troops—even lorried troops—move so fast," the driver said.

This drive to the Axis Strasse was a feint by Rommel. He drew his armor and troops back and made a second thrust, closer behind the Gazala line, and the battles of the "Cauldron" and the Knightsbridge box followed, while he bore through our main line at Gazala from both sides and thus whittled down our defenses. Afterwards came the successful attack on Tobruk, which, as I have explained, resulted more from British dillydallying than from Rommel's skill.

On the Mareth line Rommel attacked in the first week of March, intending to break through our comparatively weak positions and sweep us back as he had done twice before. He had not counted on the experience Montgomery had absorbed and was now applying. The 8th Army let the enemy come on so far, then stopped him with anti-tank fire. This round to the British.

In the last fortnight of March, Montgomery unleashed his big attack. Adopting his Alamein methods, he began with a main frontal attack. When Rommel's main force was pinned to hold the bridgehead at Wadi Zigzau, Monty scored a major tactical victory by switching the full force of his offensive in a flanking move against El Hamma, thus threatening Rommel's retreat. This round to the 8th Army.

Again, in April, we beat him at Akarit and chased him north. This round to us.

The British had won six out of eleven in the big battles waged in North Africa in the two years since the Afrika Korps first appeared. And in the Tunisian struggle, the "Killer of Coburg" swayed on the ropes as British and Americans and French, on land and in the air and on the sea, sparred for the knockout.

When Mr. Churchill used these words in speaking of the Afrika Korps commander: "We have a very daring and skillful opponent against us and —may I say across the havoc of war?—a great general" he spoke truly. A great general, but no more. Certainly not a genius; decidedly not invincible.

In the battles of the Mareth quadrilateral we not only blew more cobwebs from the Rommel myth but showed to what extent we had learned the Nazi Panzer technique and, in many ways, improved upon it. It had been a long and costly lesson, trailing all the way from Dunkirk to the mountains of Greece, from Hellfire all the weary, dusty road to Tripoli and, in the end, to the last battlefields of Tunisia as we proceeded to fling the remnants of Rommel's Afrika Korps from Africa.

Someone has remarked of Rommel: "Whatever the rest of his career, he is sure of a place in history as the general who retreated farther and faster than any other."

# "THANKS, PAL"

## by Ernie Pyle

THE Tunisian campaign was ended. Our air forces moved on farther into Tunisia, to the very edge of the chasm of sea that separated them only so little from Sicily and Sardinia and then from Europe itself. We and the British leaped upon the demolished ports we had captured, cleared out enough wreckage for a foothold for ships, and as the ports grew and grew in usefulness they swarmed with thousands of men, and ships, and trucks.

Surely before autumn we of Tunisia would be deep into something new. Most of us realized and admitted to ourselves that horrible days lay ahead. The holocaust that at times seemed so big to us in Tunisia would pale in our memories beside the things we would see and do before another year ran out.

It is hard for you at home to realize what an immense, complicated, sprawling institution a theater of war actually is. As it appears to you in the newspapers, war is a clear-cut matter of landing so many men overseas, moving them from the port to the battlefield, advancing them against the enemy with guns firing, and they win or lose.

To look at war that way is like seeing a trailer of a movie, and saying you've seen the whole picture. I actually don't know what percentage of our troops in Africa were in the battle lines, but I believe it safe to say that only comparatively few ever saw the enemy, ever shot at him, or were shot at by him. All the rest of those hundreds of thousands of men were churning the highways for 2,000 miles behind the lines with their endless supply trucks, they were unloading the ships, cooking the meals, pounding the typewriters, fixing the roads, making the maps, repairing the engines, decoding the messages, training the reserves, pondering the plans.

What I have seen in North Africa has altered my own feelings in one respect. There were days when I sat in my tent alone and gloomed with the desperate belief that it was actually possible for us to lose this war. I don't feel that way any more. Despite our strikes and bickering and confusion back home, America is producing and no one can deny that. Even here at the far end of just one line the trickle has grown into an impressive stream. We are producing at home and we are hardening overseas. Apparently it takes a country like America about two years to become wholly at war. We had to go through that transition period of letting loose of life as it was, and then live the new war life so long that it finally became the normal life to us. It was a form of growth, and we couldn't press it. Only time can produce that change. We have survived that long passage of time, and if I am at all correct we have about changed our character and become a war nation. I can't yet see when we shall win, or over what route geographically, or by which of the many means of warfare. But no longer do I have any doubts at all that we shall win.

558

The men over here have changed too. They are too close to themselves to sense the change, perhaps. And I am too close to them to grasp it fully. But since I am older and a little apart, I have been able to notice it more.

For a year, everywhere I went, soldiers inevitably asked me two questions: "When do you think we'll get to go home?" and "When will the war be over?" The home-going desire was once so dominant that I believe our soldiers over here would have voted—if the question had been put—to go home immediately, even if it meant peace on terms of something less than unconditional surrender by the enemy.

That isn't true now. Sure, they all still want to go home. So do I. But there is something deeper than that, which didn't exist six months ago. I can't quite put it into words—it isn't any theatrical proclamation that the enemy must be destroyed in the name of freedom; it's just a vague but growing individual acceptance of the bitter fact that we must win the war or else, and that it can't be won by running excursion boats back and forth across the Atlantic carrying homesick vacationers.

Our men, still thinking of home, are impatient with the strange peoples and customs of the countries they now inhabit. They say that if they ever get home they never want to see another foreign country. But I know how it will be. The day will come when they'll look back and brag about how they learned a little Arabic, and how swell the girls were in England, and how pretty the hills of Germany were. Every day their scope is broadening despite themselves, and once they all get back with their global yarns and their foreign-tinged views, I cannot conceive of our nation ever being isolationist again. The men don't feel very international right now, but the influences are at work and the time will come.

I couldn't say truthfully that they are very much interested in foreign affairs right now, outside of battle affairs. Awhile back a friend of mine in Washington wrote me an enthusiastic letter, telling of the Ball Resolution in the Senate calling for the formation of a United Nations organization to co-ordinate the prosecution of the war, administer reoccupied countries, feed and economically re-establish liberated nations, and to assemble a United Nations military force to suppress any future military aggression.

My friend told of the enthusiasm the bill had created at home, hailed it as the first definite step in winning the peace as well as the war, and asked me almost pleadingly to send back a report on what the men at the front thought of the bill.

I didn't send any report, because the men at the front thought very little about it one way or the other. I doubt that one out of ten of them remembered the thing two days, even though they may have read about it in *Stars and Stripes*. There wasn't anything specific to get their teeth into and argue about.

Our fighting equipment was the only thing that didn't stand head and shoulders above everything issued to soldiers of any other country, and that was only because we weren't ready for war at first, and for two years we have been learning what was good and what was bad. Already many of our weapons are unmatched by any other country. Give us another year and surely it can be said that our men are furnished better weapons, along with better food, health and clothing, than any other army.

Here it is June of 1943 and it seems a long time since we landed at Oran in November of 1942. Of course there were thousands of us even in those first days in Africa, and yet it seemed like a little family then. And specially so when we went on to Tunisia. In those bitter January days we were so small that I knew almost every officer on the staff of every unit, in addition to hundreds of the soldiers. Nothing was very official in our lives then; there was almost no red tape; we correspondents at the front were few and were considered by the army rather like partners in the firm. We made deep friendships that have endured.

During the winter I dropped in frequently at Corps Headquarters, buried deep in a gulch beyond Tebessa. They put up a little tent for me, and I tried to work and sleep in it, but was never very successful at either because of being constantly, paralyzingly cold throughout the twenty-four hours of the day. We ate in a tent with a crushed-stone floor and an iron-bellied stove in the center. It was the only warm place I knew, and so informal was the war in those first days that often I sat around the stove after supper and just gabbed country-storelike with Lieutenant General Lloyd Fredendall, then commander of our armies in Tunisia. I was very fond of General Fredendall, and I admired and respected him. For some unknown reason I always thought of him to myself as "Papa" Fredendall, although I don't think anybody else ever did. I still wear the Armored Corps combat jacket he gave me.

The first pioneering days of anything are always the best days. Everything is new and animating, and acquaintanceships are easy and everyone is knit closely together. In the latter part of the Tunisian war things were just as good for us correspondents—we had better facilities and the fighting Army continued to be grand to us—and yet toward the end it became so big that I felt like a spectator instead of a participant. Which is, of course, all that a correspondent is or ever should be. But the old intimacy was gone.

And then finally the Tunisian campaign was over, spectacularly collapsed after the bitterest fighting we had known in our theater. It was only in those last days that I came to know what war really is. I don't know how any of the men who went through the thick of that hill-by-hill butchery could ever be the same again. The end of the Tunisian war brought an exhilaration, then a letdown, and later a restlessness from anticlimax that I can see multiplied a thousand times when the last surrender comes. That transition back to normal days will be as difficult for many as was the change into war, and some will never be able to accomplish it.

On the day of final peace, the last stroke of what we call the "Big Picture" will be drawn. I haven't written anything about the "Big Picture," because I don't know anything about it. I only know what we see from our worm's-eye view, and our segment of the picture consists only of tired and dirty soldiers who are alive and don't want to die; of long darkened convoys in the middle of the night; of shocked silent men wandering back down the hill from battle; of chow lines and atabrine tablets and foxholes and burning tanks and Arabs holding up eggs and the rustle of high-flown shells; of jeeps and petrol dumps and smelly bedding rolls and C rations and cactus patches and blown bridges and dead mules and hospital tents and shirt collars greasy-black from months of wearing; and of laughter too, and anger and wine and lovely flowers and constant cussing. All these it is composed of; and of graves and graves and graves.

That is our war, and we will carry it with us as we go on from one battle-ground to another until it is all over, leaving some of us behind on every beach, in every field. We are just beginning with the ones who lie back of us here in Tunisia. I don't know whether it was their good fortune or their misfortune to get out of it so early in the game. I guess it doesn't make any difference, once a man has gone. Medals and speeches and victories are nothing to them any more. They died and others lived and nobody knows why it is so. They died and thereby the rest of us can go on and on. When we leave here for the next shore, there is nothing we can do for the ones beneath the wooden crosses, except perhaps to pause and murmur, "Thanks, pal."

# Part Ten: The Invasion of Europe

## DESTINATION: SICILY

### by John Mason Brown

2:40 A.M., *July 10, 1943*

WE are within five minutes of what should have been the time for "H" hour. But "H" hour has been delayed until 3:45 at the request of the Commander of Transports. Blame the choppy seas for this, and difficulties they have caused in getting the small boats out. So take time off to get your second wind.

Don't think that things have not been happening above, in spite of this delay. Do you remember those enemy searchlights which I have mentioned several times? Well, they have given us some uneasy moments. There's a hell of a lot of difference between our searchlights when they are looking for the enemy, and enemy searchlights when they are looking for us.

As far as I can make out, there have been three of these searchlights sweeping from the shore. When we were stealing in, and even after we reached our anchorage, they swept only the sky. They kept raking it back and forth, back and forth, sticking up like nervous white fingers in the darkness. They were after our planes then, and didn't seem to know we were here.

Even when they followed the transport planes out, these searchlights swung far above us—which was precisely what we kept hoping they would do. One of these beacons, however, carried its search toward the horizon until its lowered light hovered over our ships to port. Then it blinked and went out, apparently not having spotted anything of interest.

This made us breathe the easier.

But only for a while. Because in a few minutes those searchlights were in motion again. The same one that had blinked before, woke up in alarm. When it came on, it was aiming straight above it at the sky, which was still all right with us. Then it began circling its light out to sea, lower and lower each time, until it started skimming the waves. In its sweep it landed on one of our ships lying at an angle. It paused there for an awful time before starting to move again. Then it swung slowly past the other vessels ahead, seeming to halt for the same awful time on each one of them, icing them with light or showing them up as silhouettes, as neat and black as you will ever find on any Ship Identification cards.

The beacon finally reached us. Our turn came just the way it used to in school. Waiting for it wasn't pleasant. The light cut closer and closer until it was full upon us, blinding us when we looked straight at it. It wasn't hard, then, to make out the faces on the Admiral's Bridge. It would have been hard *not* to make them out. The faces of the men up there looked the way an actor's face does without make-up under a spotlight. You know that sallow look? Even the ship's gray was lighter than the sun at midday had ever made it.

I thought they had found us. I couldn't see how they had missed us.

"Can they see us?" I asked Captain Wellings, our Gunnery Officer.

"No. We can see them all right," he smiled, "but I don't think they can see us on a night like this. Anyway we are out of their range of vision."

This was good news. It still is.

4:15 A.M., July 10

The Fourth of July was never like this! These are the biggest fireworks I've ever seen. Our guns have really been speaking up, and it looks like they are much more than just big talkers. The sky is as bright as a summer parasol with the sunlight streaming through it.

The darkness is fighting a losing battle. Light is everywhere. Never for long. Always changing. Always in the swiftest motion. Then the night seeps back, only to be driven away again. Overhead it's all dots and dashes that you can see, quivering as they race to rise and fall; dots and dashes, and streamers of heat, and rockets overtaking rockets.

Light and noise. The noises are as different as the lights. There's the froglike *glump* of flak as it thuds through the water after a brief splash. There's the staccato stitching of the 20- and 40-millimeters. There's a sigh, a whine, and a whistle coming from something—I don't know what.

There are big guns, little guns, medium-sized guns—all of them fluent, and all of them demanding to be heard from, whether they are on the ships around us, in the Task Force ahead, with the enemy on shore, or the British to the east. The big guns bellow in a full, damp, dull tone. They sound the way a goldfish bowl might sound if—water and all—it exploded in your tummy.

Under this flaming cover the small landing boats have been pushing into shore. Bright as the sky is, the sea is still so dark that I have been able to see the Viking outlines of only a few of our little boats. But once in a while, in the din, the sputter of their motors has been heard.

Our big guns appear to have got two of those prying searchlights. They have been snuffed out for quite a while. It was a cruiser, I think, that scored a bull's-eye on one of them. The beacon scarcely had time to wink. Then it was done for.

7:15 A.M., July 10

We are weighing anchor now to move closer in to shore.

The Spitfires have been patrolling once more. They have come back again and again, in spite of their warm welcome.

563

Everyone topside has been nibbling on or at "K" rations and feels the better for coffee, with its illusion of breakfast.

Most of the shore batteries are silenced by now, due to the spectacular accuracy of Naval gunnery. One by one they have been snuffed out like candles.

Some jeeps have been lowered into the landing boats panting alongside of us. And the LCT's are now going in, rolling quite a bit and crowded with boys in khaki, only a few of whom look seasick and are holding their heads. These LCT's have been escorted and given fire cover by our destroyers. The Army is leaving us in large numbers. As it does so, one of our cruisers is thundering away at an inland target, and a big fire is burning on the beach to port.

8 A.M., *July 10*

For the moment, all's quiet. We have just dropped anchor. And after shaking hands with the Admiral, General Middleton of the 45th Division has gone ashore. In the same boat with him went Clark Lee, the INS correspondent. Fires are still smoking off the beaches, and guns rumbling intermittently.

The chief news is that there seems to have been no serious opposition. A message from shore says, "Considerable artillery and prisoners taken."

That's good news to sleep on. And the Chief of Staff urges that you do sleep, your duties permitting, and sleep as long as possible. You deserve that sleep and may need it tonight. It should be a happy sleep.

*July 11*

The city of Ragusa has fallen to us, and at 6:30 this afternoon Comiso airfield was captured. The leading elements of our invading forces from the 45th Division are from twelve to fifteen miles inland by now. Some of our other troops, notably the 1st Division, are progressing in spite of stiff opposition. By last night some 5,500 German and Italian prisoners had been taken. This we know definitely. From Scoglitti comes a rumor, unverified though perhaps symptomatic, which says that when we took the town we did so with the loss of only one American while 300 Italians were killed. Up until 10 this morning less than 250 injured were reported in this particular Task Force. Near us during the day a British monitor has been pounding away with ominous regularity, her big guns trained on an enemy tank concentration inland.

Of immediate concern to us all is the progress of the unloading of the transports and supply ships. The reports continue to be excellent. One transport is 100 per cent cleared. Most of the other ships are getting through a difficult job rapidly. Our air attacks on Sicilian airfields continue like an unbroken serial. A flight of eighteen B-17's passed this area, headed inland to drop their loads on enemy air centers. AA gunners with itchy fingers appear to have controlled their desire to shoot at the first plane in sight. Our air cover of Spitfires now patrols without every ship in the harbor sending up clouds of flak in appreciation. One of these patrolling Spits at about 11 A.M. this morning scored a kill on a low-flying Messerschmitt that had dodged his way in to drop bombs on the beach near Scoglitti. Earlier this morning two German bombers—JU-88's—were hit and believed to have been shot down. We had some bad moments this afternoon when several German planes swept toward the convoy and were successfully engaged by three Spitfires. Another uncomfortable few minutes came for the *Spelvin* when a JU-88 was spotted directly above us, at an altitude of 25,000 feet. Some say bombs were dropped; all agree that Spitfires drove off the JU-88.

Yesterday the Italians gave us the bird. And a very nice bird. At 9:47 P.M. a tired enemy carrier pigeon flew down to rest on one of our mine sweepers. It proved to be a comforting bird-in-the-hand. The pigeon was carrying a message from the Italian Army's 206th Division to the Italian 12th Army Corps. When translated, the message read:

"Situation 3:00 P.M.—12 o'clock Croce Camerina about to fall.... Col. Bartimo resisting.... After fifteen hours of struggle, infantrymen and artillerymen are resolutely doing their duty against overwhelming forces and means. Hundreds of anchored ships unloading material undisturbed. Our aviation absent. I have ordered shot two soldiers of the fixed defense of Pachino for being out of presence of the enemy and in civilian clothes. Please send requested pigeons."

*July 12*

On Invasion Night the enemy did not know exactly where we were. They may even have been surprised by our coming. Last night the coin was to a certain extent flipped the other way. The Germans and the Italians knew exactly where we were. It was hard, if not impossible, for us to locate their airmen in the low-hung gray clouds. From time to time only the mad hornet's buzz of their machines could be heard as they zoomed uncomfortably near. Or their many flares could be seen lanterning the sky with terror. Or their bombs could be watched as they splashed close by in the Mediterranean or exploded on the beach.

Just after dinner—at 7:50—the Task Force to the west underwent a heavy bombardment. This bombardment rumbled ahead of us like a storm sweeping down a valley. No enemy planes could be seen from our bridge, but our ears ached from the thunder of antiaircraft guns. Tracer bullets raced across the heaven, pursuing one another as if discharged from a giant's Roman candle.

By 8:10 P.M. some Messerschmitts roared shoreward to bomb the beaches. They were followed by Spitfires. Then the shore batteries began to erupt. When they were in full eruption the *Spelvin* shook for the first of many times last night; shook as if it were a muffled gong struck once but accurately. The mystery of those disquieting single quavers remains unexplained.

After all these months of preparation, these weeks of mounting suspense, and those three brief but long, crowded, and unforgettable days and nights off Scoglitti, we left Sicily last night. For us, as front line participants, the Sicilian invasion was over. Some of us came away with a few poor trophies. All of us took away our memories; memories that will grow into tales; tales that will grow faster than poplars and taller than the tallest redwoods.

We left Sicily in the kind of sunset that should have supplied a tourist with a postcard evening. The hills, the clouds, the distant mountains, and the splash of reds in the sky suggested a traveler's paradise. Yet, as if to remind us of what we had been through and why, we were given a martial farewell. At 8:15 P.M. a bomb had dropped on the beach ahead of us, after some antiaircraft had blurted out. The spot where the bomb fell was marked by a billowing cloud of smoke and a burst of flame, as if an ammunition dump had been hit. From inland, as we turned to go, came the rumble of heavy fighting.

Some of us felt guilty about leaving. We knew how the Army men on those contested beaches must feel as they saw us, their one connection with home, pull out. Our ships, as ships, were conscienceless. As they swung into the single line we joined, they seemed almost as glad to be going home as horses heading for their stables.

# GOING ASHORE

## *by George Sessions Perry*

JULY 13, 1943—The village of Scoglitti lies in the center of a scimitar of white sandy beach on the southeastern coast of Sicily. It has much the appearance of the village in Elliot Paul's Life and Death of a Spanish Town. The houses, so simple and natural that they have a kind of beautiful rightness among the dunes and dry hills around them, are low and white, made of stone and mortar with shallow sloping roofs. Scoglitti is a poor town whose people have never had much more than bread and wine and fishes, religion and the simple natural merriment of healthy hard-working folk. Bread they made in little stone igloos adjacent to their modest houses. Wine they grew in near-by fields, thankful that the vine is one of the few things that sometimes bear their best fruit in poor soil. Fishes came out of the warm blue sea that comes almost to their doorsteps and which, until the advent of Il Duce and his Fascism, could still be spoken of with affectionate pride as Mare Nostrum. As for the merriment, the lively Saturday nights in cantinas and all that, it slowly vanished as the young men of Scoglitti left their boats and fields for Ethiopia, or as still older men were called up for service in

Libya and Tunisia. Their religion was centered in the cathedral whose fine square stone tower dominated the town.

It was on July eleventh, one day after the town had surrendered to the Americans, that a group of snipers with machine guns, no doubt attracted by some notion of sanctuary as well as by the thickness of the walls, gathered in the cathedral and sprayed the streets until their position was neutralized by one of our cruisers. That was on our second day at Scoglitti.

For the ship to which I was assigned, as well as for all other American ships standing off the beach in this sector, July eleventh was a day of much greater action and strain than had been the initial day of invasion. That first day things had worked better than any of us expected because of the light resistance we encountered on the beaches. The division charged with the protection of the immediate shoreline was regional troops, poorly equipped and wanting in any real will to resist.

However, there was more determined resistance encountered a few miles from Scoglitti, near the town of Gela. Here troops equipped with tanks and artillery fought our soldiers to a standstill, once they had made their initial dash inland. And by the second day, according to a wounded American soldier brought back to one of our ships, the enemy had forced one of our battalions to retreat fourteen miles and had killed some of our men. Now the fighting was proceeding little more than four miles inland as our destroyers and cruisers fired over the heads of our own men to support them and to stem the enemy advance.

From dawn of this second day, cannonading by our warships was continuous. From the signal bridge of the ship I was on, shell bursts both from our guns and from those of the enemy were clearly visible. Nevertheless, our ships continued to move closer to this area, where supplies and reinforcements were apparently badly needed. Just to the right of this fighting was a deep ravine which wound through hills, and from it enemy bombers would periodically dart, drop their bombs over the ships and dart back into the ravine. As my ship and others in its group lay, this action was some twenty-five hundred yards distant.

Most of the planes that bombed our group during that second morning did so from high or medium altitudes. But there was such urgency to get our ship unloaded before she might be sunk that we soon dispensed with dashing into battle stations for each attack. The first phase of our job—getting men ashore in small boats—was done. The second and equally important one of landing their supplies intact largely remained to be accomplished. For the rest of the day then, except when bombers came in force, men who weren't needed for unloading were ordered to the gun pits to put up such a barrage as their numbers allowed, while the rest went on discharging cargo into whatever landing craft we could get alongside. By now many of the small landing craft we had brought with us on our decks were swamped on the beach. In any case, they bounced about so much while they were alongside, and held so little once they were loaded, that they weren't very effective cargo lighters.

By noon of the second day, with every available man bearing a hand, all holds were virtually cleared except No. 1, located up in the bow. It still contained about a hundred tons of ammunition. It was naturally this cargo of which we were most conscious each time bombs started down.

I made two trips ashore during the morning with boatloads of motorized guns and ammunition. Despite the endless lines of broached landing craft and the Gargantuan influx of supplies there was still order, people to unload boats and places to put supplies once they got ashore. The beaches were well marked; boatmen could be sure which beach was which. Steel netting ran down graded beaches and forked out into three prongs as it reached and entered the surf. Here were facilities for unloading three separate vehicle-bearing craft simultaneously.

These beaches, like the ships, were being bombed and strafed. I was there on one such occasion, dived into a ditch and though it may seem the reaction of a lunatic I felt a certain smugness, even pleasure, at feeling around me the warm, nonexplosive earth. Every other time I had been on something that if hit at all would blow up. For there are unfortunately no foxholes on an ammunition-laden transport. Each man knows that his person isn't the extent of the target he presents, but that the skin of the ship is his own skin and that he is vulnerable to all its hurts. But from the vantage point of this wonderful Sicilian ditch the planes were another and altogether less menacing thing.

On the way back to the ship we passed a tank-landing ship. Amphibious trucks called ducks were running in and out of the ship like waterbugs with windshields. By now a landing barge was alongside our ship receiving ammunition. This was in the neighborhood of two o'clock. Hardly had I gone aboard and reached the signal bridge when a flight of from twenty to forty enemy bombers roared over and dropped more than a hundred bombs, but our ship kept on unloading.

By midafternoon the ammunition barge was loaded and its lines cast away. Some fifty tons of ammunition remained. From this time until six o'clock we dribbled such loads as we could into what small landing craft were available. Many of these boats' crews hadn't left their boats since they had been lowered over the side to hit the beach the first time. Some had jugs of mud—as sailors call coffee—and sacks of sandwiches in their boats. Some had boxes of field rations. As for loading masters who had been loading boats all this time, their voices had long since vanished. Only hand signals were now being passed from loading masters to winchmen. Sporadic raiding by enemy planes in ones and twos, sometimes four or five, continued. And all of us suspected that once night fell they would swarm on this mass of ships—perhaps two hundred were in this immediate area—that they would light the sky with flares and the sea with burning ships. There was no use kidding ourselves, it was in the cards—such heavy concentrations of ships along enemy coastlines is one of the inescapable embarrassments of amphibious assaults. And for that matter none of us had ever expected this job to be as tame as the North African landing. At this stage in the operation we had no air fields closer than Malta, and the enemy had at least twenty on this island. It was therefore not hard to guess what was going to happen after nightfall.

At six in the afternoon we got good news! A tank-landing ship was coming alongside to receive the rest of our ammunition. Our small-boat problems were over. Unloading would proceed much faster, now that we had something which would hold what we had to unload without having to be constantly running to the beach itself to unload. It wouldn't be dark until after nine o'clock or so. Perhaps in that length of time with every man doing his utmost we could clear the holds and have the ship ready to get under way before mass bombings began. That way we would be in a position to maneuver and fight back, have a chance to put out such fires as bombs started, minimize our damage and fully exploit whatever possibilities a transport may have in a fight with planes. But until that ammunition was gone our job, no matter what happened, was to stay put and unload it.

At this point some thirty-five tons of ammunition remained aboard. It still covered the No. 1 hold to a depth of twelve feet. In addition many barracks bags belonging to troops who had been our shipmates remained aboard. These bags were piled ten feet deep over the portside of the boat deck and there was no way to transfer them to the opposite side and forward except for men to muscle them over there.

Now that the transfer of cargo had begun up forward every man jack not necessary to the unloading, or to stand a gun watch, formed a double line that ran the breadth of the ship down to the main deck level and forward for a hundred feet. In this line were medical officers, colored mess cooks, myself, bluejackets from every department that could spare them. The bags weighed from seventy to ninety pounds each, but once one of them was picked up it passed over the heads of all the men in line and wasn't lowered until it reached the transfer point on the main deck. Once or twice we stopped our work to go to battle stations when planes came over, dropping bombs, but that was only the barracks-bags gang. The ammunition people went right on working. Except for these crises the work never stopped. And as the number of bags passed grew from hundreds to beyond the thousand mark, some of these people who had been working furiously without sleep for three days were reeling with exhaustion. Once when the pace slowed somebody yelled, "Switch your tails and pass them bags along."

Then twenty-nine-year-old Doctor John Hope, of Mobile, said, "Let's sing," and struck up "Praise the Lord and Pass the Ammunition."

By 9:30 the bags were off the ship, but we found now that the rest of the ammunition wouldn't be unloaded until midnight, no matter how hard the men on both ships worked. Those of us not in the holds, at winches or engines, had, without knowing it, exactly fifteen minutes in which to rest, to grab sandwiches, a cup of coffee or smoke a cigarette. By now a cool night was beginning, with a bright half-moon to light the sky and sea. There was too much noise of every kind to hear the engines of the first planes as they sailed far overhead. We found they were there when flares, in all their ghastly brilliance, began to light up our ships as brightly as the sun might have. Then we knew they were up there, their own eyes shaded from the glare of flares by the parachutes that held the flares aloft. We were marvelously illuminated sitting ducks. The first bombs came down and the ships began to saw open the night.

Down in the engine room the chief water tender was watching how each time something came over the phone the men's heads would snap around with an electric movement to hear what they hoped had happened. The boilers had steam up and there was ammunition left. The ship's first lieutenant said, "Sometimes you gotta take long chances, so you take 'em and to hell with it." Those of us on deck could see that every time a bomb found its mark great sheets of enveloping flame would race out laterally and then slowly materialize into a huge, deep red spheroidal bloom. In the forward forty-millimeter gun pit, where men were begging for the order to open fire, Gunner's Mate Lee, lanky, slow-speaking, level-headed man from Mt. Vernon, Indiana, was ordering his men to be silent. "Excited people talking leads from one thing to another." Our captain withheld the order for our own ship to open up. Tied up as we were to that ammunition barge we presented a double target to which the captain wasn't eager to direct the enemy's attention. And as the night blazed with gunfire and bursting bombs our people went on unloading the usual thousands of gallons of oil in tanks.

In the sick bay it was worse. Some of the patients had been committed that day for treatment of burns, but the majority were shrapnel cases, their nerves were shot from pain and some were trying to climb out of bed, particularly when planes came so low that the roar of their engines was loud.

After a half hour there came a lull. Perhaps it lasted ten minutes. I don't think anyone knows positively. In that period those of us not unloading wandered about, watching fires burn. In passing, people made little pleasantries and passed the time of day. Nobody doubted that planes were coming back and anybody with an ounce of brains knew we were looking death by burning in the face. Yet everybody in action and word was chipper, even though the color was gone out of many a face. So far, only one person had become a little hysterical. Another had lost his power of speech.

Then the planes did come back and lighted us up and poured it on so hot and heavy that there was no longer any conceivable advantage in withholding our fire. In a matter of minutes every twenty-millimeter gun barrel was dull cherry-red as our lads watched the fire of a near-by destroyer while they enlarged and helped increase the density of its pattern.

And when forty-millimeter guns got driving with their powerful whong, whong, whong, you could feel the projectile push against the ship as it started off, and it traveled so fast that its whoosh through the air could be heard above the surrounding clamor.

Then a great orange pool of flame materialized quickly in the sky as the ships scored the first positive hit and our people cheered like hyenas. The planes must have been impressed by our lack of success with our guns during the day, for now they were pulling in close for a real kill, coming well into range of our twenties. Another plane exploded in the air. Soon we had them burning overhead, in the sea and on the shore all at once. In perhaps five minutes we bagged seven.

At the end of five minutes they either ran out of bombs or decided we were no bargain. Again action broke off. The time was roughly 11:15. Unloading hadn't even paused, but the barge with that growing pile of ammunition on deck was still tied alongside and would be there for another hour. That was the longest hour most of us have ever spent. Then finally, before the planes came back, that wonderful order to cast off lines came over the loud-speaker and was performed by willing hands. The relief with which we watched distance increase between the two craft was inexpressible. Now as soon as the first convoy of empty ships was ready to pull out we would be waiting to join it. With this consolation and the enormously satisfying knowledge that despite all the fire which the enemy could throw at us we had done our jobs, those of us with no watch to stand crawled into our bunks and slept the brick-heavy sleep of the utterly exhausted and—at least for the moment—victorious.

JULY 11: *Syracuse surrendered.*

JULY 22: *Palermo taken.*

JULY 23, 1943: *Sicily completely in Allied hands.*

# BALANCE SHEET OF A LIGHTNING CAMPAIGN

## by Ned Russell

THIS was old stuff to the American paratroopers huddled in the Forty-sevens hurtling across the Sicilian coast. They had done a lot of jumping since they dropped out of the skies over North Africa that November morning nine months ago.

Their hands were not cold and moist now. And their throats were not dry as they waited. They sat there chewing gum and grinning as the flak, hopelessly inaccurate, came up at them.

These were Colonel Edison Raff's boys—Uncle Sam's toughest birds.

And the little guy from Georgia, Sergeant Joe Moore, and his Pennsylvania sidekick, Private Joseph Moffo Junior, could see their dream taking shape. They were on the right road now. Maybe they would get to drop in on Hitler and Mussolini after all. Sicily was in the right direction.

A light flashed in each cabin of the big Forty-sevens.

The paratroopers got to their feet.

Same old stuff—just a new country.

"Geronimo," yelled the first paratrooper in line. He went out the door and down.

"San Antone," yelled another.

It was 11:20 P.M.

The Americans were in.

There had not been much rest for the Americans in the ten days since they had put foot on Sicily. At first there had been hard fighting, but once the bridgeheads were established and the Yanks moved inland, they had been going at a fast clip.

They were rolling back the Germans and Italians on the double quick.

On this hot Sunday morning of July eighteenth the Americans were over the main mountain backbone of Sicily and heading north. American tanks edged forward from fold to fold in the hills sweeping the way clear. Behind came the motorized troops.

The American advance was like lightning.

On July twenty-second more than twenty towns fell to the Allies, most of them to the American steam roller which knifed west and northwest from Agrigento through the mountainous country to take Palermo and bring all western Sicily under Allied control.

The unexpectedly fast Allied advance was achieved at almost no cost of life or equipment. The Italians made little attempt to resist. They fell back at the mere approach of the United States vanguard and gave up strong fortifications without firing a shot.

The Italian Twenty-sixth Assietta Division surrendered almost en masse. Germans fired on Italians walking forward to surrender, and Italians shot German officers.

By July twenty-third the last stage of the Battle of Sicily had been reached. General Guzzoni's Italian army was completely defeated and demoralized. Upwards of eighty thousand Axis prisoners were in Allied hands.

There remained little more than the mopping up of the island except for the northeastern peninsula jutting out from the Catania—Mount Etna— Naso line.

The battle positions much resembled the closing stage of the Tunisian campaign. The Catania bottleneck might be likened to Enfidaville, and Catania to the key base of Tunis.

Hitler knew Sicily was lost.

Mussolini listening for the sound of American Fortresses over Rome again was ready to sound the alarm that Italy had been invaded.

It was only four miles from the Sicilian port of Messina to the Italian mainland.

Yesterday it had been Sicily. Tomorrow...

JULY 25, 1943: *The King of Italy removed Mussolini from power.*

# MUSSOLINI'S FALL

## by H. R. Knickerbocker

WITH the Allied Armies near Naples, Sept. 23—(Delayed)—I have just received at first hand from a prominent anti-fascist refugee some details of events inside Italy between the fall of Mussolini July 25 and the capitulation of Italy Sept. 7.

According to this account, the anti-fascists had the immediate impression at the fall of Mussolini that the grand council of the Fascist party had intended other party men to succeed him. When Mussolini went to the King he set forth a plan to create a triumvirate with himself as head of the three men, thinking that by thus broadening his political base he could keep on.

The King, however, told him that he had already named another Prime Minister—Badoglio. Mussolini returned to the street, and found his own car gone and a car there with *Carabinieri,* who escorted him away.

"Badoglio," said my informant, "boasted six days before Mussolini fell that six months after he got power Fascism would be liquidated. But Badoglio didn't liquidate Fascism because the King realized he could not break Fascism and remain King.

"All the Italian left and middle parties are republican. The King has three forces behind him; first, the Fascists as individuals, not of course as a party; second, the clergy, and third, the army, but since the dissolution of the last ·it no longer counts."

My informant said that a good illustration of how confident the Fascists felt even after the fall of Mussolini was the fact that Count Ciano, Mussolini's son-in-law, gave an elaborate luncheon to 30 persons six days after the Duce's fall at which a toast was, "now we have our hundred days," meaning that they had only to wait and their Napoleon would return from Elba.

During this period of waiting for his return to power with the support of the Germans, Mussolini twice, Aug. 1 and 15, wrote letters to Badoglio saying he was very happy at the way he was being treated.

Badoglio's first move in foreign politics was to suggest the neutralization of Italy. The answer to this palpably German proposal was our demand for "unconditional surrender." As soon as our ultimatum was received Badoglio's foreign minister, Guariglia, called a meeting at Tervisio, which resulted in the declaration that the alliance between Italy and Germany continued in full strength, and that all military measures would be taken to continue the war.

There were in Italy at the time of Tervisio only seven Italian divisions. The conference agreed to 20 German divisions in Italy, which amounted to agreement for German occupation of Italy. The Allies' answer was the bombing of Milan. This provoked the first negotiations for surrender, but the Germans smelled the danger and threatened Badoglio with a putsch for Aug. 24. Badoglio had to arrest 700 Fascists, including Ciano and his wife, Edda, Mussolini's daughter. The point my informant was making was that while Fascists were arrested, other political parties which could form the basis of a new democratic regime were not permitted.

Nevertheless Leftist parties successfully led strikes in Milan, Brescia, Turin and other cities, calling for a republic and war against the Germans.

One lesson the anti-Fascist spokesman underlined was that the Italian surrender came too late to save Italy from the fearful consequences of being a battleground, and that quicker action, plus recognition of the Italian democratic parties could have saved many hundred thousands of lives.

SEPTEMBER 3, 1943: *Italian mainland invaded.*

SEPTEMBER 8: *Italian army surrendered unconditionally.*

SEPTEMBER 12: *Mussolini kidnaped by German paratroops.*

# ADVENTURE OF AN AMERICAN REPORTER

### by Aldo Forte

CHIASSO, Switzerland, Sept. 15—Italians in northern Italy have a burning hatred for the Germans who are occupying their soil, and men, women and children in some parts of the area that I have just visited are digging trenches and preparing to resist Adolf Hitler's troops.

They are woefully short of weapons, and some men with whom I talked during my thirteen-hour tour asked why the Allies did not parachute arms and ammunition to them. Pouring out questions on how soon the Allies could be expected in northern Italy, the people told me that the whole upper part of the country was willing and eager to fight to the last man against the Nazis, but lacked the arms to do it.

These descendants of men who fought the Germans down through the generations left no doubt of their bitter antipathy for the Nazis. They told tales of German plundering and killing, and of Germans stripping men and women of jewelry and their money in the streets.

German youths in khaki shorts, bare to the waist, were reported patrolling roads radiating from Milan, arresting all men between 18 and 50 for concentration at the central Milan station—which was patrolled by Tiger tanks —later to be shipped off in sealed box cars to unknown destinations.

Como, the center of the area through which I traveled, was flaming with the war spirit. I saw women and children helping their menfolk dig trenches in the various sections of the city itself and especially along the sector facing in the direction of Milan.

The rail station Norte Milano was patrolled by *bersaglieri,* who looked surprisingly gay in their plumed helmets. *Carabinieri* in swallow-tailed Napoleonic coats marched in the near-by streets. They allowed me to pass undisturbed—even saluted occasionally.

Disguised as a mountaineer with heavy boots, knapsack and some food, I left Chiasso at 3 A.M. Tuesday with a guide who knows every inch of the frontier passes. He should; for generations his ancestors have been smugglers. If I got caught, I planned to play the role of a lost mountain climber.

In a heavy rain we trudged through the woods and bushes, reaching Vacallo in twenty-five minutes and Sagno an hour later. After a short rest we pushed on for two hours until we reached the slopes of the Bisbino Mountains.

Ten minutes later we arrived at a three-yard-high wire fence dividing Switzerland and Italy. The guide calmly cut three strands, poked a wooden pole through, forced up the other wires and told me to crawl through. Small bells atop the fence jingled as I scrambled onto Italian soil.

The guide crawled under the wire and the bells tinkled again. I asked if the frontier guards might not hear them. He chuckled.

"No chance of an Italian sentry in this weather."

We went down the mountainside toward the hamlet of Piazzola, a cluster of seven houses. The rain stopped. The guide took me to the home of a friend, who gave us tea, bread and red wine. I gave my host a chocolate bar, which pleased him tremendously.

Proudly he showed an old hunting gun and said he had been appointed a member of civilian armed bands formed in the Milan-Comovarese district. He had twenty-five cartridges, he added.

I offered him some money, but he refused firmly when he learned I was an American.

We went down the mountain and across barren fields and in a half hour were at Piazza. We saw not a single Italian soldier and no sign whatever of the Germans.

The guide certainly knew his business. He took me to a friend, a fruit vendor, who after a few minutes' negotiation agreed to drive us to Como. He wheeled out an ancient Ford that ran on charcoal, and off we went. But the vendor refused to enter Como, for he did not know whether the Germans were there.

So we paid him off in front of the palatial Villa Olna and went on afoot. We passed a barracks but no soldiers until we reached the central Piazza Cavour, where a few cavalrymen in full war kit were basking in the sun. They took no notice of us.

The first thing I noticed was that the Piazza Cavour gardens had no flowers. Peas, beans and potatoes had been planted in the gardens.

The guide had what he called some "personal business," so we parted, agreeing to meet at the piazza at noon.

About 10 A.M. I strode through Como undisturbed. It seemed as calm as when I last saw it in the summer of 1935. The people went about their daily tasks. Some men loitered about the streets. Later I learned that their idleness was caused by the closing down of silk factories—which made parachutes—because of a strike.

The shops were open and the housewives circulated through the markets, where the principal wares were vegetables. There were lines before the few butcher shops that were open, but fish seemed plentiful.

I paused before a movie house showing a Laurel and Hardy film. Children crowded open-mouthed around the display posters.

A policeman eyed me suspiciously. I must have looked extremely dirty, even for an Italian mountain climber. With a show of confidence that I did not feel I went on by.

The only document I had was a newspaper card issued in Rome three years ago. It was signed by Carmine Senise, who was then and still is chief of the Italian police—or was until the recent upheaval.

The eleventh-century cathedral and the street scenes seemed unchanged. A few shabby cabs were stationed in the shadow of the cathedral. Youngsters played in the square, shouting the picturesque Como dialect. No great numbers of soldiers were visible, and no Germans at all.

As I was about to wander toward the *prefettura* (police station) I saw two *carabinieri* officers halt a much better-dressed man than I. I headed the other way, toward the public gardens on the shore of the lake.

When I returned to the Piazza Cavour my guide was there with two other men, one a suspicious-looking character with a closely cropped red beard. The guide hailed me and in a loud voice introduced me as *"Un amico Americano!"* scaring the devil out of me.

The men seemed pleased to meet me. They asked when the Allies were coming and said the Italians were eager to fight the Germans. Our bearded friend took us to lunch at a little place in the Via Independenta in front of the post-office.

He said he had spent four years on Ponza Island for his anti-Fascist feelings and was released after Marshal Pietro Badoglio came to power. While he was there he was told that Benito Mussolini had arrived at Ponza, but he was not permitted to see the Duce.

He had heard the German report that Mussolini had been taken away from the Italians by the Germans. He had the impression that Mussolini was taken from Ponza to La Maddalena, off Sardinia, and later to the Soratte mountaintop overlooking the small village of Santa Oreste, about thirty miles from Rome.

I was surprised to find the food quite good, except for the bread, which was bad. When I mentioned this one of the men laughed and said:

"We are not in Milan, and the Germans have not taken over here."

I slept two hours after lunch at the home of our friend, who gave us a start by bringing in word that the Germans were expected in Como from Milan at any hour. He heard reports that Marshal Erwin Rommel intended

576

to move toward Turin from Milan and that Italian troops loyal to Marshal Badoglio still were resisting.

We were advised not to go to Milan, as we had planned, because the Germans certainly would catch us.

Our bearded friend said a small motorboat was ready for us on Lake Como. After a little sightseeing we arrived at the lake at twilight. We rowed out a few miles, then the guide started the motor. In less than an hour we reached the outskirts of Cernopio, left the boat at a previously specified point and proceeded afoot.

For an hour we stumbled through the darkness along the banks of the Breggia River. We ran into a mounted regiment of Italian cavalry, which also was trying to reach the Swiss frontier. The colonel in charge told us it was useless to stay and fight because they had so little ammunition.

We left the cavalry and re-entered Switzerland a few kilometers from Chiasso.

I bade my guide farewell and told him we would go mountain climbing again in peacetime. He grinned and replied:

"Fine, *signore,* this coming Christmas."

SEPTEMBER 17, 1943: *The Germans established a fascist government in Rome.*

SEPTEMBER 18: *The bloody Battle of Salerno began.*

# SALERNO

## *by Quentin Reynolds*

IN the language of war, it was now H plus 15 on D day. To use language more understandable, this was the day we invaded the Naples area, and our assault troops had landed fifteen hours before. It was 6:30 now, and the air was soft and the skies clear, except when the raiders came, and then the sky was pock-marked with ugly black puffs where our antiaircraft shells were exploding. Either our aim was bad or the German planes were very good at evasive tactics, for, although they had already been over us five times, we had not been granted the fine sight of a single Hun plane plunging seaward in flames.

Their bombs had come very, very close to our control ship more than once. We lay there in the Bay of Salerno, a big fat ship so valuable to the success of the operation that four fighting ships had been especially assigned to protect us—if they could. We were the nerve center of the whole operation. Admiral Hewitt stayed on the bridge, directing the naval end of it, while General Mark Clark, commander of the Fifth Army, stayed in the operations room, talking by radio to his generals on the various beaches. Only by remaining here could he get the whole picture and thus shift his reserves to where they were needed. He was desperately anxious to get ashore with his staff, but up to now it had been impossible to set up a headquarters, with its complicated communications system, on land.

The main force of the American division had been forced to delay its landing because a large minefield had been discovered in shallow water just off the beaches. The assault forces of the Americans had landed right on schedule, but they had gone onto the beaches on small LCI's (Landing Craft Infantry), which slid right over the mines. The big LST's (Landing Ship Tanks), with tanks, ammunition, antitank guns and supplies, had to wait until a fairly wide channel was cleared.

Meanwhile, the boys on shore were taking it. They had dug themselves in and were merely trying to keep alive. You can't do much against tanks and 88's that are firmly entrenched in high ground, with your little Tommy guns and rifles and hand grenades.

Now, finally, the minefield had been cleared and from the port deck we watched the long line of big ships go shoreward and we breathed easier. Within an hour our lovely antitank guns would be set up on the beach; our ack-ack guns would be pointing their noses skyward; our portable hospitals would be in operation, and the kids on shore would at least have a reasonable chance of survival. The first rule of an invasion is "Establish your bridgehead." Until you have done that, you can't attack.

The night fell over the bay and the whole 24-mile field of operations as suddenly as though someone had dropped a blanket from above. It is like that here in the Mediterranean. There is very little dusk, but why this is I have no idea.

We forgot the operation for one brief hour while we had dinner. We had soup, steak smothered with onions, French fried potatoes and apple pie. It was the best meal I'd had in six months. The cheerful Negro mess boys, supremely unconscious of danger, joked among themselves and confidentially urged "seconds" on us. I had five cups of American coffee and became an object of awed interest to the mess boys. They didn't know about the coffee made of acorns I had had in Russia for months, or the French coffee made out of God-knows-what I had had in Sicily the past two months. American coffee is the best in the world and I will very gladly fight anyone at any time who thinks differently.

After dinner we listened to the news on the radio. We heard that the Italian fleet was surrendering. Then BBC came on with the news of our operation. The announcer hadn't said a dozen words when the alert screeched through the ship. Once again they were here. But we waited to hear the last of the news.

"On the whole," the smug voice from the loud-speaker said, "the operation in the Bay of Salerno is going according to plan. There is some opposition, but our men have landed and bridgeheads have been established. It may be another day before all opposition is . . ." The ship lurched. "Our air cover is keeping the Luftwaffe away and . . ."

The ship shook as though some playful undersea giant had pushed it.

The ship shuddered. The ship trembled and our ears rang with the con-cussion of a bomb that had fallen close. Then our guns spat angrily into the void of the night. A British pilot who had bailed out that afternoon, and who had been picked up by us, calmly took off his right shoe and de-liberately threw it at the loud-speaker.

"Bloody nonsense!" he said and then mimicked, " 'Our air cover is keep-ing the Luftwaffe away.' "

"Listen, chum," an American colonel put his arm around the youngster's shoulders, "take it easy. Just think what our American radio commentators are saying tonight. They're probably saying that the war is over. We're just naturally optimistic people. *We* know we are getting hell beat out of us on all sides, but they don't know that at home."

We switched to the German radio. We turned it on loud and the excel-lent music the Nazi radio provides—mostly from American records—almost drowned out the sound of the guns. When they put Bing Crosby on, singing an old but lovely song, "Time on My Hands," I laughed and thought of how The Groaner would feel if he knew that the German radio was broadcasting him. I know of no finer American than The Groaner or anyone who has given more time to the war effort than he, and now the Germans were using him to attract audiences.

This, I thought, would be one to tell Bob Hope, whom I had left in Algiers a few days before—that is, if there was anything left of Hope. He had been giving four and five shows a day for a month in Sicily and North Africa. Hope and Crosby! It was good to think of genuine down-to-earth guys like that here in this godforsaken Bay of Salerno.

Enemy planes were over us all night and then it was dawn again, and, in the language of invasion, it was D plus 1. A fast LCVI (Landing Craft Vehicles Infantry) was going ashore with messages from General Clark. I went with it. The blunt nose of our craft (it was built in Perth Amboy, New Jersey) hit the slight swell hard; the spray flew up and the sun tinted it with miniature rainbows. The spray showered us and it was cool and refreshing, for we had our shirts off.

We landed on Yellow Beach. It was a nice beach with fine white sand, extending back perhaps sixty yards. Men were unloading supplies from all kinds of craft that had been run on shore. The unloading stopped once when we all heard the scream of aircraft very low, but it resumed when we saw that they were Spitfires—four of them. They were patrolling up and down the beach at five hundred feet and very lovely they looked.

I slipped my clothes off and waded out into the clear cool water. The Mediterranean is very salty and you can float without any effort. I lay there floating and it was very peaceful. Back of the sand, there was a large white farmhouse with a red roof and beside it a whitewashed granary. A mile back of the beach I could see a collection of houses which had been getting a pasting.

I lay there floating in the cool blue water for half an hour and that was almost as good as a letter from home. Most of the men unloading were naked. Officers watched them carefully. They had to, lest the men from one outfit grab supplies assigned to another outfit. Our Army is great for that. They will steal a battleship if they can get away with it. At night, every jeep driver cannibalizes his car—removes the magneto. Otherwise, his jeep would be gone. Our boys don't call it stealing. They call it "moonlight requisitioning." My boat was due back to our control ship, so I returned with it. On the way we practiced shooting at floating boxes in the water. You've got to have some fun out of an invasion.

We had another bad night aboard, with stuff coming as close as it can come without hitting you. We had four alerts during the night, which meant, of course, that no one slept. Four times the red, streaking tracers from our ships split the night wide open. Four times the determined Luftwaffe, throwing everything it had into this all-out effort, came at us. (Note: The Navy Department does not allow us to mention ships sunk or ships damaged. If there were sinkings or damage to ships done in the Bay of Salerno, they will be announced in due course by the Navy Department.) It was a bad night as, by now, everyone was tired and weary of taking the beating without a chance of fighting back.

When dawn came to present us with D plus 2, we were met with the startling sight of a submarine not a hundred yards from us. This was an Italian submarine coming in to surrender. The captain had seen the admiral's flag flying from our mast and had rightly come alongside us. He tied up to our port side, and the crew, immaculate in blue trousers and white undershirts, gazed curiously up at us. A small dog barked joyously from the narrow deck of the sub. I went aboard and met the captain, a 24-year-old citizen of Naples who talked almost perfect English. He was happy that his country had come in on our side, but a bit rueful.

"You know," he said quite seriously, "I hadn't fired a torpedo for five weeks. Then I got the order not to fire on any American or British ships. An hour after I got that order, what happened? This big, fat convoy passes within a mile of where I had surfaced. Oh, it was a great temptation!"

"I'm glad you weren't trigger-happy," I told him, "like so many of our kids."

The expression "trigger-happy" was too much for him. I explained that our gunners, in the heat of battle, quite often just bang away at any target in sight. I had seen this happen a dozen times when sustained bombings had torn ragged nerves and had made gunners lose their sense of judgment, had made them trigger-happy or kill-crazy.

A grinning white-coated Negro messboy from our ship came down the narrow ladder with a huge tray. "With the captain's compliments, sir," he said, and placed the tray on the table. The submarine's captain blinked when he saw a huge Virginia ham lying there. The small dog smelled the ham and started leaping happily toward it. The messboy patted him, and the dog loved it.

"You want a dog?" the captain asked the messboy.

580

"Ah'm a man who loves dawgs," the Negro said happily, "and, Captain, Ah means that dogs loves me, too."

"We have four puppies aboard," the captain said. "If you would like one, take him."

He took us into the crew's sleeping quarters and there on a blanket were four incredibly small, brown-and-white puppies. This messboy grabbed one and cradled it in his hand.

"Sir, from now on, you is our mascot," he grinned. "And, Lordy, Lordy, how we need a mascot! And from now on, your name is Sir."

We took the puppy back with us. The news in the operations room wasn't good. We had captured an airport at Montecavido, near Salerno. A Spitfire had landed there and had no sooner stopped than an 88 shell from a German gun up in the hills had blasted it into eternity. Our air protection would still have to come from Sicily, 180 miles away. This whole operation was assuming the proportions of another Gallipoli. It was touch-and-go whether we would be thrown out entirely. Our casualties were heavy because the Germans held the high ground and could pour a withering fire down at us.

A group of German prisoners was brought aboard for questioning. They waited on the boat deck. They had been captured on the island of Ventotene by a very small Navy force. That was a real Dick Tracy stunt. A U.S. Navy captain, Lieutenant Commander Douglas Fairbanks, Jr., two sailors and War Correspondent John Steinbeck had landed in a PT boat and grabbed this island and the 91 German radio operators and radar men who were on it. They had come aboard during the day, tired but happy.

"They had told us that there were no Germans on the island," Steinbeck laughed. "So we landed with flashlights lit and yelling to one another, and they thought we had an army with us. Hell, the captain and Doug Fairbanks had nothing but Tommy guns with them and, so help me, they took the whole island! Two very tough citizens they are."

"We got a very good Navy, John," I said.

"We got one hell of a Navy!" the author of *The Grapes of Wrath* laughed.

One of the prisoners was seriously wounded and they took him to the sick bay below. The doctor asked me to come along to translate for him. I winced at that, because my German is the kind you learn from a Berlin menu card, but I went along. Prisoners are always given a questionnaire to fill in, and, because we treat our prisoners well, even to the extent of furnishing them with chaplains of their own particular denomination, one question to be filled out is: "What is your religion?"

I translated that for the man who lay there very close to death. He sneered at the doctor and said, "Put down Naziism. That is my religion."

He had been a tank man before being transferred to the island. He had been in Berlin only four weeks before.

"What for?" I asked.

"For a hernia operation."

There was the scar. It was encouraging to know that the German army

581

was so short of manpower that it was putting men back into combat zones only four weeks after they had been operated upon.

The news continued to be bad. A courier came from ashore to say that Jack Belden had caught it. He had been shot in the hip and the knee. Jack Belden of *Time* and *Life* went through more combat in Sicily than any other correspondent. We had a room together when we returned to Algiers. Shanghai Jack is a good man to live with. We left on the same day for this show, each being assigned to different ships, and when we left, Jack said, "Well, chum, here we go trying to beat the law of averages again."

By now, the men were haggard, wearing tired faces and frayed tempers, and their nerves were jumpy. You can take only so much sustained bombing, and then it gets you.

It got all of us. Our air cover over the land was excellent but here in the bay we were not so well protected. It's hard to protect more than 700 ships.

Only General Clark preserved his absolute calm, his good humor, and yet we knew that he suffered more than anyone on board. He had trained this Fifth Army. He had appointed its commanders, and now it was ashore fighting, and he had to remain here directing the whole show from our ship.

Lionel Shapiro of the *Montreal Gazette,* Reynolds Packard of the United Press, Sammy Schulman, the photographer from INS, and I were the only correspondents aboard.

We had written our stories, but there was no way to get them to a cable office. We were writing to ourselves and there is nothing more annoying to a correspondent. I decided to make my way to Syracuse in Sicily, if possible, for there we had censors and cable facilities.

General Montgomery had sent a fast submarine chaser to us with his aide on board. The aide was leaving now to report to Montgomery. I decided to go along. I said goodby to General Clark and, most disconcertingly, the general laughed and said, "I forgot to give you a message from Butch." ("Butch" is Commander Harry Butcher, naval aide to General Eisenhower, and one of the most popular officers in this benighted part of the world.)

"I had dinner with Butch the night we left Algiers," General Clark said smilingly. "And he asked me to give you an order. The order is: Don't get his watch wet."

I remembered now a week before when my watch had broken, Butch had lent me his. I had, of course, carefully avoided him thereafter and still wore his very fine watch on my wrist. I told General Clark that I would do my best to keep it out of salt water. I didn't mention that I had been swimming two days before with the watch on my wrist.

Then I hopped aboard that slim, fast sub chaser and headed for General Montgomery's headquarters, ten hours away. "Monty" had headquarters in an olive grove a few miles inland. Instead of commandeering a villa for his headquarters, Monty lived in his three beautifully appointed trailers. He showed me through them.

"I captured this one from General Messe in Tripoli," he said, showing the largest one. Its walls were of cedar and it held a large bed, a desk and a bathroom. The bathroom had everything including a huge bathtub.

"When I have a guest"—Monty's eyes twinkled—"I give him my guest house on wheels. Come, look at it. I captured that from Old Electric Whiskers—General Bergonzoli—in North Africa. The king found it comfortable when he stayed with me. So did my great friend, Wendell Willkie."

This one was even more elaborate. It had pictures on the wall and it, too, had a gleaming white tiled bathroom. Monty likes his headquarters to be mobile. These two huge trucks and a third smaller one containing his maps can be shifted at a moment's notice.

After the inspection, we sat outside under the trees and, for the moment, it was very pleasant being away from the hell of the Bay of Salerno.

"Notice my birds?" Monty said, pointing. A large cage hung to a tree close by, and four bright yellow canaries were singing in a joyous song. "I picked them up in Tunis. Would you like some cold lemonade? Of course. Let's have some. And have a drop of gin in yours. It'll do you good."

Then finally I realized the innate kindness of this man. He had seen that I was jittery and a little bit deaf from the sound of guns and altogether wound up like a top, and he was making me unwind by his talk of birds and his captured trucks.

I laughed and took the cold drink his orderly had brought, and I did in fact become relaxed and normal. I looked at Monty with new interest because I had never thought of him as a sensitive person. He sat in a comfortable chair, his fine teeth showing whitely when he smiled, and he talked of the Salerno operation as a general talks of military operations.

"I am running up there tomorrow," he said, "merely to ask General Clark if there is anything I can do to help. Naturally, I am anxious to reach there to join Clark and his Fifth. I suppose"—he smiled wryly—"our people at home think the war is over, now that we have landed in Italy?"

"I suppose so," I said a little bitterly, thinking of what was happening in the Bay of Salerno.

Monty leaned forward, very serious now. "Actually, the war has finally begun. The side issues, Libya, North Africa, Sicily—these have been cleared away, and now we can really get down to it. Yes, when we landed in Italy, it marked the beginning of our war against Germany. Until now, it has been Germany's war against us. We have a long, difficult fight ahead of us. The Hun is a great professional soldier, and from now on, we will fight his best divisions.

"Yes, it is going to be very difficult. Mind you, I have confidence in my army and in men like General Clark and your magnificent General Omar Bradley with whom I worked in Sicily, but it is going to be a long fight. Sometimes, you know"—he smiled ruefully—"I lose my temper when I read stories of people at home taking it for granted that the war is as good as won. Believe me, it isn't."

I left Monty and hitchhiked a ride on a British gunboat which was heading for Syracuse. I'm writing this in the tiny wardroom of the gunboat and I keep thinking of the Bay of Salerno. At last, as Monty said, this war has finally begun.

# IT WAS DARK AS HELL

### by John Steinbeck

SOMEWHERE in the Mediterranean Theater.—There is a good beach at Salerno, and a very good landing at Red Beach No. 2. The ducks were coming loaded ashore and running up out of the water and joining the lines of trucks, and the pontoon piers were out in the water with large landing cars up against them. Along the beach the bulldozers were at work pushing up sand ramps for the trucks to land on and just back of the beach were the white tapes that mean land mines have not been cleared out.

There are little bushes on the sand dunes at Red Beach south of the Sele River, and in a hole in the sand buttressed by sand bags a soldier sat with a leather covered steel telephone beside him. His shirt was off and his back was dark with sunburn. His helmet lay in the bottom of the hole and his rifle was on a little pile of brush to keep the sand out of it. He had staked a shelter half on a pole to shade him from the sun, and he had spread bushes on top of that to camouflage it. Beside him was a water can and an empty "C" ration can to drink out of.

The soldier said, "Sure you can have a drink. Here, I'll pour it for you." He tilted the water can over the tin cup. "I hate to tell you what it tastes like," he said. I took a drink. "Well, doesn't it?" he said. "It sure does," I said. Up in the hills the 88's were popping and the little bursts threw sand about where they hit, and off to the seaward our cruisers were popping away at the 88's in the hills.

The soldier slapped at a sand fly on his shoulder and then scratched the place where it had bitten him. His face was dirty and streaked where the sweat had run down through the dirt, and his hair and his eyebrows were sunburned almost white. But there was a kind of gayety about him. His telephone buzzed and he answered it, and said, "Hasn't come through yet, sir, no sir. I'll tell him." He clicked off the phone.

"When'd you come ashore?" he asked. And then without waiting for an answer he went on. "I came in just before dawn yesterday. I wasn't with the very first, but right in the second." He seemed to be very glad about it. "It was hell," he said, "it was bloody hell." He seemed to be gratified at the hell it was, and that was right. The great question had been solved for him. He had been under fire. He knew now what he would do under fire. He would never have to go through that uncertainty again. "I got pretty near up to there," he said, and pointed to two beautiful Greek temples about a mile away. "And then I got sent back here for beach communications.

584

When did you say you got ashore?" and again he didn't wait for an answer.

"It was dark as hell," he said, "and we were just waiting out there." He pointed to the sea where the mass of the invasion fleet rested. "If we thought we were going to sneak ashore we were nuts," he said. "They were waiting for us all fixed up. Why, I heard they had been here two weeks waiting for us. They knew just where we were going to land. They had machine guns in the sand dunes and 88's on the hills.

"We were out there all packed in an L. C. I. and then the hell broke loose. The sky was full of it and the star shells lighted it up and the tracers crisscrossed and the noise—we saw the assault go in, and then one of them hit a surf mine and went up, and in the light you could see them go flying about. I could see the boats land and the guys go wiggling and running, and then maybe there'd be a lot of white lines and some of them would waddle about and collapse and some would hit the beach.

"It didn't seem like men getting killed, more like a picture, like a moving picture. We were pretty crowded up in there though, and then all of a sudden it came on me that this wasn't a moving picture. Those were guys getting the hell shot out of them, and then I got kind of scared, but what I wanted to do mostly was move around. I didn't like being cooped up there where you couldn't get away or get down close to the ground.

"Well the firing would stop and then it would get pitch black even then, and it was just beginning to get light too but the 88's sort of winked on the hills like messages, and the shells were bursting all around us. They had lots of 88's and they shot at everything. I was just getting real scared when we got the order to move in, and I swear that is the longest trip I ever took, that mile to the beach. I thought we'd never get there. I figured that if I was only on the beach I could dig down and get out of the way. There was too damn many of us there in that L. C. I. I wanted to spread out. That one that hit the mine was still burning when we went on by it. Then we bumped the beach and the ramps went down and I hit the water up to my waist.

"The minute I was on the beach I felt better. It didn't seem like everybody was shooting at me, and I got up to that line of brush and flopped down and some other guys flopped down beside me and then we got feeling a little foolish. We stood up and moved on. Didn't say anything to each other, we just moved on. It was coming daylight then and the flashes of the guns weren't so bright. I felt a little like I was drunk. The ground heaved around under my feet and I was dull. I guess that was because of the firing. My ears aren't so good yet. I guess we moved up too far because I got sent back here." He laughed openly. "I might have gone on right into Rome if some one hadn't sent me back. I guess I might have walked right up that hill there."

The cruisers began firing on the hill and the 88's fired back. From over near the hill came the heavy thudding of .50-caliber machine guns. The soldier felt pretty good. He knew what he could do now. He said, "When did you say you came ashore?"

# REPORT FROM SWITZERLAND

*by Daniel T. Brigham*

BERNE, Switzerland, Sept. 20—Strongly reinforced by entire companies of regular Italian troops that overpowered their thinly spread German "captors" in the northern Po Valley, remnants of the Italian Fourth Army that have been fighting the Germans since Friday morning were reported today to have captured the town of Carmagnola, midway between Cuneo and Turin, after having killed or captured a strong German mechanized force garrisoned there.

The Italians' ranks, as they advance, are being swelled by thousands of workers and dissident Italian regulars, who in many places have had to overcome their Blackshirt officers before successfully withdrawing to the bush.

Attempts to reinforce the German garrisons on the upper Po were hampered by Fourth Army snipers, who have completely blocked the Montcenis Tunnel, the most direct route for reinforcements from France. Despite the efforts of German mountain patrols, the sappers continue their work of mining strategic roads and bridges along the frontier, rendering them all but impassable.

When the Montcenis Tunnel was exploded on Sept. 9, it was learned today, an armored German troop train attempting to block the Italians' escape was rushed into the 7.8-mile tunnel, with machine guns on a flat car ahead of the locomotive ready in case of an ambush. One mile inside a heavy mine exploded in the roof of the tunnel, killing at least thirty German soldiers and wounding hundreds more. Later a reconnaissance hand-car pushed over the wreckage was surprised 800 yards farther on. An escort of ten German soldiers and two officers was wiped out, though a French driver escaped with serious injuries.

After the Germans had withdrawn from the tunnel, the Italians blew up two more mines, bringing the walls and roofs down over three-quarters of a mile. A German report from Modane, France, said today that the continual slipping of rock, sand and water would make the reopening of the tunnel the work of at least two months.

Elsewhere in the upper Po Valley, dissidents at Monte Bracco were reported by the Guistizia e Libertà radio to have wiped out two companies of German Alpine troops ambushed in a narrow valley. German punitive expeditions, the broadcast said, retaliated by executing sixty-five hostages at Paesana, but fighting in the neighborhood continued until 3:30 P.M. today, when the report was made.

OCTOBER 2, 1943: *Naples fell to the Allies.*

# DEATH OF A LIBRARY

## by Herbert L. Matthews

NAPLES, Oct. 8—The worst example of German vandalism since the burning of the University of Louvain library in the First World War was the deliberate setting on fire, with gasoline and hand grenades, of the precious and extensive library of the Royal Society of Naples, which comprises four scientific and philosophic academies.

At the same time, with equal thoroughness and ruthlessness, the Germans burned out all the administrative offices and other rooms of the University of Naples, the third oldest and one of the largest institutions of learning in the world. This is not hearsay: I inspected the burned premises and took evidence from, among others, Professor Adolfo Amodeo, rector of the university; Dr. Arturo Imparato, administrative director; Professor Gino Bergami, a Professor of Physiology, whom the Allied Military Government placed in charge of the civilian public health services, and Professor Baldassarre de Lerma.

They will make "the most solemn protest possible" to Geneva and other world cultural centers. It is expected that the ceremony of re-dedication of the university and the Royal Society will also take place under the Allies' auspices.

On Sunday, Sept. 19, a German soldier or officer was shot by a *franc-tireur* in the Via Mezzocannone, which runs alongside the university and the Royal Society, which is attached to it and houses the university library. On Sundays, the rector and others said, no one is in the huge university building except the caretakers, who are beyond suspicion.

The Germans first closed the buildings around the university, herding together all the men, women and children found in them. One man, chosen at random, was shot before all the others. That was typical German brutality.

Three days before, some of the professors said, a sailor and a friend were returning from barracks when, on the main steps of the university, they met four German soldiers. Whatever the reason, the Germans began to beat up the Italians. The one who survived said that he had offered no resistance and had been rescued by a doughty female from across the street, who ran out and pulled him into a doorway. The other sailor tried to fight back and was shot dead. For an hour or two, the Germans stood there inviting passersby to see what happened to Italians who did not know their place.

On Sunday the Germans broke into the university after having carefully organized their procedure—squads of men, trucks with dozens and dozens of five-gallon gasoline tins and supplies of hand-grenades. Their objective was deliberate and their work was as methodical and thorough as German work always is. The university was founded in 1224 by Emperor Frederick II.

The soldiers went from room to room, thoroughly soaking floors, walls

587

and furniture, including archives that went back for centuries. The part of the university chosen was that where the rector, the dean and wholly administrative personnel worked. That it happened to contain archives and valuable documents on law and letters was beside the point.

When everything was ready, the second stage began. The soldiers went from room to room, throwing in hand-grenades. At the same time, in an adjoining building a few hundred yards up the street, an even greater act of vandalism was being perpetrated. There was something apt about it, something symbolic of the whole German attitude. It did not matter to the Germans that they were destroying the accumulated wealth of centuries of scientific and philosophical thinking.

The rooms of the Royal Society contained some 200,000 books and manuscripts, from not only Italy but every country in the world. These books were stacked neatly and soberly on shelves along the walls; in the middle of the rooms were plain wooden tables with chairs. In several rooms there were paintings—some of them by Francesco Solimene of Nocera, the great baroque architect of the seventeenth century. These had been lent by the National Museum, but they will never be returned.

Like everything else they are now heaps of ashes that I plowed through today like so much sand on a beach. Here too the Germans used the same efficient technique—gallons and gallons of gasoline and then hand-grenades.

The Germans' thoroughness, however, was not yet quite satisfied. After all, universities have professors. They went to the homes of a number of professors and burned the buildings.

Dr. Imparato took us around the university, accompanied by a number of professors. He showed us what had been his office. The floor was nothing but an uneven mass of ashes six inches deep. The walls were scarred and pitted and the ceiling had almost collapsed.

He showed us the room where the archives had been kept. It looked exactly the same. So did that whole wing of the building. The Germans had found a common denominator for everything in the cultural line: they just turned it all into ashes.

In view of what German propaganda may assert after our stories have appeared, I should state here that this damage could not possibly have been done by bombing or by ordinary fires. Nothing but gasoline and explosives placed in each room could have done it.

This became even clearer when we visited the library of the Royal Society. Every one knows how difficult it is to burn one solid unopened book thoroughly until nothing remains but a heap of fine ashes. The Germans burned some 200,000 books in that way. Of course, the fire had to rage a long time and—also of course—the German thoroughness was going to see to it that nothing interfered with the fire.

They set it at 6 P.M. Sunday. At 9 P.M. Italian fire-fighting squads came up to extinguish the flames. German guards prevented them from entering the Via Mezzocannone. For three days those fires continued burning and for three days German guards kept Italians away.

We found American troops on guard over the remains of the library. The Germans burned only the rooms on the street. Behind, on an inner court, is the university library. Fortunately, both the university and the society buildings are modern, fireproof structures and the fire did not spread. We found two rooms of the society library untouched. By coincidence they contained American publications and were set in from the street.

The huge Royal Palace is a sad wreck of what it once was. American soldiers are guarding it until the Italians take over. It is much more damaged than I realized on looking at it from the outside on the first day. Before it can ever be used again, it will have to be extensively repaired or perhaps even rebuilt.

The concert hall has been destroyed. Other rooms have holes in ceilings and broken doors. Bits of glass lie everywhere. Fortunately, all the available material in the palace had long been removed to places of safety. Most of the large paintings were left on the walls, but they were not of much value and are undamaged in many cases.

# POLITICAL STRATEGY

*by Frederick Kuh*

LONDON, Oct. 11.—The glow of satisfaction pervading the British people at the military course of the war is being dimmed by recurrent discontent concerning our political strategy.

When Parliament reassembles in the next few days after its recess, members will ask several pointed questions of the Government. These questions show a growing disquiet regarding our backward political methods in Italy.

Churchill's popularity is at its zenith and is likely to be fortified by a forthcoming event and it would be utterly wrong to read into these manifestations of discontent anything like a serious challenge to his Government's power. In the coming Parliamentary session the good fortune which has so often rallied to his great natural gifts will again come to Churchill's aid.

On the second sitting day of Commons' impending session Liberal member of Parliament Geoffrey Mander, will ask the Government to "consider the advisability of demanding from the Italian Government the surrender of Generals Ambrosio and Roatta as war criminals."

Both of these men belong to Badoglio's new Government. Ambrosio is Chief of Staff of all Italian armed forces. Roatta is Chief of Staff of the Army.

From 1936 through 1938 Gen. Mario Roatta played a big part in defeating the Spanish Republic in the civil war and clinching the victory for Hitler and Mussolini's candidate, namely, Franco. Roatta commanded the Italian *Frecci* division in Spain and the best that can be said for him is that he bears the blame for Franco's greatest military reverse—Guadalajara. He succeeded Marshal Graziani as Chief of Staff of the Italian Army in March, 1941, and stands high on the Yugoslav Government's list of war criminals.

Gen. Vittorio Ambrosio is a cavalryman who seems to have a special talent for riding the wrong horse. In April, 1942, he commanded the Second Italian Army in the invasion of Yugoslavia.

The Weekly *Economist* calls the inclusion of Roatta and Ambrosio in Badoglio's present junta "crazy politics" and recalls the reputation of both generals for ruthless terrorism in Yugoslavia.

Eight other members of Parliament are ready to put questions to the British Government demanding a clear pronouncement of whether Victor Emanuel is still recognized as Emperor of Ethiopia, which he continued to call himself in a decree Badoglio issued on Sept. 23. One member is also demanding that Badoglio be deprived of the title of Duke of Addis Ababa in view of his use of poison gas against the defenseless Abyssinians.

Dissatisfaction with our Italian policy even permeates the Conservative ranks of Parliament and a Tory member, Sir Archibald Southby, has given notice of his intention to ask the Government in Commons to "assure that use of the phrase co-belligerent implies no intention to treat Italy as an Ally against Germany, instead of a defeated enemy in view of the loss of life and suffering caused by Italy's alliance with Germany."

Another MP, Squadron Leader Fleming, intends to ask Churchill "whether he is satisfied that the activities of the Allied Military Government in Sicily are based on principles of democracy."

These currents of uneasiness find a sharp expression in the *Economist* which in discussing our political strategy in Italy declared we are "flouting political good sense in a grand manner." The magazine continues "The truth is that Military approval is being used as an alternative for political strategy because the Allies have no political strategy."

The *Economist* concludes we have only one consistent policy, "the restoration of something very like the 1939 status. The total picture is one of considerable confusion. No clear lead is being given to forces of political resistance in Europe."

It's being said that the walls of Jericho which were to have fallen at the united blast of Russian, British and American trumpets, remain unshaken at the unnerving cacophony of a couple of cornets and a police whistle.

# BLACK EAGLE GOES TO WAR

## by Edgar T. Rouzeau

SOMEWHERE in Italy.—They take death lightly, these brownskin pilots of America's first Negro fighter squadron, these pilots joking with one another in front of an operations tent sitting in a field strewn with the wreckage of German and Italian planes.

They are awaiting the roll call of those who are going over German-held territory in the day's first mission. But no one would think it, to hear their salty sallies:

"Hey, Mills—If you don't bring down the first German you meet up there, I'm going to kick you all over this field when you get back."

"Me, too," another pilot put in. "And remember, it's my plane you're flying. I don't want any bullet holes in it. If you just have to get shot at, you see to it that they get you."

A jeep pulls up. The operations officer steps out. Like all officers of the squadron from Commander down, he, too, is colored. He makes his way through the circle of pilots until he is face to face with a map of Italy mounted on a board in front of the operations tent. He refers to a list he has brought with him and reads the following:

"Capt. Hall, Lieut. Carter, Lieut. Wiley, Lieut. Rayford, Lieut. Campbell, Lieut. Knighten, Lieut. Mills...."

Several pairs of eyes look around for Lieut. Mills. The roll call over, some of the pilots walk over to congratulate and give advice.

Clinton B. Mills hails from Durham, N. C., where his father is a prominent physician. He has recently joined the squadron as a replacement and is about to go out on his first sortie, a mission over enemy territory where planes and pilots run risks from ground flak or in air combat. And where is there a veteran pilot who doesn't show interest in a recruit who is going out on his first.

"Today's target...." The operations officer is speaking again. The briefing has begun. It is the sum total of all instructions concerning the mission. The men who are going out crowd forward to see better on the target map which has now been placed beside the map of Italy.

The pilots are told to leave their base at —— time and proceed to —— place where the bombers will be awaiting them in mid-air.

The Intelligence Section takes over in the person of a Lieutenant from Boston, Mass. He points on the map of Italy to those areas where ground or air opposition may be expected. This part of the briefing is based on the experiences of other pilots who have flown the region.

There is a short pause while the group awaits the squadron commander. When his jeep arrives, all talking dies out. The C.O. is Capt. George Spencer Roberts, of Fairmont, W. Va. He, too, is on the mission. It is an unwritten law of the Air Corps that no commander may expose his pilots to risks which he himself will not undertake.

The C.O. speaks to his men in short, crisp sentences. They are cautioned to be particularly watchful "here" and to do "this" in case "that" happens. There is also a word of encouragement for the new recruit, Lieut. Mills. The C.O. then walks to the map of Italy and traces the course the mission will take to and from the target.

His last words are more of a suggestion than an order. "I think we had better go to our ships now," he says.

Lieut. Mills crowds with other pilots into one of several waiting jeeps and is taken to the flying field. Standing beside his plane is his crew chief, a staff sergeant who is chief nursemaid for that particular plane.

The crew chief makes a few observations. "Engine in good shape. Armament and Communications have checked your guns and your radio." The enlisted man salutes, half-turns, and then adds as an after-thought, "Good luck to you, Lieutenant."

The first planes are taking off. They race down the runway, two abreast, and rise as beautiful as sea gulls. Eight planes are in the air before Mills and his team-mate, a veteran of many sorties, receive the "go" signal.

As his ship begins to climb, Mills keeps an eye on his team-mate and looks around for the other planes. He soon locates them in the distance. The first four are flying abreast and are moving in a huge circle so as to give the others a chance to short-cut and catch up.

With every engine contributing its share to the harmonious hum, the squadron flies forward to the rendezvous with the bombers. The squadron formation is made up of flights which have been given color designations for this mission. The flights, in turn, are made up of teams of two planes each. The two-plane team is the smallest fighting unit of the squadron. Every effort is made to keep teams inseparable with the object of giving pilots the opportunity to acquaint themselves with each other's flying style. This intimate knowledge helps them to protect each other in air combat.

The clock system is used for all air operations. The position directly forward is 12 o'clock. Directly rear is 6 o'clock. The presence of planes, whether identified as friendly or enemy, must be reported on these clock positions by the pilot who sees them.

Now the squadron is drawing off to the right. Mills kicks his rudder to keep up with the other planes. He looks at his wrist watch and finds that they have just about covered the distance to the bomber rendezvous. He roves his eyes above and below and is thrilled by what he sees.

Several thousand feet above, a Spitfire squadron is swishing into top cover position. Down below the bombers are in formation, flying in a circle to await the escorts. The colored pilots dip their planes to the specified height for close cover and separate into flights to take up combat positions.

The three formations, flying at different levels, are now pointing towards the enemy. Mills calculates that they will be flying about twenty minutes before they reach the target. Meanwhile, he tries to think of some of the things the C.O. and others have told him during the briefing period before he left his field.

"Keep cool. If you see any Germans, don't run off and chase them. Wait until they attack. It is their object to penetrate the fighter cover so as to get the bombers. They will succeed in this aim if they can draw you out of position.

"Remember, bombers represent the striking power of our air arm and are manned by a large crew. Fighters are normally defensive weapons. If we lose one bomber because of negligence in protecting them, we will have failed in our mission even though we destroy two enemy fighters. . . ."

Lieut. Mills' thoughts are suddenly interrupted. He realizes that someone is talking. The voice is coming from the earphones in his flying headgear.

"Hello, Dunbar Red Leader. This is Dunbar Blue Four. Six boogies 10 o'clock high. . . ."

As the voice dies out, Mills' trained mind deciphers the airman's message. Red is the color designation the squadron was given for this mission. Blue is the designation for one of the flights. Boogies is air jargon for unidentified planes. Hence, the No. 4 pilot in blue flight is reporting to the squadron commander that there are six unidentified planes flying high and to the right of the No. 4 man's position.

The earphones crackle again. "Bandits," the voice says, meaning that the planes have been identified as enemies. The voice gives instructions:

"They probably haven't seen our top cover. When they do, they will probably dive fast. Blank flight will watch for this move and meet the first attackers. Other flights will stay in formation until further orders."

The expected happens. The German airmen finally spot the Spitfires above and have to "break." They are outnumbered and don't wish to fight. The nearest three are diving in the direction of the bombers and one of the flights in the close cover formation turns around to meet the expected attack. But the attack does not materialize. The Germans have noticed the defensive move by the Negro pilots and have now changed their course. They start climbing in another direction and are soon lost to sight.

Now the bombers are approaching the target area. They wheel and dive to the specified bombing level given in the briefing. The squadron assigned to close cover follows them down.

Mills feels his muscles getting tense. He sees the burst of an anti aircraft shell straight ahead. It looks just as they said it would—a rapidly widening smudge. He is unable to see much more, but he knows that the bursting shell has scattered bits of shrapnel with terrific velocity in all directions.

Mills is squeamish about looking down. But from the corner of his eye he sees that the bombers furthest to his right are weaving and turning, changing height and direction so as to confuse the ground gunners. The colored squadron follows the bombers around with the faithfulness of a watch dog. The pilots know that the larger ships cannot be left alone because sometimes enemy fighters will risk the flak and dive down to make a bomber kill.

593

Now the target comes into view. Mills looks down just in time to see the awesome sight. The bombers have opened their belly hatches and the deadly cylinders are falling out. Mills sees them for a second and then they disappear in the haze. Seconds later he sees the splashy pattern which the bombs are making on the target area. He sees what appears to be a geyser of sand. He sees a building crumble. He sees a gaping hole appear where a bridge was suspended like a slender white string a moment earlier.

Again Mills hears the authoritative voice in his earphones. This time it's instructions for the turn. Mills keeps his eye on his team-mate and executes the movement.

The bombers, freed of their bomb weight, have changed characteristics. They are much faster now. The fighter squadrons do not have to hold back so much speed to stay with them. The return journey appears so much shorter. They recross the enemy's front lines and are soon in sight of friendly landmarks. The authoritative voice speaks again in the earphones. The colored squadron wheels to the right. The bombers are close to their own field and no longer need protection. At that moment Lieut. Mills looks down and sees one of the lead bombers wag its wings in an air salute.

The engines of the colored squadron still drone harmoniously. But Mills is deep in thought. He is awed by the greatness of the Air Force, proud of his humble part in it, proud of the spirit of unstinted co-operation which permeates its fighting sons. But most of all, he thinks of the great country of which he is a citizen. It fills him with a strange feeling and he cannot seem to find words for what he feels.

# BATTLE OF VOLTURNO

## by Homer Bigart

WITH the 5th Army in Italy, Oct. 16.—The battle of the Volturno River has ended in a complete victory for the 5th Army, and the Allied troops under Lieutenant General Mark W. Clark's command have resumed their march on Rome after bridging the river at numerous places and securing a firm grip on the northern bank.

Three defeated German divisions were withdrawing today toward prepared positions in the mountains twenty miles north of the Volturno. The toll of prisoners and booty taken by the 5th Army is not considerable. The prisoners said, however, that the Germans had suffered severe casualties from the Allied artillery, whose barrage in opening the drive surpassed any other big-gun action in the Mediterranean area since the blasting of the Germans at Alamein, Egypt, almost a year ago.

The best progress was made by American troops who seized dominating heights north of Capua and relieved pressure on a British division south of the town, which the enemy had retaken Tuesday night in a surprise counterattack a few minutes before the Allied offensive began.

594

# THE SYSTEM OF ATROCITIES

*by Reynolds Packard*

NAPLES, Oct. 21—Secretary of the Treasury Henry Morgenthau is carry-ing home to President Roosevelt a list prepared by Allied Military Govern-ment officials of thirteen categories of atrocities which the Germans inflicted upon Naples before they withdrew under Allied attack.

The amazing document was edited personally by Col. Edgar Erskine Hume from Virginia, who heads the Allied Military Government in Italy.

One of the charges is that the Nazis, just before fleeing Naples, threw open the doors of thirteen prisons for dangerous criminals. Men who had been sentenced to long terms for murder, rape, homosexuality, hold-ups and other crimes—born killers and other pathological criminals—were released upon a battle-shattered populace already suffering complete disruption of its civic existence.

Thousands of these criminals were roaming the streets of Naples when the Allies entered the city but they are now being rounded up.

One portion of the report says textually:

"The Germans collectively and individually robbed shops, homes and even people in the streets.

"There were many murders, including those of a sadistic nature wherein dead bodies were mutilated, especially those of women.

"German booby traps were placed where they might be set off not only by our troops but by civilians, including children, many of whom were killed.

"There was much wanton destruction of property, with physical harm to people.

"Food supplies were destroyed or fouled. Cruel measures were taken against Italians between 18 and 35 years of age who failed to respond to the German demands for forced labor. Many people, including women, were beaten to make them disclose the whereabouts of supposed valuables."

Destruction of the University of Naples, described as "one of the oldest and most famous in existence," was detailed.

"The library of the Royal Society of Naples, one of the great learned societies of the world, was housed in the university," the report said. "It was put to the torch on the twelfth of September, a little over a fortnight before we took the city. We are collecting affidavits of faculty members and students who agree that some 600 Germans entered the university, announc-ing that they were about to burn it in retaliation for fighting by Neapolitan students against their troops.

"Cans of gasoline were brought in and the walls, furniture and books covered with it and a fire started. Firemen arrived immediately but were refused admittance.

"Two *carabinieri* who tried to halt the destruction were taken to the

595

front entrance and shot. Witnesses avow that the notorious Colonel Scholl, commander of the German troops at Naples, arrived when the work of destruction was under way and read a proclamation in German and Italian announcing that the university was being wrecked as a punishment to the city of Naples."

Here is a summary of the Hume report's thirteen categories:

1. The Germans destroyed the water supply, blowing up the main aqueduct in seven places and draining the reservoirs. "The Germans were well aware," the report said, "that we were able to bring water for the troops and therefore this was an act of cruelty against the people of Naples, old and young."

2. Pumping facilities and the sewage disposal system were destroyed, creating the danger of typhoid fever, dysentery and other contagion.

3. The Germans destroyed the generators, transformers and all other essential parts of the electrical system, depriving the Neapolitans of power to run flour mills, heat buildings, cook meals, publish newspapers. Electricity was especially important to Naples where it was in unusually widespread use.

4. The transportation system for civilians was utterly destroyed. The Germans carried off all the rolling stock from busses to horses and buggies.

5. The Nazis blew up the telephone exchange, cut lines and dynamited power plants connected with the communications system.

6. Demolition squads razed hotels including one of the most magnificent in the world. They set fire to the rubble.

7. The Germans even blew up tunnels through the hills which had been bored so the people would not have to trudge up and down the many steep hills.

8. The cunning of the Germans was shown when they planted time bombs set to go off after the Allies' arrival such as that which slaughtered many Italian women and children in the post office.

9. The Germans threw open the doors of the prisons, releasing dangerous criminals.

10. Demolition of the flour mills was a sad blow because it deprived the Neapolitans of their macaroni and bread, staples.

11. The University and library were razed, as described.

12. Germans looted the hospitals of dressings, instruments and medicines, leaving doctors and nurses almost powerless to care for the unnumbered victims of brutality.

13. In addition to many atrocities against the people of the Naples area, some of which have been described above, the Germans carried off many hostages, including the Bishop of Cava Dei Terreni and the Abbot of Badia at Corpo di Cava.

# THE ALBANIANS FIGHT BACK

## by Henry T. Gorrell

WITH a British destroyer flotilla off Durazzo, Albania, Nov. 3.—Albanian guerrillas slipped inside the German coastal batteries at Durazzo today and beheaded the Nazi gunners. They cleared the way for an uninterrupted British warship bombardment that pounded the big Axis-held Albanian seaport to a pulp.

This flotilla raced in under flares dropped by the Royal Air Force and set Durazzo ablaze with a twenty-five-minute bombardment at point-blank range, then we retired without drawing a shot from the surprised German garrison. From my vantage point on the bridge of H. M. S. *Quilliam*, flagship of the British squadron, I watched the waterfront area disappear in a burst of flame and debris.

Under the flares and the light from flaming warehouses I could see German staff officers running along the shore in their underwear, shouting orders and cursing the decapitated bodies of the gunners draped over their batteries.

Thanks to the efficiency of the Albanian knife and club artists, who cleared the way for the bombardment, the bewildered staff officers were unable to reorganize port defenses until we were miles away on our homeward run.

Then we heard German antiaircraft batteries blazing away at the now-empty skies. The *Quilliam's* crew hooted derisively at the Nazis' belated display of ferocity.

This was the first major Allied blow struck at the Germans in the Balkans with the co-operation of the guerrilla armies. The Albanian Robin Hoods who slaughtered the Nazi gunners did a perfect job.

Apparently they had made things lively for the surprised Germans before we opened fire, beheading the artillerymen with their long mountain knives, clubbing sentries to death and lighting a huge bonfire to guide us into the port.

The entire operation went like clockwork. Several hours before we reached the target, the captain of the *Quilliam* briefed his crew.

"We arrive off Durazzo at 2 A.M. and start shooting two minutes later," he said. "The targets are the warehouses, oil storage tanks, German barracks, etc., but not the town itself, in view of the friendly population.

"There are several coastal batteries that may be troublesome, although the Partisans have promised to deal with them."

This was the fleet's first real test of the German defenses in the Balkans, and everyone aboard was "sweating it out" silently until 1 A.M. when the order was passed for all hands to man battle stations.

# WHAT THE SOLDIERS THINK

*by Helen Kirkpatrick*

ALLIED Headquarters, Algiers, Oct. 27—If most of the U. S. is swinging away from isolationism the same cannot be said of the rank and file of the Army. Responsibility for this difference in outlook must be placed squarely at the door of the Army and its Special Services, in the view of this correspondent and a good many thinking soldiers to whom I have talked.

Having seen North Africa, for example, without benefit of explanation, the average soldier is going to be likely to say at home: "I know Algeria. Let me explain the Arab-Jewish problem. Hand Algeria back to the Arabs," or some other equally misinformed, superficial opinion wrung from him by admiring friends.

Listening to officers who too often are themselves haters of foreigners, he is getting the idea that the best thing Americans can do is stay at home and mind their own business.

"All we do is to hand out stuff to these people and they don't know how to use it, or they fight among themselves"—such may be the verdict of the average man. And that may become a second American if not world tragedy, which could be easily avoided if certain steps were taken now.

There are so many examples of what happens to the average American who arrives in, say Algeria, that it is difficult to choose anyone in particular. One day a few weeks ago, a red-haired GI was drowsing in front of the press building when the usual type of overloaded Arab wagon passed by and the overburdened horse slipped on the cobblestones.

The Arab driver beat the horse severely. The red-headed American leaped from his jeep and administered a severe beating to the Arab. City Arabs' treatment of horses is a subject of extreme criticism from U. S. soldiers who are equally critical, and often illogically so, of French treatment of Arabs.

At the same time, there is co-operation here among Americans and British such as has never been seen before in history between two allies. And in the field there is the same mutual respect and liking. In the back areas, however, Americans and British have separate camps and the only contact the men may have there is in cafés and on the street.

Obviously there is need for Army education, which means education and not fifth-rate entertainment. Books, speakers and discussion groups in the Army could do much to orient the American soldier without giving him a biased or slanted viewpoint.

Soldiers are hungry for facts—facts on what Fascism really did in Italy and how it came to fall; what the characteristics of various European countries are, and why things have happened as they have during the last 20 years.

The more thoughtful young officers and men will sit around for hours telling you how pernicious they believe is the influence of Hollywood and certain types of radio programs and newspapers which pander to the lowest rather than to the highest level of reader intelligence, and it is hard to escape the impression here that the Army is following faithfully in the footsteps of Hollywood, the radio and those newspapers in that respect.

The cause is not hard to ascertain—it seems to be fear of political controversy and its repercussions in the U. S. But a group of 50 soldiers discussing this the other night said in effect: "The British have two political parties, but their soldiers seem able to get reading matter and controversial subjects presented to them. Why can't we?"

# ITALY'S POLITICAL SITUATION

## by Don Hollenbeck

NAPLES, Nov. 1.—The Italian political situation today is most confusing, due to three factors:

Apathy of the people.

Our failure to begin a strenuous housecleaning of the Fascist evils.

Failure of a really strong Italian leader to emerge with the backing of most of the Italian people.

It is inadvisable to count strongly on Count Carlo Sforza, because of the impression at home that Sforza doesn't appeal to the masses. In fact, he is mostly unknown to them because his activity had been confined to intellectual circles before his exile from Italy. Many Italians are strongly disappointed at Sforza's failure to be the flaming leader of a reborn Italy.

Sforza has been forced to play a most cautious game due to his uneasy truce with the monarchy and Badoglio and the pledge of all underground leaders to co-operate with Badoglio. The chief disappointment among Italians who are most zealous for a new deal in Italy is Badoglio's delay in forming a real coalition government.

Badoglio's announcement Saturday, under the watchful eyes of Robert Murphy and Harold MacMillan, U. S. and British diplomatic representatives in Italy, that he planned to form a government which would include the members of six parties, plus the Socialists and Communists, fails to satisfy most demands for a real coalition, because Badoglio has indicated that he does not plan to relax his grasp on political matters until after the war. The presence of Murphy and MacMillan seems to be a good indication that the Allies are satisfied with the present status.

There are an estimated 300,000 minor Fascist officials throughout Italy.

Those in liberated territory are still holding on to their jobs grimly, while the people wonder where the new broom is that we promised and they show us leaflets that we dropped containing glittering promises.

For example, the customs is still collected at eight gates in Naples by fascist officials, and where the money goes it is impossible to find out. AMG is still perfecting the physical setup and so far has been unable to start checking up on such cases. But the people coming into Naples from the countryside with produce see only the same old faces at the custom gates.

There are some voices bold enough to point out the evils. For example, the Naples daily *Regimento* editorially calls on AMG to produce a better mayor, speed up reorganization and clean-up of Naples, to which AMG gives the same answer "Only temporary appointment."

But the apathy of the people shows a decided increase as the campaign slows up. They had been generally excited and eager to help the invasion and showed it by sabotaging German lines and installations and in guerilla fighting.

But as the going got tougher and we failed to produce the new broom behind the lines, such activity gradually declined and is at present practically nonexistent. Military leaders complain that the sabotage is nothing like it had been led to expect. Some of them attribute the slow forward movement partly to this factor.

Almost all political activity—even interest—is confined to Italian intellectuals who are following the traditional Italian political custom of talking a good fight. The only exception is the Italian workers movement in Naples which is run by Leopoldo Piccardi of the left center coalition.

The most hopeful group of political leaders now meeting in Naples under the name of "National Front of Liberty" includes the most liberal and leftist leaders, like those of the "Action Front."

The National Front includes leaders of all liberal parties with weaknesses that make it unlikely that it will remain a coherent group, but will split up into its former individual parties and coalitions with various leaders, due to the inability of one man to command the confidence of all.

Most members of the National Front want a republic for Italy, but they want the whole question put off until a plebiscite which would be held after the war. They realize that if the monarchy is tossed out now it would only complicate the problem. That's assuming that the monarchy could be tossed out.

One of the National Front leaders estimated that if the plebiscite could be held today the monarchy would win, due largely to the unwillingness of the people to let themselves in for another change.

# PLANNED DESTRUCTION

*by John O'Reilly*

ALLIED Headquarters, Algiers, Nov. 8, 1943—Indications that every city left behind by the Germans in their northward retreat in Italy will be subjected to destruction and sacking as was Naples were available yesterday, for 5th Army troops at the Tyrrhenian Sea end of the line could observe that the port of Gaeta was being rocked by explosions as the Germans engaged in demolition work.

Gaeta, on a peninsula across the Gulf of Gaeta from the 5th Army positions in that sector, is the next good port up the coast from Naples. It is only nine miles from the Allied lines and the 5th Army men not only could hear explosions but could see columns of smoke rising above the place.

The demolition by the Germans of Gaeta's port facilities probably means that they have little hope of remaining there much longer. The bulk of the destruction done by them at Naples began nine days before the first 5th Army units to enter that city arrived. Naples is still without most of its public utilities.

There have been various signs of a German plan of destruction in Italy, apparently designed to wreak vengeance on the Italian population as well as to impede the progress of the Allied military campaign. Not long ago German Army documents captured on the 8th Army's front showed that the German troops had been ordered to carry out a scorched earth policy to the limit of their abilities.

The German destructive work at Naples and at places south of there went beyond demolition of military and shipping facilities. The Germans destroyed or tried to destroy almost everything that contributes to normal civilian existence, and what they could not destroy they took away. In addition, time bombs were left and adjusted to explode beneath important buildings during days after the German withdrawal.

# SIDELIGHTS

*by Tom Treanor*

THESE are days that are years. Even now, long after the Germans have fled, the minutes are heavy to the bursting point with savage and comic happenings. Since our Civil War there has been no period in America which could compare with this. The pattern of life has been exploded, and emotional sensations—events, tragedies and joys—have been whistling through the air like small shrapnel.

Two hours ago I was standing at the central station when a booby trap left by the Germans exploded a hundred feet away, tearing two children half to pieces. They had been playing in a heap of rubbish and tripped the trigger.

It seemed the mother was there in a moment. One of the mothers, at least—or perhaps they were both her children. I don't know. Then two white-faced American soldiers with a jeep were picking up moaning little forms. Before the mother knew what had happened, they were whisking them off to a first-aid station while she ran screaming after them, out of her mind.

Earlier there had been one of those crazy comedies peculiar to Americans. With the water system knocked out, the only way to flush the toilets in Naples is to empty buckets of water in them.

This morning Reynolds Packard of United Press flushed a toilet with a five-gallon container one of our soldiers carried up to him. Only it turned out to be a gasoline container. Packard burst out of the bathroom bellowing, "We'll all be blown up!" While a maid ran shrieking downstairs, "Criminals, even Germans never did that!"

And out on the street, G.I.s went in a snake dance of joy when they heard what had happened to a distinguished journalist—Author Reynolds Packard.

And then after luncheon I ran across a company of G.I.s who had just returned from being cut off for two weeks behind the German lines. A complete book could be written of their harrowing experiences.

Once the hand of Providence saved them when they were so weak from lack of food they could scarcely move. Some B-25s came bombing the German concentration near where they were hiding. One stray bomb dropped in the midst of a flock of sheep, killing a couple of dozen. That's only half the story. Of course, they wouldn't dare light a fire to cook the meat for fear of disclosing their position. But the bomb set some wood afire, and they ate roasted lamb until sated.

One night they thought they'd made their way through the lines to safety and approached the sound of voices. They were about to stumble up to the supposed Allies, when the voices went into a sort of rhythmic chant, concluding, "Heil Hitler!" Then *whong!* went a German 88.

The men crept forward and saw the German gun crew sending out a quick volley, shouting, "Heil Hitler!" each time the gunner pulled the lanyard to fire the shell.

They had two such weeks of adventures beyond belief. I asked them if any one of them previously had found his life in danger of anything more serious than an automobile accident. The answer was no, but they seemed completely unshaken by the experience apart from being very lean.

There didn't seem to be a frazzled nerve in this whole crew led by a couple of Texans: First Lieutenants William W. Kellogg, 21, of Houston, and Wesley Harris, 26, of Amarillo. One of their pastimes was to have "birthday parties." Three members of the company had birthdays during the ordeal. This succeeded so well they had further parties for birthdays:

602

twin-engined Nazi bomber on patrol dipped within 200 feet of the Partisan home in which I was a guest. But I am among friends who are unafraid.

Before I set out secretly from Italy to obtain an eyewitness report from inside Yugoslavia, exiles who still are stoutly devoted to General Draja Mihailovitch warned me of the dangers.

In this newly liberated section of Yugoslavia I've found not one scrap of evidence of Partisan terror.

I am the first American (or Briton) to reach this brigade headquarters. I have been received as an important ally to whom all courtesies are due.

Coming from Italy, I reached the rendezvous point in the rainy darkness before dawn. Soaking wet, I waited in a small woods, eating hardtack very strong with cheese. Finally I was hailed by the first Partisans I had ever seen in my life—a hard-faced, unshaven blond sailor with a red star in his blue petty officer's cap, and a sixteen-year-old lad with an Italian cartridge bandolier and carbine.

The boy, I learned, is typical of the volunteers now flooding the ranks of the Partisan army. Almost the first thing he told me in broken English was that his uncle, Marin Fulmisi, lives in Los Angeles, and he, Trepan Pavlicevich, hopes to visit America some day.

My two guides took me to a deserted habitation which had been wrecked by German bombs. As the pale sun rose my khaki clothes dried quickly.

Four Partisan officers arrived presently in a steaming little Fiat with a red sickle and hammer painted on the yellow hood. One was the brigade commander, who was peasant-born and worked as a bookkeeper in a factory before he went to fight in the woods in 1941.

Another introduced himself as Ante Morovich and said two brothers, Ivan and Jozo, lived at Wellington, N. Z., and a third, Tomo Morovich, lived at Empire, La.

The third and fourth officers wore the red bars of their rank on a green background—the green indicating they were political officers not military.

I noticed what appeared to be a special medal on the chest of one of the political officers. It depicted a workingman holding aloft a red star and in the corner was the hammer and sickle insignia. He explained that it was a badge manufactured by the Soviet government in honor of the Red pavilion at the New York World's Fair and that he had received it through friends in Moscow.

The Fiat driver, carefully depositing a tommy gun inside the *tonneau,* fixed a punctured tire while the brigade commander told me that tires were among the necessities which the British-American allies should send to the Partisan Army.

We discussed the military situation for half an hour, then four officers and I got into the Fiat, which was hardly large enough for two midgets.

The engine stuttered as we climbed the mountain road through the mist. Pine and yellow blossoms of shrubbery lined the route. Once more we had a flat tire but the driver fixed it speedily.

At the edge of a mountain town we disembarked from the wheezing car and I noticed a pole from which flew a flag of red, white and blue stripes with a red star in the center of the white stripe.

"It's the Croatian national flag with the Partisan symbol of the red star," the brigade commander explained. "Each Yugoslav group has its own flag with a red star."

The commander introduced me to a group of civilian dignitaries, including a plump middle-aged gentleman in well-cut tweeds who wore no tie, and said swiftly in German: "I am the mayor."

With the commander in step on my left, I marched past an honor company of Partisan tommy-gunners who had stood impassively in the rain more than an hour awaiting my arrival. They wore pieces of Italian uniforms, all now decorated with home-made red stars, and carried themselves with the *elan* of guardsmen.

The commander paused briefly to address the tommy-gunners, telling them the doom of the Fascist enemy was drawing ever nearer and that help from Anglo-American allies was at hand.

With the precision of West Point cadets, the Partisan soldiers gave three cheers: "Long live the American nation—Long live the British nation—Long live the Soviet Russian nation!"

The commander took me past the quaint homes of limestone on which were newly painted red hammers and sickles. One bore the notice that it was a headquarters of the Communist party. Another displayed a Communist slogan.

In the town square 200 Partisan recruits were drawn up in rigid military formation for my inspection.

The Partisans, I was told, have received volunteers from the age of sixteen upward, and introduced semi-general conscription of youths more than eighteen.

During the remainder of the day I conferred with the commander for six hours, poring over maps and obtaining statements on a variety of phases of the Yugoslav military and political situation. He and the staff officers took copious notes on what was told me, and explained they would be forwarded to the Bosnian headquarters of Drug (Comrade) Tito, marshal of the Yugoslav Partisan Army.

Mainly I pressed for information on two phases: The strength and location of the Germans and Ustachis (Croat puppet storm troopers) and what kind of help and supplies the Partisans wished from the British and American forces in the Mediterranean.

What the officers said dispelled the fiction that all the Yugoslav Adriatic coast is practically in Partisan hands. The Germans control the larger towns and harbors, as well as the two trans-Yugoslavia rail lines.

Surprisingly enough, they denied that Partisan Yugoslavia has a soviet system of government. They said that the Communist party was only a political party functioning in Partisan areas, and that the system instituted by the Communist-schooled Drug Tito was that of "adbors," or authorities, not soviets.

606

They said the titular head of the National Liberation Authority was Dr. Ivan Ribar, a Belgrade lawyer and son of a Slovenian statesman who was President of post-World War Yugoslavia's first "Skupshtina" (lower house of parliament).

The head of the Croatian section of the National Liberation Authority was Dr. Vladimir Nazor, seventy-four, Dalmatian-born poet. They said Nazor once wrote a hymn in praise of Poglavnik (Fuehrer) Ante Pavelich and is typical of former Ustachi sympathizers now trying to switch sides because of a belief that Germany and her satellites are losing the war.

Partisan officers admitted that mistakes had been made at Split (Spalato) and elsewhere in arming civilians posing as Partisans who afterward attacked the Partisans when German troops approached.

The officers minimized the German strength in Yugoslavia, estimating it at six to eight divisions, including two on the Adriatic coast. They urged quick dispatch of American and British troops across the Adriatic and promised that the people would gladly tear out their vineyards to make landing strips for American and British warplanes.

They argued also for sending of grain, beans, rice and medical supplies to Partisan areas where the population is facing hunger and disease during the hard winter ahead. "But arms are the most important of all," they said. "We can fight without food but we cannot fight without arms."

The officers said the Germans undoubtedly would try fiercely to regain key positions in the long island chain now in Partisan hands from the vicinity of Fiume to Dubrovnik (Ragusa). Last week the Germans attempted to disembark from fishing boats on the Island of Mljet, near Dubrovnik, but were driven off by Partisan rifle and machine-gun fire.

The officers emphasized that the National Liberation Authority included all Yugoslav religious faiths and that a considerable number of priests were members. The priests in this town confirmed this.

The officers asserted also that the Partisan army accepted patriots regardless of their views on Communism. They brought in a Jewish soldier who said 600 from a camp of 2,000 Jewish internees on the Island of Rab had joined the Partisan forces. Seventeen from a small Jewish camp at Korcula also enlisted.

Elsewhere along the Adriatic, where the Jews fled to the safety of the Italian occupation zone from anti-Semitic terror in Zagreb and Belgrade, the Jews now have been joining the Partisans since the Italian collapse. Jewish civilians fearing further successes for the German counter offensive in Dalmatia were permitted to flee to southern Italy without hindrance from the Partisans.

The officers gave me copies of the Partisan newspaper circulating in this area. The first item was a Partisan communiqué reporting small scattered victories and how Split fell to "the enemy horde" after a prolonged Stuka bombing of fifteen days and nights.

607

Other items told of Russian triumphs on the eastern front and of the Allied advance in Italy.

Since the collapse of Italy the Yugoslav Partisan army has grown by tens of thousands. By sheer daring, commanders have won notable temporary victories and have withstood severe reverses.

As the Germans well know, the Partisans are fighting today without a single tank or plane. Rifle and machine-gun companies are led by veterans who for twenty-nine months have excelled in what they call "war in the woods."

The commander in chief of the far-flung Partisan army is a revered figure, Josip Broz, who is known as Drug Tito. (Drug, pronounced "droog," in Serbo-Croat, means "comrade." Tito is an uncommon name among the southern Slavs, although frequently encountered in Italy.)

Reputed to be a veteran of the Republican army in the Spanish civil war, Drug Tito has welded his guerrillas into a tightly disciplined and hotly idealistic force that shows more enthusiastic determination than any outfit I've seen since I met Major General Vassily Novikov's Caucasus Army during the British-Russian occupation of Iran.

# TITO'S ARMY

## by C. L. Sulzberger

DECEMBER, 1943—There are now more than 250,000 men and women organized into approximately twenty-six divisions fighting a savage war against some of Adolf Hitler's best veteran units along Yugoslavia's frontiers. That front stretches approximately 350 miles across forests, ravines and snow-covered mountains ranging between the Julian Alps of Slovenia and the forbidding crags separating bleak Montenegro from Albania and the south.

Bound together by aspirations for freedom, these soldiers, no matter what ideologists may think of them or their leaders, are as admitted by Prime Minister Churchill opposing more enemy divisions than face the Fifth and Eighth armies in Italy. As a result of their stubborn fight they are receiving American material and military aid, and accompanying them are American and British missions that soon will be joined by one from Russia.

They are openly and boastfully influenced by communism. Their chief is a Communist, and the Communist party, as he declared in a public speech, initiated and co-ordinated the peasants in their instinctive yearning for liberty. They have proclaimed themselves for a federation of the southern Slav peoples without favoring one over the other as do some of their opponents.

This force, which calls itself Yugoslav Peoples Army of Liberation, has been in process of formation for two and a half years. It began with the gradual amalgamation of nationalist and patriotic guerrilla bands and their welding together by an underground political movement, fomented by a mixture of Communist and democratic party leaders headed by a Croatian metal worker named Josip Broz, who has a Russian Soviet background.

For months M. Broz lived a furtive life in Belgrade under the eyes of the Gestapo. He sat quietly in a corner of cafes smoking endless cigarettes with a revolver in pocket, spreading his organization slowly while Nazi police and Serbian collaborationist gendarmerie hunted the capital's streets for him in scout cars mounting machine guns.

The smell of death lay heavily in that city from twisted architectural skeletons and hanging human flesh. The bodies of persons slain by the Germans dangled from lamp-posts. Sharp bursts of automatic fire occasionally rattled across the bomb-torn squares as the seeds of new rebellious movements stirred in the wreckage of the old.

Today M. Broz as Marshal Tito commands the immense popular upheaval resulting and serves as the political president of its temporary Government, which demands full recognition from the United Nations. He sends and receives important military missions to and from abroad.

Allied aircraft based in Italy are placed at the disposal of his specific commands. Sizable shipments, which now number thousands of tons of Allied war material, are being sent to his troops; guns, munitions, trucks, uniforms, medicines and special apparatus.

His army includes a regular officers' corps with special insignia, from the rank of noncom to marshal. His artillery, made up almost exclusively of captured weapons, has cannon as large as giant gun howitzers and coastal rifles. Officers' training schools, medical corps, ordnance and adjutant generals' departments have been created within his Supreme Command.

His Government, which includes a political *mélange* ranging from old-line Communists to former right-wing reactionaries, has its own banking system, printing its own money and floating its own interest-bearing loans; its own railroad, for which its own tickets are printed; its own postal system, its own agricultural department, and its own educational department, seeking to spread literacy among the peasantry.

In addition, there is a social organization that has arisen from the fires of national revolution which has its own churches with chaplain, Catholic, Orthodox and Moslem, attached to fighting units; and theaters and ballets and hundreds of small newspapers. These developments comprise the most interesting people's movement that has arisen from this war. It has now survived its terrible birth pangs, involving famine, slaughter, battle and disease to the extent to which American history has only Valley Forge to offer in comparison.

When popular anger at Yugoslavia's weakling government broke out in the *coup d'etat* March 27, 1941, and smashed the brief ties with the Axis, these young people and their small movement organized demonstrations. Colonel Dedier, who was a former foreign correspondent in Spain, London, Scandinavia, and Poland for Belgrade's biggest paper, *Politiká,* prepared a new publication, the first issue of which was ready for circulation April 6. On that day the war broke out and Belgrade was destroyed by German bombers.

Colonel Dedier joined the army as a volunteer in Sarajevo the day of capitulation. When news of the surrender came he and fifty soldiers decided to hide as many arms as possible and return to their home districts to organize resistance. He went back to Belgrade with two grenades picked up in the last minute of confusion. He worked in a vineyard belonging to his father-in-law near the German airfields at Zemun across the river from Belgrade conferring with friends disguised as common laborers.

At that time Hitler began to fulfill the anti-Slav pledges made in his book, *"Mein Kampf."* Hundreds of Serbs were shot in a mass slaughter. Latent antipathies between Orthodox Serbs and Catholic Croats were encouraged in Ustachi massacres and Chetnik retribution from mountain units organized already from the defeated army by Gen. Draja Mikhailovitch.

At the end of that first April M. Broz, under the *nom de guerre* of Tito, utilizing his hard-won experiences as a Communist organizer and political refugee from the Belgrade gendarmerie, began to try to form out of the chaos some kind of united front. During World War I he had been in the Austrian Army deserted in Russia, where he fought in a Yugoslav battalion.

After the revolution he became a Communist. His first wife was a Russian woman. Their son, Zharko, who lost an arm in the battle for Moscow, was decorated a hero of the Soviet Union.

In the mid-twenties he returned to Croatia organizing the metal workers in the Zagreb railway shops. For some years he was imprisoned as a political undesirable and after his release lived in constant fear of arrest.

On April 20 the "Slovenian front" was created. In May Marshal Tito secretly went to Belgrade and met the senior Ribar, former President of the Yugoslav Parliament, and other national leaders. A program was drafted and secret proclamations issued. The manifestos began to appear on city walls, warning the Germans they had better get out.

Digging in their vineyard Colonel Dedier's group received Marshal Tito's proclamations and prepared for action. In June when the Nazis attacked Russia, the Partisans began their active fight.

There are many people who emphasize this date as proof that Marshal Tito had no interest in Yugoslavia's defense until the Communist homeland was beseiged. Partisans claim otherwise. They admit extensive Communist influence on their movement, especially in the early days. But they point out that to begin the Soviet campaign Hitler altered the Yugoslav situation, offering advantages for the guerrilla strategy of attack.

The major portion of the Wehrmacht garrisons were withdrawn. Communist Yugoslavs saw the opportune moment to induce the people to arise on the basis of their almost mystical faith in Russianism. Finally they saw at last the Ango-Soviet alliance formed as fact.

The Communists struck first. Peasant units led by Belgrade intellectuals touched off the uprising around Valjevo, historic center of Serbian rebellions. Taking part was the son of General Mikhailovitch. He fought with the Partisans for several months before joining or being captured by his father's troops; that story is not clear.

The Valjevo insurrection began July 5 and the first German was slain by a reporter named Jovanovitch who later was killed while leading a detachment. Actions started elsewhere. In Belgrade the Young Communist League members, including young Mikhailovitch, burned thousands of copies of the new German-run paper *Novo Vreme*. Fifteen more youths were shot. In Zagreb the telephone exchange was blown up. In Serbia eighty German truckloads of oil and munitions were dynamited.

During these days Colonel Dedier was editing a secret daily paper with Olga and their little daughter. The paper was distributed in a perambulator, copies hidden in the baby's clothing.

At that time a well-known patriot, named Alexander Rankovitch, was saved from a prison hospital when a group of young patriots broke into the jail, killed two Gestapo men and whisked him off in a horse-drawn lorry, hiding his bruised and beaten face in a handkerchief. M. Rankovitch is high in the Partisan movement now.

Olga Ninchitch Humo, daughter of the former Yugoslav Foreign Minister, was freed from a Sarajevo jail, where she had been sentenced to death, by the good-will of a Czech Gestapo interpreter who died the next day for his act. Today she is an interpreter for British officers attached to Marshal Tito's supreme command.

Revolutionary moves, big and little, spread. Marshal Tito drew up special operational plans for five Partisan detachments in Serbia. In raids for firearms gendarmerie stations were ransacked. Armed with two cartridgeless rifles, a group from Kragujevac held up ten gendarmes and stole their rifles and revolvers. Today that same detachment has swollen to a brigade equipped with captured Axis tanks.

On July 13 a large uprising erupted in Montenegro and swiftly all the titanic little province except three main towns was freed of Italians. Montenegrins have always said "Together we and the Russians are 200,000,000," and now they arose to prove their fighting spirit. Major Arbo Jovanovitch of the regular Yugoslav General Staff joined the movement there with Colonel Savo Orovitch. Major Jovanovitch was a former pupil at the War College of General Mikhailovitch, studying among their subjects guerrilla tactics. Today as major general he is Marshal Tito's Chief of Staff, and heads the operational and intelligence departments of the Supreme Command.

Croatian workers, encouraged by Communist organizers, commenced a sabotage campaign, resulting in the slaughter of hundreds by Gestapo and Anté Pavelitch's Ustachi. They began to join thousands of Serbs dwelling in that province who had fled to the forest to escape massacres fostered by the Nazis.

At this time Marshal Tito was still hiding in Belgrade. Carrying a revolver and wearing dark glasses he used to watch German scout cars cruising by at snail's pace slowly swinging machine guns from side to side. When a face believed wanted by the Gestapo was spotted, short bursts sounded forth sharply.

Colonel Dedier met Marshal Tito the first time with Young Ribar in a public garden. Marshal Tito was introduced only as a "very big man in our movement." He gave Colonel Dedier a brief lecture on how to derail trains. That same July a bulletin from the Partisans' supreme command was published on wall posters. It was signed by Marshal Tito.

In August Colonel Dedier was ordered to join a detachment near Kragujevac. With a change to his best clothes, and kissing his child good-by, he traveled openly in a train compartment filled with Nazi officers, and descended on the outskirts of free Partisan territory at Gorni-Milanovac, where 600 men under Lawyer Reja Nedelkovitch controlled the region.

They did not don uniforms until they captured 400 from German trucks. They specialized in smashing lorries, blocking roads and cutting railways.

In August the Supreme Command was reorganized to embrace all Yugoslavia, and mobile headquarters for Serbia were established. Marshal Tito remained in Belgrade until September.

At this time General Mikhailovitch had headquarters at Ravna Gora. One of his detachments under an Orthodox priest, Vlado Zechevitch, fought with the Partisans against the Germans, with joint messes and a unified command at Valjevo. The Chetniks served under the Yugoslav flag bearing the picture of King Peter, the Partisans under a Yugoslav flag bearing a big five-pointed star.

Marshal Tito twice visited General Mikhailovitch at Ravna Gora in October, proposing a joint command for all, according to the Partisans. They say General Mikhailovitch refused to acknowledge the Croat Cosniaks as members of Yugoslavia, as the result of a fifth column element among them during the brief war that spring.

That autumn a mission from the Yugoslav Government in Exile, with two officers, a sergeant and an English liaison captain, arrived at Montenegro en route to General Mikhailovitch. It passed through Partisan territory and the sergeant joined the Tito movement.

On Oct. 26, 1941, Marshal Tito and General Mikhailovitch signed a treaty at Ravna Gora, under which, among other things, the Partisans agreed to furnish 5,000 rifles and 500,000 cartridges from their stores in their headquarters at Uzice, which contained an arms factory and 25,000,000 dinars, according to Marshal Tito supporters.

Shortly thereafter the open dispute between the Chetniks and Partisans began and General Mikhailovitch attacked Marshal Tito's Uzice stronghold. Efforts to end the civil war resulted in negotiations at Chachak Nov. 22. In the middle of negotiations Marshal Tito telephoned to Colonel Dedier that four German divisions were moving toward Uzice and that a joint command must immediately be arranged. The move failed, as the Germans bombarded Uzice ferociously. Colonel Dedier, previously wounded by the explosion of the time bomb, was lying in bed when a wall fell in on him. Only his huge physique preserved his life. Another bomb exploded in the Uzice bank's gold vault, where the arms factory was situated, and 112 were killed.

As the German tanks drove into the town Marshal Tito had been conferring with an English captain attached to General Mikhailovitch who had driven in for a radio set left behind previously. The two of them drove out one end of the town as the German tanks came in the other. As the road ahead was being bombed and strafed they rolled into a ditch together when a tank appeared 200 yards away. They slipped over a wall and ran. That night at Zlatiber, almost twenty miles distant, Colonel Dedier and other discouraged staff officers sat about candles in a peasant house when Marshal Tito stumbled in exhausted, and sank down saying only "Well!" and again "Well!"

Although his Uzice headquarters was gone Marshal Tito again set about organizing a patriotic movement and as the peasants fled from enemy retribution it spread slowly. M. Principe organized detachments in east Bosnia. M. Popora led an uprising in Hercegovina.

Marshal Tito went to Foca in Bosnia and remained there until May, 1942, building his movement until ousted by another German offensive. Behind him in Serbia he left small Partisan detachments for purely guerrilla activity. In Bosnia he kept with him two Serbian brigades, two Montenegrin brigades and one from Sanjak.

These were surrounded in a Nazi attack. Marshal Tito and his soldiers lived on meat often uncooked, herbs and grass. But they broke through the Nazi ring and, quickly reassembling, started a counter-attack, cutting the important Sarajevo-Mostar railway and, joining with a detail of Krajina Partisans, liberated west Bosnia and Bosanska Krajina.

At this time the first Partisan air force was proudly formed when three Croatian air force planes were deserted to the Partisans. For a very brief period of glory they satisfied themselves with strafing Nazis and dropping hand-grenades, until one plane was shot down by flak and others destroyed on the ground by German Stukas.

By the end of 1942, after a series of swift assaults and forced marches, Marshal Tito had liberated large chunks of Slovenia, Croatia, Kordun, Lika, Gorski, Cattaro, west Bosnia and much of Dalmatia.

For the first time at the town of Bihac in November, 1942, an "Anti-Fascist Assembly for the People's Liberation in Yugoslavia," or "Avnoj," met, creating executive and legislative set-ups for governing the liberated areas but not assuming any title as government. Simultaneously, the Partisans created the "People's Army of Liberation" on a formal basis from the previous loose guerrilla detachments. A regular system of officers was instituted. The political idea of unity of all Yugoslav peoples was emphasized despite terrible Ustachi massacres of Serbs and reprisal sallies of Chetniks against the Croats and Bosnians. In Dalmatia orthodox Serbian brigades fought for the Catholic Croats against the Serb Chetniks.

Early in 1943 the Germans mounted a big new offensive with four crack divisions plus Italians and Ustachi, and some Chetnik units simultaneously but independently attacked. Terrific aerial bombardments and strafings were loosed against the People's Army, which had neither fighter protection nor anti-aircraft artillery.

Around the Bihac area and in Croatia and Lika Marshal Tito left the First Bosnian Corps of four divisions and the First Croatian Corps of four divisions, and with five of his best divisions—the First, Second, Third, Seventh and Ninth—began to fight a terrible retreat southward more than 200 miles into Montenegro. With him he took 4,500 wounded rather than risk their capture.

The full tale of this retreat remains to be told. Snow whipped up by a terrible "bora" wind bit into the ragged army. Hunger was with them day and night. Their diet was raw meat and leaves. Mass hallucinations drove the troops desperate. At one stage an entire battalion fancied it saw in the distance a vast castle, with warm smoke pouring out of chimneys.

Again a whole brigade, imagining it smelled cooking food, rushed up to a barren field kitchen with battered mess tins.

At Prozor and Imotski in southwest Bosnia the People's Army, forcing a passage southward, attacked and wiped out an Italian purge division, capturing quantities of arms and clothing.

March was a savage month, cold and cheerless. The Germans commenced a new offensive from the north and Col. Gen. Alexander von Loehr flew down from Belgrade to assume command. Three Nazi divisions took part, including the Thirty-sixth Grenadiers sent from Greece.

In a desperate strategic position, Marshal Tito assembled all available munitions and started a counter-attack. Despite continual Luftwaffe bombardment, in one day the People's Army fired 3,000 captured Italian howitzer shells and drove back the Nazis.

During the month of April Marshal Tito organized a new corps in Slavonia and another in Bosanska Krajina, while the Germans prepared a fifth offensive to destroy him. Seven Nazi divisions and five of Italians as well as Ustachi troops were employed. The enemy devised a new strategy, no longer marching in large columns with vulnerable transport, but specializing in small units with heavy automatic weapon firepower which could only be supplied from the uncontested air. After careful concentration a sudden attack was launched from all sides May 15—as the Axis was expelled from Tunisia.

This action took place on the high Piva plateau in Montenegro, surrounded by declivities and steep canyons. A British military mission—the first to Marshal Tito—was scheduled to arrive and before breaking out Marshal Tito lost three days waiting for them. Gales were so stiff that the first time planes bearing paratroops neared the position the weather was too abominable for them to land.

Finally, May 27 they arrived: Six of them jumping into a terrific, slanting wind amid the steady humming and flashing of artillery rumbling through

614

the Black Mountains which give the province its name. Marshal Tito began his forced retreat prior to a counter-offensive.

As the march commenced bullets from Chetnik ambush whizzed by Marshal Tito and he said to a near-by British officer, "This is the way Mikhailovitch fights the invader."

During forty days of steady fighting Marshal Tito swung his troops northwestward, breaking through sixty kilometers of prepared German positions. Each height approached held enemy machine guns, mortars and field artillery, and the country is a mass of heights. Marshall Tito always was in the front line.

All Bosnia was liberated again just at the time the Germans were announcing that the Partisan movement had been wiped out. That was in July when there were two Nazi divisions in Sicily and seven against Marshal Tito. Winding from end to end of Yugoslavia was a long road of unmarked graves. But the movement that had grown by dogged persistence began to receive hundreds of new cohorts from ravaged areas. Homeless women and children flocked to it. When the People's Army entered the historically famous town of Jajce beneath the ancient castle of King Tvrtka of Bosnia beside a placid lake, some thousands of black-garbed peasant women clustered pitifully behind.

They were looking for salt they had done without for more than a year and for which their systems craved. In Jajce is a small chemical factory. Beside it were vast piles of salt. The miserable horde of womenfolk scrambled to it like animals and on all fours began licking it.

They came from an unbelievable, tortured hinterland of burned-down houses. The peasant had lived in makeshift shelters with jerry-built roofs. Whenever they heard the Germans were coming they destroyed roofs themselves and hid in the fields to avoid pillaging of what looked like might be their homes.

Across this landscape marched and counter-marched polyglot armies: Germans, Italians, Bulgarians, Croat Domobranci, Ustachi, Serbian fascist troops of the government and Chetniks and Partisans.

Along the Belgrade-Zagreb Railway, once Europe's main thoroughfare to the East, moved slow chugging Nazi grain convoys, warily looking out for saboteurs. Traveling only by day and at reduced speed, they were preceded by armored trains pushing ahead of the locomotive carloads of sand. Planes flew overhead and on either side were tree trunks.

Special Partisan demolition squads laid their mines carefully against these. During the early months they had only a few mines, usually rebuilt from enemy bombs that failed to explode and in which holes were drilled for the fuse. Now they had large stores of mines of their own manufacture and special Allied sent chargers. Hundreds of yards of mines were buried by night and, playing complex chargers like a piano, Partisan engineers blew up mine after mine engulfing German convoys. Tracks were littered with rotting goods. Neither side could remove the twisted locomotives. All stations were burned down.

615

During this period after June the counter-offensive of Marshal Tito's movement swelled enormously from Macedonia to Slovenia. Liaison with guerrillas in Albania, Greece, Bulgaria, Rumania and Italy was established.

By the time the capitulation of Italy arrived the Partisans were strong enough for swift action and several Fascist divisions—six in Slovenia alone —were disarmed and most of the troops sent back to Trieste. Some units joined Marshal Tito's forces.

At this time Colonel Dedier as a member of "Avnoj" was sent by Marshal Tito to Croatia accompanying two members of the Supreme Command. While crossing the Zagreb-Susak railway they heard excited firing and learned of the surrender of the Italians. Near by was an important Italian garrison.

After posting a man on slight rise with a machine gun Colonel Dedier with three Slovenes wearing British battledress dropped from a parachute and a bandaged head surmounted by a cap with a red star entered the barracks demanding the colonel who arrived haughtily with folded arms.

Speaking French, Colonel Dedier said, "Don't be a damned fool. You have three choices; fight with us, join the Germans or leave your arms with us." A Nazi reconnaissance plane cruised over as the Italian colonel requested a half hour in which to think. Colonel Dedier greeted troops standing about with *"Via Italian Libera,"* and they hailed back, *"Partizana bono."*

The colonel agreed to surrender, and three howitzers, forty mortars and many machine guns were taken over just half an hour before the first Nazi tank showed up.

After gaining vast new material resources Marshal Tito swiftly liberated the entire Dalmatian coast except Zara and Sebenico where the Germans dropped paratroops and the First Partisan tank brigade to be organized drove up to the outskirts of Trieste. The people of Slovenia arose in mass with spades and pickaxes, destroying bunkers and barbed wire.

The Germans rushed Panzer units, including Tigers, into Slovenia, but aside from destructive raids they generally were ineffective.

Following enormous new strength taken from the defeated Italians, Marshal Tito felt strong enough for decisive steps in the military and political sphere and summoned delegates to an "Avnoj" congress which met in picturesque Jajce. The word Jajce in Serbian implies masculinity and with this meeting the Partisans boasted they had emasculated the enemy.

Jajce normally is a placid, beautiful town of stone and wooden houses and cobbled street set below old King Tvtkas' castle under a waterfall beside a lake linking the Pliva and Vrbas rivers.

There in a large gymnasium across from a fortress during late November, 1943, those decisions were taken crystallizing the movement about which the world has been reading lately.

Speaking among a galaxy of homemade American, British, Soviet and Partisan flags, sketches of Marshal Tito and Premier Stalin, President Roosevelt and Prime Minister Churchill, M. Ribar and the delegates formulated

616

their program, which has both excited and perplexed the world. There Marshal Tito revealed his identity as humble Josip Broz after receiving news that the last members of his family except his second wife, Herta, who is with his army, had been slain in occupied areas. He was awarded the title of Marshal of the People's Army.

# A DYING GUERRILLA'S TESTAMENT

### by Louis Adamic

MARKO was his name, and he was a small-town man, still a young man —only a little while before the Axis turned its fury on Yugoslavia, he had married a girl named Yelena who came from a village nearby.

So begins a story people in many parts of Yugoslavia started to whisper among themselves in '42, after the country's far-flung resistance against German, Italian and Magyar occupation had taken a heavy toll of the guerrilla fighters who called themselves Partisans or the Liberation Front.

Sometimes, as the tale was told, Marko was a Serbian; sometimes a Croatian—this was not important to those who whispered it about.

What seemed to matter was that Marko was an honest man; not with any too much schooling behind him, but intelligent and able to say what went on in his head so that one who was even less well educated could understand him. In his spare time when business was slow in his shop Marko used to read newspapers and books and tell others what he read about; and evenings and Sundays he liked to talk politics and philosophy.

That is the sort of man he was, this Marko: of the people, but a little above the average in that he knew the meaning of things and could express his mind and heart in simple, honest words.

Later when the enemy occupied his town and began to seize men for hostages and, worse yet, for slave labor in Germany and Italy and behind the Russian front, Marko told his young wife Yelena, who was with child, to go back to her father's house in her native village and with God's help take care of herself as best she knew how; and he left his home and business, his friends and town, without saying a word to anyone else; and he headed for the mountains and there joined other men who felt as he did about the things that were going on under occupation.

Marko was a Partisan guerrilla and he fought in one battle after another, now against the Germans, now against the Italians, and sometimes against native dupes and scoundrels who served the Axis puppet governments; and he helped to inflict many casualties on the enemy. He was a great fighter.

But the Partisans' losses also were not small; and one day, in a fierce battle with the Axis, Marko was mortally wounded.

And as he lay on the ground with enemy metal in his torn body, knowing he was bleeding to death and no one could help him, Marko managed to get a little stub of pencil and some paper out of his coat pocket, and he started a letter to his unborn child:

My little one, curled up in the darkness, blind and unbreathing, soft and shapeless, I salute you. Now you are unhurried in the wonderful warmth; but the day of your birth is not far off and you are storing strength. When your moment comes you will be ready. Your mother, whom I love deeply, will have given you everything you need. You will twist and struggle; something within you will fight toward the light and for air, for life—no one knows why. How I wish I could hear your first gasp and see the first blink of your eyelids!

Keep burning, but always under your control, the fire of passion that tempers the steel of your young years and gives them the ring of human worth. Let the flame leap and let it be so clear that in the years of your age, when your work is over, its light will continue to shine in your eyes like a lamp in a dark-framed window, drawing and warming those who stumble in the night and are chill.

Keep your wonder and surprise, your impulse to discover, your eyes on the horizon—they are your promise of immortality. Go through storms, but fix your heart on the sun and stars above them. There is one never-changing rule in the world: dawn follows darkness.

Work as you are able, whatever the task, and keep high courage and firm faith. Do not be ashamed of fear; do not hide it; conquer it. Do not be dismayed when you see others grow tired in this confused world. There is always light around the edges of gloom; strive toward it. Think as you are able. Ponder, decide, act. Never stop the flow of thought and feeling between your mind and your heart. Let your instinct tell you what is right.

As you go on, know what is behind you. I am ashamed to leave you a world of charred hopes, of error piled upon error, blood spilled upon blood. Forgive me. Know the errors of the past, but look ahead—find the stepping-stones to the future, to a clear dawn.

Keep your love of life; but overcome your fear of death. Life is lost if it is not loved; only never love it too much. Sometimes the best thing a man can do is die.

Keep your joy in friendship, and your anger at what your instinct tells you is wrong.

Keep your pleasure in little things—a snowflake, a blade of grass, a cobweb stretched between two branches of a bush, the sheen of a bird's wing, the moisture in a linden leaf, a girl's smile. They are as big as sunlight and thunder, wind and wave on the ocean, and the greatness of heroes. There is magic in the stillness of a seed —

Vision was going from Marko's eyes; his fingers were numb and he could barely hold the little pencil. He did not finish the letter to his unborn son. In irregular lines at the bottom of the paper he scrawled: "Please deliver this to my wife Yelena," and he placed the letter under his cheek

618

so that his face served as a weight to keep the wind from blowing it away.

When his fellow Partisans found Marko, they read what he had written and they all said, "This is just as I feel." And they all copied it, making it their own letter to their unborn children, ending it themselves with "In thought, as a last benediction, I kiss your forehead," or "Good night to you, my little one—and a bright morning." Then each carried it on his person till he was killed too, and when his fellow Partisans found it on his body they copied it . . . till now every Partisan guerrilla who has a wife with child carries the letter.

It was impossible to deliver Marko's original letter to his wife Yelena, for the village where she lived was in territory which the enemy held with specially strong forces. By-and-by, however, the Partisans penetrated to that region also and liberated it. But when they reached Yelena's village, they found it destroyed. Most of the villagers had been massacred, and Yelena was among the dead.

Marko's child was never born.

But Marko's letter will be read by many a Partisan's child born under Axis occupation. It will be read the whole world over and some day "a clear dawn" *will* break over the lands of the South-Slavs, over the Balkans, over Europe, over all the earth.

*Epilogue*

# HOW IT WILL END

## *by Herbert L. Matthews*

THIS time war will lead to revolution. The defeat of the Axis will be the signal for uprisings in every occupied country of Europe—and Italy will be no exception. There can be no adaptation of Italian Fascism to a changing world. It is monolithic and infallible by definition. The movement that began without dogmas or doctrines developed them with the years and became bound by them as liberalism and democracy never have been. If our doctrines prove unworkable or undesirable, we change them, but to change Fascism is to destroy it.

But let us not delude ourselves. Italian Fascism will go, but world Fascism, international Fascism, the ideas, ideals and desires to which it responded, will remain. Fascism will be a hydra-headed monster, and we democrats can never, in our generation, lay aside our guns. "Men feel that they need an illusion," wrote Gaetano Mosca, and Fascism was a beautiful illusion to many millions. They placed their faith in it, and once a movement has a grip on the uneducated masses it dies hard. It lasts especially long when there is no substitute belief handy. There will be a "Mussolinian myth" in Italy, one of these days, just like the "Napoleonic myth" of 19th-century France.

Even in Italy we must remember, Fascism has put its men throughout the whole bureaucratic and corporative structures. No revolution can change that quickly, and any new government must retain a great deal of the Fascist set-up. The alternative would be anarchy.

But, then, what will come after Fascism?

In our day, it is Benedetto Croce who upholds the torch of Italian liberty. He wrote only a few years ago:

"No new idea has taken the place of the idea of liberty. Since the liberal ideal is the moral ideal of humanity and civilization, the new and victorious ideal should present itself as a new and more vigorous and more profound humanity and civilization, and the one-party system cannot in truth be so considered. It is a party of constriction which, in the name of this or that idol—race, State or dictatorship of the proletariat—has no creative virtues of civil and humane life, but only capacity eventually to expand the material life of some and compress that of others....

"Meanwhile, for us students and thinkers, it remains to maintain and increase the precise concept of liberty and to construct a philosophic theory upon it. That is the contribution which one has the right to ask of us in the complex work of the restoration and *risorgimento* of the liberal ideal and customs."

When everything is said and done, dictatorship is a job like any other. Mussolini and Hitler could have gone on forever, so to speak, as long as they were successful, but dictatorship is more than "a romantic form of discouragement," as Guglielmo Ferrero put it; it is an expensive luxury—like burning the candle at both ends. You can make a brighter light for a little while, but it is a form of destruction. Mussolini and Hitler solved nothing and created nothing, but they destroyed more than any other two men in history. This is a claim to fame, but it can hardly be called evidence of success.

"By their fruits ye shall know them." This is the eternal measure, and the fruits of Fascism have proved bitter to the taste.

The time has come to write "Finis" to this book and to Fascism.

# AUTHORS

ABEND, HALLETT 381

Hallett Abend was Far Eastern correspondent for the *New York Times* for fifteen years. He is the author of many books on Asiatic problems, among them being *Ramparts of the Pacific, Pacific Charter, Our Japanese Enemy,* and, recently, *My Life in China.*

ADAMIC, LOUIS 617

Louis Adamic is a Slovenian by birth and an ardent American by adoption. He has written many books and articles about his native country, and about his fellow countrymen who have emigrated to America. He is especially interested in the problem of the amalgamation of the emigrant into the melting-pot of American life.

In 1943 he published *My Native Land,* the first book which told the world the real truth about General Tito and the Partisans in Yugoslavia. While Mr. Adamic has not been a foreign correspondent, in the true sense of the word, his Yugoslav material has been included in this book because it is the best obtainable on Yugoslavia, having been secured from eyewitnesses, at first hand.

ALCOTT, CARROLL 351

Carroll Alcott was a reporter, editor, and radio commentator in Japan for fifteen years. From 1932 on he was editor of the *Shanghai Evening Post and Mercury,* an American language newspaper published in Shanghai. In 1938 he became radio commentator for Station XMHA in Shanghai. His broadcasts, in which he minced no words about the Japanese invaders, made him practically Japan's Enemy No. 1 in that city.

ALEXANDER, JACK 272

Jack Alexander is associate editor of the *Saturday Evening Post* and a frequent contributor to that periodical. In 1943 he visited England to get stories on the R.A.F. and on the American forces in England for the *Post.* He has also written articles for the *New Yorker.*

ALLEN, JAY 219

Jay Allen has been a foreign correspondent since 1924, working first for the *Chicago Tribune,* briefly thereafter for the *London News-Chronicle,* the *Chicago Daily News,* and, in 1940-41, for the North American Newspaper Alliance. He has the distinction of having secured the first exclusive interview with Marshal Pétain after the latter became dictator of France. He also achieved notice by being taken prisoner by the Germans while attempting to cross the line between occupied and unoccupied France without a permit. He was imprisoned for a time, but was eventually released and permitted to return to this country.

ALLEN, LARRY 510

Larry Allen is one of the most outstanding of the younger Associated Press correspondents. He was born in Maryland in 1908 and gained his early newspaper experience on papers in Ohio, West Virginia, and Washington, D.C. In 1942 he won the Pulitzer Prize for his reporting of the deeds of the British fleet in the Mediterranean. That same year he was captured by the Italians and confined in an Italian prison. Later, while being taken to a German prison camp, he escaped from his captors, but was badly wounded in his flight, and eventually recaptured.

## ALSOP, JOSEPH, JR.    446

Joseph Alsop, Jr., was born in 1910 and graduated from Groton and Harvard. He was on the staff of the *New York Herald Tribune* in New York from 1932 to 1935 and in the Washington office of that paper in 1936-37. Together with Robert Kintner he has written a syndicated column on politics, called "The Capitol Parade," for the North American Newspaper Alliance since November, 1937. He has been China correspondent for the North American Newspaper Alliance for several years. He is a frequent contributor to the *Saturday Evening Post,* usually jointly with Robert Kintner.

## ANGLY, EDWARD    215

Edward Angly was formerly foreign correspondent for the *New York Herald Tribune,* and, more recently, for the *Chicago Sun.* Since the beginning of our war with Japan he has been in the Southwest Pacific area.

## ARCHAMBAULT, G. H.    195

G. H. Archambault was a lieutenant with the French Army in World War I. After having participated in more than three years of active trench warfare he became a liaison officer attached to the A.E.F.

At the close of the war he became editor of the *Paris Herald,* and later of the *Paris Times.* Subsequently he became a member of the Paris staff of the *New York Sun,* and from 1933 of the *New York Times.* Since June, 1940, he has been sending his dispatches to the *Times* from Switzerland.

## ATKINSON, BROOKS    376

Brooks Atkinson was born in Melrose, Massachusetts, in 1894, and graduated from Harvard University in 1917. His repor-

torial career embraced a period as reporter on the *Springfield* (Massachusetts) *Daily News,* dramatic critic on the *Boston Evening Transcript,* editor of the book review section of the *New York Times* (1922-25), and from 1925 until 1941 dramatic critic for the same paper. At the outbreak of our war with Japan he insisted on being sent abroad as a foreign correspondent, and was accordingly dispatched to Chungking for the *New York Times.* From this city he has made many trips to air bases and front line areas in the Chinese theater of war.

## AULT, PHIL    534

Phil Ault was born in Maywood, Illinois, and graduated from De Pauw University, Greencastle, Indiana. He has been with the United Press since 1939. His experience as a war correspondent was gained in the Tunisian campaign, in which he covered the tank and infantry action, particularly in the battles at Kasserine Pass, Maknassa, and El Guettar.

## AXELSSON, GEORGE    336

George Axelsson, a native of Sweden, came to this country at the age of 17, and began his journalistic career in California. In 1926 he returned to Europe, where he worked on the Paris edition of the *Chicago Tribune,* and later as Riviera correspondent for several British and American newspapers. During the Spanish Civil War he was attached to Franco's army as correspondent for the *New York Times.* Since our entry into World War II he has covered events inside Germany from Stockholm, Sweden.

## BALDWIN, HANSON W.    466

Hanson W. Baldwin was born in 1903 and attended the Boys' Latin School, Baltimore, Maryland, and the U.S. Naval Academy. He began his newspaper career as a police reporter for the Baltimore *Sun.* He has been with the *New York Times* since 1929, and has acted as its military and naval correspondent since 1937. In

1943 he received the Pulitzer Prize for a series of articles on a tour he made through the South Pacific war area. Although not a regular war correspondent, during the present war he also visited the African battle areas for the *New York Times*.

## BARNES, RALPH W. 43

Ralph W. Barnes was born in Salem, Oregon, in 1899. His first newspaper assignment was on the *Brooklyn* (N. Y.) *Daily Eagle* in 1924. In that same year he joined the staff of the *New York Herald Tribune,* serving successively as a member of the editorial staff of its Paris bureau in 1929, its Rome correspondent in 1930, Moscow correspondent 1931-35, Berlin correspondent 1935-39, and London correspondent, 1939. He was killed in a bomber crash over Yugoslavia on November 18, 1940, while he was covering the Italo-Grecian campaign for his newspaper. He is mourned by the public as well as his colleagues as one of the outstanding foreign correspondents of our time.

## BEATTIE, EDWARD W., JR. 126, 130

Edward W. Beattie, Jr., is a graduate of Phillips Exeter Academy and Yale University. While he was on a walking tour through Germany in 1931 he became a member of the Berlin office of the United Press. Later, in the United States, he covered the Senate proceedings for the same news agency. In 1933 he went to London, and later Berlin, for the United Press. He has covered the major incidents of the present war, from the "China Incident" through the fall of France in 1940, at which time he was accredited to the B.E.F. in France. In late 1940 he returned to London as head of the United Press bureau there.

## BEATTY, JEROME G. 354

Jerome G. Beatty was a reporter on various newspapers in Kansas, New Orleans, Los Angeles, New York City, and Washington, D.C. from 1908 to 1915. From 1915 to 1928 he did motion picture publicity and advertising. Since the latter date he has been a free-lance writer. In 1938-39 he visited Arabia, the Belgian Congo, India, China, Fiji, and other far-distant points. He has published stories and articles in *Collier's, Esquire,* the *American Magazine,* the *Reader's Digest* and other periodicals.

## BELDEN, JACK 432

Jack Belden was born in Brooklyn, N. Y., in 1910 and attended Adelphi Academy, Summit, New Jersey, and Colgate University. During his college years he spent his summer vacations as a seaman, traveling all over the world. After his graduation he went to China, where he stayed for the next ten years, engaging in various occupations, and finally becoming a correspondent, in turn, for the United Press, International News Service, and *Time* Magazine. It was while he was with the latter publication that he accompanied General "Joe" Stilwell's army on its retreat from Burma, a feat which he has immortalized in his famous book, *Retreat with Stilwell*. In the early part of 1943 he was with the British Eighth Army in North Africa and later in Italy where he was wounded.

## BENNETT, LOWELL 520

Lowell Bennett, an International News Service correspondent, had had practically a lifetime of adventure before he was twenty-one: he had worked his way across the American continent, shipped to Australia, joined the R.A.F., been a sergeant in the International Brigade in Finland, driven an ambulance in France, become a member of the French Foreign Legion, volunteered as a parachutist in the Free French Army, and been captured and put into a concentration camp by the Germans after the fall of France. When he was released he became a correspondent for I.N.S. at the ripe age of twenty-three, and went through the entire Tunisian campaign. He was taken prisoner in November, 1943, while accompaning a United States Army Air Force bomber mission on the famous November raids over Berlin. Later he escaped and startled the world with accounts of what went on inside Europe, which he sent from an unknown place.

## BERKSON, SEYMOUR 40

Seymour Berkson was born in Chicago in 1905 and attended the University of Chicago. He was on the staff of the *Chicago Herald-Examiner* from 1923 to 1931, was with the New York bureau of the Associated Press in 1931, and became a staff writer for Universal Service in 1931. From 1932 to 1934 he was chief of the Rome bureau of Universal Service, and from 1934-35 chief of the Paris bureau. Later he became managing editor of International News Service in New York City.

## BESS, DEMAREE 206

Demaree Bess is an associate editor of the *Saturday Evening Post*. For many years he has covered practically every point on the globe for that magazine. During the present war he has published many articles giving his observations on all the major places of interest.

## BIGART, HOMER W. 594

Homer W. Bigart was born in Hawley, Pennsylvania, and received his education at Carnegie Institute of Technology and at New York University. His entire career as a newspaperman has been with the *New York Herald Tribune*. He began as a copy boy in 1929, and became a member of the reportorial staff in 1933. In 1942 he was sent to the *Herald Tribune's* London office, and in July, 1943, he went to Sicily to cover the activities of the United States Army there.

## BIRCHALL, FREDERICK T. 27, 123

Frederick T. Birchall was born in London, but has spent almost all of his life in this country. His career in the news-

paper world is one of the longest and most eventful of any man in the profession. After serving for twenty-seven years on the staff of the *New York Times,* the last six as its managing editor, he was, in 1932, at the retirement age. Instead of resting on his well-earned laurels, however, he then became head of the European staff of his paper, and from then on until 1939 he did perhaps the most important, and certainly the most exciting work of his career, reporting the many crises which developed in Europe during that period. These events he has recorded in one of the most distinguished books yet written by any foreign correspondent, *The Storm Breaks.* His reporting of affairs in Europe won for him the Pulitzer Prize in journalism in 1934. Since 1940 he has been on the *New York Times* staff in Canada.

## BLIVEN, BRUCE 5

Bruce Bliven was born in Emmetsburg, Iowa, in 1889, and attended Leland Stanford University. He began his editorial career on the staff of the *San Francisco Bulletin* in 1909; wrote articles and did advertising from 1912 to 1914; was director of the department of journalism at the University of Southern California from 1914 to 1916; was on the editorial staff of *Printer's Ink,* 1916-18; and with the *New York Globe,* 1919-23; and has been with the *New Republic* since 1923, latterly as its editor. During the period of his editorship he has made several trips to Europe.

## BOOTHE, CLARE 174

Clare Boothe is a well-known dramatist, journalist, traveler, and, most recently, Congresswoman from Connecticut. Her best-known plays are *The Women* (1936), *Kiss the Boys Goodbye* (1938), and *Margin for Error* (1939). In February, 1940, she went to Europe for *Time* and *Life* magazines, her husband's papers, and visited Italy, Portugal, Holland, Belgium, France, and England. Her book, *Europe in the Spring,* is the record of what she saw and heard there, in the months preceding and immediately following the invasion of the Lowlands and France. Later Miss Boothe also visited the Orient.

BOURKE-WHITE, MARGARET    306

Margaret Bourke-White was born in New York and graduated from Cornell University. She has been staff photographer for *Life* and *Fortune* magazines and has traveled over almost the entire globe taking the pictures which have won her fame. She has made many photomurals and pictures of industrial subjects, and two movies, *Eyes of Russia* and *Red Republic,* and has collaborated with Erskine Caldwell, then her husband, on three books, *You Have Seen Their Faces, North of the Danube,* and *Say, Is This the U. S. A.?* Her book *Shooting the Russian Front,* which she composed without collaborator, is an amazing pictorial record, with running commentaries, of the beginning of the Russo-German war, as seen by the author when she and her husband were in Russia in 1941.

BOYLE, KAY    228

Kay Boyle was born in St. Paul, Minnesota, in 1903 and attended the Ohio Mechanics Institute. In 1934 she won a Guggenheim fellowship, and in 1936 the O. Henry Memorial Prize. For many years she lived in France, returning to the United States only after the German victory over her adopted country in 1940. She is the author of many books, short stories, poems, and articles.

While not a foreign correspondent in the strict sense of the term, her intimate knowledge of France, gained from her long residence there, has given her a keenness of insight into the minds and hearts of its people that enables her to record with accuracy and intelligence what is going on under the surface of this subjugated country, as she has done in articles and stories since her return to this country.

BRIGHAM, DANIEL T.    586

Daniel T. Brigham was born in Massachusetts in 1901, and received most of his education in Europe—at Paris, Grenoble, and Munich. Trained in electrical engineering, he started working for the *New York Times* in 1936, on the electrical recording of telephoned copy.

His experience as a correspondent includes a period as free-lance correspondent for the *Paris Herald* and later assignments on the *Chicago Tribune* and in the Paris bureau of the *New York Times.* When France fell in June, 1940, he went to Berne, from which point he has been sending news to the *Times.*

BROCK, RAY    295

Ray Brock is one of the younger group of *New York Times* correspondents who has helped make the foreign news service of that paper famous. He went to Europe in 1939, "on a shoestring," as he himself said, landing a job as manager of the Berne bureau of Press Wireless just at the time the Germans overran Paris. When the Italians launched their attack on Greece he was sent to Belgrade by the *New York Times.* He was in Belgrade when the Germans entered Rumania, and when the Serbians staged their famous coup in rejection of the pact with the Axis. His dispatches on the latter event are considered classics in the realm of newspaper reportage.

His book, *Nor Any Victory,* is a warm and lively account of his experiences as a foreign correspondent from the time he landed in Europe, through scenes of the Greek resistance to the Italians, and the events in Yugoslavia immediately preceding and following the bombing of Belgrade by the Germans.

BROWN, CECIL    409

Cecil Brown's career has been one of adventure and hairbreadth escapes. In his younger days he "stowed away" on a cattle boat to South America, worked as a seaman on a ship making trips to Russian ports on the Black Sea, and later became a correspondent for International News Service, first in Paris and then in Rome. While still in Rome, in 1940, he became CBS correspondent there. But, following in the footsteps of many famous predecessors among foreign correspondents, he soon fell into disfavor with Mussolini on account of his distressing tendency to tell the truth about fascism as he saw it to his listeners in America, and in 1941 he was expelled from Italy. He then went to Yugoslavia, where he was arrested by the German authorities after their seizure of Belgrade. He escaped to Turkey, and was later sent to Cairo by CBS to cover the Syrian campaign. He next went to Singapore, from where he escaped shortly before it fell to the Japanese. His broadcasts from Singapore, and his book, *Suez to Singapore,* created much comment, both favorable and unfavorable, because of the sharp criticisms they contained of the British "brass hats" and their muddling in the initial phases of the war.

## BROWN, JAMES E.      332

James E. Brown, a United Press correspondent, has been a frequent visitor to Russia, in times of peace as well as war. Recently he made a trip to that country on a convoy carrying supplies to Murmansk. His book, *Russia Fights,* is a record of his impressions of Russia in the war.

## BROWN, JOHN MASON      562

John Mason Brown was born in Louisville, Kentucky, in 1900. He began his career as a teacher of the history of the theater. From 1924 to 1928 he was dramatic critic for the *Theatre Arts Monthly,* going to a similar position on the *New York Post* in 1929 and on the *New York World-Telegram* in 1941. He is now a lieutenant in the United States Navy. In 1943 he published a book, *To All Hands: An Amphibious Adventure,* dealing with his experiences in the service.

## BRUNDIDGE, HARRY T.      256

Harry T. Brundidge was born in Leavenworth, Kansas, and attended Central High School in Kansas City, Missouri. He left high school in his junior year, however, to begin work as a newspaper reporter on the *St. Louis Star,* a connection which was to continue for the next twenty-two years. During that long association Mr. Brundidge accomplished some outstanding feats of newspaper reporting for his paper. Among these are his exposé of the National Medical Diploma Mill Ring in 1924, his exposure of Jake Lingle, Chicago newspaperman, as the confederate of the underworld gangsters in that city, and his exclusive story on the assassination of Huey Long. In 1939-40 he followed the Japanese Army through Central and North China for the *Star,* and in 1941 visited England for the same paper. In 1942 he became an associate editor of *Cosmopolitan Magazine.*

## BYAS, HUGH      348

Hugh Byas was born in Scotland and did his first newspaper work there. Later, in 1909, he became a member of the staff of the *London Times.* In 1914 he went to Japan as editor of the *Japan Advertiser,* remaining in that post until 1922, when he returned to London for a brief period. In 1926 he returned to Tokyo as correspondent for the *London Times,* and a year later also became correspondent there for the *New York Times.* Mr. Byas, by reason of his long residence in Tokyo, was known as the dean of American correspondents there. He ended his long service in the Orient only in April, 1941, when he was succeeded in his post as correspondent for the *New York Times* by Otto D. Tolischus. He is the author of *Government by Assassination* and *The Japanese Enemy.*

## CALDWELL, ERSKINE      308

Erskine Caldwell has been known to the American reading public as the writer of realistic novels and short stories portraying the wretched living conditions of the Negroes and "poor whites" of the Old South. His first work as a reporter was done in collaboration with the *Life* and *Fortune* photographer, Margaret Bourke-White. In 1941 Mr. Caldwell went to Russia as a correspondent for *Collier's* and other periodicals. His book, *All Out on the Road to Smolensk,* is a complete account of his observations in wartime Russia.

## CARNEY, WILLIAM P. 101

William P. Carney started in the newspaper business in 1915, working first for the Associated Press and then for International News Service in Europe. He also worked for the *New York Evening Mail* until it ceased publication, later for the *New York Herald,* and then for the combined *New York Herald Tribune.* Before starting with the *New York Times* sixteen years ago he was on the staff of the Paris edition of the *New York Herald Tribune.* He was on the Paris bureau of the *New York Times* from 1928 to 1933, and from then until 1939 he was the *Times* correspondent in Spain. In 1939 he joined the New York staff of the *Times.*

He has written articles for *Scribner's Commentator, Collier's, Liberty,* and for several Catholic magazines, among them the *Sign.*

## CARROLL, WALLACE 318

Wallace Carroll is a former United Press correspondent, having represented that news agency at Geneva during the last years of the League of Nations. From 1938 to 1941 he was head of the London office of UP. During the heat of the German drive on Moscow he went to Russia. He was one of the group of American correspondents who covered the famous Stalin-Beaverbrook-Harriman conference there. His book, *We're In This With Russia,* is a record of this Russian visit. In 1943 he was sent to London by the O.W.I.

## CARSE, ROBERT 266

Robert Carse is a former newspaper reporter and free-lance writer, having published articles in the *Saturday Evening Post, Liberty,* and other periodicals. In 1941 he shipped on a merchant vessel to Russia. His book, *There go the Ships,* is the product of this trip.

## CASEY, ROBERT J. 201, 235, 452

Robert J. Casey saw service in World War I, emerging as a captain in the Field Artillery, only to become immediately embroiled in a newspaper career which has filled his life with adventure ever since. He has been a member of the staff of the *Chicago Daily News,* and its top feature man, for over twenty years, and has won acclaim among his colleagues for his stories of people and events, always touched with humor, always slightly sardonic, but never losing sight of the human factor in the subjects with which he dealt. As a foreign correspondent in World War II, first in England and France, and then in the South Pacific, he has shown these same qualities in abundance. *I Can't Forget,* the book in which he tells the poignant story of the crushing of the Lowland countries and France by Germany, shows Casey at his best. *Torpedo Junction* is the story of his experiences as a foreign correspondent on board a United States warship in the South Pacific.

## CASSIDY, HENRY C. 325

Henry C. Cassidy has been European correspondent for the Associated Press since 1936, when he was stationed in Paris. In 1938 he began his career as a war correspondent, covering the Battle of the Ebro on the side of the Spanish Republicans. When World War II broke out in 1939, he was accredited to the French armies, and covered the British Army and Air Force in France, remaining in Paris until after the Germans entered the city. In 1940 he went on a troop train to Berlin and from there to Moscow, where he remained as chief of the A.P. bureau. His book, *Moscow Dateline*, tells the story of that assignment.

## CLAPPER, RAYMOND 488

Raymond Clapper was born May 30, 1892, on a farm in Kansas, and grew up in Kansas City. He actually began his newspaper career here, for as a boy he sold papers on the streets for the *Kansas City World*. While he was a student at the University of Kansas he was college correspondent for the *Kansas City Star*, and left the university before his graduation to become a reporter on its staff. Later he went to the United Press, and remained with that service until 1934. In 1936 he began to write a daily column for the Scripps-Howard papers. Later his column was signed up by the United Features Syndicate. In 1942 he became a radio commentator for the Mutual Broadcasting System.

While most of his writing was done in the domestic field, he had a fling at foreign correspondence in 1930, when he covered the London Naval Conference. And in this war he made a trip to England shortly before Pearl Harbor, another to Cairo, Calcutta, and Chungking shortly thereafter, and in 1943 went on a four-months' tour of observation to England and the battlefields of Africa and Sicily. In January, 1944, he left Washington to make a first-hand survey of the war in the South Pacific. He was killed in an airplane crash there during the invasion of the Marshall Islands.

## CONGER, BEACH 194

Beach Conger was born in Copenhagen, Denmark, while his parents were returning to the United States from Germany following the break in diplomatic relations between the two countries during World War I. Conger, whose father was a well-known American foreign correspondent, was educated in Germany, and later at Cranbrook Preparatory School and the University of Michigan. During his university days he became campus correspondent for the United Press. In 1939 he was sent to its Detroit bureau, and shortly thereafter to its New York office. Early in 1940 he was assigned to Copenhagen, but after the occupation of Denmark was transferred to Berlin, where he helped cover the German campaign in the west. He was arrested and interned in Germany after the entry of the United States into the war.

## COURTNEY, WILLIAM B. 167

William B. Courtney has been associated with *Collier's* since 1925, first as associate editor and staff correspondent, and, since 1928, alternately as foreign correspondent and aviation editor. As foreign correspondent he has covered England, Russia, Finland, Sweden, France, Spain, Portugal, the Balkans, and South and Central America. He was with the Italian forces in Ethiopia in 1935-36; with the Japanese Army in Manchuria and the Chinese Army in South China and Hankow, 1938-39; with the German Army in North Europe in 1939; and in Yugoslavia in 1941. In 1943 he became the London correspondent of *Collier's*.

## COWLES, VIRGINIA 165

Virginia Cowles made her first trip to Europe as a foreign correspondent for the *New York Herald Tribune*, at the same time acting as correspondent for *Sunday Times* (London) and the *London Daily Herald*. Her work took her to Spain during the Civil War; to Russia, Germany, Czechoslovakia, and Paris, before and after Munich; and to England during the summer and fall of 1941. *Looking For Trouble* is the book in which she tells the story of what she experienced in these various theaters of war.

## DANIELL, RAYMOND 196, 247

Raymond Daniell was born in 1901 and educated at Rutgers University. His first newspaper work was with the *New York Herald*. Later he worked for the *New*

*York Post* and the Associated Press. He has been with the *New York Times* since 1928, and head of its London bureau since 1939. His book, *Civilians Must Fight,* is the story of how the people of England withstood the German raids of 1940-41.

DAVENPORT, WALTER                    437

Walter Davenport started his journalistic career on the Philadelphia *Public Ledger,* going from there to the *New York American.* Then came World War I and an interlude of service with the A.E.F. in France, from which he returned to the United States in 1919, to begin working on the *New York Sun.* In 1923 he joined the staff of *Liberty* magazine, but after only a little more than a year transferred his allegiance to *Collier's,* where he has remained ever since, and of which he is now associate editor. He has written articles on the Panama Canal Zone and on England, in the foreign field, as well as many articles on various national problems, situations, and personalities.

DAVIS, FORREST                       396

Forrest Davis, a native of Indiana, has been a newspaperman since just after the First World War, having worked in turn on the staffs of the *New York Herald Tribune* and the *New York World-Telegram,* and as general correspondent for the Scripps-Howard newspapers. He has written a number of books, among them *What Price Wall Street, Huey Long: A Candid Biography,* and *The Atlantic System,* besides contributing frequently to various periodicals. Although he is not a foreign correspondent, he has been included here because of the book *How War Came,* written jointly with Ernest Lindley, which contains an eyewitness report, supplemented by documents to which the authors were given access by government officials, of the events which led up to and culminated in our declaration of war against Japan.

DE LUCE, DANIEL                      604

Daniel De Luce was born in Yuma, Arizona, in 1911 and graduated from the University of California. He began his newspaper work on the *Los Angeles Examiner.* In 1939 he went to London for the Associated Press. He was the only newspaperman in Iran when the Allies took over that country in October, 1941. In January, 1942, he was sent to Burma, where he covered the fighting until forced into India by the advancing Japanese forces. Later he went to Italy.

He was the first American correspondent to enter the war zone of the Partisans after a sensational journey along the coast of Yugoslavia.

DENNY, HAROLD                        498

Harold Denny was born in Des Moines, Iowa, in 1899, and studied at Drake University. From 1913 to 1922 he worked on newspapers in Des Moines, St. Paul, Minneapolis, New York (the *Herald Tribune*), and on the Paris edition of the latter paper. He has been with the *New York Times* since 1922, in those years having covered the Moroccan War in 1926; the Nicaraguan crisis, 1927-28; the Cuban crisis, 1930-31; the Italian campaign in Ethiopia, 1935; the Moscow treason trials, 1936-38; the German seizure of Czechoslovakia, 1938; and the Russo-Finnish War, 1939. He was Moscow correspondent for the *New York Times* from 1934 to 1939.

During the present war he was the *Times'* accredited correspondent with the B.E.F. in France, and later covered the campaign in Libya. His capture by Rommel's forces in 1941, and his subsequent imprisonment, provided material for his book, *Behind Both Lines.* He was eventually exchanged and returned to this country on the Gripsholm. Later he became correspondent for the *New York Times* in Spain.

## DE ROCHEMONT, RICHARD 223

Richard de Rochemont was born in Boston, Massachusetts, and is a graduate of Harvard College. From 1928 to 1931, he was a reporter for Boston and New York newspapers. In 1931, he went to Paris as editor of the French edition of *Fox Movietone News.* In 1934 he became European manager for the March of Time and representative of Time Inc. publications. Residing in France, he traveled during this period through most of Europe.

The outbreak of war found him in Poland, whence he returned to Paris to become an accredited war correspondent with the French Army for *Life* Magazine. With the fall of France, de Rochemont left Paris, and returned to the United States. In 1941, he went back to Europe, visiting Portugal, Spain, and unoccupied France. During this trip he established contact with French Underground leaders, some of whom are now prominent in the French resistance movement and in the French Committee of National Liberation. At the present time, de Rochemont is the producer of the March of Time film series for Time Inc. and is active in Franco-American affairs in the United States as president of France Forever, the Fighting French committee in the United States, co-operating with the French Committee of National Liberation.

## DEUEL, WALLACE R. 141

Wallace Deuel was born in Chicago in 1905 and received his college education at the University of Illinois. For the first three years after his graduation in 1926 he was instructor in political science and international law at the American University in Beirut, Syria. In 1929 he became assistant to the foreign editor of the *Chicago Daily News,* in charge of the New York cable desk. Later he was in Washington, and then in Rome, as correspondent for the *Chicago Daily News.* In 1934 his paper sent him as corre-

spondent to Berlin with roving assignments all over Europe. He returned to this country in January, 1941. His book, *People Under Hitler,* is one of the most thoughtful and provocative analyses of the Nazi way of life.

## DEW, GWEN 442

Gwen Dew was born in Albion, Michigan, in 1907, and graduated from the University of Michigan, where she was a student of journalism. Her first work was in the field of advertising, and of writing for magazines and newspapers. In 1937 she covered the coronation of King George VI and the wedding of the Duke of Windsor. In 1940 she went to the Orient as a correspondent for the *Detroit News* and for *Newsweek.* She was in Hongkong when it was taken by the Japanese, and was among those who were imprisoned by the Japs in the concentration camp at Fort Stanley. She came back to this country on the *Gripsholm* in the summer of 1942.

## DISHER, LEO 517

Leo Disher was educated at Riverside Military Academy and Duke University. He joined the United Press in 1939 and was one of the group of U.P. correspondents who accompanied the Allied troops when they landed at Oran in November, 1942. His courage and heroism in the pursuit of his duties on that assignment won for him the Order of the Purple Heart.

## DOS PASSOS, JOHN 83

John Dos Passos was born in Chicago in 1896 and graduated from Harvard in 1916. He has won fame as an author and playwright. He became one of America's outstanding novelists. Among his best-known books are: *Three Soldiers, Manhattan Transfer, The 42nd Parallel, Nineteen Nineteen, The Big Money, Adventures of a Young Man.* Although never a newspaperman he went to Spain during the Civil War to follow the fortunes of the Loyalists, for whose cause he had great sympathy. Some of his best articles about the war there appeared in *Esquire*.

## DRISCOLL, JOSEPH 124

Joseph Driscoll was born in St. Louis in 1902. He received his education in public and private schools, and began his newspaper career on the *St. Louis Times*, later going to the *Post-Dispatch*. He has been on the staff of the *New York Herald Tribune* since 1930; chief correspondent in charge of the London office, 1935-39; chief Washington correspondent, 1939-41; and national correspondent since 1941.

## DURANTY, WALTER 60, 133

Walter Duranty was born and raised in England. During the First World War he worked for English papers as a war correspondent, and afterwards he held a job in the Paris office of the *New York Times*. He was the Moscow correspondent of the *New York Times* from 1920 to 1939. During that time he became one of the outstanding authorities on Soviet Russian affairs. Among other things Duranty was the first newspaperman to point out that a man called Stalin might one day assume international importance, and that in 1923, at a time when other correspondents had hardly ever heard that name. During the twenties Mr. Duranty also covered numerous events on the European continent, particularly in France. Aside from his outstanding work in Soviet Russia he became famous for his unwillingness to make any compromises as to how and what he wrote. He coined the phrase *"I write as I please,"* which also became the title of his outstanding autobiographical book. Other books he wrote were *The Kremlin and its People, History of the Soviet Union*. Since Mr. Duranty has left the *New York Times*, he has been a regular contributor to numerous magazines, such as *Atlantic Monthly, Harper's*, and *Collier's*. In 1932 Walter Duranty was awarded the Pulitzer Prize for distinguished foreign reporting.

## FISCHER, LOUIS 8, 57

Louis Fischer has been a free-lance European correspondent for American newspapers and periodicals for more than twenty years. In 1922 he went to Russia for the *New York Post*, and since 1924 he has been an accredited correspondent for the *Nation*. Altogether he spent fourteen years in Russia and came to be regarded as one of the outstanding experts on questions involving the Communist regime and the build-up of a socialist economic system. His two-volume work, *The Soviet in World Affairs*, became one of the outstanding source books for students of Soviet Russia. During the Civil War in Spain he spent much time at the Loyalist front. His book, *Men and Politics*, belongs among the few autobiographies of journalists which have assumed significance beyond the accounts of personal adventures. Mr. Fischer has also visited India where he spent one week with Gandhi.

## FLANNER, JANET 103

When the *New Yorker* started publication in 1925, Janet Flanner was living in Paris. She immediately became its Paris correspondent, and began writing for it, under the pen name "Genet," those "Letters from Paris" which were soon to become famous. During this period she also went occasionally to Bayreuth, Salzburg, London, and Berlin, and reported on events and personalities in those places. She returned to New York in 1939 for a conference with the editors of the *New Yorker*, expecting to go back to Europe, but was unable to do so.

Since then she has remained in the United States, using her vast knowledge of places, persons and events in Europe in the composition of profiles for the *New Yorker*. Some of the most famous of these deal with Thomas Mann, Hitler, and Marshal Petain. A collection of her letters from Paris appeared in book form under the title *An American in Paris*, in 1940.

**FLEISHER, WILFRID**                    345

Wilfrid Fleisher spent the greater part of his life in Tokyo, where his father published the *Japan Advertiser*. Later he himself was editor of the same paper, also acting as Tokyo correspondent for the *New York Herald Tribune*. His book, *Our Enemy Japan*, is an excellent portrayal of Japan as he saw it during the twenty-six years of his residence there. After December, 1941, he was in Washington as correspondent there for the *New York Herald Tribune*.

**FODOR, MARCEL W.**                    187

M. W. Fodor has been a European foreign correspondent for more than twenty years and is generally regarded as knowing more about Central Europe than any other newspaperman. He has represented the *Manchester Guardian*, the *Philadelphia Public Ledger* and the *New York Post*, and the *Chicago Daily News* as Central European correspondent. In addition he has contributed many articles on European affairs to leading periodicals such as the *Nation*, the *Atlantic Monthly*, and *Foreign Affairs*, and is the author of two books, *South of Hitler*, and *The Revolution Is On*.

**FORD, COREY**                    455

Corey Ford, author of *Short Cut to Tokyo: The Battle for the Aleutians; From the Ground Up: A Personal, Behind-the-Scenes Story of the Training of an Army Pilot from Pre-Flight to Combat* (written with Alastair MacBain); and numerous other books and magazine articles; was born in New York City in 1902. He was graduated from Columbia in 1923. From that time up to the outbreak of the war he had written nine books of humor, a great number of magazine articles and several plays. Long before the war began he knew the Aleutians from the trip he made there as the basis for a series of articles in *Collier's Weekly*. He also, in 1926, visited hitherto unexplored parts of central Borneo. Since

the beginning of the war he has been working with the Army Air Forces on specially assigned tasks. From these tasks have evolved his two most recent books. He is unmarried, and when not ranging the world in pursuit of a story he makes his home in Freedom, New Hampshire. Early in 1944 he was commissioned a major in the United States Army Air Forces.

**FORTE, ALDO**                    574

Aldo Forte was born in Boston, Massachusetts, June 12, 1910, and attended school in Brighton, Massachusetts. He went to Rome for the first time in 1933, and joined the staff of the United Press there. He became known as an expert on Vatican affairs. He left Rome several months before Italy declared war on the United States and went to Switzerland, where he remained as manager of the Berne bureau of U.P.

Early in September, 1943, Forte, disguised as an Italian mountain climber, cut his way through barbed wire on the Swiss frontier and entered German-dominated northern Italy. It was the information he gathered on this trip which enabled him to cable back to the United States his story of the desire of the Italian people to resist the Germans.

**GALLAGHER, WES**                    527

Wes Gallagher was born in Santa Cruz, California, in 1911. His first foreign newspaper assignment was in 1939, when he covered the Russo-Finnish war for the Associated Press. Later he was in Denmark, Norway, and Rumania, then covered the Italian and German campaigns in Greece, England, and the invasion of Africa. He is the author of *Back Door to Berlin*, a story of the North African campaign.

**GEDYE, G. E. R.**                    35

G. E. R. Gedye was born and educated in England. He wrote fiction and engaged in free-lance journalism before going on his first assignment as a foreign correspondent for the London *Times* in 1922. He represented that paper in the Rhineland and Ruhr districts from 1922-25, and in Central Europe, with offices in Vienna, in 1926. From 1929 to 1939 he was Central and Southeastern European correspondent for both the *London Daily Telegraph* and the *New York Times*.

He attained world fame by his dramatic coverage of the rape of Austria. Expelled from Vienna, he went to Prague, where within a short time he was to encounter the Nazis again. In 1939 his newspaper sent him to Moscow and later to Istanbul. He is the author of several books on European affairs, the most famous of these being *Betrayal in Central Europe*.

GELLHORN, MARTHA          161

As foreign correspondent for *Time* magazine, and later for *Collier's*, Martha Gellhorn has covered most of the important trouble spots throughout the world. She was in Spain during the Civil War there, visited the Finnish trenches during the Russo-Finnish campaign, and lived through the horrors of the Japanese bombings of China. Most recently she has been in England. She has published a book of American reportages, *The Trouble I've Seen*, and several novels. She is the wife of Ernest Hemingway.

GERVASI, FRANK          300, 495, 506

As correspondent for International News Service, and later as associate editor and correspondent for *Collier's*, Frank Gervasi has covered the entire scene of battle in the present war, from the Americas to Bermuda, England, South Africa, Egypt, Palestine, Libya, Turkey, Arabia, Iraq and Iran, India, Thailand, Singapore, the Philippines, and, more recently, Italy.

He has written two books about World War II: *War has Seven Faces* and *But Soldiers Wondered Why*.

GORRELL, HENRY T.          597

Henry T. Gorrell was born of American parents in Florence, Italy, in 1911. He gained his initial newspaper experience in the Mid-West and joined the United Press in Kansas City in 1930, serving later in the Washington and New York bureaus before being assigned to Buenos Aires in 1933. With the outbreak of the Italo-Ethiopian war, Gorrell was sent to Rome as assistant U.P. manager. Later he served in London, Madrid and Budapest, moving always to the currently most active front. He was shifted to the Mediterranean theater of war when the Italians invaded Greece and has been assigned to the Middle East almost continuously since.

Accompanying a U.S. bomber force raiding Navarino Bay on the Greek coast, in a plane badly crippled and riddled with fighter-plane and anti-aircraft fire, Gorrell rendered first aid to a dangerously wounded crew member, saving his life. For this "extreme gallantry in conduct under fire" he has been awarded the U. S. Air Medal. In presenting the award, Major-General Lewis H. Brereton declared his courage "typical of representatives of a free press fighting for a free world."

GRAEBNER, WALTER          328

Walter Graebner, a *Time-Life-Fortune* correspondent, was born in Columbus, Ohio, and attended the University of Wisconsin. He joined the staff of *Time* magazine soon after leaving college, eventually becoming head of its Chicago editorial office. In 1937 he went to London as head of its London office. In May, 1942, he made a trip to Russia, returning by way of Cairo just as the British Eighth Army was attacking. He brought back with him to this country a film taken on the Russian front, which was shown in the United States by the March of Time under the title "One Day of War." He is the author of several books about the present war, among them *Conversations in London* (jointly with Stephen Laird) and *Round Trip To Russia.*

GRIGG, JOSEPH W. 154

Joseph W. Grigg was born in Bangor, Maine, in 1910 and received his education at the Westminster School, London, and at Cambridge University. The son of an American foreign correspondent, he himself also entered the newspaper field in 1932, when he joined the staff of the *New York Sun.* He joined the United Press in 1934. From 1939 to 1941 he was with their Berlin bureau. He is co-author, with Frederick C. Oechsner and others, of *This Is The Enemy.*

GUNTHER, JOHN 20

John Gunther was born in Chicago in 1901 and graduated from the University of Chicago in 1922. He began his newspaper career as a reporter on the *Chicago Daily News* that same year, and served that paper as foreign correspondent in London (1924-26), Paris, Moscow, Berlin, Rome, Scandinavia, Geneva, Spain, the Near East (1926-29), Central Europe and the Balkans (1930-35), and again in London, 1935-36. He is the author of several books on foreign political affairs, notably *Inside Europe, Inside Asia,* and *Inside Latin America,* and has contributed articles to the *Nation, Harper's,* the *Reader's Digest, Asia,* the *Saturday Evening Post,* the *New Republic,* etc.

HAMILTON, THOMAS J. 105

Thomas J. Hamilton was born in Georgia in 1909 and attended the University of Georgia. Later he went to Oxford on a Rhodes scholarship, taking an honors degree in modern history there in 1930. His newspaper career began on the *Atlanta Journal* and continued in Washington, D.C., where in 1934 he became a member of the Associated Press staff. In 1936 he went to London to cover the work of the Non-Intervention Committee. He joined the staff of the *New York Times* there and was sent to Spain

at the close of the Civil War in 1939. His book, *Appeasement's Child,* is the fruit of the two years he spent there. In 1941 he returned to this country to join the Washington bureau of the *New York Times.* In 1942 he spent three months in Brazil and Chile as an exchange journalist, investigating the activities of Franco's propagandists against the United States in the Latin American countries.

HARMON, DUDLEY, II 226

Dudley Harmon was a special contributor to the *Christian Science Monitor,* in 1942 and 1943. She is the daughter of Dudley Harmon, Executive Vice-President of the New England Council. Early in 1942 Miss Harmon entered the information service of the Fighting French at Brazzaville, French Equatorial Africa. She served with them during the critical period of organization of their headquarters there, when there were practically no diplomatic facilities, and when a radio station, improvised out of spare parts, constituted one of their main sources of contact with the outside world. During this period Miss Harmon's dispatches appeared in the *Christian Science Monitor.* On her return to the United States her ship was torpedoed not far from the American coast, but she managed to get back to port ahead of the copy which she had air mailed from Africa, writing a number of political and personal-experience stories.

HARSCH, JOSEPH C. 155

Joseph C. Harsch was born in 1905 and attended Williams College and Cambridge University, England. He was at the Washington bureau of the *Christian Science Monitor* from 1931 to 1939, and then went to Europe as its foreign correspondent, in Rome and later in Berlin, 1939-41. Later he became a radio commentator over Station WTOP (CBS) in Washington, D.C. He is the author of numerous articles, as well as of a book, *Pattern of Conquest.*

## HELLMAN, LILLIAN 87

Lillian Hellman was born in New Orleans and received her education at New York and Columbia Universities. She has won acclaim as a playwright, the best-known of her dramatic productions being *The Children's Hour, The Little Foxes,* and *Watch on The Rhine.* While she has never been a newspaper correspondent in the strict sense of the term, her interest in political affairs and her sympathy with the cause of the Spanish Loyalists led her to go to Spain during the Civil War, and to write articles about what she saw there, which were published in the *New Republic* and other American periodicals.

## HEMINGWAY, ERNEST 97

Ernest Hemingway was born in Oak Park, Illinois, in 1898. He took part in the First World War. After the Armistice he settled in Paris, working as a newspaperman. Later he retired completely from journalistic work and became one of America's three outstanding modern novelists. Among his best-known books are: *Winner Take All, The Sun Also Rises, Farewell To Arms,* and *For Whom the Bell Tolls.* He has always been vitally interested in the cause of democracy in all lands. His sympathies were particularly engaged by the Spanish Loyalists, for whose cause he spent a great deal of time, energy and money. In 1937-38 he went to Spain as a correspondent for the North American Newspaper Alliance. He has been a contributor to *Esquire,* the *New Republic,* and other periodicals.

## HERSEY, JOHN 419, 462

John Hersey was born in Tsientsin, China, in 1914, the son of American missionaries. He attended schools there. Later he came to the United States and studied at Yale. In 1942 he went to England as correspondent for *Time* and *Life* magazines, later covering the Southwest Pacific war area and Italy for the same magazines. He has written two books,

*Into The Valley* and *Men on Bataan,* on his experiences in the Pacific theater, and a novel, *A Bell for Adano,* dealing with the problems of an occupied Italian town.

## HILL, RUSSELL 501

Russell Hill graduated from Columbia University in 1939. He was awarded a scholarship at Cambridge, but chose instead a journalistic career. In the same year a trip to Europe led him to Berlin, where Ralph W. Barnes, correspondent for the *New York Herald Tribune,* took him on as his assistant. He also became an assistant to William L. Shirer of the Columbia Broadcasting System. When Barnes was expelled from Germany in 1940, Russell Hill, then 21 years old, found himself the only representative of the *Herald Tribune* in Germany. Less than a year later he also had to quit the Third Reich. He went to the Balkans where he covered the Yugoslav and Greek campaigns and made a sensational escape from the Germans in a small fishing boat. Eventually he landed in Cairo.

Later he covered the events and troop movements in Syria and Iran and still later was sent to North Africa to cover the campaign of the British Eighth Army against Rommel's Afrika Korps. His brilliant books, *Desert War* and *Conquest of Africa,* contain the experiences of this youngest of all foreign correspondents.

## HINDUS, MAURICE 339

Maurice Hindus was born in Russia in 1891 and came to this country in 1901. He graduated from Colgate University, and began doing free-lance writing in 1917. In 1923 he visited Russia as a correspondent for *Century* magazine, and he has made regular visits there since that time for other periodicals. He covered the Russo-German war for the *New York Herald Tribune.* He has written many magazine articles and books about Russia and the Balkans. Some of the most recent of these are *Mother Russia, Russia and*

*Germany, We Shall Live Again,* and *Russia and Japan.*

**HOLLENBECK, DON** 599

Don Hollenbeck began his newspaper career while he was a student at the University of Nebraska. Then for nine years after his graduation he worked on the *Omaha* (Nebraska) *News-Bee,* going after that to the Associated Press and working in its New York and San Francisco bureaus. In 1940 he joined the news department of NBC in New York. Shortly after the outbreak of the war in December, 1941, he became one of the first correspondents to be assigned to the London office of the O.W.I. In March, 1942, he returned to NBC, and broadcast a "World News Roundup" every weekday morning from London. In August of that same year he was assigned to broadcast from Station AFHQ in Algiers.

**HUSS, PIERRE J.** 552

Pierre Huss was for eight years—from 1932 to 1941—head of the Berlin bureau of International News Service. He was one of the first newspaper correspondents to interview Hitler after his rise to power, and he interviewed him for the last time in November, 1941, shortly before Germany declared war on the United States. An interesting account of this interview is reported by Mr. Huss in his book, *The Foe We Face.*

**INGERSOLL, RALPH** 538

Ralph Ingersoll spent two years as a mining engineer in California, Arizona, and Mexico after his graduation from Yale University. He then came to New York, where he was first a reporter on the *New York American,* later managing editor of the *New Yorker,* and still later managing editor of *Fortune* magazine. In 1935 he became vice president and general manager of *Time* magazine, and in 1937 was appointed its publisher. In 1940 he founded a new type of newspaper, *PM.* In that same year he went to Eng-

land to observe the effects of the war there. His book, *Report on England,* tells the story of his trip. Later he traveled to all the battlefronts around the globe, recording his observations in a book, *Action On All Fronts.* Soon after his return from that extended trip, in 1942, he entered active army service, and was sent to Tunisia. From his experiences there he wrote *The Battle is The Pay-Off.*

**JACOBY, MELVILLE** 424

Melville Jacoby was a *Time* and *Life* correspondent in the Philippines during the Japanese siege of those islands. When he left Bataan he went to Australia, where he was killed in an airplane accident early in 1942. General MacArthur, when informed of his death, remarked of him that he had been a "model war reporter."

**JOHNSTON, STANLEY** 449

Stanley Johnston, an Australian by birth, enlisted in an artillery battery in the First World War at the age of 17. At the close of the war he returned to Sydney, Australia, where he obtained a degree in mining engineering at the University of Sydney in 1923. For some years thereafter he did engineering consultation work, mainly in New Guinea, where he was instrumental in establishing one of the world's first and most successful freight airlines, to haul mining machinery into, and gold out of, the island. In 1936 Johnston came to New York, where he was married. In 1937 he and his wife went to Europe, and finally settled in Paris, where in 1938 Johnston joined Press Wireless as supervisor of a "stand-by" transmitter in Bordeaux.

When France fell he joined the London bureau of the *Chicago Tribune,* and was assigned to Dover. Early in 1942 he flew to Honolulu to represent the *Tribune* in the South Pacific. His dispatches on the Battle of the Coral Sea have made newspaper history, and his book, *Queen of the*

*Flat-Tops,* has immortalized the aircraft carrier *Lexington.*

KALTENBORN, HANS V.            17

H. V. Kaltenborn has had a long experience as a newspaper reporter, editor and radio commentator. For twenty-five years he was on the staff of the *Brooklyn* (N.Y.) *Eagle,* as reporter and later as associate editor, resigning more than fifteen years ago to devote all his time to radio. Mr. Kaltenborn may be justly regarded as the dean of radio commentators. The three most famous of his radio reporting exploits are the broadcasts he made on the spot in the Spanish Civil War in August and September, 1936, the first battle broadcasts in history; his round-up of news giving a shatteringly correct picture of what went on in the world at the time of the *Anschluss;* and the radio round-up covering the conference of Munich with reporters stationed there, in Berlin, in Paris and in London. His best-known books are *I Broadcast the Crisis; Kaltenborn Edits the News;* and *Kaltenborn Edits the War News.*

KIRKPATRICK, HELEN PAULL    598

Helen Kirkpatrick was graduated from the Masters School, Dobbs Ferry, New York, and from Smith College, and at one time worked for the Foreign Policy Association at Geneva. As a newspaperwoman she has worked for leading British newspapers and magazines, including the *Manchester Guardian,* the *London Daily Chronicle,* and the *London Daily Telegraph,* besides having conducted the *Whitehall News Letter,* a weekly news digest published in London and distributed widely throughout the British Empire. At one time, too, she was foreign correspondent in Geneva for the *New York Herald Tribune.*

As the only woman on the foreign staff of the *Chicago Daily News* she has covered a great many of the important and critical points during these past most critical years: Prague, Spain, the Balkans,

Poland, Italy, Germany and France. Shortly after the A.E.F. landed in Africa Miss Kirkpatrick went there. Later she was also in Italy. She is the author of two books, *This Terrible Peace* and *Under the British Umbrella.*

KLUCKHOHN, FRANK L.        544

Frank L. Kluckhohn was born in St. Paul, Minnesota, in 1907, and received his education at the University of Minnesota and the Centro de Estudios Historicos, Madrid. He was a reporter for the *St. Paul Dispatch* from 1926 to 1928, and for the *Boston Globe* in 1929. Since 1929 he has been with the *New York Times:* he covered the Spanish Civil War in 1936; had an assignment in Mexico City in 1937-38; and spent a period as Presidential correspondent in Washington, D.C. in 1938-39. He was with the Allied forces in North Africa from the time of their landing at Oran in November, 1942, until the final victory at Cape Bon. At the conclusion of the African campaign he was transferred by his paper to the South Pacific, where he has been stationed in New Guinea.

KNICKERBOCKER,
    HUBERT RENFRO          11, 573

H. R. Knickerbocker was born in Texas in 1898 and received his education at Southwestern University in that state and at Columbia University. Later he also studied at the Universities of Berlin, Munich, and Vienna. He began his newspaper career on the *Newark* (N.J.) *Morning Ledger* in 1920, later working on the staffs of the *New York Evening Post* and *New York Sun.* His first post as foreign correspondent was in Berlin, where he was assistant foreign correspondent for the *New York Evening Post* and *Philadelphia Public Ledger,* 1924-25, and chief correspondent for those papers, 1928-1941. From 1925 to 1941 he also represented International News Service, being Moscow correspondent, 1925-27, Berlin correspondent, 1928-1933, and traveling correspondent, 1933-41. In 1941 he became chief of the foreign service department of the *Chicago Sun.* He received the Pulitzer Prize for foreign correspondents in 1931.

## KUH, FREDERICK                        589

Frederick Kuh was born in Chicago in 1895 and graduated from the University of Chicago in 1917. That same year he became a reporter on the *Chicago Herald,* and later on the *Chicago Evening Post.* From 1919 to 1924 he was Central European correspondent for the *London Daily Herald,* and from 1924 to 1942 he represented the United Press in London, Moscow, Berlin and Manchuria. In 1942 he became chief London correspondent for the Field publications.

## LARDNER, JOHN                        435

The son of the famed Ring Lardner wrote a sports column for the North American Newspaper Alliance for a number of years until shortly before our entry into the present war, when he became a war correspondent. In 1942 he accompanied the first A.E.F. to Australia, where he stayed for five months. *Southwest Passage* is the story of his experiences there. In January, 1943, he went to North Africa to cover that sector for N.A.N.A. Later he represented the Bell Syndicate in Italy.

## LAWRENCE, WILLIAM H.                        337

W. H. Lawrence was born and educated in Lincoln, Nebraska, and did his first newspaper work on the *Lincoln Star* while he was still in high school. Afterwards he worked briefly on the staffs of the *Omaha* (Neb.) *World-Herald* and the Associated Press before going to Chicago for the United Press. He made a reputation as a labor reporter with this organization by his coverage of the Michigan motor plant strikes in 1937. In 1938 he was transferred to the Washington bureau of UP. He covered the National Conventions of 1940 and was with Willkie during the entire campaign. In 1941 he joined the staff of *Newsweek* and was assigned to Moscow.

## LEE, CLARK                        402

Clark Lee was born in Oakland, California, in 1907 and received his education at Rutgers University. Like so many other newspapermen, he was born into a "newspaper" family, so to speak, since his father, mother and sister are likewise in this profession. His first assignment took him to Mexico in 1933. In 1938 he went to Honolulu, where he married a Hawaiian princess. Later he went to Tokyo for the Associated Press. He wrote the first eyewitness account of the Japanese invasion along the Lingayen Gulf to be sent from the Manila bureau on December 23, 1941. After the fall of Manila, Lee apparently disappeared. He was heard of again on January 9, 1942, from Corregidor, at a time when none of the other correspondents stationed in the Philippines had been able to contact their newspapers. He told the story of the tragic events of that month of December in *They Call It Pacific.* Later he went to Italy as a representative of International News Service.

## LESUEUR, LAURENCE E.                        321

Larry Lesueur is a native of New York City and a graduate of New York University. True to his family tradition —for his father was foreign correspondent for the *New York Herald Tribune,* and his grandfather was owner and publisher of two newspapers in the Middle West— he went into newspaper work immediately after graduating from college, joining the staff of the Associated Press in 1931. In 1937 he went to Europe as radio commentator for the Columbia Broadcasting System, covering the activities of the R. A. F. and the British army in France during the first year of the war. After the French surrender he went to the London office of CBS as assistant to Edward R. Murrow. In the autumn of 1941 he was sent to Russia, where he covered the Russian war, from the siege of Moscow to the recovery of Stalingrad. The story of these events he has recorded in his book, *Twelve Months That Changed the World*. A year later he visited Persia, Egypt, French Equatorial Africa and the Sudan.

## LIEBLING, ARNOLD J. 169

Arnold J. Liebling was born in New York City and educated at Dartmouth College, the Sorbonne and L'Ecole des Chartes in Paris. He worked briefly as a reporter on the *Providence* (R.I.) *Journal-Bulletin*. He has written many articles for the *New Yorker*, as well as for the *Saturday Evening Post* and *McCall's*, and is, in addition, the author of four books: *They All Sang* (1933); *Back Where I Came From* (1938); *The Telephone Booth Indian* (1942); and *The Road Back To Paris* (1944). Mr. Liebling knows Europe well, having visited it frequently both as a child and a young man, sent back stories of the war in France in 1939-40 to the *New Yorker*, and been later in England as correspondent for that magazine. He also covered our invasion of North Africa.

## LINDLEY, ERNEST K. 396

Ernest Lindley was born in Indiana and attended the University of Idaho. After his graduation he received a Rhodes scholarship to Oxford, where his studies on international relations earned for him the degree of Bachelor of Arts in 1923. He began his newspaper career in 1924 on the *Wichita* (Kansas) *Beacon,* coming to New York soon thereafter to work on the *New York World*. In 1931 he became a political writer for the *New York Herald Tribune,* and joined its Washington bureau in 1933. In 1937 he became Washington correspondent for *Newsweek,* and since 1938 has written a syndicated column from Washington. He also became a news commentator for NBC. He has followed President Roosevelt since the latter's days in the Governor's mansion at Albany, and is the author of several books on the Roosevelt administration and the New Deal. Among them are *Franklin D. Roosevelt—A Career in Progressive Democracy, The Roosevelt Revolution—First Phase,* and *Half-Way With Roosevelt.* While he is not a foreign correspondent, he has been included here because of the book, *How War Came,* which he wrote in co-authorship with Forrest Davis. It presents an eye-witness account of the events at the White House and the State Department which culminated in December 7, 1941.

## LOCHNER, LOUIS P. 41, 140

Louis P. Lochner was born in Springfield, Illinois, in 1897 and was graduated from the University of Wisconsin. He joined the Associated Press in 1921 and was AP correspondent in Berlin from 1924 to 1941, and chief of the Berlin bureau for the last fourteen years of his stay there. In 1939 he received the Pulitzer Prize for distinguished correspondence as foreign correspondent. After Germany declared war on the United States in December, 1941, he was interned in Bad Nauheim along with the other American correspondents there, and was later exchanged. His book, *What About Germany?* written after his return to this country, is a careful analysis of the events in Germany, and the personages behind them as he observed them during his long and intimate acquaintance with that country.

## McCORMICK, ANNE O'HARE 112

Anne O'Hare McCormick, writer and newspaperwoman, has been a contributor to the *New York Times* since 1922. A native of Cleveland, Ohio, Mrs. McCormick received her education in private schools in this country and Europe, and obtained her A. B. degree from St. Mary's College, Columbus, Ohio, and an honorary LL.D. degree from the University of Dayton. She began her newspaper career as a free-lance writer of articles on the rise of Fascism in Italy, at a time when few people had yet begun to regard Mussolini or the Fascists at all seriously. In the years that she has been writing for the *New York Times* Mrs. McCormick has made many trips to Europe, besides having traveled extensively in the Far East, and has interviewed many of the leaders of international politics. In 1936 she became a member of the *Times* editorial staff, the first woman to hold such a position on that paper. In 1937 she won the Pulitzer Prize for her work as a foreign correspondent. She is the author of a book on Soviet Russia, *Hammer and Scythe*.

MacDONALD, JAMES                    277

James MacDonald was born in Scotland in 1896, and came to the United States in 1909. His studies at Harvard University were cut short by his enlistment in the Canadian army in 1917. His newspaper career began after the war—in 1923, to be exact—on the staff of the *Yonkers* (N.Y.) *Statesman*. From 1925 to 1928 he was with the Associated Press in New York. He has been a member of the *New York Times* staff since 1928, and in its London bureau since 1938.

McMILLAN, RICHARD D.            555

Richard D. McMillan has been a United Press correspondent for sixteen years, and served in various European capitals before the outbreak of the war. He was the first correspondent to be licensed by the B. E. F., and has been with the British army in all of its important campaigns in the European and African theaters of the war. After the fall of France he was in London, staying there during the months of September and October, 1940. He was with the Greek army in Albania before he went to Africa, where he spent two years on the fighting front. His book, *Mediterranean Assignment,* is a record of the events he covered there.

MANN, ERIKA                            547

Erika Mann is the daughter of the famous author, Thomas Mann, who was exiled from Germany by the Nazis, and who now resides in this country. Miss Mann was born in Germany and studied under Max Reinhardt to become an actress. She has won fame, not only as her father's daughter, but also in her own right, as actress, lecturer, and author. Among her books are *School for Barbarians,* and, jointly with her brother, Klaus Mann, *Escape to Life,* and *The Other Germany.* She has been a resident of the United States for several years. As a correspondent for *Liberty* magazine and the *Toronto Star* she went to England, Iran and Egypt.

MATTHEWS, HERBERT L.    76, 92, 197, 587, 620

Herbert L. Matthews, one of the most famous of the large group of *New York Times* correspondents, was born in New York City in 1900 and educated at Columbia University. He has been on the staff of the *New York Times* since 1922, as reporter, foreign editor, and foreign correspondent. He was with the Paris bureau of the *Times* from 1931 to 1934; covered the Italo-Ethiopian war, 1935-36, and the Spanish Civil War, 1936-39, for that paper, and in 1939 became head of its Rome bureau. At the outbreak of the war he was interned in Siena. After his release he was sent first to India, and, after our invasion of Sicily, to Italy, again by the *Times.* He is the author of three books, *Two Wars and More To Come* (1938), *Eyewitness in Abyssinia* (1937), and *Fruits of Fascism* (1943).

MICHIE, ALLAN A.                      491

Allan A. Michie was born in Aberdeen, Scotland, and came to the United States when he was ten years old. He graduated from Ripon College, Wisconsin, and then studied law at the University of Chicago. Later he joined the staff of *Time* as foreign news editor. Shortly before the war

642

began he went to London as a member of the *Time-Life-Fortune* staff. After going through the blitz there he was ordered to Cairo, and saw most of the fighting in the Middle East. Later he returned to London to cover the war on that front. His articles have appeared in many of the leading periodicals of both England and the United States. He is the author of *Retreat To Victory*.

MIDDLETON, DREW                542

Drew Middleton was born in New York City in 1913 and attended Syracuse University. After his graduation he was sports editor on the *Poughkeepsie* (N.Y.) *Eagle-News* and later on the *Poughkeepsie Evening Star*. Later he joined the Associated Press, and was with the first B. E. F. in France. He was in England during what Robert Casey has happily christened the "bore War," going back to the continent after the German invasion of the Lowlands in May, 1940, and returning again to England after Dunkirk. In 1942 he joined the London bureau of the *New York Times*, and was immediately assigned to North Africa, arriving there in the vanguard of the troops which marched into Tunis.

MILLER, WEBB                    71

Webb Miller was born in Michigan in 1898 and began his newspaper career on a paper in the small town of Dowagiac, Michigan, in 1911, going from there to the *Chicago American* in 1912. From 1916 on he was a member of the United Press, serving first in their London and Paris bureaus; then as correspondent with the Italian army in Ethiopia in 1935, where he won the Pulitzer Prize for his forty-four-minute scoop on the announcement of the beginning of the war there; as correspondent with Franco's army in the Spanish Civil War; on the first flight of the Hindenburg in 1936; as correspondent with the British army in France in 1939; and with the Finnish army, also in 1939. He won the Pulitzer Prize for distinguished service as foreign correspondent in 1936. At the time of his death in a blackout accident in London in May, 1940, he was European chief of UP.

MOATS, ALICE-LEONE             311

Alice-Leone Moats is a young New Yorker who started her career as a foreign correspondent by "wangling" an assignment from *Collier's* to go to Russia to report that country from the "woman's angle." Her attempts to get there took her through Japan and China and down the Burma Road. The adventures she encountered on the trip, as well as her stay in Russia, where she incurred official suspicion of being a spy, are amusingly recounted in her book, *Blind Date With Mars*. After leaving Moscow, much against her will, she visited Persia, Egypt and South Africa before finally returning to New York and the amenities of civilized life. In 1943 she went off again in search of news and adventure, this time to Spain, as a correspondent for the *New York Herald Tribune*.

MOOREHEAD, ALAN                503

Alan Moorehead was born in Melbourne, Australia, in 1910, received his A.B. degree from Melbourne University, and worked as a newspaperman in that city until 1935, when he went to London for an Australian news syndicate. Later he went to Gibraltar for the *London Daily Express*. During the Spanish Civil War he went to Spain on German and Russian merchant ships that were running the blockade. From 1937 to 1938 he was in the Paris office of the *London Daily Express*. In 1939 he was in Rome, but when Italy declared war on Great Britain he moved on, first to Athens and then to Cairo. Since 1940 he has covered the campaign of the British Eighth Army in Africa; visited Persia to investigate rumors of German agents' activities there; covered the Cripps mission to India; visited Ceylon; and in November, 1942, accompanied the Allied forces on their invasion of

Africa. He is the author of *Mediterranean Front* and *Don't Blame The Generals.* Though Moorehead is not an American correspondent he was included in this collection because he is by far the most widely read English correspondent in this country.

MORGAN, THOMAS B.       284

Thomas B. Morgan has been a foreign correspondent for more than twenty years. In 1918 he covered the French War Office for the Associated Press, and was assigned to President Wilson at the Peace Conference. In April, 1919 he was sent to Italy, where in 1919 he became manager of the Rome bureau of United Press, a position he held until 1938. In the nineteen years of his stay in Italy he witnessed the growth and development of the Fascist movement from a puny child to a threatening monster. He became well acquainted with Mussolini—so much so, in fact, that in 1936 he collaborated with Il Duce in twelve articles dealing with the latter's life, and entitled "My Twenty-Four Hours—How I Live And Work." Mr. Morgan also came to be on familiar terms with the Vatican, and was thus enabled to secure a number of interesting "inside stories." He is the author of two books, both the result of years of experience in Italy, *A Reporter at the Papal Court* and *Spurs On The Boot.*

MORIN, RELMAN       362

Relman Morin was born in Illinois in 1907 but grew up on the west coast. He attended high school in Los Angeles, and graduated from Pomona College. In his senior year he was awarded a scholarship to study in China. After spending a year in that country he returned to Los Angeles, where he became sports editor on a local paper. Overcome by a nostalgia for the Orient, however, he joined the Los Angeles bureau of the Associated Press, and requested that he be sent to the Far East as soon as possible. He received the assignment in 1939. During his stay in the Orient he covered the Dutch East Indies, Malaya, Burma, Japan, China, Indo-China, and Manila. He was in Saigon when war broke out between the United States and Japan on December 7, 1941, and had the experience of being arrested as a spy. He finally returned to this country on an exchange ship in July, 1942. His book, *Circuit of Conquest,* recounts his impressions of what he saw and experienced in the Orient during the two event-laden years preceding the attack on Pearl Harbor.

MOWRER, EDGAR ANSEL    13, 25

Edgar A. Mowrer, of the famous *Chicago Daily News* family of Mowrers, was educated at the University of Michigan. When World War I broke out in 1914 he was in Paris, and he proceeded to the front, to write stories for the *Daily News.* The next year he was sent to Rome by his paper. In 1923, having fallen out of favor with Mussolini for his uncompromisingly hostile attitude toward Fascism, he was transferred to Berlin. He was thus in a front-seat position to observe the changes in that country during the next important decade. He was one of the first newspapermen abroad to realize and warn the world against the danger of the rising Nazi tide, and persisted in his fearlessly outspoken denunciations even in the face of much intimidation, at first subtle, and then frankly expressed, from Berlin. The publication of his book, *Germany Puts the Clock Back,* in 1933, incurred the great displeasure of the Nazis, and he was again forced to move on. Since the beginning of the war he has been in Washington, writing articles for the Press Alliance Syndicate. In 1933 Mr. Mowrer won the Pulitzer Prize for distinguished foreign correspondence.

MURROW, EDWARD R.       176

Edward R. Murrow was graduated from Washington State College in 1930. From 1932 to 1935 he was assistant director of the Institute of International

Education, in charge of its foreign affairs. From 1935 to 1937 he was in charge of talks in Columbia Broadcasting System's department of special events. Then he was sent to Europe as chief of the foreign news staff of CBS. His broadcasts, made from that beleaguered city during the blitz of 1940-41, have made radio history. They have since appeared in book form under the title, *This Is London.*

NEWMAN, JOSEPH                378

Joseph Newman was born in Pittsfield, Massachusetts, in 1912 and graduated from Williams College. Later he studied briefly in the graduate school of Columbia University. He worked for several newspapers in New York City and in various other cities of the United States before going to Japan in 1938 to join the staff of the *Japan Advertiser* in Tokyo. When that newspaper was taken over by the Japanese in 1940 Newman became the Tokyo correspondent of the *New York Herald Tribune.* In the same year he made a tour of the occupied sections of China. In October, 1941 he went to Honolulu to visit his wife, who had left Japan some time previously, at the request of our State Department. During his absence it was learned that the Japanese planned to arrest him on his return, using as an excuse certain alleged "unfriendly" dispatches that he had sent out. The *New York Herald Tribune* thereupon decided to close its Tokyo office, and ordered him home. He sailed on the last "peacetime" ship from Honolulu, on December 5, 1941. Later he went to Buenos Aires for the *Herald Tribune.* In 1942 he published his book, *Goodbye Japan,* based on his years of observation in the Orient.

OAKES, VANYA                359

Vanya Oakes graduated from the University of California and went to the Orient in 1932, with the vague notion of teaching English to the Chinese. She soon became a correspondent for the United Press, the North American Newspaper Alliance, and the *Christian Science Monitor.* Her assignment as a roving reporter took her to practically every corner of the Far East. She was in this trouble spot for almost ten years, returning to the United States just before Pearl Harbor. Her book, *White Man's Folly,* recounts the events of these years.

OECHSNER, FREDERICK C.        231

Frederick C. Oechsner was born in New Orleans, Louisiana, in 1903 and received his education at Williston Academy, Easthampton, Massachusetts, and at Tulane University, graduating in law in 1925. He did his first newspaper work on the *New Orleans Item.* After a trip to Central America in 1927 for a series of articles on economic and political subjects, he went abroad, working in Italy and France until 1929. Then he returned to the United States to become a member of the staff of the *Washington Evening Star.* In that same year he was appointed Berlin correspondent for the *New York Evening Sun*—Consolidated Press Foreign Service. In April, 1932 he joined the London staff of the United Press and a year later was appointed manager of their Berlin and Central European office. He continued in that capacity till December, 1941. At that time he was interned, along with the other American correspondents in Germany. While confined at Bad Nauheim Mr. Oechsner and the other UP representatives planned the writing of a co-operative book on various phases of Nazi Germany, in peace and in war. This book was published in 1942 under the title *This Is The Enemy.*

O'REILLY, JOHN                601

John O'Reilly is the son of that famous soldier of fortune, Tex O'Reilly, and seems to have inherited all of the elder O'Reilly's zest for adventure. He attended Columbia University for one year, and then joined the reportorial staff of the *New York Herald Tribune,* where he has gained fame for the humor and special style of his writing. In the fall of 1942 he flew to Africa as an accredited war correspondent for the *Herald Tribune,* going first to the Lake Chad area, where he covered the Fighting French, and later to Cairo and Iran. He was then sent to the Tunisian front, where he followed the movements of the British desert forces. After Africa he went to Sicily and Italy, landing with the Allied forces on the Salerno beachhead. In the fall of 1943 he returned from Italy to Africa, where he was hospitalized with malaria, and later came back on leave to the United States.

## PACKARD, ELEANOR 80

Eleanor Packard was born in New York City but spent her girlhood in the state of Washington. She attended the University of Washington and Columbia University School of Journalism. After three years in the advertising business she went to Paris as a reporter on the Paris edition of the *New York Herald.* A year later she went to Vienna, where she married Reynolds Packard. Now began a joint reportorial career which carried the two correspondents to Tahiti, China, India, Ethiopia, and finally to Italy, where they stayed until June, 1942. Here Mr. Packard was head of the Rome bureau of AP and Mrs. Packard was its star reporter. She is co-author with her husband of *Balcony Empire.*

## PACKARD, REYNOLDS 80, 595

Reynolds Packard was born in Atlantic City in 1903 and studied at Bucknell University. He was forced to leave college before his graduation because of injuries sustained in a football game. Later he went to Buenos Aires to study Spanish, joining the United Press while he was there. Later he went to Paris as a member of the staff of the *Chicago Tribune.* But he rejoined the United Press and covered London, Paris and Vienna. After his marriage to Eleanor Packard he and his wife pursued a joint

career as foreign correspondents in Tahiti, China, India, and, lastly, Italy, where he was chief of the UP bureau, and his wife the star reporter of the Rome staff. The Packards stayed in Italy until June, 1942, the last six months after the entry of the United States into the war being spent by Mr. Packard in internment camps. They returned to this country on the exchange ship *Drottningholm* in June, 1942. In 1943 Mr. Packard went back to Italy to cover the invasion for the United Press.

## PARKER, RALPH 331

Ralph Parker was born in England in 1907, and graduated from Cambridge University. He intended to enter the British Civil Service, but instead yielded to a *wanderlust* which carried him through Hungary, the Balkans, and Czechoslovakia. In the last-named country he was employed by President Masaryk to stimulate interest in the country abroad, especially in Britain. When the Germans entered Prague in 1938 Parker was engaged by the *New York Times* as its representative there. Later he was sent to Moscow from where he covered the Russo-German war.

## PARRIS, JOHN A., Jr. 513, 531

John A. Parris, Jr., was born in Sylvia, North Carolina, in 1914 and attended North Carolina College. He joined the United Press in 1934. He was in its London office when the Allied expedition to North Africa was being planned, and was one of the five UP correspondents chosen to accompany the Allied forces on that history-making invasion. In collaboration with Ned Russell, Leo Disher and Phil Ault he wrote an account of his experiences in North Africa which was published under the title *Springboard To Berlin.*

## PEGLER, WESTBROOK 69

Westbrook Pegler was born in Minneapolis, Minnesota, in 1894 and attended

646

Loyola Academy in Chicago. He was European correspondent for the United Press from 1916 to 1918, being attached to the A. E. F. from June, 1917 to February, 1918. At one time he was sports editor and Eastern sports correspondent for United News in New York. Since 1933 he has written a syndicated column which has appeared in the *New York World-Telegram* and many other papers. In 1936 he made a trip to Europe to attend the Olympic games at Garmisch-Partenkirchen. Although, except for his early service with the United Press in Europe, he has never been a foreign correspondent—indeed he has frequently made fun of, and even criticized the gentlemen of that profession—some of the stories of what he saw in Germany in 1936 rank with the most studious analyses of the most experienced foreign correspondents for their insight into the evils of Fascism and Nazism. In 1941 Mr. Pegler won the Pulitzer Prize for reporting.

## PERRY, GEORGE SESSIONS        566

George Sessions Perry, short story writer and novelist, is a young Texan who spent 1942 with the Army Air Force in the Southwest United States, flying with them, and living with them as their unofficial biographer. When our forces invaded North Africa, Perry, who had been in Africa in the early 30's, decided that he would like to be there, too. After the close of the African campaign Perry went to Italy. Most of his comments on the war have appeared in *Saturday Evening Post* and *Collier's*. He has published two books, *Hold Autumn In Your Hands*, and *Hackberry Cavalier*.

## POPE, ERNEST R.        114, 157

Ernest R. Pope was educated at Cornell University and later studied in Germany. Going to Munich as a free-lance correspondent, he found that he was the only American correspondent in that city. As a result, he worked, at one time or an-other, for almost every American newspaper and press association that had a foreign news service, and was thus able to score many a scoop denied to his less fortunately situated newspaper brethren. During the period of which he writes in *Munich Playground* he was also correspondent for Reuter's (London).

## PYLE, ERNEST        558

Like so many other men who have won renown in the world of journalism, and particularly in foreign correspondence, "Ernie" Pyle hails from Indiana. He attended the State University, but left before graduation to enter newspaper work, and has been at it ever since. Six years ago, while he was managing editor of the *Washington Daily News,* he became obsessed with a desire to travel, and forthwith acted as a roving correspondent for the Scripps-Howard papers.

The column that he has written for them has made his name familiar in homes all over the United States. In city and village alike his homely comments on men, places and events are relished and quoted. His observations on England under attack have been gathered together in the book entitled *Ernie Pyle in England*. Later he published his account of his experiences with the American troops in Tunisia, which he called *Here Is Your War*.

## RALEIGH, JOHN McCUTCHEON        421

John M. Raleigh was born in Helena, Montana, in 1911 and received his education at the Chicago Latin School, Purdue University and Columbia University. He was foreign correspondent for the *Chicago Tribune* from 1939 to 1940. Since 1940 he has been United Press correspondent and CBS radio correspondent in the Philippines, Shanghai, Batavia and Java. He is the author of many short stories and magazine articles, and has written two books about his work as a foreign correspondent, *Behind The Nazi Front* and *Pacific Blackout*.

RANDAU, CARL                383

Carl Randau has been a newspaperman for many years, and a foreign correspondent since the days of the Versailles Peace Conference, which he reported for the United Press. In the early spring of 1941 he and his wife, Leane Zugsmith, went to the Far East as correspondents for *PM*, their travels taking them to China, Japan, Indo-China, the Dutch East Indies, Singapore and the Philippines before they finally returned home, in the early fall of 1941.

RAWLINGS, CHARLES A.          474

Charles A. Rawlings started in newspaper work in Rochester, N.Y. Followed a brief period in the advertising business, and then an interval in Florida, during which he alternated between raising oranges and "hobnobbing with the fishermen of the sponge fleet." Out of this flirtation came his first story, "The Dance of the Bends," which he sold to *Saturday Evening Post*.

Later he left the orange groves of Florida to settle down in a little harbor town in Nova Scotia. Always a lover of the sea, in 1936 he sailed, in sub-zero weather, with some Nova Scotian fishermen, to "make a set for" cod and haddock. Out of this trip grew more stories. Late in 1942 he went to the South Pacific to cover the war there for *Saturday Evening Post*. He has sent back many notable stories from that area, among them, "We Saw the Battle of the Atlantic," "Fat Girl," and "We Skip-Bomb the Japs."

RESTON, JAMES B.            281

James B. Reston was born in Scotland in 1909, and came to this country at an early age. He graduated from the University of Illinois and then became a reporter on the *Springfield* (Ohio) *Daily News*. Later he was public relations man, first for Ohio State University and then for the Cincinnati Reds. In 1934 he joined the Associated Press as sports writer and later theater columnist. Then he was sent by AP to London, where he covered sports events in the summer and the Foreign Office in the winter. In 1939 he joined the London bureau of the *New York Times,* staying there until 1941, when he went to its Washington bureau to take charge of diplomatic and foreign affairs. Later he returned to the *Times* London bureau, this time as its acting chief. He has written *Prelude To Victory,* a book on the war.

REYNOLDS, QUENTIN   221, 261, 577

Quentin Reynolds hails from Brooklyn, New York. He has had a varied and interesting career as a newspaperman, ranging from sports editor for *Collier's* magazine to their top-flight foreign correspondent. In this latter capacity he has covered practically every spot on the globe where things have been happening these last few years—the fall of France, the Battle of Britain, the Dieppe raid, the campaign in Libya, the Russian war, and the Italian campaign, where for the first time in his wide experience with battling armies he has been with the American forces.

Some of his best-known books are *The Wounded Don't Cry, Convoy, London Diary, Dieppe: The Story of a Raid, Only The Stars Are Neutral, The Curtain Rises*.

ROBERTSON, BEN              241

Ben Robertson was born in South Carolina in 1905 and attended Clemson College in that state, and the School of Journalism of the University of Missouri. He started his newspaper work on the *Honolulu Star-Bulletin,* continuing on the *Adelaide* (Australia) *News* and, later, on the *New York Herald* and with the Associated Press. In 1940 he went to England as correspondent for *PM.*

His book, *I Saw England,* is the story of his experiences there during the blitz. He lost his life recently in a clipper crash near Lisbon.

ROBINSON, PAT 472

Pat Robinson was born in New York City and began his newspaper career as a cub reporter on a Denver (Colo.) newspaper. He was in France in World War I. Twenty-five years later, when General Douglas MacArthur arrived in Melbourne, Australia, from the Philippines in January, 1942, he saw Robinson, who was a correspondent there, and recognized him as having been on MacArthur's staff in the Rainbow Division. At the close of World War I Robinson returned to this country and was a sports writer for a number of years before joining International News Service in 1931. After Pearl Harbor he was sent to the South Pacific by INS. It was then that the meeting with MacArthur referred to above took place. He is the dean of all American correspondents in New Guinea, having served in that theater of war longer than any of the other American reporters. He has written a book, *Fight For New Guinea.*

ROMULO, CARLOS P. 426

Carlos P. Romulo is a native-born Filipino, a distinguished former editor of a Filipino newspaper, and winner of the Pulitzer Prize in journalism (1942). During the tragic days of late 1941 and early 1942 in the Philippines, Colonel Romulo, an officer in the defending forces, broadcast over "Voices of Freedom," sending messages of hope and encouragement to his hard-pressed and suffering countrymen. In recognition of his courage and devotion to the cause of freedom, and of the heroic role played by himself and his fellow Filipinos in the defense of their homeland, General MacArthur appointed Colonel Romulo his personal aide. He is the author of two books, *I Saw the Fall of the Philippines,* and *Mother America.*

ROUZEAU, EDGAR T. 591

Edgar T. Rouzeau is a veteran Negro newspaperman. He began his career as a sports writer on the college papers at Tuskegee Institute and Howard University, which he attended, and in the more than twenty years that have passed since that time he has written for the leading newspapers of his race in this country. In May, 1942, he became the first Negro correspondent to be accredited to the U.S. Armed Forces, as a representative of the *Pittsburgh Courier.* During the following eighteen months he has traveled more than 63,000 air miles and visited 26 countries in the discharge of his duties.

RUSSELL, NED 524, 571

Ned Russell was born in Baltimore, Maryland, in 1916 and began his newspaper career at the age of seventeen, as a sports writer for the *Los Angeles Examiner.* In 1936 he joined the United Press. His chief work as a foreign correspondent thus far has been in the African campaign, in the course of which he wrote many brilliant accounts of the fighting there, notably of the campaign at Enfidaville. Some of these stories are included in the book, *Springboard To Berlin,* which he wrote in collaboration with three fellow UP correspondents, Leo Disher, Phil Ault and John Parris.

ST. JOHN, ROBERT 289

Robert St. John saw service in the First World War, going to France at the ripe age of sixteen. After re-entering civilian life, he first became a reporter on the *Hartford Courant* and the *Chicago Daily News* and then took a fling at editing his own newspaper in Cicero, Illinois, the stronghold of the Capone gang. After a disastrous attempt to expose the activities of Ralph Capone, younger brother of the then imprisoned leader of the gang, "Scarface Al" Capone—an attempt which led to his being beaten up and almost killed by the gangsters—St. John gave up the adventurous life of an editor and went to work on the *Rutland* (Vermont) *Herald* and the *Philadelphia*

Record. In 1931 he joined the Associated Press, but after a few years succumbed to the lure of rural life and retired to raise chickens—and also to write—in New Hampshire. In 1939 journalism beckoned again, and he rejoined the Associated Press and went to Europe, landing in Paris just as the Germans began their invasion of Poland. He was assigned to cover the Balkans, and went through the campaigns in Yugoslavia, Greece, and Crete. His book, *From the Land Of Silent People,* is the eloquent and moving story of the resistance of the people of those countries to the German invaders.

SCOTT, JOHN 303

John Scott, the son of the famous economist and Socialist, Scott Nearing, went to Russia in the early thirties to live, and became a citizen of that country. He married a Russian girl and worked as a laborer among the Russians. Later he was Moscow reporter for the French news agency, Havas, and for the *London News-Chronicle.* In the summer of 1941 he returned to the United States, where he became foreign news editor for *Time* magazine and later its correspondent in Stockholm. He has written a number of books on Russia, notably *Behind the Urals,* and *Duel For Europe.*

SHAPIRO, HENRY 335

Henry Shapiro graduated from Harvard Law School and has specialized in international law since his admission to the New York bar. He went to Russia to study Soviet law, but while there developed an interest in journalism, and began contributing to several American newspapers and press associations. In 1937 he joined the Moscow bureau of United Press. He has been its chief since 1940.

SHEEAN, VINCENT 3, 90, 250

Vincent Sheean was born in Illinois and attended the University of Chicago. In the spring of 1922 he went to Paris and became foreign correspondent for the *Chicago Tribune.* While there he covered Lausanne, Geneva, Rome, Madrid, and London. In December, 1924, he made his way deep into Morocco, where he reported the Riff rebellion. He was the only correspondent to succeed in getting an interview with Abd-el Krim, accomplishing this scoop at great danger to himself. He was in China during the early days of the revolution there; was in Jerusalem at the time of the Arab-Jewish riots in 1929; and was in Europe again when the Germans marched into the Ruhr. His autobiography, *Personal History,* in which all these events are recorded, set the style for a host of books written subsequently by foreign correspondents, in which historical events, personal adventure, and gossip about the great and the near-great have been combined with varying degrees of readability. It is still considered the best of the *genre* by most critics. Sheean became a correspondent for the *New York Herald Tribune* during the Spanish Civil War. In the present war he has spent much time in England, covering the activities of the Royal Navy and Air Force, and with the American forces in Britain. Later he himself joined the U. S. Army Air Force, and took part in the invasion of Italy. Besides *Personal History* he has written several other books based on his experiences as a foreign correspondent, notably *Not Peace But a Sword* and *Behind the Thunder and the Sun,* and besides many magazine articles.

SHERROD, ROBERT 484

Robert Sherrod has been a correspondent for *Time* magazine for more than nine years, in New York, Chicago, and Washington. Six months before Pearl Harbor he abandoned political writing and started covering the Army, in anticipation of the coming war. He was the first of *Time's* many correspondents to go abroad with the United States forces, leaving with one of the first convoys for Australia in February, 1942. He was in New Guinea for six months, and then, in

May, 1943, was sent to Attu. He was there at the time of the Japanese breakthrough, and also witnessed the invasion of Kiska. Later he was sent to the South Pacific. His book, *Tarawa: The Story of a Battle,* tells the rest of the story.

## SHIRER, WILLIAM L. 108, 212

William L. (Bill) Shirer was born in Chicago and educated at Coe College, Cedar Rapids, Iowa. After finishing college he worked his way to Europe on a cattleboat, intending to stay for the summer, and remained for fifteen years. From 1925 to 1932 he was European correspondent for the *Chicago Tribune,* covering assignments all over Europe, the Near East, and even India. In 1934 he became chief of the Berlin bureau of Universal Service, and in 1937 Continental representative for CBS, with headquarters in Berlin. He remained there until December, 1940, when he returned to the United States to write and to do broadcasting for CBS. *Berlin Diary,* the record of his years in Europe, stands in first place as the book which gave the American reading public the inside story of many of the important events which had filled the years of his residence in Europe, particularly in Germany.

## SMEDLEY, AGNES 363

Agnes Smedley was born in Missouri, but her childhood was spent in the camps of the Rockefeller Fuel and Iron Company in Colorado, where her father was employed as a laborer. Her formal education was practically nonexistent, as her family was very poor, and she began to work at a very early age in order to help out with the family finances. When she was sixteen her mother died and she thereupon left home, to begin the wandering life which has been hers ever since: from Colorado to southwest Arizona; from stewardess on a Russia-bound boat to Berlin and a meeting with a cultured Hindu, an ardent worker for the freedom of India, with whom she main-

tained a close relationship for eight years, and from whom she imbibed a deep interest in India and its problems; then visits to Moscow in 1921 and 1928; also in 1928, a trip to China, where she remained until her return to this country in the summer of 1941. She became deeply interested in the part the common people were playing in the war against Japan, and she went about with their guerrilla armies, helping them in their schools and setting up medical units for the care of their wounded. While there she was a correspondent for the *Manchester Guardian* and also contributed articles to the *Nation* and other American periodicals. She is the author of *Daughter of Earth, Chinese Destinies, China's Red Army Marches, China Fights Back,* and *Battle Hymn of China.*

## SMITH, HOWARD K. 313

Howard Smith was born in New Orleans, Louisiana, and was graduated from Tulane University in 1936. He went to Europe that summer, to see for himself what was going on in Hitler's Germany. Returning to the United States, he worked for a time on the *New Orleans Item,* and then went to Oxford on a Rhodes scholarship. On the day that war was declared against Germany by Great Britain he went to London as correspondent for the United Press, and later was in Germany. During the latter half of 1941 he was assistant to Harry Flannery, CBS radio correspondent in Berlin, and successor to William Shirer, and after Flannery's return to the United States he became CBS's sole Berlin correspondent. Like so many other American journalists, he fell into disfavor with the Nazis, and it was arranged to have him transferred to Berne. He crossed the border into Switzerland on December 7, 1941, quite literally on the last train from Berlin for Americans, and remained in Berne after the war as radio correspondent for CBS. His book, which he called *Last Train From Berlin,* tells the story of those last few tension-laden months in Germany before the declaration of war against the United States.

## SNOW, EDGAR  367

Edgar Snow was born in Missouri and received his baptism in newspaper work on the *Kansas City Star,* later working for the *New York Sun.* For thirteen years he was Far East correspondent for the *London Daily Herald,* and his two important books on China, *Red Star Over China* and *Battle For Asia,* are outstanding testimonials of his knowledge and understanding of the embattled peoples of that country and their problems. Later he has been in Russia as a correspondent for the *Saturday Evening Post,* of which he is an associate editor.

## SPIVAK, JOHN  47

John Spivak was born in 1897 and gained his early reportorial experience on the *New York Sun* and the *Call.* In 1922-23 he was International News Service correspondent in Moscow. Since 1924 he has devoted his time to free-lance writing, and has made frequent visits to Germany, Poland, Russia, Spain, and other European countries. Some of his best-known books are *Plotting America's Pogroms, America Faces the Barricades, Europe Under the Terror,* and *Secret Armies.*

## STADLER, GLEN M.  217

Glen M. Stadler was born in Indiana in 1911 and received his education at Indiana University and Toledo University. He worked on many newspapers in Indiana and Ohio before and after his graduation from college. In 1936-37 he made a trip around the world for the *Evansville* (Indiana) *Courier,* covering the Olympic Games in Germany and going down the Burma Road. In 1937 he joined the United Press at Lansing, Michigan, and was subsequently stationed on the New York cable desk. In 1940 he was in France, and after its fall went to Berlin. He covered the remainder of the war, before December, 1941, there and on the Finnish front. He is co-author, with Frederick C. Oechsner and others, of *This Is The Enemy.*

## STEEL, JOHANNES  52

Johannes Steel was educated at Heidelberg, Geneva, and Oxford. He has traveled widely throughout Europe, Asia, and South America. During the early 1930's he was foreign editor for the *New York Post,* where his inside stories of Nazi Germany and his accurate predictions of things to come created many a sensation. Later he became war correspondent for *Liberty* magazine. He is now a widely syndicated columnist and a radio commentator over Station WMCA in New York. He is the author of *Hitler As Frankenstein, The Second World War, Europe to the Present,* and *Men Behind the War.*

## STEELE, ARCHIBALD T.  353

A. T. Steele was born in Canada in 1903 and came to the United States in 1916. He attended Leland Stanford University, and then became in turn reporter, editor, and owner of various newspapers on the Pacific Coast. In 1932-33 he was correspondent for the *New York Times* in Manchuria and North China, and from 1933 to 1935 represented the Associated Press in Shanghai. Since 1937 he has been Far Eastern correspondent for the *Chicago Daily News.* He has contributed articles to many leading American periodicals.

## STEINBECK, JOHN  584

John Steinbeck was born in Salinas, California, in 1903, and attended Stanford University. He is considered one of America's outstanding novelists, the most famous of his novels being *Of Mice and Men, The Grapes of Wrath,* and *Tortilla Flat.* Although he has never been a newspaperman, he went abroad in 1943 as correspondent for the *New York Herald Tribune* syndicate, and has written many human-interest stories of high literary merit from England, Africa, and Italy.

## STEVENS, EDMUND 186

Before the war Edmund Stevens lived for five and one-half years in Moscow, where he was correspondent for the *Christian Science Monitor*. Since then, however, he has been in most of the important theaters of war: he was in Vilna before the Russians entered that city; covered the Russo-Finnish war; saw the betrayal of Norway from within; and covered the campaigns in Greece, Yugoslavia, and the Near East. In 1941 he went to Africa, accompanying General Montgomery's army on its march from El Alamein to Tripoli. Later he returned to Moscow as staff correspondent for the *Christian Science Monitor*.

## STONEMAN, WILLIAM H. 258

William H. Stoneman was born in Grand Rapids, Michigan, in 1904 and was educated at the University of Michigan. His entire career in the newspaper field has been with the *Chicago Daily News:* as reporter, 1925-28; foreign correspondent in Scandinavia, 1928-29; Rome correspondent, 1929-32; Moscow correspondent, 1932-35; Ethiopia and the Near East, 1935-36; and, since 1936, London.

## STOWE, LELAND 178, 298

Leland Stowe was educated at Wesleyan University. Immediately after his graduation in 1921 he joined the reportorial staff of the *Worcester Telegram*. In 1922 he went to the *New York Herald,* and from 1924-26 he was foreign editor of Pathé News. In 1926 he became a member of the foreign staff of the *New York Herald,* for which paper he covered assignments all over Europe, as well as in North and South America. In 1939 he wanted to go abroad again to cover the war, but his managing editor thought he was too old. The *Chicago Daily News* foreign news service did not share this opinion, however, and so he became one of their outstanding war correspondents, covering the campaigns in Finland, in Norway, where he made his tremendous scoop on the invasion of Oslo, in Rumania, and in Greece. Later he was in the South Pacific and in Italy. He has written several books on European affairs, among them *Nazi Germany Means War, No Other Road To Freedom,* and *They Shall Not Sleep*. In 1930 he received the Pulitzer Prize in journalism for his coverage of the Young Reparations Conference in Paris.

## SULZBERGER, CYRUS L. 608

Cyrus (Cy) Sulzberger was born in New York City, received his education at Harvard University, and started his newspaper career on the *Pittsburgh* (Pennsylvania) *Press*. In 1935 he went to Washington for United Press, and in 1938, during the Albanian crisis, he covered Bulgaria and Greece for U.P. He joined the foreign news staff of the *New York Times* in 1939, and was assigned to the Balkans, and later to Russia. In 1941 he received the Overseas Press Club award for his reporting of the war from Russia. Among his journalistic feats was the first complete coverage of the story of Tito and his Yugoslav partisans, early in 1944.

## SWING, RAYMOND GRAM 118

Raymond Gram Swing was born in 1887 and educated at Oberlin College. He obtained his first newspaper assignment on a newspaper in Cleveland, Ohio, in 1906, working thereafter on various midwestern newspapers, until in 1913 he was sent to Berlin as foreign correspondent for the *Chicago Daily News*. He remained there for a number of years, becoming correspondent for the *New York Herald* from 1919 to 1922. From 1924 to 1934 he represented the *Philadelphia Public Ledger* and the *New York Evening Post* in London. He was radio commentator for CBS from 1935-36, and for MBS, 1936-42, thereafter for NBC. He is the author of *How War Came* and

*Preview of History,* besides a number of articles which have appeared in leading periodicals.

## TAYLOR, EDMOND L.      172

Edmond Taylor was born in St. Louis in 1908. He was a reporter on the *St. Louis Globe-Democrat* and the *St. Louis Times* in 1926. From 1928 to 1930 he was a reporter and assistant manager of the European edition of the *Chicago Tribune,* and from 1933 to 1940 chief of its Paris bureau. In 1940 he became CBS correspondent in France. He is the author of *Strategy of Terror,* the first book of the present war period to describe the war of nerves as it was being waged by the Germans.

## THOMPSON, DOROTHY      31, 192

Dorothy Thompson was born in 1894 and studied at Lewis Institute, Chicago, at Syracuse University, and the University of Vienna. She was foreign correspondent for the *Philadelphia Public Ledger* and the *New York Evening Post* from 1920 to 1928, being stationed in Vienna from 1920 to 1924 and in Berlin as chief of the Central European Service from 1924 to 1928. From 1936 to 1941 she conducted a column of political comment for the *New York Herald Tribune* syndicate. She is now a radio commentator for NBC, and writes a widely syndicated column for the *New York Post.* Although in the very earliest days of Nazism, before Hitler came to power, she did not feel that he constituted a great danger for the world, she soon became convinced of the contrary when she saw what he was doing in Germany; and she became one of the most indefatigable writers and speakers against the Nazis, conducting a campaign that was for a time practically single-handed in an attempt to arouse public sentiment in this country against them. How admirably she succeeded may be judged by the fact that she became perhaps the most hated of all American correspondents and writers in Germany. A collection of her articles appeared under the title *Let the Record Speak.*

## TOLISCHUS, OTTO D. 65, 149, 390, 400

Otto D. Tolischus was for many years chief representative of the *New York Times* in Berlin, until he was expelled by the Nazis in 1940. In the same year he received the Pulitzer Prize for his work as a foreign correspondent. After a brief interlude in Stockholm he went to Tokyo in the spring of 1941, to replace Hugh Byas as head of the Tokyo office of the *Times.* He was imprisoned by the Japanese after December 7, 1941, and subjected to terrible torture. He returned to this country in July, 1942. *They Wanted War,* the book he wrote on Nazi Germany, is one of the least hysterical, and presents one of the clearest and coolest analyses of the Nazi danger of any yet made by any foreign correspondent. And the same characteristics mark his *Tokyo Record,* which he wrote following his stay in Tokyo in 1941-42.

## TOMARA, SONIA      209

Sonia Tomara is on the staff of the *New York Herald Tribune.* She was in the Paris office of this paper from the late 1930's until after the fall of France. Later she went to India and Cairo. At the end of 1943 she covered Spain and in the beginning of 1944 French North Africa.

## TREANOR, TOM      601

Tom Treanor began his journalistic career as a reporter on the *Los Angeles Times.* In 1942 his paper sent him to the east coast to write a column, "The Home Front." But Treanor asked his editor whether he would mind sending him to the war fronts, on the same expense account. The editor did not mind; and so he popped up, unaccredited, in Africa, wearing a self-pronounced trademark: "The only American foreign correspondent from west of Chicago." Throughout the Italian campaign he wrote a number of articles which appeared in *Collier's.*

## TREGASKIS, RICHARD 459

Richard Tregaskis was born in Elizabeth, New Jersey, on November 28, 1916, and educated at the Pingrie Day School for Boys, Elizabeth, New Jersey, at Peddie School, Hightson, New Jersey, and at Harvard University. During his senior year at college his work as a member of the editorial board of the *Harvard Crimson* attracted the attention of Jack Malloy, then managing editor of the *Boston American,* who hired Tregaskis as campus correspondent and gave him a position on the editorial staff of the *American* when he left school. For more than three years he worked on the *American,* as reporter, feature, and special writer, and then he went to the cable department of International News Service.

When the United States entered the war he was immediately groomed for foreign service, at length being assigned to the U.S. Navy at Pearl Harbor and accompanying the Marines on their initial invasion of the Solomons. His *Guadalcanal Diary* is a personalized account of the terrific fight the U.S. forces put up there. Later Tregaskis was with the U.S. forces in Italy, receiving wounds there for which he was invalided back to the United States.

## VILLARD, OSWALD GARRISON 145

Oswald Garrison Villard was born in 1872 and graduated from Harvard University. He was a reporter on the *Philadelphia Press* from 1896 to 1897, and editorial writer and, in the later years, also president of the *New York Post* from 1897 to 1918. From 1918 to 1932 he was editor and owner of the *Nation.*

He has traveled widely in Europe and written several books as well as many articles for other periodicals besides the *Nation.*

## WELLER, GEORGE 415

George Weller was born in Boston in 1907 and received his education at Roxbury Latin School and Harvard University. Later he won an exchange fellowship in Austria and studied at the University of Vienna and the Max Reinhardt School of the Theater. He traveled extensively in Central and Mediterranean Europe and spent some time in Mexico. His newspaper work includes a period as Sunday feature writer for the *Boston Post* and almost four years—October, 1932, to May, 1936—as Balkan correspondent for the *New York Times.* In 1941 he became Balkan correspondent for the *Chicago Daily News.* He was in Greece when the Germans came, and was the last American correspondent to leave burning Salonika, escaping to Athens by traveling in small fishing boats, only to be "quarantined" by the Germans when he reached Athens and brought to Berlin under the "protection" of the Gestapo. He was held there for more than two months, but finally escaped to Africa, where he secured an exclusive interview with General De Gaulle.

When the Japanese started their conquest of the Pacific area Weller flew to Singapore. After the fall of that city, the story of which he tells in his book, *Singapore is Silent,* he went to Java, Batavia and Bandoeng, and finally Australia. He was awarded the Pulitzer Prize in 1943 for one of his stories from that area.

## WHEELER, KEITH 479

Keith Wheeler is a correspondent for the *Chicago Times* who has covered the entire war between the United States and Japan, from Pearl Harbor to the Aleutians. He was, in fact, the first correspondent to get to the Aleutians. The story of his coverage is told in the book *The Pacific Is My Beat.*

## WHITAKER, JOHN T. 286

John Whitaker was born in 1906 and educated at the University of the South,

Sewanee, Tennessee. He began his newspaper career as a reporter on the *Chattanooga* (Tennessee) *News,* and later was on the staff of the *New York Herald Tribune.* He covered the League of Nations, and was a war correspondent in Ethiopia and Spain. Later he was correspondent for the *Chicago Daily News* in Europe, the Near East, South America, and Italy, from which latter country he, like so many of his predecessors, was finally expelled. He has written several books, among them *Americas to the South, And Fear Came,* and *We Cannot Escape History.*

### WHITE, WILLIAM L.                            244

W. L. White is another foreign correspondent who has been nourished on printers' ink since his childhood. He is the son of the famous William Allen White, the late editor of the *Emporia* (Kansas) *Gazette.* He was born in 1900 and attended Kansas University and Harvard. He was on the staff of the *Washington Post* in 1935, a correspondent for *Fortune* in 1937, and from 1939 to 1940 was CBS European correspondent. He was in the South Pacific area during the fight for the Philippines.

He has contributed articles to *Life,* the *Atlantic Monthly,* the *Reader's Digest, Cosmopolitan,* the *New Republic,* and the *Saturday Evening Post,* besides having written three books, *Journey For Margaret, They Were Expendable,* and *Queens Die Proudly.*

### WINCHELL, WALTER                            477

Walter Winchell was born in New York City in 1897. In his young boyhood he was on the vaudeville stage. When World War I came he was in the Naval Reserve. After the war he went into newspaper work, writing for *Vaudeville News,* and serving as columnist, dramatic critic, and finally dramatic editor of the *Evening Graphic* from 1924 to 1929. Since 1929 he has written a daily column for the King Features Syndicate. His sensational success also extended to his broadcasts. After Pearl Harbor he entered the Naval Reserve Intelligence and was on duty until early in 1943. Although never officially a war correspondent, he gave some lively accounts of his missions for the Navy which rank with some of the best reporting done by regular correspondents.

### WOLFE, HENRY C.                            404

Henry C. Wolfe was born in Newcomerstown, Ohio, in 1898 and attended Phillips Andover Academy and Kenyon College. He was with the American Relief Administration in Russia in 1922 and the American Red Cross Mission in Greece in 1923. He has been a writer, traveler, and a lecturer on international affairs for many years. He has been a frequent contributor to the *Atlantic Monthly, Harper's, Current History,* the *Saturday Evening Post,* and other magazines. Among his best-known books are *The German Octopus, Human Dynamite,* and *The Imperial Soviets.*

### WOLFERT, IRA                            463

Ira Wolfert is a graduate of Columbia University and lives (when he is not being a foreign correspondent) in Brooklyn. He has been with the North American Newspaper Alliance since 1929. He was the only newspaperman to accompany the Free French expedition which ended in the capture of St. Pierre and Miquelon. Early in October, 1942, he was sent by N.A.N.A. to the Pacific area, where he witnessed, among other conflicts, the Battle for the Solomons, which he has told about in his now famous book of the same title. In 1943 he won the Pulitzer Prize for his articles on this heroic struggle.

### ZUGSMITH, LEANE                            388

Leane Zugsmith (in private life Mrs. Carl Randau) started her writing career as a novelist and teller of short stories. Her work as a newspaper correspondent was done for *PM* on the trip which she took with her husband, also a *PM* correspondent, through the Far East in the early months of 1941. Miss Zugsmith and her husband are co-authors of *The Setting Sun of Japan,* the book which tells the story of what they saw in Japan, China, Indo-China, the Dutch East Indies, Singapore, and the Philippines in the months just before Pearl Harbor.

## PULITZER PRIZE WINNERS

### "For Distinguished Service as a Foreign Correspondent"

| YEAR | | PAGE | YEAR | | PAGE |
|---|---|---|---|---|---|
| 1930 | Leland Stowe | 178, 298 | 1940 | Otto D. Tolischus | |
| 1931 | H. R. Knickerbocker | 11, 573 | | | 65, 149, 390, 400 |
| 1932 | Walter Duranty | 60, 133 | 1941 | No award | |
| 1933 | Edgar Ansel Mowrer | 13, 25 | 1942 | Laurence Edmund (Larry) | |
| 1934 | Frederick T. Birchall | 27, 123 | | Allen | 510 |
| 1935 | No award | | | Carlos P. Romulo | 426 |
| 1936 | Webb Miller | 71 | 1943 | Ira Wolfert | 463 |
| 1937 | Anne O'Hare McCormick | 112 | | Hanson W. Baldwin | 466 |
| 1938 | No award | | 1944 | Daniel De Luce | 624 |
| 1939 | Louis P. Lochner | 41, 140 | | Ernest Taylor (Ernie) Pyle | 558 |

# INDEX OF SOURCES

Title        Page

Adventure of an American Reporter. *Forte.* "Dispatch on Trip to Italy," *United Press,* Sept. 15, 1943    574

Albanians Fight Back, The. *Gorrell.* "Dispatch on Guerilla Fighting," United Press, Nov. 3, 1943    597

Aleutian Campaign. *Wheeler. The Pacific Is My Beat,* 1943    479

Algiers. *Parris. Springboard to Berlin,* 1943    513

Allies Evacuate Namsos. *Stevens.* "Evacuation from Namsos," *Christian Science Monitor,* May 3, 1940    186

American Paratroopers. *Bennett. Assignment to Nowhere,* 1943    520

And Not a Tear Was Shed. *Gallagher. Backdoor to Berlin,* 1943    527

Anniversary. *Lawrence, W. H.* "Anniversary of Russian Revolution," *N. Y. Times,* Nov. 7, 1943    337

Anschluss. *Shirer. Berlin Diary,* 1941    108

Assassination of a Prime Minister. *Byas. Government by Assassination,* 1942    348

At the Finnish Front. *Gellhorn.* "Blood on the Snow," *Colliers,* Jan. 20, 1940    161

Augury of Death. *Clapper.* "Augury of Death," *New York World Telegram,* Feb. 15, 1944    488

Badoglio Enters Addis Ababa. *Matthews. Two Wars and More to Come,* 1938    76

Balance Shift of a Lightning Campaign. *Russel. Springboard to Berlin,* 1943    571

Battle of Midway. *Casey. Torpedo Junction,* 1942    452

Battle of the Atlantic, The. *Sheean.* "Shepherds of the Sea," *The Saturday Evening Post,* July 12, 1941    250

Battle of Volturno. *Bigart.* "Battle of Volturno," *N. Y. Herald Tribune,* Oct. 17, 1943    594

Before the Deluge. *Tolischus. Tokio Record,* 1943    390

Bitter End, The. *Flanner.* "Letter from Perpignan," *The New Yorker,* Mar. 11, 1939    103

Black Eagle Goes to War. *Rouzeau.* "Black Eagle Goes to War," *Pittsburgh Courier,* Oct. 6, 1943    591

Blackout in Berlin. *Courtney.* "Darkest Continent," *Colliers,* Dec. 9, 1939    167

Blitz, The. *Robertson. I Saw England,* 1941    241

Blitzkrieg. *Tolischus. They Wanted War,* 1940    149

Bloodpurge, The. *Birchall. The Storm Breaks,* 1940    27

Bomb Explodes, A. *Pope. Munich Playground,* 1941    157

Bombs Over Belgrade. *Brock. Nor Any Victory,* 1942    295

Break-Through at the Meuse, The. *Fodor. The Revolution Is On,* 1940    187

| Title | Page |
| --- | --- |
| British First Army. *Russell. Springboard to Berlin*, 1943 | 524 |
| British Victory and Defeat. *Michie. Retreat to Victory*, 1942 | 491 |
| Buna Victory. *Robinson.* "Ordeal in New Guinea," *International News Service*, Jan. 15, 1943 | 472 |
| Burma Road. *Oakes. White Men's Folly*, 1943 | 359 |
| Casablanca Conference. *Parris. Springboard to Berlin*, 1943 | 531 |
| Chamberlain in Berchtesgaden. *Pope. Munich Playground*, 1941 | 114 |
| Chinese Guerrillas. *Smedley. A Battle Hymn of China*, 1943 | 363 |
| Christmas in the Maginot Line. *Liebling.* "They Defend Themselves," *The New Yorker*, Feb. 10, 1940 | 169 |
| Chungking. *Atkinson.* "Where Tomorrow Is Bright Day," *N. Y. Times Magazine*, Jan. 17, 1943 | 376 |
| City in Prison. *Alsop.* "City in Prison," *The Saturday Evening Post*, Jan. 9, 1943 | 446 |
| Compiègne. *Shirer. Berlin Diary*, 1941 | 212 |
| Conquest of Crete. *Gervasi.* "Hell From on High," *Colliers*, July 26, 1941 | 300 |
| Convoy. *Brundidge.* "Nazi-Subs Attack Convoys," *St. Louis Star-Times*, Feb. 4, 1942 | 256 |
| Counterattack! *Brown. Russia Fights*, 1943 | 332 |
| Coup, The. *St. John. From the Land of Silent People*, 1942 | 289 |
| Day in Spain, A. *Hellman.* "A Day in Spain," *The New Republic*, Apr. 13, 1938 | 87 |
| Death of a Library. *Matthews.* "German Vandalism in Italy," *N. Y. Times*, Oct 12, 1943 | 587 |
| Defeat. *Cowles. Looking for Trouble*, 1941 | 165 |
| Depression. *Mowrer. Germany Puts the Clock Back*, 1939 | 13 |
| Destination: Sicily. *Brown. To All Hands*, 1943 | 562 |
| Dieppe. *Reynolds.* "Boat Trip to Dieppe," *Colliers*, Sept. 19, 1942 | 261 |
| Dollfuss Assassinated. *Gedye. Betrayal in Central Europe*, 1939 | 35 |
| Dragon Licks His Wounds, The. *Snow.* "The Dragon Licks His Wounds," *The Saturday Evening Post*, Apr. 30, 1940 | 367 |
| Dunkerque. *Daniell. Civilians Must Fight*, 1941 | 196 |
| Dying Guerilla's Testament, A. *Adamic. My Native Land*, 1943 | 617 |
| End of the Beginning. *Reston.* "England Under Bombardment," *N. Y. Times*, Oct. 22, 1943 | 281 |
| England Goes to War. *Villard.* "London Blackout," *The Nation*, Sept. 16, 1939 | 145 |
| Europe Holds Its Breath. *Beattie. Freely to Pass*, 1942 | 130 |
| Fall of Nanking. *Steele.* "Siege and Fall of Nanking," *Chicago Daily News*, Dec. 15, 137 | 353 |
| Fall of Sedan. *Archambault.* "Fall of Sedan," *N. Y. Times*, May 15, 1940 | 195 |
| Farewell to Bataan. *Jacoby.* "Farewell to Bataan," *Life*, Mar 30, 1942 | 424 |
| Fascism Died There, Too. *Whitaker.* "The Truth About Italy," *Chicago Daily News*, 1941 | 286 |
| Fascism in the West. *Steel.* "Is England Going Fascist?" *The Nation*, Apr. 4, 1934, and "Fascism in France," *New York Post*, Oct. 30/Nov. 5, 1935 | 52 |
| Fate of the Dutch East Indies, The. *Raleigh. Pacific Black-Out*, 1943 | 421 |

| Title | Page |
|---|---|
| Fear Comes to Cairo. *Gervasi. But Soldiers Wondered Why,* 1943 | 506 |
| Fear in Germany. *Bliven.* "Germany in Fear," *New Republic,* Nov. 18, 1931 | 5 |
| Fifth Battle of the Solomons, The. *Wolfert. The Battle for the Solomons,* 1943 | 463 |
| Fighting French, The. *Harmon.* "The Far-Flung Fighting French," *Christian Science Monitor,* Oct. 3, 1942 | 226 |
| Fire, The. *Gunther. Inside Europe,* 1937 | 20 |
| First Guadalcanal Notes. *Tregaskis.* "Guadalcanal Landing," *International News Service,* Sept. 7, 1942 | 459 |
| First Interview with Reich Chancellor Adolf Hitler. *Kaltenborn.* "Heil Hitler," *New Republic,* Feb. 15, 1933 | 17 |
| Flight to Guadalcanal. *Baldwin.* "Flight to Guadalcanal," *New York Times Magazine,* Nov. 1, 1942 | 466 |
| France Under the Nazi Heel. *Stadler. This Is the Enemy,* 1942 | 217 |
| Franco's Revolt. *Packard. Balcony Empire,* 1942 | 80 |
| French Morale. *Boothe. Europe in the Spring,* 1940 | 174 |
| French Reasoning. *Taylor. Strategy of Terror,* 1940 | 172 |
| From Moscow to Kuibyshev. *Carroll. We're in This with Russia,* 1942 | 318 |
| From Saigon to Singapore. *Randau.* "Saigon and Singapore," *P.M.,* Sept. 4, 1941 | 383 |
| From the White House. *Davis and Lindley. How War Came,* 1942 | 396 |
| German Counterattack. *Ault. Springboard to Berlin,* 1943 | 534 |
| Germany at War. *Deuel. People Under Hitler,* 1942 | 141 |
| Germany Prepares for War. *Fischer.* "Germany Prepares for War," *The Nation,* Mar. 11, 1936 | 57 |
| Going Ashore. *Perry.* "Forty Hours on a Sicilian Beach," *The Saturday Evening Post,* Aug. 19, 1943 | 566 |
| Great Migration, The. *Beatty.* "China Moves on Yankee Power," *Esquire,* Jan. 1939 | 354 |
| Greek Tragedy. *Stowe. No Other Road to Freedom,* 1941 | 298 |
| Greeks Meant Business, The. *Morgan. Spurs on the Boot,* 1941 | 284 |
| Hanging of Zoya, The. *Hindus. Mother Russia,* 1943 | 339 |
| Hell in Shanghai. *Alcott. My War with Japan,* 1943 | 351 |
| Hellfire. *Gervasi. War Has Seven Faces,* 1942 | 495 |
| Heroes. *Hersey. Into the Valley,* 1943 | 462 |
| Hill 609. *Middleton.* "Hill 609," *N. Y. Times,* May 6, 1943 | 542 |
| Hitler's "Victory." *Smith. Last Train from Berlin,* 1942 | 313 |
| Hongkong, 1942. *Dew. Prisoner of the Japs,* 1942 | 442 |
| How It Began. *Sheean. Personal History,* 1934 | 3 |
| How It Will End. *Matthews. Fruits of Fascism,* 1943 | 620 |
| Indo-China. *Abend. Pacific Charter,* 1943 | 381 |
| Inside Warsaw. *Grigg. This Is the Enemy,* 1942 | 154 |
| International Brigade. *Sheean. Not Peace But a Sword,* 1939 | 90 |
| Invasion, The. *Miller. I Found No Peace,* 1936 | 71 |
| It Was Dark as Hell. *Steinbeck.* "Landing at Salerno Beach," *N. Y. Herald Tribune,* Oct. 4, 1943 | 584 |

| Title | Page |
|---|---|
| Italy's First Defeat. *Matthews. Two Wars and More to Come,* 1938 | 92 |
| Italy's Political Situation. *Hollenbeck.* "Political Situation in Italy," *P M.*, Nov. 3, 1943 | 599 |
| Japanese Generals. *Hersey. Men on Bataan,* 1942 | 419 |
| Jewish Children, The. *Pegler. T'aint Right,* 1936 | 69 |
| Last Day of the Phony War. *Murrow. This Is London,* 1941 | 176 |
| Last of the *Repulse,* The. *Brown.* "Stand by, Torpedoes," *Colliers,* Jan. 17, 1942 | 409 |
| *Lexington* Goes to Glory, The. *Johnston. Queen of the Flat-Tops,* 1942 | 449 |
| Logic and Death. *Harsch. Pattern of Conquest,* 1941 | 155 |
| London in Flames. *Casey. I Can't Forget,* 1941 | 235 |
| Lone Wolves of the RAF. *Alexander.* "Lone Wolves of the RAF," *The Saturday Evening Post,* July 12, 1943 | 272 |
| Loyalist, The. *Hemingway.* "Hemingway Reports Spain," *The New Republic,* Jan. 12, 1938 | 97 |
| Luftwaffe Over Moscow. *Caldwell. All Out on the Road to Smolensk,* 1942 | 308 |
| MacArthur. *Wolfe.* "The Man Japan Fears Most," *This Week,* Nov. 30, 1941 | 404 |
| Made in Japan. *Newman. Good-bye, Japan,* 1942 | 378 |
| Madrid Bombed. *Dos Passos.* "Room and Bath in the Hotel Florida," *Esquire,* Jan., 1938 | 83 |
| Man Who Didn't Quit, The. *Reynolds.* "The Man Who Didn't Quit," *Colliers,* Aug. 10, 1940 | 221 |
| Man Who Quit, The. *Allen.* "Interview with Marshal Petain," *N.A.N.A.,* Jan., 1941 | 219 |
| Manchurian Incident, The. *Fleisher. Our Enemy Japan,* 1942 | 345 |
| Manila. *Lee. They Call It Pacific,* 1942 | 402 |
| Mediterranean Fleet. *Allen.* "Dispatch On the Mediterranean Fleet," *Associated Press,* Oct. 6, 1942 | 510 |
| Mission Over Kiska. *Ford. Short Cut to Tokyo,* 1942 | 455 |
| Mr. Churchill Goes to Moscow. *Cassidy. Moscow Dateline,* 1943 | 325 |
| Moscow Trials, The. *Duranty.* "The Riddle of Russia," *The New Republic,* July 14, 1937 | 60 |
| Munich. *Birchall.* "Signing of the Munich Pact," *N. Y. Times,* Sept. 30, 1938 | 123 |
| Mussolini's Fall. *Knickerbocker.* "Mussolini's Downfall," *P.M.,* Oct 11, 1943 | 573 |
| Nazis Crack, The. *Huss.* "I Saw the Nazis Crack," *Cosmopolitan Magazine,* August, 1943 | 552 |
| Nazis Enter Stalingrad, The. *Parker.* "The Nazis in Stalingrad," *The N. Y. Times,* Sept. 27, 1942 | 331 |
| Neither Guns Nor Butter. *Hamilton. Appeasement's Child,* 1943 | 105 |
| New Guinea. *Lardner. Southwest Passage,* 1942 | 435 |
| On a Paris Railway Station. *Thompson.* "On a Paris Railway Station," *N. Y. Herald Tribune,* May 13, 1940 | 192 |
| On the Roads of France. *Tomara.* "Flight of the Refugees," *N. Y. Herald Tribune,* June 15, 1940 | 209 |
| On the Way to Murmansk. *Carse.* "We Fought Through to Murmansk," *The Saturday Evening Post,* Nov. 7, 1942 | 266 |

Title                  Page

One Year Later. *McCormick.* "Austria One Year Later," *N. Y. Times Magazine* Mar. 12, 1939    112

Oran. *Angly.* "Seizure of the French Fleet," *N. Y. Herald Tribune,* July 4, 1940    215

Panama Patrol. *Davenport.* "Panama Patrol," *Colliers,* May 16, 1942    437

Partners, The. *Duranty.* "The Russo-German Partnership," *The Atlantic Monthly,* March, 1940    133

Party in Control, The. *Lochner. What About Germany,* 1942    41

Peace in Our Time. *Driscoll.* "Chamberlin's Reception in London," *N. Y. Herald Tribune,* Oct. 1, 1938    124

Persecution of the Jews. *Mowrer. Germany Puts the Clock Back,* 1939    25

Plains Beyond Gafsa, The. *Ingersoll. The Battle Is the Pay-Off,* 1943    538

Planned Destruction. *O'Reilly.* "Blowing-up of Port Gaeta," *N. Y. Herald Tribune,* Nov. 9, 1943    601

Pogrom, The. *Tolischus.* "Nazis Loot, Smash and Burn," *N. Y. Times,* Nov. 11, 1938    65

Political Strategy. *Kuh.* "Political Situation in Italy," *Chicago Sun,* Oct. 11, 1943    589

Prague, September 1938. *Swing.* "Hotel Room in Prague," *Ken,* Dec. 1, 1938    118

Prisoner of the Axis. *Denny. Behind Both Lines,* 1942    498

Protector, The. *Beattie. Freely to Pass,* 1942    126

PT's to the Front. *Rawlings.* "In the Dark of the Solomons Moon," *The Saturday Evening Post,* Jan. 2, 1943    474

Rebirth of Stalingrad. *Shapiro.* "Dispatch on Stalingrad," *United Press,* Feb. 3, 1943    335

Refugees. *Casey. I Can't Forget,* 1941    201

Report from Switzerland. *Brigham.* "Italian Guerillas," *N. Y. Times,* Sept. 21, 1943    586

Retreat with Stilwell. *Belden. Retreat with Stilwell,* 1943    432

Road to Hitler, The. *Fischer. Men and Politics,* 1936    8

Rommel in Tobruk. *Moorehead. Don't Blame the Generals,* 1943    503

Russia and Japan. *Scott. Duel for Europe,* 1942    303

Russia Invaded. *Bourke-White. Shooting the Russian War,* 1942    306

Russo-Japanese Clash. *Morin. Circuit of Conquest,* 1943    362

Salerno. *Reynolds.* "Bloody Salerno," *Colliers,* Oct. 23, 1943    577

Scorched Earth. *Moats. Blind Date with Mars,* 1943    311

Sevastopol. *Lesueur. 12 Months That Changed the World,* 1943    321

Shakeup in the General Staff. *Axelsson.* "Recall of General Bock," *N. Y. Times,* Sept. 23, 1943    336

Shame of Nuremberg, The. *Barnes.* "The Nuremberg Laws," *New York Herald Tribune,* Sept. 16, 1935    43

Sidelights. *Treanor.* "Neopolitan Notes," *Colliers,* Nov. 27, 1943    601

Siege of Barcelona, The. *Carney.* "The Siege of Barcelona," *N. Y. Times,* Jan. 28, 1939    101

Silent Women, The. *Boyle.* "Europe's Women Fiercely Silent," *Vogue,* Apr. 1, 1942    228

Title                                                                                    Page

Something Is Rotten. *Thompson.* "Goodbye to Germany," *Harper's,* December,
    1943                                                               31
Stab in the Back, The. *Matthews. Fruits of Fascism,* 1943                               197
Story of the Partisans, The. *De Luce.* "Dispatch on the Partisans," *Associated
    Press,* Oct. 3, 1943                                              604
Stresa: End of an Era. *Berkson.* "Stresa Conference," *International News Service,*
    Apr. 15, 1935                                                      40
Surrender of Holland. *Conger.* "Surrender of Holland," *N. Y. Herald Tribue,*
    May 14, 1940                                                       194
System of Atrocities, The. *Packard.* "Dispatch on German Atrocities," *United
    Press,* Oct. 21, 1943                                             595
Tarawa. *Sherrod. Tarawa,* 1944                                                          484
Target: Berlin. *McDonald.* "With 7 Men in a Bomber," *N. Y. Times Magazine,*
    Feb. 7, 1943                                                       277
Teamwork. *Stoneman.* "Teamwork of British Navy and Air Force," *Chicago
    Daily News,* Jan. 10, 1942                                         258
"Thanks, Pal." *Pyle. With the Yanks in Africa,* 1943                                    558
They Could Take It. *White. Journey for Margaret,* 1941                                  244
This Man Rommel. *McMillan. Mediterranean Assignment,* 1943                              555
Tito's Army. *Sulzberger.* "Yugoslavs Drawn to Tito," *N. Y. Times,* Dec. 21, 1943      608
Tobruk Liberated. *Hill. Desert War,* 1942                                               501
Tokyo: December 7th. *Tolischus. Tokyo Record,* 1942                                     400
Topic of Conversation, A. *Zugsmith.* "Uneasy Laughter," *P.M.,* Sept. 14, 1941         388
Tour of Duty. *Winchell.* "Tour of Duty," *Daily Mirror,* Jan. 25, 1943                 477
Two Worlds. *Mann.* "Two Worlds," *Tomorrow,* December, 1943                             547
Unconditional Surrender. *Weller. Singapore Is Silent,* 1943                             415
Underground 1935. *Spivak.* "The Underground Speaks," *The New Masses,*
    Dec. 31, 1935                                                       47
Underground France. *De Rochemont.* "Underground France," *Life,* Aug. 20,
    1942                                                               223
Waiting for Der Tag. *Lochner. What About Germany?,* 1942                                140
War in Norway. *Stowe. No Other Road to Freedom,* 1941                                   178
Warlord, The. *Oechsner. This Is the Enemy,* 1942                                        231
We Have Done Our Best. *Romulo. I Saw the Fall of the Philippines,* 1942                 426
We Take Tunis and Bizerte. *Kluckhon.* "Twin Drive Scores," *N. Y. Times,*
    May 8, 1942                                                        544
Wendell Willkie in the Kremlin. *Graebner. Roundtrip to Russia,* 1943                    328
What the Soldiers Think. *Kirkpatrick.* "What the Soldiers Think," *Chicago
    Daily News,* Oct. 28, 1943                                         598
When the Raids Were Over. *Daniell. Civilians Must Fight,* 1941                          247
Winter 1931-1932. *Knickerbocker. German Crisis,* 1932                                    11
With Their Hands in Their Pockets. *Bess.* "With Their Hands in Their Pockets,"
    *The Saturday Evening Post,* Aug. 31, 1940                         206
Wounded Are Waiting, The. *Disher. Springboard to Berlin,* 1943                          517

# ACKNOWLEDGMENTS

The editor wishes to thank Mr. Ralph M. Nunberg, with whom he collaborated closely in bringing about this book. Mr. Nunberg's extensive knowledge of world affairs as well as contemporary non-fiction literature proved to be extremely helpful.

Thanks also go to Miss Mildred C. Kuch, who together with Mr. Nunberg conducted the extensive research. Her methodical mind and her training in index work helped overcome seemingly never ending difficulties during the time of compilation.

The editor is forever grateful to Miss Caroline Sauer of G. P. Putnam's Sons, who made literally thousands of telephone calls and wrote hundreds of letters as well, handling among other matters the extremely involved copyright situation.

Any anthology of such length and ambition is necessarily the result of team work. The editor wishes to acknowledge and give thanks for the help of a number of friends who concentrated on and specialized in certain phases to be covered by this book. Mr. Adolf Caspary attended to the Balkans and to Soviet Russia, Mr. W. M. Citron to the Far East, Miss Maria Eisner to France, Mrs. Valerie Engelsrath to England and the Battle of the Atlantic, Miss Nina Lowenstein to prewar Central Europe.

The editor cannot possibly attempt to include all those without whose kindness and friendly help he would have had a very difficult time. His deepest gratitude, however, goes to the American book publishers who with great understanding for the idea of this compilation and its educational possibilities did everything in their power to facilitate its coming into being. Without their generosity and friendship this book would never have been possible. Acknowledgment is here made to the following authors, publishers, newspapers, and magazines:

Jack Alexander for "Lone Wolves of the RAF" which appeared in *The Saturday Evening Post,* copyright 1943, by Curtis Publishing Co.

Jay Allen for "The Man Who Quit," copyright 1941, by New York Times Company.

J. Alsop for "City in Prison" which appeared in *The Saturday Evening Post,* Jan. 9, 1943, copyright 1943, by Curtis Publishing Co.

Associated Press for "Mediterranean Fleet" by Larry Allen, published in the *Boston Daily Globe,* Oct. 6, 1942; "The Story of the Partisans" by Daniel de Luce, copyright 1943.

Dorothy Bess for Demaree Bess' "With Their Hands in Their Pockets" which appeared in *The Saturday Evening Post,* copyright 1940, by Curtis Publishing Co.

Bruce Bliven for "Fear," copyright 1931, by *The New Republic.*

The Bobbs-Merrill Company for "London in Flames" from *I Can't Forget* by Robert J. Casey, copyright 1941; "Battle of Midway" from *Torpedo Junction* by Robert J. Casey, copyright 1942.

Kay Boyle and *Vogue* for "The Silent Women" by Kay Boyle, copyright 1942, by Condé Nast Publications, Inc.

666